Annals of Information Systems

Volume 13

For other titles published in this series, go to
www.springer.com/series/7573

Frada Burstein • Patrick Brézillon
Arkady Zaslavsky
Editors

Supporting Real Time Decision-Making

The Role of Context in Decision Support on the Move

Springer

Editors
Frada Burstein
Centre for Organisational and Social Informatics
Faculty of Information Technology
Monash University
Melbourne, Australia
Frada.Burstein@monash.edu

Patrick Brézillon
Laboratoire d'Informatique de Paris 6,
Université Pierre et Marie Curie
Paris, France
Patrick.Brézillon@lip6.fr

Arkady Zaslavsky
Department of Computer Science and Electrical Engineering
Luleå University of Technology
Luleå, Sweden
arkady.zaslavsky@ltu.se

ISSN 1934-3221 e-ISSN 1934-3213
ISBN 978-1-4419-7405-1 e-ISBN 978-1-4419-7406-8
DOI 10.1007/978-1-4419-7406-8
Springer New York Dordrecht Heidelberg London

Printed on acid-free paper

Springer is part of Springer Science+Business Media (www.springer.com)

Frada Burstein • Patrick Brézillon
Arkady Zaslavsky
Editors

Supporting Real Time Decision-Making

The Role of Context in Decision Support on the Move

Springer

Editors
Frada Burstein
Centre for Organisational and Social Informatics
Faculty of Information Technology
Monash University
Melbourne, Australia
Frada.Burstein@monash.edu

Patrick Brézillon
Laboratoire d'Informatique de Paris 6,
Université Pierre et Marie Curie
Paris, France
Patrick.Brézillon@lip6.fr

Arkady Zaslavsky
Department of Computer Science and Electrical Engineering
Luleå University of Technology
Luleå, Sweden
arkady.zaslavsky@ltu.se

ISSN 1934-3221 e-ISSN 1934-3213
ISBN 978-1-4419-7405-1 e-ISBN 978-1-4419-7406-8
DOI 10.1007/978-1-4419-7406-8
Springer New York Dordrecht Heidelberg London

Printed on acid-free paper

Springer is part of Springer Science+Business Media (www.springer.com)

Foreword

Over the past 25 years, decision support systems (DSS) have become so widely deployed – from individual to organizational to interorganizational levels – that they are often taken for granted. Aside from common adherence to the generic architecture of DSS, they have become amazingly diverse in their implementations and applications. Across much of the world, they have come to a point of seamlessly blending into ordinary decisional activities of individuals and organizations. Now, with the relentless march of technology and the trend toward hyper-competition, we must look beyond ordinary decisional activities to those that are remarkable in the sense of demanding (or potentially benefiting from) real-time support. Growth, high performance, and even survival will increasingly depend on DSS that can provide needed knowledge to decision makers to fuel their efforts toward decisional processes and outcomes that are more productive, more agile, more innovative, and more reputable – all within the context of a modern world of high velocity punctuated with crises and underscored by incessant movement of ideas, people, and products.

This book is the first concentrated guide to understanding the emergence of real-time DSS as a phenomenon and as a generator of interesting issues for researchers, practitioners, vendors, and educators.

The international array of contributors to the book covers the nature of this phenomenon in ways that will provoke and stimulate the reader. They offer insightful explanations about the characteristics needed for DSS to be relevant and helpful for supporting decisions that must be made along the frontier of events as they unfold – some decisions sparking those events and others extracting value from them. The book discusses various technologies that can underlie the realization of systems that are essentially "aware" of the context within which they collaborate with users for real-time decision making along emergent frontiers. The wide applicability of such decision support is amply demonstrate through a diverse set of examples – emphasizing real-time decision making in the cases of emergencies, mobile situations, and medical events.

In general, DSS differ from other kinds of information systems (e.g., transaction systems, management information systems) in terms of both purpose and features. Their *purpose* is quite simply to support decisional episodes (rather than to handle transactions or keep records for management reporting). According to scholars involved in the development of the DSS field, their distinguishing *features* include satisfying ad hoc knowledge needs (proactively and/or reactively), deriving knowledge, discovering knowledge, direct interaction with those who need knowledge (i.e., without the requirement of intermediaries), system customization for functionality and interfaces, fostering collaboration among multiple decision participants, and learning from prior decisional experiences. Now, we must realize that many such features were largely visionary at the time of their original introduction. Over time, progress has been made along each of these lines. It is very interesting that, in this book, we see the visions becoming real as the features coalescing into real-time DSS – a phenomenon driven by pressing needs in today's world.

The march toward support for real-time decision making is intertwined with other developments in the discipline of information systems: organizational computing, electronic business, and pervasive computing. Not only have these developments enriched transaction processing and management record keeping/reporting, they have added substantial wealth to progress in the DSS field. In this book, we can see many examples of the results and prospects for this value added for dealing with temporal, spatial, and environing facets of decisional contexts. Such contexts form turbulent frontiers in which a decision maker is buffeted by waves of rapid and unceasing change with respect to such considerations as global markets, interorganizational connections (e.g., supply chains), mass customization, continuous learning, sociopolitical diversity, culture shifts, and advances in distributed and intelligent systems. Competitiveness with respect to such contextual waves requires dynamic capabilities on the part of decision makers, and DSS are an integral component of such capabilities. According to the nascent *science of competitiveness*, the decision maker is confronted not only with contextual waves, but also with contextual storms and quakes – terrorist acts, natural disasters, financial calamities. Competitiveness with respect to such contextual waves requires improvisational capabilities on the part of decision makers, and here is where real-time decision support truly shines and holds great promise for further progress.

Clyde W. Holsapple
Fellow, Decision Sciences Institute
Rosenthal Endowed Chair
University of Kentucky

Preface

This special volume of Annals of Information Systems explores the issues associated with the design and use of real-time DSS in ubiquitous, mobile and distributed computing environments with the focus on the importance of context for successfully addressing dynamic decision-making processes.

The idea of the book on real-time decision support was born as a result of international collaboration on the topic of context-aware computing as part of the Task Force of the Australian Research Council initiative called Research Network in Enterprise Information Infrastructure [EII].[1] This unique initiative supported a series of events and activities, which brought together academics and practitioners keen on promoting an integration of ubiquity and mobility of devices, applications and users in order to significantly improve business processes and to reduce operational costs. This initiative is also aiming at establishing a focal point for bringing together researchers and practitioners working in the area of context-awareness in pervasive computing in Australia and worldwide. This collaboration gave us an opportunity to reflect and consolidate many years of research results in the use of intelligent technologies for decision support. We were able to establish the boundaries of current approaches to applying advanced technology for supporting context-specific and personalised information needs of field workers. One of such boundaries was established in the area of real-time decision support. The invitation from the Annals of Information Systems for the issue in the topical area of decision support provided us with a fortunate opportunity to put together this book with the aim of crossing this boundary and extending this exciting cross-disciplinary research area.

Sponsored by the Association for Information Systems, Special Interest Group on Decision Support, Knowledge and Data Management Systems (AIS SIG DSS), we organised a workshop "Supporting real-time decision-making: The role of context in decision support on the move" as a part of the International Conference in Information Systems ancillary events (pre-ICIS DSS workshop) in December 2008 in Paris. The call for papers for the event invited authors to contribute related theories, tools and techniques, as well as to share some case studies from their

[1]http://www.eii.edu.au/

experience. We were interested in collecting cases in which the real-time decision support was successfully provided based on context-aware information systems, as well as those where time-critical support failed due to the shortcomings of technology or social components of the information systems. Some of the chapters in this book are based on the presentations from that workshop. The authors came to present and discuss their research ideas on the role of context in real-time DSS. The presenters debated advantages of and obstacles to real-time DSS and the role of context in it. The workshop included a key note and a panel discussion on the future research required to successfully advance the DSS field, capitalising on the opportunities of the ubiquitous technologies and addressing the challenges of making better decisions 'on the move'.

The review of the recent literature on decision support and submissions to the workshop reconfirmed to us that there was no other source, which would systematically cover theory, technologies and techniques applicable to capture dynamic context for the needs of real-time decision support. Hence, the need for this book has become even more evident.

Based on the identified themes, an open call for book chapters was issued, which resulted in multiple submissions not only from the participants of the workshop, but from other active researchers in the field. Each chapter of the book underwent at least three rounds of peer and editorial review. Although not all submissions found their way into this book, we do appreciate the effort of all the authors.

The overarching research question this book aims to address is: How discovering, extracting, interpreting, predicting and managing context can assist in real-time decision support? The volume's focus is on the challenges of context modelling and management as a component of knowledge management for decision making and support. We collected a number of case studies and example projects where such technologies were successfully applied. A number of authors describe potential innovations which could support real-time decision making processes. In particular, the book contains a few examples of the use of innovative approaches for dealing with context in crisis and emergency management situations.

The volume focuses on the role of context for time-critical decision support. It includes chapters describing theory and practice of real-time decision support, and decision support 'on the move' in particular. The topics covered in the book include theoretical and technical aspects and application case studies of:

- Context-based decision-making methods and tools
- Contextualising information for time-critical decision making
- Processes and procedures of extracting contextual information for decision support
- Identifying context in decision making/support process
- Managing the contextualization process of decision making/support
- Dynamic filtering of information for real-time decision making and support.

The chapters describe concrete and constructive research results on the topics as well as more broad theoretical frameworks about the role of context in decision-making and support, a comprehensive review of the available approaches to mobile real-time decision support.

The book is organised around three themes, which can be broadly labelled as theories in, technologies for and application cases of real-time context-aware DSS. The final theme covers a wide range of sample applications among the many that have been successfully implemented to deal with the contextual needs of decision-makers in various applications. It is represented by ten chapters. First three chapters of the final theme explore the real-time decision support for groups in emergency and crisis management. They are followed by four chapters looking at the real-time decision support in medical and business contexts. The remaining three chapters explore the issues related to mobile decision support.

The first theme provides a solid foundation by exploring paradigms and methods associated with real-time DSS, and how they fit with other studies and theories of computerised decision-making support. The theme is represented by an introductory note from the editors and two full chapters, which establish the ontology of the field of real-time decision support and establish foundations and new outlooks for enabling such systems and supporting organisations in realising the full potential of opportunities provided by the *anywhere, anytime computing* paradigm.

Chapter 1 by Dan Power looks at the problem of successful implementation of real-time decision support systems (DSS) emphasising on three major categories of challenges: technical, organisational and social/psychological. The author justifies why these are the challenges that the managers should be aware of in order to successfully implement real-time DSS and what benefits such awareness brings.

In Chapter 2, Eric Stein explores the concept of improvisation as a framework for understanding real-time dynamic decision making and systems support for it. He introduces a framework that classifies improvisational contexts according to problem structure and foreseen consequences, identifies the elements necessary for effective individual and team improvisation, and lists the design requirements necessary to support improvisational behaviours and conversations.

The second theme consists of five chapters that explore various innovative approaches trailed by the authors and offered as potentially beneficial technical solutions when making time-critical decisions.

Chapter 3 by Arkady Zaslavsky and Andrey Boytsov addresses the problem of context prediction and subsequent proactive adaptation. The authors start by developing and justifying the principles to analyse and compare various context prediction methods, followed by analysing the development in the area and comparing different context prediction techniques to identify their benefits and shortcomings. They conclude their empirical research by identifying current challenges in the area and proposing the potential solutions to address these.

In Chapter 4, Patrick Brézillon proposes modelling of real-time decision making in order to support the self-training of actors to modify weaknesses of their behaviour during task realisation. The author introduces a contextual methodology composed of a series of ten steps that cross the four levels of human behaviour known as policy, strategy, tactic and operation. Such contextual methodology proposes a unified framework that brings together aspects that are generally contrasted – procedure versus practice, task versus activity, logic of functioning versus logic of use – and explains the two types of contextualisation in a context-oriented model with three layers. The contextual methodology and the framework are applied in the road safety domain.

In Chapter 5, Seng Loke uses a declarative programming approach to the situation programs that encapsulate and modularise the way context is aggregated to infer various situations. The author treats the situation programs as first-class entities, describes the initial prototype LogicCAP-S based on the language LogicCAP, and discusses how it could be further applied in the mobile environment.

In Chapter 6, Florence Aligne and Juliette Mattioli explore crisis management as a typical situation in need for real-time decision support. The authors outline the importance of the contextualisation of information in the situation understanding process. They propose a crisis management cycle structured along three crucial steps: information gathering, situation understanding and decision making. For each step, the authors describe the processes involved and propose some relevant techniques to implement them.

In Chapter 7, Norita Ahmad and Reza Barkhi attempt to establish how various contextual and collaborative approaches influence human decision makers through interface manipulations. Focusing on the Second Life (SL) technology that creates a virtual world, the authors design an experiment where they explore the SL context, user behaviour and perceptions about SL. Experiment results provide empirical evidence of the use of SL and the future of this technology for human interaction in the real-time decision-making context.

For the last theme, we have selected a range of case studies covering a range of opportunities and challenges associated with providing time-critical decision support on the move. Some of the case studies look specifically into the role of context in their cases and reflect on some lessons learnt in dealing with context in a particular way. We start this section of the book with three chapters addressing case studies in emergency, disaster and crisis management, which were identified in the previous section as one of the obvious areas in need of real-time decision support.

Chapter 8 by Tung Bui and Ina Sebastian explores the crisis scene and proposes that under extraordinary conditions that information provided to the decision makers should help them in dealing with emotions and stress, reinforce motivation to help and nurture a sense of altruism. In their research, the authors step outside of the rational decision-making paradigm and provide a new perspective on what constitutes effective decision support to the volunteer helpers.

Chapter 9 by Murray Turoff, Connie White and Linda Plotnick looks at the Threat Rigidity Syndrome and information overload as the genesis of various design problems of the emergency decision support systems. The authors investigate how these problems can be overcome using the example of High Reliability Organisations (HRO) that utilise a set of practices to manage low-probability/high-consequence events.

In Chapter 10, the authors Linda Plotnick, Murray Turoff and Connie White explore how the use of electronic communications allows Partially Distributed Emergency Teams (PDET) accomplish various tasks remotely instead of face to face. The authors discuss how such teams, being empowered by the new technologies, form virtual communities of practice, and identify strategies that can help build and nurture these virtual communities by looking at the ways to further utilised new technologies.

Chapter 11 by Fergal Carton, Frederic Adam and Patrick Brézillon opens a subsection concerned with real-time decision support in business context. The authors look at the problems of providing real-time decision support to managers in the context of a case study of a multinational manufacturing firm that relies on an ERP (enterprise resource planning) package for transaction processing. Aligning the ERP system with the reality of doing business proves to be a real challenge and a subject to constraints arising from both the business and virtual context of the firm. By analysing the emerging gaps between the inflexible ERP system and the decision support needs of managers, the authors offer a theoretical framework for the relationship between real-time transaction processing and decision support.

Chapter 12 by Robert Baksa and Murray Turoff contrast continuous auditing systems with the emergency management and response systems that integrate continuous auditing's detection and alerting functions with the tracking of decisions and decision options for situations that could be more effectively handled by human judgement. The authors propose using emergency management and response systems as a prototype to help overcome some of the implementation obstacles of the auditing systems. The authors suggest possible architectures for the continuous auditing systems, list some common implementation challenges, and provide a case study to illustrate a few successful implementations.

Chapter 13 by a team of researchers and practitioners from Canada consisting from Ziad Kobti, Anne W. Snowdon, Robert D. Kent, Gokul Bhandari, Shamual F. Rahaman, Paul D. Preney, Carol A. Kolga, Barbara Tiessen and Lichun Zhu is concerned with the real-time decision support in medical context. The authors discuss challenges faced by semiautomated decision support systems in health care, mainly in generating evidence-based recommendations in a short critical timeframe. They report on a multidisciplinary project between computer and health sciences resulted in a cumulative framework that encapsulates innovative distributed data collection methodology, coupled with an intelligent multi-agent, socially driven decision support system.

In Chapter 14, Shane Grigsby, Frada Burstein and Nyree Parker discuss the role of decision context within time-critical decision support in medical triage. The authors believe that establishing a decision context in time-critical decision support could assist in provisioning time-critical information to improve decision outcomes. They look at the safety measures and risk mitigation in the clinical health care setting, and how decision support systems can refine contextual guidelines on the task being undertaken in such settings. They identify contextual elements of a task being undertaken as a means to establish rules that can influence provided decision support in the given settings and subsequently improve decision-making outcomes.

Three final chapters of the book look at the approaches specific to mobile decision support. Chapter 15 by Yves Vanrompay and Yolande Berbers looks at how the current and future context of the system affects the quality of support provided by that system. The authors propose to run a DSS on top of a middleware that helps the decision maker to contextualise information. They provide a set of requirements the middleware should fulfil to learn, detect and predict patterns in context to optimise the information flow to the decision maker, and validate their findings in the medical health care domain.

Chapter 16 written by Supavich Pengnate, Ramesh Sharda, David Biros, Michael Hass and Upton Shimp looks at the military domain where availability of needed ammunition information is critical for decision making, especially in a war zone. The authors use a case study where the extension of a web-based ammunition multimedia encyclopaedia (AME), developed for the US Army Defence Ammunition Center (DAC), used mobile handheld technology to provide Quality Assurance Specialist Ammunition Surveillance (QASAS) personnel access to needed ammunition information via a personal digital assistant (PDA).

The final Chapter 17 of the book by Pedro Antunes, Claudio Sapateiro, Gustavo Zurita and Nelson Baloian describes the development of a model and tool supporting collaborative construction of situation awareness. The model organises awareness information elements according to situation dimensions, dimensional elements and correlations between dimensional elements, while the developed tool supports collaborative information management using mobile devices and pen-based interaction. The reported case study illustrates implementation of the developed model and tool in the support to disaster recovery of business operations.

From the above description, the reader can gain a fair idea of the breadth and the depth of the material covered in the book. We believe that this book will to have a wide range of appeal to the readers who recognise the importance of providing relevant knowledge on the move in timely manner. It is written by academics and practitioners for academics and practitioners. It does not require the reader to have specific background in information systems in general and decision support in particular. It targets to reach four audiences:

- Practitioners involved with the design of real-time DSS
- Users of various levels concerned with effective use and management of these systems
- Technologists searching for empirical evidence and feedback on opportunities and drawback associated with the use of real-time DSS
- Researchers and students interested in study and further research in the area of context-aware DSS

The goal of this book is not to bring a final point to the current state on DSS on the move, but rather emphasise the importance of this new field for extensive research in the near future.

Acknowledgements

This book would not have been possible without the efforts of many people. We would like to thank the contributors for their inspiring research and hard work under extreme pressure to satisfy the requirements of thorough and professional reviewers. We appreciate the efforts of the reviewers that have contributed to the quality of this book. Some of the authors of the chapters have also served as reviewers of other chapters, so their contribution is doubly appreciated. We would like to thank Ms Kate Lazarenko for her assistance in keeping this project on track and attention to detail in achieving the quality of this publication.

The Springer publishing team's support, patience and assistance are greatly appreciated.

We would like to acknowledge the Australian Research Council Research Network in Enterprise Information Infrastructure (EII) initiative for the sponsorship of this book project. We also express gratitude to our respective universities for providing time and resources to complete this international project.

Finally we thank you, the research community, for your interest in this emerging field of real-time decision support and we hope that this book will be a worthwhile addition to the DSS body of knowledge.

Monash University, Melbourne, Australia — Frada Burstein
Université Pierre et Marie Curie, Paris, France — Patrick Brézillon
Luleå University of Technology, Luleå, Sweden — Arkady Zaslavsky

Contents

Part III Case Studies

Contributors

F. Adam
Business Information Systems, University College Cork, Ireland
FAdam@afis.ucc.ie

N. Ahmad
School of Business and Management, American University of Sharjah, Sharjah, UAE
nahmad@aus.edu

F. Aligne
Thales Research and Technology, France
florence.aligne@thalesgroup.com

M. Alles
Rutgers Business School, Department of Accounting, Business Ethics & Information Systems, Newark, NJ, USA
alles@business.rutgers.edu

P. Antunes
Faculty of Sciences, University of Lisbon, Portugal
paa@di.fc.ul.pt

R. Baksa
New Jersey Institute of Technology, Newark, New Jersey, USA
rbb25@njit.edu

N. Baloian
Department of Computer Science, University of Chile, Santiago de Chile, Chile
nbaloian@gmail.com

R. Barkhi
Pamplin College of Business, Virginia Tech, Blacksburg, VA, USA
reza@vt.edu

Y. Berbers
Department of Computer Science, Katholieke Universiteit Leuven, Leuven, Belgium
Yolande.Berbers@cs.kuleuven.be

G. Bhandari
Odette School of Business, University of Windsor, Windsor, Ontario, Canada

D. Biros
Department of Management Science and Information Systems, Oklahoma State University, OK, USA

A. Boytsov
Computer Science and Electrical Engineering Department, Luleå University of Technology, Sweden
Andrey.Boytsov@ltu.se

P. Brézillon
Laboratoire d'Informatique de Paris 6, Université Pierre et Marie Curie, Paris, France
Patrick.Brézillon@lip6.fr

T. Bui
Pacific Research Institute for Information Systems Management (PRIISM), Shidler College of Business, Honolulu, HI, USA
tung.bui@hawaii.edu

F. Burstein
Centre for Organisational and Social Informatics, Monash University, Melbourne, Australia
Frada.Burstein@monash.edu

F. Carton
Business Information Systems, University College Cork, Ireland
f.carton@ucc.ie

M. De Silva Borges
Universidade Federal do Rio de Janeiro, Brazil
mborges@nce.ufrj.br

S. Grigsby
Centre for Organisational and Social Informatics, Monash University, Melbourne, Australia
sagri2@student.monash.edu

M. Hass
Department of Management Science and Information Systems, Oklahoma State University, OK, USA

R. D. Kent
School of Computer Science, University of Windsor, Windsor,
Ontario, Canada

Z. Kobti
School of Computer Science, University of Windsor, Windsor, Ontario, Canada
kobti@uwindsor.ca

C. A. Kolga
Kingston General Hospital, Kingston, Ontario, Canada

S. W. Loke
Department of Computer Science and Computer Engineering,
La Trobe University, Melbourne, Australia
S.Loke@latrobe.edu.au

J. Mattioli
Thales Research and Technology, France
juliette.mattioli@thalegroup.com

D. Nicklas
Juniorprofessur Datenbanken und Internettechnologien, Universität Oldenburg,
Department für Informatik, Oldenburg - Germany
nicklas@offis.de

N. Parker
School of Nursing and Midwifery, Monash University, Peninsula Health,
Frankston Vic, Australia

S. Pengnate
Department of Management Science and Information Systems, Oklahoma
State University, OK, USA
fone.pengnate@okstate.edu

L. Plotnick
Jacksonville State University, Jacksonville, Alabama, USA
lplotnick@jsu.edu

D. J. Power
College of Business Administration, University of Northern Iowa,
Cedar Falls, Iowa, USA
power@uni.edu

P. D. Preney
School of Computer Science, University of Windsor, Windsor, Ontario, Canada

S. F. Rahaman
School of Computer Science, University of Windsor, Windsor, Ontario, Canada

H. Rahman
Institute of Computer Management & Science (ICMS), Bangladesh
email@hakik.org

C. Sapateiro
Systems and Informatics Department, School of Technology, Polytechnic Institute of Setúbal, Portugal
csapateiro@est.ips.pt

I. Sebastian
Pacific Research Institute for Information Systems Management (PRIISM), Shidler College of Business, Honolulu, HI, USA
isebasti@hawaii.edu

R. Sharda
Department of Management Science and Information Systems, Oklahoma State University, OK, USA
ramesh.sharda@okstate.edu

U. Shimp
The U.S. Army Defense Ammunition Center, OK, USA

A. W. Snowdon
Odette School of Business, University of Windsor, Windsor, Ontario, Canada
snowdon@uwindsor.ca

E. W. Stein
Penn State Great Valley School of Graduate Professional Studies, Malvern, PA, USA
ews3@psu.edu

B. Tiessen
Leamington District Memorial Hospital, Leamington, Ontario, Canada

M. Turoff
New Jersey Institute of Technology, Newark, New Jersey, USA
turoff@njit.edu

Y. Vanrompay
Department of Computer Science, Katholieke Universiteit Leuven, Leuven, Belgium
yves.vanrompay@cs.kuleuven.be

C. White
Jacksonville State University, Jacksonville, Alabama, USA
connie.m.white@gmail.com

J. Xie
Centre for Organisational and Social Informatics, Monash University, Melbourne, Australia
Jue.Xie@monash.edu

A. Zaslavsky
Computer Science and Electrical Engineering Department, Luleå University of Technology, Sweden
Arkady.Zaslavsky@ltu.se

L. Zhu
School of Computer Science, University of Windsor, Windsor, Ontario, Canada

G. Zurita
Management Control and Information Systems Department, Business School, Universidad de Chile, Chile
gzurita@fen.uchile.cl

Author Biographies

Frédéric Adam is Associate Professor of Business Information Systems at University College Cork in Ireland and visiting research fellow in the School of Economics and Management at Lund University (Sweden). He holds Ph.D.s from the National University of Ireland and Université Paris VI (France). His research interests are in the area of decision-making and decision support and in the area of ERP. He has authored and edited six books and has over 20 journal papers published in international journals including *Information and Management*, the *Journal of Strategic Information Systems*, *Decision Support Systems*, and the *Journal of Information Technology*. He is the Editor-in-Chief of the *Journal of Decision Systems* and is Vice-Chair of the Working Group 8.3 on DSS of the International Federation for Information processing (IFIP).

Norita Ahmad is Assistant Professor of MIS at American University of Sharjah, UAE. She received her Ph.D. in Decision Science Engineering Systems from Rensselaer Polytechnic Institute (RPI), and an M.S. and a B.S. in Telecommunications and Network Management and Computer Sciences, respectively, from Syracuse University. Her research interest includes decision analysis, database management systems, and knowledge management. She has presented research internationally and published in a variety of scholarly journals such as *International Journal of Information Technology & Decision Making*, *Journal of Intelligent Manufacturing*, *Journal of Business Ethics, International Journal of Enterprise Information Systems*, and *International Journal of Services Operations and Informatics*.

Florence Aligne, Research engineer in applied maths and statistical modelling, holds an M.Sc. in Statistical and Stochastic modelling at Orsay University (France). She worked two years as a research engineer in INRETS, national traffic research centre, on road traffic control optimisation. She obtained her Ph.D. in signal analysis in 1999 at Supélec (France), focusing on data analysis, statistics and optimisation to build a global maritime traffic image. From 1999 to 2006, she was in charge in Eurocontrol of statistic modelling of air-traffic controllers' workload and of the data analysis of ground and air experiments. Since 2006, she works in Thales on classification, languages identification and decision support analysis for crisis management.

Pedro Antunes is Associate Professor (with Habilitation) at the University of Lisbon's Department of Informatics. He received his Ph.D. degree in electrical and computer engineering from the Technical University of Lisbon and is interested in the design, development and evaluation of collaborative technology with the main purpose to increase flexibility, transparency, awareness, latitude of decision, safety and resilience. He has edited several special editions of journals and conference proceedings, published more than 120 scientific papers and also has been a consultant for governmental agencies in e-health, document management, information security, quality management and electronic voting.

Robert Baksa has been a Director at Gupton Marrs International, a boutique management-consulting firm that specialises in performance and risk management, since 2006. He has helped Fortune 500 companies achieve their compliance objectives and strengthen their internal control structures. Mr. Baksa has an M.B.A. from the Stern School of Business, an M.Sc. in Information Systems from New York University, and a B.Sc. in Computer Science and Business from the University of Pittsburgh. Currently, he is a Ph.D. candidate in Information Systems at New Jersey Institute of Technology.

Nelson Baloian is Associate Professor at the Department of Computer Science at the Universidad de Chile, Santiago, Chile. He obtained his Ph.D. in 1998 at the University of Duisburg in Germany. Since then his main research topics have been computer supported collaborative work in general and computer supported collaborative learning, developing technologies and methodologies for using computer and information technologies, which support learning inside and outside the classroom. He is author and coauthor of more than 70 scientific articles. He is also a regular visiting professor at the University of Waseda, Tokyo, and at the University of Duisburg-Essen, Germany.

Reza Barkhi is an associate professor and faculty research fellow of Information Systems at Pamplin College of Business at Virginia Polytechnic Institute and State University. He received a B.Sc. in Computer Information Systems, and an M.B.A., M.A., and Ph.D. in Business Focusing on Information Systems, Operations Management and Decision Sciences, all from The Ohio State University. His current research interests are in the areas of collaborative technologies and problem solving, and topological design of telecommunication networks. He has published in journals such as *Location Science*, *European Journal of Operational Research*, *Computers & OR*, *Group Decision and Negotiation*, *Decision Support Systems*, *Communication Research*, *Communications of AIS*, *Information Technology and Management*, *Information & Management*, and *Journal of Management Information Systems*.

Yolande Berbers obtained her M.Sc. degree in Computer Science from the Katholieke Universiteit Leuven in 1982. In 1987, she received a Ph.D. degree in Computer Science at the same university. Since 1990 she has been an associate professor in the department of computer science. She spent five months during 1985–1986 at the National Institute for Research in Computer Science and Control

(INRIA), France. She teaches advanced courses on software for real-time and embedded systems and on computer architecture. Her research interests include software engineering for embedded software, ubiquitous computing, middleware, real-time systems, component-oriented software development, distributed systems, and environments for distributed and parallel applications. She is cofounder of EuroSys, a European association for the advancement of systems research in Europe, linked with ACM SIGOPS. She has more than 40 scientific publications in the last five years.

Gokul Bhandari is Assistant Professor of MIS at the Odette School of Business, University of Windsor, Canada. He received his Ph.D. is Management Science/ Information Systems and M.A. in Economics from McMaster University and M.B.A. from the University of Minnesota. He has published more than a dozen journal articles and conference proceedings in the area of information systems, finance, and economics.

David Biros is Assistant Professor of Management Science and Information Systems at Oklahoma State University. He is a retired United States Air Force Lieutenant Colonel who worked in the fields of communications and information assurance. His research interests included knowledge management, information assurance, deception detection and system trust. He has been published in *MIS Quarterly*, *Decision Support Systems*, *Group Decision and Negotiation*, *MISQ Executive*, and the *Journal of Digital Forensics Security and Law*. He is also an associate editor for the *Journal of Digital Forensics Security and Law* and is an adjunct professor at Edith Cowen University in Australia.

Andrey Boytsov is employed as a Ph.D. student at the ICT division of Computer Science and Electrical Engineering Department in Luleå University of Technology, Sweden. He received an M.Sc. degree in Computer Science at Saint Petersburg State Polytechnical University (Russia, June 2008). There he was awarded the Polytechnical Medal for 100 per cent achievement (all excellent grades) during the entire period of studies. He has coauthored several papers and received multiple diplomas for research achievements. He worked as a senior software developer at Motorola (Saint Petersburg Development Center, January 2006–November 2008). Work mostly concerned development of infrastructure of mobile telecommunication systems. Coauthored one paper. Current research interests involve context awareness and context prediction in pervasive computing and socioeconomic systems. His Web home page is http://staff.www.ltu.se/~andboy

Patrick Brézillon defended his Thèse d'Etat (6-year duration) in 1983. He now belongs to the Laboratoire d'Informatique de Paris 6 for 20 years. His research focuses on context modelling and management applied to human reasoning (and especially decision making). He proposes now a coherent conceptual framework based on the concepts of generic frame and of situation dressing, framework implemented in a context-based formalism – called contextual graphs – for representing in a uniform way elements of reasoning, of knowledge and of contexts. This formalism is used in applications belonging to more than 20 different domains. This work will conclude soon on a contextual methodology for modelling actors accomplishing a task in a given situation, in a given domain and a given context. The next step is a focus on context-based intelligent assistant systems in which context plays a role of same importance as the decision-making process itself.

Tung X. Bui is Matson Navigation Company Endowed Chair of Global Business and Professor of Information Technology Management at the Shidler College of Business of the University of Hawaii at Manoa. Bui's current research interests include the cost-effective use of information and communication technologies in organisations with special focus on negotiation and crisis management support. Prior to joining the University of Hawaii, Bui was on the faculty at New York University, the US Naval Postgraduate School, the Universities of Fribourg and Lausanne, Switzerland, and the Hong Kong University of Science and Technology. Website: http://shidler.hawaii.edu

Frada Burstein is Professor in the faculty of Information Technology at Monash University in Melbourne, Australia. She holds an M.Sc. (Applied Math) degree from Tbilisi State University, Georgia, USSR, and a Ph.D. in Technical Cybernetics and Information Theory from the Soviet Academy of Sciences. Her current research interests include knowledge management technologies, intelligent decision support, and real-time decision support. Her research appears in such journals as *Decision Support Systems*, *Journal of the American Society for Information Science and Technology*, *Journal of Organizational Computing and Electronic Commerce*, *Information Technology & People*, *Knowledge Management Research and Practice* and others. Professor Burstein is Co-Editor of the *Journal of Decision Systems* and *VINE: The Journal of Information and Knowledge Management Systems*. Website: http://www.infotech.monash.edu.au/about/staff/Frada-Burstein

Since 2002, **Fergal Carton** has been a college lecturer in Business Information Systems at University College Cork in Ireland. With 15 years experience as an Information Systems consultant, starting with the Boston Consulting Group in London, he has worked for over 30 major clients on projects concerning IT strategy, enterprise software selection and implementation. With a primary degree in Computer Science (University College Dublin), and an MSc in Management from the European School of Management Studies (ESCP-EAP) in Paris, Fergal's research output focuses on the impact of ERP integration on management control.

Shane Grigsby is currently a Research Assistant, working on an emergency coordination ontology as part of the Australian Research Centre collaborative Linkage project within the Centre for Organisational and Social Informatics, Monash University. Prior to this, he received a Bachelor of Network Computing degree in 2003 and consecutively an honours degree in the same field in 2004. Both were completed at Monash University, Peninsula Campus, Australia. He was awarded a scholarship to undertake a Ph.D. project at Monash University, Caulfield Campus, Australia under supervision of Professor Frada Burstein. His Ph.D. was in information management and systems, exploring mobile decision support systems in health care. The project involved the development of a knowledge based, mobile triage decision support system prototype. He has recently submitted his Ph.D. thesis for examination. His research interests include mobile decision support systems, business intelligence and health care-oriented information systems.

Michael Hass is a doctoral student enrolled in the Management Science and Information Systems department at Oklahoma State University. A former major in the Air Force, he has over 12 years of experience in program management, information assurance, and IT policy. Research interests include design science and social network analysis approaches to information system development. He is a frequent guest speaker for undergraduate classes and local high schools on the topics of system analysis and design and information assurance and has published in the Cutter IT Journal, the Hawaii International Conference on System Science, and the Americas Conference on Information Systems.

Robert D. Kent is a Full Professor in the School of Computer Science, since 1982, and cofounder of the High Performance and Grid Computing group and Intelligent Systems for Health Management group at University of Windsor. He received his PhD in theoretical Physics in 1979 from Windsor and B.Sc. (Hons.) in 1972 from the University of British Columbia. His research is currently focused on design and construction of intelligent decision support systems, but his active interests range from security and scheduling in distributed systems, to subjective and higher order logics, complex systems modelling and other matters.

Ziad Kobti is a tenured Assistant Professor with the School of Computer Science and director of the Centre for Applied Social Intelligent Systems (CenAppSIS). He is also an adjunct researcher with Washington State University specialising in multi-agent systems, simulating artificial societies and artificial cultural evolution. He received his Ph.D. in 2004 from Wayne State University and M.Sc. in 1999, and B.Sc.H. 1996 from the University of Windsor.

Carol A. Kolga completed her Master's in Nursing at the University of Ottawa. As a professor in the Collaborative Nursing Program at St. Clair College, Windsor, she was engaged in a variety of research initiatives. Most recently, she has joined the Kingston General Hospital in Kingston, ON, as the director of Professional Practice Nursing. As a Ph.D. (student) at the University of Western ON in Health and Rehab Science, her focus remains in health promotion and injury prevention within the older adult demographic.

Seng W. Loke is a reader and associate professor at the Department of Computer Science and Computer Engineering in La Trobe University, where he leads the Pervasive Computing Group. He has authored *Context-Aware Pervasive Systems: Architectures for a New Breed of Applications* published by Auerbach (CRC Press). He has coauthored more than 200 research publications and has been on the PC of numerous conferences/workshops in the area, e.g., Pervasive '08 and Percom '10. His research has been published in *IEEE Pervasive, Knowledge Engineering Review, Elsevier's Pervasive and Mobile Computing Journal, IEEE Transactions on SMC*, and *Theory and Practice of Logic Programming*.

Juliette Mattioli has a Ph.D. in Applied Mathematics (1993), with a focus on signal analysis, pattern recognition, mathematical morphology, set valued analysis and neural networks. She has been in charge of various research projects and activities at the corporate research centre of Thales, led the PLATON Team. She is now the head of the Decision Technologies and Mathematics Laboratory in Thales Research and Technology, including research activities covering high-level information fusion including heterogeneous classifier fusion, problem solving, operation research, decision theory and viability theory.

Nyree Parker is a practising registered nurse working in the Emergency Department of Peninsula Health since 1995. Various roles during this time include practising as a clinical nurse specialist, nurse educator, clinical research assistant, external emergency management coordinator, a volunteer coordinator and to date, nursing workforce planning and strategy manager. Academic achievements involve Diploma Applied Science Nursing 1989–91; Bachelor of Nursing 1993; Graduate Diploma of Nursing Critical Care 1995–96; Masters of Nursing 1998–2000; Graduate Certificate in Health Professional Education 2005; Graduate Certificate in Emergency Health 2007–08; and Masters in External Emergency 2009 onwards. Courses completed at Monash University at various campuses. A Graduate Certificate in Health Promotion was completed at Deakin University Burwood campus around 1997. Current interests are in nursing workforce strategies and practice and external emergency management practices.

Supavich Pengnate is a doctoral student enrolled in Management Science and Information Systems in the Spears School of Business at Oklahoma State University. His research interests include e-commerce-related adoption, mobile technologies issues related to information privacy and security, and information visualisation and interface design for interactive environments. He holds an M.Sc. degree in Information Systems and Operations Management from The University of North Carolina at Greensboro, has nine years experience in computer graphic design and information systems design and development, and has published in the Americas Conference on Information Systems.

Linda Plotnick is Assistant Professor in the Mathematical, Computing and Information Sciences department at Jacksonville State University, Jacksonville, AL. Her research interests include leadership and trust in partially distributed teams; public warning; using Web 2.0 technologies in emergency management; and implications of the threat rigidity thesis for emergency management system design.

Daniel J. Power is Professor of Information Systems and Management at the College of Business Administration at the University of Northern Iowa, Cedar Falls, Iowa and the editor of DSSResources.COM, the web-based knowledge repository about computerised systems that support decision making, and the editor of *DSS News*, a bi-weekly e-newsletter. Dan writes the column “Ask Dan!” in *DSS News*. Also, he is the Decision Support Expert at the Business Intelligence Network. Since 1982, Dan Power has published more than 50 journal articles, books, book chapters and proceedings papers. His most recent book with Business Expert Press is titled *Decision Support Basics* (2009). His Web home page is http://dssresources.com/vita/djphomepage.html

Paul D. Preney is a doctoral student at the School of Computer Science, University of Windsor.

Shamual F. Rahaman is a doctoral student at the School of Computer Science, University of Windsor.

Since 2001, **Cláudio Sapateiro** has been a teaching assistant at the Systems and Informatics Department of the School of Technology of the Polytechnic Institute of Setúbal, Portugal. Under the scope of ongoing Ph.D. activities, his research interests have been focused on mobile support to teams that must perform under critical disruptive events.

Ina Sebastian is currently a doctoral student in International Management, with a focus on Management Information Systems, at the Shidler College of Business, University of Hawaii. She earned a Bachelor in Business Administration from the RWTH Aachen University, Germany and an M.B.A. from the University of Hawaii. Prior to pursuing her doctoral research, Sebastian worked as an industry analyst at Jupiter Research, California. Website: http://shidler.hawaii.edu

Ramesh Sharda is Director of the Institute for Research in Information Systems (IRIS), ConocoPhillips Chair of Management of Technology, and a Regents Professor of Management Science and Information Systems in the Spears School of Business at Oklahoma State University. His research has been published in major journals in management science and information systems including Management Science, Information Systems Research, Decision Support Systems, Interfaces, INFORMS Journal on Computing, Computers and Operations Research, and many others. His coauthored text book (Decision Support and Business Intelligence Systems by Turban/Sharda/Delen, 9th edition, Prentice Hall) has just been released. He serves on the editorial boards of journals such as the INFORMS Journal on Computing, Decision Support Systems, Information Systems Frontiers, and OR/MS Today. Ramesh is also a cofounder of a company that produces virtual trade fairs, iTradeFair.com.

Upton R. Shimp is Director of training at the Defense Ammunition Center (DAC), McAlester, Oklahoma. Dr. Shimp earned a B.Sc. degree in Education (Mathematics and Elementary Education) from the University of Missouri. For several years after graduation, Dr. Shimp worked in the Missouri public schools as a secondary and elementary education teacher. Dr. Shimp also holds an M.Sc. degree in management from Southern Nazarene University and Doctor of Philosophy in Education from Oklahoma State University. He began his career as a civilian employee of the US Army in January 1980. During his 30 years in federal service, Dr. Shimp's awards include two Meritorious Civilian Service Awards, the Superior Civilian Service Award, the Commanders Award for Civilian Service, the European Association of the United States Army Commendation, Ammunition Manager of the Year, and numerous Special Service Awards.

Anne W. Snowdon is a Full Professor at the Odette School of Business and is cross-appointed to the Faculty of Engineering at the University of Windsor. She holds adjunct appointments at McGill University and Ivey School of Business in the Centre for Health Innovation and Leadership. Her research focuses on innovative approaches to Safety and Injury Prevention, specifically injury prevention for children in vehicles and Decision Support Systems for the Health Sector. She received a Ph.D. in 2000 from the University of Michigan, an MSc in 1985 from McGill University, and a B.Sc.N. in 1981 from the University of Western Ontario.

Eric W. Stein is Associate Professor of Management Science and Information Systems at Penn State's Great Valley School of Graduate Professional Studies. His areas of research and expertise are organizational memory, learning, experts, decision support, business design, creativity and improvisation, and high tech ventures. He served as director of the New Ventures and Entrepreneurial Studies M.B.A. concentration for several years. Dr. Stein has published in the *Journal of Management Information Systems*, International Journal of Expert Systems, International Journal of *Information Management*, *Information Systems Research*, and Expert Systems with Applications and serves as a reviewer for several MIS journals and conferences. Dr. Stein received his doctorate in Managerial Science from the Wharton School of the University of Pennsylvania and has a degree in physics from Amherst College.

Barbara Tiessen is the Executive in Residence for Healthcare at Odette School of Business, University of Windsor. She is a registered nurse whose 40-year career in health care includes middle management and senior executive positions in Ontario hospitals. She holds a Master in Social Work degree from Wilfrid Laurier University (1985), and an M.Sc. in Administration (Health Services) from Central Michigan University (1997).

Murray Turoff designed the first online emergency response information systems in 1971 for the Wage-Price-Freeze. It was a collaborative decision support system. He has been a designer and researcher in collaborative decision support and computer conferencing systems for over 35 years. He has worked on applications of group communications for project management, policy analysis, online learning and forecasting. Since 2004 he returned to working in the design of emergency preparedness and management systems for distributed group collaboration and command and control.

Yves Vanrompay is a Ph.D. student and Research Assistant in the DistriNet research group of the Katholieke Universiteit Leuven's Department of Computer Science. He received his M.Sc. degree in Informatics in 2003, and his M.Sc. in artificial intelligence in 2004 from the Katholieke Universiteit Leuven. His research interests include context-aware systems, adaptation, context reasoning and learning. He works in the European FP6 project MUSIC, which provides a middleware, methodology and tools for developing self-adaptive applications.

Connie White teaches and conducts research in the emergency domain examining a variety of topics with graduate students who are practitioners from the field. Her primary research is on building an online real-time Delphi system to support decision making by large groups of experts: http://delphi.sahanafoundation.org/delphi/. Other research interests of hers include leveraging social media for emergency management, high reliability organisations, virtual communities, emergency notification systems, collaborative international online system development, homeland security (S&T), social media and Web 2.0 technologies, GIS in EM, The Virtual USA Project, communities of practice, cyber security, collaborative decision making, and emergency scales/threat assessment tools.

Arkady Zaslavsky is holding a Personal Chair (Chaired Professor) at Luleå University of Technology, Sweden. He worked at Monash University, Australia for 17 years before joining LTU. He received M.Sc. in Applied Mathematics majoring in Computer Science from Tbilisi State University (Georgia, USSR) in 1976 and a PhD in Computer Science from the Moscow Institute for Control Sciences (IPU-IAT), USSR Academy of Sciences in 1987. His research interests include mobile and pervasive computing; distributed and mobile agents and objects; wireless networks; distributed computing and database systems; distributed object technology and mobile commerce. Currently his research is focussed on context- and situation-awareness, context prediction, validation and verification as well as on context quality metrics. He, along with his Ph.D. students and colleagues, developed a theory of context spaces for representing and reasoning about context. His Web home page is http://staff.www.ltu.se/~arkady/

Lichun Zhu is a graduate student at the School of Computer Science, University of Windsor.

Since 2004, **Gustavo Zurita** has been an Assistant Professor at the Information Systems and Management Department of the University of Chile in Santiago, Chile. He obtained his Ph.D. in Mobile Computer Supported Collaborative Learning in 2003. Since 2008, he has been research director of the Information Systems and Management Department and also of the Business School. His current research areas are learning and motivation in face-to-face learning supported by mobile computing, decision-making systems supported by mobile computing, mobile meeting support systems, mobile commerce, knowledge management and mobile computing, mobile geo-collaborative systems, utility and usability.

Introducing Context into Decision Support on the Move

Frada Burstein[1], Patrick Brézillon[2], and Arkady Zaslavsky[3]

[1]Centre for Organisational and Social Informatics, Monash University, Melbourne, Australia
[2]Laboratoire d'Informatique de Paris 6, Université Pierre et Marie Curie, Paris, France
[3]Computer Science and Electrical Engineering Department, Luleå University of Technology, Sweden

Abstract This chapter offers a short entre to the book by reviewing the major concepts related to real-time decisions support. It aims to introduce to the reader three basic themes that are covered in this book. These themes are then expanded in the respective book sections. In a nutshell, this chapter helps to justify the need for any-time-any-space decision support, explain the semantics and definition of what constitutes "context" and clarify why it is essential to capture the context to address personalised needs of decision makers on the move. We supply some seminal definitions and references for studies in this area. In conclusion, some future research directions and challenges are also suggested.

Keywords Real-time • decision support • context modelling • ubiquitous computing • pervasive systems

Introduction

Decision support systems (DSS) are computerised interactive systems that are widely used to support decision-making activities (Beynon et al. 2002). The main purpose of decision support--> systems is to deliver the data/information which is most relevant to the current decision-making context. In dynamic environments, only real-time data can provide decision makers with such relevant knowledge (Delic et al. 2001). The ability to access real-time knowledge opens an exciting new opportunity to enhance the quality and timeliness of decision support due to the widespread use of the Internet, the wider accessibility of wireless sensor technology and mobile communications (Burstein et al. 2008).

The phenomenal growth of mobile technologies over the last decade, along with the 'anytime, anywhere' connectivity in conjunction with the low cost of mobile devices, presents an unprecedented opportunity for mobile DSS. Such growth enables real-time decision making on the move when access to desktop computers is not available. In dynamic, high-risk and uncertain mobile environments, it is equally important to study and propose approaches for making time-critical (namely in real time) operational decisions in the best possible way.

Recent development of information and communication infrastructures and sensor technologies has resulted in an opportunity to create a class of systems which are capable of recognising the environmental changes and of acting accordingly by adjusting their functionality to best suit the context of their operation. Such systems are often referred to as *context-aware pervasive systems-->*, or in short, context-aware systems (Padovitz et al. 2008). These systems are aware of not only the computational environment, but also, notably, of the physical environment, of human users, places, locations and other factors, which in combination represent the context of their operation. More importantly, they can respond intelligently to such context information when responding to the user's requirements. Quite often it is expected that such systems are pervasive and ubiquitous from the user and environmental perspectives, which should make interactions with them "transparent" and "unobtrusive".

Decision Support in Real Time: Can It Be Achieved?

Decisions and actions are deeply intertwined. A decision usually leads to an action and an action modifies the environment. The environmental changes trigger the need for making some new decisions, which have to take into consideration and fit a new, revised decision context. Such a view on the decision-making process is much more dynamic and is no longer suitable to be modelled in a linear manner within a/the traditional decision analysis paradigm. In reality, there is little chance to plan all possible decision alternatives and to explicitly assess them in real time when the decision-making environment is constantly changing and decision outcomes are time critical. Hence, the emphasis for the real-time decision support is shifting from complex modelling of the alternative decisions, to representation of the context in which these decisions are situated. The complexity, multiple goals and various time-critical imperatives associated with such decision support, increases the importance of identifying, modelling, learning and managing the right context for making efficient decisions.

In dynamic and uncertain environments where instances of context elements constantly change, context-awareness is crucial for enabling applications, including decision support systems, to tailor their behaviours according to the contextual/situational changes and to better meet user and application needs (Salber et al. 1999).

The advantages of real-time, context-sensitive decision support have been investigated in several projects such as mobile business applications (Nelson and Wright 2004; Burstein et al. 2008), healthcare emergency decision-support (Burstein et al. 2005; Fitzgerald et al. 2008), and dynamic data driven application systems (DDDAS) (Darema 2004; Gaynor et al. 2006). Effective emergency and crisis management often depend on access to real-time information and decision support tools have been created for safe and successful rescue and recovery operations (Turoff et al. 2004; Wallace and De Balogh 1985). Context-awareness enables decision support systems to assist the users in an efficient and intelligent manner and enhance their experience by increasing productivity and satisfaction with the process and outcomes of the decision-making process (Henricksen et al. 2002).

Why Context and Context Awareness Is Important for Timely Decision Support?

In our view, making context explicit is a way to model the environment and create an interface between the decision maker and the tools needed to assist in real-time decision making. Context provides a representation of the environment as a set of contextual elements (CEs). This contextual information presents the decision makers with the necessary knowledge to react and respond as soon as they obtain the context instances. Some contextual elements will have a known instance, and thus can be taken into account in the decision-making process. Some other CEs will be known, but their instantiations may not be pre-defined. In the latter case, known as context-awareness, the instance of CE will change or will be known only in real time. Based on the new instance of CE obtained in real time, the decision maker will be able to react and make new decisions in an informed way. Aiming to support such real-time decisions requires continuous reflections on the environmental changes and explicit knowledge of the current context.

Context is a powerful and multifaceted concept. Context information can be sensed, derived, reasoned, computed, calculated or explicitly entered by users. There is a flurry of definitions of context in current literature. A general definition by Dey (2001); one adopted by most researchers, describes context as "any information that can be used to characterise the situation of an entity" (p. 5). Brézillon and Pomerol (1999) suggest that context consists of two types of knowledge, including external and contextual knowledge. External knowledge is the part of the context that is not relevant to the decision-making process on hand, and contextual knowledge is the other part of the context that is relevant to the decision. A subclass of contextual knowledge is called proceduralised context that is invoked and structured with respect to the task at hand and the decision-makers involved in the decision-making process (Brézillon and Brézillon 2008). It is essential for the decision support system to identify and obtain the contextual information as the decision-making situation changes, rather than focusing on the external knowledge.

Context can have different aspects and characteristics as follows (Delir Haghighi et al. 2008):

- Dynamic and static context – context can be dynamic, like heart rate; or static, like user-name or e-mail.
- Continuous data streams – context can be continuous like sensor data streams.
- Uncertain and imperfect context – context information is liable to imperfection and can be erroneous, ambiguous or incomplete.

- Temporal context – context can be associated with temporal data, which enables representation of histories of context.
- Situational context – contextual information can be used to represent a situation such as a user activity.

Quality of Context (QoC) – the same context information about an entity can be of different quality. To indicate this feature of the context a special measure of QoC marks such precision that, according to Buchholz et al. (2003), can be defined as "any information that describes the quality of information that is used as context information" (p. 5).

There is an abundance of approaches in the literature proposed for modelling of, and reasoning about, the context. These approaches apply well-known concepts and principles such as Bayesian reasoning methods (Fox et al. 2003), Dempster-Shafer theory (Wu et al. 2003), fuzzy logic (Delir Haghighi et al. 2008; Mäntyjärvi and Seppanen 2002), graphical modelling (Henricksen et al. 2002), and basic ontology-based modelling approaches (Chen et al. 2003; Ranganathan and Campbell 2003; Truong et al. 2005). Ontologies provide a formal representation of concepts and their relationships within a certain domain that can be used for knowledge sharing and reasoning about context. To improve context-management capabilities, different modelling approaches can also be used for predicting future context of mobile applications. A number of different techniques such as classification, neural networks, Bayesian networks and statistics-based techniques can be useful in predicting the future context.

One of the main application domains that can benefit from context-awareness is crisis and emergency management. The crisis and emergency management process heavily relies on the availability and quality of the crisis context, and requires in-time contextualisation to enhance the overall process of crisis management. The complex nature of emergency events, coupled with time-constraints, emphasises the importance of using real-time decision support systems. Due to the dynamic nature of disasters like fires or floods, ground commanders and central command officers need to gather and analyse data/information on a wide range of emergency management activities, and make instant and split-second judgments. The need for up-to-date information and data are critical in emergency management DSS, to determine the priorities for operation and resource allocation and management. Examples of such systems include the NSW Fire Brigades I-Zone planning system (Byrne 2009) and Gold Coast DSS for flood emergency management (Mirfenderesk 2009). Emergency responders depend on the availability of up-to-date information to guide them in making timely and effective decisions (Gaynor et al. 2006). In the emergency management environments, real-time decision support systems assist emergency managers in formulating, analysing and interpreting disaster-related issues. Management of safe and successful rescue and recovery operations requires access to real-time situational information and effective decision support tools (Kaloudis et al. 2005).

Where to From Here?

It is known that the inclusion of real-time knowledge enables DSS to actively adapt themselves according to current available information and environmental conditions (Holsapple et al. 1993; Shim et al. 2002). There are a number of adaptive decision support systems introduced in the literature that aim to improve the decision quality and user experience. These include, for example, ADAPTOR (Paranagama et al. 1998), the adaptive DSS for real-time scheduling of a flexible manufacturing system (Piramuthu et al. 1993), the adaptive DSS for science and finance management (Fazlollahi et al. 1997), and the adaptive model based on multi-agent system for flood forecast (Georgé et al. 2009).

In dynamic and changing environments such as air traffic controlling, large amounts of information need to be processed in a very limited time, and consequently, decision makers need to solve new problems and adapt to new situations whilst preserving the evolving progress of decision-making tasks in their minds (Gonzalez 2004). Dynamic decision making (DDM) systems enable real-time, continuous and interrelated decisions in highly dynamic and complex environments (Edwards 1962; Gonzalez 2004, 2005).

In the context of business decision making, real-time decision support provides timely support to the decision makers. As an emerging trend, real-time data warehousing offers industry and IT managers the following values: (1) immediate information delivery by shortening the time-span between business events and information process and delivery; (2) data integration across the enterprise; (3) future vision from historical trends; (4) tools for looking at data in new ways to enable creative problem solving and posing new questions; (5) end-user empowerment with regards to writing queries and building reports; (6) consistency, timeliness and credibility of information delivered (Nelson and Wright 2004).

From the brief review provided in this chapter, it is clear that there are tremendous opportunities and challenges associated with the implementation of such context-aware systems. However, there are also clear benefits that can evolve from such implementation – ranging from, for example, context-aware mobile phones that know what to do with incoming calls; context-aware printing, which would be mindful of the resources constraints; context-aware enterprises that respond with agility to an understanding of physical circumstances; to context-aware toys that interact with children and have an understanding of their special needs and expectations; and context-aware bookshops that interact with personalised computer assistants to mine some profiles of users interests; from context-aware parking areas that tell drivers where to go, to context-aware road intersections that warn drivers of dangerous situations. We can envisage a proliferation of such systems in different walks of life once the theoretical and technical challenges are appropriately addressed.

References

Beynon, M., Rasmequan, S., and Russ, S., "A new paradigm for computer-based decision support," Decision Support Systems, 33, 2002, 127–142.

Brézillon, P. and Brézillon, J., "Context sensitive decision support systems in road safety," *Handbook on Decision Support Systems 2 – Variations*, F. Burstein and C. Holsapple (eds.). Berlin: Springer, Vol. 2, 2008, pp. 107–123.

Brézillon, P. and Pomerol, J.C., "Contextual knowledge sharing and cooperation in intelligent assistant systems," *Le Travail Humain*. Paris: PUF, Vol. 62, No. 3, 1999, pp. 223–246.

Buchholz, T., Kupper, A., and Schiffers, M., "Quality of context: What it is and why we need it," Proceedings of the Workshop of the HP OpenView University Association 2003 (HPOVUA 2003), Geneva, 2003, pp. 1–13. URL= www.nm.ifi.lmu.de/pub/Publikationen//bks03/PDF-Version/bks03.pdf

Burstein, F., Cowie, J., Zaslavsky, A., and San Pedro, J., "Support for real-time decision making in mobile financial applications," Information Systems and E-Business Management, 6(3), 2008, 257–278.

Burstein, F., Zaslavsky, A., and Arora, N., "Context-aware mobile agents for decision-making support in healthcare emergency applications," Proceedings of the 1st Workshop on Context Modeling and Decision Support, Paris, France, 2005.

Byrne, G., "I-Zone planning: Supporting frontline fire-fighters," The Australian Journal of Emergency Management, 24(1), February 2009, 48–58.

Chen, H., Finin, T., Joshi, A., "Using OWL in a pervasive computing broker," Workshop on Ontologies in Agent Systems (AAMAS 2003), Melbourne, Australia, July 2003.

Darema, F., "Dynamic data driven applications systems: A new paradigm for application simulations and measurements," Workshop on Dynamic Data Driven Applications Systems, Arlington, 2004. Lecture notes in Computer Science, Vol. 3038. Berlin: Springer, 2004, pp. 662–669.

Delic, K.A., Douillet, L., and Dayal, U., "Towards an architecture for real-time decision support systems: Challenges and solutions," Proceedings International Symposium on Database Engineering and Applications, Grenoble, 2001, pp. 303–311.

Delir Haghighi, P., Krishnaswamy, S., Zaslavsky, A., and Gaber, M., "Reasoning about context in uncertain pervasive computing environments," 3rd European Conference on Smart Sensing and Context (EuroCSS 2008), Zurich, Switzerland, October 29–31, 2008. Lecture Notes in Computer Science (LNCS), Vol. 5279, Springer, Berlin, 2008, pp. 112–125.

Dey, A.K., "Understanding and Using Context," *Personal and Ubiquitous Computing*, Vol. 5, No. 1, February. London: Springer, 2001, pp. 4–7, ISSN 1617-4909.

Edwards, W., "Dynamic decision theory and probabilistic information processing," Human Factors, 4, 1962, 59–73.

Fazlollahi, B., Parikh, M.A., and Verma, S., "Adaptive decision support systems," Decision Support Systems, 20(4), August 1997, 297–315.

Fitzgerald, M., Farrow, N., Scicluna, P., Murray, A., Xiao, Y., and Mackenzie, C.F., "Challenges to Real-Time Decision Support in Health Care," Advances in patient safety: New directions and alternative approaches. Henriksen, B.J., Keyes, M.A., Grady, M.L., AHRQ Publication No. 08-0034-2. Rockville: Agency for Healthcare Research and Quality, Vol. 2, August 2008, pp. 1–14.

Fox, D., Hightower, J., Liao, L., Schulz, D., and Borriello, G., "Bayesian filtering for location estimation," IEEE Pervasive Computing, 2(3), July–September 2003, 24–33.

Gaynor, M., Seltzer, M., Moulton, S., and Freedman, J., "A dynamic, data-driven, decision support system for emergency medical services," International Conference on Computational Science, Vol. 2, 2006, pp. 703–711.

Georgé, J.-P., Peyruqueou, S., Régis, C., and Glize, P., "Experiencing self-adaptive MAS for real-time support systems," 7th International Conference on Practical Applications of Agents and Multi-Agent Systems (PAAMS 2009), Salamanca, Vol. 55, 2009, pp. 302–309.

Gonzalez, C., "Decision support for real-time, dynamic decision-making tasks," Organizational Behavior and Human Decision Processes, 96, 2005, 142–154.

Gonzalez, C., "Learning to make decisions in dynamic environments: Effects of time constraints and cognitive abilities," Human Factors, 46(3), 2004, 449–460.

Henricksen, K., Indulska, J., and Rankotonirainy, A., "Modelling context information in pervasive computing systems," 1st International Conference on Pervasive Computing (Pervasive'02), Zurich, January 2002. Lecture Notes in Computer Science (LNCS), Vol. 2414. Berlin/ Heidelberg: Springer, 2002, pp. 79–117.

Holsapple, C.W., Pakath, R., Jacob, W.S., and Zaveri, J.S., "Learning by problem processors: adaptive decision support systems," Decision Support Systems, 10, 1993, 85–108.

Kaloudis, S.T., Lorentzos, N.A., Sideridis, A.B., and Yialouris, C.P., "A decision support system for forest fire management," An International Journal of Operational Research, 5(1), 2005, 141–152.

Mäntyjärvi, J. and Seppanen, T., "Adapting applications in mobile terminals using fuzzy context information," Proceedings of 4th International Symposium on Mobile Human-Computer Interaction, Pisa, 2002. Lecture Notes in Computer Science, Vol. 2411. Berlin: Springer, 2002, pp. 95–107.

Mirfenderesk, H., "Flood emergency management decision support system on the Gold Coast, Australia," The Australian Journal of Emergency Management, 24(2), May 2009, 17–24.

Nelson, G. and Wright, J., "Real time decision support: Creating a flexible architecture for real time analytics," Proceedings of the 29th SAS User Group Conference (SUGI29), Montréal, May 9–12, 2004, pp. 109–29. URL=http://dssresources.com/papers/features/nelson&wright/nelson&wright11182005.html

Padovitz, A., Seng, W., Loke, A., and Zaslavsky, A., "The ECORA framework: A hybrid architecture for context-oriented pervasive computing," Pervasive and Mobile Computing, 4, 2008, 182–215.

Paranagama, P., Burstein, F., and Arnott, D., "ADAPTOR: A personality-based adaptive DSS generator," Proceedings of the Thirty-First Hawaii International Conference on System Sciences, Hawaii, Vol. 5, 1998, pp. 54–63.

Piramuthu, S., Raman, N., Shaw, M.J., and Park, S.C., "Integration of simulation modeling and inductive learning in an adaptive decision support system," Decision Support Systems, 9, 1993, 127–142.

Ranganathan, A. and Campbell, R.H., "An infrastructure for context-awareness based on first order logic," Personal Ubiquitous Computing, 7(6), 2003, 353–364.

Salber, D., Dey, A.K., and Abowd, G.D., "The Context Toolkit: Aiding the Development of Context-Enabled Applications," Proceedings of the SIGHI Conference on Human Factors in Computing Systems, (CHI'99), Pittsburgh, May 1999. New York: ACM, 1999, pp. 434–441.

Shim, J.P., Warkentin, M., Courtney, J.F., Power, D.J., Sharda, R. and Carlsson, C., "Past, present, and future of decision support technology," Decision Support Systems, 33, 2002, 111–126.

Truong, B.A., Lee, Y. and Lee, S., "Modelling uncertainty in context-aware computing," Proceedings of the 4th Annual ACIS International Conference on Computer and Information Science (ICIS'05), Jeju Island, July 14–16, 2005, pp. 676–681.

Turoff, M., Chumer, M., Van de Walle, B. and Yao, X., "The design of a dynamic emergency response management information system (DERMIS)," Journal of Information Technology Theory and Application, 5(4), January, 2004, 1–35.

Wallace, W.A. and De Balogh, F., "Decision support systems for disaster management," In Petak, W.J. Emergency management: a challenge for public administration, special issue, Public Administration Review, 45, January 1985, 134.

Wu, H., Siegel, M., and Ablay, S., "Sensor fusion using Dempster-Shafer theory II: Static weighting and Kalman filter-like dynamic weighting," Proceedings of the 20th IEEE Instrumentation and Measurement Technology Conference Technology Conference (IMTC'03), Vol. 2, Vail, 2003, pp. 907–912.

Part I
Theories of Real-Time Decision Support

Chapter 1
Challenges of Real-Time Decision Support

Daniel J. Power

Department of Management, College of Business Administration, University of Northern Iowa, Cedar Falls, Iowa, USA

Abstract Real-time computerised decision support is providing timely support to business decision makers. Real-time decision support systems (DSS) can support operational and tactical decisions, and may enhance strategic decision making in some situations. Current systems can deliver needed data, results, and communications with essentially no processing delay. When evaluating implementation of these systems, managers need to consider and respond to three categories of continuing challenges: (1) technical, (2) organisational and (3) social/psychological. Potential benefits include faster response, improved efficiency, reduced risk, and reduced operating costs. Real-time technological can be disruptive and likely threatens the competitive position and success of many organisations.

Keywords DSS • Challenges • Disruptive technological • Real-time decision support

1 Introduction

Technological innovations such as the telephone, radio, television, and, now, smart phones and text messaging, have speeded up awareness of current events and happenings. This broader societal change has created a perceived need for more timely information delivered in a "real-time" way to help people make business decisions. Speeded-up response can create competitive advantage for companies and predictions from real-time data can help managers anticipate responses and needed actions. Improved communications using voice, video, and text can improve coordinated responses and help people share analyses and observations. Some tactical and operational decisions will especially benefit from improved

D.J. Power (✉)
College of Business Administration, University of Northern Iowa,
Cedar Falls, Iowa, USA
e-mail: power@uni.edu

F. Burstein et al. (eds.), *Supporting Real Time Decision-Making*,
Annals of Information Systems 13, DOI 10.1007/978-1-4419-7406-8_1,

situational awareness and relevant data exchange. Many strategic decisions do not need real-time data, but decision makers may benefit from improved rich media, real-time communications. Choosing when and how to deploy real-time decision support is an important decision that creates opportunities and challenges for managers and organisation stakeholders.

Pushing real-time, "zero latency" information to decision makers is now realistic and practical. People can communicate from almost anywhere to anyone anywhere using voice, video, and messages. People can also "pull" extensive information as needed. According to Margulius (2002), a major need of the anticipated real-time enterprise is integrating public and proprietary company information in appropriate, "right-time" feeds that enhance decision making.

Managers and organisations face challenges in transforming work processes with real-time decision support. Some challenges and obstacles threaten successful implementation; other obstacles are minor impediments that are easily overcome. Technical challenges are perhaps the most manageable obstacles and the easiest to overcome. Organisational challenges are harder to deal with; and, some social/ psychological challenges may be major, relatively permanent barriers in some organisations. Managers need to understand the various challenges at a general level to direct resources to resolve them.

Challenges encountered in designing any information system are magnified with real-time systems. Also, when response time or delay in retrieving data impacts decision-making timeliness and effectiveness, managers are faced with a trade-off between technological expenditures, decision quality, and decision risk. As the cost of technological expenditures decreases, the trade-off equation changes.

The next section defines real-time decision support. Then the third section reviews some possible tactical and operational decision support applications. The fourth section discusses the three major categories of implementation challenges. The final section draws some conclusions relevant to managers, especially information technological managers.

2 Defining Real-time Decision Support

Decision support is a broad concept that prescribes using computerised systems and other tools to assist in individual, group, and organisational decision making. Thierauf (1982) argued that "any system that processes and stores data or reports them as they are happening is considered to be an on-line real-time system (p. 20)." His broad definition seems appropriate for current discussions of real-time decision support.

Demarest noted in an email (Power 2002) that the adjective real-time means that informational inputs to decision-making processes are available as soon as there are changes in the environment that alter those informational inputs. "Real time also means 'near real time' in practice because there is always some latency between

(a) the actual state change, (b) the reflection of that state change in data in one or more systems of record and (c) the availability of the changed data to decision makers." Real time is not the same for every decision task.

Managers and technologists have discussed real-time decision support in articles and books for more than 30 years, but as computing, sensor, and networking technologies improves and provides new capabilities, our expectations for real-time DSS continue to increase. At a fundamental level, the hope has always been that our information and decision support system (DSS) would help decision makers monitor events and evaluate, choose, and act on alternatives as events actually unfold. Constraining factors like data availability, data capture, and transmission speeds are less of a problem and technological advances provide new tools to receive and access real-time data. Technological progress continues to facilitate real-time decision support innovation.

Real-time decision support has six major capabilities:

1. Monitoring activity using decision rules to send alerts. A sensor or data-gathering instrument captures actions/data and individual data elements, or groups of observations are processed using rules and messages, or alerts are sent. The data may or may not be captured and stored.
2. Fast exchange and transmission of data to systems and decision makers. Information systems may exchange data or data is exchanged with one or more people.
3. Information available to a decision maker as soon as a change occurs. Data is updated and processed as change occurs and the information is immediately accessible to a decision maker. The decision maker is always accessing and using current data. The data is stored and updated.
4. Processes and stores data and reports raw or summarised data as events happen. The new data is streamed or pushed to decision makers.
5. Provides analytics or knowledge at the point of use. Data is perhaps not rapidly changing, but the decision support user can perform analyses or obtain advice immediately and as needed.
6. Provides synchronous exchange from data origination to data use. The exchange may be using voice, video and/or text. The exchange may be initiating and confirming a transaction or supporting collaboration.

3 Operational and Tactical Decision Support

A major issue facing managers and technologists is when to build and then use any type of real-time decision support. This issue generates a number of questions. Is the capability needed in potential crisis and emergency situations? Is the capability widely needed at the operating level in most organisations? Is the perceived need urgent and pervasive or more discretionary? In general, today all six types of real-time decision support are needed and appropriate at the operation and tactical decision-making levels in organisations.

Let us now examine three decision situations. First, emergency response is an important and needed use of real-time decision support. Assuming highly reliable, redundant systems, data-driven, real-time DSS can help monitor the volume and intensity of events, abrupt or sudden change, and changes in the external or internal environment of an organisation. Model-driven, real-time DSS can help identify vulnerabilities and evaluate crisis scenarios. Communications-driven DSS can reduce potentially the negative effects of time pressure in a crisis. Web portals, text messages, and Web-based DSS can help organisations share information with the media, the stakeholders, and the public during a crisis. Improved communications technologies and handheld and portable computing technologies make it possible for first responders to bring decision support technologies into a crisis management setting whether that is in a nearby hotel room, a tent or at the scene of an incident. A commander at the scene of an incident or crisis can conceivably have access to the entire range of DSS.

Second, let us examine a customer service situation. An airplane coming from Europe is going to arrive an hour late at JFK Airport, and there are 165 passengers on that flight who have to make connections. An active data warehouse application could prepare all their flight schedules, all their seat assignments, all their new gates, all their baggage transfers, and even provide flight attendants the information in order to communicate with premier and regular customers (Power 2003; Watson 2005).

Finally, envision support for call centre staff who must make decisions in less than a minute: "Should I try to keep this customer?" "Should I bargain with this customer on price or service?" Real-time decision support can provide relevant information and guidance to the staff person.

Real-time data can be pushed to sales people as they are meeting with a client or customer. Product or service pricing can change as needed for business reasons and the change can be rapidly disseminated. Demand forecasts can be rapidly updated and the impact on production determined almost instantaneously. Managers can chat with colleagues in a synchronous group meeting from wherever participants happen to be. As national and state laws change, tax planning knowledge-driven DSS can be quickly updated. New business documents and videos can be quickly created and made available and potential readers can be notified easily of the availability. Managers can be tracked and warned and notified. Decision makers should have more awareness of their surroundings and others will be more aware of what a specific decision maker is doing. Smart phones can deliver data in real time to managers, sales staff, and emergency personnel.

There are four broad application areas for operational data-driven, real-time DSS:

- First, customer relationship management applications. For example, revising passenger schedules for passengers on a delayed plane or supporting call centre staff who are trying to make decisions (Swift interview by Power 2003);
- Second, DSS that support sales people using a smart phone. For example, a salesperson accesses an operational business intelligence system to recommend the best-fit fertilizer to a farmer (Violino 2008);

- Third, monitoring operations; for example, Suzuki uses dashboards to highlight warranty claim and external customer satisfaction data (TDWI.com). Also, companies like Papa Gino's and Hillman Group monitor operations in real time;
- Fourth, consolidating historical and current data and creating alerts. For example, in real time it is possible to integrate customer reservations data and generate security alerts.

Aberdeen Group (Hatch 2008) identifies three types of operational, real-time decision support: (1) real-time analytics with business rules applied to data as it is captured; (2) near real-time analytics at the point of use; and (3) business activity or process monitoring. Hatch (2008) generalises that "operational business intelligence is about delivering information to people when and how they need it in the context of business need."

Decision making at the operational level in organisations will benefit first and most from real-time decision support. Real-time decision support cannot reduce the problems caused by missing, inaccurate or incomplete data. The subjective data often used in more strategic decision situations is hard to capture and transmit. Real-time collaborative technologies may, however, help increase the situational awareness of senior managers.

4 Challenges

Although deploying technologies for real-time decision support has become more affordable, there remain challenges. Use of real-time technologies in personal decision making using smart phones may speed up adoption of new capabilities, but prior experience by early adopters will not necessarily reduce organisational and social challenges. Examining the processing of Twitter and RSS feeds suggests the need for effective filtering to manage information load. Organisational changes resulting from the adoption of real-time decision support will be substantial. If these technologies are used inappropriately to provide more data and communication faster when that is not needed, then technological may actually hurt responses and increase stress on decision makers. Having too much real-time information may lead to poor decisions, rather than better decisions.

The context of decision making and computerised decision support in most organisations is increasingly complex, interdependent, and interrelated. The real-time challenges are demanding and stimulate change and innovation (Davis and Meyer 1998). Challenges are sometimes confused with problems, and if not confronted, challenges may become problems. Five factors magnify the challenges of implementing real-time decision support: (1) high frequency of information change, (2) high frequency of decision making, (3) high timeliness requirement for information, (4) high need for synchronicity, and (5) high stress of managing in real time. The connected, global economy drives the current focus on real-time decision support and operations (Davis and Meyer 1998).

4.1 Technical Challenges

Information technological used for real-time decision support continues to change, improve, and evolve. Real-time decision support involves access to diverse data sources in different formats, including spatial data, use of dynamic-high resolution displays (Batty 2004), high-speed wireless remote access to applications, rapid analytics, automated data collection, dynamic processing, and rapid distribution. Real-time systems must accommodate a wide variety of processing objectives (Masters and Welch). In some situations, a small amount of current data is retrieved predictably, like customer status. In some situations, a large amount of continuously refreshed data is needed under a tight deadline. Data may be collected and processed using multiple hardware and software components with a dynamic range of processing loads. In general real-time decision support must be very reliable and continuously available. The data and capabilities also must be secure. These technological requirements and technical challenges seem applicable for any large, globally distributed organisation. Meeting these objectives requires sophisticated technological and enhanced infrastructure. Some technical challenges like data capture are solvable, while some like security seem more intractable.

4.2 Organisational Challenges

Many organisations have become larger, global, and more bureaucratic. If these organisations want to effectively use real-time decision-support capabilities, managers must strive to make their organisations more agile and adaptive. Managers in these organisations must become more aware of speed and rapid response issues. Many bureaucratic organisations will need to undergo extensive changes to become agile and responsive. Such a change helps exploit real-time decision support. Also, many current organisations are limited by insufficient data-gathering systems for real-time use, poor data-gathering processes, overlapping or poorly defined decision-making responsibilities, poorly managed information assets, poorly defined key performance indicators and weak management systems, including processes, policies, and procedures. Overcoming these weaknesses requires changes in processes, leadership, and employee development. Moving into a real-time tactical decision-support environment involves restructuring organisational arrangements, retraining human resources, adjusting task priorities, and potentially making organisational culture changes.

4.3 Social/Psychological Challenges

Real-time decision support may increase information load and create social and psychological disruption for individuals and groups. Changing the attitudes of employees and the culture of the organisation and relations with customers, stakeholders and especially suppliers may be the major challenges to adopting real-time decision support. Managers need to gain support for change, deal with increased work-related stress, overcome resistance to change, understand training needs, provide rewards, develop incentive-based compensation, and recognise that real-time decision support may disrupt relationships. People have social expectations about how organisations can or must operate, like the need for a change in chain of command and direct superior/subordinate relations that can be altered with real-time decision support. People, work groups, and stakeholders need to learn positive coping behaviours to deal with the ambiguity, the changed interpersonal dynamics, the varied responses of family and co-workers, and the "work fast" cultural changes that are likely to occur.

5 Conclusions

Real-time decision support has many new uses in organisations, even where it has been hard to implement for technological reasons. Today, because technological has improved, historical expectations for supporting decision-making seem more realistic. In general, real-time technologies for supporting decision making will continue to improve and become more sophisticated. This change in technological utilisation will be disruptive of traditionally accepted behaviours, organisational structures, industries, and interpersonal relationships. Some organisations will receive few benefits from real-time decision support, while others will achieve very significant competitive benefits. From my vantage point, I observe that individuals using social computing are demonstrating the value and addiction of real-time communication and computing. Increasing economic complexity and the existence of large, global organisations create a need to exploit this technological to develop more real-time information and DSS in organisations.

When is real-time decision support desirable and needed? First, real-time decision support is desirable when the decision maker and the organisation are likely to benefit. The benefit may be faster response to customer requests or to competitor actions. Second, real-time decision support improves understanding in a situation without creating information overload. Third, the support must be cost effective. The anticipated benefits must justify the investment in new technologies. Fourth, real-time information needs to "make a difference" and it must accurately reflect what is happening in the decision situation. Finally, real-time decision support and data analysis are definitely important for some operational decisions.

We are seeing the "dawn of the real-time enterprise" (Margulius 2002). In general, organisational activities will continue to be performed at a faster speed; product time horizons and lead times for inputs and outputs will continue to contract; products and services will change more frequently; customers will expect rapid responses to problems and questions; and information technological will support complex interorganisational relationships across time and space. For some managers, the stress will lead to burnout; for others, the changes will create opportunities, invigorate them, and validate their visions. The potential benefits of a real-time enterprise include faster response, improved efficiency, and reduced costs.

Best-in-class organisations need to be prepared for a disruptive technological that threatens a firm's competitive position or marketplace (Baldridge Quality Award criterion, www.baldrige21.com). A recent example of such a technological is the personal computer that replaced the typewriter. To cope with the potential disruption, organisations need to be scanning the environment inside and outside their immediate industry to detect such challenges at the earliest possible point in time. Real-time decision support, especially using a personal digital device like the smart phone, is a disruptive technological.

Challenges exist in implementing real-time decision support. Workplaces will change when employees receive text messages or visual directions to assist in action taking. Using more video communication and even virtual world technologies will change employee behaviours. Data that is available on demand or automatically pushed to employees will be part of an organisation's operational system. To meet the technical, organisational, and social/psychological challenges of real-time decision support, organisations need knowledgeable, entrepreneurial leadership. Many current firms will not prosper in an information-rich, real-time decision support environment.

Acknowledgment My views on real-time decision support benefited from the email comments of Marc Demarest, Nigel Pendse, Neil Raden, and Ron Swift. The material in this chapter is derived from columns in *DSS News*.

References

Batty, P., Technical challenges for real-time spatial systems, *Tech Time*, September, posted on: 9/1/2004, URL = http://www.geoplace.com.

Davis, S. and C. Meyer, *BLUR: The Speed of Change in the Connected Economy*. New York: Perseus Books, 1998.

Hatch, D., Operational BI: Getting 'real time' about performance, *Intelligent Enterprise*, January 28, 2008, URL = http://www.intelligententerprise.com/showChapter.jhtml?articleID=205920233, retrieved on 2008-09-03.

Margulius, D.L., Dawn of the real-time enterprise, *Infoworld*, January 17, 2002 URL = http://www.infoworld.com.

Masters, M. and L.R. Welch, Challenges for Building Complex Real-time Computing Systems, URL = http://www.nitrd.gov/subcommittee/sdp/vanderbilt/position_papers/michael_masters_challenges _for_building.pdf, retrieved on 2008-09-03.

Power, D., What is 'real-time' decision support? *DSS News*, Vol. 3, No. 24, November 24, 2002, URL = http://dssresources.com/faq/index.php?action=artikel&id=31, retrieved 2008-10-29.

Power, D., When is 'real-time' decision support desirable and needed? *DSS News*, Vol. 3, No. 25, December 8, 2002, URL = http://dssresources.com/faq/index.php?action=artikel&id=32, retrieved 2008-10-29.

Power, D., Interview: Ron swift comments on decision support and CRM, DSSResources. COM, posted11/07/2003, URL = http://dssresources.com/interviews/swift/swift11072003.html, retrieved 2008-10-29.

Power, D., How does organization level impact decision support? *DSS News*, Vol. 9, No. 16, August 10, 2008 URL = http://dssresources.com/faq/index.php?action=artikel&id=170, retrieved on 2008-09-03.

Power, D., What is operational business intelligence? *DSS News*, Vol. 9, No. 18, September 7, 2008, URL = http://dssresources.com/faq/index.php?action=artikel&id=174, retrieved 2008-10-29.

Power, D., What are challenges of real-time decision support? *DSS News*, Vol. 9, No. 22, November 2, 2008, URL = http://dssresources.com/faq/index.php?action=artikel&id=178174, retrieved 2008-11-04.

Thierauf, R.J., *Decision Support Systems for Effective Planning and Cont*rol. Englewood Cliffs: Prentice-Hall, Inc., 1982.

Violino, B., Operational BI: Digging deeper for data, *CIO Insight*, 08-27-2008, URL = http://www.cioinsight.com/c/a/Strategic-Tech/Operational-BI-Digging-Deeper-for-Data/?kc=CIOMINUTE09032008CIO1, retrieved on 2008-09-03.

Watson, H.J., 2005, Real time: The next generation of decision-support data management, *Business Intelligence Journal*, September 15, 2005 URL = http://www.tdwi.org/Publications/BIJournal/display.aspx?ID=7667, retrieved 2009-07-06.

Chapter 2
Improvisation as Model for Real-Time Decision Making

Eric W. Stein

Penn State Great Valley School of Graduate Professional Studies, Malvern, PA, USA

Abstract This work explores the concept of improvisation as a framework for understanding real-time dynamic decision making (RTDDM) and systems support for it. The contexts for RTDDM and those in which agents improvise are remarkably similar according to several parameters. The foundations of improvisation are built on management theory, practice, and education. The work provides a rich definition of improvisation and a typology of different improvisational contexts based on two key dimensions. This framework illustrates how seemingly diverse contexts such as emergency management and jazz performance are related. The work then explores the antecedents of improvisation, degrees of improvisation, the elements for individual and team improvisation, and effective improvisation. The work then explores the design of Real-Time dynamic decision support systems (DSS). These are broken into pre- and postperformance support, as well as Real-Time support. The conclusion is that our knowledge of improvisational contexts can shed new light on RTDDM systems design and development.

Keywords Real-time dynamic decision making • Improvisation • Jazz • Decision support systems

1 Introduction and Research Objectives

The purpose of this research is to apply emerging models of organisational improvisation to better understand Real-Time decision making and explore the implications for the design of decision support systems (DSS). Real time in this case is defined as decisions that must be made within seconds or minutes. As will be shown, improvisation

E.W. Stein (✉)
Penn State Great Valley School of Graduate Professional Studies,
Malvern, PA, USA
e-mail: ews3@psu.edu

F. Burstein et al. (eds.), *Supporting Real Time Decision-Making*,
Annals of Information Systems 13, DOI 10.1007/978-1-4419-7406-8_2,

and Real-Time decision making are inter-related concepts and contexts. Improvisation has often been likened to a "conversation." This distinction has implications for the design of DSS to support Real-Time decision making in context. Unlike systems that deliver pre-planned routines, knowledge and scripts, helping decision makers to respond to situations in real time by engaging in improvisational behaviours and "conversations" requires different design principles and information systems with different features. Systems must deliver Real-Time information and knowledge to decision makers to support a range of problem-solving behaviours. Our goal is to flesh out these specifications by looking at this problem from the vantage point of the literature on improvisation.

There are several objectives to this work. Specifically:

- To discuss the real-time dynamic decision making (RTDDM) support context and the relationship of improvisation to RTDDM,
- To discuss the history of research in organisational and team improvisation and the definition of improvisation,
- To introduce a framework that classifies improvisational contexts according to problem structure and magnitude of consequences (MoC),
- To discuss the antecedents of improvisational behaviours and degrees of improvisation,
- To define the concept of performance,
- To identify the elements necessary for effective individual and team improvisation, and
- To flesh out the unique design requirements necessary to support improvisational behaviors and conversations.

I begin with a discussion of the relationship between Real-Time decision making and improvisation, and then discuss the elements of improvisation in greater depth.

2 Real-Time Dynamic Decision Making Contexts and the Relationship with Improvisation

The literature (e.g., Lerch and Harter 2001; referencing Brehmer 1990, 1992; Edwards 1962) suggests that four primary factors define RTDDM contexts:

- Tasks require a series of decisions,
- Decisions are interdependent,
- The environment changes autonomously and as a result of the decisions taken by members, and
- Decisions are made in real time.

Let us contextualise these parameters in the context of a fighter pilot engaged in evasive action as he or she makes decisions regarding the flight path of the aircraft. To begin with, the task environment requires a series of decisions, many of which have been pre-programmed. These decisions are interdependent, i.e., each choice leads to other choices processing down a decision tree. As decisions are selected, the hostile craft may change direction in response, thus changing the texture of the environment.

The pilot (along with the on-board computer systems) makes decisions in real time, i.e., in the fraction of a second. As can be seen, all conditions for RTDDM are met in this context.

Interestingly enough, we do not typically think of the pilot as improvising. We describe the evasion in terms of procedures and "expertise." Yet, the pilot must modify the "script" to respond to Real-Time changes in the environment. It can be shown that improvisation and Real-Time decision making are inter-related constructs, and that improvisational contexts meet the requirements proposed above.

Let us take another example that clearly is an improvisational context: a jazz group. Jazz musicians begin together and end together, but in between, they modify the key parameters that define the "song" (e.g., melody, harmony, rhythm); in short, they improvise. Is a jazz performance a case of RTDDM? Table 1 clearly indicates that this is the case, going by an application of the criteria proposed by Lerch and Harter (2001).

As can be seen above, all the criteria are met. Jazz musicians execute choices in real time in the fraction of a second during a solo performance. The choice of notes and rhythms influences and is influenced by the other members of the group. Interestingly, the quality of the performance is determined by elements that are recognisable by the audience interspersed with elements that are surprising or unpredictable. Although it may not seem so to someone new to the art form, the experimentation that occurs during performance is not random but is based on underlying patterns and themes that are a part of the immediate context as well as the broader context of jazz music (we will discuss this issue in greater depth in the next section). One difference, however, between jazz contexts and other Real-Time contexts (e.g., emergency management) is that environmental changes during a jazz performance are almost always internal (e.g., actions taken by the performers) and rarely external (e.g., a failed microphone, an earthquake). During emergency management situations on the other hand, external changes in the environment (i.e., events) are frequent and expected.

Furthermore, as an instance of RTDDM, jazz can be further described in terms of the task framework provided by Lerch and Harter (2001). They argue that RTDDM contexts can be characterised in terms of the clarity of the goals, task

Table 1 Improvisation as an instance of RTDDM

RTDDM	Improvisation - jazz example
Tasks require a series of decisions	Yes. Team must decide what tune to play, its style, the tempo, the order of soling, etc.
Decisions are inter-dependent	Yes. As each player performs, he or she is influenced by the choice of notes (courses of action) by other players
The environment changes autonomously and as a result of the decisions made by members	Yes. Each player can interject new musical events at any time during performance, forcing the other players to respond (internal change)
Decisions are made in real time	Yes. Each performance is completed within minutes. At a tempo of 120 beat/min., notes are chosen at the rate of 0.125–0.5/s

Table 2 RTDDM task parameters applied to jazz context

RTDDM task parameter	Improvisation - jazz example
Clarity of goal	Goal is clear: produce a quality performance. Measures of success include audience/client feedback, communication between members, error detection/correction during or after performance.
Structure of task	Task is structured by referent and norms of performance mitigated by familiarity of members with each other and experience in task.
Task complexity	Complexity is variable depending on underlying referent and experience of players. Causal relationships are fairly well understood by experienced members.
Level of uncertainty	Uncertainty is a function of the experience of the members, familiarity, training, availability of referents (e.g., SOPs), and audience.
Time pressure	Notes are typically chosen at the rate of 0.125–0.5/s and even faster in some cases.

structure, task complexity, level of uncertainty, and time pressure. Table 2 elaborates the Real-Time decision-making aspects of a jazz performance in terms of this framework.

The conclusion we can draw from the preceding framework suggests that improvisation is an instance of RTDDM. In keeping with the alignment of these contexts, the goal of this chapter is to re-interpret RTDDM in light of the rich body of knowledge that has emerged regarding the concept of improvisation. Put another way, we can use the rich descriptions of improvisation and improvisational contexts (e.g., jazz performances; emergency management situations) to obtain new insights into RTDDM and how to design systems support for it.

In the next section, we discuss the nature of improvisation in greater detail.

3 Towards a Shared Understanding of Improvisation

3.1 *History of Interest in Improvisation*

Despite the appeal of Peter Drucker's (1985) view of the organisation as a "symphony" and leaders as "conductors," there has emerged a sense that organisations rarely follow the "score." Organisations sometimes operate as places of rationality, scripts, and routines, but this is not true in every context. They frequently improvise to manage and capitalise on changing conditions and needs. As environmental complexity (i.e., multiple stakeholders) and the velocity of change have increased (Huber 1984), interest in improvisation has grown.

We see the penetration of the concept of improvisation in several areas of the management literature including management theory, management practice, and education (see Fig. 1).

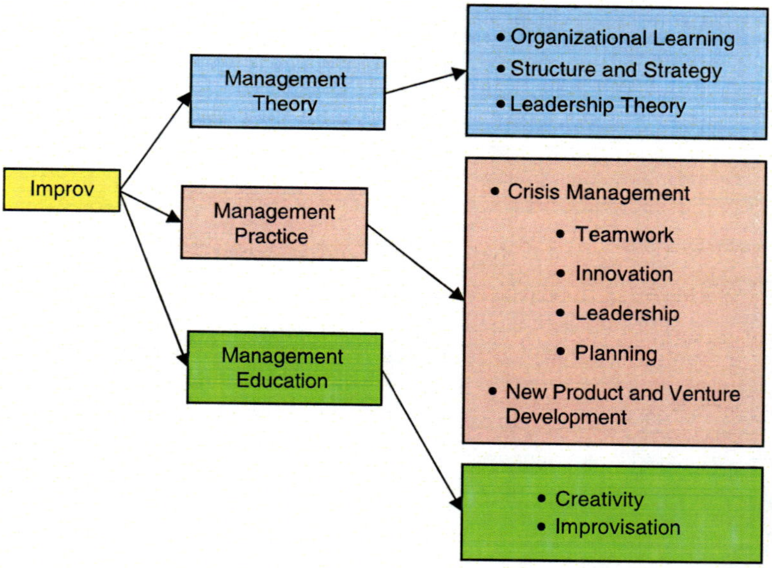

Fig. 1 Emphasis of improvisation in the management literature

A major milestone for research in organisational improvisation occurred at the Academy of Management (AoM) meeting held in 1995 in Vancouver. A special event was organised by Hatch, Barrett, and Havlovic of the AoM 1995 LAC to explore the use of jazz as a metaphor for understanding organisation and improvisation. The interest generated at this meeting motivated several research studies which, in 1998, resulted in a special issue of *Organization Science* devoted to organisational improvisation. Since then, a stream of articles has poured into the literature on issues ranging from organisation to product innovation to systems design, e.g., Zack (2000), Kamoche and Miguel Pina e Cunha (2001), McKnight and Bontis (2002), and Morazzoni (2005) to name a few.

3.2 Defining Improvisation

Some common definitions of improvisation include:

- To invent, compose, or perform something extemporaneously,
- To improvise music, and
- To make do with whatever materials are at hand.

The roots of the idea come from the Latin derivative "proviso" which means to stipulate beforehand or to foresee. "Im" means "not", i.e., the negation. Hence, the word *improvisation* can be interpreted to mean *unforeseen* or to take action in the moment.

This notion dovetails with the ideas of Real-Time decision making and making decisions "on the move" and fits nicely with the theme of this book. Quoting Berliner, Weick writes:

> Improvisation involves reworking pre-composed material and designs in relation to unanticipated ideas conceived shaped and transformed under the special conditions of performance, thereby adding unique features to every creation
>
> Berliner (1994, p. 241)

Or, put another way by Barrett (1998): "Improvisation involves exploring, continual experimenting, tinkering with possibilities without knowing where one's queries will lead or how action will unfold" (p. 606).

Furthermore, the sometimes mistaken notion that during improvisation, the decision maker simply makes things up in the moment without rigor or structure is inaccurate; many would argue that nothing could be further from the truth:

> The popular definitions of improvisation that emphasise only its spontaneous, intuitive nature…are astonishingly incomplete. This simplistic understanding belies the discipline and experience on which improvisers depend, and it obscures the actual practices and processes that engage them. Improvisation depends… on thinkers having absorbed a broad base of… knowledge, including myriad conventions that contribute to formulating ideas logically, cogently, and expressively.
>
> Berliner (1994, p. 492 cited by Weick)

In order to be able to respond effectively in context, the improviser must have at his or her disposal sets of routines and packets of knowledge that roughly match that context. In other words, "you can't improvise on nothing; you got to improvise on something" (C. Mingus appearing in Kernfeld 1995, p. 119 as cited by Weick 1998). A decision is made then to modify the routines to fit the novel conditions that exist for a given situation.

Making effective decisions in real time requires the decision maker (DM) to make sense of what is being communicated by others straight off and to self-reflect (or hear) the words and behaviors of the DM himself or herself. Weick refers to this as retrospective sense making. The latter requires the ability to self-monitor and listen to one's own voice. It also requires extensive memory to assess resources and make choices. "If you are not affected and influenced by your own notes [or ideas] when you improvise then you're missing the whole point" (Konitz, cited in Berliner 1994, p. 193 as cited by Weick 1998).

Finally, improvisation is *process oriented* as opposed to *output oriented.* This distinction is made clear by comparing improvisation to innovation. Although Drucker defines innovation as change that results in new levels of performance (1985), he is referring to the outputs of such change (e.g., the creation of goods or services) rather than to the performance itself. Luecke and Katz (2003, p. 2) clarify this idea of innovation: "Innovation is the embodiment, combination, or synthesis of knowledge in original, relevant, valued new products, processes, or services." Improvisation, on the other hand, focuses on the quality of the performance of the agents (and the resultant outcomes) as opposed to the artifacts that they may use or create.

3.3 A Typology of Improvisational Contexts

We see examples of improvisation in many different fields ranging from music to business to medicine. In Table 3, we outline several areas of activity aligned with improvisation. We contrast this with *design* or *composition*. The latter are non-Real-Time decision-making contexts that result in the creation of ideas, activities, and artifacts. Design and improvisation are related by output but differentiated by process.

There are many types of improvisational contexts as illustrated above. We can differentiate contexts by classifying them according to one or more underlying dimensions. Such classification can be done from a variety of perspectives; however, I have chosen two dimensions that provide a useful first cut at delineating the various seemingly disparate types of improvisation. Again, this classification is a starting point, and further subdivision will be the subject of future research.

The two dimensions identified for the initial typology are: (a) the degree of structure of the problem space and (b) the degree of risk of actions taken, where risk is defined as the likelihood of outcomes that bear consequences for direct recipients and other stakeholders. For example, in jazz, the recipient is the listener. In health care, the recipient is the patient and his or her family.

Simon (1960) defined the degree of structure of the problem space (e.g., structured to unstructured) to evaluate different problem-solving contexts, a framework that was subsequently used by Gorry and Morton (1971) to categorise DSS. Structure in this case refers to the degree to which the problem-solving domain can be conceptualised and the procedures, methods, and decision aids that can be developed to support the decision maker. For example, frequently performed surgical procedures tend to become structured problem spaces over time as the surgery is refined and standards evolve. On the other hand, administering an experimental new drug is considered a low-structure context as limited experiential knowledge is available to the decision makers.

The second dimension, outcome risk, is referred to as the MoC by theorists in the study of business ethics. MoC is a component of moral intensity as defined by

Table 3 Areas recognised for improvisation

Area	Sub-area	Design (Composition)	Improvisational Behaviours
Performing arts	Music	Classical	Jazz music
	Theatre	Opera	Improve theatre
	Dance	Ballet	Jazz dance
	Comedy	Comedy shows	Improve comedy
Visual arts	Art	Finished works of art	Doing art studies, sketches
Literary arts		Novels, poems, essays	Telling stories
Engineering		Buildings, products	Building models
Management		New product development, e.g., iPod	Responding to crisis, e.g., Tylenol; problem solving
Medicine		Routine surgical procedures or protocols	"Unexpected" and complex surgeries

Table 4 Typology of improvisational contexts

Structure	**Hi**	**High structure/low risk** Examples: Traditional jazz music Business simulations	**High structure/high risk** Examples: Surgical procedures Military operations
	Lo	**Low structure/low risk** Examples: "Free" jazz music Free form brainstorming	**Low structure/high risk** Examples: Emergency management Fixing the world financial system
		Lo	**Hi**
		Magnitude of consequences	

Jones (1991). MoC captures the notion that actions that result in more severe consequences (e.g., death, dismemberment, etc.) are deemed to have higher moral intensity, all other things being equal. MoC is defined as "… the sum of the harms (or benefits) done to victims (or beneficiaries) of the moral act in question" (Jones 1991, p. 374).

Improvisational contexts may be delineated by these two dimensions, thus giving rise to the following typology (see Table 4).

The four quadrants allow us to categorise different improvisational contexts. For example, traditional jazz music is considered a high structure, low-risk context. Traditional jazz (e.g., Dixieland) has a well-defined set of rules and structures that define the music within which the improviser can take liberties. This is contrasted with "free jazz" that minimises most structures for the performer. For the audience, this is the most challenging type of jazz to listen to and requires the most active interpretation and sense making. Both are considered low risk in that the consequences of a poor choice are minimal. While it may result in embarrassment to the performer and some dismay on the part of the listeners, these "damages" are temporary and easily recovered. Other low-risk environments include most forms of the performing arts (although dance could result in physical injury), the visual and literary arts (although inflammatory material can carry civil and criminal penalties), and simulations used in business, engineering, and health care. Lower MoC contexts encourage decision makers to take risks of increasing magnitude and to push the envelope of what is "expected." We see this occurring in jazz on a frequent basis.

High-risk environments are typical in business, medicine, and engineering practices such as emergency management, crisis management, complex surgical procedures, and logistics. In these cases, poor decisions can result in physical, psychological, and financial harms to one or more stakeholders (Stein and Ahmad 2009). Although some high-risk contexts such as doing complex surgeries or executing a military mission benefit from a fair degree of problem structure, they are nonetheless risky. The biggest problem oftentimes here is the variance in the characteristics of the recipient, e.g., the patient.

High-risk contexts typically constrain decision makers who will be more cautious and attempt to rely on existing routines. This is typical when doing complex surgical procedures. The surgeon and his or her team adhere to well-constructed protocols and routines; deviation is not desirable. This type of improvisation is different, becoming the "flexible treatment of pre-planned material" (Weick 1998 quoting Berliner 1994, p. 400).

However, in the absence of routines and conditions of high MoC, the decision maker must perform under the most trying conditions and may be forced to take more risks by necessity. Indeed, evidence suggests that some DMs will fail in these contexts, i.e., overcome by the MoC and unable to control feelings of panic, some manage in crises and some do not. Decision makers may be forced to improvise given a deficit of knowledge or experience or both.

3.4 Antecedents of Improvisation

There are several antecedent conditions that lead to opportunities for improvisation. These include but are not limited to:

- Unexpected problems,
- New or revised goals,
- Changes in the structure of the problem space,
- Changes in the environment, and
- Knowledge limitations.

Problems that emerge unexpectedly can trigger improvisational behaviors by the agents. The case of Apollo 13 dramatically illustrates the role of antecedent conditions. The explosion in the fuel line of the spacecraft sent the crew and ground support group into a frenzy of improvised problem solving. In Table 5, we see how the values of these factors changed.

At the onset, the explosion imposed severe time constraints on the agents because the lives of the crew depended on swift diagnosis and treatment. The structure of the problem space abruptly changed from "routine" to "novel" because of the unspecified damage to the ship. There were now limited structures or routines available to help the agents. The state of the agents' knowledge went from relatively complete to incomplete. Agents now found themselves in a turbulent environment (Emery and Trist 1965) of multiple interconnected problems. Goals were quickly revised from mission duties such as research and data collection to survival. Agents thus went from performing a relatively routine set of activities to a mode of improvisation in order to survive. Very quickly, the crew and ground support

Table 5 Illustration of the change in antecedent conditions in case of Apollo 13

Condition	Before	After
Unexpected problems	None	Numerous
Structure of the problem space	Well known	Limited structures or routines
New or revised goals	No	Yes
The environment	Stable	Turbulent
Knowledge limitations	Well-articulated base of knowledge	Limited or no knowledge by agents
Constraints	Within range	Time and resource constrains

diagnosed the problem and crafted a strategy to deal with it. In general, they developed new solutions based on existing knowledge and constructed hypotheses on the spot; they had no choice.

Although transitions from high-structure/high-risk situations to low-structure/high-risk contexts rarely occur so dramatically in more down-to-earth settings, there is considerable variation in terms of the degree of improvisation over the course of a performance. In other words, whether the context changes or not, the degree of improvisation is not static and may change over a given time period (i.e., during performance).

In the next section, we discuss degrees of improvisation in response to changes in antecedent conditions as well as throughout a given performance when agents change goals.

3.5 Degrees of Improvisation

At its simplest level, improvisation is a set of design or problem-solving behaviours that involve the modification of a *referent*. A referent is declarative knowledge, procedural knowledge, a representation or schema that guides and constrains an improviser's choices. For example, a referent can be a score or a set of procedures, routines, or scripts. In business, it can be a standard operating procedure (*SOP)*; in medicine, a *protocol*; and in music, a *score*.

To be clear, when we discuss improvisational behaviors, we refer to a set of behavioral types, not a single behavioral type. There is considerable difference between what is referred to as an "improvisation" in one context versus another. Those differences are a consequence of the degree to which the referent is modified by the improviser.

Thus, improvisation can be classified by the amount of variation of the referent. Although these variations properly fall on a continuum, we can discern at least five different categories along that continuum (see Fig. 2):

- Replication (i.e., no improvisation),
- Interpretation,
- Embellishment,
- Variation, and
- Improvisation (i.e., full improvisation).

Replication is the opposite of improvisation, i.e., there is no change in the referent. Replication is just a simple copying of the original with all its structural and functional features intact. *Interpretation* involves subtle changes to the referent. This is evidenced by conductors who interpret a work by Bach or Mozart. The score or "instruction set" is given and meant to be replicated but with slight stylistic changes by the orchestra leader, thus giving rise to a characteristic sound of a particular orchestra, e.g., the Philadelphia Orchestra under Eugene Ormandy. *Embellishment* is an active and purposive act of changing the referent, but within well-defined

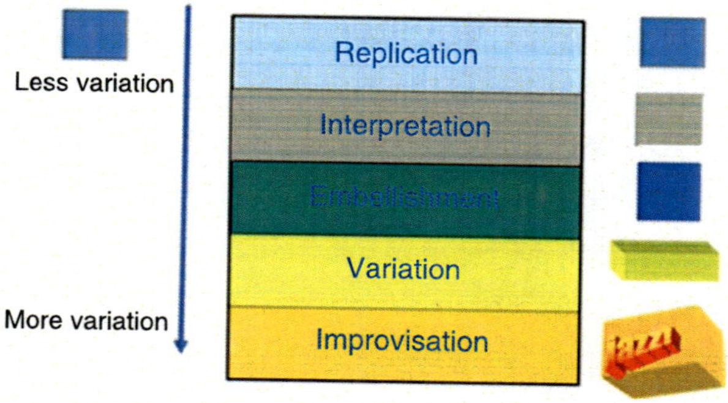

Fig. 2 Degrees of improvisation

boundaries imposed by the genre. Embellishments typically enhance the major qualities of the referent by reinforcing them and accentuating them, rather than diminishing them. A cartoonist or storyteller embellishes to highlight certain features of the image or storyline. A *variation* is an active modification of the original referent to achieve a certain result. The variation may accent certain features and diminish others all the while keeping the identity and coherence of the original form. Finally, *improvisation* allows the agent to modify all structural and functional features of the referent under certain guidelines imposed by the domain. In jazz music, these are the rules of harmony and rhythm. The improviser is careful to make modifications that still retain the outline and identify of the original, even if those boundaries are tenuous. The difference between staying "in" or going "out" in jazz is a measure of how far the improviser strays from the referent. In emergency management situations, the improviser is still aware of key social and technical rules and boundaries that constrain choices as modifications are made to procedures and routines.

In the next section, I discuss the meaning of performance and how the degree of improvisation may change over the course of a performance.

3.6 Performance and the Episodic Nature of Improvisation

A *performance* happens in a finite period of time, during which a set of agents execute a sequence of actions. In music, this would include the beginning, middle, and end of a concert piece or song. In an emergency management (EM) context, it would be the onset of the crisis, containment, and the transition to a noncrisis or routine state.

Performances are situated in time between an *initialisation* phase and an *epilogue* phase. In the initialisation phase, members agree on a referent and other parameters of performance. The epilogue phase occurs at the completion or near completion of the performance. The epilogue is the final opportunity for new ideas, modification of referent, or closing pattern. In music, this is referred to as a *cadenza*. See Fig. 3.

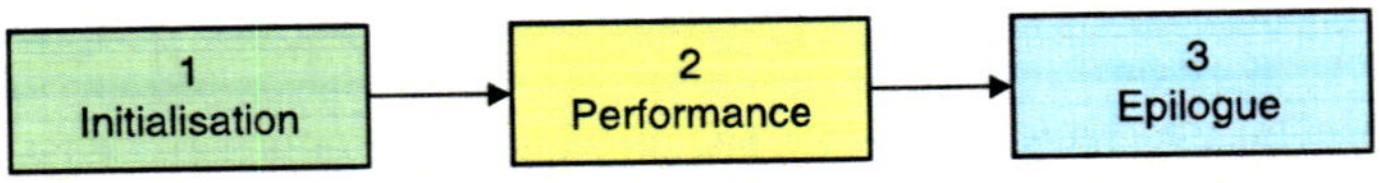

Fig. 3 The performance context

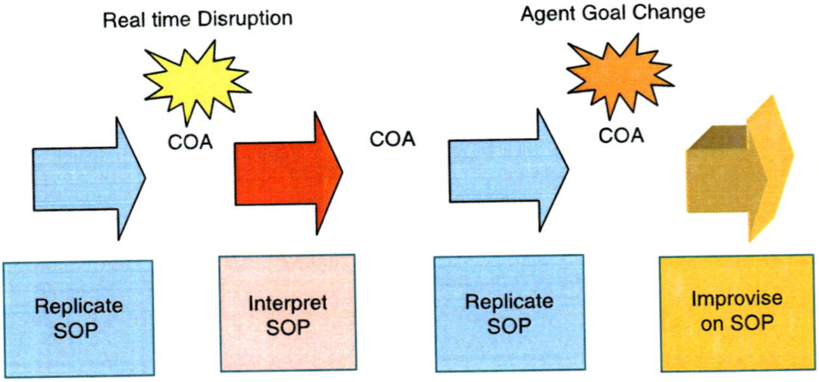

Fig. 4 Episodic nature of improvisation during performance in problem-solving contexts

Within a typical performance, there are usually three subsections. Initially, there is a starting pattern based on the referent. Next is the improvisation section. real-time changes are made to referent as antecedent conditions warrant or as the goals of the agents change. Typically, the performance returns to some restatement of the referent or underlying pattern; the latter provides a sense of coherence.

Each performance is thus a unique *realisation* of the referent. The performance may contain episodes of improvisation alternating with the performance of scripts and routines based on changes in the conditions or the goals of the agents. See Fig. 4.

3.7 *Elements Necessary for Individual and Team Improvisation*

To summarize what has been suggested in the previous sections, we identify the elements necessary for individuals and teams to engage in improvisational behaviors. See Table 6.

3.8 *Improvising Effectively*

In order to improvise effectively, the team must have cultivated several skills, abilities, and conditions (see Table 7).

Table 6 Necessary elements for individual and team improvisation

Element	Description
Goals	Goals are selected to respond to antecedent conditions
Agents	One or more agents
	Agents are brought together to achieve goals, e.g., perform a musical piece; contain an emergency situation; perform a surgical operation
	Each agent must possess knowledge of the task and of the norms that govern team behaviour
	Each agent accepts risk and uncertainty of task setting
Set of COAs	Agents will choose appropriate courses of action (COAs) from available set to meet goals
Referents	A *referent* is a cognitive tool that constrains the task and COAs
	In music, it is the harmony or score. In organisations, routines, SOPs
Opportunity to Perform	Each "performance" is a *realisation* or variation of the referent that is unique to that situation

Table 7 Cultivating effective improvisation

Element	Description
Ability to communicate	Improvisation in a team is a conversation
	Requires excellent listening skills
	Agents must have a "vocabulary" of "words/phrases" to communicate
Relationships of trust	Agents must trust each other to promote free and open communication
Ability to self-monitor	Requires ability to self-monitor and listen to self, i.e., engage in retrospective and real-time sense making (Weick 1998; Berliner 1994)
Knowledge base	Agents must have complementary bases of knowledge and expertise
	Agents must share a common base of knowledge related to task environment
	Requisite variety of knowledge helps handle discontinuities
Working memory	Agents need extensive working and/or external memory to perform
Leadership	Each team has a de facto leader
	Leadership may be temporarily shared amongst the group members during performance
Client/recipient awareness	Members of the team must be aware of the unique characteristics of the client/recipient and tailor responses and procedures, accordingly.

To begin with, the team should have developed effective communication capabilities. Effective communication is defined as communication that produces the intended effect in the recipient, not just simply sending the message from one point to the next (Tagiuri 1972, 1993). For example, effective communication requires excellent listening skills and the members of the team should have developed a vocabulary of words, phrases, and ideas specific to the domain, to establish meaningful conversations. In jazz music, these are the note sequences that fit specific harmonic structures. In surgery, it would be the vocabulary that identifies the tools, methods, and aspects of human anatomy that intersect during complex tasks.

The second requirement is that the members of the team must trust each other. This is absolutely critical. Trust is a key aspect of team and organisational performance (e.g., Six and Sorge 2008) and especially so in Real-Time decision making contexts. Third, the members of the team must be able to self-monitor. As was stated earlier, "If you are not affected and influenced by your own (notes) when you improvise then you're missing the whole point" (Weick 1998, using Konitz cited in Berliner 1994, p. 193). Self-reflection in real time is also key. While engaged in conversation with other members of the team, the agent must also listen to himself or herself speak the vocabulary of the domain as the interaction unfolds and make modifications accordingly. Fourth, the team must possess a base of common knowledge specific to the domain as well as other referent domains. This knowledge guides and constrains the choice of "permitted" courses of action selected by the team. Fifth, the team must have at its disposal both in context memory (i.e., memory of the earlier parts of the current performance) and of previous performances.

Sixth, the members of the team may rotate and share leadership throughout the performance. For instance, when jazz groups perform, there is a "passing of the baton" of leadership from one member to the next as each soloist takes his or her turn. The transition from one to the next is swift and effortless. Shared leadership allows each member to perform at his or her highest level of ability, while alternating between "sideman" to featured "soloist." Together, these factors drive teams to be effective in their improvisations. On the other hand, it should be pointed out that most groups have a *de facto* leader, and although leadership may temporarily shift during performance, the primary leader may assume control at any point during, preceding, and following the performance. This understanding is implicit amongst the members.

Finally, the team must tailor the performance to the unique characteristics (and limitations) of the client or recipient. In jazz music, this is relatively trivial (i.e., the performers must take into account the responses of the audience, who may boo or usher the performers off the stage). In health care, this is of crucial importance and can mean the difference between success and failure. Although all patients are human beings of a certain age and gender, the variance between patients of a given class may be significant, based on different life-styles and environmental factors. The "performers" must, therefore, adapt existing routines to match the unique characteristics of a given individual.

4 Implications for Real-Time Dynamic Decision Support Systems (DSS)

DSS continue to represent an important part of IS research and practice (Burstein and Holsapple 2008). The concept of improvisation as "conversation" and other qualifying conditions that have been identified in this work have implications for the design of DSS that support Real-Time decision-making in context. Conventional (i.e., nonReal-Time) DSS typically deliver data and preplanned routines, knowledge, and scripts to decision makers. Many Real-Time decision systems (RTDS) are designed for semiautonomous control systems that serve to assist or replace human operators (Seguin, Potvin, Gendreau, Crainic, and Marcotte 1997). We suggest an alternative set of design specifications, i.e., we want to help human decision-making teams to respond to situations in real time by engaging in improvisational behaviors and "conversations." This goal requires different design principles and information systems with different features. In short, we want to support *performances* as opposed to just tasks. We break requirements into pre-performance, performance, and post-performance support components.

4.1 Pre-performance Support

Contrary to common thought, improvisers from Second City comics to jazz musicians train extensively to provide them with the facility to create in real time. This paradox of preparation to enable more freedom is not widely understood. However, when a surgical team improvises out of necessity, we instinctively understand the role and importance of prior experience and knowledge. In light of this need, we identify several design requirements. See Table 8.

This pre-performance support component has many aspects of a learning management system (e.g., Yueh and Hsu 2008; Lytras and Pouloudi 2006; Hall and Paradice 2005). We see the system providing support for extensive learning drills and preparation in the procedures of the domain. Easy access to videos and other multimedia illustrations by domain experts will be very useful. Simulations in a variety of contexts would also prepare the user for several scenarios. Fast access to the declarative knowledge of the domain is also necessary for study and preparation, especially for newcomers. Finally, the pre-performance component should have a social networking feature like MySpace or LinkedIn to facilitate communications amongst users. This facility will increase trust and familiarity with current or potential team members. It also will be a means by which novices and peers learn from experts or other peers by cultivating a community of practice (Stein 2005).

Table 8 Pre-performance support

Support area	Support method
▪ Rehearsal support	▪ Drills and training methods and procedures
▪ Feed-forward	▪ Reviews of experts in similar contexts
▪ Domain learning	▪ Simulations
▪ Referent support	▪ Declarative knowledge libraries
▪ Trust	▪ Build trust of members through social networking

Table 9 Performance support

Support area	Emphasis	Support method
Referent support	Historical	▪ Libraries of routines, SOPs, scripts ▪ Decision tree logic libraries
Case support	Historical	▪ Histories of previous cases
Knowledge support	Historical	▪ Knowledge base of task domains
Supporting real-time sense making	Real time	▪ Real-Time data feeds and representations of current data according to task environment
Conversation analysis and support	Real time	▪ Natural Language (NL) processing of encoded conversation streams ▪ Detect and anticipate problem situations, errors ▪ Verbal cues, emotions ▪ Allow agents to issue verbal /non-verbal commands to system to execute tasks

4.2 *Performance Support*

The performance component of the support system must support the episodic nature of improvisation during the performance, i.e., it must support varying degrees of improvisation throughout the performance. See Table 9. See Table 9.

In support of relatively routine contexts where replication is the goal, making available libraries of patterns, routines, SOPs, and scripts will be useful. Other useful forms of external history-based support will include case support and a knowledge base of the task domain. Support for the Real-Time aspects of the performance include data feeds and representations of current data indicators, such as a Real-Time executive information system (e.g., Watson, Kelly Rainer Jr., and Koh 1991) or business intelligence system (e.g., Turban, Aronson, Liang, and Sharda 2007). The most important feature of the system will be an ability to analyse conversations of the team members and to make assumptions about changing needs. The system will utilise natural language (NL) processing of encoded conversation streams to detect and anticipate problem situations and errors. Verbal cues, emotions of the team members, and other verbal and nonverbal behavior analysis will be used. This feature is essential to anticipate the need of the team to move from executing routine procedures to higher degrees of improvisation. Because of the multitasking requirements of the team, the system should be able to respond to verbal/non-verbal commands issued by the members to execute commands and tasks.

4.3 *Post-performance Support*

The primary goal of post-performance support is to support retrospective sense making, reflection, after-action reviews, error analysis, and feedback. The consequences of these support features for the organisation and team are individual and organizational learning and memory (Stein 1995; Stein and Zwass 1995) (see Table 10).

Table 10 Post-performance support

Support area	Post-support type
▪ Retrospective sense making ▪ After-action reviews ▪ Error analysis ▪ Feedback	▪ Rich data and video capture of events ▪ Data on recipients and outcomes ▪ Templates for knowledge capture ▪ Records indexing to enable the review of event data to support after-action reviews, feedback, error analysis ▪ Social networking support ▪ Access to libraries of procedures and knowledge for comparison to actual

Many have stressed the importance of reflection (e.g., Garner 1993) and sense making (e.g., Weick 1998) to help people to learn and interpret prior experience. Members of Real-Time task teams need time to process the rich experiences they encounter in RTDDM contexts, in order to learn. Decision support should, therefore, include the use of rich media (e.g., video) to capture events for later review and reflection. Given the intensity of Real-Time situations, it is even likely that participants fail to remember details given a complete immersion in "flow" (Csikszentmihalyi 1991, 2000). Providing Real-Time capture of events is therefore critical. The data can then be used to support sense making, after-action reviews, and error analysis. These activities are indispensable to both individual and organizational learning. The provision of a social networking feature promotes social learning within the team and community of practice (Stein 2005). Finally, feedback on recipients and their outcomes (e.g., patients) is crucial for after-action learning.

4.4 Systems and Organisational Implications

While it is outside the scope of this work to articulate a full description of the system features, architectures, and organisational attributes required to support improvisation, we can summarise our general observations. As described above, the system will have the following features and components.

- Database component
  - Access to databases of declarative knowledge pertaining to the subject matter
  - Access to case histories
  - Access to SOPs, scripts, and decision trees
  - Access to rich media libraries that feature video clips and images of events, procedures, and interviews with content experts
- Social networking component
  - Facilitates networking with other professionals in and out of context
- Simulation component
  - Allows for trying out various "what-if" scenarios

- Training component
  - Supports repetitive training in methods and procedures with feedback
- Real-Time data component
  - Provides access to live data feeds on Real-Time events and news
  - Real-Time event capture
- Natural language-processing component
  - Real-Time analysis of actor conversations
  - Real-Time action-taking in response to verbal cues
- Learning and knowledge-management component
  - Provides a "scratch-pad" for agents to perform after-action reviews and make explicit learning from each event

Together, these components will provide a supportive environment for improvisational behaviours amongst the agents in context. Organisations that support the development of these systems will benefit from certain characteristics. Improvisation will likely flourish in the context of learning organisations (Argyris and Schon 1978). Learning organisations encourage knowledge testing and refinement. Agents in a learning organisation are relatively free of defensive routines and are simply motivated to serve clients more effectively over time. Clearly, more research is needed to flesh out the full range of organisational attributes that support improvisational behaviours.

5 Summary and Conclusions

Improvisation and RTDDM are inter-related concepts and contexts. Although emergency response teams and jazz groups do not seem to have much in common, they are, indeed, examples of teams operating in dynamic Real-Time choice environments. Dynamic Real-Time decision-making contexts are fluid,and the nature of problem solving around which decision support is built is both changeable and episodic.

What distinguishes one context from others is the structure of the problem space and most importantly, the MoC of the decision space. MoC is a construct defined by Jones (1991) to describe the impact of decision outcomes on external stakeholders in the realm of ethics. For instance, MoC clearly differentiates jazz contexts from emergency response contexts in terms of risk.

What they share, however, is the delivery of a *performance*. During performance, the degree of improvisation varies. We have shown that the degree of improvisation falls along a continuum, with at least five categories identified: replication – interpretation – embellishment – variation – improvisation. Periods of replication are punctuated with periods of improvisation based on changing conditions and revised goals of the team members. Agents are constantly slipping into and out of various contexts; so, it is not sufficient to simply characterise a team's performance as "by the book" or improvised; it is likely to contain elements of both.

The nature of improvisation has implications for the design of DSS. These requirements have been broken into pre-performance, performance, and post-performance specifications. The goal of pre-performance support is to provide access to declarative and procedural knowledge about the domain and to enable team members to sharpen their knowledge about the domain and train in skills required for the domain. Social learning is encouraged through features found in social networking sites. The goal during the performance phase is to support Real-Time information representation and to anticipate changes in the problem/decision context in both problem structure and MoC. Additional research is needed to explore the episodic nature of performance (i.e., RTDDM) as contexts change. Finally, the goal of the post-performance phase is to support retrospective sense making, learning, and the development of organisational memory (Stein 1995; Stein and Zwass 1995). Future research needs to be conducted to implement these ideas with the use of appropriate systems technologies.

Another area of future research is to explore the development of semi-autonomous agents that would (a) help recognise improvisational contexts and (b) intervene in improvisational contexts to increase the variety of choices and to help generate context-appropriate outcomes for team members.

References

Argyris, C. and D.A. Schon, *Organizational Learning: A Theory of Action Perspective*, Reading: Addision-Wesley, 1978.

Barrett, F. J., Creativity and improvisation in jazz and organizations: Implications for organizational learning, *Organization Science*, 9(5), 605–622, Sept–Oct, 1998.

Berliner, P., *Thinking in Jazz: The Infinite Art of Improvisation*, Chicago: University of Chicago Press, 1994.

Brehmer, B., Strategies in Real-Time, dynamic decision making, In R.M. Hogerth, ed., *Insights in Decision Making*, Chicago: University of Chicago Press, 1990, pp. 262–279.

Brehmer, B., Dynamic decision making: Human control of complex systems, *Acta Psychologica*, 81(3), 211–241, 1992.

Burstein, F. and C.W. Holsapple, New horizons at the core of information systems: Decision support system advances, *Information Systems and eBusiness Management*, 6(2), 109–115, 2008.

Csikszentmihalyi, M., *Flow: The Psychology of Optimal Experience*, New York: Harper Perennial, 1991.

Csikszentmihalyi, M., *Beyond Boredom and Anxiety: Experiencing Flow in Work and Play*, New York: Jossey-Bass, 2000.

Drucker, P., *Innovation and Entrepeneurship: Practice and Principles*, New York: Harper & Row, 1985.

Edwards, W., Dynamic decision theory and probabilistic information processing, *Human Factors*, 4, 59–73, 1962.

Emery, F. and E. Trist, The causal texture of organizational environments, *Human Relations*, 18, 21–32, 1965.

Garner, H., *Creating Minds: An Anatomy Of Creativity As Seen Through The Lives Of Freud, Einstein, Picasso, Stravinsky, Eliot, Graham, And Gandhi*, New York: Basic Books, 1993.

Gorry, A. and Morton, M.S.S. A framework for management information systems, *Sloan Management Review*, 13(1), 55–70, Fall, 1971, Massachusetts Institute of Technology.

Hall, D.J. and D. Paradice, Philosophical foundations for a learning-oriented knowledge management system for decision support, *Decision Support Systems*, 39(3), 445–461, 2005.

Huber, G.P., The nature and design of post-industrial organizations, *Management Science*, 30(8), 928–951, 1984.

Jones, T.M., Ethical decision making by individuals in organizations: An issue-contingent model, *The Academy of Management Review* 16(2), 366, 1991.

Kamoche, K. and Miguel Pina e Cunha, Minimal structures: From jazz improvisation to product innovation, *Organization Studies*, 22(5), 733, 2001, Berlin.

Lerch, F.J. and Harter, D.E., Cognitive support for Real-Time dynamic decision making, *Information Systems Research*, 12(1), 63–82, 2001.

Luecke, R. and R. Katz, *Managing Creativity and Innovation*. Boston: Harvard Business School Press, 2003.

Lytras, M.D. and A. Pouloudi, Towards the development of a novel taxonomy of knowledge management systems from a learning perspective: An integrated approach to learning and knowledge infrastructures, *Journal of Knowledge Management*, 10(6), 64–80, 2006.

McKnight, B. and N. Bontis, E-improvisation: Collaborative groupware technology expands the reach and effectiveness of organizational improvisation, *Knowledge and Process Management*, 9(4), 219, Oct–Dec 2002, Chichester.

Morazzoni, A.M., Challenging wisdom, *European Journal of Information Systems*, 14(5), 522, Dec 2005, Basingstoke.

Seguin, R., J.-Y. Potvin, M. Gendreau, T.G. Crainic, and P. Marcotte, Real time decision problems: An operational research perspective, *The Journal of the Operational Research Society*, 48(2), 162–174, 1997.

Special issue of *Organization Science*, 9(5), Sept–Oct, 1998.

Simon, H.A., *The New Science of Management Decision*. New York: Harper & Row, 1960.

Six, F. and A. Sorge, Creating a high-trust organization: An exploration into organizational policies that stimulate interpersonal trust building, *The Journal of Management Studies*, 45(5), 857, 2008.

Stein, E.W., Organizational memory: Review of concepts and recommendations for management, *International Journal of Information Management*, 15(1), 17–32, 1995.

Stein, E.W., A qualitative study of the characteristics of a community of practice for knowledge management (KM) and its success factors, *International Journal of Knowledge Management*, 1(3), 1–24, Jul–Sept 2005.

Stein, E.W and N. Ahmad, Using the analytical hierarchy process (AHP) to construct a measure of the magnitude of consequences component of moral intensity, *The Journal of Business Ethics*, 89,391–407, 2009.

Stein, E.W. and V. Zwass, Actualizing organizational memory with information technology, *Information Systems Research*, 6(2), 85–117, 1995.

Tagiuri, R., *On 'Good' Communication*, Boston: Harvard Business School Publishing, 1972, 1993, #9-475-013.

Turban, E., J. Aronson, T.P. Liang, and R. Sharda, *Decision Support and Business Intelligence Systems*. Upper Saddle River: Prentice Hall, 2007.

Watson, H.J., R. Kelly Rainer, Jr., and C.E. Koh, Executive information systems: A framework for development and a survey of current practices, *MIS Quarterly*, 15(1), 13, 1991.

Weick, K.E, Improvisation as a mindset for organizational analysis, *Organization Science*, 9(5), 540–545, Sept–Oct 1998.

Yueh, H.-P. and S. Hsu, "Designing a learning management system to support instruction," association for computing machinery, *Communications of the ACM*, 51(4), 59, 2008.

Zack, M.H., Jazz improvisation and organizing: Once more from the top, *Organization Science*, 11(2), 227, Mar/Apr 2000.

Part II
Tools and Technologies for Context-aware Real-Time Decision Support

Chapter 3
Context Prediction in Pervasive Computing Systems: Achievements and Challenges

Andrey Boytsov and Arkady Zaslavsky

Computer Science and Electrical Engineering Department, Luleå University of Technology, Sweden

Abstract Context awareness is one of the core principles of pervasive computing. Context prediction is also recognised as a challenge and an opportunity. Numerous approaches have been applied to resolve context prediction. This work develops and justifies the principles of analysis and comparison of context-prediction methods, analyses the development in the area, compares different context prediction techniques to identify their benefits and shortcomings, and, finally, identifies current challenges in the area and proposes the solutions.

Keywords Pervasive computing • Context awareness • Context prediction • Sequence prediction • Markov model • Bayesian network • Neural network • Branch prediction • Expert system.

1 Context and Context Prediction

Pervasive computing paradigm is a relatively recent approach where computing systems are integrated into everyday life and the environment in a transparent, graceful, and nonintrusive manner. An example of a pervasive computing system can be a smart home that adjusts lights and temperature in advance before the user enters the room, which increases the efficiency of energy and water consumption. Or, it can be an elderly care system that decides whether the user needs advice or assistance. Or, it can be a smart car that proposes the best route to the destination point, and that assesses its own condition and provides a maintenance plan. Many pervasive computing systems are now being introduced into our lives.

A. Boytsov (✉)
Computer Science and Electrical Engineering Department,
Luleå University of Technology, Sweden
e-mail: Andrey.Boytsov@ltu.se

F. Burstein et al. (eds.), *Supporting Real Time Decision-Making*,
Annals of Information Systems 13, DOI 10.1007/978-1-4419-7406-8_3,

One of the grounding principles of the pervasive computing system is context awareness. Earlier works on context and context awareness proposed numerous different definitions of the context. A. Dey and G. Abowd, writing in Dey and Abowd (2000), performed a comprehensive overview of those efforts. From now on, their definitions of context and context awareness will be used: "Context is any information that can be used to characterise the situation of an entity" (Dey and Abowd 2000). So, in fact, every piece of information a system has is a part of that system's context.

"A system is context-aware if it uses context to provide relevant information and/or services to the user, where relevancy depends on the user's task" (Dey and Abowd 2000). Or, in more simple words, the system is context-aware if it can use context to its benefit. Context awareness is one of the main principles of pervasive computing.

Reasoning about the context is the process of obtaining new information from the context. Context model, in that case, becomes an intuitively understandable term that can be formally defined as a way of context representation that is used for further reasoning. Context prediction, therefore, does not need any special definition and merely means the activities to predict future context information.

Context awareness and context prediction are relatively new areas. However, they already have some methods developed for reasoning about the context and prediction of the context.

Cook and Das (2004) give quite a comprehensive overview of the context prediction area with a focus on smart home environments and location prediction. Pichler, Bodenhofer, and Schwinger (2004) provide a context prediction overview, focusing on artificial intelligence-based techniques; they discuss not only the examples, but further possibilities as well. Ziebart, Maas, Dey, and Bagnell (2008) contains another context-prediction overview with the focus on user-behaviour modelling; Hong, Suh, Kim, and Kim (2009) focuses on user preferences, inference, and utilisation of the context history; Cook, Augusto, and Jakkula (2009) focuses on ambient intelligence systems; and Boytsov, Zaslavsky, and Synnes (2009) focuses on machine learning-based techniques. One of the most comprehensive works regarding the general approach to context prediction is Mayrhofer (2004), which is explained in more detail below.

2 Context Prediction Task

2.1 Context Prediction Task

Context awareness is one of the core features of any pervasive computing system. Context prediction is acknowledged as a challenge and an opportunity. Some works provide comprehensive lists of context prediction use case scenarios. Those use cases include (list partially based on Nurmi, Martin, and Flanagan 2005; Mayrhofer 2004):

1. Reconfiguration. Sometimes configuration-related tasks take a while to complete. This includes installation of updates, loading and unloading libraries, starting

new applications, processing the infrastructure changes related to node mobility, searching in large databases. If the system can predict the need for those tasks in advance, it can perform the work beforehand and avoid unnecessary delays. An application-specific example was presented in Mayrhofer (2004). When the key appears near upper-class BMW cars, the car predicts that it is going to be started and the on-board navigation system initiates boot-up. Therefore, when the user enters the car, the navigation system is already fully functional. Otherwise, it would have taken an extra 30s to complete.

2. Device power management. Devices that are unused and will not be used in the near future can be shut down or switched to sleep mode. There are other scenarios that fall under that category as well. For example Nurmi et al. (2005), if the user attempts to send a large multimedia message while in an area of bad radio reception, the system can predict that the user is going to enter a better reception area soon and will delay sending the message (thereby saving power).
3. Early warning of possible problems. Context prediction can determine whether the system is about to enter an unwanted state and act accordingly. For example, a pervasive system can predict that it is going to run out of memory or computation power soon and act proactively to counter that problem – for example, find the devices to share the computations, offload the data, and drop unnecessary applications. Or, for example, a pervasive system can predict that user is going to enter a traffic jam soon. In that case, the system can find a way around the traffic jam and provide it to the user before the traffic jam area is entered. Different cases of accident prevention also fall under the category of early warning of possible problems.
4. Planning aid. If a user's needs can be predicted, a pervasive system can meet them proactively. For example, an air conditioner in a smart home can be launched in advance to have a certain air temperature when the user returns from work. Or, in a smart office, the door can be opened just before the person enters.
5. Inferences on other's future contexts. User can actually be influenced by the future context of another user. For example Nurmi et al. (2005), a user may have confidential information on the screen. Therefore, when someone passes by, the screen should be hidden. Prediction of other people's interference can help to hide the image proactively and in a timely fashion.
6. Early coordination of individuals. This can be viewed as a consequence of the previous point. If the needs of several users in a group can be predicted, the system can act to satisfy the interests of the group as a whole.

Future context can be predicted using a large variety of models. However, implementation of context prediction faces challenges that distinguish context prediction from many other kinds of prediction tasks. The challenges include the following (partially based on Nurmi et al. (2005); Mayrhofer (2004):

1. Pervasive systems work in real time.
2. Pervasive systems need to predict human actions. This is one of the main reasons why most of context prediction techniques are grounded in machine learning.

Human actions depend on human habits and personal features which, in turn, often cannot be guessed beforehand but can be inferred during the run time.
3. The systems work in discrete time. All context data are provided by sensors and sensors work in an impulse manner which provides the measurements in certain points of time.
4. The data are highly heterogeneous. Lots of data of different nature and different types come from different sources. Context data can be numerical and non-numerical; context data can come periodically or when a certain event occurs, etc.
5. Sometimes, hardware capabilities are limited. The use of lots of small and preferably inexpensive devices is very common in pervasive computing. Many devices have to be relatively autonomous and use wireless interfaces for interactions. Devices of this kind have limited power supply and limited computational capacity.
6. Connectivity problems, which can cause problems including data loss and sensor unavailability, are possible.
7. The learning phase should be kept to a minimum. Often, a pervasive computing system needs to start working right away. Ability to incorporate prior assumptions about the system is also highly desired in order to achieve a fast system start.
8. Sensors are uncertain. Not taking that into account can lead to reasoning and prediction problems.
9. There is a need for automated decision making.

There are, at present, some techniques that address context prediction challenges, but there still is a definite lack of a universal approach to the problem.

In this chapter, context prediction techniques will be classified according to the formal models and approaches that inspired them. This is an insightful way that can provide a direction for new techniques research. Sometimes those approaches can overlap and, therefore, some approaches can be associated with several classes.

2.2 From Task Definition to Evaluation Criteria

To develop a basis for context prediction methods classification, we need a formal definition of the context prediction task. It will help to identify criteria for classification and evaluation of context prediction approaches.

Let S_1, S_2 be the context data at a certain moment in time. As usual, every portion of context data S_i is a vector that contains sensor data and the results of sensor data pre-processing.

A context predictor, in the most general sense, can be viewed in the following manner:

$$\Pr = G(S_1, S_2, \ldots, S_t)$$

where t is the current time and Pr is the prediction result; the prediction result can be either just a set of expected future context features, or their distribution, or a

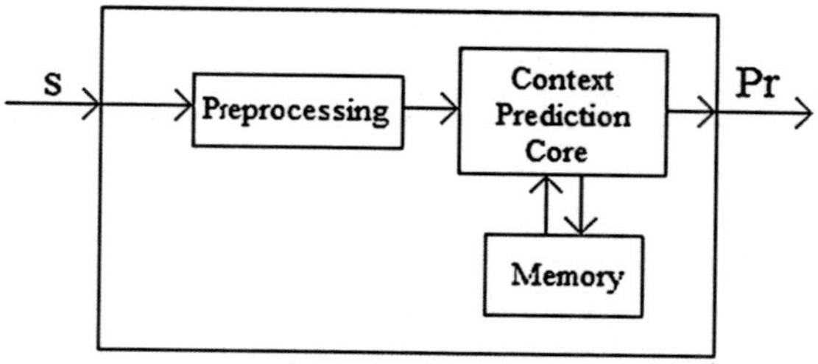

Fig. 1 Context prediction – general structure

future event, or a future state, etc. Context prediction operation is represented by operator *G*. Initial knowledge and assumptions about the system are also included in G. To summarise, context prediction results depend on the context-prediction method and possibly on context history and current context data. Questions of context history awareness are addressed later in this section.

The context predictor can be viewed in more detail in the following manner: (See Fig. 1).

Several parts of the context predictor can be identified.

Part 1. Context prediction core. It implements the exact context prediction method. This can be an ad hoc method defined for an exact case or any kind of well-known approach (such as neural network, Markov model, Bayesian network, sequence predictor, etc.). Actually, the method used as the context prediction core is the main criterion while distinguishing one method of context prediction from another.

To define the context-prediction method, we need to define its main principle (e.g., Bayesian network, Markov model, neural network, etc.) and its parameters. Those parameters can be, for example, transition probabilities for Markov chain, neural network coefficients, or distributions for Bayesian network. The context predictor can obtain the parameters as prior knowledge or infer the parameters during run time. Here are the suggested evaluation criteria:

Criterion 1. Determine whether prior estimations about a pervasive system can be incorporated into the method. If the method cannot do that, it might result in low effectiveness at the start-up. Sometimes, prior training can be a workaround for that problem: to pre-train the context predictor, the trainer system needs to generate training data according to prior estimations and present it as pre-training before the system actually starts.

Criterion 2. Determine, whether context predictor can learn during the runtime. In pervasive computing systems, the problem of having numerous unknown parameters is quite common. For example, pervasive computing systems often involve user-behaviour prediction. User behaviour depends on user habits; the system usually cannot guess those habits in advance and needs to learn them during the run time. Thus, there are, in practice, hardly any methods in pervasive computing that are incapable of incorporating run-time knowledge.

Criterion 3. Determine whether the method is a white box/black box. Another criterion, closely correlated with the two aforementioned ones, is whether the method is a "black box" or a "white box." If the method is a white box, method parameters usually show how the system really works in quite an insightful manner. By looking at system parameters the expert can tell what exactly the system has learnt or, in turn, having some prior estimation, the expert can configure the system parameters accordingly. If the method is a black box, it is capable of prediction, but an expert cannot see the underlying reasons for the current prediction even if that expert knows the complete set of method parameters. Black box methods are generally unlikely to be able to incorporate prior knowledge about the system.

For example, transition probabilities of the discrete time Markov chain explicitly reveal the chance for the system context to be in a particular state at a particular time; the state, in turn, corresponds to certain context features. And, with the transition probability, the expert can easily understand what kind of regularity is found (at least in terms such as "if context at current time t has features a_1, a_2, a_3, ..., that means that it will have features b_1, b_2, b_3, ... at time $t + t'$ with probability p"). So, Markov chain-based methods are white box methods. As for neural networks, even though the expert knows all the weights for every neuron, it is usually impossible to tell what kind of regularities it corresponds to. So, neural network-based methods are black box methods.

Criterion 4. Determine whether estimation of prediction reliability is incorporated into the method. In practice, if the method is capable of estimating its own reliability, the predictor usually returns the distribution of the predicted value (e.g., Markov models, Bayesian networks), not just the value itself. If reliability estimation is not possible in the method, such a method usually returns just the predicted value and no probabilistic estimations.

Criterion 5. Determine outlier sensitivity. All sensors have some degree of uncertainty. Moreover, the sensors can become unavailable or the measurement results can be lost in transfer. In that case, an outlier appears. The outlier can significantly alter the prediction results. In a very general sense we can classify outlier sensitivity in the following groups.

- *No sensitivity.* Outliers will not affect prediction effectiveness in any way. No examples so far. It is possible theoretically, if, for example, we have just a prediction formula, which does not take any current data into account:

$$\Pr = G(S_1, S_2, \ldots, S_t) = G(t)$$

But practically, that kind of predictor is very inflexible and, therefore, is not used.

- *Moderate sensitivity.* Outliers do affect prediction effectiveness, but over time the influence of the outlier fades. For example, the neural network of the Markov predictor learns over time, and if there is an outlier in the training sequence, it will have an effect. However, the amounts of data in the training sequence will be growing and the influence of the outlier will be decreasing.

- *High sensitivity*. One outlier can significantly influence subsequent results of context predictions; the effect of the outlier will not decrease until the outlier value is completely excluded from the history. For example, the values of sensor measurements over time can be treated as function and interpolated. Later that function can be extrapolated to the future and it will be the prediction result. But outlier presence can significantly alter the resulting function and the effect will not be reduced until that point is out of the history range (which will happen practically, at least due to memory limitations).

Criterion 6. Determine what types of incoming data are supported by the context predictor. Context can contain data of several types: real, integer, and non-numerical (e.g., room in smart office or the position of the switch). If some data type of the context is not accepted by the context prediction method, pre-processing needs to be performed.

Part 2. Pre-processing block. The pre-processing block transfers incoming sensor data to the format that is applicable to the context prediction core. In a very general sense, it can be represented in the following manner:

$$S' = \mathrm{Prep}(S)$$

where S is the current received context data, and S' is pre-processed context data for further usage by the context prediction core. Prep(S) represents the pre-processing operator. The pre-processing operation also can theoretically be dependent on historical data, but practically it is not likely.

Criterion 7. Determine pre-processing information loss. The more information lost during pre-processing, the greater the chance to miss significant information, not use it during context prediction, and therefore, get reduced context prediction capability. So, here is one more context prediction method evaluation criterion: whether the information is lost during pre-processing.

- *No information loss*. For example, the context can be left as is (it can be represented as a state-space model with later prediction using filter theory, or context data can be used directly as an input for the neural network). Or, new context attributes can be introduced during pre-processing (e.g., one of the environmental characteristics can be estimated in two different manners to detect sensor failure or use filtering to combine two sources of data). So, processing, in this case, can require some efforts as well. The criterion for the method to be included in this category is as follows: for every S', there should be, at the most, one value of S.
- *Information loss present*. Denotes all other cases. For example, some values can be aggregated, or context can be completely reduced to a finite number of states of the Markov model or probabilities of Bayesian network nodes, or the context can be decomposed into event flow and timing information can be lost, and many more examples.

Usually, the presence of information loss depends both on the prediction method and on the sensor data the system obtains. For example, if there are only a few sensors with a small set of discrete non-numerical data coming from them, the Markov model can be created without information loss – every predictor state (S') will correspond to every possible combination of sensor values (S). However, even if the system has just one real-valued sensor, creating the Markov model without information loss is impossible – there is an infinite number of possible values of S and it cannot be covered by any finite number of states in S'.

Part 3. Memory. The predictor might need to store history or parameters in an applicable manner. Some methods require only current value and do not store history in any manner. Some of the methods are capable of handling all the history and using it to its benefit.

Criterion 8. Determine constant or variable amount of memory needed. For example, a neural network needs only memory to store weight coefficients for neurons. The Markov model needs only a fixed amount of memory to store transition probabilities and some intermediate data to obtain them. However, an expert system based context predictor that constantly introduces new rules or a sequence predictor-based approach with growing prediction tree requires a variable amount of memory and the memory demand can grow over time.

In summary then, here are the defined criteria for evaluation of context prediction methods:

1. Prior knowledge accumulation? Yes/No.
2. Real-time knowledge accumulation? Yes/No.
3. "Black box"/"White box"?
4. Prediction reliability estimation? Yes/No.
5. Outlier sensitivity? No/Medium/High.
6. Types of data supported?
   6.1 Real? Yes/No.
   6.2 Integer? Yes/No.
   6.3 Non-numerical? Yes/No.
7. Information loss on pre-processing? Yes/No (usually it depends on certain conditions).
8. Memory amount needed? Fixed/Variable.

3 Context Prediction Methods

In practice, the methods used most frequently are:

1. Sequence prediction approach.
   This approach to context prediction is based on the sequence prediction task from theoretical computer science and can be applied if the context can be decomposed into some kind of event flow.
2. Markov chains approach.
   Context prediction techniques based on Markov chains are quite widespread. Markov chains provide an easily understandable view of the system and can be

applied if the context can be decomposed into a finite set of nonoverlapping states.

3. Bayesian network approach.
   This can be viewed as the generalisation of the Markov models. It provides more flexibility but requires more training data in turn.

4. Neural networks approach.
   Neural networks are biologically inspired formal models that imitate the activity of an interconnected set of neurons. Neural networks are quite popular in machine learning. Context prediction approaches based on neural networks exist as well.

5. Branch prediction approach.
   This approach initially comes from the task of predicting the instruction flow in a microprocessor after the branching command. Some context prediction systems use similar algorithms.

6. Trajectory prolongation approach.
   Some context prediction approaches treat the vector of context data as a point in multidimensional space. Then, the context predictor approximates or interpolates those points with some function, and this function is extrapolated to predict future values.

7. Expert systems approach.
   Based on expert systems and rule-based engines, the expert systems approach appears in some works on context prediction. The goal of the approach is to construct the rules for prediction. It provides a very clear view of the system.
   Subsequent chapters address those approaches in more detail.

3.1 Sequence Prediction Approach

The sequence prediction task is quite a researched problem in theoretical computer science. Generally, the problem is as follows: having the sequence of symbols <$S(1)$, $S(2)$, …, $S(t)$>, received at the time from 1 to t, the task is to predict the next symbol $S(t + 1)$.

If the context of pervasive computing systems can be represented as a flow of symbols (e.g., flow of events or state of Markov model in a particular time), the context prediction problem can be viewed as a sequence prediction task.

D. Cook et al. provided quite a comprehensive overview of sequence prediction techniques used in context prediction (particularly in smart home environments) in Cook and Das (2004).

The earliest works that treated the problem of user-activity prediction as sequence prediction tasks were the works related to command prediction in the UNIX environment (Davison and Hirsh 1997; Davison and Hirsh 1998). Those works inspired subsequent research in the area of user activity prediction, including context prediction in pervasive computing systems and particularly smart home systems.

In a number of works (Mayrhofer 2004; Bhattacharya and Das 1999; Das, Cook, Bhattacharya, Heierman and Lin 2002; Roy, Bhaumik, Bhattacharya, Basu, Cook, and Das 2003), algorithms from the Lempel-Ziv family were suggested as means of context prediction. In practice, the LZ78 algorithm was a baseline for a set of context prediction algorithms. For more details, refer to Ziv and Lempel (1978) for the description of the algorithm; to Feder, Merhav, and Gutman (1992), for subsequent researches; and to Gopalratnam and Cook (2003), for the overview of enhancements related to context prediction.

In Bhattacharya and Das (1999), the authors introduced the LeZi update, which addressed the problem of predicting the next location of the user in a cellular network. Proactivity in this case could benefit the cellular system by enhancing paging and location updates. Bhattacharya and Das (1999) also inspired the work (Das et al. 2002), where the use of the LeZi update algorithm for the smart home environment was presented. This work was described in more detail and further enhanced in Roy et al. (2003). Here, the questions of energy consumption prediction based on path prediction were addressed as well.

Compared to the classical LZ78 approach, the LeZi-Update approach tried to keep a track of all contexts within a phrase. The idea of enhancement is as follows: at every step, update frequency – not only for every prefix, as in LZ78, but for every suffix of this prefix. E.g., if the received phrase is "ABC," then the frequency should be updated not only for "ABC," but for "C" and "BC" as well.

LeZi-Update inspired further enhancements including Active LeZi. In Gopalratnam and Cook (2003), the authors introduced the Active LeZi algorithm in order to predict the actions of inhabitants in smart home environments. Authors identified several shortcomings of the initial LZ78 algorithm:

1. The algorithm will lose any information that will cross the boundary of the phrase.
2. There is a low rate of convergence.

The authors proposed a solution to the shortcomings. Using the LeZi Update as a basis, they introduced a sliding window of previously seen symbols to be able to detect patterns that cross phrase boundaries. During a testing scenario without any noise or sensor uncertainty on highly repetitive data, Active LeZi reached almost 100% prediction rate after around a 750-symbol training sequence. However, when noise was introduced into testing scenarios in practical implementations, the prediction rate began to float around 86%. Testing on real data has shown that Active LeZi has around 47% prediction rate after around 750 symbols. In Mayrhofer (2004), the author suggested using Active LeZi in a more general case of context prediction task. More details on this work are given in Sect. 4.

Therefore, sequence prediction turns out to be a feasible and widely used approach for context prediction and this approach has shown good performance practically. Moreover, some theoretical enhancements in the sequence prediction area were made while researching the context prediction problem (e.g., Active LeZi development). However, the sequence prediction approach has several shortcomings. Generally, reduction of the entire context to the mere sequence of symbols introduces the possibility of losing valuable information on pre-processing. Another problem is that the system cannot deal with levels of confidence when a situation has occurred. Prediction reliability can be computed, but the reliability of observed data cannot be taken into account. One more major shortcoming is that this approach generally does not deal with time (although some exceptions do exist). It does not detect timing-dependent regularities such as "If engine is overheated, it will break down in 10 min." The duration of a situation's occurrence can also be important. This is not considered in the sequence learning approach, either. However, although the sequence prediction approach has its shortcomings, it still turns out to be a good choice for many practical tasks.

3.2 Markov Chains for Context Prediction

The discrete time first order Markov chain is a model that consists of following parts:

1. Finite number of possible model states:

$$S = \{S_0, S_1, \ldots, S_{n-1}\}.$$

2. The probability of the system to transition from one state to another:

$$P_{ij} = P(S(t+1) = S_j \mid S(t) = S_i), i, j \varepsilon [0..n-1], t = 0, 1, 2, \ldots$$

Markov property is the property of the system's future states to be dependent on the current state only (and not on the history). In a more general case of Markov chains of order K, transition probabilities depend not only on current state, but on the history of states down to time $t-(K-1)$.

The transition probabilities are stationary – P_{ij} does not depend on time.

3. Initial probability of the model to be in certain state: $P(S(0)=S_i)$ $i = 0,1,\ldots,n-1$

Pervasive systems usually employ discrete time models due to the nature of sensory originated data, which usually arrive at certain moments in time, either in some period or at the occurrence of some event. So, from now on, we are going to refer only to discrete time Markov chains, unless it is explicitly stated otherwise.

Markov chains are widely researched formal models that were applied to numerous practical tasks. See, for example, Russell and Norvig (2003) for more details on

Markov chains, and Baum and Petrie (1966), Rabiner (1990) for more details on hidden Markov models.

Some projects applied Markov chains to address context prediction problems. For example, in Kaowthumrong, Lebsack, and Han (2002), the authors addressed an active device resolution problem. A device resolution problem is a problem when the user has a remote control to interact with a set of devices, but there are always several devices in user proximity. The system needs to determine to what device the user is referring. The proposed solution was to predict the next device to which the user is likely to refer and use this information to resolve ambiguity on the next step. The authors proposed the hypothesis that the next device depended on the current device only. That hypothesis is actually Markov property. The context prediction system constructs the Markov chain, where states represent devices and transition between the states represent the order of device access. E.g., if the user turns on the light (state L) and then turns on the TV (state T) that means that the model transitioned from state L to state T. The model continued being in that state until a new action was performed by the user. The goal was to infer user habits from observed action sequence. Initially, transition probabilities were unknown. During the run time, the system inferred transition probabilities by calculating relative transition frequency.

$$P_{ij} = \frac{N\left(\forall t > 0, S(t-1) = S_i, S(t) = S_j\right)}{N\left(\forall t \geq 0, S(t) = i\right)}$$

where N is the count of cases.

Having several devices in proximity to a remote control, the system chose the one with the highest probability among them. Prediction accuracy was estimated at 70–80%.

Another example is Krumm (2008) where the author used discrete time Markov chain for driving route prediction. Road segments were states in the Markov chain and the transitions were the possibilities to enter another road segment, e.g., at the crossroad. Probabilities were inferred from the history in a manner similar to Kaowthumrong et al. (2002). The author used Markov chains of different orders and compared the results. One-step prediction accuracy exceeded 60% for first order Markov model. Prediction accuracy exceeded 80% and tended to 90% when Markov model order grew to 10. Overall, the system was able to predict one segment ahead (237.5 m in average) with 90% accuracy and three segments ahead (712.5 m in average) with 76% accuracy. In Zukerman, Albrecht, and Nicholson (1999), the authors used Markov models for prediction of next user request on WWW.

Using discrete time Markov chains in context prediction is plausible and an easy way when the system is fully observable and when the context can naturally be represented as a limited set of possible states changing over discrete time. However, more complicated cases require the extension of Markov chain approach.

The hidden Markov model (HMM) extends Markov chains to the case of partial observability. HMMs were introduced in Baum and Petrie (1966). HMMs can be defined as Markov models where the exact state of the system is unknown. One of the very popular examples is urns with coloured balls (according to Rabiner (1990), introduced by J. Fergusson in his lectures on information theory). Each urn contains many balls of different colours, and the distribution of colours is different between the urns. The user sees the colour of the ball, but he/she does not know which urn the ball has been taken from. In this example, the right urn stands for a hidden state and the colour of the ball stands for output. Compared to fully observable Markov chain description, HMM also requires the following distribution:

$$P'_{jk} = P(Y(t) = k \mid S(t) = S_j)$$

P_{jk} represents the probability of seeing output k in state j at time t.

Several tasks are quite common for HMM:

1. Given the model and the output, identify underlying sequence of states and transitions.
2. Given the model and the output, identify the probability of an output to correspond that model. One of the special cases of that task is following: given a set of possible underlying models, choose a model that matches the output sequence best.
3. Given a model without transition probabilities and given some output, find the missing probabilities. The process of detecting those probabilities is usually referred to as training HMM. This HMM use case is the most common one for context prediction task.

For more information on the algorithms for different tasks, refer, for example, to Rabiner (1990).

HMMs were used for context prediction in several projects. For example, in Gellert and Vintan (2006), the authors used HMMs to obtain the prediction of the next room a person was likely to visit. The resulting HMM represented every room as a possible state. In Simmons, Browning, Zhang, and Sadekar (2006), the authors used HMMs for route prediction. The prediction system represented the road structure as a graph where nodes were crossroads and edges were roads between crossroads. The state of HMM was the combination of the position on the road (which was observed) and destination point (which was not observed, but could be guessed). According to the authors, prediction accuracy was up to 98% in most cases. HMMs are rather popular for cases where the Markov model is applicable and the system is partially observable; partial observability often appears due to sensor uncertainty or due to parameters such as user intentions or user emotions being taken into account, which are not directly measurable.

One more extension of the Markov chain is the Markov decision process (MDP). MDP is a formal model that consists of the following parts:

1. Finite number of possible model states:

$$S = \{S_0, S_1, \ldots, S_{n-1}\}.$$

2. A set of possible actions to be taken in state

$$S_i : A(i) = \{a_{i1}, a_{i2}, \ldots\}, i = 0,1,\ldots,n-1,\ i = 0,1,\ldots,n - 1.$$

3. The probability of the system to transition from one state to another on a particular action:

$$P_{ij}(k) = P(S(t+1) = S_j \mid S(t) = S_i, \quad a(t) = k), \quad i, j \varepsilon [0..n-1], \quad t = 0,1,2,\ldots$$

4. Initial probability of the model to be in certain state: $P(S(0) = S_i)$ $i = 0,1,\ldots,n - 1$.
5. A reward or cost for transferring from state S_i to S_j on choosing certain action a: $R(S_i, S_j, a)$.

There are often considered simpler cases when the reward depends only on next state and action ($R(S_j, a)$) or even next state only ($R(S_j)$).

Partially observable MDP (POMDP) is an extension of MDP idea for partially observable systems. POMDP extends the concept of MDP in the same manner like HMM extends the concept of the Markov chain. POMDP also requires the distribution of possible observations depending on the state:

$$P'_{jk} = P(Y(t) = k \mid S(t) = S_j).$$

Usually, the goal of MDP processing is to find a policy or principles of choosing the action to maximise the rewards. Policy can be defined as $\pi = \{\pi_0, \pi_1, \pi_2, \ldots\}$, where $\pi_i = \pi_i(h_i)$ is a probability distribution of choosing certain actions on the basis of observed history.

Sometimes, the objective is to resolve an inverse problem with the following consideration: the system needs to find cost or reward function $R(i,a)$ that explains user behaviour. This task is usually referred to as apprenticeship learning. Refer to Abeel and Ng (2004) for more details on the apprenticeship learning problem.

To compare different policies, several methods are available:

1. Discounted expected total reward.

$$R = R(S_0) + \sum_{i=1}^{L} \beta^i R(S(i-1), S(i), A(i))$$

where β [0,1] is a discount factor, $S(t)$ stands for the state at time t, $A(t)$ stands for action at time t, R stands for reward function, and L stands for horizon (it is often infinite).

2. Average reward criterion.

$$R = \lim_{N\to\infty} \left(\frac{R(S_0) + \sum_{i=1}^{N} \beta^i R(S(i-1), S(i), A(i))}{N} \right)$$

Refer to Russell and Norvig (2003) for more details on MDP theory.

Markov decision processes were used in location prediction and gained some popularity in driving route prediction. For example, in Ziebart et al. (2008), the authors proposed the Probabilistically Reasoning from Observed Context-Aware Behaviour (PROCAB) method and used it for vehicle navigation. More specifically, the authors addressed three issues: turn prediction, route prediction, and destination prediction. The system represented user-behaviour as sequential actions in a Markov decision process. The authors adopted an apprenticeship learning approach: at first, the system observes driver actions and infers driver preferences. After some training, the system is able to predict driver actions. Inferred cost function is used to compare the significance of route benefits and shortcomings according to the opinion of the driver (which is very different from person to person). For apprenticeship learning, the authors adopted the approach presented in Abbeel and Ng (2004). As a result, the system became capable of predicting route, turn, or destination, and provided services and suggestions proactively. In Hoey, Von Bertoldi, Poupart, and Mihailidis (2007) the authors used POMDP in systems for the care of the elderly, for people with dementia. The system tracked the process of hand-washing of people with dementia and decided whether to call a caregiver, give advice, or just not interfere. Using the camera, the elderly care system could observe some activities such as the stage of the hand-washing process (turned the water on, washed the hands, soaped the hands, etc.), and some information such as the stage of the disease was considered to be hidden state.

So, MDPs are a plausible and practically effective way to predict the context in the situations where Markov models are applicable and control actions can significantly affect prediction results.

3.3 Neural Networks for Context Prediction

Neural networks are formal mathematical models that imitate biological neural structures. Starting back in the 1940s with the first models of neuron, they became one of the most popular ways of solving artificial intelligence-related tasks. Learning capability allows neural networks to solve a variety of problems including pattern association, pattern recognition, and function approximation. For a comprehensive neural networks overview refer, for example, to Russell and Norvig (2003).

Neural networks were used for context prediction as well. For example, in Mozer (1998), the author described a smart house that predicts expected occupancy patterns in the house, estimates hot water usage, estimates the likelihood for a zone to be entered soon, etc. In that project the authors used feedforward neural networks trained with back propagation. Indoor movement prediction related projects considered the neural network approach as well. For example, in Vintan, Gellert, Petzold, and Ungerer (2004), the authors addressed the problem of finding the next room the person is going to visit. Predictor took the current room number as an input and was expected to give the most probable next room number as an output. For the prediction method, the authors chose multilayer perceptron with one hidden layer and a back propagation learning algorithm. The system used a log of movement for training. In Al-Masri and Mahmoud (2006), the authors suggest using artificial neural networks for providing mobile services. The authors presented a SmartCon application that is capable of learning user needs and dynamically providing applicable mobile services. Authors elicited relevant information by training a neural network with device-specific features (all the information about the user's device: hardware type, terminal browser, software platform), user-specific features (learned user preferences) and service-specific features (service provider preferences). Later this information is used to suggest proper mobile service to the user. Lin et al. suggested using a neural network for smart handoff in Lin, Wang, and Lin (2008). The process of handoff occurs when a mobile device is moving away from the coverage area of one base station to the coverage area of another. The handoff decision is usually based on characteristics such as signal strength, bit error rate, signal to noise ratio, etc. However, sometimes a user is moving close to the borders of the coverage areas of different base stations and lots of unnecessary handoffs appear. The goal is to predict whether a user is likely to move under the coverage area of any base station completely. Prediction results will affect the handoff decision. The authors proposed to use a multilayer perceptron to detect the correlation between packet success rate and a certain set of metrics. According to Lin et al. (2008), their algorithm outperforms current common handoff algorithms.

As a result, neural networks turned out to be a feasible way of context prediction for many practical use cases. There are various types of neural networks available, and they can provide a flexible trade-off between complexity and effectiveness. The major shortcoming of the neural network approach is that it is a black box – by examining the neural network structure, it is not possible to say exactly what regularities are detected.

3.4 *Bayesian Networks for Context Prediction*

The approach of Bayesian networks generalises Markov models and avoids some of the Markov model shortcomings. The Bayesian network is a direct acyclic graph where every node is associated with a fact and every directed edge represents the influence on one fact by another. Nodes of the Bayesian network have local Markov property: each variable is independent of its non-descendants, given its parent variables. For basic information on Bayesian networks refer, for example, to Russell and Norvig (2003).

A classic example of a Bayesian network is the sprinkler and rain network depicted in Fig. 2.

The following interpretation begins by examining three facts – whether there is rain (node R), whether the sprinkler is working (node S), and whether the grass is wet (node W). Every node has probability distribution depending on its parents; for example, if it is raining and the sprinkler is working as well, then the grass is wet with a probability of 99%; if it is just raining – there is a 95% probability of the grass being wet; if just the sprinkler works – 90% probability; and if there is no rain and the sprinkler is off – a probability of 3%. Nodes with no parents have only prior

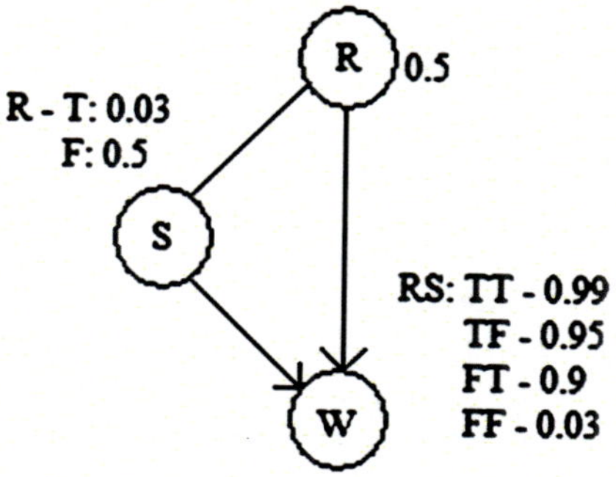

Fig. 2 Bayesian network example

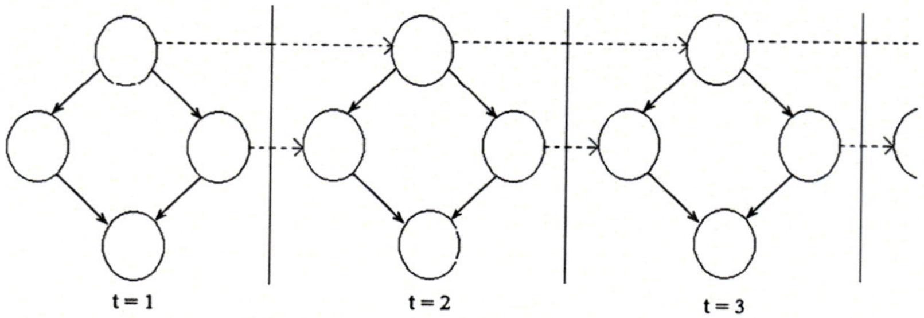

Fig. 3 Dynamic Bayesian network example

probability (for rain, it is 50%). Some facts are directly observed (e.g., we see or hear that the sprinkler is working). The system can compute the posterior probabilities of unobserved facts using either the formula of Bayes (up the graph – whether it is raining) or direct probability calculations (down the graph – whether the grass is wet).

A learning task is quite common for Bayesian networks. Users sometimes do not have complete information about the network and need to infer probability distributions of the nodes (parameters learning task) or even the structure of Bayesian network graph itself (structure learning task). For more details, refer to Russell and Norvig (2003).

A dynamic Bayesian network (DBN) is a special version of BNs that takes timing into account. Considering time as discrete (t = 1,2,3….), the DBN can be defined as a pair of B_1,$B_{->}$, where B_1 is the BN which defines all prior probabilities on time $t = 1$ and $B_{->}$ defines several-slice (as usual, two-slice) temporal BN, where all time dependencies are represented in terms of directed acyclic graph. For example, it can look like this (see Fig. 3).

Broken lines in Fig. 3 represent temporal dependencies. B_1 is the initial graph of $t = 1$ with all the necessary starting probability distributions, $B_{->}$ being a combined graph of $t = 1$ and $t = 2$ (with all the necessary distribution functions).

Learning tasks in DBNs are the straightforward generalisation of learning tasks for simple BNs: parameter learning and structure learning. In context prediction, the tasks structure of a DBN is usually known and the system needs to infer parameters. For more information on DBNs see, for example, Russell and Norvig (2003).

Numerous projects have used DBNs for context prediction. For example, in Petzold, Pietzowski, Bagci, Trumler, and Ungerer (2005), the authors used DBNs to predict a person's indoor movement. The context is represented as DBN, where the current room depends on several rooms visited previously and the duration of staying in the current room depends on the current room, time of the day, and day of the week. The context predictor achieved high prediction accuracy (ranging between around 70% and around 90% for different persons and tasks). However, retraining the system in case of user habit change turned out to be cumbersome. DBNs were also widely used to recognise user plans and infer user goals. The work by Albrecht, Zukerman, and Nicholson (1998), is an example of user modelling and user goal inference using a BN. The authors used DBNs to predict further user actions in an adventure game. This task can still be viewed as context prediction – the fact that context is completely virtual does not really affect the essence of the method. Horvitz, Breese, Heckerman, Hovel, and Rommelse (1998) describes another example of DBNs – the Lumiere project. The project intended to predict the goals of software users and provide services proactively. Nodes of DBN were user profile, goals, and actions.

Numerous projects have used BNs for context prediction. BNs have a broad range of possible use cases and good opportunities to incorporate any kind of prior knowledge.

3.5 Branch Prediction Methods for Context Prediction

Historically, branch prediction algorithms are used in microprocessors to predict the future flow of the program after branch instruction. By their nature, branch prediction methods are fast and simple and designed for fast real-time work. Refer to Yeh and Patt, (1992) for more details on branch prediction techniques.

In Petzold, Bagci, Trumler, and Ungerer (2003), the authors used branch prediction algorithms for context prediction in pervasive computing systems. Authors used branch prediction to predict moving of the person around the house or office. The system described in Petzold et al. (2003) used several kinds of predictors: state counter-based predictor; local two-level context predictors; and global two-level context predictors. Counter-based predictors were much faster in training and retraining while two-level predictors were much better at learning complicated patterns. The authors also developed some suggestions for enhancements that can take into account time and confidence level.

Context prediction using branch prediction algorithms is not a widespread approach. Algorithms are generally very simple and fast, but they can detect only very simple behaviour patterns.

3.6 Trajectory Prolongation Approach for Context Prediction

Context prediction by trajectory prolongation works in the following manner:

1. Consider every context feature as an axis and construct multidimensional space of context features.
2. Consider the observed context features at a certain moment in time as a point in that multidimensional space.
3. Consider the set of those points collected over time as a trajectory in multidimensional space.
4. Interpolate or approximate that trajectory with some function.
5. Extrapolate that function further in time to get the prediction results.

Some projects have used this approach to context prediction. For example, in Anagnostopoulos, Mpougiouris, and Hadjiefthymiades (2005), the authors suggest a special architecture and approach for context prediction. The authors validate their approach on location prediction methods for longitude and latitude. For validating and testing, the authors used GPS trace files. According to the authors, Newton and Lagrange's interpolation methods proved to be inappropriate for the purpose due to oscillatory behaviour on a high number of points. Cubic Bezier splines in turn appeared to be promising and moreover had the complexity only $O(n)$. Regression-based techniques are also a part of trajectory prolongation approach. For example, Karbassi and Barth (2003) addressed vehicle time of arrival estimation. The system built linear regression between a congestion factor and time of arrival and inferred the parameters from the history. Some works (Sigg, Haseloff and David 2006; Mayrhofer 2004) suggested use of autoregressive models to resolve context prediction task.

Trajectory prolongation approach initially comes from a location prediction area, which is adjacent to context prediction and can be viewed as its subtask. However, trajectory prolongation can face numerous shortcomings when applied to a general context prediction task. The most important shortcoming for the trajectory prolongation approach is that it is not capable of handling non-numerical data, which is quite common for pervasive computing environments.

3.7 Expert Systems for Context Prediction

Expert systems theory is a branch of the artificial intelligence area, which attempts to imitate the work of a human expert. Usually, an expert system represents the regularities in terms of rules. For example, it can look like this: $(t > 37°\mathrm{C})\&(cough) \rightarrow (ill)$ which means that "if the person's body temperature is over 37°C and he has a cough, he/she is ill."

A large number of projects applied expert systems to different fields. For more details on expert systems refer to Giarratano and Riley (2004). Expert systems are sometimes used for context inference and context prediction. For example, in

Hong et al. (2009), the authors use rule engines for context prediction. The system inferred rules in the runtime to determine user preferences and provide services proactively. For example, with user age, gender, and family status, the engine can infer what kind of restaurant a user is likely to look for this evening. It is done in terms of rules like: $(age > 23)\&(age < 32)\&(gender = male)\&(familyStatus = married) \rightarrow (preference = familyRestaurant)$

Then, for example, the system can predict that the user is going to the restaurant in the evening and proactively provide the choice, find the route in advance, etc. A context-aware system employs decision tree learning techniques to mining for user preferences. Decision tree is a tree-like structure used in decision support. A simple example can be found in Fig. 4. For more details on decision trees, refer to Russell and Norvig (2003).

In Hong et al. (2009), the authors provide several reasons to use decision trees: they are easily understandable; they are capable of processing nonlinear interactions among variables; they have very low sensitivity for the outliers; they can handle large amounts of data; and they can process both categorical and numerical data.

The system described in Hong et al. (2009) used the algorithm called "apriori". It is a classic algorithm for decision tree learning. Initially that algorithm was developed to mine the data from database transactions and find sets of features that appear together. The main idea of the algorithm is to find the subsets of facts of different length incrementally, starting from single facts. On every step, bigger subsets are generated and subsets with frequency below some thresholds are dropped. For more details on the algorithm and its enhancements, refer to Agrawal and Srikant (1994).

In Williams, Mohammadian, Nelson, and Doherty (2008), the authors discuss forecasting a person's location using the context prediction approach. The system collects the log of household activities and elicits sequential association rules using a generalised sequential patterns (GSP) technique. See Srikant and Agrawal (1996) for more details on the rule mining method.

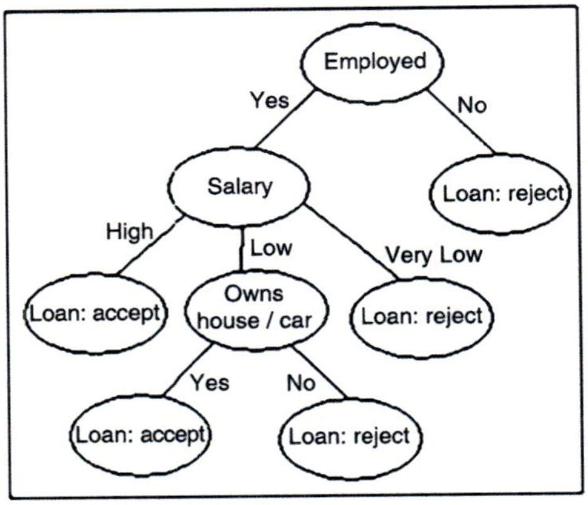

Fig. 4 Decision tree example

In another example (Vainio 2008), the authors considered mining the rules to learn user habits and implement fuzzy control in smart home environments. The pervasive system learns by example from user actions. In brief, their approach looks like this: all the day is divided into the set of timeframes. The system detects association rules within the timeframe. Every rule has sensor conditions as an input and triggered actuators as an output. The system also maintains a weight coefficient for every rule: triggering the rule increases the weight, not triggering the rules decrease the weight. Rules with 0 weights are removed. If both the weight and the degree of membership for the rule are high enough, the system starts executing the actions proactively, instead of the user, according to the rule.

One more notable work in the area of rule-based systems is Loke (2004). The questions of proactivity and the questions of action consequences were addressed. The author proposed to determine whether the action was worth performing by comparing the uncertainty of the context and the severity of the action in the form of a rule:

$$\text{IF Uncertainty(Context)} < \text{U AND Severity(Action)} < \text{S THEN DO Action}$$

That work addresses not just rules for taking actions, but different argumentation techniques to define those rules (based on different sources of knowledge) and to determine what action to take.

To summarise, the approach to context prediction based on expert systems is quite promising. It allows quick and natural integration of prior knowledge, it allows relatively easy integration of adaptation actions, and it can contain learning and self-correcting capabilities.

3.8 Context Prediction Approaches Summary

Table 1 presents the comparison of context prediction approaches, according to the criteria identified in Sect. 2. It should be noted that different kinds of predictors can be combined to improve prediction quality, enhance each other's strength, and compensate for each other's weaknesses.

4 General Approaches to Context Prediction

One of the context prediction research challenges is the development of a general approach to context prediction. Many context prediction approaches were designed to fit one particular task and most of them were not designed to be generalisable (although some of them have generalisation capability).

Quite a notable attempt was made by R. Mayrhofer to look at the context prediction problem in general; he developed a task-independent architecture for context prediction (Mayrhofer 2004).

Table 1 An overview of context prediction approaches

Approach	Prior knowledge inference	Run-time knowledge inference	Reliability estimation	Outlier sensitivity	Observability	Information loss on pre-processing	Data supported			Memory amount needed
							Integer	Real	Non-numerical	
Pattern matching	Yes	Yes	Yes	Moderate	White box	Yes	No	No	Yes	Variable
Markov models	Yes	Yes	Yes	Moderate	White box	Yes	No	No	Yes	Fixed
Bayesian networks	Yes	Yes	Yes	Moderate	White box	Yes (usually)	Yes	Yes	Yes	Fixed
Neural networks	No	Yes	No	Moderate	Black box	No	Yes	Yes	No	Fixed
Branch predictors	Yes	Yes	Almost no	Moderate	White box	Yes	No	No	Yes	Fixed
Trajectory interpolation	No	Yes	No	Moderate or High	Black box	No	Yes	Yes	No	Variable
Trajectory approximation	Yes	Yes	Yes	Moderate	White box	No	Yes	Yes	No	Usually fixed
Expert systems	Yes	Yes	Yes	Moderate (practically – low)	White box	Yes	No	No	Yes	Variable

As a result, the context-prediction process consists of several steps:

1. Sensor data acquisition. This step takes data received from multiple sensors and arranges them into the vector of values.
2. Feature extraction. This step transforms raw sensor data for further usage. From vector of sensor data, vector of features is formed.
3. Classification. Performs searches for recurring patterns in context feature space. Growing neural gas was considered to be the best choice. See Fritzke (1995) for more details on that algorithm. The result of the classification step is a vector of values that represents degrees of membership of current vector to certain class.
4. Labelling. This is the only step that involves direct user interaction. The frequency of involvement depends on the quality of the clustering step: if classes are often overwritten and replaced, it will result in more frequent user involvements.
5. Prediction. This step takes the history of class vectors and estimates an expected class membership vector for the future. For this step, the author researched numerous prediction approaches and, according to evaluation results presented in Mayrhofer (2004), an active LeZi – combined with a duration predictor – slightly outperformed other evaluated algorithms.

Many context prediction applications provided the architecture for particular context prediction tasks. The work presented in Mayrhofer (2004) was one of the first works that addressed the context prediction task in a general sense and provided complete architecture to handle that challenge. The architecture is well-developed and well-reasoned, and it ensures pluggability of different context prediction methods, and non obtrusiveness for the user. The author put large research efforts into estimating the effectiveness of different context prediction approaches and provided quite comprehensive overview of those. The shortcoming here is that the problem of acting on predicted context was not recognised as a challenge and, moreover, using the rules to act on predicted context was considered the only option without any reasoning. That drawback is quite common throughout many general case context predictors. One more minor shortcoming is that feature extraction was restricted only to clustering of sensor data and no other pre-processing was considered.

Several other works addressed general case of context prediction as well. For example, in Nurmi et al. (2005), the authors developed their architecture for context prediction for a MobiLife project. The authors suggested that the process of context prediction consists of several steps: data acquisition, pre-processing, feature extraction, classification, and prediction. Actually, the view is quite similar to the one provided in Mayrhofer (2004). However, there are some differences. One of them is that in Nurmi et al. (2005), the authors introduced a pre-processing step. As the authors noticed, in Mayrhofer (2004) some pre-processing was included into the sensor data acquisition step. However, separating pre-processing and data acquisition can provide a more insightful view on the system and make it more flexible. Also, in Nurmi et al. (2005), the authors merged a labelling step into the classification step and provided some techniques to make labelling even less obtrusive. The shortcomings are generally the same compared to Mayrhofer (2004). The problem of acting on predicted context was briefly mentioned, but no exact solution was proposed.

One more notable work on context prediction architecture is the Foxtrot framework described in Sigg et al. (2006). Here, the authors presented quite a different view of the context prediction problem. They focused their efforts on treating the context as time series and applying time series forecasting techniques such as Markov predictors, an autoregressive moving average model or alignment methods. The Foxtrot project represented the context as a multilayered structure where higher level context information was obtained from lower level context information using pre-processing. Context prediction worked on every context layer and provided the prediction for every layer. The approach itself was quite novel. The authors conducted extensive research to theoretically estimate the possible error of such an approach. Also, the authors defined a context prediction task in a very general sense and did not make any unnecessary assumptions (such as restricting pre-processing to clustering or having only high-level context features and low-level context data); therefore, they implicitly assumed only two context layers. The Foxtrot framework implemented prediction on every layer of context data and did not restrict it to higher level context only. However, the choice of possible context prediction methods was relatively small (just autoregressive methods, alignment methods or Markov predictor) and the architecture itself took almost no context prediction specifics into account. The problem of how to use predicted information (including the questions of labelling context classes to achieve meaningful and understandable output of predicted information and the questions of acting on predicted context) was not considered at all.

In Anagnostopoulos et al. (2005), the authors present another general approach to context prediction. They treat context data as time series, interpolate the trajectory, and extrapolate it further for prediction. However, although stated as a general context prediction method, the approach was derived from location prediction techniques validated on location prediction problems and does not take into account general context prediction specifics. Prediction methods were restricted to interpolation (which generally has numerous shortcomings, see Sects. 3.6 and 3.8), the questions of pre-processing and different layers of context were not taken into account, and the questions of meaningful output or acting on predicted context were not considered as well.

Context prediction and proactivity problems were also addressed in the works regarding context spaces theory. The overview of theory of context spaces can be found in Padovitz, Loke, and Zaslavsky (2008). The theory itself represents the context as a multidimensional space and uses geometrical metaphors to improve context awareness. The situations are represented as subspaces. Context spaces theory was used as a basis for some context prediction and proactive decision-making mechanisms. In Padovitz, Loke, Zaslavsky, and Burg (2008), the authors discuss the questions of proactive behaviour of a mobile reasoning agent that migrates between different information sources to collect additional information and reason about the situations. In Padovitz, Loke, Zaslavsky, and Burg (2007), the authors provide the concept of natural flow – pre-defined likely sequence of situations over time. Natural flow was used as a verification technique if there were uncertainty about the current situation. Situations that fit the flow are considered to be more likely. Although not used for context prediction directly, the natural flow concept has definite context prediction potential. Another work regarding context prediction and proactivity in context space theory is the work of Boytsov et al. (2009). Here the authors provide the techniques to adopt different machine learning-based context prediction techniques to context spaces theory.

To summarise, there do exist some projects that address the problem of context prediction in a general sense. However, their number is small and still the development of a general approach to context prediction task is a challenge. The most serious common shortcoming is that acting on predicted context is not recognised as a problem and either is not mentioned at all or considered as a task subsequent to the context prediction step. Meanwhile, in many cases, system actions can influence prediction results and therefore, treating context prediction and acting on prediction as independent sequential tasks can severely limit the scope of possible use cases.

5 Research Challenges of Context Prediction

Context prediction is a relatively new problem for computer science. The area of context prediction is just being developed, and there are numerous challenges yet to be addressed. Those challenges include:

1. Lack of general approaches to the context prediction problem.

   Most current solutions predict context for particular situations. There have been only a few attempts to define and solve the context prediction task in general.

2. Lack of automated decision-making approaches.

   Most context prediction-related work focused the efforts on prediction itself, but proper acting on prediction results was usually not considered. Most context prediction systems employed an expert system with pre-defined rules to define the actions based on prediction results. With the notable exception of MDPs, hardly any system considered problems such as "learning to act."

3. Mutual dependency between system actions and prediction results is not resolved.

   This challenge is somewhat related to the previous one. Many context prediction systems considered the tasks of predicting the context and acting on predicted context in sequence: predict and then act on prediction results. That approach can handle only simplified use cases when actions do not affect prediction results. For example, in a smart home, the system can employ any policy for switching on the light or opening the door in advance, depending on user-movement prediction results. But whatever the system does, it will not affect user-intentions to go to a particular room. However, in a general case system, actions do affect prediction results. For example, consider a pervasive system which is capable of automatic purchases to some degree and which needs to plan the expenses, or in a more serious use case, consider a pervasive system that is capable of calling the ambulance and that needs to decide whether to do it or not depending on observed user conditions. In those and many more use-cases, prediction results will clearly depend on what the system does. However, there is almost no work that has considered the problem of mutual dependency between system actions and prediction results. So far, the only works which did address that problem were the works on the MDPs (see Sect. 2.3). But actually the task of resolving the dependency is the special case of a reinforcement learning task. In our opinion, although, compared with most reinforcement learning tasks, pervasive computing systems have their own specifics (e.g., relatively obscure cost and reward functions, high cost of errors and, therefore, very limited exploration capabilities, etc.), recent advancement in the reinforcement learning area can help to overcome that problem.

If all those context prediction challenges are resolved, it will enable pervasive computing systems to handle more sophisticated use-cases, enhance the applicability and the effectiveness of context prediction techniques and, therefore, enhance the overall usability of pervasive computing systems.

References

Abbeel, P. and A.Y. Ng, "Apprenticeship learning via inverse reinforcement learning," in *Proceedings of the Twenty-first International Conference on Machine Learning, Banff, Alberta, Canada*, 2004, pp. 1–8.

Agrawal R. and R. Srikant, "Fast algorithms for mining association rules," in *Proceedings of the 20th International Conference on Very Large Data Bases*, VLDB, Santiago de Chile, Chile, 1994, p. 487–499.

Al-Masri, E. and Q.H. Mahmoud, "A context-aware mobile service discovery and selection mechanism using artificial neural networks," in *Proceedings of the 8th International Conference on Electronic Commerce: The New e-Commerce: Innovations for Conquering Current Barriers, Obstacles and Limitations to Conducting Successful Business on the Internet, Fredericton, New Brunswick, Canada,* 2006, pp. 594–598.

Albrecht, D.W., I. Zukerman and A.E. Nicholson, "Bayesian models for keyhole plan recognition in an adventure game," *User Modeling and User-Adapted Interaction*, Vol. 8, 1998, pp. 5–47.

Anagnostopoulos, C., P. Mpougiouris and S. Hadjiefthymiades, "Prediction intelligence in context-aware applications," in *MDM'05: Proceedings of the 6th International Conference on Mobile Data Management*. New York: ACM Press, Ayia Napa, Cyprus, 2005, pp. 137–141.

Baum, L.E. and T. Petrie, "Statistical inference for probabilistic functions of finite state Markov chains," *The Annals of Mathematical Statistics*, Vol. 37(6) 1966, pp. 1554–1563.

Bhattacharya, A. and S.K. Das, "Lezi update: An information-theoretic approach to track mobile users in PCS networks," in *Proceedings of the 5th annual ACM/IEEE Conference on Mobile Computing and Networking, Seattle, Washington, USA,* 1999, pp. 1–12.

Boytsov, A., A. Zaslavsky and K. Synnes, "Extending context spaces theory by predicting run-time context," in *Proceedings of the 9th International Conference on Smart Spaces and Next*

Generation Wired/Wireless Networking and Second Conference on Smart Spaces. St. Petersburg: Springer, Saint-Petersburg, Russia, 2009, pp. 8–21.

Cook, D.J. and S.K. Das, *Smart Environments: Technologies, Protocols, and Applications*, Wiley, Hoboken, New Jersey, USA, 2004.

Cook, D.J., J.C. Augusto and V.R. Jakkula, "Ambient intelligence: Technologies, applications, and opportunities," *Pervasive and Mobile Computing*, Vol. 5, Aug. 2009, pp. 277–298.

Das, S.K., D.J. Cook, A. Bhattacharya, E.O. Heierman and T.Y. Lin, "The role of prediction algorithms in the MavHome smart home architecture," *IEEE Wireless Communications*, Vol. 9, 2002, pp. 77–84.

Davison, B.D. and H. Hirsh, "Toward an adaptive command line interface," *Advances in Human Factors Ergonomics*, Vol. 21, 1997, pp. 505–508.

Davison, B.D. and H. Hirsh, "Probabilistic online action prediction," in Smith, M.J, Koubek, R.J. and Salvendy, G. (eds.) *Advances in Human Factors/Ergonomics Volume 21B – Design of Computing Systems: Social and Ergonomic Considerations*, Elsevier, North Holland, The Netherlands, 1998, pp. 148–154.

Dey, A.K. and G.D. Abowd, "Towards a better understanding of context and context-awareness," *CHI 2000 Workshop on the What, Who, Where, When, and How of Context-Awareness*, The Hague, The Netherlands, 2000, pp. 304–307.

Feder, M., N. Merhav, and M. Gutman, "Universal prediction of individual sequences," *IEEE Transactions on Information Theory*, Vol. 38, 1992, pp. 1258–1270.

Fritzke, B., "A growing neural gas network learns topologies," *Advances in Neural Information Processing Systems* Vol. 7, 1995, pp. 625–632.

Gellert, A. and L. Vintan, "Person movement prediction using hidden Markov models," *Studies in Informatics and Control*, Vol. 15, 2006, p. 17.

Giarratano, J.C. and G. Riley, *Expert Systems: Principles and Programming*, Course Technology, International Thomson Publishing, USA, 2004.

Gopalratnam, K. and D.J. Cook, "Active LeZi: An incremental parsing algorithm for sequential prediction," in *Proceedings of the Florida Artificial Intelligence Research Society Conference*, 2003, Pensacola, Florida, USA, pp. 38–42.

Hoey, J., A. Von Bertoldi, P. Poupart, and A. Mihailidis, "Assisting persons with dementia during handwashing using a partially observable Markov decision process," in *Proceedings of the International Conference on Vision Systems*, Bielefeld, Germany, 2007, p. 66.

Hong, J., E.H. Suh, J. Kim and S.Y. Kim, "Context-aware system for proactive personalized service based on context history," *Expert Systems with Applications*, Vol. 36, 2009, pp. 7448–7457.

Horvitz, E., J. Breese, D. Heckerman, D. Hovel and K. Rommelse, "The Lumiere project: Bayesian user modeling for inferring the goals and needs of software users," in *Proceedings of the Fourteenth Conference on Uncertainty in Artificial Intelligence*, Madison, Wisconsin, USA, 1998, pp. 256–265.

Kaowthumrong, K., J. Lebsack and R. Han, "Automated selection of the active device in interactive multi-device smart spaces," The Spontaneity Workshop at *UbiComp'02: Supporting Spontaneous Interaction in Ubiquitous Computing Settings*, Göteborg, Sweden, 2002.

Karbassi, A. and M. Barth, "Vehicle route prediction and time of arrival estimation techniques for improved transportation system management," in *Intelligent Vehicles Symposium*, Columbus, Ohio, USA, 2003, pp. 511–516.

Krumm, J., "A Markov model for driver turn prediction," *Society of Automative Engineers (SAE) World Congress*, Detroit, Michigan, USA, 2008.

Lin, T., C. Wang and P.C. Lin, "A neural-network-based context-aware handoff algorithm for multimedia computing," *ACM Transactions on Multimedia Computing, Communications, and Applications (TOMCCAP)*, Vol. 4, 2008, pp. 1–23.

Loke, S.W., "Facing uncertainty and consequence in context-aware systems: Towards an argumentation approach," in *Proceedings of the Workshop on Advanced Context Modelling, Reasoning and Management @ Ubicomp 2004*, Tokyo, Japan, 2004. URL = http://citeseer.ist.psu.edu/loke04facing.html

Mayrhofer, R., "An Architecture for Context Prediction," Ph.D. thesis, Johannes Kepler University of Linz, Austria, October 2004. URL = http://www.mayrhofer.eu.org/downloads/publications/PhD-ContextPrediction-2004.pdf

Mozer, M.C., "The neural network house: An environment that adapts to its inhabitants," in *Proceedings of the American Association for Artificial Intelligence Spring Symposium on Intelligent Environments*, Stanford, California, USA, 1998, pp. 110–114.

Nurmi, P., M. Martin and J.A. Flanagan, "Enabling proactiveness through context prediction," in Proceedings of the Workshop on Context Awareness for Proactive Systems (CAPS, Helsinki, June, 2005), Helsinki University Press, 2005, pp. 159–168.

Padovitz, A., S.W. Loke, A. Zaslavsky and B. Burg, "Verification of uncertain context based on a theory of context spaces," *International Journal of Pervasive Computing and Communications*, Vol. 3(1), 2007, pp. 30–56.

Padovitz, A., S. Loke and A. Zaslavsky, "Multiple-agent perspectives in reasoning about situations for context-aware pervasive computing systems," *IEEE Transactions on Systems, Man and Cybernetics – Part A: Systems and Humans*, Vol. 38(4), 2008, pp. 729–742.

Petzold, J., F. Bagci, W. Trumler and T. Ungerer, "Context prediction based on branch prediction methods," Technical report, 2003. URL=http://www.informatik.uni-augsburg.de/lehrstuehle/sik/publikationen/reports/2003_14_pet/2003_14_pet_pdf.pdf

Petzold, J., A. Pietzowski, F. Bagci, W. Trumler and T. Ungerer, "Prediction of indoor movements using Bayesian networks," *Location-and Context-Awareness (LoCA 2005)*, Oberpfaffenhofen, Germany, 2005, pp. 211–222.

Pichler, M., U. Bodenhofer and W. Schwinger, "Context-awareness and artificial intelligence," *Österreichische Gesellschaft für Artificial Intelligence (ÖGAI)*, 23/1, ISSN 0254-4326, April 2004, pp. 4–11. URL=http://www.schwinger.at/PUBLICATIONS/08_2004_OeGAI_ContextAwareness_and_ArtificialIntelligence.pdf

Rabiner, L.R., "A tutorial on hidden Markov models and selected applications in speech recognition," *Readings in Speech Recognition*, Vol. 53, 1990, pp. 267–296.

Roy, A., S.K. Bhaumik, A. Bhattacharya, K. Basu, D.J. Cook and S.K. Das, "Location aware resource management in smart homes," in *Proceedings of the First IEEE International Conference on Pervasive Computing and Communications*, Fort Worth, Texas, USA, 2003, pp. 481–488.

Russell, S.J. and P. Norvig, *Artificial Intelligence. A Modern Approach*, 2nd edition. Upper Saddle River: Prentice Hall, 2003.

Sigg, S., S. Haseloff and K. David, "A novel approach to context prediction in UBICOMP environments," in *Proceedings of the 2006 IEEE 17th International Symposium on Personal, Indoor and Mobile Radio Communications*, Helsinki, Finland, 2006, pp. 1–5.

Simmons, R., B. Browning, Y. Zhang and V. Sadekar, "Learning to predict driver route and destination intent," *IEEE Intelligent Transportation Systems Conference – ITSC'06*, Toronto, Ontario, Canada, 2006, pp. 127–132.

Srikant, R. and R. Agrawal, "Mining sequential patterns: Generalizations and performance improvements," *Advances in Database Technology – EDBT'96*, Avignon, France, 1996, pp. 3–17.

Vainio, A.-M., "Proactive fuzzy control and adaptation methods for smart homes," *IEEE Intelligent Systems*, March 2008, pp. 42–49.

Vintan, L., A. Gellert, J. Petzold, and T. Ungerer, "Person movement prediction using neural networks," *First Workshop on Modeling and Retrieval of Context*, Ulm, Germany, 2004.

Williams, C.A., A. Mohammadian, P.C. Nelson and S.T. Doherty, "Mining sequential association rules for traveler context prediction," in *Proceedings of the 5th Annual International Conference on Mobile and Ubiquitous Systems: Computing, Networking, and Services*, Dublin: ICST (Institute for Computer Sciences, Social-Informatics and Telecommunications Engineering), Ireland, 2008, pp. 1–6.

Yeh, T.-Y. and Y.N. Patt, "Alternative implementations of two-level adaptive branch prediction," in *Proceedings of the 19th International Symposium on Computer Architecture*, Gold Coast, Queensland, Australia, 1992, pp. 124–134.

Ziebart, B.D., A.L. Maas, A.K. Dey and J.A. Bagnell, "Navigate like a cabbie: Probabilistic reasoning from observed context-aware behavior," in *Proceedings of the 10th International Conference on Ubiquitous Computing*, Seoul, South Korea, 2008, pp. 322–331.

Ziv, J. and A. Lempel, "Compression of individual sequences via variable-rate coding," *IEEE Transactions on Information Theory*, Vol. 24(5), 1978, pp. 530–536.

Zukerman, I, D.W. Albrecht and A.E. Nicholson, "Predicting users' requests on the WWW," in *Proceedings of the Seventh International Conference on User Modeling*, Banff, Alberta, Canada 1999, pp. 275–284.

Chapter 4
A Contextual Methodology for Modelling Real-Time Decision-Making Support

Patrick Brézillon

Laboratoire d'Informatique de Paris 6, Université Pierre et Marie Curie, Paris, France

Abstract Human behaviour must be described on the four levels known as policy, strategy, tactic, and operation. From the upper level (policy) to the lower (operation), the corresponding decision-making process goes through two successive contextualisations. At the first level, decision making has a fixed part (policy and strategy) and a dynamic part (tactic and operation), at the second level. Real-time aspects of decision making are on the dynamic part, i.e., in strong connection with the context in which an actor makes a real-time decision. We propose a modelling of real-time decision making by a contextual methodology that is composed of a series of 10 steps crossing the four levels. The aim is to support the self-training of actors to modify weaknesses of their behaviour during task realisation. The contextual methodology here proposes a unified framework on aspects that are generally contrasted – procedure versus practice, task versus activity, logic of functioning versus logic of use – and explains the two types of contextualisation in a context-oriented model with three layers. The contextual methodology has been applied in a road-safety domain (in which the car driver is continuously in a situation of real-time decision making) and is now used in another application in Open Source domain.

Keywords Decision making • Context management • Contextual graphs • Road safety • Drivers' behaviours modelling • Practice • Activity • Task • Procedure

1 Introduction

Leplat (Leplat and Hoc 1983) pointed out the gap between task and activity (as well prescribed and effective tasks). Similar observations were made in other domains to differentiate procedure. and practices, logic of functioning and logic of use, etc.

P. Brézillon (✉)
Laboratoire d'Informatique de Paris 6, Université Pierre et Marie Curie, Paris, France
e-mail: Patrick.Brezillon@lip6.fr

F. Burstein et al. (eds.), *Supporting Real Time Decision-Making*,
Annals of Information Systems 13, DOI 10.1007/978-1-4419-7406-8_4,

(Richard 1983). Numerous examples were exhibited to illustrate this gap, some explanations were proposed to explain the gap, but no practical solution was offered to fill this gap.

Brézillon (2007) goes one step further on the topic of gap management by showing that first, the difference between prescribed and effective tasks comes from the organisation of the domain knowledge: that is, the procedure relies mainly on the natural structure of the domain knowledge. For example, in the diagnosis of a DVD reader, the domain knowledge (e.g., electrical part, mechanical part, video part, etc.) is organised for the diagnosis in a parallel structure corresponding to the usual paradigm "divide and conquer". The practices have a use-oriented organisation of the domain knowledge in the user's task. To see a movie on a DVD reader, the user first switches on the TV and the DVD reader (and thus power supply problems appear first). Second, the user introduces a DVD in the reader (and thus mechanical problems are considered). Third, the user starts the DVD (and thus video and audio problems may occur). If a procedure has a parallel structure, practices have more sequential structures due to the high contextualisation of the task by the user. Thus, it is better to prefer a model of the practices than to apply only a generic procedure model for a better understanding of the user's concern, not only that of the designer's concern. In our study, we deal with the viewpoint of the actor that accomplishes a task in a given situation and environment that constitutes the context of the task realisation.

Context is always relative to something called a focus (Brézillon 2005). We went a step further: first, by assimilating the relevant part of a context to a set of contextual elements (CEs), and second, by distinguishing the focus definition and its different expressions in real-world situations corresponding to a dressing of the focus (Brézillon and Brézillon 2007). The dressing takes into account the contextual specificity of the situation at hand. For example, a crossroads has a unique definition, but there are never two real identical crossroads in the world. In other words, a generic frame can be defined for representing the class of crossroads by a set of CEs (location, number of roads, traffic lights, etc.), but all the elements will not have the same importance for each real crossroad. This finding is exploited in the contextual methodology that is discussed hereafter.

We also distinguish a CE and its instantiations. An instantiation is the value that a CE can take for a specific instantiation of the focus. For example, I want to take friends out for dinner (the focus). Among different CEs, I have the CE "choice of the restaurant". This CE has generally different instantiations like "French restaurant", "Japanese restaurant", "Italian restaurant", etc. Once the CE "choice of the restaurant" is instantiated, the focus moves towards "Go to the restaurant". This first instantiation in the domain (e.g., Japanese restaurant) must be instantiated itself to address the concrete question "Which one?" (e.g., the Japanese restaurant that is on Avenue Auguste Blanqui in Paris).

The three steps of this example of decision-making process (e.g., go to a restaurant, choose a Japanese restaurant, and go to the Japanese restaurant that is on Ave. A. Blanqui) can be easily explained in the usual policy, strategic, tactical, and operational levels. These levels are used for describing any human behaviours when we consider the focus (i.e., invite friends for a dinner) at the policy level, the way to satisfy the focus (i.e., invite them at a restaurant) at the strategy level, the first instantiation (i.e., a Japanese restaurant) at the tactical level, and the second instantiation (i.e., location of the Japanese restaurant on Ave. A. Blanqui) at the operational level. Often, the policy level (the upper level) is supposed to stay the same all along the task realisation and thus is left implicit. We think that making this policy level explicit allows the organisation of items at lower levels in a more understandable way across different domains.

Existing proposals for context modelling (e.g., Neto and Pimentel 2005; Henricksen and Indulska 2005) establish generally a static and predefined set of entities in a specific domain and therefore, model the context directly as static attributes associated with these entities, which are often obtained through sensors. However, context is a very subtle concept and has an infinite dimension (McCarthy 1993). Thus, one cannot think about context management in a totally generic way without defining and limiting the scope of what will be characterised. A generic and reusable context model cannot be established from a limited set of CEs related to a specific problem prior to its use. The key point is the development of a generic frame composed of all the CEs that are relevant to all the known instantiations of the focus, the user, the task, the situation at hand, and the given environment. This generic frame is open in the sense that it can be enriched incrementally when a situation is partially new. However, this generic frame needs to be instantiated for representing a specific situation.

Hereafter, the chapter is organised in the following way: Sect. 2 presents the background of the contextual methodology, especially concerning the difference procedure versus practice, the notions of CEs, the four levels for describing human behaviour, and the three layers of the context-oriented model that is the bed of contextual methodology (hereafter quoted c-methodology). Section 3 presents the 10 steps of the c-methodology and an application of the c-methodology in road safety.

2 Background of the Contextual Methodology

2.1 Modelling of Procedure and Practice

Enterprises establish procedures based on their experience in order to guide actors' reasoning in a goal of efficiency. Procedures are collections of secure action sequences developed to address a given focus in any case. These procedures are decontextualised in order to cover a large class of similar focuses (generally differing by their contexts of occurrence). Such procedures describe the expected behaviour that actors would adopt to address the focus, i.e., the task model. Generally, there are different methods for task realisation, but the choice of the method does not matter here.

Conversely, the activity model corresponds to the effective behaviours displayed by actors facing the task realisation (i.e., the focus) in a specific context (under some constraints, in a given situation, in a specific environment). Differences between the task model and the activity model arise mainly from the actors' perception of the context. The choice of a method for the task realisation depends on different CEs and mainly on the values (instantiations) that these CEs have when the task must be realised (i.e., in the context at hand). Generally, this granularity is too fine for a task but could be essential for the actor (Brézillon and Brézillon 2007).

A final difference between the task model and the activity model is when a new situation arises. This supposes the revision of the whole structure within the task model when, in the activity model, it necessitates the addition of a few elements such as a new CE and a few actions. Thus, the activity model is incrementally enriched, but, in some domains, may move away from the task model.

We are not concerned here with the theoretical aspects of these notions, only with their use, from a user-centred viewpoint.

2.2 A Context Representation by Contextual Elements

In a previous work on incident management for subway lines, Pomerol, Brézillon, and Pasquier, (2002) showed that context-based reasoning has two parts: diagnosis and action. The diagnosis part analyses the situation at hand and its context in order to extract the essential facts for the actions. The actions are undertaken in a predictable order to realise the desired task. Sometimes actions are undertaken even if the situation is not completely analysed (or even not analysed at all). Other actions are carried out before the proceduralisation of a part of contextual knowledge. Thus, diagnosis and actions constitute a continuous interlocked process, not two distinct and successive phases in context-based reasoning. Moreover, actions introduce changes in the situation or in knowledge about the situation and imply a revision of the diagnosis, and thus of the decision-making process itself. As a consequence, there is a need for a context-based formalism for a uniform representation of diagnosis and actions.

For Brézillon and Pomerol (1999), context is "what constrains something without intervening in it explicitly". We now consider the "something" by extension as a focus of attention for an actor. Several elements justify this definition, the three main elements being that (1) context is relative to the focus of attention, (2) as the focus of attention evolves, its context evolves too, and (3) context is highly domain dependent. As a consequence, one cannot speak of context in an abstract way. Next, we can show that the focus of attention allows the division of context into external knowledge and contextual knowledge (Brézillon 2005). The latter constitutes a kind of tank where the CEs are to some extent related to the focus of attention in a flat way, whereas the former has nothing to do with it. The focus of attention evolves because a new event occurs (e.g., an unpredicted event) or as a result of a decision made at the previous stage of the focus of attention. Consequently, the notion of context impacts more on the relationships between knowledge pieces than upon the pieces themselves (and thus impacts reasoning too).

Brézillon and Brézillon (2007) introduce the concept of focus dressing to represent the fact that, if there is a unique focus, the ways to address that focus are generally different, at least in some details. Thus, we describe all the objects intervening in a context (the actor, the task, the situation, the environment) by a list of CEs that may differ in two ways from the list describing another approach of the focus: (1) by the CEs that are present in the list, and (2) by shared CEs common to the two lists that may have different values. This leads us to develop the notion of generic frame that is the sum of all the CEs known to intervene in some description of the actor, the task, the situation, and the environment.

A generic frame allows the description of a class of objects. The frame is composed of CEs that may be organised according to the domain structure. An object of the class will be described by a subset of the CEs of the generic frame in relationship with the focus for which this object is considered. For example, if a focus is to reduce health risks linked to pollution, one way is to attack cars in cities. The CE "pollution" of the frame for cars will be relevant for usual cars but generally not for electric cars. In a second step, the CE "pollution" of a specific normal car may take different values: "normal", "high", "dangerous". Thus, there are two successive instantiations of the generic frame: (1) selection of the relevant CEs, and (2) identification of the values of the relevant CEs. The first instantiation is at the abstract levels (policy and strategy) and the second instantiation is at the concrete levels (tactic and operation). The value of a CE may be either a value or another CE depending on the focus.

Moreover, the instantiation of a CE may lead to another CE being triggered or inhibited by the value taken by another CE. For example, if the CE "period of the day" has the instance "night", as a consequence, the CE "car light" must be present and have the value "switch on", and the instance "sunny" of the CE "weather" can be eliminated. This implies the first category of rules: the integrity rules. There is the second category of rules that is concerned with the expected behaviour in the contextualised domain. For example, with the instance "rainy" of the CE "weather", one expectation is that a driver will (1) reduce the speed of his car, and (2) increase the distance from the car in front of him. This constitutes the expected behaviour that actors must display in the specific context of the situation, i.e., for the given situation dressing (e.g., a crossroads on a rainy night). Note that this expected behaviour model of the actors is more complete (contextualised) than rules such as those in highway laws. We spoke of a contextualised task model in Brézillon and Brézillon (2008).

2.3 *The Four-Level Representation of Human Reasoning*

In crisis management, Canton (2007) organises a crisis response into three rough categories:

- Operational or field response consists of the systems and resources needed to respond directly to the impact of an event. These systems and resources include first responders (i.e., police, fire, emergency medical personnel) and manage response at the field level.

- Tactical response manages the overall response to the event by coordinating the activities of multiple responding agencies, anticipating the resources needed, and coordinating public information.
- Strategic response manages the crisis by examining long-range implications of the event, determining long-term goals and objectives, and establishing priorities that will guide operational response.

Each level determines planning assumptions, level of detail, and resources required. However, the three levels are considered in the same framework of the management of a crisis that corresponds to the policy level.

In the military domain, Clausewitz (1873) considers the same levels but introduces the operational level between the strategic and tactical levels in order to insist on two parts, namely an abstract part (policy and strategy) and a concrete part (operation and tactic). Thus, the political level generates the purpose of war. The strategic level provides the overall idea of how to fight the war by transforming ambiguities of the political nuances into directives to the next level. The operational level is responsible for the deployment of the armies, navies and air forces for the war. Field elements are orchestrated to achieve the objectives of command strategy and ensure that tactical actions are coordinated to achieve strategic objectives. The tactical level is responsible for the manoeuvres, which bring the military units in contact with the enemy. Objectives are defined in the material terms of boundaries, time, numbers, and resources.

These levels constitute a continuum. We do not want to enter into the discussion for the respective position of the tactical and operational levels. In our view, we just have to make our choice clear at the beginning. We have decided to follow the ordering of the more generally accepted (policy, strategy, tactic, and operation).

2.3.1 Policy Level

A policy is related to the interest of the organisation and its natural values, and is more specifically a key point for the organisation facing the environment. The policy statement describes what is unique about the organisation's ability to execute on its mission statement. The policy provides guidelines to the members of the organisation for deciding a course of action. A policy statement helps make an organisation predictable and eventually prevents some serious problems for the organisation. Policies are generally expressed in a qualitative, conditional or general way. Policies ensure that all decisions are mutually consistent, uniform, and viable.

The mission addresses critical policy issues affecting the organisation. If the policy defines the fundamental objective of an organisation or an enterprise, the intention of a mission statement is to keep members and users aware of the organisation's objective. The mission statement concentrates on the present and takes into account the complexity of the situation in the domain. It defines the actors and the critical processes. This requires a complex combination of resources, competences, and a sensibility to contextual differences.

2.3.2 Strategic Level

Organisational mission and objectives are the starting points of strategy formulation. The policy gives a sense of direction while the strategy gives a sense of purpose in a given context. A strategy is a long-term plan of action focused on achieving a goal that supposes a part of anticipation. A strategy is a statement of why (the policy). The strategy is established at a high level and is the connection between the determination of the basic long-term goals and objectives of an organisation and the adoption of the course of action and allocation of resources necessary for carrying out these goals. The process of environmental analysis includes collection of relevant information from the environment, interpretation of its impact on the future organisational work, and determination of what opportunities and threats – positive and negative aspects – are offered by the environment. A strategy looks inward at the organisation but it also looks outward at the competition and at the environment and business climate.

A strategy is a course of action through which an organisation relates itself with the environment so as to achieve its objectives (mission statement). There is not a unique way, but the strategy defines the direction in which the organisation must go to stay within the policy and respect the mission statement. This allows the organisation to be proactive (tactics are reactive) in a kind of planning of the mission statement. A strategy is a set of actions and sequencing commitments, consistent with doctrine and driven by the unique features of an action domain that constrains but does not define plans and schedules. Strategies focus on action and imply deployment of resources for their implementation. They are well thought out and a long-range plan aims at goal achievement.

2.3.3 Tactical Level

Tactics correspond to specific actions, sequences of actions (procedures), and schedules to fulfil the strategy. A tactic is an abstract action that can be applied in any of a large class of situations. Tactics are flexible. If a tactic isn't working, actors can adjust it and try again. Tactics are goal-oriented because each action is planned according to the global picture given at the strategic level. A tactic is a conceptual action, a kind of guideline at the lower level of operation that will have to be implemented. A tactic describes, in a logic of functioning, how to achieve the accomplishment of the goal as one or more tasks (or procedures). This is the viewpoint of leadership, which is mainly interested in task organisation, timing, and articulation of different tactics.

2.3.4 Operational Level

Operation is the discipline of realising strategy in the context of a background of infrastructure systems and resources. The tactic specifies a general organisation of the tasks to be executed (a kind of abstract workflow), provides a type of resource but does not specify which one exactly. Operation contextualises the tactic by choosing a given method for accomplishing each task and selecting a specific resource that is needed in the current context for respecting all the practical constraints. An operation is lead in a logic of use and is developed in one or more activities (or practices) which are fully contextualised. The operation specifies the contextualisation of the task architecture to be processed (a kind of concrete workflow) and the selection of the better resource in the context. This is provided by a given person (or a group of persons) in a given situation and a given environment. If a tactic is a first level of contextualisation (giving meaning to entities in the chosen domain and for the focus at hand), then operation is the second level of contextualisation that transforms the entities of the domain to specific objects in a specific situation in the domain. This is the viewpoint of the actor accomplishing the task.

2.3.5 Summing Up

Policy and strategy are at an abstract level while tactics and operation are at an implementation level. This sheds some light on the well-known duality of task versus activity, procedure versus practice, etc., because it addresses the same problem from two different viewpoints. A task is an abstract description of what must be done. Often, different methods may be used to execute the task and the choice of one method over the others depends on the actor executing the task taking into account the situation, the actor, and the environment. An activity (or a practice) is a contextualisation of the task (or the procedure) made by the (operational) actor. It is interesting to note that this twofold aspect of decision making appears in two places, first between strategy and tactical levels, and second between tactical and operational levels. The first stage corresponds to the selection of the CEs that are relevant for a specific application of the focus, while the second stage corresponds to the instantiation of the retained CEs. This shows that we can consider two types of contextualisation. In our view, it is a key point when we study real-time decision making because this shows that there is a stable part (the abstract one) and a dynamic one (the contextualised one). Thus, it is essential to make context explicit for analysing real-time decision making.

Another point is that the two actors (the tactical actor and the operational actor) are able to speak of the same thing, each with his or her mental representation of the problem. For example, in an application for the subway, the responsible actor of a subway line (the tactical actor) says to the driver of the train (the operational actor): "Empty your train of travellers". For the former, it is a simple action, while the latter considers it as a complex action (make an announcement in the train, stop at the next station, etc.)

2.4 *A Three-Layer Model*

In the realm of Brézillon and Pomerol's work (1999) and Vieira, Tedesco, Salgado, and Brézillon (2007), we propose a context-oriented model approach that considers

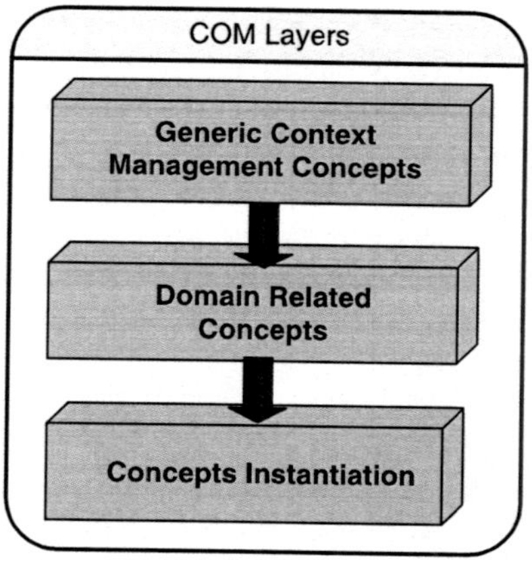

Fig. 1 The three layers of the context-oriented model

the modelling of decision makers' behaviours in three layers (Fig. 1). The upper layer characterises the generic (i.e., domain-independent) context management-related concepts and can be qualified as a meta model since it is used for creating individual models. The upper level is a high level domain-independent layer where concepts can be managed in a generic manner without worrying about the domain particularities. The middle layer defines the domain-specific context-related concepts in accordance with the upper layer. This is the level where the generic frame is introduced in the previous section. The lower layer represents the instantiation of the domain concepts according to a specific application, incrementally acquired during the system usage.

The context-oriented model relies on five main concepts: entity, CE, focus, rule, and action.

Focus is a central concept in the context-oriented model since the context is always related to a focus of attention. It is an objective to be achieved, such as a task in problem solving or a step in decision making. The focus allows the determination of the relevant CEs to use and instantiate in a specific situation.

An entity is anything in the real world that is relevant to describe the domain. An entity is characterised by one or more CEs.

CE identifies the atomic part of the context of an entity. A CE may be composed of one or more entities, meaning that an entity is related to the CE.

Rule is associated with the CEs and supports the building of the proceduralised context in the focus. Each rule has one or more conditions but returns one action. Conditions are represented by instances of type of CE and the returned action is an instance of the class action.

Action indicates what a context-sensitive system is supposed to trigger when a rule is activated; thus, the rules are specified according to defined actions.

To represent the concepts in the context-oriented model, we are using a combination of extended ontology and topic maps based on the model presented in Fig. 1.

Ontology enables knowledge sharing between human and software agents, easy knowledge reuse between systems, and can be easily used by inference engines for reasoning. Thus, they are appropriate to represent the hierarchical structure between the CEs and its instances. Topic maps can be used to organise large sets of information to build a structured semantic link network over existing resources (Power 2003). This representation formalism allows easy and selective navigation to the requested information. An interesting characteristic of topic maps is that topics can have relationships (associations) with each other and topics can play different roles in different associations.

3 The Contextual Methodology

3.1 The 10 Steps

Contextual methodology has 10 interdependent steps organised along the four levels of policy (at steps 1 and 2), strategy (at steps 3–8), tactics (step 9), and operations (step 10). This methodology was applied successfully in the domain of road safety and currently is used in the open source domain (for the assembling of software components). We describe each of the 10 steps here in a unique format (goal, means, results, comments). The application in road safety is used in the next section to illustrate the c-methodology.

Step 1: Select the domain (Policy level)

Goal(s): Select a domain where there is a crucial problem for the organisation or, by side effect, in other domains of interest for the organisation.

Means: General information (statistics, major events, etc.) and specific information (e.g., highway code), choices of the people responsible for the policy of the organisation, such as the CEO of a company.

Results: The domain that is important for the organisation or the society, its importance, and the need to smooth things.

Comments: Steps 1 and 2 must be considered jointly.

Step 2: Fix the focus (Policy level)

Goal(s): Select a problem encountered by the organisation and identify the key issues relating to that problem.

Means: New laws, new technology, information, new rules, actors' training, and self-training.

Results: Selection of a way for problem solving and coordination with other challenges of the organisation or the society.

Comments: The focus will lead to a move of the organisation or the society that is necessary for facing a change in its environment. The choice of the objects in the domain depends on the focus in the domain. General elements of the generic frame are chosen during steps 1 and 2.

Step 3: Select a situation (Strategy level)

Goal(s): Choose a situation where the problem is particularly visible.
Means: General knowledge on the domain, problem characteristics, statistics, expected consequences.
Results: A representation in terms of CEs of the relevant situation.
Comments: The situation is chosen because of its appearing frequently and being general enough. If there is a unique definition of this situation, there are numerous variants of the situation; there is always at least one CE that differs between the two instantiations of the situation. The generic frame is supposed to collect a large number of CEs covering known instantiations of the situation. Because we cannot know in advance all that will be needed, the representation formalism must allow the incremental acquisition of new CEs (and/or their values) at any time for enriching the generic frame.

Step 4: Choose a task (Strategy level)

Goal(s): Choose a task realised in the situation that is described at the right granularity (the observation level).
Means: The situation, knowledge on the task, methods used in the task, performances, weaknesses, crucial steps in the task realisation that are related to the problem, means for studying actors' behaviours.
Results: The task model is described in terms of CEs in the generic frame for its static part, and in terms of contextual graphs for the dynamic part concerning actor's behaviour.
Comments: Tasks are specified at an abstract level, such as procedures, routines, and rules. In the following, the task will be considered through its contextualisation in the situation. The task realisation will be studied through actor's behaviour.

Step 5: Establish integrity rules for the generic frame (Strategy level)

Goal(s): Establish the internal coherence of the generic frame and the possibility of automatically propagating CE instantiation.
Means: Analysis of the relationships between CEs and their values, common sense, procedures, routines.
Results: A set of integrity rules to trigger during CE instantiation.
Comments: The generic frame contains a description of the focus, the domain, the situation and the task in terms of CEs, eventually organising them according to the sources of context (physical elements, technical elements, etc.) Because CEs are interdependent, the choice of a CE or its value in a specific situation may influence other CEs as expressed by integrity rules.

Step 6: Model the expected behaviour of actors (Strategy level)

Goal(s): Establish the expected behaviour of actors for the given environment, focus, situation, and task.

Means: Body of legal knowledge, common sense, the generic frame, known constraints, contextual graphs, procedure, routines.

Results: A model of the expected behaviour of actors that will be a guideline for modelling effective behaviours.

Comments: The expected behaviour corresponds to a standard user. A system applying such rules holds model-based reasoning. The model tries to be as exhaustive as possible but, nevertheless, is at a very abstracted (decontextualised) level.

Step 7: Model effective behaviours of actors (Strategy level)

Goal(s): Collect usual practices

Means: The situation, the task, record of variables on actors' behaviours, inquiry, questionnaires, the generic frame, contextual graphs.

Results: A representation of the known practices for accomplishing a given task in a given situation according to the actors' viewpoints. An extension of the generic frame along the human dimension and the real constraint resources. The representation includes any type of behaviour, good as well as bad with respect to the initial problem.

Comments: The generic frame is enriched here by the human dimension and ephemeral conditions (e.g., the weather). The practice model is a way to measure the distance with respect to the expected behaviour. It represents the compatibility of what exists compared to what is done with it. The practice model may be used to explain to a subject his or her behaviour as the result of a combination of CEs and actions, what mistake was made, why the subject made the mistake, and to train the subject to give more importance to the CE(s) corresponding to the mistake. Effective behaviours allow defining the status of each instantiation of the situation (normal, critical, pre-critical).

Step 8: Establish classes of actors (Strategy level)

Goal(s): Analyse variables (i.e., CEs of the generic frame), leading actors to have behaviours related to the identified problem.

Means: Questionnaire, trace analysis, the practice model, the generic frame, statistical tools.

Results: A class corresponds to a combination of variables representing a type of behaviour that can be a cause of the problem. Classes are organised in order to have only one negative variable that is different between two connected classes. The organisation is realised in two ways along general characteristics (age, sex, etc.) and along the interdependency of the variables.

Comments: We check the external coherence of the generic frame here according to actors' viewpoints. The class categorisation with respect to general characteristics allows us to allocate a given actor to a starting class, when the categorisation with respect to the interdependency of the variables is used to allocate the subject from the observation of his/her effective behaviour, determine sensible variables for the identified problem, and the path to correct "negative" variables one by one. All the classes are relevant for explaining different behaviours leading to the problem in the focus.

Step 9: Design scenarios (Tactical level)

Goal(s): Find scenes and scripts where a subject will be placed to check the negative variables of the class in which he/she is supposed to be, and then establish scenarios.

Means: Classes, practice model, generic frame, questionnaire, a simulator, and a real-world situation.

Results: A set of scenarios to determine if the subject exhibits the planned negative variables associated with his/her class (for checking, validation, and training purposes).

Comments: A simulator is used if a focus implies dangerous behaviours of actors.

Step 10: Analyse a subject's behaviour (Operational level)

Goal(s): Select a negative variable of the starting class for correction, convince the subject that his/her behaviour is responsible for the problem to be corrected, show him/her how to correct it, validate the correction, and reiterate for treating another variable.

Means: Scenarios, classes, practice model, the generic frame, questionnaire, a simulator, real-world experiments.

Results: A subject is aware of the mistake associated with the negative variable, why it is a mistake, and how to correct it. The validation of the training is made on a similar scenario in another context.

Comments: There is a better integration of the problem and its correction because we take the actor's viewpoint, we exhibit how the actor shows a bad behaviour, why, and then we explain how to correct it and go back progressively to a normal behaviour (i.e., not abruptly with a punishment).

3.2 *Application in the Modelling of Drivers' Behaviour*

The contextual methodology has been elaborated, initially using our application in road safety (Brézillon 2009). The Goals for Driver Education (GDE) matrix (see Table 1), with results of a European project, was the first attempt to describe human behaviour in terms of variables (our CEs) and to classify them at four levels,

Table 1 The GDE matrix with contextual elements corresponding to drivers' behaviours (Hatakka et al. 1996)

	Knowledge and skills	Risk increasing factors	Self-evaluation
Political Goals for life and skills for living (general)	*Knowledge about/ control over how life goals and personal tendencies affect driving behaviour:* • Lifestyle/life situation • Group norms • Motives • Self-control, other characteristics • Personal values • etc.	*Risky tendencies:* • Self-enhancement through driving • High level of sensation seeking • Complying with social pressure • Use of alcohol/ drugs • Values, attitude towards society • etc.	*Self-evaluation/ awareness of:* • Personal skills for impulse control • Risky tendencies • Safety negative motives • Personal risky habits • etc.
Strategic Goals and context of driving (trip related)	*Knowledge and skills concerning:* • Effects of trip goals on driving • Planning and choosing routes • Evaluation of social pressure in the car • Evaluation of necessity of trip • etc.	*Risks connected with:* • Driver's condition (mood, blood alcohol, etc.) • Purpose of driving • Driving environment (rural/urban) • Social context and company • Extra motives (competing, etc.) • etc.	*Self-evaluation/ awareness of:* • Personal planning skills • Typical goals of driving • Typical risky driving motives • etc.
Tactical Mastery of traffic situations	*Knowledge and skills concerning:* • Traffic rules observation/selection of signals • Anticipation of course of • Situations • Speed adjustment • Communication • Driving path • Driving order • Distance to others/ safety • Margins • Distance to others/ safety margins • etc.	*Risks caused by:* • Wrong expectations • Risk increasing driving style (e.g., aggressive) • Unsuitable speed adjustment • Vulnerable road users • Not obeying rules/ unpredictable behaviour • Information overload • Difficult conditions (darkness, etc.) • Insufficient automatism/ skills • etc.	*Self-evaluation/ awareness of:* • Strong and weak points of basic traffic skills • Personal driving style • Personal safety margins • Strong and weak points for hazard situations • Realistic self-evaluation • etc.

(continued)

Table 1 (continued)

	Knowledge and skills	Risk increasing factors	Self-evaluation
Operational Vehicle manoeuvring	*Knowledge and skills concerning:* • Control of direction and position • Tyre grip and friction • Vehicle properties • Physical phenomena • etc.	*Risks connected with:* • Insufficient automatism/skills • Unsuitable speed adjustment • Difficult conditions (low friction, etc.) • etc.	*Awareness of:* • Strong and weak points of basic manoeuvring skills • Strong and weak points of skills for hazard situations • Realistic self-evaluation • etc.

corresponding more or less to policy, strategy, tactic, and operation. It was shown that difficulty encountered by novices in the driving task was due to a training limited to the lower level (vehicle manoeuvring at the operational level) and sometimes the level above (mastery of traffic situations at the tactical level) but never moving to the two upper levels (strategy and policy).

Step 1: Select the domain

The chosen domain was road safety. Road safety is one important challenge of our society. Fatalities on the road are due to bad driving habits, infrastructure (secure highway), and car design. Road safety is also to be considered with other challenges of the society (economy, market, oil, etc.).

Step 2: Fix the focus

The chosen focus was to "reduce the number of fatalities on the road by favouring self-training of car drivers". There are several ways for improving road safety by acting on drivers: limit car speed (e.g., radar), develop information for drivers, increase road signals, improvement of the road network. Generally, behind each option there are big industrial groups (car makers, oil companies, etc.), and thus a strong lobby against the focus. Self-training in the driving task is a way to learn the highway code from the practical viewpoint of the driver, to complement the theoretical viewpoint of the driving licence. Existing approaches such as the highway code are based on notions of punishment that are not well-perceived. (Punishments address the effects, not the causes.) Here, the idea was to design software in the spirit of "serious games".

Step 3: Select a situation

The situation is a crossroads. There are different sources of contexts that allow organisation (roughly) of CEs. In road safety, the main classes of elements of a situation are: physical elements (e.g., environment), technical elements (e.g., structure of the crossroads), moment elements (e.g., day, season, weather), context of the task execution (e.g., vehicles, traffic, visibility, etc.), human elements (e.g., physical and cognitive aspects, journey).

Step 4: Select a task

The given task is "Turn left at a crossroad" because a number of fatalities may occur during this task execution. For instance, in France, if a car coming from the opposite direction also wants to turn left, you and the other driver must turn one after the other (see Fig. 2a). However, if this situation does not imply two cars but two lines of cars, drivers fall in a dead-end because each line stops the other. Legally, there is a second rule "Do not stop in the central area of a crossroads" (and then wait at the entrance of the area) to avoid this dead-end. Practically, drivers find a private solution (i.e., a practice that is a translation of the procedure satisfying everybody) of type B in Fig. 2. Thus, the first driver who can operate will turn, whatever the length of the line on the other side. However, this is a practice, not the procedure.

Step 5: Establish integrity rules for the generic frame

A large part of the integrity rules come from the Highway Code such as:
IF a car is coming from your right at a crossroads,
THEN let it give way
Other rules are common sense knowledge:
IF value (period_of_the_day) = "Night"
THEN suppress the value "sunny" of the CE "weather" (in France)
Another part comes from drivers' experience such as:
IF at night time, lights on the right road mean a car is coming
THEN I must let it "give-way"
(note, that this is not an absolute rule because this does not concern bikes, hay cart, tractors, etc.).

Step 6: Identify the expected behaviour of drivers

Most of the rules comefrom the Highway Code such as:
IF value(weather) = "Rainy" or value(ground) = "Wet"
THEN the driver must reduce the speed of his/her car.
But also from the driver's experience: "I had an accident at this crossroads in the past, so now I must pay attention".

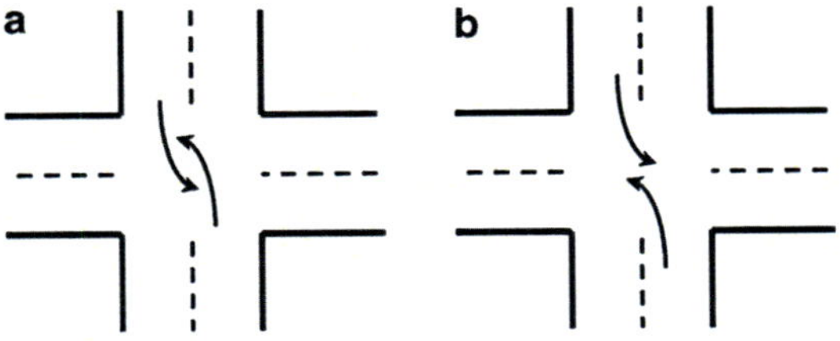

Fig. 2 Turn left task at a crossroads

Step 7: Model effective behaviours of drivers

The GDE matrix (Hatakka, Keskinen, and Laapotti 1996) organises CEs in cells. The four lines of the matrix are close to the usual approach – policy-strategic-tactical-operational levels – found in other domains. The redundancy of the CEs appearing on several levels implies that the drivers' decision-making processes must be analysed on all these levels and not at the tactical or operational level only. A bad (especially risky) behaviour may have different reasons at upper levels that are important to identify precisely for correcting the bad behaviour.

From this study, the lessons learned are the following (see Brézillon 2009 for details):

- numerous CEs must be collected for describing car drivers' behaviours for a given objective (identification and correction of risky behaviours in our application)
- CEs come from numerous sources and are related to one another, and
- the four levels description (policy, strategic, tactical. and operational) shows that the instantiation of the CEs at one level depends on CEs at upper levels.

We have analysed the variables of the GDE matrix in terms of CEs to describe drivers' behaviours. Table 1 represents the GDE matrix as found in Hatakka et al. (1996). However, such a work is specific to a domain and does not exist everywhere. Thus, a preliminary work must be to collect CEs corresponding to decision makers' behaviours in the domain.

A situation corresponding to the arrival of a driver at a T-intersection with a right-of-way is described by this set of practices, and then Fig. 3 shows eight different (good and bad) practices (paths in the graph).

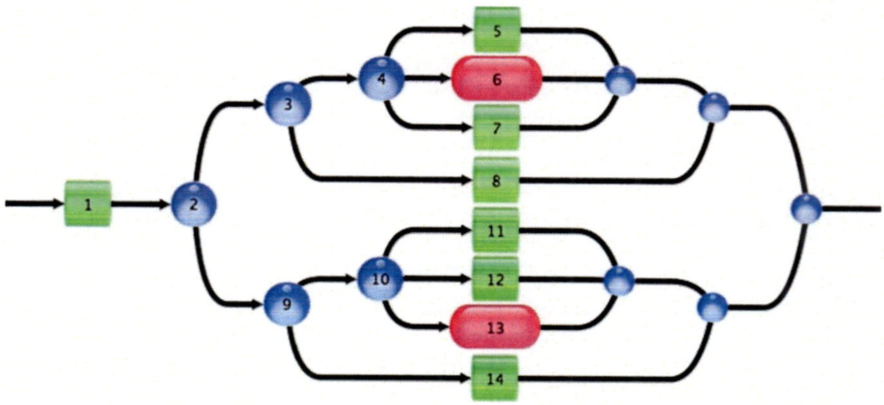

Fig. 3 The practice model, which is represented in the contextual graphs formalism, corresponds to a driver arriving at a crossroads with another car coming from his right (Brézillon 2009)

(a) 1: Arrive to a T-intersection with the right-of-way
(b) 2: Look at right?
(c) Yes 3: Is there a car at right?
(d) Yes 4: Pay attention to Car-B?
(e) No 5: Cross the T-intersection
(f) Yes 6: Activity « Car-B Management »
(g) Stop7: Brake strongly
(h) No 8: Cross the T-crossroad
(i) No 9: Expectation?
(j) Unpredicted event 10: Decision?
(k) Stop 11: Brake strongly
(l) Keep right-of-way 12: Cross the T-intersection
(m) Take care 13: Activity « Car-B Management »
(n) Correct 14: Cross the T-intersection

This is the model of all the collected practices, not a statistical model. Each practice can be explained relative to others. This includes the initial task model, some interpretations such as in Fig. 2b, but also bad and dangerous behaviours (e.g., "I have time to cross before the other driver does something" or, conversely, "The other has a give-way but I prefer to stop just in case", forgetting, say, the car behind). However, a driver may have different reasons for showing a bad behaviour. This is the object of the next step.

This practice model is used to explain to a subject who makes a mistake, to point out why the subject makes this mistake, and to train the subject to give more importance to the concerned CE. Another interesting result is that an action can correspond to good decision making or bad decision making depending on the context in which this action is executed. This includes also some socially implicit rules such as at a crossroads with two long lines of cars one coming from the right of the other. One observes that cars of each line alternate to cross the intersection, and never all the cars of the line without priority allow all the other cars to cross first.

Step 8: Establish classes of drivers

For identifying and classifying the different classes of bad behaviours of car drivers, a questionnaire was designed according to the focus and put on the Web. The questionnaire had 162 questions on 61 variables (the CEs). We obtained 419 full answers on 600 visits to the website and thus we were able to identify 15 classes. A class is defined by a combination of negative variables (i.e., leading to a bad or dangerous behaviour of drivers with respect to the focus). Table 2 provides 4 of the 15 classes of effective behaviours.

For each class, we then identify the "negative variables" corresponding to risky behaviours (e.g., "aggressive", but for another focus like "save energy", a bad behaviour could be "Does not evaluate the need of a trip"). Afterward, we organise classes in two ways. The first one (see Fig. 4 for the variable "age") is based on general variables. The goal is to be able to associate a new subject with a class from general characteristics (age, sex, education, etc.). The second way (see Fig. 5) corresponds

Table 2 : Some classes that were identified for drivers (Brézillon 2009)

1	Man
	35–45 years old
	Working
	Uses car daily
	Has had driving licence more than 15 years
	Does not respect safety margins
	On information overload
	Does not respect driving rules
5	Man
	55–65 years old
	Retired
	Uses car regularly
	Has had driving licence more than 15 years
	Drives for another reason than going somewhere
	Does not respect safety margins
	Does not have the basic skills for driving
	Has stress while driving
	Is not objective in auto evaluation
	Do not drive in case of ice on the road
	Does not evaluate the necessity of the trip
	Has personal driving style
	Attains self-enhancement through driving
	Drives as fast as possible
	Do not take care of his car
	Drives usually in urban environment
7	Woman
	18–25 years old
	Drives for another reason than going somewhere
	Does not care about gasoline economy
	On information overload
	Does not have basic skills for driving
	Lack of automatisms
	Does not evaluate the necessity of the trip
	Has personal driving style
9	Man
	18–25 years old
	Working
	Does not have licence for the first time
	On information overload
	Does not have basic skills for driving
	Drives in a bad mood
	Does not evaluate the necessity of the trip
	Has personal driving style
	Does not consider his car as purely functional
	Has work not related to driving but obliges him to drive daily

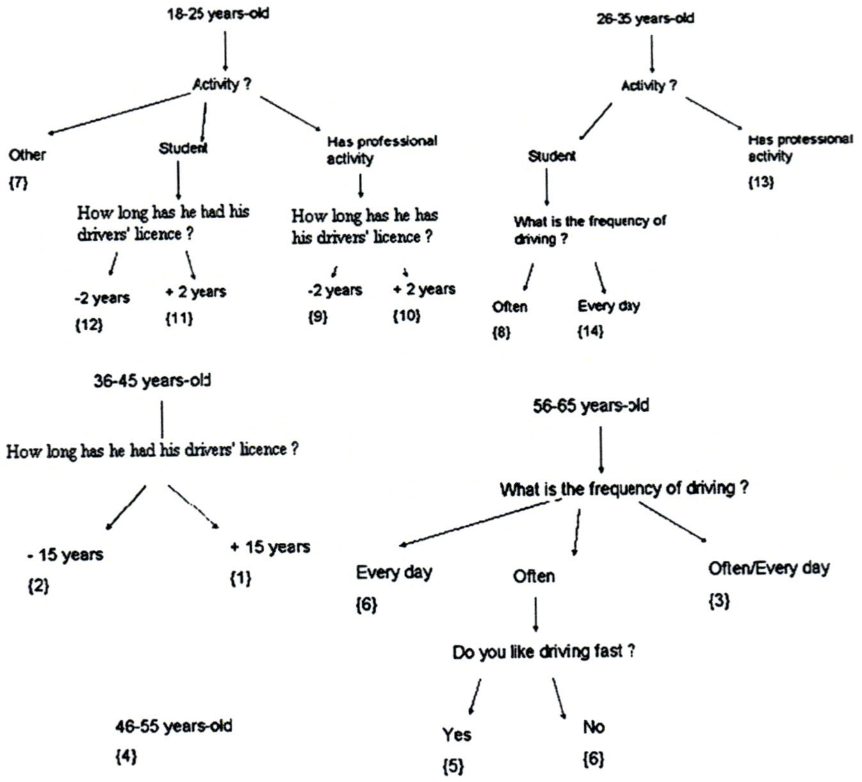

Fig. 4 Class organisation by drivers' age intervals (Figures between brackets correspond to the class numbers as the examples given in Table 2)

to an organisation based on the negative variables corresponding to the mistakes a driver may make. For explanation and for training purposes, the way from one class to another corresponds to the change of value of a unique negative variable. We thus obtained the "expected behaviour" from the first way and the "effective behaviour" of a given subject by the second way.

Step 9: Design scenarios

Figure 6 presents the following scenario: The vehicle preceding the subject indicates that the driver plans to turn right, this driver brakes suddenly and stops before turning on the right. The competences that are concerned are basic competences for driving, good prediction, lack of automatism, respect for safety interval between cars.

Step 10: Analyse a subject's behaviour

Suppose we plan to correct an aggressive behaviour. We thus propose a first scenario corresponding to a turn-left when there is a continuous line of cars coming from the opposite way and with intervals that look "almost" sufficient to turn. Some subjects

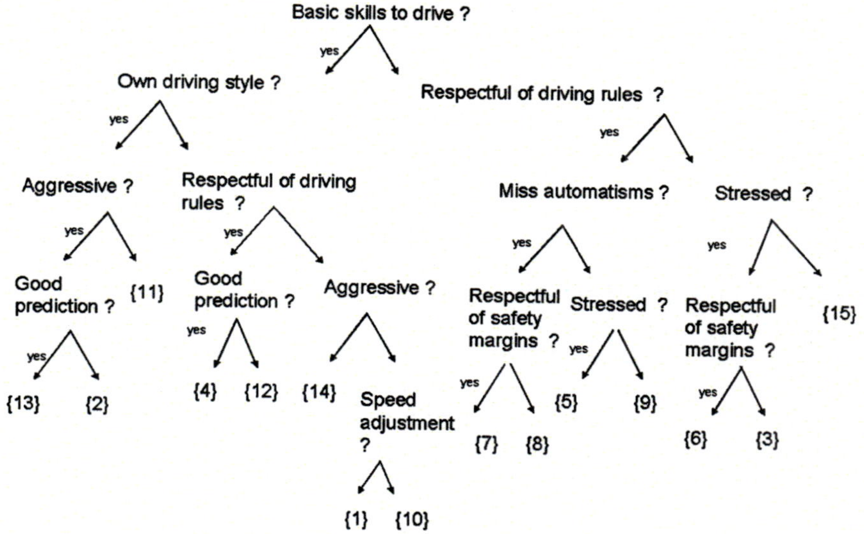

Fig. 5 Class organisation by drivers' errors (Figures between brackets correspond to the class numbers as the examples given in Table 2)

Fig. 6 Screen copy of the scenario in which the car ahead indicates that it is turning right but stops totally before turning, obliging the subject to react

wait quietly, even if surprised, when other subjects try to break through the line of cars, expecting that a driver will let him/her to turn left. The procedure here is the following:

1. General question (age, sex, etc.) to determine the initial class.
2. Deduction of the expected errors associated with this class.
3. Proposition of a scenario associated with this class.
4. Recording of the effective behaviour when the subject processes the scenario.

5. Research of the class corresponding to the effective errors.
6. The experiment ends with a questionnaire to increase the situation awareness of the subject.

We have conducted an experiment in real conditions with 45 individuals and 11 scenarios.

4 Conclusion

The notion of criticality of a situation is *relative* to the context: it may appear critical in one context and not in another. Indeed, making context explicit in our methodology first allows the making of any behaviour explainable, and, second, allows the decision maker to learn why his or her behaviour may lead to the problem that is in focus and how such an undesirable behaviour may be modified by pointing out the easiest path between the bad behaviour and the nearest good behaviour through identification of the CE(s) misinterpreted.

The contextual methodology has two main parts – pretreatment and treatment. The pretreatment phase occurs only once for each actor, followed by a series of treatments applied to subjects. In the pretreatment phase, we first establish a conceptual description of decision-makers' behaviours that addresses the initial objective of behaviour management (the description is given by a set of CEs). Then, we try to have as many as possible instantiations of this conceptual description (the instantiations are obtained by a questionnaire). These instantiations help us to identify classes of behaviours that are relevant to our initial objective.

The next step is (a) to express quantitatively the objective in each class (e.g., if the objective concerns the correction of errors, CEs that correspond to errors specific to each class are pointed out), and (b) to establish the paths between classes corresponding to smooth changes (i.e., when two classes differ by the value of a unique CE). These paths will guide decision makers in their training to evolve from a "bad" behaviour to a "good" behaviour. This is implemented by the use of scenarios. In a treatment phase (i.e., for each subject), we first look for the class in which the subject can be initially considered to determine his or her "expected behaviour". Before beginning to train the subject to correct these expected errors, we validate our allocation by applying a scenario to obtain the "effective behaviour" of the subject. The comparison between "expected" and "effective" behaviours allows adjusting our model of the decision-maker's behaviour. The next step is the training itself, with identification and explanation of errors committed by the subject, the path to follow to evolve towards a good behaviour (through intermediary classes) and use of new scenarios addressing the same errors in different contexts. There are thus two different validations.

Our contextual methodology concerns mainly two notions: the notions of behaviour and of situation. For a given situation (e.g., a crossroads), a decision maker (e.g., a driver) may present different behaviours (e.g., quiet or aggressive) in a given activity (e.g., crossing the intersection) according to CEs (e.g., it is raining, or the driver is in a hurry). Because some behaviours are dangerous (e.g., the driver does not give way to a car at right), a normal situation may become a critical situation (e.g., a collision). We identify a third situation between the normal and critical situations called the pre-critical situation. It is the last situation in which a person can make a decision to return in a normal situation. We conclude our analysis by building the behaviour space (corresponding concretely to the practice model associated with the given situation) and the situation space (all the possible variants from the chosen situation according to the degree of criticality of the situation), and then we associate the situation space with the behaviour space. We thus refine a statistical result such as "critical situation" by explaining the type of criticality and the type of behaviours associated with this criticality. Results confirm the interest of the context-based methodology for this application in road safety as well as in other domains where it is more important to work on behaviours of decision makers than decision makers themselves.

The c-methodology has been applied in the domain of road safety but can be extended easily to domains in which a population of actors that have to frequently make decisions in an environment evolving dynamically and eventually dangerously for these actors. However, the notion of critical situation can have different meanings. For instance, this could include the wrong decision of the board of a bank that may lead to bankruptcy. Domains in which the context-based methodology can be applied concern any population of decision makers realising – in a coordinated way or not – the same task. They could be people looking for information on the Web, travellers using public transportation, supporters at sports events, people arriving in a foreign country, hackers concerning computer security. In all these domains, there is a "normal behaviour" according to the focus, but also persons who do not behave "normally". The methodology could help to identify such abnormal behaviours (risky or not, for the concerned person or the others, etc.) and either help the concerned persons correct their behaviours (e.g., a foreigner in a country) or prevent their bad action for the community (e.g., the hacker in the computer area).

References

Brézillon, P., "Task-realization models in Contextual Graphs," in A. Dey, B. Kokinov, D. Leake, R. Turner (Eds.), *Modeling and Using Context* (*CONTEXT-05*), Springer, Berlin, LNCS 3554, 2005, pp. 55–68.

Brézillon, P., "Context modeling: Task model and model of practices," in B. Kokinov et al. (Eds.), *Modeling and Using Context* (CONTEXT-07), Springer, Berlin, LNAI 4635, 2007, pp. 122–135

Brézillon, J., "Context-based learning for improving decision making in a driving activity," *Revue d'Intelligence Artificielle*, RSTI-RIA-23/2009, Human-Centered Processes, 2009, pp. 539–553.

Brézillon, J. and P. Brézillon, "Context modeling: Context as a dressing of a focus," in B. Kokinov et al. (Eds.), *Modeling and Using Context* (*CONTEXT-07*), Springer, Berlin, LNAI 4635, 2007, pp. 136–149.

Brézillon, P. and J. Brézillon, "Contextualized task modelling," *Revue d'Intelligence Artificielle*, Vol. 22, No. 5, 2008, pp. 531–548.

Brézillon, P. and J.-C. Pomerol, "Contextual knowledge sharing and cooperation in intelligent assistant systems," *Le Travail Humain*, PUF, Paris, Vol. 62, No. 3, 1999, pp. 223–246.

Canton, L.G., *Emergency Management: Concepts and Strategies for Effective Programs*. Wiley, New York, 2007.

Clausewitz, C., *On War*, Translation by J.J. Graham, 1873. URL = http://www.clausewitz.com/index.htm.

Hatakka, M., E. Keskinen and S. Laapotti, "Professional and private driver training in Finland – Evaluation of results," *International Conference on Traffic and Transport Psychology*, Handbook of paper and poster presentations in short version, Valencia, May 22–25, 1996.

Henricksen, K. and J. Indulska, "Developing context-aware pervasive computing applications: Models and approach," *Pervasive and Mobile Computing Journal*, Vol. 2, No. 1, 2005, pp. 37–64.

Leplat, J. and J.M. Hoc, "Tâche et activité dans l'analyse psychologique des situations," *Cahiers de Psychologie Cognitive*, Vol. 3, 1983, pp. 49–63.

McCarthy, J., "Notes on formalizing context," in *Proceedings of the 13th International Joint Conference on Artificial Intelligence (IJCAI)*, Vol. 1, 1993, pp. 555–560.

Neto, R.F. and M.G.C. Pimentel, "Toward a domain-independent semantic model for context-aware computing," in *Proceedings of the 3rd IW3C2 Latin American Web Congress*, IEEE Computer Society, Buenos Aires, 2005, pp. 61–70.

Pomerol, J.-Ch., Brézillon, P. and Pasquier, L., "Operational knowledge representation for practical decision making," *Journal of Management Information Systems*, Vol. 18, No. 4, 2002, pp. 101–116

Power, R., "Topic maps for context management," in *Proceedings of the 1st International Symposium on Information and Communication Technologies – Workshop on Adaptive Systems for Ubiquitous Computing*, Dublin, 2003, pp. 199–204.

Richard, J.F., Logique du fonctionnement et logique de l'utilisation, *Rapport de Recherche*, INRIA, No. 202, 1983.

Vieira, V., P. Tedesco, A.C. Salgado and P. Brézillon, "Investigating the specifics of contextual elements management: The CEManTIKA approach," in B. Kokinov et al. (Eds.), *Modeling and Using Context (CONTEXT-07)*, Springer, Berlin, LNAI 4635, 2007, pp. 493–506.

Chapter 5
Towards Real-Time Context Awareness for Mobile Users: A Declarative Meta-Programming Approach

Seng W. Loke

Department of Computer Science and Computer Engineering, La Trobe University, Melbourne, Australia

Abstract We envision a future with thousands of publicly available context sources acquired via sensors supplying real-time information about mobile users' current circumstances with information on the Web. Such information can be harnessed for real-time decision making in daily life. Since context sources and information can be combined in myriad ways and be reasoned about in different ways, there is a need for some means to represent such aggregations, to create new aggregations, or to reason with such aggregations. Our basic idea is that the way context is aggregated to infer situations can be encapsulated and modularised in what we call "situation programs." As we use a declarative programming approach, situation programs are readable, yet executable – a situation program encapsulates rules and queries to context sources, which can be executed to determine if a particular situation is occurring. Situation programs are treated as first-class entities and can be exchanged or loaded to increase the repertoire of situations an application can detect, or to provide alternative ways for an application to detect a situation or reason about situations. We describe our initial prototype Logic Programming for Context-Aware Programming System (LogicCAP-S) based on the language LogicCAP, and discuss extensions towards the mobile environment.

Keywords Context awareness • Mobile users • Declarative programming • Situation programs • Sensor mashups • Context mashups

1 Introduction

Information is required for decision making, but with an increasing proliferation of sensor infrastructure and information services, there are tremendous opportunities for better decisions. The mobile platform provides an unprecedented tool for providing

---

S.W. Loke (✉)
Department of Computer Science and Computer Engineering,
La Trobe University, Melbourne, Australia
e-mail: S.Loke@latrobe.edu.au

F. Burstein et al. (eds.), *Supporting Real Time Decision-Making*,
Annals of Information Systems 13, DOI 10.1007/978-1-4419-7406-8_5,

contextually relevant information to users, and for users to share contextually indexed information with others. Such information ranges from those already available on the Web to information provided real-time via sensor network infrastructures.

The advantages are many. For example, an information user, driving through the city at night after a late evening meeting, might want a selection of restaurants for a late dinner. A system would provide the user with a list of nearby restaurants still open, with suitable closing times, not too busy and sporting a preferred atmosphere. Or, a cyclist may want to be warned of substances in the air space ahead to which he or she is allergic. Drivers could be informed of traffic conditions early enough to decide how to avoid relevant hazards, or be aware of three different areas close enough where there is a high likelihood of available parking at the time. Anyone who has experienced getting stuck in the heavy congestion inside a multi-storied car park of a large shopping centre would like to be warned ahead of time. Another might be warned about a sudden violent demonstration or riot just breaking out a few blocks away but not currently visible. In health care, provided privacy and legal issues could be avoided, the location of people with Swine Influenza (A1N1) virus could be tracked (for better or worse) or affected areas be brought to the attention of people more vulnerable to the virus. Tourists could be warned that certain areas tend to have a higher rate of crimes at certain times of the day or that certain activities or events are about to take place.

There is much context information one can extract, aggregate, and reason with in order to enable users to be much more aware of their surroundings, akin to having "super-senses" perceiving the surroundings beyond what is normally possible today. Just as the Web enabled tremendous scalability as people began to put up information and more importantly link that information to what already exists, we envision growing information services and sources of context information that could be combined in myriad ways. For example, from 20 context information sources there are potentially thousands of combinations of context that one can create. Such combined context sources can then inform or influence our daily life decisions in real time. There are two ends to the flow of context information: the source can be static information already on the Internet or information picked up real time by sensors, and the destination can be repositories (stationary servers or mobile devices) or users who will consume the information immediately.

We have been exploring a declarative programming paradigm for describing different combinations of context information, proposing an integration of logic programming with context-aware middleware to provide a declarative programming platform for sensor-based situation-aware applications. The use of logic programming is aimed at providing ease of programming. A unique feature of LogicCAP (Logic Programming for Context-Aware Programming) is its treatment of situations as logic programs comprising rules that describe how different context information are combined; in this chapter, we view a situation as an aggregation of current context information. Our approach, hence, provides a more elaborate representation of situations and the manipulation of situations via meta-programming.

Here, we provide implementation of the approach outlined in theory in Loke (2004, 2006a) called LogicCAP. By integrating the popular logic programming language Prolog with the Context Toolkit software (2003), first introduced in Loke (2008), we expand on the work first presented there. While our implementation is on a desktop, we discuss the use of LogicCAP for the mobile environment with the view of context being much more diverse for mobile devices, and we also describe our vision of LogicCAP running on mobile platforms. We also propose LogicCAP as a declarative language for (context or sensor) mashups, the analogy being with Web mashups which aggregate data from multiple websites onto one site. The LogicCAP idea of representing situations as logic programs is a modularity and an encapsulation – all context information required to describe a situation is encoded within a corresponding logic program. Such programs can then be exchanged or added to the system on a mobile device (essentially to increase the set of situations that the device can reason with).

Below we use the operational definition of context from Dey (2001): "Context is any information that can be used to characterise the situation of an entity. An entity is a person, place, or object that is considered relevant to the interaction between a user and an application, including the user and applications themselves." Also, our use of the situation abstraction, which views the situation roughly, as aggregation of context, conceptualises situations as first-class entities in our programs in the spirit of work such as situation theory (Barwise and Perry 1983) and situation calculus. We note the primacy of the situation abstraction, namely that humans can individuate a situation and that one can effectively "carve the world up" into "pieces," each of which might be recognised via a collection of sensors. Such pieces can be integrated to construct complex representations of situations. We use a broad definition of sensor as in Loke (2006a), which is taken to mean not only temperature, heat or motion sensors but any device or mechanism that is used to provide contextual information. Our approach clearly differentiates between sensor readings, context, situations, and applications that use situations in this model.

An extensive survey of work showing the originality of our approach is given in Loke (2004, 2006a). But we also note that of late, the notion of reasoning about situations using explicitly represented relationships between situations has been employed (Ye, Coyle, Dobson, and Nixon 2008), demonstrating that situation is a useful abstraction for building applications at a high level of abstraction.

In Sect. 2, we provide a brief overview of LogicCAP and Sect. 3 outlines the architecture and prototype implementation, including several ongoing extensions. Section 4 outlines modes of usage in the mobile environments of the proposed approach. Section 5 reviews related work and Sect. 6 concludes with future work.

2 A Brief Introduction to LogicCAP

This section provides an outline of the LogicCAP formalism, comprising the notion of situation programs, and an extension of Prolog.

2.1 LogicCAP Situation Programs

Queries to underlying sensors are abstracted as predicates, which we term *sensor predicates* of the form:

```
<sensor_id>*(<inputs>, <output_readings>)
```

The output from a sensor is represented by a variable, and inputs to sensors by parameters (for more than one inputs, we use the functor i(..)) to encapsulate the inputs, and similarly, for more than one output variables, the functor o(..); otherwise, we simply use the variable names without these terms, and also, we use underscore "_" if there are no inputs, or outputs – i.e., returning true or false). For example, the following represents a query to the sensor locationGPS to get Tom's location:

```
locationGPS*("Tom", L)
```

A *situation program*, each having its own identifier, relates context information acquired from sensors with a situation and is defined as a collection of rules (or a logic program), each rule of the form: *A –e-> G* where the operator "–e->" denotes either an abductive reading, i.e., a situation "is a possible explanation for" a set of (inter-related) observed context information, or an interpretive reading, i.e., a situation "is an interpretation of" a collection of (inter-related) context information (we rely on context of use of the operator to decide which reading); in Loke (2004), we only used an abductive reading, but more generally, a situation may not explain a set of readings, but could also simply be a label, "interpreting" the collection of context information or sensor readings. And *G* is given (in EBNF) by:

```
G ::= A | S  | (G,G)  | Sit*>E
```

A is an atomic goal formula (an ordinary Prolog-style term), *S* is a sensor predicate, "," denotes conjunction, *Sit* is a situation program identifier and *E* is an entity (e.g., user, device, or software agent) identifier. We call the operator "in-situation" denoted by "*>." A goal of the form Sit*>E is read as a query "is *E* in situation *Sit*?", is a meta-level goal which succeeds if provable from *Sit* in the way we describe later. A situation program has one distinguished rule (which we call the *situation rule*) whose premise is a predicate naming the situation and, optionally, has a parameter denoting the entity. For example, a rule such as the following in the situation program `fire_in_room`:

```
fire_in_room(L) -e->
  smoke_detector*(L,positive),
    thermometer*(L,R), R> 90.
```

specifies that a fire in room L is a possible explanation for an observed positive reading on the smoke detector in room L, and the temperature reading to be above 90 degrees Celsius. As the predicate smoke_detector*/2 is a sensor predicate, it obtains its values from querying the sensor (i.e., the smoke detector). So also, the temperature*/2 predicate. The abductive reading is due to our perspective of sensor readings as functioning to provide context information, which needs to be integrated to provide a "picture" of what is happening, i.e., each piece of context information provides a "hint" or an "indicator" of some situation that is occurring. The occurrence of some situation is hence an explanation for why one is detecting this collection of "hints" or "indicators." In other words, it is because some situation is occurring that the sensors are taking on particular readings and certain context information is being acquired. The situation `fire_in_room` could explain the given smoke detector and temperature sensor having those readings at the same time. Both sensors malfunctioning could be another (albeit, least likely) explanation:

```
sensors_malfunction(L) -e->
  smoke_detector*(L,positive),
  thermometer*(L,R), R> 90.
```

Predicates of the form *S*>E* allow more complex reasoning to be specified, where a situation occurring might also explain why some other situations might be occurring (through other abductive rules). For example, taken from Loke (2006b), the following rule says that E being in a situation `sleeping/1` is a possible explanation for E being in situation `not_answering_calls/1` and E being in situation `motionless/1`:

```
sleeping(E) -e->
  not_answering_calls*>E, motionless*>E.
```

There could be other reasons why E is not answering calls and E is motionless, as in:

```
dead(E) -e->
  not_answering_calls*>E, motionless*>E.
```

Several possibilities might be equally likely answers, or the system might choose the best explanation based on some strategy; here, we do not discuss strategies for choosing explanations. Also, we note that the same situation (e.g., "dead", "sleeping", or "fire in room") could be explanations for a different collection of sensor readings (or context information) – this also suggests a way of modelling different ways of recognising the same situation.

The above syntax of rules allows situation programs that refer to other situation programs. The advantage of being able to split rules into separate situation programs is a modularity, which encourages reuse, i.e., one can build up a collection of situation programs and use them in different applications. Note also that the situation programs are decoupled from the actual sensors that instantiate the sensor predicates. Hence, we have another level of abstraction here.

2.2 LogicCAP Prolog: Meta-Programming with Situation Programs

The in-situation operator "*>" can be embedded into Prolog programs (such an extended Prolog we simply call *LogicCAP Prolog*) as a distinguished predicate, evaluated to infer whether an entity E is in a situation defined by a situation program S.

The following example are rules that state a meeting is currently not possible amongst a list of individuals when any one of them is at home or the meeting room is on fire:

```
meeting_not_currently_possible(Es,_L) :-
  member(E,Es), at_home*>E.
meeting_not_currently_possible(_Es,L) :-
  fire_in_roomm#>L.
```

Prolog backtracking search applied with the rule will go through every member of the list Es and returns true for the goal "meeting not currently possible" if any one of the members of Es is found to be at home, determined by evaluating against the situation program at home. Note that normal Prolog evaluation will be employed for evaluating such rules, except when evaluating the in-situation goals (`e.g., at_home*>E`), where a different evaluation strategy (as noted later) will be employed for these goals. Another example rule specifies if an individual E is in any of the situations from a given list `Ss`:

```
any_situation(Ss, E) :-
  member(S, Ss), S*>E.
```

These rules illustrate meta-programming, with situation programs manipulated as first-class entities. A situation program represents how a situation should be recognised and relationships amongst situations can be expressed at the meta-programming level. In applications, it may be useful to talk about relationships between situations. The following relationships may be observed between situations and can be modelled as relationships between situation programs:

- One situation includes another
- One situation precedes another.
- Two situations always co-occur
- Two situations are incompatible (and cannot occur at the same time).
- One situation causes or induces another.
- One situation is a generalisation of another.
- One situation is a specialisation of another.

For example, the following are Prolog facts modelling situations.

```
isa(lecture, meeting).
isa(seminar, meeting).
isa(gathering, meeting).
isa(supervisor_student_meeting, meeting).
```

And we have a situation program meeting which says that a meeting occurring is a possible explanation for two or more people in the same room, using the people sensor in the room (denoted by people*):

```
meeting(R) -e->
people*(R,N),
N > 1.
```

For any relationship between two situations, there could of course be exceptions, and even exceptions can be stated as a Prolog rule. In Prolog, we can also state that two situation programs are equivalent (e.g., if they describe two different ways of aggregating similar or different contexts to infer the same situation).

We also note that our use of Prolog supports rule-based reasoning about situations, which is a useful platform for rule-based decision-making applications, which need to employ context information.

Loke (2004), has given an operational semantics for LogicCAP. We discuss in more detail how LogicCAP programs are executed in the next section.

3 Prototype Implementation

In this section, we discuss implementation issues with the LogicCAP paradigm. We first outline an initial prototype implementation that we have built and then discuss three extensions under development. It is possible to implement an integration of Prolog with context and sensors in different ways; our approaches leverage on existing middleware and logic programming platforms. But whatever be the choice of context middleware or logic programming system, the principles of integration remain the same and the exchange and use of modular situation programs is the key idea.

3.1 Architecture of LogicCAP-S with the Context Toolkit

We have built an initial prototype implementation of the LogicCAP-S by integrating SWI-Prolog with the Context Toolkit, via our own custom-built Java program called a mediator (and are continuing to extend its capabilities). This choice was prompted not only by the popularity of the above two systems, but also by their ease of use and functionality they provide, i.e., we wanted to quickly build a functioning prototype. Our prototype implementation comprises three main components: a Prolog system (i.e., SWI-Prolog), which contains the LogicCAP interpreter and a knowledge base of situation programs; the Context Toolkit (i.e., a running instance of it); and a mediator between Prolog and the Context Toolkit instance with example context widgets encapsulating sensors, as illustrated in Fig. 1.

While our current implementation is on a desktop, we see an important future in having LogicCAP-S running on a mobile device, applications of which we discuss later.

Vanila Metainterpreter in LogicCAP-S. *LogicCAP metainterpreter is given below, presented in a simplified form as an extension of pure Prolog (it could be*

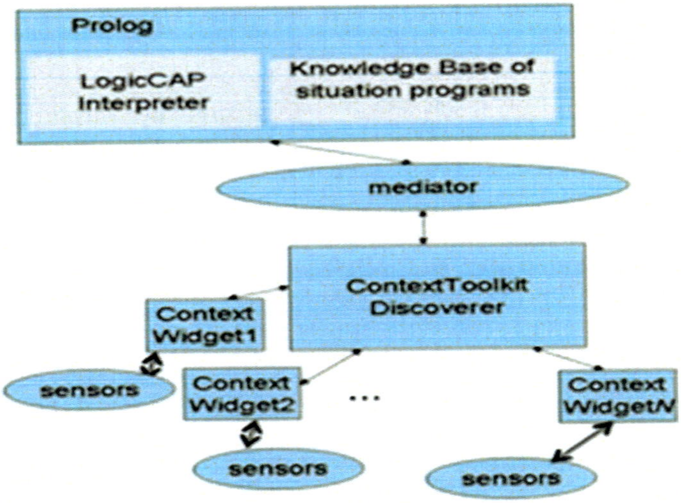

Fig. 1 Architecture of the prototype system

easily extended to accommodate calls to SWI-Prolog built-in libraries from LogicCAP programs):

```
%%% as a pure Prolog extension
solve(true).
solve((A, B)) :-
  solve(A), solve(B).
solve(Sit*>E) :-
ssolve(Sit,Sit*>E).
solve(A) :-
  (A :- B), % clause(A,B)
  solve(B).
solve(builtin(A)) :-
  call(A).
%%% for situation programs
ssolve(_Sit,NewSit*>E) :- !,
  load(NewSit),% load the situation pgm
  (A=..[NewSit,E]),
ssolve(NewSit,A).
ssolve(Sit,(A, B)) :- !,
  ssolve(Sit,A), ssolve(Sit,B).
ssolve(_Sit,F*(I,O)) :- !,
  query_sensor(F,I,O).
ssolve(_Sit,builtin(A_) :-
  call(A).
ssolve(Sit,A) :-
```

```
   Sit:(A -e-> B),
  ssolve(Sit, B).
```

The solve/1 predicate represents a metainterpreter for pure Prolog extended to evaluate goals with the "in situation" operator. This rule delegates evaluation of such goals to the ssolve/2 predicate:

```
solve(Sit*>E)  :-  ssolve(Sit,Sit*>E)
```

The ssolve/1 predicate represents a metainterpreter for situation programs. The query_sensor/1 predicate will bind to a sensor, i.e., in the system, it will result in queries being sent to the appropriate sensors, outside of Prolog; in our case, the query is issued to the sensor via the Context Toolkit, via the Discoverer to context widgets encapsulating sensors. We assume at this point that the sensor to which the query is issued to obtain the required context information has been predefined, but later discuss general ways of binding a sensor predicate to a sensor. We note that this can be viewed as a "pull" model of obtaining information from a sensor, i.e., the current reading of the sensor is returned via this call, even if it is negative (e.g., if the query is about whether someone is in the room, the query returns "yes" or "no" depending on the result at the time the positioning sensor is queried). In examples, we will often omit the builtin(..) functor when it is understood to be a built-in predicate.

3.2 Extension 1: Extending the Vanila Metainterpreter in LogicCAP-S with Concurrent Event-Driven Behaviour

Returning the current reading of a sensor is not necessarily always useful; we might want to have more "event-driven" behaviour in the sense that the query should block (perhaps for some pre-specified period of time) while waiting for the person to be in the room (i.e., wait for the sensor to return a "yes" result). We support this behaviour via a small extension to sensor predicates to another type of sensor predicate of the following form:

```
<sensor_id>*[Timeout](
  <inputs>, <output_readings>,
  <required_output_conditions>, <TimeStamp>)
```

i.e., suppose the query was issued at time *T*, then we allow a duration timeout parameter which waits up till time *T* + *Timeout*, for the <output_readings> to satisfy the <required_output_conditions>. The query evaluates to true instantiating a <TimeStamp> when the output conditions have been satisfied (if so), and false with <TimeStamp> being null, otherwise. Note that we require that actual parameters be supplied for the formal parameters <inputs>, <output_readings>, and <required_output_conditions>. This means, for example, that a query issued at some time T, such as

```
location*[300]("Tom",L,[L="Room 142"], S)
```

if false at the time of evaluation, will block for up to 300s, waiting for the output to satisfy the output condition, i.e., the predicate returns true if Tom enters "Room 142" at some time S, with S instantiated with a timestamp within the time interval [T,T+300], or false, if it is otherwise. The implementation must use an asynchronous block by default so that other goal evaluations can proceed, but the final goal evaluation is not complete until all sensor predicate goals have timed out or returned true. Such queries map to publish/subscribe queries to context widgets encapsulating particular sensors in the Context Toolkit.

By default, the timeout is 0s, and for completeness, we define a special symbol "@" to mean wait forever. So, the corresponding rule in the metainterpreter is modified to be:

```
ssolve(_Sit,F*[D](B)) :- !,
  current_time(T), % assume a built in
  new_thread(query_sensor(F,B,wait([D,T+D]),ThreadID),
  register_thread(ThreadID).
```

Note that D is duration before timeout. To support asynchronous blocking, a new thread is created to handle each sensor query, and the thread ID is remembered. Each such sensor predicate goal will have its own thread.

In an evaluation of a goal, there could be several such sensor predicates being evaluated, each with its own timer. Such a mechanism could be used to program event-driven behaviours, together with temporal operators similar to those in [13] that can be used to compare the relative time of occurrence of events. Suppose we have predefined built-in predicate `within_duration(Ts,D)` takes a list of timestamps Ts and a duration D, and returns true if the timestamps are all within D, i.e., `max(Ts) - min(Ts) < D`. For example, consider the goal

```
?- danger_in_room*>("Room 142").
```

and the following rules defined in its own situation program danger_in_room, which states that there is danger in the room if the there is a fire in the room and the room is not empty, at roughly the same time (i.e., danger in room is an interpretation of these events):

```
danger_in_room:
danger_in_room(L) -e->
  fire_in_room(L,T1,T2),
not_empty(L,T3),
  within_duration([T1,T2,T3],300).
fire_in_room(L,T1,T2) -e->
 smoke_detector*[@](L,SR,[SR=positive],T1),
  thermometer*[@](L,TR,[TR > 90],T2).
not_empty(L,T) -e->
 people_sensor*[@](_,Count, [Count > 0], T).
```

The goal will, hence, wait "forever" until, for the room, the smoke detector reads a positive value and the temperature goes above 90 degrees Celsius, and the people sensor counts at least one person in the room. The condition `within_duration([T1,T2,T3],300)` ensures that the three events of the smoke detector being positive, the temperature being above 90 degrees, and at least one person in the room, occur no more than 300s within each other (i.e., at roughly the same time). The goal can then be viewed as simply setting up an event-driven or reaction rule. Note that the goal will return false if the three events occur more than 300s apart from each other, and this is by definition.

Evaluation of the above goal results in two phases:

1. *Tree expansion*, where the proof tree mainly expands (mainly, since some sub-goals can be resolved) as sub-goals (and sub-goals of sub-goals, etc.) are identified, until blocking sensor predicate queries are encountered, and
2. *Tree contraction*, where the proof tree contracts when the sensor predicate queries return (or timeout), and sub-goals are evaluated.

Figure 2 shows an expanded tree for the above goal, assuming a time when no sensor predicate query has returned results. The dotted lines show the dependencies between the `within_duration/2` sub-goal and the other sub-goals – the dependencies between sub-goals are traced by observing the use of common variables by the sub-goals (for example, `T1`, `T2`, and `T3` are used by the `within_duration/2` sub-goal and the earlier two sub-goals, so that there is a dependency between the `within_duration/2` sub-goal and each of the two sub-goals `fire_in_room/3` and `not_empty/2`). Each sensor predicate query (three in total in this case) is managed by its own thread, so that while waiting for results from the smoke detector query, goal evaluation can proceed, in this case, to initiating the thermometer query, and eventually to the people sensor query, and finally to the `within_duration/2` sub-goal. In typical Prolog goal evaluation, a goal implicitly depends on completion of its sub-goals (so that the solid lines in Fig. 2 are also dependencies). However, the dependencies are recorded so that the `within_duration/2` sub-goal will not complete until all the sub-goals it depends on also are complete, and the root goal will not complete until all its sub-goals are completed. The expanded tree, hence, maintains its shape until the sensor predicate

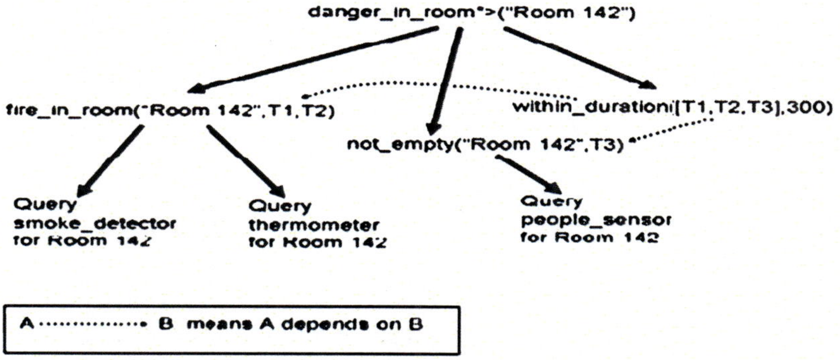

Fig. 2 An expanded proof tree

queries begin to timeout or suitable outputs from sensors arrive. A user initiating the goal resulting in this "waiting" tree, effectively, can be viewed as representing the user "registering an interest" in a collection of inter-related events. The tree contracts as sensor predicate queries begin to return results. The context widgets in the Context Toolkit supports asynchronous publish/subscribe mode of communication when waiting for sensor data, which these event-driven sensor predicate queries can be mapped to. Our expanded proof tree has some similarities with the operator graphs in Solar (Chen, Li, and Kotz 2008), though our proof trees are created at run-time.

Note that we could have modularised our program into three (individually reusable) situation programs as follows:

```
danger_in_room:
danger_in_room(L) -e->
  fire_in_room*>(L,T1,T2),
not_empty*>(L,T3),
within_duration([T1,T2,T3],300).
fire_in_room:
fire_in_room(L,T1,T2) -e->
 smoke_detector*[@](L,SR,[SR=positive],T1),
  thermometer*[@](L,TR,[TR > 90],T2).
not_empty:
not_empty(L,T) -e->
 people_sensor*[@](_,Count,[Count > 0], T).
```

The phase of tree contraction begins as either a sensor-predicate query timeout or a result arrival where the output conditions are satisfied. The contraction occurs from leaf nodes up to their parents, and to their parents' parent nodes, recursively, until the root goal resolves. In the example above, if the sub-goal (of the root goal) `fire_in_room/3` completes with suitable sensor readings, but `not_empty/2` is unresolved (e.g., if the room remains empty), then the root goal cannot complete. But there is no loss of generality since at the top level, one could initiate detection of different types of situations (even situations within situations). For example, one can initiate two top-level goals:

```
?- danger_in_room*>("Room 142").
```

and (perhaps in a separate Prolog thread):

```
?- fire_in_room("Room 142",T1,T2),
builtin(within_duration([T1,T2],120)).
```

With these two goals, there would be two expanded proof trees, both trees waiting on common sensor inputs, since they employ the same sensor predicate queries. This means that if there is a fire in the room but no one in the room, the first top-level goal remains unresolved (and still waiting), with its tree only partially contracted, while the second top-level goal will resolve returning presumably true (with its tree fully contracted). More generally, there could be several top-level goals sharing common sensor predicate queries and so, multiple expanded trees waiting for the same sensor readings. Arrival of sensor-suitable readings then could then trigger the resolution of multiple top-level goals, which in turn, could be programmed to trigger actions, thereby, effecting an event-driven approach.

Apart from timing out on sensor predicate queries, we can add distancing out on sensor predicate queries, i.e., we consider a spatial temporal boundary within which we are willing to wait for output conditions to be satisfied. To do this, we extend the sensor predicate queries with an additional parameter, which we define as the distance from where the user currently is (we assume a positioning technology that can provide such information).

Consider a moving user in which queries are being evaluated on a mobile device (we assume, say, with a version of the LogicCAP-S system implemented on a mobile device). We support this behaviour via a small extension to sensor predicates to another type of predicate of the following form:

```
<sensor_id>*[Timeout,D](
<inputs>, <output_readings>,
<required_output_conditions>, <TimeStamp>)
```

I.e., suppose the query was issued at time *T*, at location *L*, then we allow a time-out and distance-out parameter which waits up till time *T*+*Timeout*, and waits as long as the user is in the zone defined by a radial distance of *D* from *L*, for the <output_readings> to satisfy the <required_output_conditions>. This means that even if it has not timed out but the user is at an (Euclidean) distance larger than *D* from *L*, then the query is failed. A "tolerance period" $t << T$ can be preset so that if the user is to move further than a distance *D* away from *L*, for a period no more than *t*, i.e., returning within the radial distance *D* in time, then the query does not fail. The query evaluates to true instantiating a <TimeStamp> when the output conditions have been satisfied (if so), within the timeout period and within the area boundary, and false with <TimeStamp> being null, otherwise. This additional parameter allows a spatial temporal window of relevance (or of waiting constraints) to be expressed. If not specified, then *D* is infinite. We discuss goal evaluations and applications for LogicCAP in the mobile environment later.

It is not difficult to allow the user to specify global constraints on the entire top-level goal evaluation, which can be propagated down to each sensor predicate query (overriding any individual constraints).

3.3 *Extension 2: Levels of Abstraction, Dynamic Situation Program Binding, Dynamic Sensor Binding, and Goal Evaluations in the Mobile Environment*

We distinguish three levels of abstraction in our system:

- A collection of LogicCAP Prolog programs,
- A collection of LogicCAP situation programs, each used by one or more LogicCAP Prolog program(s),

- Sensors: each sensor may be used by one or more situation program(s). Note that in LogicCAP-S, sensors are encapsulated and queried via context widgets, which are, in turn, registered with, and discovered via the Context Toolkit's Discoverer facility.

Figure 3 illustrates these three layers with the operator that connects between the layers. An "in-situation" goal within a LogicCAP Prolog program invokes a situation program, and a sensor- predicate query within a situation program results in sensors being queried.

The advantage of such a decoupling is to facilitate reuse, e.g., the same situation program can be used in different LogicCAP Prolog programs or even by different situation programs, and the same sensor predicate queries can be issued from different situation programs. Moreover, three layers allow two levels of dynamic binding: the first level is from in-situation goals in LogicCAP Prolog programs and the second level is from sensor predicate queries in situation programs to actual sensors that could be used to answer the queries.

Another advantage of the decoupling is to allow distributed processing. Consider the execution of a LogicCAP Prolog program on a mobile device. In a mobile environment, the available set of sensors are either those of the mobile device and/or those in the vicinity of the user, or accessible to the user, but in the surrounding infrastructure of the user (including fixed hosts or even other mobile hosts within range). Sensor predicates can, therefore, bind to whatever suitable sensors are available at that time.

This dynamic binding of sensor predicate queries to sensors is similar to the idea of `LocationProvider` in the J2ME Location API (JSR-179 2009), which wraps above the underlying positioning technology (which, for example, can be a GPS-based or a Bluetooth positioning system), and different underlying positioning technologies can be chosen at run time depending on the program-specified criteria. The mechanism for such binding can range from a simple keyword matching (sensor predicate names) – which is our prototype implementation at the moment – to a sensor lookup table, where each sensor is identified by one or more key phrase(s), to more elaborate directory listings or semantic-based matching, which requires, e.g., where

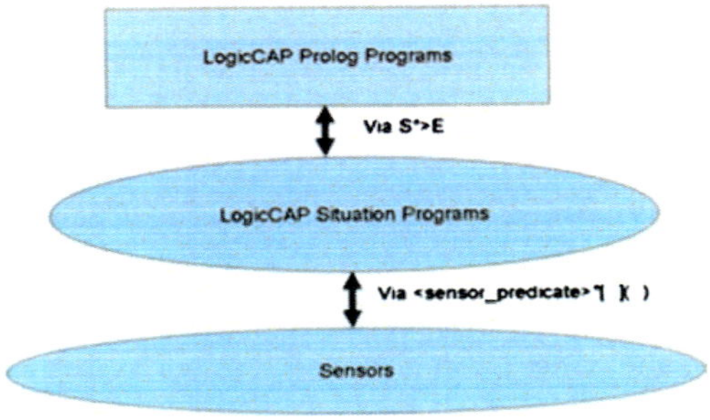

Fig. 3 Three layers of abstraction

sensors are described more comprehensively using, for example, SensorML (Sensor 2010) and sensor predicates have more parameters to provide more comprehensive sensor search criteria. Alternative semantics-based matching of sensor criteria in a sensor predicate query with sensors is via a semantic services language such as W3C's OWL-S. Ontologies of context can also be constructed and employed, which map between different types of contexts (e.g., "location", "position", etc.) that correspond to sensor predicate queries. Future standardised descriptions of what have been termed context sources can also be employed.

In the same way, the mechanism for dynamic binding of "in-situation" goals to situation programs can range from simple keyword matching (with names of situations) to more sophisticated search criteria, complex descriptions of situation programs, and ontology-based matching. In a mobile environment, the available set of situation programs are either those on the knowledge-base of the mobile device and/or those in the server in the vicinity of or accessible to the user, or a combination thereof. Evaluation of a goal of a LogicCAP Prolog program can result in situation programs on the mobile device and in another server being used, and evaluation of a situation program may result in sensors, both on the mobile device and in the surrounding infrastructure being employed. But at a different location, the in-situation goals and sensor predicate queries may rebind to a different knowledge-base and/or different sensors.

Consider a top-level query, evaluated on a mobile device of a cyclist C, to detect danger in the environment for the cyclist, such as the following program:

```
caution(C) :-
  slippery_road*>C
  ; hazardous_air*>C
  ; heavy_traffic*>C.
```

with situation programs:

```
slippery_road(C) -e->
 locationGPS*(C,L),
  wet_road_condition*(i(L,1000),_).
  hazardous_air(C) -e->
```

allergy(C,A),

```
  air_sensor*(A,_).

heavy_traffic(C) -e->
  locationGPS*(C,L),
  traffic_threshold(Th),
  traffic_count_ahead*(i(L,1000),Cnt),
  Cnt > Th.
```

A query `caution(..)` might first bind to particular situation programs and then to suitable sensors in the environment. Note that the operator ";" represents OR. As yet, there seems to be no widely accepted standard way to describe context or sensors, though there have been working proposals (e.g., the NEX-OF (Nexof 2010) and XCML (Robinson and Indulska, 2007)); hence, the example above assumes available matching situation programs and sensors. The query `wet_road_condition*(L,1)` determines if the stretch of the road 1,000 m around location L is wet. We assume `allergy(C,A)` facts that provide information about the substances (e.g., pollen) that the cyclist is allergic to, and `air_sensor*(A)` returns true if the air contains the substance A. The query `traffic_count_ahead*(L,T)` returns the count of cars within 1,000 m radius of location L, which is then compared with a pre-determined threshold. Note that the meaning of the conjunctive goal

```
traffic_count_ahead*(i(L,1000),Cnt),
Cnt > Th
```

differs from that of the goal

```
traffic_count_ahead*[@](i(L,1000),Cnt,
[Cnt > Th], T)
```

The latter will wait indefinitely for the count to be more than the threshold whereas the other will not.

Rebinding of sensors and situation programs need not only happen for the purpose of mobility or binding to more relevant resources in the current vicinity, but can also be used upon failure of particular sensors or failure of connections to context sources, in order to rebind to other available sources. We discuss further the modes of usage for the mobile environment in Sect. 4.

3.4 Extension 3: Control of Goal Evaluation – Persistent Queries, Forced Contraction, and Partially Complete Evaluations

Earlier, we described an evaluation that takes a goal (starting with a top-level goal), a LogicCAP Prolog program, an associated set of situation programs, and a model of a set of sensors (as streams of time-stamped data), and outputs a tree. The tree is said to be expanded when there are sensor predicates waiting (assuming that sensor predicates with 0 timeout duration "waits" even if for an instant). In Fig. 2, suppose that all the sensor predicate queries are waiting, then the tree remains expanded as shown. Now, consider the top-level goal again:

```
?- danger_in_room*>("Room 142").
```

And consider this goal as persistent, i.e., equivalent to an infinite number of calls to this same goal, regardless of whether it returned true or false the previous time. We define a predicate peval/1 that takes a goal and initiates it again after the goal returns, irrespective of the previous result, using Prolog's built-in repeat/0, which always succeeds on backtracking:

```
peval(G):-
repeat, solve(G), get_result(G)), fail.
```

where get_results(G) may merely store the time-stamped bindings when G succeeds:

```
get_result(G) :-
current_time(T), assert(result(T,G)).
```

So, a goal such as

```
?- peval (danger_in_room*>("Room 142")).
```

We also define another predicate `forced_terminate(G, Duration)` which terminates the goal execution, i.e., `solve(G)`, `Duration` seconds from the start time, regardless of any waiting sensor predicate queries. All still-waiting sensor predicate queries at the time of termination are considered to return false, and evaluation of the top-level goals uses these "false" results. Such a goal, terminated prematurely in this way, however, is considered to be merely partially evaluated in that insufficient time was given.

In the case where not all the conditions that a situation recognition requires are satisfied, it can still be useful to interpret the partial results. For example, in Fig. 2, it may be that all the sensor predicate queries return true except for the thermometer, which returns a false value (temperature was 80 degrees) for example. A question is then how one should treat this scenario. One possibility is to gradually relax the constraints so that they can be satisfied. For example, if the constraints are simple inequalities (e.g., `Cnt > Th`), we can reduce gradually the threshold Th when the query has timed out until the constraint is satisfied. Hence, the query is partially satisfied but with a more relaxed constraint. But there must now be a way to say that the situation is occurring but to a certain degree (with a fuzzy measure) or the situation is occurring with an estimated probability (with a probabilistic measure). Whether it is the case that there is 80% chance that a dangerous situation is occurring or a dangerous situation is occurring to an extent of 80% is arguable. Moreover, relaxing constraints is less trivial if they are non-numerical. We consider interpreting partial matching an avenue for future work.

4 Modes of Usage in Mobile Environments

4.1 Situation Programs As Mobile Context (and Sensor) Mashups

Many mobile devices are now equipped with sensors (or can be augmented with sensors) and an API to access sensor inputs (iPhone has sensors, and so do many new mobile phones, which support the JavaME JSR 256 Mobile Sensor API (and Bluetooth discovery and GPS inputs can be viewed as sensors for an application)) and we imagine a greater sophistication and a variety of sensors on mobile devices on the user as well as on vehicles. There has been a number of websites providing map-based visualisation of real-time data acquired via sensors at different geographical locations, many of which have been contributed by the public and are community-based; for example, see the sites *www.contextwatcher.com*, *www.pachube.com*, *http://atom.research.microsoft.com/sensewebv3/sensormap/* and *http://sensorbase.org/*. There are others with more specific information such as real-time information about bus arrivals in the Cambridge TIME project (TIME 2010). Some sites provide visualisations of GPS-tracked cycling and walking routes from voluntary contributors (e.g., see *http://www.motionbased.com* and *http://www.msslam.com/slamxr/slamxr.htm*) and car routes (CarTel 2010). Sensors have to be described to the visualization framework in a markup language such as SensorML or EEML (*www.eeml.org*). Other work permits users to manually associate information (and even photos and videos) with physical sites or locations, e.g., see *www.contextwatcher.com*.

In summary, whether it is information manually added or data generated from sensors (on the mobile device or in surrounding infrastructure), there will be an increasing amount of information available at a particular location, which a user may want to be aware of, or which should be aggregated and correlated to infer interesting semantic content and/or situations on behalf of users. Or, users may want to write their own aggregations (or mashups) or inter-relations of context information, some of which are for visualisation purposes, and others constitute interpretations or explanations of aggregated or inter-related context, i.e., to infer situations. Our approach addresses the latter uses of integrating publicly available context and sensor data (and perhaps combining that with locally available information from sensors on the mobile device itself, or even from sensors in the clothing worn by the user and in the vehicle which the user is travelling in, and perhaps even binding temporarily to sensors in other vehicles or other mobile entities in the vicinity at the time), providing a declarative language for this purpose. In effect, a situation (expressed as a situation program) is a context/sensor mashup in the sense that it aggregates context/sensor information in a particular way.

Queries about situations can be used in numerous ways and can be particularly interesting for mobile users whose environment and circumstances change due to location. We consider two types of users who may utilise information about situations: human users and nonhuman users, i.e., autonomous entities (including software agents, robots, and devices capable of autonomous behaviours), and either of the two modes of usage: (1) The user simply "tunes in" (or opts in) to "listen in" (giving some constraints to reduce overload) on information about situations that are occurring or not occurring based on predefined situation programs on the server-side; this mode of usage does not now require the entity to have predefined queries, LogicCAP programs or situation programs, and does not need knowledge about what to query in the first place. (2) The user comes with his/her/its own predefined queries (and LogicCAP and situation programs) in their mobile devices, and on evaluation, may bind to some local sensors and context sources.

We envision a scenario where a person passes through a region (a floor, building, street, or a larger area) at a given time, and could opt in (perhaps, selecting from a menu) with an information provider to "listen in" on results of queries to situation programs predefined by the information provider. The set of situations that a mobile user should listen to is itself situation dependent. For example, if the mobile user is in a large shopping complex, the user could start to run situation programs that listen to information relevant within the shopping complex, ranging from contextually motivated marketing information (e.g., nearby offers and promotions, which can be exploited by retailers to clear goods, and advertisements issued when the number of people nearby the shop is above a given threshold, and varies over time) to advice on "green shopping", wait times at particular restaurants, and potential hazards. When the mobile user is out of the shopping complex and on the street, a different set of situation programs can be loaded and executed to listen to a different set of situations.

Hence, there are rules which can be encoded to launch different situation programs on detecting new situations – so-called "meta-situation rules", since they install and execute new situation programs on detecting new situations. For example, the following rule first checks the mobile user's location to see if he/she is now on a street known for its crime rates, and if so, invokes the situation program danger_in_sheet to continually check for dangers:

```
alert_to_danger :-
  my_id(Me),
  location*(Me,L),
  street_name(L,S),
  notorious_street(S),
  peval(danger_in_street*>(S )).
```

which can be coded also as follows, assuming a dangerous_street situation program:

```
alert_to_danger :-
  my_id(Me),
  dangerous_street*>(Me,S),
  peval(danger_in_street*>(S )).


dangerous_street:
dangerous_street*>(Me,S)  :-
  location*(Me, L),
  street_name(L,S),
  notorious_street(S).
```

However, the user may also wish to use his/her/its own context mashups (or situation programs) in goal evaluations. With event-driven time-outs and distance-outs, initiating an "in-situation" goal or a sensor predicate query effectively "registers" the user's interest in particular situations, events or sensor outputs. Hence, service providers can either provide information about available sensors (which can be queried directly by the user via sensor predicate queries), and available situation programs (which can be queried by the user via in-situation goals).

5 Related Work

There have been explorations of the declarative style of programming for sensor-based and sensor network applications (Whitehouse, Zhao, and Liu 2006; Tavakoli, Chu, Hellerstein, Levis, and Shenker 2007; Henricksen and Indulska 2006; Ranganathan and Campbell 2003). Henricksen and Indulska (2006) use first-order logic predicates to represent situations and to relate named situations to context attributes. However, they do not have the notion of situation programs as we do here, which we think are more expressive than simple situation predicates.

In Ranganathan and Campbell (2003), first-order logic rules are used to map context attributes and values to appropriate actions to be taken. This work is perhaps close to our use of rules to map situations to actions. However, while they represent different types of contexts using different predicate names, they do not have the notion of situations that we do. The notion of situations, we contend, provides a convenient conceptual mechanism to capture aggregations or combinations of context information, which otherwise would be difficult to capture.

Tavakoli et al. (2007) use logic programs to program the global behaviour of sensor networks, but do not consider context attributes or the notion of situations explicitly in their programs as we do here. Whitehouse et al. (2006) use logic programs to model wrap sensor data sources and to relate processing modules for sensor data streams – they provide a notion of linking modules that are used to process streams of sensor data, but do not use the high level notions of situations.

There has also been work on acquiring and using context information on mobile platforms (Raento, Oulasvirta, Petit, and Toivonen 2005; Riva 2006; Nurmi, Kukkonen, Lagerspetz, Suomela, and Floréen 2007). Also, there has been a trend of what can be called sensor and context mashups (Neely, Stabeler, and Nixon 2008), where information from geo-tagged sensors are aggregated and "pushed out" on the Web to be visible. Such mashups mechanisms do not make use of a logic-based declarative programming language as we do here. The advantage of using a full programming language (as we propose with LogicCAP) is expressiveness in describing situations, yet maintaining a formal operational semantics. Of interest is that modern mobile phones have an array of sensors built-in including compass, accelerometer, GPS, and Bluetooth (the use of Bluetooth discovery can be viewed as sensing Bluetooth-enabled devices nearby). More types of sensors could be embedded into such devices in the future.

While new platforms such as Google's Android and the popular JavaME platform support event-driven programming and have libraries to enable mobile sensor programming, there is a need to (1) program such applications at higher level of abstractions using notions of situations and context as first-class entities, and (2) simplify programming of applications (that deal with and reason with sensor data or context information) and a declarative paradigm, as we argue, can serve this purpose.

6 Conclusion and Future Work

We discussed LogicCAP, its prototype system called LogicCAP-S, and discussed extensions to LogicCAP-S, which is ongoing work, towards the mobile environment. Uncertainty in reasoning with situation programs is an avenue of future work since there is often a measure of uncertainty with acquiring context-information and also a measure of timelines (or time validity) of real-time information. Applications need to know when such context information would expire. Moreover, we hope to extend LogicCAP-S to query sensors with WiFi or Bluetooth interfaces and to allow LogicCAP-S (when running on a mobile environment) to bind to sensors (and other Context Toolkit instances or context other middleware) running in the surrounding fixed infrastructure of hosts or on other mobile devices in the vicinity. We would also need sensor discovery protocols (similar to and based on Bluetooth device discovery protocols) and lease-based sensor binding and rebinding for this purpose – JINI leasing would be a guiding idea in this work.

LogicCAP allows aggregation of context as situations to be represented and programmed. We addressed the question of how to represent and reason with different possible context sources and information in order to infer the current situation of mobile users. We envision that a LogicCAP-S installed on the user's mobile device will continually inform the user or his/her applications of different situations and some of these applications will take actions for the users, suggest actions for users, or simply inform the users of situations. With the ability to treat situation programs as first-class entities, a user will also be able to extend the set of situations he/she is interested in by downloading new situation programs or writing his/her own situation programs to connect to available context sources. How users will now change their behaviours and make decisions in daily life, given such an increased awareness of surrounding situations, is a question that remains open.

Also interesting is getting context information via manual data entry as opposed to using sensors. For example, twitter technology can be used by users to "report" on what they are doing – to those who "follow" the user. Such reports basically provide real-time information, sometimes in meaningful words, compared to raw sensor data. It would be interesting to mine such twitter comments for useful context information.

It is contended that a programming language can be used for context mashups, and that a Prolog-based approach or a declarative programming approach is a good candidate (being at a high-level of abstraction) for context mashups, and should be given serious consideration.

There are numerous issues on reasoning with context (Bettini, Brdiczka, Henricksen, Indulska, Nicklas, Ranganathan, and Riboni 2009) that have not been addressed here, including the uncertainty and quality of context information. There is a need to deal with missing, imprecise or wrong values (Padovitz, Loke, and Zaslavsk 2004) – fuzzy logic (as implemented in Fuzzy Prolog (CiaoProlog 2004) for example) can be employed to represent fuzzy descriptions of situations where there is vagueness to model. Probabilistic inferences can be done in a version of Prolog called PRISM (2010), which allows reasoning with predicates with assigned probabilities. Hence, our approach of being Prolog-based can leverage on extensions of Prolog with both fuzzy and statistical/probabilistic reasoning for context-aware and situation-aware applications; further work is required, however, to explore such languages on mobile platforms.

With heterogeneity, the approach assumes a system that is technically, syntactically, and semantically homogenous. There is a need of ontologies for contexts and situations (Ye, Coyle, Dobson, and Nixon 2007), and there are Ontology Web Language (OWL) parsers in Prolog already developed (e.g., Thea 2010) but resource-constrained reasoning might call for alternative techniques beyond traditional desktop Prolog implementations (e.g., see Steller, Krishnaswamy, Cuce, Newmarch, and Loke 2008).

We deal with discrete context information, but continuous and concurrent sensor streams should also be considered as in Gurgen, Roncancio, Labbé, Bottaro, and Olive (2008); stream-based Prolog and parallel Prolog systems (Lindgren 2010) can be explored for this purpose. And finally, privacy and security are an issue; personal context information is inherently sensitive and there should be some means for users to control how their context information should be handled as noted in Hong (2005).

Crucial to decision making in real time is reasoning with contexts and situations. For context/situation-aware computing, leveraging on the myriad reasoning mechanisms already developed within the declarative logic programming setting would provide a key advantage though further explorations are needed to prove their value. This chapter has endeavoured to provide initial steps in this direction, and to provoke future developments along these lines.

Acknowledgements The author thanks Do Manh Thang for implementation of the current desktop prototype, and anonymous reviewers for their valuable input. This chapter contains portions reprinted, with permission, from the paper "Towards declarative programming for sensor-based situation-aware applications: The LogicCAP approach", published in the *Proceedings of the International Conference on Intelligent Sensors, Sensor Networks and Information Processing*, 2008, ISSNIP'08, pp. 447–452, ©2008 IEEE.

References

Barwise, J. and J. Perry, *Situations and Attitudes*. Cambridge: MIT Press, 1983.

Bettini, C., O. Brdiczka, K. Henricksen, J. Indulska, D. Nicklas, A. Ranganathan and D. Riboni, "Survey of Context Modelling and Reasoning Techniques", *Pervasive and Mobile Computing*, 6, 2, 2009, 161–180.

CarTel, *Project Overview*, 2010, URL = http://cartel.csail.mit.edu/doku.php

Chen, G., M. Li and D. Kotz, "Data-Centric Middleware for Context-Aware Pervasive Computing," *Pervasive and Mobile Computing*, 4, 2, 2008, 216–253.

CiaoProlog, *Fuzzy Prolog*, 2004, URL = http://clip.dia.fi.upm.es/Software/Ciao/ciao_html/ciao_113.html

ContextToolkit, *Context Toolkit User's Guide*, 2003, URL = http://contexttoolkit.sourceforge.net/documentation/UserGuide.html

Dey, A.K., "Understanding and Using Context," *Personal and Ubiquitous Computing Journal*, 5, 1, 2001, 4–7.

Gurgen, L., C. Roncancio, C. Labbé, A. Bottaro and V. Olive, "SStreaMWare: A Service Oriented Middleware for Heterogeneous Sensor Data Management", in *Proceedings of the Fifth International Conference on Pervasive Services*, Sorrento, Italy 2008, 121–130.

Henricksen, K. and J. Indulska, "Developing Context-Aware Pervasive Computing Applications: Models and Approach," *Pervasive and Mobile Computing*, 2, 1, 2006, 37–64.

Hong, J.I., "An Architecture for Privacy-Sensitive Ubiquitous Computing", Ph.D. Thesis, University of California at Berkeley, Computer Science Division, Berkeley, 2005, URL = http://www.cs.cmu.edu/~jasonh/publications/jihdiss.pdf

JSR-179, *Location API for J2ME*, 2009, URL = http://jcp.org/en/jsr/detail?id=179

Loke, S.W., "Representing and Reasoning with Situations for Context-Aware Pervasive Computing: A Logic Programming Perspective", *The Knowledge Engineering Review*, 19, 3, 2004, 213–233.

Loke, S.W., "On Representing Situations for Context-Aware Pervasive Computing: Six Ways to Tell If You Are in a Meeting," in *Proceedings of PerComWorkshops*, Pisa, Italy 2006a, 35–39.

Loke, S.W., *Context-Aware Pervasive Systems: Architectures for a New Breed of Application.* Auerbach (CRC), http://www.amazon.com/Context-Aware-Pervasive-Systems-Architectures-Applications/dp/0849372550 2006b.

Loke, S.W., "Towards Declarative Programming for Sensor-Based Situation-Aware Applications", in *Proceedings of the International Conference on Intelligent Sensors, Sensor Networks and Information Processing (ISSNIP 2008)*, 2008, Sydney, Australia 447–452.

Neely, S., M. Stabeler and P. Nixon, "SensorMash: Exploring System Fidelity through Sensor Mashup", Poster at the *Sixth International Conference Pervasive Computing*, Sydney, 2008.

Nexof (Reference Architecture), *Context Model and Universal APS*, 2010, URL = http://www.nexof-ra.eu/context_model_universal_APIs

Nurmi, P., J. Kukkonen, E. Lagerspetz, J. Suomela and P. Floréen, "BeTelGeuse – A Tool for Bluetooth Data Gathering", in *Proceedings of BodyNets '07*, Florence, Italy 2007, URL = http://betelgeuse.hiit.fi/articles/betelgeuse_bodynets07.pdf

Padovitz, A., S.W. Loke and A. Zaslavsk, "On Uncertainty in Context-Aware Computing: Appealing to High-Level and Same-Level Context for Low-Level Context Verification", in *Proceedings of the International Workshop on Ubiquitous Computing*, Porto, Portugal 2004, 62–72.

Lindgren, List of Parallel Prolog Implementations, 2010, URL = http://user.it.uu.se/~thomasl/par-prolog.html

PRISM Prolog System, PRISM: Programming in Statistical Modeling, 2010, URL = //sato-www.cs.titech.ac.jp/prism

Raento, M., A. Oulasvirta, R. Petit and H. Toivonen, "ContextPhone – A Prototyping Platform for Context-Aware Mobile Applications," *IEEE Pervasive Computing*, 4, 2, 2005, 51–59.

Ranganathan, A. and R.H. Campbell, "An Infrastructure for Context-Awareness Based on First Order Logic," *Personal and Ubiquitous Computing*, 7, 2003, 353–364.

Riva, O., "Contory: A Middleware for the Provisioning of Context Information on Smart Phones," in *Proceedings of the Seventh ACM International Middleware Conference*, Melbourne, Australia 2006, 219–239.

Robinson, R. and J. Indulska, "XCML: A Runtime Representation for the Context Modelling Language," in *Proceedings of PerCom Workshops*, White Plains, New York City, USA 2007, 20–26.

Sensor, ML, *Sensor Model Language*, 2010, URL= http://www.opengeospatial.org/standards/sensorml

Steller, L., S. Krishnaswamy, S. Cuce, J. Newmarch and S.W. Loke, "A Weighted Approach for Optimised Reasoning for Pervasive Service Discovery Using Semantics and Context", in

Proceedings of the International Conference on Enterprise Information Systems (ICEIS), Barcelona, Spain 2008, 113–118.

Tavakoli, A., D. Chu, J. Hellerstein, P. Levis and S. Shenker, "A Declarative Sensornet Architecture," *ACM SIGBED* Review, Special Edition on International Workshop on Wireless Sensor Network Architecture, 4, 3, Cambridge, Massachusetts, USA 2007, 55–60.

Thea, A., *Web Ontology Language – OWL Parser for (SWI) Prolog*, 2010, URL= http://www.semanticweb.gr/TheaOWLParser/

TIME (Transport Information Monitoring Environment), *The TIME Project*, 2010, URL = http://www.cl.cam.ac.uk/research/time/

Whitehouse, K., F. Zhao and J. Liu, "Semantic Streams: A Framework for Composable Semantic Interpretation of Sensor Data," in *Proceedings of the Third European Workshop on Wireless Sensor Networks*, Zurich, Switzerland 2006, 5–20.

Ye, J., L. Coyle, S. Dobson and P. Nixon, "Ontology-based Models in Pervasive Computing Systems," *Knowledge Engineering Review*, 22, 4, 2007, 315–347.

Ye, J., L. Coyle, S. Dobson and P. Nixon, "Representing and Manipulating Situation Hierarchies Using Situation Lattices," *Journal of Revue d'Intelligence Artificielle*, 22, 5, 2008.

Chapter 6
The Role of Context for Crisis Management Cycle

Florence Aligne and Juliette Mattioli

Thales Research and Technology, France

Abstract This chapter establishes the major role of the sense making and situation-understanding process in crisis management, and outlines the importance of the contextualisation of information in this process. As a result of a wider analysis of past crisis-management feedback, we define the term *crisis* and propose a crisis-management cycle, along with a set of decision support activities. From a system point of view, crisis management functionalities are structured along three crucial steps: information gathering, situation understanding, and decision making. For each step, the processes involved are described and for each one some relevant techniques are proposed to implement the processes. For the information-gathering step, the use of ontology allows the building and structuring of a coherent situation model. The initial overall picture of the situation, obtained by some on-line information extraction and fusion, is then consolidated in the situation understanding step to provide meaningful real-time situation awareness. This provides the essential base to derive the final decision-making step. In the decision phase, the context has a dual impact on the decision-making process; the context first constrains the resolution of the resource allocation problem, but it also contributes to discriminate between several resource allocation solutions. It is thus shown that each step of the crisis management process relies on the availability and quality of the crisis context, and that this in-time contextualisation is required to enhance the overall process of crisis management.

To summarise, this chapter highlights the key role of situation understanding for crisis management and reveals the crucial necessity of in-time contextualisation at each step of the crisis management process.

Keywords Information contextualisation • Situation understanding • Decision support • Crisis management • Ontology • Information fusion • Complex event processing

---

F. Aligne (✉)
Thales Research and Technology, France
e-mail: florence.aligne@thalesgroup.com

F. Burstein et al. (eds.), *Supporting Real Time Decision-Making*,
Annals of Information Systems 13, DOI 10.1007/978-1-4419-7406-8_6,

1 Introduction

It is asserted that in the future the number, intensity, and diversity of crises will increase (due, for example, to new asymmetric threats, environmental changes, globalisation, and migrations), and that there is a keen necessity to provide crisis managers with efficient decision support. This need has been identified by the European States, and is present in the security theme of the European Research Framework Programme (FP7 security call 2).

Anticipating, responding, or recovering from a disaster, an incident, a crisis, or an emergency (called later in the chapter as DICE) in a timely and effective manner can reduce deaths and injuries, contain secondary effects, and mitigate the resulting economic losses and social disruption. Implementation of those activities involves information management, decision making, problem solving, tasking and planning, resource management, monitoring, and coordination. These activities are complex multidimensional processes involving a large number of inter-operating entities (teams of humans and systems) and are affected by various social, medical, geographical, psychological, political, and technological factors. From the information technology viewpoint, those processes can be hindered by a lack of adequate, comprehensive and timely information; the presence of conflicting goals, policies, and priorities; or a lack of effective coordination between different rescue operations. Therefore, the situation understanding issue is one of the cornerstones of the DICE management process. To underline that purpose, consider that during the first hours post-incident, the Crisis Response Coordination Team (CRCT) is confronted with uncertainties in making critical decisions. There is a real need to gather, in-time, situational information (e.g., information on casualties), together with contextual information (e.g., medical facilities, rescue and law enforcement units). Then, the sense-making process allows the CRCT team to develop a picture of the overall impact of a DICE and establish priorities for response and recovery efforts. Moreover, the analysis of past crises, such as the Madrid train bombings, Gustav hurricane, or the poliomyelitis propagation, illustrates the need for in-time situation understanding in crisis management based on situational and contextual information.

This need to get a global and contextual situation understanding to mitigate DICE impacts has been illuminated in a study carried out by Thales Research & Technology, aimed at identifying adapted decision support tools to facilitate the decision-making of crisis managers. This situation understanding is required through the crisis cycle; thus, a main decision-support goal is to provide real-time contextualised information. Real-time in this chapter refers to the notion of on time. It could be only a few seconds or several hours or even some days, depending on the DICE type. For example, in case of a bomb explosion, every second is important to assess the damage and send rescue operations to save lives. Alternatively, in case of a pandemic, the situation evolution is more on a day timescale.

This chapter thus highlights the role of sense making and situation understanding to enhance crisis management decision support. More specifically, it reveals the need of real-time context availability in the crisis management process. The chapter is structured as follows: Sect. 2 illustrates the need for timely context in crisis management using the analysis of past crisis feedback. In Sect. 3, as a pre-requisite, the definition of the crisis concept is proposed, together with the key functions required for a crisis-management decision-support system. Section 4 presents the overall process of DICE management through its three phases – information gathering, situation analysis, and decision making – and highlights the need to get contextual information for each phase. Finally, it states that in-time contextual information is also required in the overall upgrade process of DICE management, which includes feedback analysis and training. The conclusion is presented in Sect. 5.

2 Need of Context for Crisis Management

Efficient DICE management requires a good, accurate understanding of the situation to improve chances of a successful outcome. Significant challenges include coordination of information amongst entities involved, needs, sharing situation awareness amongst all relevant units, and having an efficient adaptive organisational structure that can change to suit the needs presented by the dynamic situation. This imposes very accurate knowledge of the situation and a keen necessity to correlate the events amongst each other: that is, to get some contextual information. This correlation has to be performed in real time so as to provide an overall and updated understanding of the situation. To illustrate that purpose, here are some real cases.

Poliomyelitis propagation, World, 2003–2005: The international propagation of the poliovirus in 2003–2005 was a shock, as it was considered to be dying out. Due to resurgence of the virus, a wide monitoring infrastructure was created to trace any poliomyelitis cases detected throughout the world. This infrastructure also monitors many other diseases that can be prevented by vaccine. A holistic situation awareness picture is mandatory to watch the world health, to raise the alarm for potential threat, and to anticipate the response. This picture is not only based on situational information (e.g., diseases information) but also on contextual information (e.g., available infrastructures and drugs).

Heat wave, France 2003: As a result of one of the most severe heat waves, more than 14,000 people died in France, mostly elderly people in the northern part of the country where people were not used to the heat. One of the main problems was locating the old people who needed assistance. While trying to minimise the crisis, the French administration was blamed for a lack of reactivity and for ignoring warnings from health and emergency professionals. This heat wave, together with an unusual increase of the paediatric epidemic diseases in winter 2003–2004, outlined the necessity to reinforce the sanitary watch and get some tools to monitor and control hospital emergency services. These events led to the creation of a new regional centre to monitor and drive emergency services, the Centre Régional de Veille et d'Action sur les Urgences (CERVEAU) in the Île-de-France region (CERVEAU 2006; Lepée and Camphin 2007). The two main missions of CERVEAU are to insure:

- sanitary monitoring of emergency services (situational information), and
- monitoring of care resources (contextual information, e.g., number of available hospital beds…).

These missions confirm the necessity of getting a real-time global context of the sanitary situation to handle the crisis response.

Madrid train bombings, Spain, 2004: A series of coordinated bombings in four Madrid commuter trains occurred during rush hour on the morning of Thursday, 11 March 2004. Soon after, the communication network shut down. Thanks to the knowledge of the context, the emergency units could build a first raw estimation of the damage and severity level. In this case, the context enabled them to provide an assessment of needs despite the lack of communication.

As for organisation of the dispatch of victims to the hospitals, instead of going to the Fire-Emergency Medical Services (EMS) triage centre, about 80% of the casualties by-passed it and went directly to the closest hospital. This self-evacuation resulted in an over-triage rate of 68%, with the closest hospitals being over-run. In case of a nuclear or biological attack, these hospitals could have been contaminated (Peral-Gutierrez de Ceballos, Turégano-Fuentes, Pérez Díaz et al. 2005; Turégano-Fuentes, Pérez-Díaz, Sanz-Sánchez, and Ortiz Alonso 2008). Here, lack of a real-time overall view and context of the situation impeded the coordination of the rescuers, prevented the optimal crisis response, and could have increased the mortality.

Hurricane Gustav, New Orleans, USA, 2008: Gustav, the second major hurricane of the 2008 Atlantic hurricane season, caused serious damage in Haiti, the Dominican Republic, Jamaica, the Cayman Islands, Cuba, and the USA. In the USA, there were 138 deaths attributed to Gustav. Due to the anticipation of meteorological conditions, two million people were evacuated to mitigate the risk. Therefore, in the case of the USA, accurate knowledge of the context and anticipation of the threat enabled the evacuation of people and saved lives.

Aftermath of the terrorist attack, USA, 11 September 2001: The 2001 terrorist attacks illustrate the difficulties of governments to tackle a new threat and adapt their defence to a new form of terrorism (isolated cells no longer linked to any state). For J.-L. Bruguière, a French judge specialising in antiterrorism, governments have to face a diffluent and mutant system, which forces one to have a clear and holistic understanding of the situation and the ability to isolate weak signals from amongst a huge amount of information. He insists that it is compulsory to have a geopolitical watch, which implies having a good knowledge of the context (Bruguière 2008). As, by definition here, a "weak" signal refers to some events that, taken independently, would not allow the identification of a risk, but that, when the context is taken into account, are able to reveal some threat through their relations to other events.

Road traffic jam, France, 1999: It started to snow in the late afternoon over the Île-de-France region, when rush hours commenced. Due to a lack of anticipation and the heavy traffic load, it was impossible to clear the road network. Several million people remained blocked until well into the night. To avoid such situations, seven regional centres are now in charge of road traffic monitoring and coordination.

Their mission is to provide traffic and road information to the users, inform and advise authorities in charge of crisis management, and coordinate emergency traffic response. As for the coordination, it is essential to anticipate the consequences of any actions on the road traffic load (e.g., it is essential to anticipate lane-closing consequences). Also, these centres today benefit from a large amount of traffic data reporting, although according to an operator, they still lack some efficient tools to compare relief roads and estimate the impact of DICE on the traffic.

These examples reveal the critical necessity to get the right information in the right place at the right time. It confirms that the lack of the relevant information in time can have tremendous impact, and that even for events of a long duration, such as a pandemic, the mitigation of DICE relies on the availability and timeliness of an overall and contextualised understanding of the situation.

This, thus, underlines the major role of sense making to support overall crisis management, and shows that real-time information contextualisation is a cornerstone in each phase of the global process from the early watch to the decision.

The next section defines the crisis and crisis management concepts and outlines the main crisis management support functionalities. This provides a framework to analyse the role of context for crisis management (Sect. 4).

3 Crisis Management

A research study, carried out in Thales between 2007 and 2008, investigated decision tools for crisis management support (Gabaix and Gavard 2008). Indeed, even if there are some experts specialised in crisis management, there exist few studies that put the crisis systems in the centre of the analysis (systems such as those used in crisis response units). Users' needs are still partially stated and specified; the users rely on basic tools to manage the crises and are not aware of the potential provided by the new information technologies. Thus, there is a necessity to tackle the subject with a wider open-mindedness in order to multiply the usages and the concepts. To achieve this goal, the Thales study has been carried out upon many past crises analysis and through the interviews of about 15 crisis managers from the following organisations: RATP – France Parisian underground, SNCF – French National Railway Company, DDSC – French Direction of the Civil Defence and Security. The main results are presented hereafter.

3.1 Crisis Characteristics

Dealing with decision tools for crisis management support immediately raises the question of crisis definition and characteristics, which in turn raises some paradoxes.

To define the crisis concept, we retain – from the etymology analysis – the notions of bifurcation, lack of time, the decisive nature, the stakes, the breakdown aspect, and the alert signals, as associated with the crisis.

Nevertheless, the analysis of feedback from past crises experience shows that crises differ by their duration, their spatial extent, and their type (terrorist attack, natural disaster…). The multiplicity, the specificity, and the variety of past crises are large; so the Thales approach is not meant to be exhaustive, and instead, prefers to grab some pinches of the crisis characteristics in several domains. (This method is referred to by Rosier as an approach by "touches" (Rosier 2007).)

To get an indication of the variability of past crises, the study covered several types of crises, such as *terrorist attacks* (like the events of 11 September 2001 in the USA, the bomb attacks of 11 March 2004 in Madrid, the sarin attack in Tokyo subway on 20 March 1995, and attacks in a Paris subway in 1995); *natural disasters* (with the analysis of the tsunami in Asia in 2004 and hurricane Katrina in Louisiana in 2005 (Lagadec 2007)); *industrial accidents* (with the explosion of AZF factory in Toulouse (France) in 2001, the electrical blackout in the Northeast of the USA and Canada in 2003, and the power cut in Italy in 2003); and *sanitary crises* (with the study of SARS in 2003, the mad cow disease (BSE) in 1996, the heat wave in France in 2003, the epidemic of chikungunya at Reunion Island in 2005–2006 (Ministère de la Santé et des Solidarités 2007)). Other types of crises were also considered in the study, together with situations with high potential to turn into crisis ("crisogen" situations), in particular social situations, through the analysis of big gatherings (for example football meetings, demonstrations), of drug trafficking and of independent armed groups (such as the increase of forces of opposition groups as the FARC in Colombia), the cybernetic attacks (Estonia 2004), and the attacks on banking systems.

So, using the feedback on these past experiences, we have retained the criteria proposed by Doctor General Crocq to characterise crises (Crocq 2007):

- A break (disorder, disturbance),
- A bifurcation (transition period, decisive moment, choice),
- A threat (danger, severity),
- An important stake (large number, large scale),
- The urgency (surprise, miss time),
- A degraded, unordered situation (means shortage), and
- A difficulty, a psychological tension.

The validation of one or more of these criteria is then a sufficient condition to qualify the event as a crisis (to a certain level, of course).

Based on the previous analysis, let us retain the following crisis definition (Aligne 2009):

> A situation of break [from a normal situation] with regard to the previous events, which threatens the functioning and the values of the individual and/or the community, and where [there] appears an urgent necessity to act despite the degradation of the means, the information and the control. The characteristic of a crisis is that it is unpredictable, out of frame, that it exceeds the existing means, and that it cannot be anticipated by scenarios.

This definition identifies the crisis as an exceptional situation because of its unpredictable character and the underlying overtaking of means; and as thus, most of the usual methods of intervention will not be adapted. What is crucial for the resolution of the crisis is the capacity and ability to get some tactical reflection and intelligence that can be mobilised. This need was well understood by Lagadec (Beroux, Guilhou, and Lagadec 2007) with his concept of "strengths of fast reflection" units, set up in EdF (French Electricity board). These structures aim at facilitating work of reflection. This outlines the important and essential role of reflection and intelligence in the resolution of the crises. It reveals the necessity of having some information systems and decision-making supports to assist and facilitate reflection.

Let us now characterise such a system.

3.2 *From Crisis Management Concept to Crisis Management Support*

To approach the notion of crisis management, let us first model the crisis. Based on past crisis feedback analysis, we propose a crisis cycle model (Fig. 1) (Aligne and Mattioli 2008), adapted from the *Disaster Risk Management Cycle* (DRMC) Diagram proposed by Barnier and Baas et al. (Barnier 2006; Baas, Ramasamy, Depryck, and Battista 2008). This crisis cycle is divided into three phases: Pre-disaster, Response, and Post-disaster.

In the Pre-disaster phase, we identify the activities of watching, monitoring, intelligence gathering, detection, identification of the crisis, and assessment of induced risks.

Fig. 1 Crisis management cycle (adapted from Baas et al. 2008 crisis cycle)

Unless the crisis is avoided, the next phase is the Response phase, which starts with the alert and possibly evacuation procedures. Activities for this phase are evaluation, rescue commitment, and crisis management of different aspects (human, material, financial, and legal). This phase can borrow some methods from defence services, such as the preliminary sorting of the victims to manage a large number of victims. This phase leads back to a normal (stabilised) situation, and is more or less long and expensive depending on the resilience capacity of the organisation. From the beginning of the crisis, experience feedback procedures must be applied to enable an accurate analysis of the crisis in the third phase, the Post-disaster phase.

In the Post-disaster phase, experience feedback is analysed so as to better anticipate and forecast potential problems, to identify the risks and to revise planned procedures. We then enter a process of preparing, teaching, simulating, and training.

It is manifest that this cycle hides some subtleties; for example, the analysis of the experience feedback will start before everything is solved; also, during long term and progressive crises like pandemics or sanitary crises, identification of risks or evaluation of damage must be continuously performed and revised throughout the DICE.

Using this crisis management cycle representation, and based on past crisis analysis (Dautun 2004; Lagadec 1993; Lagadec 2007; Ministère de la Santé et des Solidarités 2007), a set of functionalities for crisis management decision support had been identified. To collect some users' requirements, this work was completed by some operational risk manager interviews in several domains: public transport, hospitals, fire brigades, civil safety administration, and food chain suppliers. The outcome of the study was a set of decision support functionalities that are of particular interest for crisis management, such as information gathering, information updating, information sharing, situation analysis and understanding, situation monitoring, detection and identification of crisis, issuing alerts, decisions set elaboration and presentation, resources allocation, analysis of decision impact (Fig. 2).

These functionalities can be structured into the three main steps of the decision support processing: *information gathering*, *situation analysis and understanding*, and *decision-making support*.

Information gathering: These are the functions allowing the description of the real world in the form of numeric data, which can be worked out by a computer (video, audio, satellites, radars data, etc.), but also of data collected by someone (intelligence gathering). These data have to satisfy certain qualitative criteria so that they can be used. In many domains, the data are still manually entered by an operator into the systems. The functionalities involved are thus information gathering, information updating, and information sharing.

Situation assessment and understanding: These are the functions that enable the processing of data into relevant information to achieve an objective and with regard to the asked question. It includes, for example, functions provided by

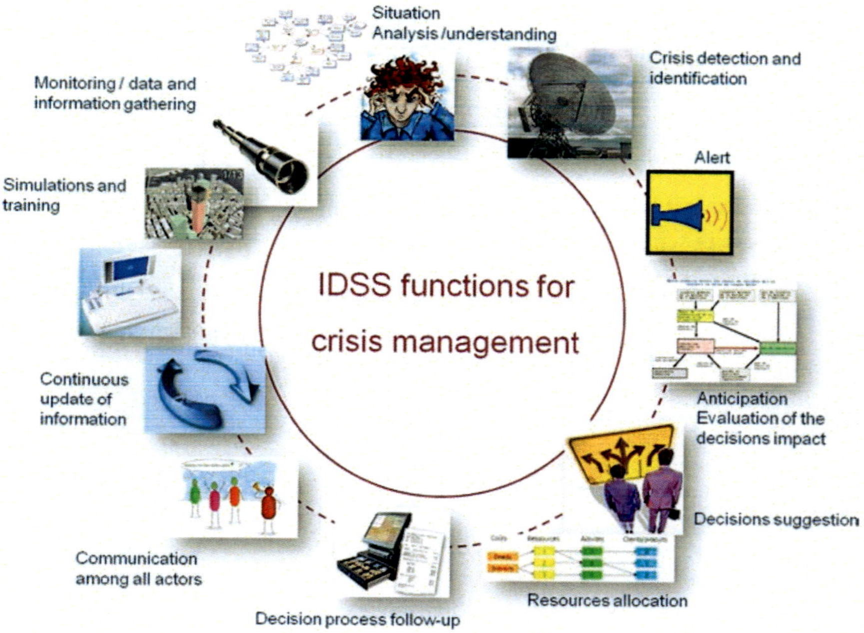

Fig. 2 Crisis management functionalities

geographical information systems (GIS), by the information systems of command centres, biometric systems, and statistical tools of analysis. The assessment and understanding of the situation will provide the user with a clear and synthetic vision of the situation, enable the organisation and analysis of the information, and facilitate the decision-making process. This, thus, comprises the production of key indicators, dashboards, etc. The functionalities involved are situation analysis and understanding, situation monitoring, detecting and identifying the crisis, and issuing alerts.

Decision-making support: These functions assist decision makers to overcome the complexity of the situation by suggesting or supporting decisive alternatives. We can mention, for example, the planning and scheduling systems of enterprise resource management (ERP). This domain still has much to explore. The decision making very frequently relies on the combination of expert assessments and complex logics. Although we do not aim to replace the expert, to support him in his decision task can turn out to be very delicate and complicated. Some systems, used in well-delimited domains, nevertheless have already proven their effectiveness. The functionalities involved are thus the elaboration and presentation of the decision set, resources allocation, and analysis of decision impact.

In the following section, we describe the processes involved in these three steps and propose some relevant techniques for implementation of each one. This will highlight the key role of "context" in crisis management.

4 Contextualisation Use in the Three Phases of DICE Management

4.1 Contextualisation for Information Gathering

The specific term “situation awareness”, most commonly used by the Human-Computer Interaction community (Endsley 1995), is defined as “the perception of the elements in the environment within a volume of time and space, the comprehension of their meaning, and the projection of their status in the near future”. Furthermore, a situation can provide answers to some but not all questions induced by the decision problem. Therefore, situation awareness plays a central role in cognition, which spans the entire spectrum of cognitive activities from situation analysis (perception + comprehension) to near-future forecast. To efficiently support humans in their situation understanding in such decision-making processes and particularly in the induced cognitive overload context, there is a crucial need to provide in time only the critical information required. In such situation, the decision makers have to deal with a huge amount of heterogeneous information that comes from different sources and thus is often redundant, if not conflicting.

It is therefore necessary to model and specify the context and situation to provide support functions for cognitive overload mitigation such that the stakeholders can easily exchange, share, and re-use their knowledge. Situation understanding is not only a matter of knowing the objects that are present in the external world, but also to make sense of the situation assessment achieved by specifying and representing the relations amongst it. To design such support systems, one of the major challenges is to construct a situation model from which crisis management operations can be planned and updated. A situation model is a representation of the situation that will serve as a reference for each participating user; it allows a complete cognitive understanding of the situation (Mattioli, Museux, Hemaissia, and Laudy 2007). It includes the representation of all events, actions, actors, past experiences, and items which explain, impact or are impacted by the situation (note that in this chapter, actors are the individuals involved in the DICE mitigation). Therefore, the situation model provides a cognitive representation of the situation context.

To build a situation model, we use ontology concepts as they are used to capture knowledge about some domain of interest. Matheus, Baclawski, and Kokar (2003a) advocate the use of formal ontologies to describe the fundamental events, objects, and relations of a situation’s domain and logical rules. This is in order to define ways of fusing information and identifying higher order relations relevant to the situation (Matheus, Baclawski, and Kolar 2003b). Smirnov, Pashkin, Shirov, and Levashova (2007) also propose to include ontology for mega disaster management.

Therefore, the situation model contains a knowledge-level view of DICE using some specific ontology, such as Crisis Response Management (CRM) ontology. The model is created and updated by a constant flow of events and reports collected from the operational space. These events include both human and artificial intelligence. Because of the large amount of raw data being collected, the event stream needs to be processed and correlated to produce situational events, i.e., events at the domain level. This reduction and inference step is performed by an information-fusion stage. Thanks to the OASIS consortium, most of the relevant situation items (class, property or individual) can be described through the definition of the Tactical Situation Object (TSO) (OASIS Project 2006), which contains at least the following information.

- Identification information: it shall be identified in an unambiguous way. It shall also describe who the originator of the information is and when the information was created.
- Description of the case: the TSO is one solution to provide to other entities its own view of the case such as the type of the case, its extent, the number of casualties, the consequences on the environment, its criticality, etc.
- Description of the context: the CRCT is interested to know which resources are already used, which resources are available (including the human resources), their availability, their position, and their capabilities.
- Description of the actions: it is also very important to inform the others of the activities which are in progress or which are foreseen, so that the coordination is efficient. Information on the past, future, and ongoing tasks must be available (their status, the teams, and resources that are engaged on a task, their planning, etc.).

Following OASIS guidelines, the Interactive Collaborative Information Systems (ICIS) project (2003) provides crisis response management ontology composed of three modules: *situational*, *contextual*, and *decisional* (Figs. 3, 4 and 5). The situational information provides a view of the crisis case, such as, for example, the type of crisis, its extent, number of casualties, environmental impact, and criticality. The contextual information addresses the status of resources, which includes list of resources, their availability, position, and capabilities. The decisional information concerns the tasks that are ongoing. This comprises their status, the team, and resources involved and their planning (Mattioli et al. 2007).

Based on this situation model, the *information extraction* consists of the analysis of data coming from different sources so that these data become meaningful. The objective is to extract information from the available data. The techniques we use are text mining, audio mining, and image processing. The notion of text mining has been widely spread by the search engines though these do not allow the performance of sense making on the data. Text mining, as used here, seeks to find relations between blocks of text data contained in a text to provide information. Audio mining allows the extraction of information from an audio stream (speech or noise analysis). In particular, speech analysis is reinforced today by the background sounds analysis that can provide much additional information to optimise the sense-making processing. Information extraction methods, either in text, audio or images, usually use ontology to structure the input data, and supervised classification methods to analyse and extract relations amongst entities. Thus, this is very much correlated with the above modelling phase. The capability of the method to extract relationships amongst entities and model the crisis situation context is a key factor of the information extraction phase.

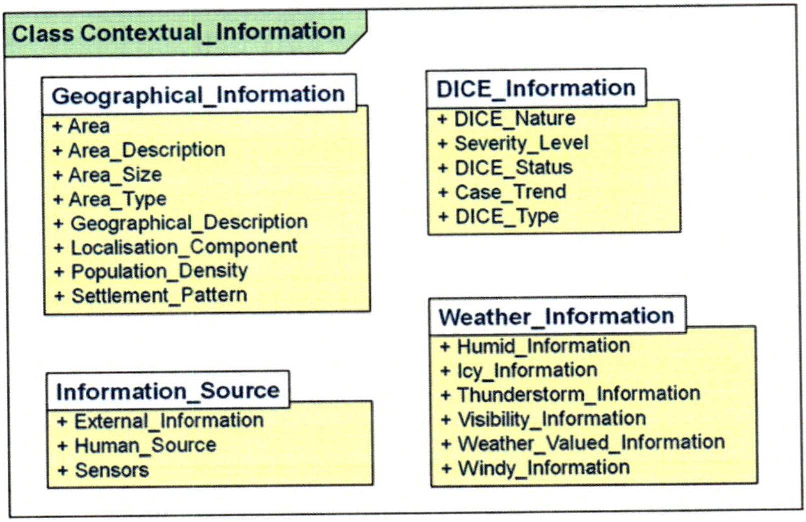

Fig. 3 Contextual information modelling, from ICIS project (ICIS project 2003)

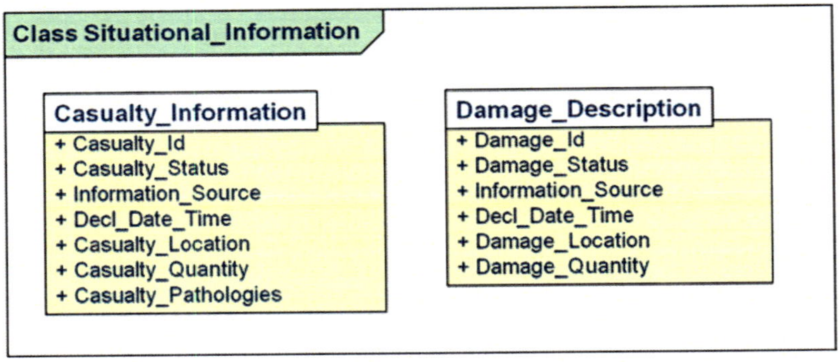

Fig. 4 Situational information modelling, from ICIS project (ICIS project 2003)

Following the information extraction, the construction of a coherent overall situation picture will require some fusion of heterogeneous and redundant information techniques. Most of the time, because information is coming from a wide range of sources including both human and signal sources, the pieces of information must be combined and correlated in accordance with

- The objectives of the crisis response (for example, for early crisis response the objectives can be immediate life saving, search and rescue, medical aid),
- The information reliability and relevance, and
- The information temporality (obsolescence and update).

The processing and correlating of all available information is performed by an information-fusion stage. The information items, stored as graph structures, are combined using fusion heuristics. The fusion algorithm is based on a graph homomorphism

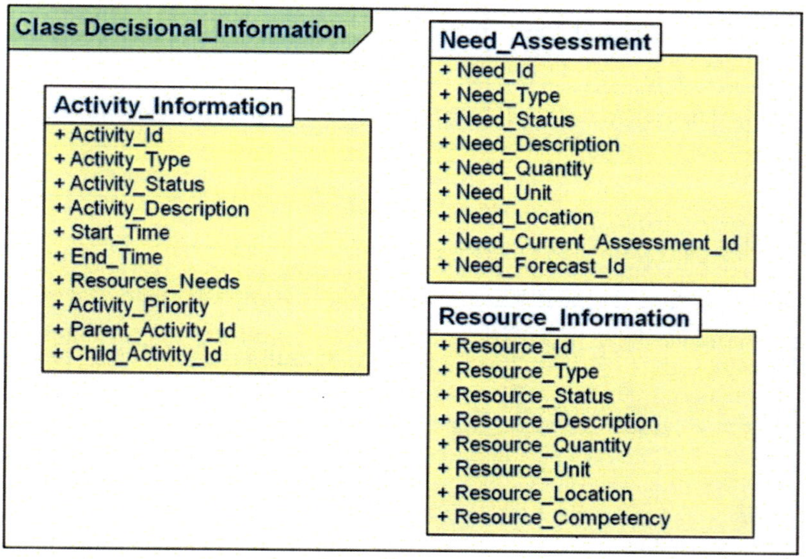

Fig. 5 Decisional information modelling, from ICIS project (ICIS project 2003)

algorithm where we look for compatible subgraphs (i.e., fusible). The compatibility is processed thanks to the fusion heuristics – called fusion strategies – that contain both a part to test the compatibility of two observations and a part to compute the fused observation (Laudy and Ganascia 2008a,b; Laudy, Ganascia, and Sedogbo 2007).

This early overall situation picture then has to be consolidated with some situation understanding process and sense-making analysis. This is to provide a meaningful situation awareness, the basis on which the final decision-making step can be performed. These two steps are presented hereafter.

4.2 *Contextualisation to Get a Meaningful Situation Awareness*

Situation understanding is used to manage, in real time, crisis situations of critical infrastructures (such as production line breakdown, network intrusion or attack of public area). For example, an alert can be raised only if responsible actors have a clear understanding of the global situation. The situation understanding has to be as complete as possible and has to consider the information from different points of view, from the smallest standpoints to wider perspectives. For example, the detection of weak signals amongst a huge amount of information is of major importance for information intelligence activities. This implies a capability of analysing the situation down to its smallest component using a well-established global situation analysis. This should enable the detection of small pieces of information that – put back into the context – are of prior interest.

The situation understanding process is a cognitive and analytical process by which we can take some information and synthesise it with previously held information. It is then used in a new context, or used in a different way to that envisioned when first collected. The difference between situation understanding and information gathering is the difference between learning and memorising as compared to this ability to transform information through experience and know-how. Thus, the situation understanding depends not only on the information content but also on its contextualisation.

It should be pointed out that context also impacts the frequency at which information used to get meaningful situation awareness is constantly updated. As already mentioned in the introduction, real-time here refers to the notion of on time and can range from a few seconds to many days depending on the DICE type (example of bomb explosion vs. pandemic situations). The need for real-time information for situation awareness is indeed very dependent on the context, as shown in the following example which is very illustrative, though not directly linked to DICE management.

When enhancing air traffic management (ATM) procedures and tools, new concepts have to be validated through real-time simulation exercises. During an air traffic simulation session, pilots were asked to deal with a new ATM procedure that involved an automatic adaptation of the aircraft speed with regard to the preceding aircraft speed and position. The modified simulator displayed the value of the aircraft speed taking into account the new requirements in real time. However, after a few training exercises, this speed value displayed in real time had to be averaged and smoothed so as to display a stabilised value of the speed. This was because pilots were unable to get a comprehensible situation awareness from a constantly changing speed. It is therefore important to adapt the notion of real time to the use, context, and decision need. Thus, real-time here implies the notion of *on time*, or as referred to (Nelson 2004) *time to decision*.

This outlines the crucial role of contextualisation in the previous information-gathering step to building a contextualised situation understanding, and emphasises that this information gathering requires real-time updates. Complex event processing (CEP) is widely used for situation analysis and understanding. It allows the identification of relevant information to provide answers, in real time, to the crisis managers' needs. It consists of the detection of complex events, the correlation, and analysis of hierarchical events and events relations (such as causality or temporality) (Museux, Mattioli, Laudy, and Soubaras 2006).

With a keen, updated, and contextualised situation awareness, a coherent and efficient crisis management plan to mitigate and resolve the DICE can be envisaged and elaborated.

4.3 Dual Impact of the Context on Decision Making

Decision-making support is used in the response planning and implementation phase to optimise resource allocation and scheduling. This aims to first meet specific relief objectives and later to fulfil recovery and development goals. Because of the high combinatory complexity of resource allocation and scheduling problems, we use a hybrid method, combining an optimisation algorithm with a meta-heuristic algorithm. This enables us to split the problem into subproblems. To be efficient and operational, the selected decision has to correctly tackle the operational constraints in the optimisation problem. These constraints then are to be included into the Situation Model. The final decision also takes into account some potential conflicting goals. This last issue can be addressed by the use of some negotiations in the optimisation algorithm (Hemaissia et al. 2006).

Crisis response requires the management of all relevant resources (infrastructures, material, human); a lack of resources can lead to the abortion of the whole response. It is thus very important to have an updated knowledge of the availability of resources and of the procedures required to use them. Besides, in order to support the decision makers, the shared situation awareness picture has to materialise the "decisional environment" and so makes it clear why emergency operation planning is necessary.

Once some allocation or scheduling of resources has been performed, and before the commitment to the crisis response tasks has been made, there is a great necessity to analyse what would be the impact of the response operations. This impact should be analysed in terms of results as well as risk involving the crisis mitigation. Between two responses, it might be wiser not to choose the more efficient one (efficient with regard to some predefined criteria such as time and/or cost) if its level of risk is very high compared to the other one. The efficiency and risk can be evaluated by the modelling of the situation evolution. The final response selection thus requires a time projection of the situation understanding process. We call it the "dual impact of the context for the crisis management decision support". The context first constrains the resolution of the resource allocation problem (or scheduling), but it also helps discriminate amongst several resource allocation solutions.

To measure the impact of a decision to the context, some simulation tools to "play" the decision in advance are used to analyse its consequences. As an example, some recent research carried out by the multiagent community is now presented.

This research aims to define a simulation tool for road traffic crisis management and uses the context as a key function for the agent to take his/her decisions. Environment as active support of interaction (EASI) is a multiagent model of interaction conceived by the *Laboratoire d'Analyse et de Modélisation des Systèmes pour l'Aide à la Décision* (LAMSADE), which is based on a reification of implicit and explicit rules to enable the interaction of a multiagent system with the environment. The objective is to model the link between the perception domain and the activities of the agent, and so to allow the use by the agent of this knowledge to reach its objective. More recently, a new contextual simulation multiagent model has been studied by F. Balbo and F. Badeig. The objective is to extend the EASI contextual principle of interaction to a contextual activation of the simulation agents (Saunier, Balbo, and Badeig 2007). This model, called Environment as Active Support of Simulation (EASS), separates the simulation process from the activation process of the agents. The approach used is the study of the context and the interactions between the actors

(Badeig, Balbo and Pinson 2007). A first application of this work concerns crisis management in the transport domain. The goal is to simulate the complexity of a crisis for better analysis and understanding. The simulation of different scenarios for the same crisis will help the conception of new intervention plans and the validation and adaptation of existing plans (Badeig and Balbo 2008).

The above description of the decision-making process thus shows that the situation understanding process is essential and that a decision has to be correlated to its context.

4.4 Contextualisation of the DICE Management Upgrade Process

A very important point to take full advantage of DICE management processes and to improve them is to regularly train all the actors who may have to play a role in the DICE mitigation. It must be stressed that people involved in the process during a DICE management might not be people usually in charge of the process. The training should thus be large enough to familiarise the people with a large event of practices. Training sessions aim at getting the people used to the tools and practices, often through life-sized exercises of simulated DICE events. The goal is to put people in some degraded situations already encountered by others, in order to develop individual best practices. This implies getting the actors accustomed to different contexts (Gauthey 2008).

The upgrade of the DICE management process also relies, of course, on the analysis of the feedback from past events so as to learn and capitalise from past mistakes. As stated by Cheila Duarte-Colardelle, most of the incident report forms do not allow for catching the "why" and "how" of the acts and decisions. The situation perception is ignored, which is a limitation to the understanding of some events. Dysfunction and misleads are analysed with the aim of understanding not only the "how", but also especially the "why". When someone makes a decision, several choices are available; the decision and the resulting action might not be understood by others. "Why has he done this?" There is always some reason that can be explained by the context (Duarte-Colardelle 2006).

Rescue plans have also been defined step-by-step and adapted with regard to some evolution of the context. These evolutions are detected and analysed to capitalise on and benefit from them. In the work of Duarte-Colardelle (2006), the author explains how to trace and analyse the dynamic progress of each case study. This method, called positive feedback (*REX positif*), aims no longer at learning from accidents or dysfunctions, but at detecting the good practices and at strengthening them; the notion of "key moment associated with a cycle of decision" is the most significant contribution of the method. The comparison between the decisions that make the situation worse, with "good" decisions that could have saved the situation, is the basis of the process. We agree with Sarant that this is an important contribution, provided the decision making contexts are taken into account (Sarant 2003).

5 Conclusion

This chapter has established the major role of sense making and situation understanding process in DICE management and has outlined the importance of real-time information contextualisation in this process.

The efficiency and effectiveness of DICE management responses are deeply correlated with the availability and quality of the relevant contextualised information. The appropriate update of this information is a key issue to enhance the DICE management process. Many examples, taken from past crisis experience feedback, outline the keen necessity to get the right information at the right place and in-time. Thus, in the watch process the need to get a holistic situation awareness based on updated situational and contextual information is illustrated by the poliomyelitis example. The necessity to get a holistic geopolitical watch correlated to the context is also stressed by the antiterrorism judge Bruguière on the analysis of the 11 September event.

To summarise, the aim of this chapter has been to present application domain crisis management and to show the importance of the real-time context in this domain. To introduce the subject, past crisis analysis examples were presented in Sect. 2 to illustrate the need of contextualisation at various stages of the crisis management process. Section 3 presents the meaning of crisis management process and the main functionalities involved along three axes: information gathering, situation understanding, and decision making. Using this structure, an analysis of the role of context in the DICE management process was derived in Sect. 4. This analysis demonstrates that contextual information is required at every stage of the DICE management process. It also shows that nowadays some emergent technologies are able to deal with real-time contextualised information to fulfil the requirements of the identified DICE management support tools functionalities. Thus, for the information-gathering step, the use of ontology allows us to build and structure a coherent situation model that enables DICE managers to build and share a real-time contextualised situation representation. The initial overall picture of the situation, obtained by information extraction and fusion and with real-time updates, must then be consolidated in the situation-understanding step to provide meaningful situation awareness. This provides the essential base to derive the final decision-making step. In this last step, we have outlined that the context has a dual impact on the decision-making process: the context constrains the resolution of the resource allocation problem and also helps discriminate amongst several resource allocation solutions.

The variety of actors involved and the unpredictability of the situations are the main specificities of the DICE management application domain. The importance and impact of real-time context throughout the DICE management process have been carefully established here, and emergent technology has been identified for each step of the DICE management process to take the context into account. Yet, more research should be conducted for a deeper insight into the robustness of this contextualisation and insure that the foreseen solutions are coherent across the large variety of stakeholders and throughout the DICE management processes. DICE management endeavours to deal with a very large variety of actors (medical units, fire brigades, police forces, but also, electricity, water, road infrastructures services…), and situations (located events or disasters that impact a large geographical area, natural events, human mislead or intend attacks…). This implies the need to take into account a broad set of contexts and to enable adaptation in real time the decision support tools for any new situation. The solutions envisaged here are meant to be as generic as possible; there has been no focus on a specific type of DICE as we tackled the problem from the analysis of DICE characteristics. Yet, the adaptability of the solutions for different contexts that occur randomly should be further investigated. In particular, it is expected that there would be great benefit in considering the outcomes of recent researches on the use of improvisation to provide real-time decision making (Stein 2008).

Currently, in Thales Research and Technology we apply this contextualisation process to improve the DICE operations deployment at the DICE management strategic level in a new study carried out within the Descartes project (project of the French "pôle de compétitivité" Infom@gic). This study addresses the crisis cell at the council level and aims at optimising the resources allocation of the first crisis responders (emergency medical units, fire brigades, and police). Following the recommendations presented here, the context is taken into account through the modelling of rescue plans. Though this still requires more theoretical work in the planning domain, the results are promising and enable us to cross different contexts for different actors, both at different space and time scales.

Lastly, we mention another area of research that should be addressed to enhance the whole process of DICE management: the resolution of conflicting goals. It is indeed another major issue to be resolved when many actors are implicated in the decision process. How could the use of context anticipate and prevent the occurrence of conflicting situations, and could it facilitate their resolution?

References

Aligne, F., Which information and decision support system for the crisis management? in *NATO RTO-MP-IST-086*, May 2009, Romania.

Aligne, F. and J. Mattioli, Situation understanding process: The cornerstone for crisis management support, in *RTDMC 08 Proceedings*, 2008, Paris.

Baas, S, S. Ramasamy, J.D. Depryck and F. Battista, *Disaster Risk Management System Analysis. A Guide Book*, FAO, Rome, January 2008, URL=ftp://ftp.fao.org/docrep/fao/010/ai504e/ai504e01.pdf.

Badeig, F. and F. Balbo, La gestion de crise dans les transports, Un simulateur multi-agent centré environnement, in *Atelier Systèmes d'Information en Transport, Inforsid 08*, 2008.

Badeig, F., F. Balbo and S. Pinson, Contextual activation for agent-based simulation, in *Proceedings, 21st European Conference on Modelling and Simulation*, 2007, Prague.

Barnier, M., *Pour une force européenne de protection civile: Europe aid*, 2006, URL=http://ec.europa.eu/commission_barroso/president/pdf/rapport_barnier_20060508_fr.pdf

Beroux, P., X. Guilhou and P. Lagadec, Implementing rapid reflection forces, *Crisis Response*, Vol. 3, No. 2, March 2007, pp. 36–37.

Bruguière, J., Le terrorisme, nouvelle menace, Conference held at Polytechnic, 24 January 2008, France.

CERVEAU, Centre Régional de Veille et d'Action sur les Urgences en Île-de-France, *Charte de partenariat*, 2006.

Crocq, L., Médecin Général des Armées, *Formation et sensibilisation NRBC*, Haut Comité Français pour la Défense Civile, 2007.

Dautun, C., Organisation de la gestion de crise « Les secours face à une crise de grande ampleur, Thèse professionnelle, mastère Sécurité Industrielle et Environnement, Ecole des Mines d'Alès et INERIS, France, 2004.

Duarte-Colardelle, C., Analyse de la dynamique organisationnelle en temps de crise, Thèse de doctorat en Ingénierie et Gestion – Sciences de Gestion, Ecole Nationale Supérieure des Mines de Paris, France, 2006.

Endsley, M., Toward a theory of situation awareness in dynamic systems, *Human Factors*, Vol. 1, No. 37, 1995, pp. 32–64.

Gabaix, J.-C. and C. Gavard, Exploration d'un domaine d'innovation dans un marché émergent: systèmes d'information et d'aide à la décision pour la gestion de crise, Master Projet Innovation Conception de l'Ecole Polytechnique, Mention Economie et Gestion, Polytechnique, France, 2008.

Gauthey, O., Le retour d'expérience, Etat des pratiques industrielles, *Les cahiers de la sécurité industrielle*, ICSI, Institut pour une culture de sécurité industrielle, France, 2008-02.

Hemaissia, M. et al., Cooperation-based multilateral multi-issue negotiation for crisis management, in *AAMAS'06 International Workshop on Rational, Robust and Secure Negotiations in Multi-Agent Systems (RRS 2006)*, May 2006, Hakodate, pp 77–95.

ICIS project, D6 – A survey on situation theory and CEP focusing on emergency situation understanding, ICT project selected for by the BSIK programme, ICIS-ESA cluster, Interactive Collaborative Information Systems, 2003–2008, URL=www.icis.decis.nl.

Lagadec, P., *Apprendre à gérer les crises*, Editions d'Organisation, 1993.

Lagadec, P., *Katrina: Examen des rapports d'enquête*, 2007, URL=http://www.patricklagadec.net/fr/pdf/2007-25.pdf

Laudy, C. and J.G. Ganascia, Information fusion in a TV program recommendation system, in *Proceedings of the 11th International Conference on Information Fusion (FUSION 2008)*, July 2008a, Cologne, pp. 1455–1462.

Laudy, C. and J.G. Ganascia, Information fusion using conceptual graphs: A TV programs case study, in additional *Proceedings of the 16th International Conference on Conceptual Structures (ICCS 2008)*, P. Eklund and O. Haemerlé (Eds), July 2008b, Toulouse, pp. 158–165.

Laudy, C., J.G. Ganascia and C. Sedogbo, High-level fusion based on conceptual graphs, in *Proceedings of the 10th International Conference on Information Fusion (FUSION 2007)*, July 2007, Québec.

Lepée, M. and P. Camphin, Le centre régional de veille et d'action sur les urgences d'île-de-France (Cerveau): Une information partagée pour une action concertée, *Gestion hospitalière*, No. 462, 2007, pp. 60–65, France.

Matheus, C., K. Baclawski and M. Kokar, Derivation of ontological relations using formal methods in a situation awareness scenario, in *Proceedings of SPIE Conference on Multisensor, Multisource Information Fusion*, April 2003a, pp. 298–309.

Matheus, C., K. Baclawski and M. Kolar, *Phase I Final Report: A Formal Framework for Situation Awareness*, AFRL Funding number: F30602-02-C-0039, January 2003b.

Mattioli, J., N. Museux, M. Hemaissia and C. Laudy, A crisis response situation model, in *10th international Conference on Information Fusion*, 2007, Quebec.

Ministère de la Santé et des Solidarités, *Chikungunya: gestion d'une crise longue, société française de médecine de catastrophe*, rapport, France, 2007.

Museux, N., J. Mattioli, C. Laudy and H. Soubaras, *Complex Event Processing Approach for Strategic Intelligence*, FUSION 2006 Technical Program, Paper Number: 200, Tuesday, 11 July 2006, Special Session: Situation Management I.

Nelson, G.B., Real time decision support: Creating a flexible architecture for real time analytics, in *SUGI 29 Proceedings*, Montréal, May 9–12, 2004.

OASIS Project, *Open Advanced System for Disaster and Emergency Management Definition of the OASIS Tactical Situation Object*, EU- FP6 – OASIS project – Part of the D-TA2_06 (OASIS external interfaces), 2006. URL=http://www.oasis-fp6.org/documents/OASIS_TA21_DDD_041_DSF.pdf

Peral-Gutierrez de Ceballos, J., F. Turégano-Fuentes, D. Pérez Díaz et al., Casualties treated at the closest hospital in the Madrid, March 11, terrorist bombings, *Critical Care Medicine*, Vol. 33, 2005, pp. S107–S112.

Rosier, R., Stratégies et organisations des processus d'exploration: le cas de la pile à combustible chez Axane/Air Liquide, Thèse, Université de Paris-Est Marne-la-Vallée, U.F.R. science et gestion, 2007.

Sarant P.-M., Retour d'expérience sur la prise de décision et le jeu des acteurs: le cas du cyclone Lenny dans les Petites Antilles au regard du passé, Programme 'Evaluation et Prise en compte des Risques naturels et technologiques', Ministère de l'écologie et du développement durable, France, 2003.

Saunier, J., F. Balbo and F. Badeig, Environment as active support of interaction, in *Proceedings Environments for Multiagent Systems*, LNCS 4389, 2007, pp. 87–105.

Smirnov, A., M. Pashkin, N. Shirov and T. Levashova, Intelligent support of context-based megadisaster management: Hybrid technology and case study, in *Proceedings of the 4th International Conference on Intelligent Human-Computer Systems for Crisis Response and Management ISCRAM 2007*, 13–16 May 2007, Delft.

Stein, E.W., Supporting real time decision-making: The role of context in decision support on the move, SIG DSS Pre-ICIS Workshop on Real Time Decision Support – RTDMC 2008, 13 December 2008, Paris.

Turégano-Fuentes F., D. Pérez-Díaz, M. Sanz-Sánchez and J. Ortiz Alonso, Overall assessment of the response to terrorist bombings in trains, Madrid, 11 March 2004, *European Journal of Trauma and Emergency Surgery*, 2008, Æ No. 5, Urban & Vogel.

Chapter 7
The Contextual and Collaborative Dimensions of Avatar in Real-Time Decision Making

Norita Ahmad[1] **and Reza Barkhi**[2]

[1] School of Business and Management, American University of Sharjah, Sharjah, UAE
[2] Pamplin College of Business, Virginia Tech, Blacksburg, VA, USA

Abstract Technology, combined with the changing nature of work, has created a new environment where individuals have significant options for communication, interaction and real-time decision making. An interesting research question is how various contextual and collaborative approaches influence human decision makers through interface manipulations. We focus on Second Life (SL), a virtual world with media rich context in which avatars interact and make real-time decisions. Even though the decisions in virtual worlds currently have limited impact and consequences, we make the case that it is a good laboratory to study real-time decision making. We study how a sense of presence and a sense of context can be achieved through SL. We design an experiment to study the contextual dimensions of the avatars in SL, user behaviour and perceptions about SL. The results of this study support an assertion that when individuals feel that SL is useful in a real-time decision-making context, it can influence the SL experience and together with SL experience can impact the attitude towards use of SL in real-time context.

Keywords Second Life • Virtual world • Real-time decision making • Context • Collaboration • Technology acceptance model • Avatar • Presence

1 Introduction

The way people work is evolving towards virtual workplaces where connectivity is enabled by electronic networks technology. Technology, combined with the changing nature of work, has created a new environment where individuals have significant options for communication and interaction. One of the possibilities that

N. Ahmad (✉)
School of Business and Management, American University of Sharjah, Sharjah, UAE
e-mail: nahmad@aus.edu

F. Burstein et al. (eds.), *Supporting Real Time Decision-Making*,
Annals of Information Systems 13, DOI 10.1007/978-1-4419-7406-8_7,

manifests from such new advancements is effective support for real-time decision making. Making high quality decisions is the most important managerial skill for organisational effectiveness (Heller, Drenth, Koopman, and Rus 1988) and the Internet is increasingly recognised as an enabling technology. The next generation of the Internet is characterised by user participation, openness, and network effects (O'Reilly and Musser 2006) where organisations create and access information in a way that has not formerly been possible.

We focus on Second Life (SL), a virtual world that is designed for real-time interaction between people. SL is a media-rich context that provides an artificial platform to learn and study real-time human decision making and interaction. It creates a simulated environment where the normal impact and consequences of wrong decisions in real-time scenarios are not as catastrophic as real life and hence can provide an excellent learning tool. It provides an environment to study how virtual space influences human cognition, judgements, decision process, and outcomes in real-time decision-making contexts. In this study, we illustrate how SL can be used to study the perceptions of real human decision makers who control the behaviour of the avatars they represent in a virtual world. For example, the experience of presence in a virtual world (Lombard and Ditton 1997) can influence the attitude of the humans controlling their avatars. Presence is the feeling of "being there" and can influence the decision and action of the avatars in the virtual world. While presence is perceived by the human who controls the avatar, context can be viewed as shared knowledge about physical, social, historical, or other circumstances within which an action or event occurs (Borges, Brézillon, Pino, and Pomerol 2005). To illustrate the influence of context in a virtual world, we focus on context variables that have practical implications and are of theoretical interest in computer-supported group decision-making situations (Fjermestad and Hiltz 1998).

Interaction in SL is done via avatars, and what we learn about presence in SL may have parallels in real life (first life). The presence in a virtual world can be used as a substitution for physical presence because it mimics presence in first life where the person's body is "captured" by the avatar representation. While humans increasingly travel between virtual spaces and physical spaces for communication (i.e., email, SL and social networks), the influence these mixed spaces have on human decision making in real time and their impact on human cognition, judgement, and decision process and outcomes is unknown. SL provides a natural setting for us to study human interaction in virtual space and compare and contrast that with real-time decision making in the physical world or emerging mixed worlds (i.e., both virtual and physical).

Learning about this enabling technology can help in developing new models for real-time decision support and virtual co-presence. We design an experimental study to illustrate how the contextual dimensions of the avatars in SL can influence the behaviour and perception of humans controlling the avatars in SL. We propose a simple illustrative model that describes the contextual dimensions of the avatars and their effect on antecedents of human attitude as it relates to SL. We utilise Theory of Reasoned Action (TRA) (Ajzen and Fishbein 1980), and Technology

Acceptance Model (TAM) (Davis 1986) to guide the development of the model that we hope can capture the dynamics of the decision in a virtual environment. The major contribution of our study, and what makes it unique, is its examination of the latest technology that allows individuals and organisations to manage real-time decision making effectively. In a period where it is more socially and professionally desirable than ever to rapidly adapt to a changing business environment, the need to incorporate the latest breed of technology to increase the effectiveness and automation of the decision process has never been greater.

2 Background

Second Life (SL) is growing throughout the business sector, as well as in educational environments (Lagorio 2007; Maher 1999; Metz 2007; Ringo 2007; Smith 2008; Boulos, Hetherington, and Wheeler 2007; Jarmon and Sanchez 2008). Companies on the cutting edge – and even those not traditionally seen as technology based – are using SL to provide additional benefits to their employees, customers and the general population (Metz 2007; Cheal 2007). SL creates a new workplace that is unlike any we have experienced before where individuals control their avatars in real time. Gradually, every person will increasingly have the capacity to customise his/her work, locations, information sources, and tools for conducting online work unbound by traditional constraints of location and time. This new working paradigm raises the question about the impact of identity and presence on human communication and collaboration and subsequently on our decision-making process and outcomes. The real-time nature of avatars in SL and the fact that each avatar is controlled by a human in real time suggests that SL can influence real-time decision making.

2.1 Second Life

Second Life (SL) is a 3-D digital world created by Linden Research, Inc. in 2003. SL residents offer diverse backgrounds in terms of culture, ethnicity, nationality, age group, profession and education amongst others. Since opening to the public, SL has over 16 million registered users as of October 2009 (Second Life official website).

SL residents, by virtue of having originated from different backgrounds, have formed active and heterogeneous communities (Rymaszewski, Wallace, Winters, and Au 2006). These communities are global because the residents literally log in from different parts of the globe. SL allows its residents to own and retain the copyright of their own object creations. This encourages residents to unleash their creativity, build unique products and sell them to others. It supports residents who want to offer some services and build their own businesses (Berman, Abraham,

Battino, Shipnuck, and Neus 2007; Au 2008). All of these simulate a virtual online economy with its own currency. The Linden dollar is tradable for real US dollars with a specific exchange rate, i.e., 1 USD = 265 LD (Second Life official website). This means the income generated in SL virtual world corresponds to actual money that is usable in real life and the exchange rate fluctuates in real time.

Residents log in to SL via their avatars. An avatar is the user's graphic resembling human beings in the form of a two-dimensional or three-dimensional image or character (see Appendix I for detail). Residents perform activities and communicate with one another in real time by controlling their avatars. Communication can be done either through text messaging where users communicate by typing, or through voice chatting using specially designed microphone technology (Second Life official website), as well as through body movements such as waving hands or even dance movements.

Avatars can move around within SL spaces and can face each other, performing a range of other humanlike activities such as communicating with body language and tone of voice (Seyama and Nagayama 2007; Nowak and Rauh 2005; Boellstorff 2008; Smith 2008). Since avatars and their actions are controlled by real people in real time, their actions reflect the action of humans who control them. In addition, each SL resident can manipulate his/her own avatar (see Appendix I for detail) and certain objects in the environment (Tapley 2007; Boellstorff 2008). Any actions performed by avatars are reflected and communicated in real time to all the other avatars that are present in the same environment at the same time.

A sense of presence can influence perception and action as well as contextualisation (Thie and Wijk 1998). Contextualisation is the ability of the environment to respond autonomously to events that are beyond one's control and this is a characteristic of SL due to the presence of others whose own contextualised experience cannot be predicted. Context can be defined as physicality of the experience, as well as the social and cultural mood (Lave 1988). It has also been defined as "any information that can be used to characterise the situation of an entity" (Dey and Abowd 1999). An entity can be a person, place, or object that is considered relevant to the interaction between a user and an application (Dey and Abowd 1999). Therefore, context-aware applications need facilities for recognising and representing context, reasoning on it and adapting to it accordingly (Lave 1988; Dey and Abowd 1999; Ondrejka 2004).

We view context as constraints or factors that explain human decision making and behaviour in a real-time virtual world. We believe that in order for us to use context effectively, we must understand both what context is and how it can be used. An understanding of context will enable us to choose the best context to use to support real-time decision making. On the other hand, an understanding of how context can be used will help us become more aware of what is needed to support the efficient use of any given context for effective real-time decision making.

SL is an example of a virtual context that is becoming increasingly popular for facilitating interaction between avatars in a three-dimensional real-time environment. Hence, as an ideal example for virtual interaction, we study SL and its implications as an environment to support real-time decision making.

2.2 *Second Life as an Environment for real-time Decision Making*

SL provides a place where the environment is constantly redefined by user interaction. This makes it an ideal improvisational real-time setting for human interaction, opening many windows for business opportunity (Cagnina and Poian 2008). The ability to make decisions in real-time is critical in today's highly competitive and automated business environment. The term real-time itself has become synonymous with one's ability to become more agile and responsive. In business, this agility undoubtedly can bring business benefits such as agile software development and pair programming. However, many are still struggling to find the right technologies that can help them react in a timely fashion to business needs in a real-time context. Decision making in real time is a dynamic process that depends on the decision context (Beroggi, and Wallace 1997) such as physical, emotional, social, and cultural factors (Kaenampornpan and O'Neill 2004). In addition, a real-time decision is different from conventional decisions because it requires that the decision is made very quickly (Chaturvedi, Hutchinson, and Nazareth 1993).

In SL, users are able to make a quick decision since SL provides a platform for users to communicate and interact collaboratively in real time. It allows for real-time voice communication, and motions, from a simple handshake to fancy dance moves and body gestures. Thus in SL, a user makes a real-time decision to control his or her avatar to participate in constructing a collaborative context. For example, in 2007, a virtual conference was held in SL to discuss teaching in a virtual world where 1,300 unique avatars from around the world attended the event (Cheal 2007). Most participants described the experience as better than teleconferences or email because of the opportunity to mingle, chat and get to know each other instantly.

Today, there are more than 300 colleges and universities including Harvard, New York University, Pennsylvania State, San Diego State, Stanford and Texas State University that use SL as an educational resource (Second Life official website). SL offers both students and educational bodies a new context in which to teach and collaborate (Boulos et al. 2007; Jarmon and Sanchez 2008; Jarmon, Traphagan, and Mayrath 2008; Zhu, Wang, and Jia 2007). Some of these colleges and universities use SL to carry out entire distance learning courses while others use it to supplement classes (Second Life official website; Jarmon and Sanchez 2008; Jarmon et al. 2008; Lee, Ahmad, and Hudson 2007). Students interact instantaneously and work together in real-time fashion. The education experience in SL is largely beneficial for distance learning. Mentors and students do not just send instant messages; they see one another in the form of avatars inside their computer monitors. Students, for example, can collaboratively build a computer program, design the prototype of an automobile, draw the layout of a plan, or build the blueprint of a structure (Jarmon et al. 2008; Lee et al. 2007). Recently, Manchester Business School in the United Kingdom (UK) celebrated the first graduation ceremony for the British Petroleum (BP) Managing Projects distance-learning course in SL (McGahern 2009). BP employees from around the world such as the UK, United States (US), Canada, and Russia who completed a distance learning course attended the graduation ceremony and received their certificates from the dean of the Business School in real time in SL.

The collaborative and social context of SL motivates and encourages participation in communication and interaction. The open flow of discussion and the absence of heightened presence – as well as the availability of chat using text in addition to verbal communication – help ideas and thoughts to come up in a less linear fashion than they do in a regular classroom (Jarmon and Sanchez 2008; Jarmon et al. 2008). SL proves to be an appealing medium for students to get together and work with one another (McGahern 2009). It also serves as a motivating environment to proactively research and discover new things as well as conduct some experimentations and testing. One of the most interesting examples is the ability for medical students, potentially from any number of medical schools, to study surgical techniques by observing virtual operations performed by doctors who may be geographically distant from the students' schools in real time (Boulos et al. 2007). Another interesting breakthrough for medical students is the project called PIVOTE carried by St George's University of London (SGUL). PIVOTE is an open-source authoring system for learning in virtual worlds to help paramedics learn. It provides a structured framework in which SGUL has replicated life and death in medical situations in real time (Linden 2009).

While many companies are still figuring out the best way to make use of virtual worlds (Cheal 2007; Smith 2008), a few trends are starting to emerge in how businesses are using the virtual environments (Metz 2007). Some of the trends are brand and service expansion, human resources, business-to-business opportunities, online collaboration and an opportunity to get ahead on the learning curve for future demand for immersive online retail experiences (Berman et al. 2007; Rymaszewski et al. 2006). The real-time context that a virtual world facilitates has significant business applications.

There are a number of ways that companies use SL to help increase the awareness of their brand, ensure brand loyalty, and drive customers to utilising other services that a company offers. Currently, there are more than 50 major corporations that have established a presence in SL such as IBM, Dell, Cisco, Coca-Cola, News Corp, and Royal Philips Electronics (Second Life official website). By establishing a presence in SL, these companies offer real-time services such as product consulting through knowledgeable employees that a customer might not get from a company's website. For example, Dell Computers sells real PCs to customers through its virtual store in SL and provides a live service for system selection or troubleshooting without customers going to a physical location to have it be more interactive than just a website (Metz 2007; Cheal 2007).

Reebok provides a service where customers can customise sneakers for their avatars which can then be manufactured and purchased in real life (Metz 2007). This type of brand expansion can be useful, especially in a 3-D environment, in getting customers engaged in some level of product development. Circuit City has established an area in SL where avatars can experience home theatre setups based on their real world measurements. Customers enter the area which can be configured to match the customer's home environment so that they can try out, virtually, how different screen sizes would appear in their environment (Metz 2007).

Another area that is quickly gaining momentum in SL is the concept of hiring and interviewing virtually (Berman et al. 2007). SL provides potential employers an opportunity to interact with potential employees virtually. A natural, or at least easier, expansion of this concept is enabling companies with specific contract needs (such as software development needs) to identify and communicate with potential service providers (independent contractors) in real time, saving potential communication costs associated with collaboration. Virtual human resource services in SL are in the early stages of development and it is unclear as to how effective they can be in getting people real-world positions. However, as with brand or service expansion, it gives companies a new way to bring people in virtually and get them to buy their real world services as well (Berman et al. 2007).

There is also a large benefit in using SL for companies that operate in business-to-business (B2B) industries to promote their brands or services (Metz 2007). SL gives these companies an opportunity to interact in real time with their customers (other businesses). A large, global IT services company, for example, could have a virtual sales meeting with a number of potential clients in SL, show its products or services to those clients interactively, with subject matter experts who may be spread out across the world. Companies can also make use of SL to save their customers money by hosting real-time virtual events such as trade shows, media conferences, and training seminars (Ringo 2007; Smith 2008). These services could drive additional revenue at a fraction of the marketing cost compared to live events. This has been shown to be true through virtual events that have been hosted by some of the largest B2B companies such as Cisco, IBM, SUN and others (Smith 2008). Cisco, for example, uses SL to have spontaneous interaction with customers that would otherwise be impossible to achieve. Customers can meet and talk to Cisco's employees at Cisco SL Island in real time. In addition, Cisco provides customer education and training in SL, holds meetings with customers, business partners, and amongst its own staff, and holds seminars or events that combine people in the real world with avatars in SL. Christian Renaud, chief architect of networked virtual environments for Cisco, described SL as a way for companies to come together and talk with their business partners and customers (Wagner 2007).

Another significant benefit of SL comes from the ability to collaborate online (Ringo 2007; Mania and Chalmers 1998; Jarmon and Sanchez 2008). The ability for diverse groups of people from a global perspective to interact in real time is a key to ensure success of any global venture (Mania and Chalmers 1998; Kumar, Chhugani, Kim, Kim, Nguyen, Dubey, Bienia, and Kim 2008). SL facilitates this by providing a live, 3-D environment for the interaction to take place. Virtual meetings and virtual training sessions are two of the many examples of real-time collaboration that occur in SL (Ringo 2007; Mania and Chalmers 1998; Boulos et al. 2007; Jarmon and Sanchez 2008, Perlin 1995). Collaboration is a great opportunity for businesses to improve their relationships (Berman et al. 2007; Mania and Chalmers 1998; Maher 1999). Recently, Children's Memorial Hospital Chicago in Illinois/USA held disaster preparedness training in SL providing staff with a true-to-life immersive training environment that improved emergency response planning without interfering with hospital operations.The success of the project has inspired the hospital to expand its training in SL and share the positive experience with others (Second Life Success Stories 2009). These examples show that SL is a virtual environment, with real people with real perceptions and attitudes who can make real-time decisions via their avatars; their decisions, however, may or may not have consequences in real life as we will discuss later and explain the potential impact of consequences on real-time decisions.

3 Research Model

Figure 1 illustrates our proposed research model.

We first study the relationship between individuals' experience in using SL and their actual attitude towards SL. The relationship suggests that when individuals have positive experience using SL, they are likely to develop positive attitude towards SL. On the other hand, when they have negative experience with SL, they are likely to develop a negative attitude towards using SL. Earlier studies on virtual world suggest positive results (higher attitude towards using the virtual world) when individuals experience the feeling of presence (Thie and van Wijk 1998; Barfield and Weghorst 1993; Witmer and Singer 1998). However, the feeling of presence will arise only if the individuals have emotional and social connection with the environment. Therefore, we can also argue that the interpretation of SL will be influenced by these emotional states. Based on this understanding, we operationalised the construct "Second Life Experience" to represent individuals experience in using SL. We defined the construct in terms of a five-item questionnaire that measures five factors relevant to individuals experience with SL, namely: (1) A sense of "being there",

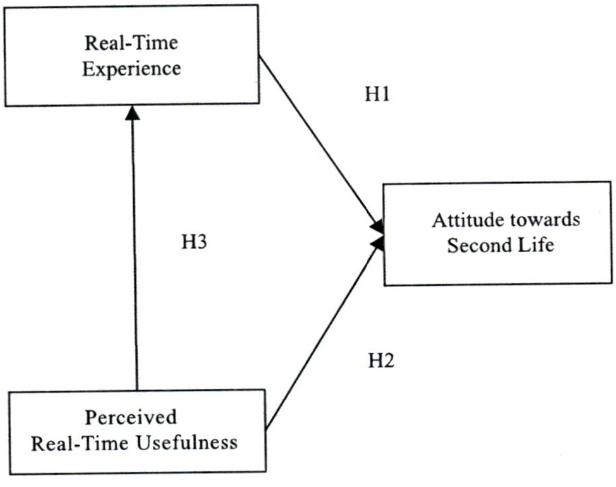

Fig. 1 Proposed research model operationalised in SL

(2) A sense of "reality", (3) A sense of "social presence", (4) A sense of "excitement", and (5) A sense of "acceptance" (Will you continue using Second Life?). We measured these items using a seven point Likert scale. Based on the arguments above captured by the relationship depicted in Fig. 1, we propose the following hypothesis:

H1: real-time Experience positively affects Attitude towards SL.

Building on the theory of reasoned action (TRA), Davis (1986) developed the Technology Acceptance Model (TAM) which attempts to explain why individuals choose to adopt or not adopt a particular technology when performing a task. According to TAM, perceived usefulness and perceived ease of use are causally linked to attitudes, intentions, and actual use (behaviour). "Perceived usefulness" refers to the degree to which an individual believes that using a particular technology would enhance his or her job performance (Davis 1989). "Perceived ease of use" refers to the degree to which an individual believes that using a particular technology would be free of physical and mental effort (Davis 1989). The validity and reliability of the perceived usefulness and perceived ease of use variables in TAM have been supported by many studies (Subramanian 1994; Hendrickson, Massey, and Cronan 1993). TAM has also been expanded and adapted by many information systems researchers (Mathieson 1991; Straub, Limayem, and Karahanna-Evaristo 1995; Segars and Grover 1993; Szajna 1996); several researchers have used TAM to study the adoption of online systems (Featherman and Pavlou 2003; Gefen, Karahana, and Straub 2003; Gefen and Straub 2000; Moon and Kim 2001). Because SL provides a very natural user interface where individuals can move their avatars easily in a three-dimensional space similar to the real space, the subjects normally find that it is a very easy software interface to use. Hence, we did not find much variability in the ease-of-use construct and therefore we decided to omit this TAM construct for our study given that it is not directly applicable to the SL interface. In other words, perceived ease-of-use is more relevant for technology that traditionally was very cumbersome to use. SL has a natural interface and is very easy to use. Hence, we use only perceived useful in developing our model for SL. This section explains how perceived usefulness fits into the model of virtual space in SL as shown in Fig. 1. Hence, we propose the next two hypotheses:

H2: Perceived Usefulness positively affects Attitude towards SL.
H3: Perceived Usefulness positively affects SL Experience.

4 Research Methodology

To evaluate the proposed research model shown in Fig. 1 and to test the hypotheses generated from the model, we drew upon validated instruments that were developed and tested in prior research. Perceived usefulness has been used before by other researchers to understand the use of computers and other technologies (Subramanian 1994; Doll, Hendrickson, and Deng 1998; Grover and Segars 1993; Dennis et al. 1992). Therefore in this study we simply change the phrase "computer systems" with the phrase "Second Life" in questions that measure user perception about computer systems. For example, instead of measuring participant perception about "usefulness" of the computer systems, we measured participant perception about "usefulness" of SL. We used SL as it is one of the most popular virtual worlds where avatars can interact with other avatars in virtual space. Attitude towards using SL was adopted from Taylor and Todd (1995), Hiltz (1988), Barki and Hartwick (1994) and Culnan (1993).

As discussed earlier in the chapter, we operationalised the SL experience using five factors: sense of being there, sense of reality, sense of social presence, sense of excitement, and whether they will continue using SL. The subjects responded on a seven point Likert scale to these five questions.

As described in the following section, we performed a variety of statistical techniques to assess the validity of the questions measuring the various model constructs. We used multiple items to measure each construct. Most items were measured on a seven point Likert type scale ranging from "strongly agree" to "strongly disagree". A few constructs had similar scales but the choices at the extremes represented the answers such as seldom/often, and like/dislike. We refined the initial version of our survey instrument through extensive pre-testing and discussions. The questions from the final instrument are shown in Appendix II.

4.1 Subjects

A total of 123 surveys were collected. However, we had to drop 17 surveys because some information was missing. Therefore, we had a total of 106 participants who completely answered all the questions in the survey that provided the usable data for our statistical analysis. We used students who were enrolled in several sections of a management information systems (MIS) course taught by the authors. The participants had experience with the Internet and computers, and hence were representative of Internet users. The data we gathered from this convenience sample of subjects can guide us about human decision making in real-time contexts. In addition, the course was a core requirement for all business majors so it focused primarily on the organisational foundation of management information systems by establishing a link between business processes and information technology. Given that it was a core requirement, the subject pool represented all majors rather than being dominated by one major. All participants were enrolled in the undergraduate programme in a major American university in the United Arab Emirates. The university is modelled after American institutions of higher education, and hence, the students are acculturated in the American culture but at the same time are grounded in the Arab culture. The average age of the students was 20. Please see Table 1 for participant demographics. The participants received class participation credit for completing the survey.

An issue often raised by researchers is whether the use of students for a study limits the external validity of the results obtained. Some may feel that the students' perceptions are different than those of the general population. However, prior

Table 1 Breakdown of study participants

Demographic categories	Range	Percentage
Gender	Male	33
	Female	67
Major	Finance/accounting	50
	Management/marketing	23
	MIS	8.5
	Economics	1.9
	Other	16
Academic rank	Freshman	34.9
	Sophomore	53.8
	Junior	9.4
	Senior	1.9
Frequency of using virtual worlds (including Second Life)	Daily	1.9
	Weekly	17.0
	Monthly	16.0
	Rarely	39.6
	Never	25.5

research illustrates that there are no statistically significant differences between students' and general consumers' beliefs and attitudes (Durvasula et al. 1997), especially when student subjects have the appropriate experience and can relate to the task they face. Also, surveys of Internet users reveal that young people with above average education form the majority of users; therefore, they also form the majority of potential Web users (Second Life official website).

5 Results

In this section, we test the three hypotheses that resulted from our proposed model about the constructs related to the perception and use of SL. Table 2 provides the summary of the significance levels we obtained from running General Linear Model (GLM) using SPSS software. The actual results obtained from running GLM for each hypothesis are presented in Appendix III. The results of GLM showed no significant two-way or three-way interactions and hence we removed those from Table 2 (and Appendix III as well) to ease illustration. Since our proposed hypotheses are one-sided, we obtained the significance levels reported in Table 2 by converting the significance levels to fit each one-sided hypothesis by dividing each by 2.

As shown in Table 2, there is evidence to support all of the three hypotheses that we proposed in Sect. 3. That is, SL Experience positively affects attitude towards SL (H1), perceived real-time usefulness positively affects attitude towards real-time SL (H2), and perceived real-time usefulness positively affects SL real-time Experience (H3).

Table 2 Summary of hypotheses testing (GLM)

	Mean	Std. deviation	*P-value (1)	*P-value (2)
H1: Second Life experience (SLE) → attitude (AT)				
SLE1	4.40	1.270	0.076	–
SLE2	3.99	1.464	0.003	–
SLE3	4.52	1.382	0.004	–
SLE4	4.95	1.450	0.012	–
SLE5	4.26	1.635	0.007	–
**H2: Perceived usefulness (PU) → attitude (AT) (*P*-value 1)				
***H3: Perceived usefulness (PU) → Second Life experience (SLE) (*P*-value 2)				
PU1	3.82	1.590	0.089	0.089
PU2	4.01	1.577	0.037	0.037
PU3	3.94	1.672	0.021	0.021
PU4	3.62	1.582	0.004	0.004
PU5	3.24	1.705	0.011	0.011
PU6	3.70	1.736	0.007	0.007
PU7	4.97	1.533	0.013	0.013
PU8	3.48	1.646	0.027	0.027
PU9	5.31	1.469	0.000	0.000

Note: *Significant value based on Roy's longest root, **H2 is based on *P*-value (1), ***H3 is based on *P*-value (2)

6 Discussion and Implications

We focus the discussion on the results of the experiments about real-time use of SL. However, we ask the reader to keep in mind that behind every avatar in SL is a real person, and hence, what we report about SL can have implications for real-time decision making in real life. We will discuss a major difference between real-time decision making in SL and in real life with respect to the consequences of decisions. We elaborate on the implications of this SL study on real life decision making after we discuss the results and implications of the study.

The results of this study support the assertion that when individuals have positive real-time experience using SL, they are likely to develop positive attitude towards real-time use of SL. On the other hand, when they have negative real-time experience with SL, they are likely to develop negative attitude towards real-time use of SL. From the results, we can also see that individuals have higher positive attitude towards using real-time SL when they experience the feeling of presence. That is, when they have emotional and social connection with the SL environment resulting from real-time interactions with high levels of social presence, they are more likely to develop positive attitude about real-time use of SL. Hence, sense of presence perceived by humans behind avatars defines a context that facilitates real-time interaction and decision making. The real-time interactions of avatars in SL make it a suitable environment for supporting real-time decision making of individuals or organisations. For example, organisations can have real-time help centres in SL to respond to customer questions or use the SL environment for real-time meetings and expert advice.

When individuals believe that they can actually benefit from using SL, they are likely to have better experience with SL. On the other hand, when they feel that SL is not going to be useful to them, they are likely to have negative experience with SL. Given that in SL virtuality is reality, the objective reality in SL is actually the subjective reality of the human users behind the avatars. For example, when two individuals with different perceptions of usefulness about SL use it, they are likely to differ in their attitudes towards real-time use of SL. As we can see from the results of this study and the above arguments, when individuals feel that real-time SL is useful, they are likely to develop positive attitudes towards real-time SL and this reinforces their continued use of SL for real-time decision making and interaction.

6.1 Implications for Research

This research extends the technology acceptance model--> by proposing and testing a model which demonstrates that individuals develop different attitudes towards a virtual world according to their experience and perceived usefulness. The results of our study indicate that when users feel that SL is useful, it can influence SL experience and together with SL experience can impact the attitude towards adoption and use of SL to support real-time collaborative decision making. This study has significant implications for personalisation, collaboration and ecommerce. For example, by developing applications that make SL more useful, we can expect to have users gain more positive experience with SL and develop a more positive attitude about the use of SL so that shopping malls can have effective real-time presence in this virtual world. Avatars can try on a dress or a suit and see the latest in fashion industry, identify the latest electronics and automobiles. While the technology can provide a real-time virtual environment, the question of the usefulness of the avatar for applications of real-time electronic commerce is not fully explored. Future research should investigate the individual differences as a way to explain the appeal of SL to users for an environment for real-time decision making. In addition, understanding the contexts influencing behaviour that are discussed in this study will help educators and businesses to best utilise virtual worlds and continue to create innovative, user-focused services for real-time decision contexts.

6.2 Implication for Practice

The results obtained in this study imply that user perceptions about real-time use of SL can be manipulated by personalising the context such that users feel comfortable with the SL environment. Therefore, the results shown here can guide strategy formulation, technology design, and marketing policy for real-time decision-making contexts. Since SL is still in the infancy stage, businesses can gain a competitive edge if they can properly utilise this environment for facilitating real-time decision making contexts. SL is a highly imaginative and creative world that businesses can use to help employees, customers and business partners collaborate and learn. SL has potential for business communication, interaction and collaboration in real-time when people cannot be physically in the same place but still need to perceive a sense of presence using their avatars.

If businesses can creatively enhance the perceived usefulness of SL for their customers, the customers are more likely to use SL for their real-time business transactions. Although businesses may find it difficult to attract customers through SL initially, there are actions that businesses can take in order to appeal to the customers and increase traffic. This seems to happen when customers view SL not as an imaginary world, but rather as a medium for real-time communication to access goods and services. Customers' experience within the environment can improve when they feel the sense of presence. For example, the ability to view a particular dress on their avatar, interact with objects in the environment, and also interact in real-time with other avatars can certainly enhance their positive experience of presence.

7 Conclusions and Future Work

Virtual spaces have the capacity to facilitate real-time decision making for collaborative groups whose members are physically dispersed. It can also be an environment for testing how humans would behave in different real-time decision contexts. SL provides a natural setting for us to study human interaction in a real-time context – in virtual space – and compare and contrast that with the physical world where social presence impacts various aspects of human interaction. We expect this type of technology to be utilised increasingly in the business world for human interaction, especially for education and real-time electronic commerce. Given that virtual worlds mimic the physical world by creating avatars of representing the physical body and movements of individuals, the increased sense of presence may have positive applications in real-time decision contexts. While in this study we propose a very simple model of interaction with the virtual world, our results provide important insights about future use of this technology for human interaction and commerce for real-time decision making. At this early stage in the development of virtual space technology, the questions should focus on how this technology can be adopted and how it can influence the decision dynamics of avatars in real-time contexts. Future research should investigate other issues that study the factors that make virtual worlds useful for real-time decision-making contexts.

We studied whether sense of presence and real-time experience in SL, along with perceived real-time usefulness, can enhance the use of SL for real-time decision-making context. We believe studying this technology, which is increasingly utilised by individuals who make avatars of themselves, can enable new business models for supporting real-time decision making when individuals are not physically present. Our results suggest that when users feel SL is useful in a real-time decision making context, it can influence real-time SL experience and together with SL experience can impact the attitude towards use of SL in a real-time decision-making context. Hence, by developing applications that make SL more useful in a real-time decision-making context so that users perceive high usefulness, we can expect to have users gain more positive experience with SL and develop more positive attitude about the use of SL in real-time decision-making context.

7.1 Future Work

This research may be expanded in a number of different directions. First, it can use additional data by including more participants covering a wider range of backgrounds rather than the convenient sample of undergraduate students. Having participants from different countries with different cultures can illustrate the utility of the virtual world for supporting real-time decision making on a global scale. Future research can develop meaningful metrics for measuring decision quality of avatars in virtual worlds. For example, in order to develop a multi-dimensional and generic measure of decision quality, future research can investigate the applicability of data envelopment analysis (DEA). DEA is a non-parametric programming technique that provides a comparative monitoring that identifies variations, and hence, guides performance improvement (Charnes, Cooper, Lewin, and Seiford 1994). DEA can help measure decision efficiency in the virtual world and translate it to the decision efficiency in real world of humans behind the avatars.

We note that there is one significant difference between real-time decision making in a virtual world and in the real world: the consequences of decisions in these two worlds. While the consequences of decisions in real world can be significant, in the virtual world the consequences are often less significant. For example, the consequence of making the wrong decision in real-time context in real life such as emergency medical care can result in death. On the other hand, the wrong decision in SL can influence the avatar and unless there is a clear link between the welfare of the avatar and the human behind the avatar, the consequence is marginal. Hence, those experimenting with virtual worlds should be cautious about the impact of the consequences on the quality of their real-time decision. Despite this limitation, for many decision contexts, proper design of experiments can help us learn about real-time decision making in real life by operationalising real-time studies in SL.

References

Ajzen, I. and M. Fishbein, *Understanding Attitudes and Predicting Social Behavior*. Englewood Cliffs: Prentice Hall, 1980.

Au, W.J., *Notes from the New World: The Making of Second Life*. New York: HarperCollins, 2008.

Barfield, W. and S. Weghorst, "The Sense of Presence within Virtual Environments: a Conceptual Framework," in *Proceedings of the Fifth International Conference on Human-Computer Interaction*, 2, 1993, 699–704.

Barki, H. and J. Hartwick, "Measuring User Participation, User Involvement, and User Attitude," *MIS Quarterly*, 18, 1, 1994, 59–79.

Berman, S.J., S. Abraham, B. Battino, L. Shipnuck and A. Neus, "New Business Models for the New Media World," *Strategy & Leadership*, 35, 4, 2007, 23–30.

Beroggi, G.E.G. and W.A. Wallace, "The Effect of Reasoning Logics on real-time Decision Making," *IEEE Transactions on System, Man, and Cybernetics – Part A: Systems and Humans*, 27, 6, 1997, 743–749.

Boellstorff, T., *An Anthropologist Explores the Virtually Human: Coming of Age in Second Life*. Princeton: Princeton University Press, 2008.

Borges, M.R.S., P. Brézillon, J.A. Pino and J.-C. Pomerol, "Groupware System Design and the Context Concept," *Lecture Notes in Computer Science*, 31, 68, 2005, 45–54.

Boulos, M.N.K., L. Hetherington and S. Wheeler, "Second Life: An Overview of the Potential of 3-D Virtual Worlds in Medical and Health Education," *Health Information & Libraries Journal*, 24, 4, 2007, 233–245.

Cagnina, M.R. and M. Poian, "Second Life: A Turning Point for Web 2.0 and E-Business?" in D'Atri, A., De Marco, M., and Casalino, N. (eds.), *Interdisciplinary Aspects of Information Systems Studies: The Italian Association for Information Systems*. Heidelberg: Physica, 2008, 377–383.

Charnes, A., W.W. Cooper, A.Y. Lewin and L.M. Seiford, *Data Envelopment Analysis: Theory, Methodology, and Application*. Boston: Kluwer Academic, 1994.

Chaturvedi, A.R., G.K. Hutchinson and D.L. Nazareth, "Supporting Complex real-time Decision Making Through Machine Learning," *Decision Support Systems*, 10, 22, 1993, 213–233.

Cheal, C., "Second Life: Hype or Hyperlearning?" *On the Horizon*, 15, 4, 2007, 204–210.

Culnan, M.J., "How Did They Get My Name?: An Exploratory Investigation of Consumer Attitudes Toward Secondary Information Use," *MIS Quarterly*, 17, 3, 1993, 341–364.

Davis, F.D., "A Technology Acceptance Model for Empirically Testing New End User Information Systems: Theory and Results," in Ph.D. Thesis, Sloan School of Management, MIT, Cambridge, MA, 1986.

Davis, F.D., "Perceived Usefulness, Perceived Ease of Use, and User Acceptance of Information Technology," *MIS Quarterly*, 13, 3, 1989, 318–340.

Dennis, A., et al., "Perceived Usefulness, Ease of Use, and Usage of Information Technology: A Replication," *MIS Quarterly*, 16, 2, 1992, 227–247.

Dey, A. and G. Abowd, "Towards a Better Understanding of Context and Context-Awareness," *GVU Technical Report* GIT-GVU-00–18, Georgia Institute of Technology, 1999.

Doll, W.J., A. Hendrickson and X. Deng, "Using Davis's Perceived Usefulness and Ease of Use Instruments for Decision Making and Multi-Group Invariance Analysis," *Decision Sciences*, 29, 4, 1998, 839–869.

Durvasula, S., et al., "Advertising Beliefs and Attitudes: Are Students and General Consumers Indeed Different?" *Journal of Asian Business*, 13, 1, 1997, 71–84.

Featherman, M.S. and P.A. Pavlou, "Predicting E-Services Adoption: A Perceived Risk Facets Perspective," *International Journal of Human-Computer Studies*, 59, 4, 2003, 451–474.

Fjermestad, J. and S.R. Hiltz, "An Assessment of Group Support Systems Experimental Research: Methodology and Results," *Journal of Management Information Systems*, 15, 3, 1998, 7–150.

Gefen, D., E. Karahana and D. Straub, "Trust and TAM in Online Shopping: An Integrated Model," *MIS Quarterly*, 27, 1, 2003, 51–90.

Gefen, D. and D. Straub, "The Relative Importance of Perceived Ease-of-Use in IS Adoption: A Study of E-Commerce Adoption," *Journal of the Association for Information Systems*, 1, 8, 2000, 1–20.

Grover, V. and A.H. Segars, "Re-examining Perceived Ease of Use and Usefulness: A Confirmatory Factor Analysis," *MIS Quarterly*, 17, 4, 1993, 517–526.

Heller, F., P. Drenth, P. Koopman and V. Rus, *Decisions in Organizations*. Beverly Hills: Sage, 1988.

Hendrickson, A.R., P.D. Massey and T.P. Cronan, "On the Test-Retest Reliability of Perceived Usefulness and Perceived Ease of Use," *MIS Quarterly*, 17, 2, 1993, 227–230.

Hiltz, S.R., "Productivity Enhancement from Computer-Mediated Communication: A Systems Contingency Approach," *Communications of the ACM*, 31, 12, 1988, 1438–1454.

Jarmon, L. and J. Sanchez, "The Educators Coop Experience in Second Life: A Model for Collaboration," *The Journal of the Research Center for Educational Technology*, 4, 2, 2008.

Jarmon, L., T. Traphagan and M. Mayrath, "Understanding Project-Based Learning in Second Life with a Pedagogy, Training, and Assessment Trio," *Educational Media International*, 45, 3, 2008, 153–171.

Kaenampornpan, M. and E. O'Neill, "Modelling Context: An Activity Theory Approach," in Markopoulos, P., Eggen, B., Aarts, E. and Croeley, J. L. (eds)., *Ambient Intelligence: Second European Symposium on Ambient Intelligence, EUSAI 2004*, volume 3295 of *Lecture Notes in Computer Science*. Berlin: Springer, 2004, 367–374.

Kumar, S., J. Chhugani, C. Kim, D. Kim, A. Nguyen, P. Dubey, C. Bienia and Y. Kim, "Second Life and the New Generation of Virtual Worlds," *IEEE Computer Society*, 41, 9, 2008, 46–53.

Lagorio, C., "The Ultimate Distance Learning," *The New York Times*. January 7, 2007, URL = http://www.nytimes.com/2007/01/07/education/edlife/07innovation.html

Lave, J., "The practice of learning: The problem with context," in Chaiklin, S. and Lave, J. (eds.), *Understanding Practice: Perspectives on Activity and Context.* Boston: Cambridge University Press, 1988, 3–32.

Lee, P.D., N. Ahmad and A. Hudson, "The Use of Second Life in Graduate Education," *Decision Sciences Institute Annual Meeting*, 2007.

Linden, A., "Three Questions about PIVOTE by Daden, as used by St. George's University London (SGUL) in Second Life," October 28, 2009, URL = //blogs.secondlife.com/community/workinginworld/blog/2009/10/28/three-questions-about-pivote-by-daden-as-used-by-st-george-s-university-london-sgul-in-second-life

Lombard, M. and T. Ditton, "At the Heart of It All: The Concept of Presence," *Journal of Computer-Mediated Communication*, 3, 2, 1997.

Maher, M.L., "Designing the Virtual Campus as a Virtual World," in *Proceedings of the Computer Support for Collaborative Learning*, Hoadley, C. and Roschelle, J. (eds.). Palo Alto: Stanford University, 1999.

Mania, K. and A. Chalmers, "A Classification for User Embodiment in Collaborative Virtual Environments," in *Proceedings of the 4th International Conference on Virtual Systems and Multimedia*. Amsterdam: IOS/Ohmsha, Ltd., 1998, 177–182.

Mathieson, K., "Predicting User Intentions: Comparing the Technology Acceptance Model with the Theory of Planned Behavior," *Information Systems Research*, 2, 3, 1991, 173–191.

McGahern, R., "Manchester Business School Hosts First UK Virtual Graduation," February 19, 2009, URL = http://www.trainingjournal.com/news/1953.html

Metz, C., "The Emperor's New Web: Some of the Biggest Names in High Tech Are Convinced That Second Life and Other Virtual Worlds Are the Future of the Net. Are They Fooling Themselves?" *PC Magazine*, 26, 9, 2007, 70–77.

Moon, J. and Y. Kim, "Extending the TAM for a World-Wide-Web Context," *Information and Management*, 28, 2001, 217–230.

Nowak, K.L. and C. Rauh, "The Influence of the Avatar on Online Perceptions of Anthropomorphism, Androgyny, Credibility, Homophily, and Attraction," *Journal of Computer-Mediated Communication*, 11, 1, 2005, 153–178.

Ondrejka, C., "Escaping the Gilded Cage: User Created Content and Building the Metaverse," *New York Law School Law Review*, 49, 2004, 81–101

O'Reilly, T. and Musser, J., *Web 2.0 Principles and Best Practices*. Sebastopol: O'Reilly Media, 2006.

Perlin, K., "Real-time Responsive Animation with Personality," *IEEE Transactions on Visualization and Computer Graphics*, 1, 1, 1995, 5–15.

Ringo, T., "IBM Explores New Frontiers in Collaborative Innovation," *Research Technology Management*, 50, 5, 2007, 6–7.

Rymaszewski, M., M. Wallace, C. Winters and W. J. Au, *Second Life: The Official Guide*. New York: Wiley, 2006.

Second Life official website. January 2010, URL = http://www.secondlife.com

Second Life Success Stories, December 2009, URL = http://work.secondlife.com/en-US/successstories/case/chmc/

Segars, A.H. and V. Grover, "Re-Examining Perceived Ease of Use and Usefulness: A Confirmatory Factor Analysis," *MIS Quarterly*, 17, 4, 1993, 517–525.

Seyama, J. and R.S. Nagayama, "The Uncanny Valley: Effect of Realism on the Impression of Artificial Human Faces," *Presence*, 16, 4, 2007, 337–351.

Smith, S. "Second Life Mixed Reality Broadcasts: A Timeline of Practical Experiments at the NASA CoLab Island," *Journal of Virtual Worlds Research*, 1, 1, 2008.

Straub, D.W., M. Limayem and E. Karahanna-Evaristo, "Measuring System Usage: Implications for IS Theory Testing," *Management Science*, 41, 8, 1995, 1328–1341.

Subramanian, G.H., "A Replication of Perceived Usefulness and Perceived Ease of Use Measurement," *Decision Sciences*, 25, 5/6, 1994, 863–874.

Szajna, B., "Empirical Evaluation of the Revised Technology Acceptance Model," *Management Science*, 42, 1, 1996, 85–92.

Tapley, R., *Designing Your Second Life*. Berkeley: New Riders, 2007.

Taylor, S. and P.A. Todd, "Understanding Information Technology Usage: A Test of Competing Models," *Information Systems Research*, 6, 2, 1995, 144–176.

Thie, S. and J. van Wijk, "A General Theory on Presence: Experimental Evaluation of Social Virtual Presence in a Decision Making Task," in *Presence in Shared Virtual Environment Workshop*, University College London, UK, 10–11 June 1998.

Wagner, M., "Using Second Life as a Business-to-Business Tool," *Information Week*, April 2007, URL = http://www.informationweek.com/blog/main/archives/2007/04/using_second_li_2.html;jsessionid=GGSANGEHOLJK3QE1GHPCKHWATMY32JVN

Witmer, B.G. and M.J. Singer, "Measuring Presence in Virtual Environments: A Presence Questionnaire," *Presence: Teleoperators and Virtual Environments*, 7, 3, 1998, 225–440.

Zhu, Q., T. Wang and Y. Jia, "Second Life: A New Platform for Education," *Information Technologies and Applications in Education*, ISITAE, 23, 25, 2007, 201–204.

8 Appendix I: Example of Avatars

1. One of the authors is changing her avatar's appearance

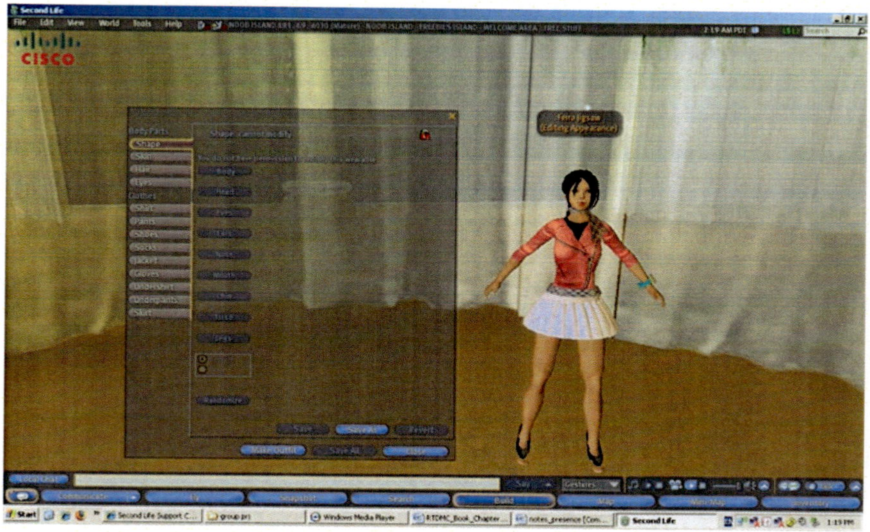

2. Image after changing appearance

9 Appendix II: Survey Questions

Part A: Answer the following questions
Demographics

1. Major?
   - MIS
   - Finance/Accounting
   - Management & Marketing
   - Economics
   - Others: ___________
2. Your current standing:
   - Freshman
   - Sophomore
   - Junior
   - Senior
3. What is your gender?
   - Male
   - Female
4. Your experience with Second Life (SL) or other similar applications such as World of War Craft, and SimCity:

Not at all			Moderately		Totally	
1	2	3	4	5	6	7

5. If yes, how often do you use them?
   - Daily
   - Weekly
   - Monthly
   - Rarely
   - Never

Part B: Answer the following questions
Perceived Usefulness (PU)

1. Using SL adds value to my learning.

Strongly disagree 1 2 3 4 5 6 7 Strongly agree

2. Using SL helps me to expand my skills.

Strongly disagree 1 2 3 4 5 6 7 Strongly agree

3. Using SL is beneficial to me

Strongly disagree 1 2 3 4 5 6 7 Strongly agree

4. Using SL makes me more effective

Strongly disagree 1 2 3 4 5 6 7 Strongly agree

5. Using SL makes my life easier

Strongly disagree	1	2	3	4	5	6	7	Strongly agree

6. Using SL can be useful in my future job.

Strongly disagree	1	2	3	4	5	6	7	Strongly agree

7. Using SL can expand my network.

Strongly disagree	1	2	3	4	5	6	7	Strongly agree

8. Using SL is a waste of time.

Strongly disagree	1	2	3	4	5	6	7	Strongly agree

9. Using SL can be fun.

Strongly disagree	1	2	3	4	5	6	7	Strongly agree

Second Life Experience (SLE)

Please rate *your sense of being in* SL, on the following scale from 1 to 7, where 7 represent your *total agreement* with the statement.

For Question 1–4: During my experience in Second Life, I felt …

1. A sense of "being there":

Not at all	1	2	3	4	5	6	7	Totally

2. A sense of "reality"

Not at all	1	2	3	4	5	6	7	Totally

3. A sense of "social presence"

Not at all	1	2	3	4	5	6	7	Totally

4. A sense of "excitement"

Not at all	1	2	3	4	5	6	7	Totally

5. Will you continue using Second Life

Not at all	1	2	3	4	5	6	7	Totally

Attitude towards Second Life (AT)

1. Using SL is a (good/bad) idea.

Bad	1	2	3	4	5	6	7	Good

2. Using SL is a (foolish/wise) idea.

Foolish	1	2	3	4	5	6	7	Wise

3. I (like/dislike) the idea of using SL.

Dislike	1	2	3	4	5	6	7	Like

4. Using SL would be: (pleasant/unpleasant).

Unpleasant	1	2	3	4	5	6	7	Pleasant

10 Appendix III: General Linear Model

GLM for hypothesis H1: Second Life experience (SL) à attitude (AT)

		Value	*F*	Hypothesis df	Error df	Sig.
Intercept	Pillai's trace	0.997	1.979E2	4.000	2.000	0.005
	Wilks' lambda	0.003	1.979E2	4.000	2.000	0.005
	Hotelling's trace	395.732	1.979E2	4.000	2.000	0.005
	Roy's largest root	395.732	1.979E2	4.000	2.000	0.005
SLE1	Pillai's trace	1.198	0.665	12.000	12.000	0.755
	Wilks' lambda	0.143	0.506	12.000	5.583	0.849
	Hotelling's trace	3.788	0.210	12.000	2.000	0.970
	Roy's largest root	3.149	3.149[b]	4.000	4.000	0.146
SLE2	Pillai's trace	1.985	1.232	16.000	20.000	0.326
	Wilks' lambda	0.009	1.534	16.000	6.748	0.296
	Hotelling's trace	17.783	0.556	16.000	2.000	0.803
	Roy's largest root	11.804	14.755[b]	4.000	5.000	0.006
SLE3	Pillai's trace	2.271	1.094	24.000	20.000	0.423
	Wilks' lambda	0.006	1.133	24.000	8.187	0.453
	Hotelling's trace	19.761	0.412	24.000	2.000	0.891
	Roy's largest root	14.103	11.753[b]	6.000	5.000	0.008
SLE4	Pillai's trace	1.387	0.531	20.000	20.000	0.917
	Wilks' lambda	0.067	0.478	20.000	7.583	0.911
	Hotelling's trace	8.011	0.200	20.000	2.000	0.983
	Roy's largest root	7.326	7.326[b]	5.000	5.000	0.024
SLE5	Pillai's trace	1.912	0.916	20.000	20.000	0.577
	Wilks' lambda	0.020	0.852	20.000	7.583	0.639
	Hotelling's trace	12.245	0.306	20.000	2.000	0.941
	Roy's largest root	9.482	9.482[b]	5.000	5.000	0.014

GLM for hypothesis H2: Perceived usefulness (PU) à attitude (AT)

Effect		Value	F	Hypothesis df	Error df	Sig.
Intercept	Pillai's trace	0.915	1.296E2	4.000	48.000	0.000
	Wilks' lambda	0.085	1.296E2	4.000	48.000	0.000
	Hotelling's trace	10.796	1.296E2	4.000	48.000	0.000
	Roy's largest root	10.796	1.296E2	4.000	48.000	0.000
PU1	Pillai's trace	0.310	0.714	24.000	204.000	0.835
	Wilks' lambda	0.719	0.699	24.000	168.662	0.848
	Hotelling's trace	0.354	0.685	24.000	186.000	0.862
	Roy's largest root	0.183	1.556[b]	6.000	51.000	0.179
PU2	Pillai's trace	0.349	0.812	24.000	204.000	0.720
	Wilks' lambda	0.686	0.802	24.000	168.662	0.730
	Hotelling's trace	0.410	0.794	24.000	186.000	0.742
	Roy's largest root	0.243	2.062[b]	6.000	51.000	0.074
PU3	Pillai's trace	0.437	1.041	24.000	204.000	0.416
	Wilks' lambda	0.619	1.034	24.000	168.662	0.426
	Hotelling's trace	0.528	1.023	24.000	186.000	0.439
	Roy's largest root	0.278	2.361[b]	6.000	51.000	0.043

(continued)

Effect		Value	F	Hypothesis df	Error df	Sig.
PU4	Pillai's trace	0.503	1.223	24.000	204.000	0.225
	Wilks' lambda	0.568	1.237	24.000	168.662	0.217
	Hotelling's trace	0.642	1.244	24.000	186.000	0.210
	Roy's largest root	0.391	3.326[b]	6.000	51.000	0.008
PU5	Pillai's trace	0.424	1.008	24.000	204.000	0.457
	Wilks' lambda	0.624	1.018	24.000	168.662	0.446
	Hotelling's trace	0.529	1.024	24.000	186.000	0.437
	Roy's largest root	0.325	2.760[b]	6.000	51.000	0.021
PU6	Pillai's trace	0.407	0.964	24.000	204.000	0.515
	Wilks' lambda	0.633	0.983	24.000	168.662	0.492
	Hotelling's trace	0.516	0.999	24.000	186.000	0.469
	Roy's largest root	0.355	3.020[b]	6.000	51.000	0.013
PU7	Pillai's trace	0.375	0.879	24.000	204.000	0.631
	Wilks' lambda	0.661	0.887	24.000	168.662	0.619
	Hotelling's trace	0.462	0.895	24.000	186.000	0.609
	Roy's largest root	0.312	2.653[b]	6.000	51.000	0.026
PU8	Pillai's trace	0.329	0.763	24.000	204.000	0.780
	Wilks' lambda	0.699	0.761	24.000	168.662	0.781
	Hotelling's trace	0.392	0.760	24.000	186.000	0.783
	Roy's largest root	0.264	2.241[b]	6.000	51.000	0.054
PU9	Pillai's trace	0.487	1.179	24.000	204.000	0.264
	Wilks' lambda	0.566	1.244	24.000	168.662	0.212
	Hotelling's trace	0.674	1.306	24.000	186.000	0.164
	Roy's largest root	0.516	4.387[b]	6.000	51.000	0.001

GLM for hypothesis H3: Perceived usefulness (PU) à Second Life experience (SLE)

Effect		Value	*F*	Hypothesis df	Error df	Sig.
Intercept	Pillai's trace	0.915	1.296E2	4.000	48.000	0.000
	Wilks' lambda	0.085	1.296E2	4.000	48.000	0.000
	Hotelling's trace	10.796	1.296E2	4.000	48.000	0.000
	Roy's largest root	10.796	1.296E2	4.000	48.000	0.000
PU1	Pillai's trace	0.310	0.714	24.000	204.000	0.835
	Wilks' lambda	0.719	0.699	24.000	168.662	0.848
	Hotelling's trace	0.354	0.685	24.000	186.000	0.862
	Roy's largest root	0.183	1.556[b]	6.000	51.000	0.179
PU2	Pillai's trace	0.349	0.812	24.000	204.000	0.720
	Wilks' lambda	0.686	0.802	24.000	168.662	0.730
	Hotelling's trace	0.410	0.794	24.000	186.000	0.742
	Roy's largest root	0.243	2.062[b]	6.000	51.000	0.074
PU3	Pillai's trace	0.437	1.041	24.000	204.000	0.416
	Wilks' lambda	0.619	1.034	24.000	168.662	0.426
	Hotelling's trace	0.528	1.023	24.000	186.000	0.439
	Roy's largest root	0.278	2.361[b]	6.000	51.000	0.043
PU4	Pillai's trace	0.503	1.223	24.000	204.000	0.225
	Wilks' lambda	0.568	1.237	24.000	168.662	0.217
	Hotelling's trace	0.642	1.244	24.000	186.000	0.210
	Roy's largest root	0.391	3.326[b]	6.000	51.000	0.008

(continued)

Effect		Value	*F*	Hypothesis df	Error df	Sig.
PU5	Pillai's trace	0.424	1.008	24.000	204.000	0.457
	Wilks' lambda	0.624	1.018	24.000	168.662	0.446
	Hotelling's trace	0.529	1.024	24.000	186.000	0.437
	Roy's largest root	0.325	2.760[b]	6.000	51.000	0.021
PU6	Pillai's trace	0.407	0.964	24.000	204.000	0.515
	Wilks' lambda	0.633	0.983	24.000	168.662	0.492
	Hotelling's trace	0.516	0.999	24.000	186.000	0.469
	Roy's largest root	0.355	3.020[b]	6.000	51.000	0.013
PU7	Pillai's trace	0.375	0.879	24.000	204.000	0.631
	Wilks' lambda	0.661	0.887	24.000	168.662	0.619
	Hotelling's trace	0.462	0.895	24.000	186.000	0.609
	Roy's largest root	0.312	2.653[b]	6.000	51.000	0.026
PU8	Pillai's trace	0.329	0.763	24.000	204.000	0.780
	Wilks' lambda	0.699	0.761	24.000	168.662	0.781
	Hotelling's trace	0.392	0.760	24.000	186.000	0.783
	Roy's largest root	0.264	2.241[b]	6.000	51.000	0.054
PU9	Pillai's trace	0.487	1.179	24.000	204.000	0.264
	Wilks' lambda	0.566	1.244	24.000	168.662	0.212
	Hotelling's trace	0.674	1.306	24.000	186.000	0.164
	Roy's largest root	0.516	4.387[b]	6.000	51.000	0.001

b = Mean value

Part III
Case Studies

Chapter 8
Beyond Rationality: Information Design for Supporting Emergent Groups in Emergency Response

Tung X. Bui and Ina Sebastian

Pacific Research Institute for Information Systems Management (PRIISM), Shidler College of Business, Honolulu, HI, USA

Abstract Acknowledging that real-time information is central to emergency response, we advocate that information provided to decision makers – especially the emergent groups who happen to be at the crisis scene and are called upon to help under extraordinary conditions – should not just be designed to support problem-solving in a rational behaviour. Based on a framework of cognitive, affective and situational information support, we call for inclusion of information that helps deal with emotion and stress, reinforces motivation to help, and nurtures a sense of altruism. To illustrate our discussion, we sketch a set of information templates as successive conceptual instantiations of our theoretical exploration. As authorities are still debating on how to use emergent groups effectively, our attempt to outline a foundation of information analysis beyond the rational decision-making paradigm is a systematic and necessary step towards effective decision support to the volunteer-helpers.

Keywords Information requirements • Disaster management • Emergent groups • motivation • Information processing • Template • Decision support

1 Introduction

The purpose of this chapter is to use the context of supporting emergent groups engaging in emergency response, as a case discussion to advocate the need for expanding theoretical foundations for information requirement analysis for real-time decision support. In particular, we argue that information provided to

---

T.X. Bui (✉)
Pacific Research Institute for Information Systems Management (PRIISM), Shidler College of Business, Honolulu, HI, USA
e-mail: tung.bui@hawaii.edu

F. Burstein et al. (eds.), *Supporting Real Time Decision-Making*,
Annals of Information Systems 13, DOI 10.1007/978-1-4419-7406-8_8,

decision makers – especially the rescuers – should not only be framed to support rational problem solving, but also to support other elements that affect the decision-making process and outcome. In the context of emergency response, these cognitive, affective and situational aspects include helping behaviour, stress management, effective problem solving and social interaction.

A response-focused practitioner defines disasters as situations or events that overwhelm local rescue capacity (CRED 2008). Rescuers find themselves in situations characterised by unique combinations of dynamic and complex natures, uncertainty, stress and dissonance. The necessity to support real-time decision-making is particularly relevant for crisis and disaster management because of the possible loss of human lives and other valued assets during periods when rescuers have restricted time to decide and act. Indeed crises are serious threats to the basic structures or the fundamental values and norms of a social system, which require critical decision-making under time pressure and highly uncertain circumstances and outcomes (e.g., Boin 2005).

While waiting for large-scale efforts to get organised and fully deployed, citizens and groups not belonging to any formal authority structures or emergency response plans are often the first to deal with on-the-spot disaster relief and humanitarian assistance. These emergent groups take a variety of forms. For example, in immediate response to Hurricane Katrina, groups emerged to participate in search and rescue (e.g., collaboration of civilian boat operators with the Coast Guard and other response agencies), to provide shelters and first aid (e.g., privately run shelters before approval from the Red Cross), and to communicate important information (e.g., knowledge dissemination and information sharing through the Katrina Help Wiki) (Majchrzak, Jarvenpaa, and Hollingshead 2007; White, Plotnick, Addams-Moring, Turoff, and Hiltz (2008); White, Hiltz, and Turoff 2008). Local volunteer help was critical, as professional responders were in many cases not able to join rescue efforts because physical infrastructure and formal response coordination had broken down. Volunteers' help is even more needed in the absence of authorities. It was reported that an increased number of emergency personnel and police force did not report to work, or appeared to have abandoned the disaster scene (Fischer, Gregoire, Scala, Letukas, Mellon, Romine, and Turner 2006).

In acknowledging the role of emergent groups in humanitarian assistance and disaster relief (HA/DR), the issue here is what kind of information we should provide to these volunteers to help them help others. This is an issue of decision support in high-stress situations in which information can affect the cognitive capabilities and affective state of the decision makers. Assuming a more or less effective distribution of problem-centred instructions by professionals with prior emergency training, we are interested in processes that must be recognised "beyond rationality", which may contribute to real-time decision-making of stakeholders implicated in a crisis.

This chapter is structured as follows. Section 2 provides a contextual overview of the emergence phenomenon in disaster situations. Section 3 introduces an information framework to help us set the conceptual context for information requirement analysis according to rational and "beyond rational" perspectives. Section 4 concludes the chapter and offers a short discussion of other important aspects of information and decision support in disaster situations such as the dynamic nature of information.

2 Emergency Assistance, Emergent Groups and Context-Based Decision Support

Scope and magnitude of disasters tend to be positively related to the phenomenon of emergence (Drabek and McEntire 2003). Existing authorities may not be able to meet urgent rescue demands due to rigidity and slowness of public institutions and inappropriateness of organisational structures and tasks (Drabek and McEntire 2003). In unexpected crises, volunteers often find themselves to be the only available resources (Tierney, Lindell, and Perry 2001).

Authorities responsible for disaster response still contemplate how to use emergent groups effectively, partly because it is difficult to predict what types of emergent groups with which skill sets will be available or required. The centralised approach to response considers ad-hoc emergence as counterproductive (Fritz and Mathewson 1957). However, disaster sociology researchers have repeatedly argued that the command-and-control approach is too static – particularly for large disasters – and that its narrow view of crisis management and assumptions about behaviour in the emergency phase tends to lead to misguided conclusions at the expense of needed flexibility (Drabek and McEntire 2003). Due to the inherent unpredictability of large-scale disasters, formal plans and communication links break in unexpected and unrehearsed ways and formal organisations are prone to paralysis from overwhelming lack of certainty and structure (Lanzara 1983). Failure of central disaster response structures has been observed consistently across large crises (Majchrzak et al. 2007). Hurricane Katrina emergency responders noted that formal emergency preparedness structures, including interagency and inter-organisational coordination, failed within hours of landfall with the loss of infrastructure and equipment and lasted up to two weeks (Fischer et al. 2006; Van de Walle and Turoff 2007). Therefore, the horizontal model of response (including local communication links and emergent groups) tends to work more effectively in extreme conditions. Despite the reservations of some professional rescuers, experience from recent crises strongly suggests that involvement of emergent groups is a critical contribution to immediate large-scale disaster response (Sutton, Palen, and Shklovski 2008). Local volunteers are the first potential helpers in close proximity to the most urgent needs. Moreover, their knowledge of the area and community may enhance the ability to improvise and respond effectively in the absence of professional training (Palen, Hiltz, and Liu 2007).

Few attempts, however, have been made to extend organisational theory to explain the unique organisational behaviour of emergent groups, whose characteristics require non-traditional approaches to expertise and knowledge coordination. Recent research proposes an extension of Transactive Memory Systems (TMS) theory which traditionally seeks to explain how groups with known group membership perceive cognitive interdependence and share goals, learn, store, use, and coordinate knowledge (Majchrzak et al. 2007). As the cognitive structure of emergent groups centres on immediate action instead of deep domain knowledge and task-relevant expertise of members, Majchrzak et al. (2007) propose that task assignment and specialisation should be based on the group's collective knowledge of relationships, tools, and tasks, willingness to act on that knowledge through capability (resources), motivation, and knowledge flexibility. In the absence of a shared meta-structure, knowledge coordination is based on observing action scenarios, joint on-the-spot sense making, simple coordination mechanisms, and community-developed narratives and observable records. Credibility in expertise is replaced by the concept of swift trust through action, known from research on ad-hoc project teams, which is highly dynamic and based on group dynamics rather than situations (Majchrzak et al. 2007).

Researchers also examine the opportunity provided by the Internet for involvement of local and geographically removed citizens in disaster response. Examples include citizen-led online forums and other "backchannel" response activities that emerged following Hurricane Katrina, the Southern California wildfires (Palen et al. 2007; Sutton et al. 2008), and the Virginia Tech shooting (Vieweg, Palen, Liu, Hughes, and Sutton 2008). As Palen et al. note, ICT reveals the role that citizens have always taken as first responders in emergency situations (Palen et al. 2007). Indeed, emergent behaviours observed on social networking sites and blogs may be catalysts of change for future disaster response (Sutton et al. 2008).

In the next section, we present a theoretical discussion of concepts that correspond to the framework of cognitive, affective, and situational support. We discuss several mainstream decision-centred approaches to information support, and then introduce a selected set of theoretical backgrounds inspired from sociology, psychology and communication sciences, which we believe contribute significantly to an increased understanding of more effective interaction with volunteers. We sketch a set of templates, which successively integrate additional theoretical approaches as instantiations of our theoretical exploration.

3 Theoretical Perspective on Information Requirements for Emergent Group Support

Information is the central structural support for all activities in extreme conditions with high uncertainties (Van Someren, Netten, Evers, Cramer, de Hoog, and Bruinsma 2005). Members of emergent groups report that they often do not know the specifics of what to do and how to do it (Lanzara 1983). As such, there is a valid justification for deploying decision support technology. In general, a decision support system (DSS) can take many forms and differ regarding capabilities, targeted users or user groups, purpose (i.e., general or function- or industry-specific), and enabling technology (Power 2002). For example, Simon's Intelligence-Design-Choice (IDC) process model conceptually applies to individual and group decision making with practical accommodations for the communication aspects of cooperative problem-solving in group processes (Forgionne 2002; Bui 1987). Choo (2006) proposes an information framework for organisations that seek to create meaning, knowledge and action and suggest any organisational knowledge should take into account the cognitive and affective elements as well as the context in which the knowledge is being used. From a decision support perspective, we advocate the need for looking at the cognitive, affective and situational factors that determine the information needs and use for emergent first responders both at the individual and collective levels.

- *Cognitive Support:* Norman notes that without external aids, decision makers find themselves constrained in their ability to remember, think, and reason (Norman 1993). Sprague and Carlson (1982) propose an information requirements analysis for building effective Decision Support Systems (DSS), i.e., the Representations-Operations-Memory Aids-Control Mechanisms (ROMC) approach. As discussed later, any effective DSS should provide its user with a right representation of artifacts, right set of operational tools, and means to use external data sources to support his/her mental ability to recall and manipulate information.
- *Situation Awareness and Affective Support:* The concept of situation awareness is concerned particularly with environmental perception of decision makers in complex, dynamic systems, such as emergency response. Situation awareness is the perception and interpretation of environmental elements in the context of time and space, and the projection of what is likely to occur in order to define an appropriate action (Endsley and Garland 2000). Situation awareness is typically based on (1) the decision maker's prior knowledge and understanding about the problem at hand which helps identify the problem and the possible solutions, and (2) the ability to scan the environment to formulate a context-sensitive approach to problem solving (Kulyk, van der Veer, and van Dijk 2008). The role of emotional aspects of information processing on the individual level is gaining increasing importance in information systems design; for example, with the concepts of "affective revolution" and information seeking and use as part of sense making (Nahl 2007; Dervin 1983). The decision maker engages in a cue extraction process to make plausible sense of an uncertain or ambiguous situation (Weick, Sutcliffe, and Obstfeld 2005). As gathered cues are analysed from the decision maker's own perspectives (identity, experience and cultural background), emotion tends to arise – either positively or negatively. It is thus important for the DSS to help the decision maker continue his sense making until he feels comfortable enough with the possible course of actions to achieve his perceived goals. On a collective level, social support research interprets convergence behaviour as a tendency of people to (1) engage in social embeddedness or emotional attachment to others, (2) enact support or the awareness of the number of supportive behaviours that people have received from each others, and (3) accept support that has yielded satisfaction (Barrera 1986; Fisher and Lerner 2004). For many DSS researchers, situational support primarily deals with supporting Context-Based decision-making. In a social context, rallying situational support for the ephemeral group is essential.

With this framework as a guideline, information requirement analysis for problem-centred emergent group support should not only address specifics of relevant disaster types, but also the dynamics of emergent groups from an organisational perspective. An analysis of collective characteristics of the emergent groups in action should provide information support that can leverage their strengths and mitigate their weaknesses in disaster response.

3.1 Template as Means of Information Support to Emergent Groups

An instinctive outcome of the discussion on emergent group characteristics is template-driven processing, i.e., design of a mechanism to support the creation and use of templates for representing, extracting, organising, and acting on relevant information (Bui and Tan 2007; Sebastian and Bui 2009). Templates are tools to categorise and adapt actions on a scenario basis which makes it easier to compare multiple cases and infer generalisations. Templates provide a flexible, structured medium to locate relevant information in an easier and timely manner with simple, clear and intuitive presentations of instructions that support proactive information processing, are easily transferable amongst group members, and allow for documentation (Bui and Tan 2007). They are modular, scalable, and can be used for multiple protocol activations (Lee 1997). In this chapter, we refer to the template as a conceptual information requirements framework. Once the required information is identified, the template can be designed, standardised and delivered by any possible communication means deemed appropriate at the decision-making time. These may include cell phones and SMS, paper flyers, online databases, or online social networks and social media technologies such as IM, blogs and tweets (e.g., Plotnick, White, and Plummer 2009).

In a less than ideal world, instructions should focus on task completion rather than maximum efficiency and enable quick ad-hoc decision making. Each task within a given disaster response operation is represented as a set of descriptive templates (Bui and Tan 2007; Sebastian and Bui 2009). For example, Fig. 1 shows a generic template with a basic standardised set of placeholders as representation of the activity details. A similar template design was proposed by Xu, Yuan, and Ji (2008) as a framework for decision analysis of emergency notification strategies. The template consists of only the necessary information to establish a conceptual framework for rational and affective information requirements. An actual instantiation would require the expansion of the template with information regarding the roles of the users (e.g., names and IDs of those who fill in the fields), information related to time (e.g., time and frequency of updates) and sources of information (e.g., general situation update), and other operational issues.

Analysis and design of a template is based on detailed case-based and action-driven descriptions of concrete instances of crisis situations and relief operations. Templates may be categorised (e.g., Group Assignment, Task Execution, and Communication) for a more precise representation of activities. Normative templates are derived

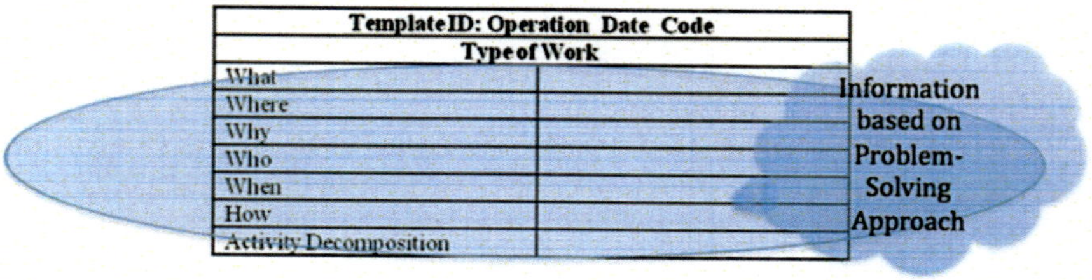

Fig. 1 An example of a generic template for emergent group support with the problem-solving DSS approach

from descriptive templates specified as successful or failed, by generalising the values of the descriptive slots, such as "Where", "When", and "Who", to the appropriate level (Bui and Tan 2007; Sebastian and Bui 2009).

The template process is embedded as part of the information/action flow in various phases of the emergency management process. Preparedness is widely recognised as critical (Bui and Sankaran 2001) because urgency combined with the consequences of one's actions result in heavy stress, often causing simple errors and non-optimal behaviours (Billings, Milburn, and Schaalman 1980). Template preparation should include definitions of all routine protocols, selection and customisation according to descriptive (what happened) and normative (what should have happened) examples, and establishment of temporal sequences, context-sensitivity based on disaster taxonomies, and performance measures. During disasters, templates are used to increase effectiveness of execution – or at least to reduce execution flaws and adjust and adapt to the competencies of existing emergent groups. After disasters, the effectiveness of templates is debriefed for analysis with particular attention to lessons from successes and failures (Bui and Tan 2007).

3.2 *Problem-Solving Approach*

Decision Support Systems (DSS) can be defined as a computer-based problem-solving method that attempts to support decision makers for unstructured, ill-structured or underspecified problems that cannot be automated (e.g., Bui 1987). Decision support focuses on key decisions and tasks with the goal of improving the effectiveness (i.e., what should be done, as opposed to improved efficiency as in operations) of the decision makers' problems-solving process. The structure of such semi-structured tasks is sufficient to make analytic aids valuable, but managerial judgement is critical and therefore supported rather than replaced (Keen and Morton 1978). Decision Support Systems should accommodate human reasoning from strategic to granular levels in order to serve as models for action that reflect the appropriate complexity of the decision process (Adam and Humphreys 2008). The question is how well human reasoning is captured with a pure problem-centred approach to decision making.

The Problem-Solving Approach, which is the theoretical foundation for the first possible approach to information support, is central to the DSS field. Keen and Morton (1978) provide an overview of the basic assumptions underlying the design of DSS. With strong emphasis on developing problem-solving techniques, the dominant view of decision making in DSS research focuses primarily on structure and analytical methods, decision content, and the assumptions of a rational decision maker. March and Simon's "bounded rationality" concept, also known as the satisficing, process-oriented view of decision making, represents the prevailing organisational decision paradigm in building DSS (March, Simon, and Guetzkow 1958). According to this school of thought, decision makers are "intendedly rational" (Simon 1955), but possess limited knowledge and skills, and therefore rely on heuristics and "good enough", rather than optimal, solutions. While Simon has modified and greatly improved the very normative ideas of rationality introduced by the economic rationality model, the concept is nevertheless limited to a rational perspective of the decision-making process.

The DSS field has largely ignored more descriptive viewpoints on decision-making, such as those advanced by the organisational procedures view, the political view, or the individual differences approach according to Keen and Morton's typology of approaches (1978). Indeed, perspectives that look at decision-making beyond rationality contain a wealth of interesting alternative theoretical ideas that may be more appropriate for ill-structured problems, but whose implications are unfortunately only little explored in DSS research. For example, Lindblom (1959) views decision making as a political process in which the decision maker should utilise remedial strategies of marginal incrementalism in order to reduce complexity and achieve feasible goals based on the assumption of limited intellectual capabilities (Lindblom 1959). Tversky and Kahneman (1974) show the reliance on a limited number of heuristic principles to decrease the complexity of assessing probabilities of events, which constitute the basis for many decisions. The "garbage can model" suggests adoption of random search and choice rules under severe lack of knowledge (e.g., Cohen, March, and Olsen 1972; Bui 1987). Cognitive style research of the individual differences perspective emphasises the psychology of individual differences in problem solving. Therefore, it seems necessary to diagnose which perspectives, or combinations of perspectives, are relevant for a particular situation (Keen and Morton 1978; Bui 1987).

Following the rational decision making paradigm, the majority of DSS research anchors analysis and design in Simon's Intelligence-Design-Choice (IDC) process model of the human decision-making process (Simon 1960). In the intelligence phase of this general and fundamentally sequential model, the decision maker observes reality, gains an understanding of problems and opportunities, and systematically acquires information. In the design phase, decision criteria and alternatives are developed, uncontrollable events are identified, and relationships specified. The choice phase contains the logical evaluation of alternatives and development of actions. In the implementation phase, which represents a later extension of the model suggested by empirical testing, the decision maker ponders analyses and recommendations, weighs consequences, gains sufficient confidence in the decision, develops an implementation plan, secures resources, and puts the plan into action (Forgionne 2002).

As presented earlier, we use templates as a means to instantiate our information requirement analysis. Figure 1 illustrates a basic example of a problem-centred information support approach aimed at providing intelligence within Simon's IDC framework. The template seeks to provide rescuers with artifacts that support the representational, reasoning and computational tasks (e.g., "what" task to be performed, "where" to help, "why" to execute a specific task, "who" to communicate to), based on real-time information compiled from past or current data.

While information should help the group to identify existing expertise and opportunity, the template should ultimately focus on providing knowledge and guidelines on activities, which are at the centre of the emergent group's cognitive structure. Assuming lack of expertise and presence of high stress, instructions must not only be simple but outside expertise should be made accessible when possible. Because of the potential for unstable ICT, information support should help groups quickly develop and communicate a simple coordination mechanism that does not rely on individual expertise but on a documented narrative of actions to enable assessment on what further help is needed, and to counteract the lack of organisational memory and intelligence.

3.3 Action-Resource-Based Approach to Defining Information Needs

The action-resource-based approach to problem representation and problem solving posits that a decision problem requires the decision maker to identify actions to be taken, as well as input resources that are consumed and output resources that are generated in relation to the actions within the problem constraints. The resulting activity triplet (e.g., input resources/action/output resources), which can represent a portfolio of actions, can be viewed as a "primitive" process component that should increase the decision makers' awareness of the relevance of appealing alternative actions based on their feasibility (Bui, Bodart, and Ma 1998). From a real-time perspective, the search of an optimal activity triplet is the result of a constant scanning of the decision-making environment, the prioritisation of actions, and a negotiated set of allocated resources.

Based on the dynamics of ongoing rescue processes and organisational characteristics of the involved emergent groups, the determination of such activity triplets is even more challenging. Emergent response groups can be viewed here as groups of individuals who use non-routine resources and activities to apply to non-routine domains and tasks using non-routine organisational arrangements (Drabek and McEntire 2003; Tierney et al. 2001). They are distinctly different from disaster response groups with pre-existing structures, because they are transitory organisations that form to address particular ad-hoc situations. They are "dynamic" insofar as they shift in response to events, information and people, and that their goals can

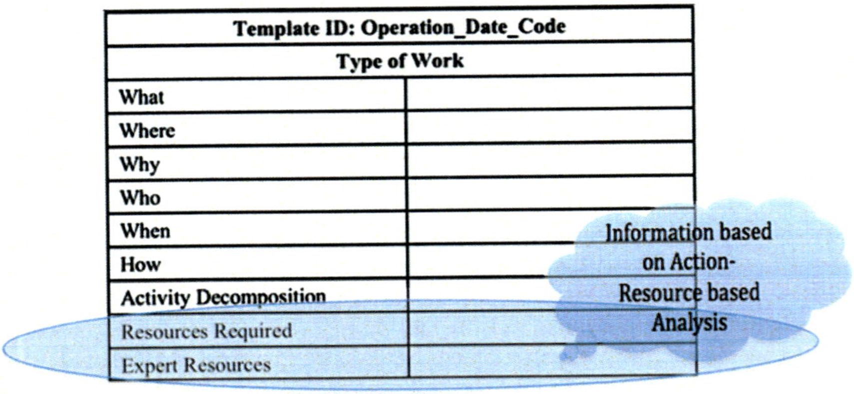

Fig. 2 Example of a generic template for emergent group support with the action-resource based approach

change (Saunders and Kreps 1987). Based on a field study of emergent groups during the 1980 earthquake in Southern Italy, Lanzara (1983) proposes eight characteristics of emergent organisations, taking into account the wide variety of organisational structures and behaviours, including variable boundaries and memberships, distributed leadership, heterarchical configuration, spontaneous activities and context-driven rules, short-term organisational memory and ephemeral and exchangeable roles. Lack of memory paradoxically adds to the appeal of emergent groups (e.g., routines may be ineffective, outdated, misleading for the current situation), but knowledge translated into best practices for future reference can prove useful. Given the scarcity of resources, the unique nature of emergent groups, and the dynamics of rescue operations, the action-resource-based approach would provide a critical mechanism for a more formalised and cost-effective approach to resource allocation, decision making, and problem solving.

Figure 2 incorporates the logic of the action-resource-based approach by adding information categories related to chosen actions and their needed resources for each of the identified tasks.

3.4 Control and Monitoring Approach to Managing Complex Organisations

Anthony, Dearden, and Bedford (1984) advocate the necessity to implement a management control system to assure that the organisation carries out its strategies as envisioned. As such, task control can be seen as the process that monitors efficient and effective implementation of planned activities. Urgency and error-prone stress in disaster operations suggest benefits from a certain amount of system automation with constant human monitoring and the ability to override (Sebastian and

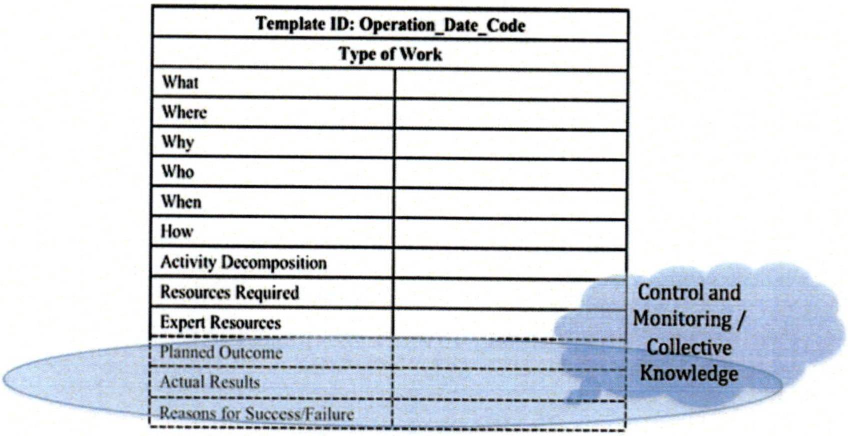

Fig. 3 Example of a generic template for emergent group support with control and monitoring

Bui 2009; Bui and Tan 2007). Effective information support requires constant or periodic monitoring in order to evaluate progress of the volunteer operations (e.g., search and rescue), ensure timely delivery of critical information and resources, and maintain a sustained level of motivation and morale in line with the discussed behavioural models. Real-time monitoring during disasters should therefore be enforced to reassign templates based on field performance and status of involved emergent groups (Bui and Tan 2007).

For example, templates can be embedded in an ad-hoc or collaborative workflow-type process management system as a tool for simulations, monitoring progress, and providing quick feedback on previous decisions (Housel, El Sawy, and Donovan 1986). While existing ad-hoc workflow models are too inflexible – if not at all possible – for emergent group support, they offer some interesting features such as frequent amendments of process definitions and low priority of throughput (Stohr and Zhao 2001). Regardless of the implementation of the monitoring mechanism, Fig. 3 provides an example of integration of control and monitoring information requirements within a template approach.

3.5 Motivational Approach Based on the Altruistic Community Model

So far, we have given examples of information support to the decision makers (in our case the volunteer rescuers), which cover intelligence needs for problem-centred "rational" decision making in Simon's IDC framework (Simon 1960). In the following two sections we introduce examples of behavioural models, which we believe also address critical aspects of information needs that focus more on supporting the decision makers themselves. As we cannot assume that rescuers in the field will solely act as rational decision makers according to the bounded rationality model, we posit that consideration of a multidisciplinary behavioural theoretical background will improve the amount and quality of information support – for the rescuers themselves and – perhaps more importantly – for an effective outcome for the overall rescue operation.

The first concept is that of motivational support. Fritz and Mathewson (1957) describe five types of informal convergence behaviours immediately following disasters, which refer to dynamic dominant motivations and potential social roles: helpers, returnees, the anxious, the curious, and the exploiters. "Helpers", often surviving community members who are present or nearby, initiate crucial disaster response activities (Lowe and Fothergill 2003).

Barton's research on the determinants of helping behaviour in communities under collective stress, i.e., situations that arise from large-scale deprivation of conditions relative to the standards of a given social system (Barton 1969), is relevant to our goal of improving response effectiveness because it addresses the formation and operation of emergent groups at the disaster scene. His "altruistic community model" advocates for social mechanisms that produce helping behaviour amongst victims of collective stress situations. Seventy-one propositions, clustered around social processes, describe the relationships amongst individual-level variables, contextual relationships to corresponding aggregate-level variables and global variables (which characterise impact, community structure, and role of media), and collective-level relationships (Barton 1969; Barton 2005).

We are predominantly interested in the cluster of propositions that is organised around the determinants of individual-level motivation to help victims which comprises the variables of sympathetic identification with victims, individual feelings of moral obligation, and perception of a "helping community" norm (Barton 1969, 2005). Figure 4 shows direct relationships of major factors in the model with individual-level motivators, based on Barton's propositions as detailed in (Barton 1969).

Because Barton's propositions are also oriented towards analysis of larger social systems and production of helping behaviour for remote victims, some of the motivating factors are beyond the control of disaster management managers, and the altruistic community model may have the strongest potential related to disaster preparation (e.g., establishing a prior expectation of a helping community norm). Nevertheless, we believe that it is to some extent possible to encourage and support effectiveness of emergent group formation and operation with an information design that nurtures altruism through awareness of the nature and severity of the disaster and ongoing help efforts for increased personal identification and a sense of moral obligation.

Empirical research is needed to verify the net impact of these factors and their direct and indirect relationships with a multilevel analysis, as well as the role of information in their stimulation. The examples in Table 1 serve as an illustration of the opportunity related to designing information support based on Barton's model and behavioural research in general.

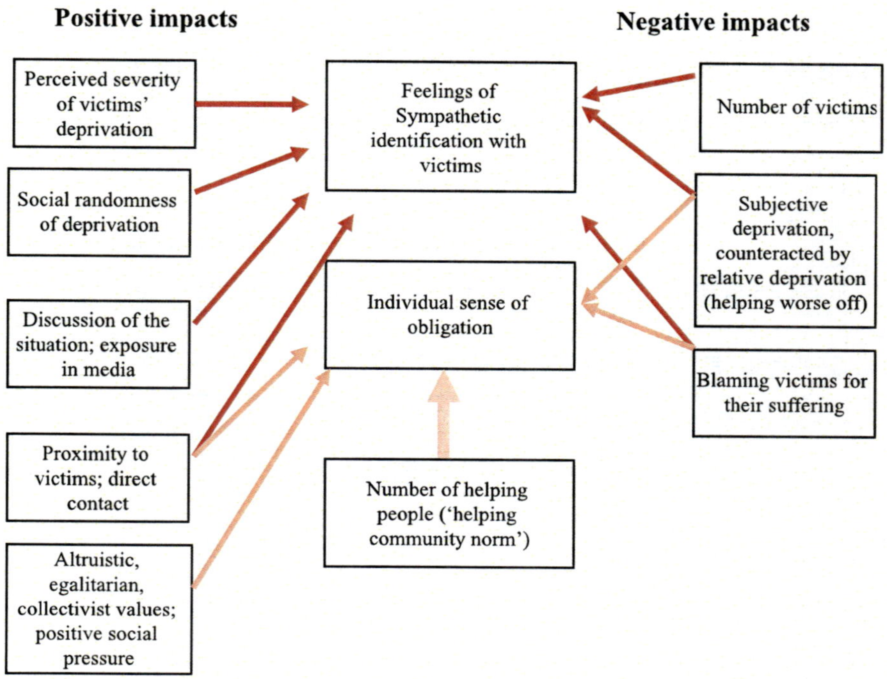

Fig. 4 Major direct impacts on the motivational basis of a helping community (*Source*: Adapted from Sebastian and Bui 2009)

As such, information could be provided to encourage and reinforce the motivation to help with the following categories introduced in Table 1:

- *Others Helping*: Positive reinforcement of the 'helping community norm' has a strong potential to heighten the personal sense of obligation and creates a snowball effect of motivated volunteers. Green and Pomeroy (2007) found that social support had significant positive effect on successful outcomes of stressful situations. Asking local helpers or even the victims who could be helpful based on past incidents (if any) assures the rescuer and provides him with resources.
- *People in Need of Help*: Information should be specific to the community with sensitivity to the potential of overwhelming helpers by sheer number of victims. Specific local information should boost motivation with awareness of proximity and severity, and facilitation of direct contact.
- *General Situation Update*: Information regarding the crisis characteristics has the potential to touch upon all positive impact variables, thereby – if balanced to avoid overwhelming recipients – increasing the potential of reinforcing the motivational basis. A question for continued research is how much information is enough for motivating and executing a task, but not overwhelming in a decentralised/distributed management approach (e.g., Sengupta and Abdel-Hamid 1993). Updates on upcoming arrival of professional help may mitigate low morale.

Table 1 Motivational information design opportunities (*Source*: Information adapted from Barton 1969)

Impacting Factors	Examples of Information Categories That May Trigger Helping Behavior
Perceived severity of victims' deprivation (Impact characteristic)	*The worse off the victims, the stronger others sympathize* → 'People in need of help' (e.g., information on expected needs and injuries in an area), 'General information update
Social randomness of deprivation (Impact characteristic)	*Random impact in relation to social categories tends to decrease relevance of prior social status and relationships compared to current fate, all can identify* → 'General information update (disaster characteristics)
Proximity to victims (Impact characteristic)	*The closer and more similar victims are, the more others sympathize; individual's sense of obligation is strongest when victims are nearby (group loyalty)* → 'People in need of help' (e.g., information about volunteers' immediate surroundings), 'General information update'
Discussion of the situation (Communication)	*Intense word-of-mouth increases sympathy in absence of direct contact, supplements or replaces media* → 'People in need of help', 'General information update', Encourage communication of the information
Media exposure (Communication)	*Coverage of victims' plight increases sympathetic identification* → Generally more relevant for motivation of remote volunteers → 'General information update', potential integration of mass media feature (e.g., if template is distributed on website)
Direct contact with victims (Communication)	*Direct, firsthand perception of need is most potent for sympathy, counteracts stereotypes* → 'People in need of help', 'General information update' (e.g., facilitate contact by specific location information regarding victims /strongest impact)
Altruistic/egalitarian/collectivist values	*Group culture, or ideologies and values of individuals may strengthen or weaken sense of moral obligation (social pressure)* → Factor is more relevant in disaster preparation, varies among communities
Helping community norm (number of helping people)	*Generates perception of being expected to help (indication of moral standards), increases with the number and proportion of helpers* → 'People who are helping' (e.g., information on number of helpers)
Number of victims (beyond threshold)	*Others are overwhelmed by the size of the problem, threatened by potential sacrifice of own living conditions* → 'People in need of help', 'General situation update' (balance information e.g., as localized as possible)
Subjective deprivation	*Priority to one's own problems; obligation to help competes with sense of looking after oneself/immediate family (counteracted by relative deprivation mechanism, which decreases perception of severity of own suffering (the more others feel better off, the more they sympathize)* → 'People in need of help', (e.g., information on expected needs and injuries in an area), 'General information update'
Blaming victims for their suffering	*Blame reduces sympathy and moral obligation, counteracted by situational factors 'social randomness', 'sudden deprivation'* → 'General information update' (disaster characteristics), 'People in need of help', (e.g., facilitate direct contact with localized information), 'People who are helping' (perception of community consensus)

Following the discussion above, information requirements based on the altruistic community model are reflected in the template example shown in Fig. 5.

3.6 *Sense Making and an Affective Approach to Deal with Disaster-Induced Stress*

As mentioned throughout this chapter, emergent groups are likely to operate under significant stress and urgency, particularly in a search and rescue scenario. People's

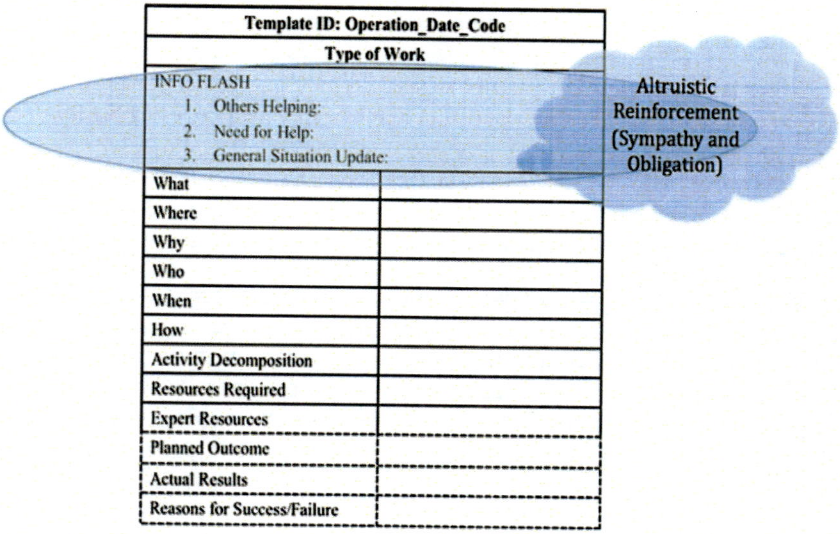

Fig. 5 Example of a generic template for emergent group support integrating motivational support

cognitive abilities tend to reduce under stress (Bui and Sankaran 2006). Information support for volunteers should therefore also approach stress as an issue related to information processing. Furthermore, sociological research suggests that citizens generally react positively and constructively under the stress of immediate response contrary to "disaster myths" that imply panic reactions (Tierney et al. 2001). Recent empirical research finds that social interaction is crucial for affected citizens as it helps to cope with the stress based on the severity of the situation and uncertainty of information (Sutton et al. 2008).

Sense making is a potentially important concept to disaster research, as it is a process of search for meaning to deal with uncertainty. Studies on sense making in the context of decision making in formal disaster response describe it as a social and collaborative process, in which the social context affects selection and interpretation of cues, and therefore actions (Landgren 2005; Van de Ven and Neef 2006; Grant 2005). In a study related to emergent groups, Vieweg et al. (2008) observe the existence of altruistic online communities with characteristics of collective distributed problem solving and sense making in their analysis of social media use related to the Virginia Tech shooting. Recent IS research suggests that crisis management and IS design should support the sense making process particularly in ongoing crises, as it – more effectively than rational decision-making – addresses characteristics of crisis situations (e.g., discontinuity, dissonance, ambiguity and ill-structured problems) (Muhren, van den Eede, and van de Walle B 2008).

Dervin (1983) conceptualises information seeking and use as part of sense making, with a central affective component that impacts motivation. Recent research finds variations in the perceived value of cognitive and affective help sources depending on situational characteristics (Nahl and Bilal 2007). These variations constitute interesting guidelines for information requirements in crises because they suggest an integration of more affective, interactive and encouraging information support in addition to cognitive instructions. For example, according to affective load theory, successful information behaviour in a situation of increased "affective load" (an affective satisficing procedure combining uncertainty and time pressure) depends on counterbalancing procedures related to coping skills, consisting of self-efficacy and optimism (Nahl and Bilal 2007).

Moreover, several research streams in Information Science-related fields and Human-Computer Interaction (HCI) emphasise the importance of emotion in information processing and information system design (Nahl 2007). Affective control theory focuses on the control mechanism of emotions on cognitive operations and explains mental processes related to receiving and using information through interaction of three human biological systems with each other and with technology (Nahl and Bilal 2007). Nahl's unified theory of information behaviour, while not tested in crisis situations, provides valuable insight for the design of interface and instructions for volunteers by considering the biological procedures of how users notice, think, and intend when interacting with technology.

Based on the concepts of stress, affective information processing and sense making, information requirement analysis should embed affective information processing in order to maximise information reception and reduce the potential of miscommunication in a context highly charged with emotion and complex social situations.

- A design for inexperienced volunteers in high-stress situations must be simple, intuitive, concise and unequivocal, enabling immediate noticing and understanding of critical content, and providing a simple tool for documenting and communicating experiences and needs. The design must mitigate potential adverse reactions to unfamiliar instructions and their presentation (e.g., overwhelmed and intimidated feelings), based on the assumption that affective and cognitive procedures are learnt group practice-based skills and require adaptation to new situations (Nahl and Bilal 2007).
- The provision of the "Info Flash", with real-time assessment of the situation and upcoming availability of rescue staff (in addition to addressing the motivational support of volunteers) should reduce environmental uncertainty and increase the plausibility of meanings related to instructions and context, thereby supporting the cognitive and situational components of sense making process as conceptualised by Choo (2006).
- Components of reassurance and interaction should be integrated into information support in order to alleviate crisis-induced stress, support an increased in perceived helpfulness of affective help sources in challenging situations, and address issues related to the affective sense making components of ambiguity and doubt (Mak, Mallard, Bui, and Au 1999). Specific information on the availability of expert resources, online operating procedures and matched-up volunteer networks seek to mitigate stress by reducing uncertainty and to create opportunities to get help and encouragement. Whenever technologically feasible,

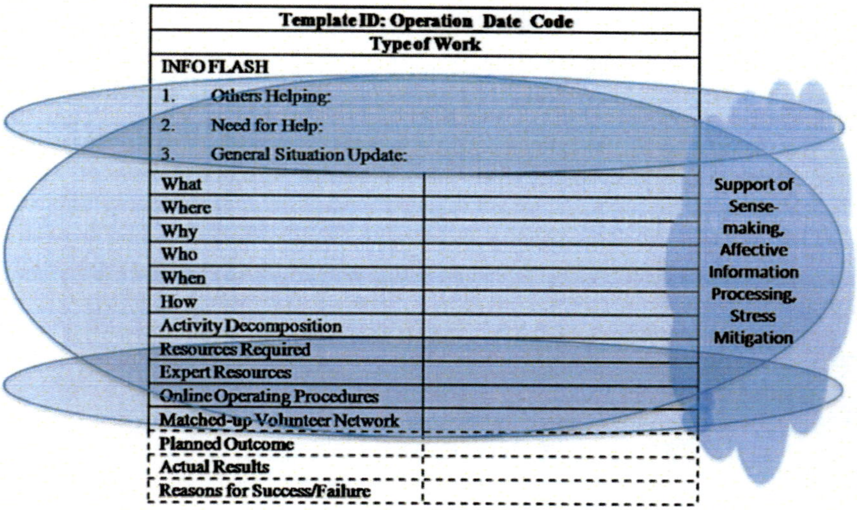

Fig. 6 Generic template for emergent group support integrating stress management, affective control, and sense making

any suggested rescue action should be assisted by a remote professional via telecommunication means, and a matched-up volunteer network should create a sense of community amongst the rescuers (White et al. 2008).

- Based on the dynamic nature of the probable action-based swift trust structure within and amongst emergent groups, low trust levels and potential conflicts should be expected. Information support should consider a potentially helpful effect of a core member and trust-augmenting measures (Majchzrak et al. 2007), as long as flexibility is preserved.

Figure 6 illustrates an attempt to incorporate stress mitigation features and acknowledgement of heightened affective information processing into information support for emergent groups.

4 Conclusion

Lessons learnt from recent crises strongly suggest that involvement of ordinary individuals or groups of people in emergency response is a critical and necessary contribution to large-scale disaster relief, especially at the beginning of the crisis. While not meant to displace response from trained professionals, these emergent groups should be regarded as immediately available and valuable assets. Instead, the issue is to find ways to support these emergent first responders when formal responders have yet to arrive at the scene and information is scarce, confusing, depressing, and not informative enough to support rescue work.

Information is recognised as one of the most critical aspects for all crisis management activities. Therefore, from a real-time decision support perspective we offer an extended view of what types of information should be collected and disseminated to support the cognitive, affective and situational conditions of the rescuers. In this conceptual chapter, we outline a stepwise approach to understanding the information needs of emergent groups during emergency response. We begin with the predominant approach to decision making, one that seeks to provide information to the rescuer-decision maker with the aim to improve his/her cognition, and subsequently, his/her problem-solving effectiveness. We next extend this approach to underscore the needs for supporting emergent groups from an organisational perspective, highlighting the necessity for economic efficiency (what action to take and what resources to commit in the overall context) and control and monitoring. Based on a framework of cognitive, affective and situation information support, we further call for inclusion of information that helps deal with emotion and stress, reinforce motivation and nurture a sense of altruism in extreme crisis situations.

At the individual level, it seems natural and sensible to boost the sympathetic identification with victims and the sense of obligation to help. Also, based on the affective perspective on information processing, we posit that information to best help the individual helpers should take into consideration both situation-sensitive cognitive activity and affective intentionality. At the collective level, information design should pay attention to innovative and flexible mechanisms that enable collaboration and coordination of non-professionals in extreme environments.

Admittedly, the discussion in this chapter is a truncated analysis of the identification of real-time information for the emergent groups. We purposely chose in this chapter a couple of leading theories to make a case of our "beyond rationality" theme. Also, we have utilised templates to illustrate several important issues related to the identification and design of information to support emergent groups in emergency response. As expected, these illustrations are not meant to be comprehensive in identifying all the possible information constructs that instantiate the approaches of information requirement analysis discussed in this chapter. The point is that DSS research should look beyond the rationality assumption. Furthermore, any attempt to integrate various decision support paradigms should require careful identification of constructs and their operationalisation, as well as assessment and validation of the interactive effects amongst these constructs. As an example, we need to address the selection of physical media to deliver the information to the emergent groups (e.g., voice vs. text; Internet vs. telephony). In any case, going beyond the rationality paradigm offers the hope of recognising and realising the opportunity associated with effective participation of emergent groups in exceptional emergency situations.

References

Adam, F. and P. Humphreys, *Encyclopedia of Decision Making and Decision Support Technologies*. London: IGI Global, 2008.

Anthony, R.N., J. Dearden and N.M. Bedford, *Management Control Systems*, Fifth Edition. Homewood: Richard D. Irwin, Inc., 1984.

Barrera, M. Jr., "Distinctions Between Social Support Concepts, Measures and Models," *American Journal of Community Psychology*, 14, 4, 1986, 413–445.

Barton, H.A., *Communities in Disaster: A Sociological Analysis of Collective Stress Situations*. Garden City: Doubleday & Company, Inc., 1969.

Barton, A.H., "Disaster and Collective Stress," in R.W. Perry and E.L. Quarantelli (eds.), *What Is a Disaster? New Answers to Old Questions*, International Research Committee on Disasters, 2005, 125–152.

Billings, R.S., T.W. Milburn and M.L. Schaalman, "A Model of Crisis Perception: A Theoretical and Empirical Analysis," *Administrative Science Quarterly*, 25, 2, 1980, 300–316.

Boin, A., "From Crisis to Disaster: Towards an Integrative Perspective," in R.W. Perry and E.L. Quarantelli (eds.), *What Is a Disaster? New Answers to Old Questions*, International Research Committee on Disasters, 2005, 153–172.

Bui, T. X., *Co-op: A Group Decision Support System for Cooperative Multiple Criteria Group Decision Making*. Berlin: Springer, 1987.

Bui, T. and S. Sankaran, "Design Consideration for a Virtual Information Center for Humanitarian Assistance/Disaster Relief Using Workflow Modeling," *Decision Support Systems*, 31, 2, 2001, 165–179.

Bui, T. and A. Tan, "A Template-Based Methodology for Large-Scale HA/DR Involving Ephemeral Groups," in *Proceedings of the 40th Hawaii International Conference on System Sciences*, Big Island, 2007, 34a.

Bui, T., F. Bodart and P. Ma, "ARBAS: A Formal Language to Support Argumentation in Network-Based Organizations," *Journal of Management Information Systems*, 14, 3, 1998, 223–237.

Choo, C.W., *The Knowing Organization: How Organizations Use Information to Construct Meaning, Create Knowledge, and Make Decisions*. New York: Oxford University Press, 2006.

Cohen, M.D., J. March and J. Olsen, "A Garbage Can Model of Organizational Choice," *Administrative Science Quarterly*, 17, 1, 1972, 1–23.

CRED (Center for Research on the Epidemiology of Disasters, EM-DAT Emergency Events Database), April 7, 2008, URL = http://www.emdat.be/glossary/9

Dervin, B., "An Overview of Sense-Making Research: Concepts, Methods, and Results to Date," *International Communication Association Annual Meeting*, Dallas, May 1983.

Drabek, T.E. and D.A. McEntire, "Emergent Phenomena and the Sociology of Disaster: Lessons, Trends and Opportunities from the Research Literature," *Disaster Prevention and Management*, 12, 2, 2003, 97–112.

Endsley, M.R. and D.J. Garland (eds.), *Situation Awareness: Analysis and Measurement*. Mahwah: Lawrence Erlbaum, 2000.

Fisher, C.B and R.M. Lerner, *Encyclopedia of Applied Developmental Science*. Thousand Oaks: Sage, 2004.

Fischer, H.W., K. Gregoire, J. Scala, L. Letukas, J. Mellon, S. Romine and D. Turner, "The Emergency Management Response to Hurricane Katrina: As Told by the First Responders – A Case Study of What Went Wrong & Recommendations for the Future," *Quick Response Research Report 189*, Center for Disaster Research & Education, Millersville University of Pennsylvania, 2006.

Forgionne, G.A., "An Architecture for the Integration of Decision Making Support Functionalities," in M. Mora, G.A. Forgionne and J.N.D. Gupta (eds.), *Decision Making Support Systems: Achievements and Challenges for the New Decade*. Hershey: Idea, 2002.

Fritz, C.E. and J.H. Mathewson, "Convergence Behavior in Disasters: A Problem in Social Control," *Committee on Disaster Studies, Disaster Research Group*. Washington, DC: National Academy of Sciences – National Research Council Publication, 1957, 476.

Grant, T., "Integrating Sensemaking and Response Using Planning Operator Induction," in *Proceedings of the 2nd International Conference on Information Systems for Crisis Response and Management (ISCRAM)*, Brussels, 2005, 89–96.

Green, D.L. and E.C. Pomeroy, "Crime Victims: What Is the Role of Social Support?," *Journal of Aggression, Maltreatment and Trauma*, 15, 2, 2007, 97–113.

Housel, T.J., O.A. El Sawy and P.F. Donovan, "Information Systems for Crisis Management: Lesson from Southern California Edison," *MIS Quarterly*, 10, 4, 1986, 389–401.

Keen, P.G.W. and M.S.S. Morton, *Decision Support Systems: An Organizational Perspective*, Addison-Wesley Series on Decision Support. Reading: Addison-Wesley, 1978.

Kulyk, O., G. van der Veer and B. van Dijk, "Situational Awareness Support to Enhance Teamwork in Collaborative Environments," in *Proceedings of the 15th European Conference on Cognitive Ergonomics: The Ergonomics of Cool Interaction*, Funchal, 2008.

Landgren, J., "Shared Use of Information Technology in Emergency Response Work: Results from a Field Experiment," in *Proceedings of the 2nd International Conference on Information Systems for Crisis Response and Management (ISCRAM)*, Brussels, 2005, 35–40.

Lanzara, G.F., "Ephemeral Organizations in Extreme Environments: Emergence, Strategy, Extinction," *Journal of Management Studies*, 20, 1, 1983, 71–95.

Lee, J., "Design Rationale Systems: Understanding the Issues," *IEEE Expert: Intelligent Systems and Their Applications*, 12, 3, 1997, 78–85.

Lindblom, C.E., "The Science of 'Muddling Through,'" *Public Administration Review*, 19, 2, 1959, 79–88.

Lowe, S. and A. Fothergill, "A Need for Help: Emergent Volunteer Behavior after September 11," in *Beyond September 11th: An Account of Post-Disaster Research*, Program on Environment and Behavior, Special Publication #39, Institute of Behavioral Science, Natural Hazards Research and Applications Information Center, 2003.

Majchrzak, A., S.L. Jarvenpaa and A.B. Hollingshead, "Coordinating Expertise Among Emergent Groups Responding to Disasters," *Organization Science*, 18, 1, 2007, 147–161.

Mak, H-Y, A.P. Mallard, T. Bui and G. Au, "Building Online Crisis Management Support Using Workflow Systems," *Decision Support Systems*, 25, 3, 1999, 209–224.

March, J., H.A. Simon and H.S. Guetzkow, *Organizations*. New York: Wiley, 1958.

Muhren, W., G. van den Eede and B. van de Walle, B., "Sensemaking Methodology for ISCRAM Research: Information Processing in an Ongoing Crisis," in *Proceedings of the 5th International Conference on Information Systems for Crisis Response and Management (ISCRAM)*, Washington, DC, 2008, 315–323.

Nahl, D., "Social-Biological Information Technology: An Integrated Conceptual Framework," *Journal of the American Society for Information Science and Technology*, 58, 13, 2007, 2021–2046.

Nahl, D. and D. Bilal (eds.), *Information and Emotion: the Emergent Paradigm in Information Behavior Research and Theory*. Medford: Information Today, 2007.

Norman, D.A., *Things That Make Us Smart: Defending Human Attributes in the Age of the Machine*. Reading: Addison-Wesley, 1993

Palen, L., R. Hiltz and S.B. Liu, "Online Forums Supporting Grassroots Participation in Emergency Preparedness and Response," *Communications of the ACM*, 50, 3, 2007, 54–58.

Plotnick, L., C. White and M. Plummer, "The Design of an Online Social Network Site for Emergency Management: A One-Stop Shop," in *Proceedings of the 15th Americas Conference on Information Systems*, San Francisco, 2009, Paper 420.

Power, D.J., "Categorizing Decision Support Systems: A Multidimensional Approach," in M. Mora, G. Forgionne and J.N.D. Gupta (eds.), *Decision Making Support Systems: Achievements and Challenges for the New Decade*. Hershey: Idea, 2002, 20–26.

Saunders, S. L. and G.A. Kreps, "The Life History of the Emergent Organization in Times of Disaster," *The Journal of Applied Behavioral Science*, 23, 4, 1987, 443–462.

Sebastian, I. and T. Bui, "Emergent Groups for Emergency Response: Theoretical Foundations and Information Design Implications," in *Proceedings of the 15th Americas Conference on Information Systems*, San Francisco, 2009, Paper 638.

Sengupta, K. and T.K. Abdel-Hamid, "Alternative Conceptions of Feedback in Dynamic Decision Environments: An Experimental Investigation," *Management Science*, 39, 4, 1993, 411–428.

Simon, H.A., "A Behavioral Model of Rational Choice," The *Quarterly Journal of Economics*, 69, 1, 1955, 99–118.

Simon, H.A., *The New Science of Management Decision*. New York: Harper & Row, 1960.

Sprague, R. and D. Carlson, *Building Effective Decision Support Systems*. Englewood Cliffs: Prentice-Hall, 1982.

Stohr, E.A. and J.L. Zhao, "Workflow Automation: Overview and Research Issues," *Information Systems Frontiers*, 3, 3, 2001, 281–296.

Sutton, J., L. Palen and I. Shklovski, "Backchannels on the Front Lines: Emergent Uses of Social Media in the 2007 Southern California Wildfires," in *Proceedings of the 5th International ISCRAM Conference*, Washington, DC, 2008, 624–632.

Tierney, K., M.K. Lindell and R.W. Perry (eds.), *Facing the Unexpected: Disaster Preparedness and Response in the United States*. Washington, DC: Joseph Henry, 2001.

Tversky, A. and D. Kahneman, "Judgment Under Uncertainty: Heuristics and Biases," *Science*, New Series, 185, 4157, 1974, 1124–1131.

Van de Walle, B. and M. Turoff, "Decision Support for Emergency Situations," in F. Burstein and C. Holsapple (eds.), *Handbook on Decision Support Systems*, International Handbook on Information Systems Series. Berlin: Springer, 2007.

Van de Ven, J. and M. Neef, "A Critical Thinking Environment for Crisis Response," in *Proceedings of the 3rd International ISCRAM Conference*, Newark, 2006, 223–229.

Van Someren, M., N. Netten, V. Evers, H. Cramer, R. de Hoog and G. Bruinsma, "A Trainable Information Distribution System to Support Crisis Management," in *Proceedings of the 2nd International ISCRAM Conference*, Brussels, 2005, 203–206.

Vieweg, S., L. Palen, S.B. Liu, A. Hughes and J. Sutton, "Collective Intelligence in Disaster: Examination of the Phenomenon in the Aftermath of the 2007 Virginia Tech Shooting," in *Proceedings of the 5th International Conference on Information Systems for Crisis Response and Management (ISCRAM)*,, Washington, DC, 2008, 45–54.

Weick, K.E., K.M. Sutcliffe and D. Obstfeld, "Organizing and the Process of Sensemaking," *Organization Science*, 16, 4, 2005, 409–421

White, C., Plotnick, L., Addams-Moring, R., Turoff, M. and Hiltz, S.R. (2008), Leveraging A Wiki to Enhance Virtual Collaboration in the Emergency Domain, in Ralph. H. Sprague, Jr. (Ed.) Proceedings of the 41st Hawaii International Conference on System Sciences.

White, C., Hiltz, R. and Turoff, M. (2008), United We Respond: One Community, One Voice, Information Systems for Crisis Response and Management, in Frank Fiedrich and Bartel van de Walle (Eds.) Proceedings of the 5th International ISCRAM Conference, Washington, DC, USA, May 2008, 25–33.

Xu, Z., Yuan, Y., and Ji, S. (2008), A Decision Analysis Framework for Emergency Notification, in Ralph. H. Sprague, Jr. (Ed.)Proceedings of the 41st Hawaii International Conference on System Sciences.

Chapter 9
Dynamic Emergency Response Management for Large Scale Decision Making in Extreme Hazardous Events

Murray Turoff[1], Connie White[2], and Linda Plotnick[2]

[1] New Jersey Institute of Technology, Newark, New Jersey, USA
[2] Jacksonville State University, Jacksonville, Alabama, USA

Abstract This chapter begins by discussing the nature of large groups and subgroups of crisis experts who are involved in the decision-making process during a disaster. This is followed by an examination of how to best support these efforts. Subsequently, we describe design problems inherent in emergency decision support systems, the genesis of such issues, and how to overcome them. In particular, this chapter describes the impact of the threat rigidity syndrome and information overload and how to mitigate their effects. We describe current research efforts to promote effective decision making. Characteristics of High Reliability Organisations (HROs) enable their effective response by utilising a set of practices to manage low probability/high consequence events, focusing on the best feasible solutions using the concept of "muddling through" (Weick and Sutcliffe 2001, 2007; Lindbolm 1959). Finally, we provide concluding observations in which we reiterate some of the most critical tactics needed to promote effective decision making by large groups responding to and recovering from a disaster or catastrophic event.

Keywords Emergency management • Emergency information systems • Threat rigidity syndrome • Emergency preparedness

1 Introduction

Effective management of a large scale extreme event requires a system that can quickly adapt to changing needs of the users. There is a critical need for fast decision making within the time constraints of an ongoing emergency (Rodriguez 1997;

M. Turoff (✉)
New Jersey Institute of Technology, Newark, New Jersey, USA
e-mail: turoff@njit.edu

F. Burstein et al. (eds.), *Supporting Real Time Decision-Making*,
Annals of Information Systems 13, DOI 10.1007/978-1-4419-7406-8_9,

Kowalski-Trakofler, Vaught, and Sharf 2003). Extreme events are volatile, change rapidly and can have unpredictable outcomes (Danieisson and Ohisson 1999). Real-time, effective decisions are required of experts collaborating on management and response. Without effective response, outcomes can be catastrophic, with more dire consequences than expected or previously experienced. Judgemental errors from command and control yield poor decisions worsening the situation, resulting in greater injury, loss of life, and/or an increased financial toll (Brinkley 2006). Lessons learned from experiences provide a feedback mechanism in which the processes of an event can be critiqued and further utilised to promote a learning opportunity by closely examining the failures. Characteristics of success need to be identified and integrated into the information system. Anticipating and managing unexpected events successfully call for a dynamic system with features supporting group collaboration on a large scale. Large, ad-hoc groups of experts with no prior work history need a system that will expedite the response and recovery to any unforeseen event.

The problem of designing emergency decision support systems to function in real time involves many more factors than merely the analysis of the given decision problem and the appropriate decision support aids. There are many other requirements that result from the various aspects of group collaboration, coordination and cooperation that need to be a part and parcel of any associated decision support augmentation that can be supported by computer-mediated communications. These include considerations of both individual and group behaviour.

2 The Nature of Emergencies

Extreme events are complex and difficult to understand (Skertchly and Skertchly 2001). Managing such diverse and unpredictable situations calls for many people to interact together in the form of groups; tens, hundreds, or more likely, thousands of individuals working collaboratively (Hiltz and Turoff 1978; White, Hiltz, and Turoff 2008b). These groups have dynamic membership whereby individuals come and go as the problems and response evolve over the life of the disaster. For any particular problem, only a small number of individuals of the total membership may be required. Even though emergency specialised functions can be predetermined to a certain degree, the unique requirements cannot be foreseen, given these extreme events have never been experienced up to that time. Consequently, the unique roles required to satisfy the needs of any given problem cannot be predetermined before the actual event occurs. Only when the problem occurs can various members identify that they can be contributing members to the needs of that particular problem. An example would be after a large train derailment has occurred, a hazardous material has spilled into a tunnel going through a populated area. Not until the chemical is identified and the surrounding infrastructure evaluated for identifying potential threats and risk can a team of experts be identified to respond and manage the situation in the most effective manner. There could be a set of pre-existing conditions that combine with the event to create a new set of threats. For example, the chemical spill could occur during high ill-patterned winds where toxic material is now a plume floating over a residential area with rain intensifying the outcomes.

These small concerned groups are professionals working together – sometimes for the first time – from several unique organisations, often from different areas with assorted domains of expertise. They are groups of individuals with no prior collaborative work experience who come together with a common goal: to attempt to save lives and lessen the negative consequences of an emergency or disaster. As the event unfolds, the groups will evolve to fit the new needs of the present state since the prior problem no longer exists, or is not considered important anymore. The next problem-solving group to form will have some considerable degree of change given that the roles required of this next problem will have changed. They will not follow any long-term pattern of emergent groups. Only when the group exists within a single organisation is there any real chance of becoming permanent. We argue that it is due to these dynamic and spontaneous requirements that this limitation can be overcome by establishing long-term large virtual groups that plan and train together continuously through modern asynchronous collaborative technology (Turoff, Chumer, Van de Walle, and Yao 2004a; Turoff and Hiltz 2009a). It will take fundamental changes in cooperation and collaboration amongst the established organisations in emergency management processes to bring this about. All emergencies are local to the people and the places they affect and to the emergency management officials hired within that jurisdiction to coordinate such response efforts (Radvanovsky and McDougall 2010). Right now those who do the planning are not those who execute the plans; this dichotomy leads to the same sort of problems we have in software development where those who design the software requirements are often not those who undertake the development work, nor are they the actual users of the system. Without real collaboration amongst all the stakeholders, many potential problems go undetected. The larger the disaster, the more individual roles become involved. The 24-h nature of the response requires multiple people to back up one another and to be able to replace one another in any given role (Danieisson and Ohisson 1999). New problems to solve are constantly occurring and who is concerned with a given problem at a given moment is equally unpredictable or unknowable (Weick and Sutcliff 2001,2007). The problems must be revealed as open information to those involved in the process so they learn that something of concern to them is going on. The system must allow temporary solving groups to gather around a problem, exchange information and viewpoints on options that are available, and collectively evaluate the advantages and disadvantages of each feasible option (White, Turoff, and Van de Walle 2007a). Results of this activity should be made available to the person in the role with the authority and responsibility for executing one or more of the options. Although many people contribute or collaborate to provide solutions for any given problem, in the end decisions in an emergency are the responsibilities of a single individual. This is the same concept supporting the United States National Response Framework which dictates that someone should be held accountable for meeting predetermined goals

(Radvanovsky and McDougall 2010). There is always a need for accountability and to be able to ultimately evaluate the decision process in emergency management compared to the final outcomes (Turoff, Chumer, Hiltz, Klashner, Alles, Vararheyi, and Kogen 2004b). Lessons learned are used from these outcomes to improve the process in the future. This is the crux of developing a High Reliability Organisation (HRO) where an error is viewed as a learning opportunity (Weick and Sutcliff 2001).

A typical problem is the relative shortage of some resource relative to the demand for it. Out of the hundreds or thousands involved, there are subgroups of anywhere between five and 50 that are concerned with allocation of resources. This also includes those who are responsible for analysing the situation and conducting oversight of the allocations, as well as those maintaining the resource and those identifying new sources of the resource. All of these are defined as common roles in the process and normally should be identified in a comprehensive collaboration system. A typical unpredictable decision problem is that a resource is in short supply (e.g., fuel being limited) and this establishes a dynamic group of those concerned with this particular resource allocation problem. An important function of any decision support system is to aid in the dynamic formation of this dynamic community of concern for solving this particular problem.

This formation of a problem-solving group to suggest and evaluate the decision options does not change the need for one individual to make the decisions on the actual allocation. In the collaboration system, the stakeholder who needs a resource can put it in as a decision option with his or her current requirements and disposition and can further comment on each option and/or propose the change of options. Everyone needing the resource, then, has a chance to make the case for receiving it, and can indicate his or her judgement of the cases of the others in the group. This does not change the fact that one person will make the final decision for a given part of the requirements and someone else might authorise an allocation as a percentage of the cluster of requirements. However, it is important that all concerned with the outcome has an equal chance to make their needs known and can justify their case since everyone involved is ascribing to some common goals to save lives. All should recognise that some options might be better than others. Those who can present the best set of observations and provide an accurate description of their situation are most likely to have a higher rating in the resulting exchange. The ability to do this is usually tied to their prior experience with such situations. Everything is being done with a high degree of uncertainty, an urgency of acting in a time-urgent manner, and hopefully, a mutual respect and trust of each other's performance ability.

Crisis and disaster events have no respect for manmade boundaries: geographical, political, organisational or functional. Emergency plans often conform to those very boundaries. Meaningful plans must cut across these boundaries with respect to roles, actions and collaboration requirements. Even snowstorms cutting across many rural towns and counties have demonstrated many of the same problems we saw in larger events such as Katrina or 9/11, where both local command and control centres disappeared at the start of the disaster (Chen, Sharman, Rao, Upadhyaya, and Cook-Cottone 2010). The Federal Emergency Management

Agency (FEMA) acknowledges this in the National Response Framework (NRF), desiring more collaboration between divided entities (www.fema.gov). All these considerations impact the design of decision support systems supporting all the emergency phases: mitigation, preparation, response and recovery.

Katrina can be viewed as an extreme event that was both natural and manmade if one considers the actions of mankind over the past 100 years that destroyed natural mitigating conditions. This resulted in short-sighted decisions about the use and design of the land and the waterways (Brinkley 2006). In the case of Katrina we had, and have, numerous problems arising from the lack of coordination throughout the area in planning, mitigation, response and consistency of recovery (Moss and Shelhamer 2007). Although the local control centre went out with the break in the levees, many of the real problems that began to occur would not have been manageable by a fixed single physical command and control centre (White et al. 2007a). For example, there was no way for the Coast Guard, volunteer boat owners and the Red Cross to act as a single coordinated unit to carry out the processes to get the rescued victims from the freeway. The Coast Guard delivered the victims by boat to where the Red Cross could carry out its mission of organising and maintaining shelters (Brinkley 2006). There were no plans in place to enable these three units or other emergent groups as such to communicate.

Many decisions in a disaster have strong elements of disagreement (White, Plotnick, Turoff, and Hiltz 2007b) – for example, how to allocate mobile emergency generators since there are never enough to satisfy all those who want them. However, the important point is that those who feel they need one should be able to make their case for getting one, so that all those in that situation can see how their needs stack up against the others. In addition, a changing situation can easily change the priorities of this sort of decision for allocation of a scarce resource. For example, after Hurricane Katrina made landfall, the hospitals in New Orleans didn't have electricity, but they had generators. However, by nightfall, 80% of the city was flooded and so too were the generators in the hospitals. This life or death situation can be a persuasive arguement for resources.

As we will also see, we need to design for an atmosphere where the professionals and stakeholders involved will come to trust the problem-solving process as a fair one which provides the ultimate decision maker with the best information available when the decision must be made. However, everyone in emergency management realises that any delay in a decision will have some negative impact on some aspect of the situation that may, or may not, be overcome by the benefits of waiting for better information. Using a computer-based system to allow direct lateral contact amongst those most concerned with a given decision, rather than going through command and control, the person-to-person hierarchies can make a considerable improvement in the normal situation. There is no single variable that can be optimised as these are all multi-criteria problems. There is no time to expose and consider every possible option that is possible.

Extreme events have task structures which are categorised as wicked. Wicked problems are volatile and of a very dynamic nature with considerable uncertainty and ambiguity (Churchman 1967). Wicked problems are ongoing and have no stopping rule (Rittel and Webber 1973). They are never resolved and change over time (Conklin 1998). Wicked problems are solved per se when they no longer hold interest to the stakeholders, when resources are depleted or when the political agenda changes. There are many stakeholders with multiple value conflicts who redefine what the problem is repeatedly, reconsider what the causal factors are, and have multiple views of how to approach and hopefully deal with the problem (Conklin and Weil 1998). Getting and maintaining agreement amongst the stakeholders is most difficult as each has his or her own perception and thus, opinion of what is best (Rittel and Webber 1973).

> An emergency is by definition a unique an unpredictable event, and it is seldom possible, even in retrospect, to assess what the outcome of an emergency response would have been if alternative measures had been followed (Danieisson and Ohisson 1999, p. 92).

Traditional management styles of one or two people in charge of word making all the decisions must be changed whereby the person in charge more often defers to the expertise of the members of the problem-solving group during the analysis part of the response effort. One shouldn't make decisions when he or she is not familiar with a subject area, has little expertise or experience in a situation. Leaders should surround themselves with qualified experts and defer to their expertise during times of uncertainty. As the magnitude of an event grows, so too does the size of the group of people needed to contribute to the consideration of the situation grow. It has been suggested that implementing an incident command system as a hierarchical network is the best solution for managing a large and unknown situation, allowing for flexibility for those in charge (Moynihan 2006). We differ very much with this view and offer the challenge of how to turn a large scale team of professionals into an instant High Reliability Organisation (HRO) (Weick and Sutcliff 2001) even when there is no prior work history. An HRO posses five qualities which minimise low risk/high consequence outcomes from the unforeseen in disasters by providing a mindful framework of:

1. A preoccupation with failure.
2. A reluctance to simplify.
3. Sensitivity to operations.
4. Commitment to resilience.
5. Deference to expertise.

It's by following these five principles that a more efficient and effective solution set will be implemented not only after a disaster, but more importantly, before one occurs. It is a critical component that a place has the capability to bring itself back to the prior state promoting resilience. This can only be accomplished by a group practicing mindfulness by implementing these principles as an overall guide (Weick and Sutcliff 2001). Problems occur when someone expects something to happen and it doesn't, or if someone expects something not to happen and it does or when something occurs that was totally unexpected. Large and unforeseen events create a host of unique problems which must be addressed spontaneously and expeditiously.

> A commander must continually face situations involving uncertainties, questionable or incomplete data, or several possible alternatives. As the primary decision maker, he, with the assistance of his staff, must not only decide what to do and how to do it, but must also recognise if and when he must make a decision (Clausewitz 1976, p. 383).

Learning how to manage and expect the unexpected (Weick and Sutcliff 2001) calls for an approach to be implemented by management that has a trickle down effect for abstract thinking and quick improvisations in new or unexpected situations. This calls for teams of experts to form as many subgroups as may be necessary in order to address the extreme event. A system must be designed to allow for adequate representation of needed expertise, and management must defer to that expertise.

Time and time again, it has been seen that in unexpected problems, decision authority flows down to those closest to the situation in either location or knowledge. The role of upper management becomes the important one of conducting oversight and seeking additional resources to meet demands (Turoff et al. 2004a). One person is in charge of making the final decision for action, but this is a collaborative effort of numerous stakeholders sharing numerous overlapping tasks.

> As complexity increases, it becomes impossible for a single individual with the limited information processing capacity to gain control (Danieisson and Ohisson 1999, p. 93).

We believe what is needed is a virtual distributed command and control centre. Who should be involved at any time in a large-scale emergency is very unpredictable, as is their location. Those in closest proximity to a situation often best make decisions or, at least, their observations should be given a high degree of consideration by all those involved. However, those in the trenches do not have the time to consider conflicts and alternatives with current command and control systems, which often severely limits who can be brought into the largely verbal communication process. Even coordination amongst different entities such as medical, law enforcement, public works and fire units is often completely verbal and on a one-to-one basis. Taking advantage of expert volunteers, citizens with resources, and observations from citizens on-site is impossible in current command and control structures. The high priority currently given to planned access is contrary to what is really needed in an emergency. In a well-designed system it should be possible to bring into the command and control structure, in a very quick and dynamic way, any individual located anywhere who has something useful to contribute. This synthesises the concepts of deferring to expertise and recognition that there needs to be final decision makers who are cognisant of all the factors relevant to the decision and who hold that authority.

A dynamic decision-making approach is a much needed method due to the inherent nature of chaos characteristic of extreme events (Danieisson and Ohisson 1999). Extreme events need to be managed using structure with flexibility to improvise or adapt where necessary and achieve agility (Harrald 2009).

Decision making cannot be statically in the hands of a few centrally located individuals. As the situation changes, delegation of decision making should adapt to allow for those experts best suited to make decisions to have authority. At best, in an extreme event, we can know who, with what talents, is available, but we won't know everyone who should be called into a state of active participation until events and problems begin to unfold. The concurrent need for a fully dispersed command and control centre where anyone can participate from wherever they happen to be, without having a single physical centre (Turoff et al. 2004a), was clearly demonstrated by the events of Katrina, the terrorist attacks of 9/11, and the Haitian Earthquake.

When individuals are not actively involved, they are often on stand-by and need to be kept apprised of the situation, maintaining a readiness to contribute their expertise when the situation demands it. These teams of experts work collaboratively in the form of virtually distributed teams, addressing subsets of the problem by incorporating a "divide and conquer" strategy in order to focus on and address all problem areas to the best of their ability. A virtual organisation is created from the overall available experts, dynamically using those who are needed at any particular time (Mowshowitz 2002).

2.1 Large Groups and Subgroups of Decision-Analysis Teams

When a specific problem occurs, there is no way to predict who needs to be involved and the system must provide open access to this new problem to be solved as it occurs (Turoff et al. 2004a). While thousands might be involved, the number of professionals, managers, politicians and decision makers who are interested in a particular problem is probably in the range of five to 20 in most cases. The system needs to be designed to allow the people involved to gather, to propose solution options and to evaluate them. This is done for the benefit of the decision maker or action taker who will need, at some point in time, to actually make a decision or trigger an action. Time is precious and accurate decisions must be made along a timeline at particular points in time over the duration of the event as a disaster evolves (Brehmer 1988; Danieisson and Ohisson 1999).

> The operational commander continually faces an uncertain environment (Rodriguez 1997, p. 5).

The person designated as the decision authority for a particular problem is largely based upon the nature of most unexpected problems for which one can enumerate expertise and roles required once the problem is known (Turoff et al. 2004a, b). Usually this person is someone close to the situation or a professional with expertise in the problem domain.

3 Formulating Group Viewpoints

Thurstone's Law of Comparative Judgement (Thurstone 1927, 1928; Torgerson 1958) helps to best reflect a groups' opinion by breaking complex situations down into a manageable set of characteristics. Thurstone's method takes paired comparisons or rank orders by individuals and uses N for such inputs to create an interval scale out of the resulting N ranking scales where the interval distances represents how much agreement exists. The farther apart two options are on the scale, the more agreement there is that one of the options is preferred more than the other. If two options are at the same point on the scale, then they are equally preferred by the group voting on them.

We have made a major theoretical modification to Thurstone's method that allows complete dynamic voting, the introduction of new items and a different number of voters possible on any subset of preference items in the list (White et al. 2007a, b). As is encouraged in most Delphi-like processes, professionals are asked to express their preferences amongst options when they feel they know enough about the two options they are comparing to make an informed judgement. Therefore, we modified the Thurstone procedure to allow incomplete voting; the scale at any moment only reflects those who have voted and indicates that number. The interim calculation of the probability that one option is preferred to another only counts the actual comparisons made. This allows people to visualise the interval scale of the options from highest preference to lowest. The zero point for any probability is the value of 0.5 (which literally indicates no information or the condition of "maybe").

Our modification of Thurstone's method, where not everyone has to compare every pair, is based upon the Delphi observation that only those who are confident in their judgement should vote on a given pair. Since they can change their vote at any time, comments made by others may make members feel more competent to vote or to change their vote. One may use the frequency of comments made and vote changes made to determine when no further activity is taking place. Comments made may not always be anonymous, but voting needs to be so that people can take initial positions freely without regard to current status and so that evidence is based upon comments which focus on voting that shows disagreement, not the status of the person making the comments. The reasons and support for this are found in prior work on the Delphi method (Linstone and Turoff 1975).

In emergency management, we usually have highly interdisciplinary collaborators who are working on subjective judgements based upon their given areas of expertise. They form heterogeneous groups and are best served by a collaborative system that makes everything explicit in terms of their comments, their organisation, their relationships and their voting. Only by voting to expose disagreement can ambiguities be uncovered and resolved so that the true uncertainties can be made clear to all and allow those with relevant expertise to make their case for resolving the uncertainty to whatever degree is possible. Some proposed options will not be resolvable within the time limits of making the given decision. One of the measures of the quality of a Delphi process is the number of vote changes made (Linstone and Turoff 1975). By tracking the rate of vote changes, we can provide an indication of how long it is going to take to get a reasonable input of votes to be able to reduce any large uncertainty in the most favoured options in the ongoing list. In fact, as allocation choices for a resource are being made, we can dynamically remove the options that have been chosen, and continue to rate new ones as more of the resource becomes available.

The work on this approach includes the development of a new uncertainty scale based upon those who have not voted on particular pairs but who have shown interest by voting on other items. It assumes they vote contrary to the current trend for a given pair to produce an uncertainty scale that will always be shorter than the current one and more tightly cluster the options that have missing votes. Less distance between options means less agreement on which is preferred to the other. As a result, the critical contribution to this approach is a new measure of uncertainty that results in a separate Thurstone scale that shows the worst possible uncertainty condition that results from some items having only a few votes and other items having many more votes. This is done in the following manner:

1. We take the item with the most paired comparisons to provide a current maximum for the number of potential votes.
2. For any other paired comparison, we subtract the total number who have voted on that comparison from the maximum votes possible to get the current number of potential new votes possible in the paired comparison being examined.
3. We assume that those potential voters will vote opposite to the trend the current voters of that paired comparison to force it back towards a probability of .5 for the two items being compared.
4. If the calculated value has not reached .5, we use that value for the uncertainty value or we stop if the value of .5 is reached, or it goes in the other direction, and make that the current value.

These assumptions result in a second Thurstone scale that can be lined up with the first scale to show the potentially large changes that can occur for items that are new and/or have currently only a small number of evaluations. With this method, then, anyone can change their vote at any time based upon the discussion that has occurred about what appear to be meaningful disagreements. The interval scale provides a visual measure of the degree of agreement on the relative preference of any two items. With this feedback, and the visual information provided by the second scale that shows the relative possible changes as described above, experts have a more complete understanding of the level of agreement and status of opinions for decision making.

People may choose to vote via "paired comparisons", rank order, "yes", "no", "no judgement", or "no judgement at this time", thus showing their intention to vote in the future. The feedback mechanisms of the voting scheme allow participants to see just how many vote changes have occurred for any one item in the list. We are adapting the standard Delphi design practice of only encouraging those who are confident in their judgement to express a preference at that time (Linstone and Turoff 1975). Also, the frequency of vote changes in time tends to inform the users and the system when the processing of certain options has really been completed.

Thus, this new method allows for providing a group reflection of individual experts to vote, revote or not vote at all on a given situation, depending upon the relevance of the decision to the experts' domains of knowledge. These subsets of experts can then work more effectively given the dynamic nature of the event, and can work from anywhere, anytime, asynchronously. Characteristics of a continuous Delphi type system (i.e., no round structure) to aid in the dynamic decision-making conducive for best reflecting expert group opinions include (Linstone and Turoff 1975; Turoff 2002; White et al. 2007a):

- Asynchronous interaction by an individual
- Anytime, anywhere participation in decision processes
- Informative visual feedback of present group state on issue
- Ability to vote on an issue, not vote, wait for more information to vote, or change a vote based on the changes in merit from evolving information input
- Visual feedback system on real-time vote outcome
- Anonymous voting
- Total vote changes on any item and histogram of recent vote changes over time
- Contribution to any part of the above decision process by any team member

Figure 1, next, provides an example of a decision process that could be used in conjunction with the above set of characteristics. Note the directions of the arrows between the processes. These demonstrate that anyone can participate in any part

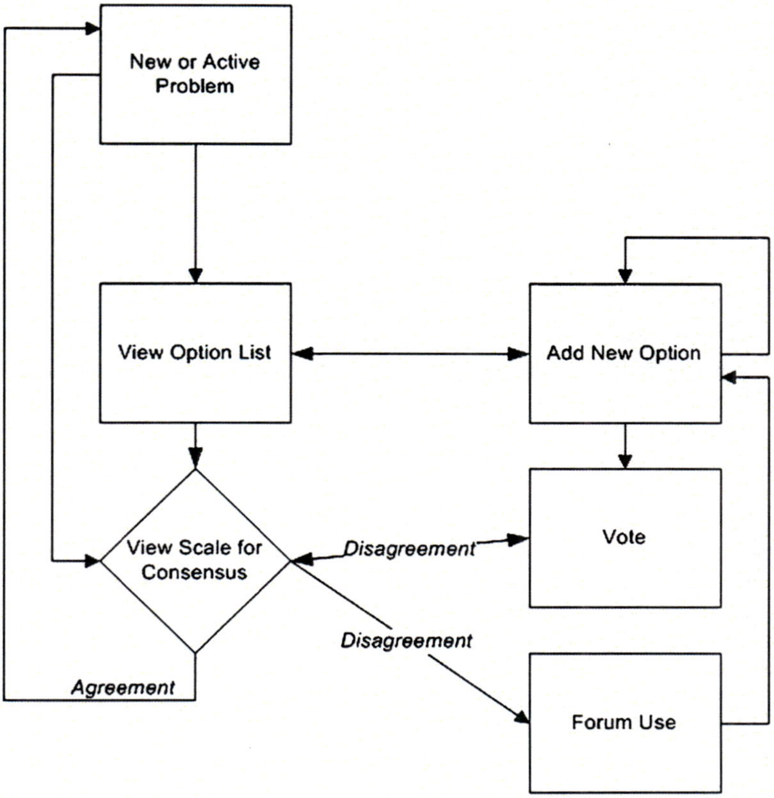

Fig. 1 Continuous real-time collaborative decision analysis: Dynamic Delphi process (White et al. 2007b, 2008a; Turoff et al. 2006)

of the process at anytime; this is crucial as the experts can change their minds and change a vote on a given decision based on the changes in merit of the arguements. Discussion is stimulated by disagreements made salient to the participants by a visual voting feedback system. This discussion amongst experts furthers understanding of a given situation and lessens ambiguity. In many cases, the individuals converging on a specific problem will have different professional backgrounds and represent different viewpoints. In such situations, the quick recognition of differences in meaning (ambiguity) is critical to reaching the stage where the more difficult issue of uncertainties can be dealt with.

4 Theory and Use of Emergency Management Systems

There are various theories that support emergency management and the design of systems. These include the "Science of Muddling Through" (Lindblom 1959), High Reliability Theory (Weick 2001), the Law of Requisite Variety (Van Den Eede 2009), and associated general systems theories of loosely and tightly coupled systems. Their support for some of the assumptions made in this chapter is detailed in Turoff, Hiltz, White, Plotnick, Hendela,and Yao (2009b); Weick and Sutcliff (2001); and Lindblom (1959, 1979).

Expertise is used when and where it is most needed. Teams of experts should be in a standby mode ready for disaster when disaster strikes, anytime. However, the system must be used by the participants in the interim because having a history of using the system regularly will promote ease of use. Waiting until a disaster to use a system impedes making full use of its capabilities (Turoff et al. 2004a). Only when a system is used on a day-to-day basis will the experts and teams be able to interact efficiently and effectively to use it as a means to communicate and solve problems. This means that the thousands of people involved, who come from a great many different organisations and affiliations, must have access to the system between emergencies. This is for the purpose of replacing the need for a physical system as the basis for an HRO (e.g., nuclear power plant, aircraft carrier) with a virtual command and control system that they can fine tune and train with on a part-time basis (Turoff, Chumer, and Hiltz 2006). They can become part-time participants in a virtual organisation where they can also develop the social relationships and other factors necessary to evolving a team and develop the trust in each other's capabilities necessary to allow for the sharing of roles and responsibilities in any event lasting more than one work period.

4.1 Groups as High Reliability Organisations

A high reliability organisational approach is best suited for the low risk/high consequence environments in which the smallest of errors can prove disastrous. It includes the following operational principles:

- Where the knowledge building from the preoccupation with failure is provided by examining in detail lessons learned
- In the open environment where problem identification and reporting is desired and even rewarded
- Where there is a keen mindfulness to the operations where success must also be questioned and not be strictly a source of comfort
- Where there is a dedication to the level of preparation in the situation to bounce back *(resilience)* and continue operations back to normal as soon as possible
- And where deference to expertise is practiced and implemented into action for the realisation and the quality of those outcomes (Weick and Sutcliff 2001)

Characteristics of high reliability organisations that contribute to their ability to manage the unexpected include a preoccupation with failure such that it is watched for and learned from, and deference to expertise. The solution to handling extreme events well must include the use of a system that supports those characteristics. Today it is extremely difficult, if not often impossible, to get information on mistakes because of liability or political concerns. This long-term hindrance is being ignored.

4.2 Building Knowledge, Experts Voting

Groups of crisis experts can use voting to make decisions, build knowledge and categorise the abstract (White et al. 2007a, b, 2008b; Plotnick, Gomez, White, and Turoff 2007). Voting can be used as a way to reflect an expert's opinion (White et al. 2007a). Using paired comparisons to rank opinions during time critical situations can be beneficial in that paired comparisons can simplify a complex situation and increase accuracy in the intended judgement of the expert. This holds true even when numerous alternatives exist along with many ongoing problems (White, Turoff, and Hiltz 2010). Paired comparisons are a method used for voting (Thurstone 1927).

The objective or goal of voting in this decision analysis process is not to make a decision but to focus the discussion on the items the group disagrees about so individuals can make useful comments that might influence others, rather than discussing items there is already agreement about. Voting, when used with Thurstone's Law of Comparative Judgement, takes in many individual experts' opinions, and creates a single group calculation demonstrating where the group stands on alternative solutions given some particular problem (Thurstone 1927). In many emergency decision processes like allocating resources, it is not a matter of one option but which options you are going to do in the time you have. So what is presented to the decision maker is an ordered set of options with rationales for those for which there was some disagreement. One might view the resulting list as informing the decision maker of which items should be done now with current resources; which should be done as resources become available if it is still useful to do; and which options should not be done at all.

5 Other Design Problems for Emergency Decision Support Systems

It is not sufficient to build merely something that performs by providing collaborative decision support for emergency information systems. There are many associated behavioural problems in emergency management that the designer must be aware of and try to provide solutions for.

How does one ensure that improvisation or creativity is allowed in the context of the system? One does this by ensuring the user can dynamically create new templates for the system during an emergency. One may need new roles and people to fill them, new actions that can be triggered for this particular situation, or new members for roles created on the fly like a citizen observer at a critical site able to report dynamically on a quickly changing situation. This is a wide open area for design and it has not received a great deal of attention outside of some of the more exploratory tabletop exercises.

How does one develop and promote trust amongst the participants? It is clear that everyone is usually dedicated to doing an effective job and is motivated to try to take actions that will save lives; collectively this is a community of interest (CoI). A CoI is a community where the membership is fuzzy but it is held together by like-minded people desiring access to the same information contribution and exchange process. The purpose is to keep the community informed as the group evolves and ends organically (Wenger, McDermott, and Snyder 2002). However, there are conflicts for resources and there are sometimes conflicts for authority. There is also the question of whether everyone is equally competent. Will someone trust someone else to take over his or her role after they have been working for 18 h and then be able to come back and find that this other person from a different organisation did as good a job as he or she was doing? Is one jurisdiction more prepared and resilient than its neighbour when the impact zone crosses borders and must be managed as one? This is what sometimes keeps people working to the point of exhaustion. These and other factors bring us to a very well known problem in emergency management, the threat rigidity syndrome.

6 Threat Rigidity Syndrome

Under the stress of a large or new threat, groups and individuals often react with well-learned behaviours, whether or not they are appropriate for the current situation. This rigid response, identified by Staw, Sandelands, and Dutton (1981), is known as "threat rigidity". Threat rigidity is a result of restriction of information and constriction of control, which comes about in an attempt to focus limited resources and centralise control when dealing with the threat (Staw et al. 1981; Plotnick and Turoff 2010). While in some cases habitual response may be appropriate (e.g., a pilot dealing with a stalled plane), if the threat is new or larger enough, a response that is habitual will not likely address the reality of the situation and, therefore, will be maladaptive.

Many factors can lead to this syndrome setting in and causing a person to start making the wrong decisions. For example, information overload can result in feelings of stress which can lead to threat rigidity. One common coping mechanism is to "ignore" some new incoming information (cognitive simplification), thus causing important information to be bypassed. Systems can be designed to avoid information overload. An emergency response system should be designed to allow a monitor to determine if any person in a role might be entering a state of threat rigidity. Self-monitoring of the decision maker's ability and capacity to manage is a critical factor found in good decision making. If this is done properly, a monitor should be able to request that a user relinquish his or her role if factors he or she can monitor indicate this is necessary. Items that can be monitored, for example, are time without sleep, food, syntactic error rate, ineffective and/or late decisions. There are a number of other factors that influence the occurrence of this syndrome. That is why it is important to have a comprehensive understanding of this syndrome when designing such systems. Some of these factors can be affected directly by the design of the interaction process for the user. For example, allowing a user who is going to undertake a role to monitor the screen of someone carrying out the role, and being able to review the associated transactions before his or her turn at the role.

Figure 2 below is a dynamic process diagram that shows how various factors can either lead to threat rigidity and ultimately poor decision making or can lead to flexibility and innovativeness of decision making and appropriate responses. This diagram (from Plotnick and Turoff 2010) is a result of an analysis of threat rigidity and related theories such as cognitive absorption (Agarwal and Karahanna 2000), sensemaking and HRO theory (Weick and Sutcliff 2001). It is a meta-analysis piecing together potential associated factors from a variety of different areas. For example, a large amount of irrelevant information can lead to an increase in information overload which can ultimately lead to a loss of cognitive attention. If one is not focused, the perception of information overload can actually increase. This ultimately leads to higher stress levels which can increase fatigue and lead to increased threat rigidity syndrome with the ultimate outcome of maladaptive decision making. But, awareness of this process can lead to better system design. For example, user controlled filtering can help reduce information overload. For a more complete discussion, see Plotnick and Turoff (2010). There are a number of possible experiments that would aid in refining this model.

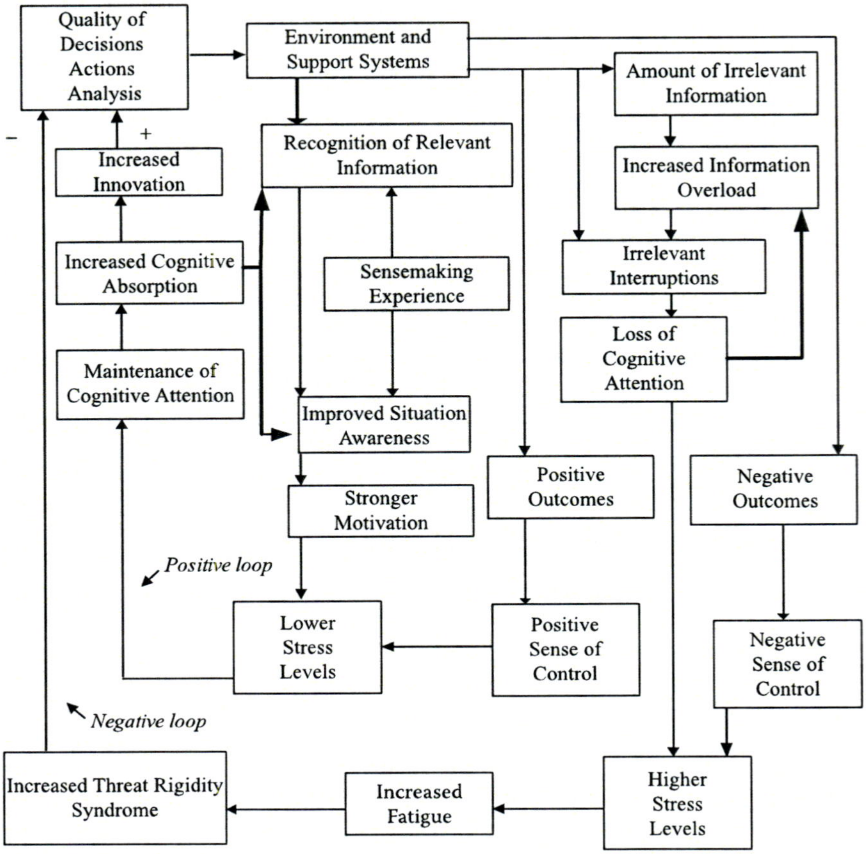

Fig. 2 Dynamic process diagram for the individual threat rigidity syndrome as a cognitive process (Plotnick and Turoff 2009)

7 Information Overload in Emergency Management

When experts work collaboratively with a goal of learning from one another and sharing common interests, a community of practice (Wenger et al. 2002) can emerge, which can strengthens the likelihood of good performance in situations of great stress. If the system has been used previously and is well understood, attention can be focused on the emergency and not diverted to issues of system use.

A virtual community of practice can form with each player having a role that can be called upon as the need arises. Like a library in a programming language, teams of experts are needed that are specific to a problem and its needs as the crisis evolves and a list of priorities expands and contracts as the merits of the decisions change over time. Thus, a system must be able to manage dynamic changes in roles used and the people filling those roles (White, Plotnick, Addams-Moring, Turoff, and Hiltz 2008a).

The formation of the Department of Homeland Security and the incorporation of FEMA into that agency created a situation where the responsibilities for specific aspects of natural disasters were still divided up and scattered in many different federal agencies. The ability of FEMA to coordinate these activities was severely hampered by this reorganisation. Removing FEMA's direct link to the president, added another layer of bureaucracy to go through in attempts to get the same job done. As a result, hundreds of documents have inundated many local practitioners and academic professionals in emergency preparedness and management every month. They believe they are somehow responsible for being cognisant of this flood of material. This has resulted in a situation of information overload (Hiltz and Turoff 1985; Turoff and Hiltz 2002, 2008a, b, 2009a). This has become a serious problem inhibiting the development of emergency management as a professional field. It also impacts the effectiveness of local planning and operations in obtaining relevant and precise information. It is in fact a highly interdisciplinary field when one considers the variety of expertise that may be needed and the very different organisations that must work together (Turoff, Hiltz, Cho, Li, and Wang 2002 and Hiltz 2008a, b, 2009a): tribal, local, state, regional, governments, military units, medical facilities, public health offices, non-profit community groups, the Red Cross, utilities, construction companies, etc.

This is a far more serious problem than is commonly recognised and the recent mushrooming of research and degree programmes in emergency management, that are often isolated in various specific disciplines with accompanying rigid policies and procedures and which ignore the interdisciplinary nature of this area, is not providing an adequate academic solution for the future. In fact, given all of the new avenues for disseminating information (*email, sites, twittering*), it is becoming a major contributor to the fundamental information overload problem.

8 High Reliability Organisations and Muddling Through

The theory of operation for organisations responding to an emergency has been High Reliability Organisations (HROs) (Weick and Sutcliffe 2007). Usually, this is thought of as an operational approach when the organisation has a complex physical system to deal with such as an aircraft carrier or a nuclear power plant or the mass of equipment needed for large wild fires. However, there is a great deal of similarity between HRO theory and the one developed by Lindblom (1959, 1979) in *The Science of Muddling Through*. "Muddling Through" was developed to apply to any type of government operation. The use of HRO theory was developed for organisations having complex physical systems. The theory of "muddling through" provides the same organisational guidance without any need for an organisation to have a complex physical system. Some of these strategies have important consequences for the design of decision support systems. Lindblom characterised a set of properties for what he called "disjointed incrementalism" (Lindblom 1979, p. 517).

The first aspect common to both concepts is the idea of lateral communications amongst all those concerned with any problem to be solved. HRO refers to "the deference to expertise" so that it is not even necessary that the people involved belong to the same team; anyone with useful knowledge can be part of the solution process. In the muddling through process, there is the need for "fragmentation of analytical work to many (partisan) participants in policy making" (Lindblom 1979, p. 517). This was even more clearly stated as:

> A frequent opinion that the inequalities of partisan mutual adjustment are so great that more central decision making can simply be assumed to be an improvement is simply naive. Strong central authority can be – and historically is, in case after case – an instrument for protecting historically inherited inequalities (Lindblom 1979, p. 523).

In the current public administration literature, this has become the concept of "networking" (Moynihan 2008). In the computing literature, it is tied up with the concepts of virtual organisations and virtual communities (Mowshowitz 2002). This is why we have asserted the need for an open design and a free flow of information about ongoing problems to all those involved in the governance of and reaction to the current crisis. This will prompt the development of trust and follows theoretical guidelines on the deference to expertise espoused by both Lindblom (1959) and Weick and Sutcliff (2001) as well as Delphi approaches to heterogeneous groups. Both concepts imply open networking across functional areas, which, in turn, means in emergency management integration over all the phases such as planning, mitigation, preparedness, response and recovery.

HRO theory requires that anyone in the organisation at any level who detects an error, mistake or problem immediately bring it to light and that everything be done to correct even a small error before it grows into a bigger one. Lindblom (1979) calls for:

> A greater analytical preoccupation with ills to be remedied rather than positive goals to be sought (p. 517).

Lindblom extrapolates this policy to point out that it is much easier to make major changes or improvements in organisations by a series of small changes, rather than through the establishment of major goals. This is also associated with the age-old observation that emergencies often offer an opportunity for desirable changes.

Both sources speak about the use of empirical aspects of any problem and the use of individual and team wisdom to focus on a limited number of solution options or alternatives, rather than trying to establish all possibilities. In HRO theory the term used is "sensemaking".

Today, the paradox we are faced with is that we do not really use any of this advice. Emergency teams made up of individuals from many different organisations do not exist until the emergency occurs. There is no continuous activity today to tie together all those who need to learn to be a team and to carry out these processes (Banuls, Turoff, and Lopez 2010, Yao, Turoff, and Chumer 2009). Furthermore, all too often errors are buried because of possible political consequences or fears of liability consequences which means they cannot be corrected. It is a wonder sometimes that we do as well as we actually do in many disaster situations. However, Katrina is an example we are going to be doomed to repeat if we do not make some fundamental changes to the way we handle preparedness for extreme disasters. The latest example of this is how the same mistakes were made in response to Haiti after the earthquake.

Supplies stayed stockpiled at the airport. Countless people died day after day while the medical supplies remained on the runway. The race to be a first responder organisation and the absence of a national command and control structure to integrate the response process was clearly a significant cause of this bottleneck.

9 Observations and Conclusions

We have mainly focused on the lack of integration across man-made boundaries which, if integrated, would compensate for the fact that disasters transcend these man-made boundaries. However, there is an equally important problem and that is the lack of integration of all the phases that must go on before and after a disaster that cross the same artificial boundaries (Turoff, Van de Walle, and Hiltz 2010). Those phases include:

- Planning (for all phases of a function)
- Mitigation (long-term reduction of risk)
- Training (for all phases)
- Detection and warning (for all disaster types)
- Preparedness (pre disaster event readiness)
- Response (to a disaster event usually short term)
- Recovery (which is dependent on all the other phases)

The professionals and managers who participate in the response must also be the ones who develop the plans. If this is not the case, it is unlikely the plans will ever work well. These same individuals should participate in all the phases. In large scale disasters that cut across even local organisations, we have many examples of impacts that create errors and significant delays in the response process (Chen et al. 2010). Based upon historical studies, we know that every effective mitigation option usually pays for itself in savings of three to five dollars for every dollar invested (Turoff et al. 2010).

Many of the proposed automated approaches to handling events in disasters are ineffective. What we need is creative and dedicated individuals trained and motivated to deal with the unexpected. This view is shared by others as well (French and Turoff 2007; Carver and Turoff 2007). Where we need automation is in helping to reduce information overload in the emergency management field. This field is growing a lot faster in the volume of documents than in the wisdom we are seeking. One of the biggest problems facing professionals in emergency management is the resulting information overload and the associated feeling that they cannot easily obtain the information they need to make better decisions in an emergency (Turoff and Hiltz 2009a). Too much that is obvious as to what needs to be done is not being done because of reasons such as our increasingly ageing infrastructure and a lack of emphasis on mitigation in emergency preparedness. Perhaps the one effort that might turn this around is the creation of an emergency preparedness and business continuity audit that would create a comparative measure for a given type of organisation or facility of how well prepared it was for an emergency event (Turoff et al. 2004b; Baksa and Turoff 2010). Finding agreement on the components of such an audit measure would be an excellent application of the voting technique by large, heterogeneous groups of professionals as discussed in this chapter. Many of the broader concepts discussed in this chapter have been more thoroughly covered in a recent *Handbook* chapter on "Decision Support for Emergencies" (Van De Walle and Turoff 2007).

Emergency preparedness and management, as well as business continuity and facilities management, is clearly an interdisciplinary area involving professionals from management, public administration, engineering, medicine and public health, the physical sciences and the social sciences. These divisions occur even in the universities and colleges. This compartmentalisation of the field into different disciplines results in research approaches that rarely look at the total problem. Research sponsorship by government bodies is also largely lacking any real interdisciplinary perspective. Those of us in computing often find what we can do to design more useful systems is forbidden because of these artificial divisions that prevent a general approach to the real problems of integration across the man-made physical, geographical and political boundaries. Added to this are the boundaries and barriers to interdisciplinary efforts that cross discipline boundaries. It is not so much that we cannot design real-time integrated decision support systems for this field, but more that the need for it is neither understood in the emergency community, nor in the computing community itself.

There is no way in the design of emergency preparedness and management and information systems that we can create effective decision support systems unless the problem is also viewed as tightly coupled to the communication properties of all the phases of emergency management and how they ultimately integrate with the need for supporting real-time decision analysis and actions.

References

Agarwal, R. and E. Karahanna, "Time Flies When You're Having Fun: Cognitive Absorption and Beliefs About Information Technology Usage," *MIS Quarterly*, 24, 2, 2000, 665–694.

Banuls, V.A., M. Turoff and J. Lopez, "Clustering Scenarios Using Cross Impact Analysis," in *Proceedings of the Seventh International Conference on Information Systems for Crisis Response and Management (ISCRAM)*, Seatle Washington, May 3–6 2010.

Baksa, R. and M. Turoff, "The Current State of Continuous Auditing and Emergency Management's Valuable Contribution," in *Proceedings of the Seventh International Conference on Information Systems for Crisis Response and Management (ISCRAM)*, Seatle meeting publisher online ISCRAM.ORG 2010.

Brehmer, B., "Organization for Decision-Making in Complex Systems," *Communications of the ACM*, 1988.

Brinkley, D., *The Great Deluge: Hurricane Katrina, New Orleans, and The Mississippi Gulf Coast*, William Morrow, Harper Collins Publishers 2006.

Carver, L. and M. Turoff, "Human Computer Interaction: The Human and Computer as a Team in Emergency Management Information Systems," *Communications of the ACM*, March 2007, 33–38.

Chen, R., R. Sharman, H.R. Rao, S.J. Upadhyaya and C.P. Cook-Cottone, "Coordination of Emergency Response: An Examination of the Roles of People, Process, and Information Technology," in Van de Walle, B., Turoff, M. and Hiltz, S.R. (eds.), *Information Systems for Emergency Management*. Armonk: M.E. Sharpe, Inc., 2010.

Churchman, C.W., "Wicked Problems", *Management Science*, 14, 4, December 1967. Guest Editorial

Clausewitz, C.V., *On War*. Princeton: Princeton University Press, 1976.

Conklin, J. and W. Weil, "Wicked Problems: Naming the Pain in the Organization." 3M Meeting Network, October 1998. http://www.leanconstruc/on.org/pdf/wicked.pdf

Danieisson, M. and K. Ohisson, "Decision Making in Emergency Management: A Survey Study," *International Journal of Cognitive Ergonomics*, 3, 2, 1999, 91–99.

French, S. and M. Turoff, "Decision Support Systems," *Communications of the ACM*, March 2007, 39–40.

Harrald, J., "Achieving Agility in Disaster Management," *International Journal of Information Systems and Crisis Management*, 1, 1, 2009.

Hiltz, S.R. and M. Turoff, "Structuring Computer-Mediated Communication Systems to Avoid Information Overload," *Communications of the ACM*, 28, 7, July 1985, 680–689.

Hiltz, S.R. and M. Turoff, *The Network Nation: Human Communication via Computer*, First Edition: Addison-Wesley, 1978; Revised Edition: MIT Press, 1993.

Kowalski-Trakofler, K., C. Vaught and T. Sharf, "Judgment and Decision Making Under Stress: An Overview for Emergency Managers," *International Journal of Emergency Management*, 1, 3, 2003, 278–289.

Lindblom, C., "The Science of Muddling Through," *Public Administration Review*, 1959, 79–88.

Lindblom, C., "Still Muddling, Not Yet Through," *Public Administration Review*, November/December 1979, 517–526.

Linstone, H. and M. Turoff, *The Delphi Method: Techniques and Applications*, Addison-Wesley Advanced Book Program, 1975, URL = http://is.njit.edu/turoff

Moss, M. and C. Shelhamer, "Communications and Catastrophe: Improving Robustness and Resiliency. The Stafford Act: Priorities for Reform," *The Center for Catastrophe Preparedness and Response*, New York University, April 20, 2007, URL = http://www.nyu.edu/ccpr/pubs/Report_StaffordActReform_MitchellMoss_10.03.07.pdf

Mowshowitz, A., *Virtual Organization*: Toward a Theory of Societal Transformation Stimulated by Information, Quorum Books, Westport, CT.

Moynihan, D., "From Forest Fires to Hurricane Katrina: Case Studies of Incident Command Systems," *Networks and Partnerships Series*, IBM Center for the Business of Government, 2006.

Moynihan, D., "Learning Under Uncertainty: Networks in Crisis Management," *Public Administration Review*, March/April 2008, 350–365.

Plotnick, L., E.A. Gomez, C. White and M. Turoff, "Furthering Development of a Unified Emergency Scale Using Thurstone's Law of Comparative Judgment, A Progress Report," in *Proceedings of the Fourth International Conference on Information Systems for Crisis Response and Management (ISCRAM)*, Delft, Netherlands, May 13–16, ISCRAM.ORG 2007.

Plotnick, L. and M. Turoff, "Mitigating Threat Rigidity in Crisis," in Van de Walle, B., Turoff, M. and Hiltz, S.R. (eds.), *Information Systems for Emergency Management*. Armonk: M.E. Sharpe, Inc., 2010.

Radvanovsky, R. and A. McDougall, *Critical Infrastructure: Homeland Security and Emergency Preparedness*, 2nd Edition, CRC Press/Taylor & Francis Group, 2010.

Rittel, H.W.J., and Webber, M.M., "Dilemmas in a General Theory of Planning," *Policy Sciences*, 4, 2, June 1973, 155–169.

Rodriguez, D.M., "Dominating Time in the Operational Decision Making Process, Final Report," *Naval War College*, Newport, June 1997.

Skertchly, A. and K. Skertchly, "Catastrophe Management: Coping with Totally Unexpected Extreme Disasters," *The Australian Journal of Emergency Management*, 16, 1, Autumn 2001.

Staw, B., L.E. Sandelands and J.E. Dutton, "Threat Rigidity Effects in Organizational Behavior: A Multilevel Analysis," *Administrative Science Quarterly*, 26, 1981, 501–524.

Thurstone, L.L., "The Method of Paired Comparisons for Social Values," *Journal of Abnormal and Social Psychology*, 21, 1927, 384–400.

Thurstone, L.L., "Attitudes Can Be Measured," *The American Journal of Sociology*, XXXIII, 4, 1928, 29–33.

Torgerson, W.S., *Theory and Methods of Scaling*, John Wiley and Sons, 1958.

Turoff, M., "Past and Future Emergency Response Information Systems, *Communications of the ACM*, 45, 4, April 2002, Hawaii, January, IEEE Press 29–33.

Turoff, M., S.R. Hiltz, H-K Cho, Z. Li and Y. Wang, "Social Decision Support Systems," in *Proceedings of the 35th Hawaii International Conference of System Sciences (HICSS)*, 2002.

Turoff, M., M. Chumer, B. Van de Walle and X. Yao, "The Design of a Dynamic Emergency Response Management Information System (DERMIS)," *Journal of Information Technology Theory and Application (JITTA)*, 5, 4, 2004a, 1–35.

Turoff, M., M. Chumer, S.R. Hiltz, R. Klashner, M. Alles, M. Vararheyi and A. Kogen, "Assuring Homeland Security: Continuous Monitoring, Control & Assurance of Emergency Preparedness," *Journal of Information Technology Theory and Application (JITTA)*, 6, 3, 2004b, 1–24.

Turoff, M., M. Chumer and S.R. Hiltz, "Emergency Planning as a Continuous Game," in *Proceedings of the Third International Conference on Information Systems for Crisis Response and Management (ISCRAM)*, Newark, New Jersey, May, ISCRAM.ORG 2006.

Turoff, M. and S.R. Hiltz, "The Future of Professional Communities of Practice," in Weinhardt, C., Luckner, S. and Stöâer, J. (eds.), *WeB 2008*, LNBIP, Vol. 22. Berlin: Springer, 2009a, 144–158.

Turoff, M., S.R. Hiltz, C. White, L. Plotnick, A. Hendela and X. Yao, "The Past as the Future of Emergency Preparedness and Management," *Journal of Information Systems for Crisis Response and Management*, 1, 1, January–March 2009b, 12–28.

Turoff, M., B. Van de Walle and S.R. Hiltz, "Emergency Response Systems: Past, Present, and Future," in Van de Walle, B., Turoff, M. and Hiltz, S.R. (eds.), *Information Systems for Emergency Management*, Armonk: M.E. Sharpe, Inc., 2010.

Turoff, M. and S.R. Hiltz, "Information Seeking Behavior and Viewpoints of Emergency Preparedness and Management Professionals Concerned with Health and Medicine," *Final Report for the National Library of Medicine*, March 6, 2008a, URL = http://is.njit.edu/turoff

Turoff, M. and S.R. Hiltz, "Assessing the Health Information Needs of the Emergency Preparedness and Management Community," *Journal of Information Services and Use*, 28, 2008b, 269–280.

Van de Walle, B. and M. Turoff, "Decision Support for Emergency Situations," in Burstein, F. and Holsapple, C. (eds.), *Handbook on Decision Support Systems, International Handbook on Information Systems Series*, Springer, 2007.

Van Den Eede, G., "Two Cases in High Reliability Organizing: A Hermeneutic Reconceptualization," Thesis, Tilburg University, 2009.

Weick, K. and K. Sutcliff, *Managing the Unexpected: Assuring High Performance in an Age of Complexity*, Jossey-Bass, 2001.

Weick, K. and K. Sutcliffe, Managing the Unexpected: Resilient Performance in an Age of Uncertainty, Jossey-Bass, 2007

Wenger, E., R. McDermott and W. Snyder, *Cultivating Communities of Practice: A Guide to Managing Knowledge*. Boston: Harvard Business School Press, 2002.

White, C., M. Turoff and B. Van de Walle, "A Dynamic Delphi Process Utilizing a Modified Thurstone Scaling Method: Collaborative Judgment in Emergency Response," in *Proceedings of the Fourth International Conference on Information Systems for Crisis Response and Management (ISCRAM)*, Delft, Netherlands, May 13–16, ISCRAM.ORG 2007a.

White, C., L. Plotnick, M. Turoff and S.R. Hiltz, "A Dynamic Voting Wiki," in *Proceedings of the 13th Americas Conference on Information Systems (AMCIS)*, 2007b.

White, C., L. Plotnick, R. Addams-Moring, M. Turoff and S.R. Hiltz, "Leveraging a Wiki to Enhance Virtual Collaboration in the Emergency Domain," in *Proceedings of the 41st Hawaii International Conference of System Sciences (HICSS)*, Hawaii, January, IEEE Press 2008a.

White, C., S.R. Hiltz and M. Turoff, "United We Respond: One Community, One Voice," in *Proceedings of the Fifth International Conference on Information Systems for Crisis Response and Management (ISCRAM)*, 2008b.

White, C., M. Turoff and S.R. Hiltz, "A Real Time Online Delphi Decision System, Version 2.0: Crisis Management Support During Extreme Events," in *Proceedings of the Seventh International Conference on Information Systems for Crisis Response and Management (ISCRAM)*, Seattle meeting publisher online ISCRAM.ORG 2010.

Yao, X., M. Turoff and M. Chumer, "Designing a Group Support System to Review and Practice Emergency Plans in Virtual Teams," in *Proceedings of the Sixth International Conference on Information Systems for Crisis Response and Management (ISCRAM)*, Gothenburg, Sweeden, May 19–14, ISCRAM.ORG 2009.

Chapter 10
Partially Distributed Emergency Teams: Considerations of Decision Support for Virtual Communities of Practice

Linda Plotnick[1], Murray Turoff[2], and Connie White[1]

[1] Jacksonville State University, Jacksonville, Alabama, USA
[2] New Jersey Institute of Technology, Newark, New Jersey, USA

Abstract Emergency situations often require cross-organisational response and planning by groups that are geographically distant from one another. Increasingly, individuals and these groups are leveraging technology to support a variety of communication and decision-making needs. This is creating an opportunity for groups, who traditionally worked in face-to-face environments, to accomplish these same tasks remotely using electronic communications resulting in new group dynamics. These groups, known as partially distributed emergency teams (PDETs), are managing crises, working together as a team of geographically dispersed collocated groups. This forms a flatter organisation which supports greater collaboration. Technology can be used to support creative ways that replace and enhance the gaps that are left from the transition of a F2F environment to a virtual one. There are underexplored methods that can be further developed to support virtual communities of practice communication and decision-making needs. We identify these gaps and suggest strategies to help build and nurture these communities. We conclude the chapter by describing the strength of online citizen participation and describe how using a global population can change the way some decision- making efforts can be enabled and enhanced.

Keywords Partially distributed emergency teams • Communities of practice • Trust • Social media

1 Introduction

When organisations work together to respond to, plan for or prepare for an emergency, they may well do so in partially distributed teams. This has implications for communication resources. Communication is critical to the building of trust and

L. Plotnick (✉)
Jacksonville State University, Jacksonville, Alabama, USA
e-mail: lplotnick@jsu.edu

F. Burstein et al. (eds.), *Supporting Real Time Decision-Making*,
Annals of Information Systems 13, DOI 10.1007/978-1-4419-7406-8_10,

team cohesion and the use of communications technology may reduce interpersonal and process conflict within a virtual team (Wakefield, Leidner, and Garrison 2008).

Research has suggested that communications media choices for partially distributed teams may vary within subteam and between subteam use and that trust is associated with frequency of use of those choices (Plotnick, Hiltz, and Ocker 2010). Media synchronicity theory (MST) suggests that media supporting lower synchronicity is best for the conveyance of information while for convergence (reaching agreement), higher synchronicity is called for (Dennis, Fuller, and Valacich 2009). This suggests that the system design should incorporate a variety of communications channels, both asynchronous and synchronous, and that all members be equally comfortable with all of the choices (Plotnick et al. 2010).

For emergency management ad hoc teams that cross organisational boundaries, this insight is especially important as within organisation communication media may not be compatible across organisations. This, again, points to the need to use a system before the emergency arises. For subteams from different organisations to effectively communicate and build trust, the common communication channels provided by the system must be used during times of low stress.

2 Partially Distributed Emergency Teams

Team coordination strategies often depend upon the situation the team is currently in. Team coordination strategies will evolve from explicit coordination under low workload conditions to implicit coordination as workload increases. Large-scale emergency operations imply distributed decision making in that decisions are disseminated amongst many stakeholders, amongst whom no single individual has complete knowledge of the current situation (Danieisson and Ohisson 1999; Mitchell 1999; Kowalski-Trakofler, Vaught, and Sharf 2003). Larger problems are better managed when command and control defers to expertise and delegates these subproblems to those in the field who can accomplish the task. This process often results in a distribution of small teams where some members may be located on the same site, while others are based somewhere geographically different Yet, both the dispersed members and those at the same site will need to be able to communicate across organisations and distance.

Often these groups are partially distributed teams (PDTs). A PDT is a hybrid team whereby there are some individuals collocated in subgroups, and the subgroups are distributed from one another (Huang and Ocker 2006). These subgroups must then work as a team using communication technologies, trusting these technologies and each other no matter the proximity. It is the objective of this chapter to discuss how the groups effectively work together to create a community of practice (CoP). It is important to identify and support the needs for these CoPs to have and sustain trust amongst the members of the team. A "primary product is a cultural commodity: civic and market trust in its managers' and experts' competencies" (Weick and Sutcliffe 2007, p. 44). In an emergency, people from each organisation that is involved in the response, be it one or many, may form such distributed subgroups. We describe such PDTs as partially distributed emergency teams (PDETs), extending the definition to be "a team that has subteams, some of which are distributed from others geographically and/or organisationally, but within a subteam the members are working together on a common goal." Therefore, within a subteam in a PDET, some members may be collocated or geographically distributed (or some combination thereof), but they tend to be in the same organisation, discipline or area of expertise (e.g., law enforcement, public works, medical, etc.). Thus, subteam identity is more easily developed than whole team identity as any two subgroups are likely to be distributed by a faultline that is geographic, organisational or functional. Electronic communication allows for the variety in team structures and allows for the fluidity with which these teams are formed and changed. In a PDET, membership is fluid with the nature of problems within the emergency and subteam membership can change such that members can have multiple roles and are part of more than one PDET group. Our extension of the PDT definition used in the literature is to recognise that organisational distributedness can create a faultline such that strong subteam identity can develop even when at a given time the members may not be physically collocated. However, we propose that in-group/out-group effects may still be manifest in such teams as subteam loyalty may occlude team identity. The challenge is for the subgroups to form an effective unified team.

A system must enable the teams to overcome the inherent difficulties of working in such PDTs. For example, collocated members may tend to have "collocation blindness" (Bos, Olsen, Nan, Shami, Hoch, and Johnson 2006) whereby they will resist reaching out to distributed members even when the best expertise lies outside of the collocated group. Deferring to expertise is something too often lacking in extreme events. Additionally, for deference to expertise to be effective, trust in both the system and in the distributed team must be in place. For this reason, the system must be available and used before an emergency in day-to-day communications so that people will already be familiar and comfortable using the system during time critical emergent situations (Turoff, Chumer, Van de Walle, and Yao 2004a).

2.1 *Trust and PDETs*

Trust is a critical factor for successful collaboration. It has been shown in PDTs to affect outcomes such as performance and satisfaction. Trust in PDTs has been shown to be different for early trust, when the team members first begin working together as a team, than for the longer term trust when the team has had experience working together (Plotnick, Hiltz, and Ocker 2009). Early on, before distributed members have an opportunity to get to know one another, trust may need to be based upon such characteristics as role and reputation forming a trust called "swift trust." As the members work together, they use their experiences to form feelings of trust of the other members. Both early and longer term trust are critical for groups whose lives are dependent upon one another. Teamwork, enabled by trust and inhibited by lack of trust, is essential in the efforts of teams such as fire fighters and SWAT teams.

Early trust has three dimensions: personal trust, process trust and expertise trust, all of which should be promoted by system design. Personal trust is based upon the interactions of the team; process trust is based upon inferences made from the process of the team members working together; and expertise trust is based upon a trustor's judgement of the trustee's expertise. While early personal trust and process trust are based upon actual early experiences, what is of particular interest is expertise trust which is a form of "swift trust" (Meyerson, Weick, and Kramer 1996) based upon cues other than experience (e.g., role, reputation). After the members have been working together, (longer term trust), expertise trust becomes subsumed by personal trust as the members have then had experience with the trustee's expertise and can form or maintain trust based upon that experience. A system should be designed to support and promote the development of all three dimensions of early trust and should be designed to promote the development of and maintenance of longer term trust. Expertise trust, for example, can be promoted by having profiles for each team member that list the affiliation, experience and areas of expertise of the member. In addition, homepages providing further credentials such as résumés, experience, publications and military background and deployments provide each other the detailed information that one may desire to know about another when considering their expertise.

Personal and process trust can be enhanced when people have a chance to express their views and compare them when difficult choices are being made. Ambiguities are reduced and better clarity in communications is gained which helps groups make better decisions (White, Plotnick, Turoff, and Hiltz 2007a). In an emergency, "swift trust" is common amongst the emergency workers seeking to cooperate in an overall effort to best manage a situation and reduce the potential of further harm and casualties. Information system design that allows people to know what others are doing and thinking, providing open participation and other associated characteristics, is very important for the development of trust.

2.2 Role Management to Support PDETs

Design considerations for a dynamic emergency system have been identified by Turoff, Chumer, Hiltz, Klashner, Alles, Vararheyi, and Kogan (2004b) Turoff, Chumer, and Hiltz 2006. These propositions describe the support needed for dynamically changing teams of experts as they respond to or plan for extreme events. By focusing on roles, changes in personnel assigned to the roles can occur seamlessly and not adversely impact the effectiveness of the team. Each individual needs to have access to information that is relevant to his or her effective response. Flexibility, robustness and a dynamic nature are keys to effective handling of such emergencies. It is proposed (White, Plotnick, Addams-Moring, Turoff, and Hiltz 2008) that a dynamic voting Delphi-like process can further increase effectiveness and ameliorate some of the problems that are inherent in rapidly changing, critical environments.

The people who will be the responders from many different organisations should be involved in the continuous process of planning and training together in an asynchronous virtual environment before the occurrence of emergencies. Users will meet one another and have a means of building trust within a virtual social network (Turoff et al. 2004a). Currently, large scale or unexpected events will result in numerous participants in the command, control, and analysis process who have not interacted before and/or don't have a plan that fits the circumstances. The secret for planning in emergencies is having a process that works and known resources that can be commanded, not in designing decisions ahead of time. Trust may need to develop quickly as swift trust, and/or have challenges not present in more static, well-defined situations (Iacono and Weisband 1997; Coppola, Hiltz, and Rotter 2004).

A person in a decision role may be reluctant to hand over that role to someone they don't know well enough to trust to carry out the role as well as they do. This is what leads to individuals working until exhaustion becomes a problem for making reliable decisions. Roles have to function on a 24 h, 7 day basis. This also requires systems that track accurately the status of any response so that those taking over roles can have all the information dealing with an open response event. Familiarity with a system is a critical factor, especially when the participants in a crisis are further challenged with duress from psychophysical symptoms (Turoff et al. 2004a) such as the threat rigidity syndrome.

In a PDET, leadership roles may be distributed in a number of ways. For example, there may be a leader in each subteam but no overall designated leader. Or, there may be an overall leader while the subteams are self-managed. There may be subteam leadership and overall team leadership or any combination of leadership configuration. Being distant from one's subordinates creates challenges for leadership. A leader must create "telepresence" to overcome the lack of cues available in face-to-face situations that make members aware of the leader's presence and position (Zigurs 2002). Just as the members need to have an awareness of the distant leader, leadership must have awareness, through system notifications, etc., of the distant subordinates so that expertise can be identified and decision making delegated to the right people at the best time.

It should be noted that PDETs are fluid by nature. Who is on the team and what subteams are involved are not static but need to be dynamically responsive to the situation. Additionally, the distant members may come together face-to-face depending upon the phase of the emergency (e.g., training exercises). Trust must be engendered both in the face-to-face meetings and through system support for virtual collaboration.

A significant problem that can face any PDT is group team dynamics where there is strong subteam identity and a distrust of distant subteams (Panteli and Davison 2005; Polzer, Crisp, Jarvenpaa, and Kim 2006). The face-to-face interaction within a subteam promotes subteam cohesion and shared identity. However, the strong identity with a subteam can result in preferential treatment of subteam members so that between subteams are dynamics that lead to distrust, threaten team cohesion and impede team effectiveness (Armstrong and Cole 2002; Hinds and Mortensen 2005). Given that within a subteam there is often a shared organisational culture that is not shared with the distributed subteams, this divide can be exacerbated. The goal, of course, is to develop trust across distance, both organisational and geographic, and to develop a shared team identity. System designers need to be cognisant of these goals and build into the system that which will promote the trust and development of shared identity. Leaders need to model trusting behaviours and make clear that the collaboration is necessary and expected to be effective.

In cross-organisational emergency response teams today, for the most part only the organisation leaders (subteam leaders) have communication with distant subteams (i.e., with leaders of other organisational groups in the team). Communication is the key to the development of trust and so this mode of operation may do little to promote mitigating in-group dynamics or little to promote whole team identity. A system that supports cross-communication between members, however, can help to promote whole team identity. It may be that communication between members of distributed subteams can also be advantageous for identifying expertise and deferring to that expertise. If members of subgroup A are lacking expertise in an area but have knowledge of a member in subgroup B who has the needed skills, if collocation blindness is avoided through the development of whole team identity, the expertise can be readily tapped to solve the existing problem.

Clearly defined roles are key as well. An emergency management information system should have templates that describe the relationships of roles and actors and the communication processes between the roles. Who will fill the roles may not be able to be determined ahead of time, but through templates, the support will be there. These templates can be filled in when planning a response to the particular disasters relevant for a given location or situation (Turoff et al. 2004a, b). Examples of roles for the general function of allocating resources are:

- A resource allocate who can allocae some portion of a resource for a certain set of targets, areas, etc.
- An observer who has important information on the situation for the group of roles concerned with the problem of allocating a resource.
- An expert or experts who have insights relevant to the resource allocation.
- A requestor who is concerned with getting that resource for use by the resource consumers he or she represents.
- An analyst who is concerned with trying to determine how long the resource will last.
- An oversight monitor who can veto an allocation if he or she believes that the addition of the resource amount is best used somewhere else or held in reserve until more information comes in.
- An acquirer who is trying to get more of the resource before the current supply runs out.
- A communications monitor concerned with finding others who need to be involved with a given situation for problem solving and ensuring that they know about the problem so that they can participate.

The larger the disaster, the more likely more unique roles are needed. There may be many resource allocators for the same resource handling different areas, for example.

Using templates enables the creation of new roles and actions during a disaster as needed. For example, one might dynamically include citizen observers at key locations in an ongoing disaster response. Thus, a system should support the flexibility of response needed to adapt and react to the changing environment of the disaster.

3 Training Members of PDETs

There are many challenges to consider when designing real-time decision support for PDETs. One particular theory is that, in order for people to best use a system for emergent stressed situations successfully, they need to use the system on a regular basis (Turoff et al. 2004a). One of the least effective ways to try to use a system is to use it when you have a dire need, but are unfamiliar with its protocol. We forget our login names and passwords, we forget how to do specific functions that require a sequence that may not be deemed logical by the user, and other high stress outcomes of rejection are likely. The system is only as good as the person who can use it. There are a number of ways this effort can be implanted into the design.

3.1 Wikis

One of our current efforts is focused on a dynamic voting wiki with quick access to group support tools for real-time information distribution across the Internet. Extreme events can span the globe and cross natural boundaries and given the multi-cultural, multi-lingual environment in which we live, a wiki should be considered. A wiki that can support many languages, thus lessening the interpretative burden that comes with not speaking the native language of the location where the most damage may be occurring, is proposed to be a suitable platform. For example, in response to the 2006 tsunami, many people and organisations came together, requiring great variation in languages, to make a rapid, timely response more manageable for a diverse group (White, Turoff, and Van de Walle (2007b); White et al. 2008). Some of the best wikis are free. For example, wikimapia (wikimapia.org) is an online editable map that is already in use in a few localities for letting citizens contribute to a preparedness database. They can indicate resources and potential trouble spots (e.g., locations that always flood, intersections that always clogs, location of contractors' bulldozers, boats available, etc.). Thus wikis are a Web 2.0 application that can support not only professional responders but the involvement of dispersed members of the public as well.

3.2 Gaming

A related effort has been to seek an appropriate multiplayer gaming environment where people may take on roles of defence or offence with respect to countering threats or making them worse. This would lead to an iterative cycle of improved plans with the uncovering of flaws on the defence and offensive side. Such games could be played continuously and asynchronously and offer the challenge to the participant of actually making it a part-time recreational occupation for training (Hendela, Yao, Turoff, Hiltz, and Chumer 2006). Unfortunately, none of the current generation of asynchronous groupware really provides the underlying knowledge structure needed. Therefore, we have currently been working on a system to allow for true collaboration in the formation and specification of any threat or defence scenario (Yao and Turoff 2007; Yao, Turoff, and Chumer 2009; Hendela et al. 2006). Once such a system is demonstrated, we have the key tool to develop a game that allows such scenarios to be played off against one another (Banuals, Turoff, and Lopez 2010). Choosing reactive options in such a game would function much like the decision support systems we have described throughout this chapter.

The recognition of the need for professionals who can adopt different roles at different times in an emergency argues for the importance of "role playing games" over the Web, which can allow professionals from many different agencies to be able to engage asynchronously in this activity as a continuous form of training. This is a natural extension of involving the practitioners in an emergency in a continuous planning process. This type of regular collaboration across organisations would involve the development and evolution of the fundamental scenarios of concern. One of the ignored problems in recent times has been the tremendous turnover of the people who need to be involved and trained. In corporate context, this is the classic problem of "organisational learning" and the lore of any operation that exists only in the minds of those involved in executing the operation.

The practitioners need to be made aware of the conflicts and different priorities of others supplying information and rationales for differing and conflicting options they may have to deal with. They must be made to realise that others in different roles will be facing the same challenges and that they may have different but valid rationales as to how and why a decision may have to be made and how that decision may affect other outcomes. There are very few "ideal" decisions that can be made in extreme disasters and one is only hoping for the best alternative as determined by the available information.

3.3 Collaborative Scenario and Exercise Generation

Scenarios are the best method for guiding the planning process and ultimately for explaining the plans to others. Collaborative scenario development on a continuous asynchronous basis, across all the organisations that might be involved in any given disaster, would serve a significant number of objectives:

- Training in how to use the same decision aids for real time decision analysis and support.
- Establishing a working team amongst those who will be the core of the response team in an actual disaster.

- Eliminating possible trust and conflict issues.
- Developing a working social group with all the desirable properties for a collaborative team able to cope with the difficulties of an extreme disaster.
- Using convenient hours for each participant by an asynchronous operation for the development of scenarios and the resulting plans.

Only by involving those who will execute the plans and people with expertise in user behaviour in a continuous process, will we overcome the limitations of current planning processes. We saw in the attempts at city evacuation in both New Orleans during Katrina and later in Texas how the lack of any understanding of human behaviour, possible ethical conflicts, and mistrust of government actions combined to defeat the objectives of the evacuations and assumptions of how it would occur. Gas stations, food stores and other services necessary to support the evacuation route were closed as owners and employees focused their efforts on helping their own workers and families. In Katrina, a large number of public employees chose to save their families before considering reporting for duties. There were also role abandonment problems with a large number of personnel of the New Orleans police department. Bus drivers who could not take their families on the bus chose to drive their families out in the family car instead of reporting for duty. In Katrina, the local governments waited too long to issue a mandatory evacuation order to the public. As a result, in Texas, the public left as soon as they could and did not consider waiting for the staggered area evacuation planned by the local government which was a key part of the plan to avoid congestion of the highways. Planning for real-time decisions is a highly interdisciplinary undertaking and the execution of the plans in real time will involve highly interdisciplinary inputs from a heterogeneous team of professionals.

4 The Gold Mine: Citizen Participation

Citizen participation is one of the most underutilised resources of emergency management. We will explore many different ways in which the community should be used in emergency response and the design issues that should be considered when information systems for crisis decision making are created.

4.1 Warning System Development

The overall goal of emergency management is to protect the citizens of our communities. Just as in planning and preparedness, the community should be considered and utilised when creating systems – especially when these systems are designed for the community members themselves.

We have been researching design issues and implementations of a disaster scale that would be more meaningful to the average citizen in a local area. For example, much criticism has been made of Homeland Security's Threat Assessment Level concerning its ambiguity and lack of ability to provide a message of warning of any real value. The scale we designed utilised the public from its inception. Further development of the scale is needed and many ideas should be tested. For example, on this given research effort, the scale would be scored in a local area by professionals and citizens who have lived and experienced similar disaster events in the past. It would be a collaborative online process for any of the typical disasters in the given local area. It would collect estimations on the types of damage that would take place locally (Plotnick, Gomez, White, and Turoff 2007). If we are going to take many types of extreme events seriously, we have do much more about meaningful citizen involvement as they are the ones who need to be prepared and are also the true first responders (Palen, Hiltz, and Liu 2007).

In one exercise, we took a graduate class in Emergency Management that had a majority of working professionals, and had them work through a Delphi process to come up with the most important measures of a disaster that could be used before, during and after the actual occurrence of the disaster. Such a scale would be dynamically changed based upon new information and the judgement of local professionals. The result of this is summarised in Table 1. The scale evaluated the importance of different measures of disaster to the nature of local emergency

Table 1 A Thurstone scale for the relative importance of measures of disaster impact (Plotnick et al. 2007)

Scale Rank	Scale Value	Disaster Damage Dimensions
20	20.00	Casualties and fatalities
19	–	–
18	18.00	Utilities impact
17	–	–
16	16.60	Potential to spread
	15.90	Ability of local response adequacy
15	15.43	Loss of command and control
	15.40	Infrastructure damage
	15.40	Resources for aid/containment
	15.38	Time needed for response
14	14.82	Duration of disaster
13	13.09	Public reaction
12	12.96	Geographic impact
11	–	–
10	10.07	Time to return to normal
9	–	–
8	8.61	Chance of imminent reoccurrence
7	–	–
6	–	–
5	–	–
4	4.70	Financial loss
3	–	–
2	–	–
1	0.01	Financial recovery costs

management. Note that what is reported in the news, financial loss, is represented by the two bottom items in the scale. For emergency management concerns, these are the least important criteria and had a group rating of 20 linear units less important than the top rated "Casualties and Fatalities." Any real measure tied to an anticipated or detected disaster needs to be a multi-dimensional scale with estimates of the most important parameters in this scale being part of a public meter for the current anticipated or occurring disaster.

It would be useful to repeat this sort of exercise with an interdisciplinary group of professionals in all the concerned areas of emergency preparedness and management. This should include an examination of the best ways to visualise the most important dimensions and recommendations to get a composite picture. This is the problem of visualising weighted multi criteria. One example of a visualisation method could be the circular population spokes of a polar type graph used to measure the relative values of plants and animals in a food chain or spoke diagram. In this case, the length of the base line spokes would be proportional to the weights determined by the use of the Thurstone's method, to incorporate the subjective judgements, and ordered in size to provide a spiral type boundary for the enclosed area. The current value along each linear dimension would be the subjective judgements, counts and/or samples being made before, during and after a given emergency.

4.2 Social Media and Citizen Participation

In recent years, there has been considerable use of social software systems by citizens to participate in the response to disaster situations. Many local groups have used systems like Facebook and Twitter to coordinate and gather information during an actual disaster. Some recent studies have recorded and presented specific examples of demonstrations of collective intelligence by citizen groups. Collective intelligence (Vieweg, Palen, Liuk, Hughes, and Sutton 2008; Hiltz and Turoff 1978) is a group arriving at a result which is better than any member might have made alone without the group interaction and contributions. Most groups that are new rarely have such an outcome and many face-to-face meetings fall victim to the outcome of "group think" due to the many possible process losses in a face-to-face group process.

In the aftermath of the Virginia Technology shootings, a Facebook group had all the names of the wounded and killed many hours before they were released by the police. This was a result of the students and the parents in Facebook pooling their information. While we cannot be sure of when the police had the result, we do have the interesting paradox that the police could not release what they had until every family had been notified, while many parents had already learned about their sons or daughters through Facebook. So, the public learned of the victims' names sooner by the social network site than from the administration or police (Vieweg et al. 2008).

Recent studies (Palen et al. 2007; Vieweg et al. 2008), have shown that citizen group collaborative intelligence is both timely and accurate, often leading to the dissemination of information before it is revealed by administrative or governmental agencies.

> For the inductively-derived issue of distributed problem-solving in times of disaster, the research objective is showing that the phenomenon of collective intelligence does, in fact, exist, and can exist in a directed fashion around focused tasks with self – regulated and accurate results. Furthermore, the phenomenon runs counter to popular mythology around disaster behaviour of civic post-disaster engagement as hysterical, prone to error and even dangerous – a view that pervades current disaster management policy and technological orientations (Vieweg et al. 2008, p. 46).

There is much more to be done here because citizens who are interested and particularly those who have experienced prior disasters in their area often can bring insights to not only the response phase but also to earlier planning and training phases, as well as suggestions for future mitigation activities or investments. The caution that is needed here is that the social network systems were not designed for this purpose and there needs to be an investment in the tools that will help to more directly support the collective intelligence process (Hiltz and Turoff 1978, 1993) and make it a great deal easier for it to occur.

4.3 Global Community Participation

Another study demonstrated more benefits to utilising the community, not only on the local level, but also including a global audience. Texas Border Neighbourhood Watch invited the Internet community to monitor and report surveillance cameras along the Texas/Mexico border. In one month, 230,000 users enrolled and generated over 27.5 million hits. The community provided the following critical components to success summarised in Table 2:

One can hypothesize that the dynamic Delphi described earlier is an ideal system for citizen use and one that will encourage collective intelligence outcomes. There is at least one experimental result where online Delphi teams had statistically significant better improvisation in their discussions than the same online discussion system without a Delphi communication structure imposed (Turoff et al. 2006).

Citizens do not just participate from afar. When a disaster occurs, before the first responders arrive, volunteers (citizens) may form ad-hoc teams to respond. These teams are emergent and the membership of the group depends on the situation at hand (Sebastian and Bui 2009). The concept of "helping communities" is as old as disasters encountered by tribal, rural or ghetto communities. Helping communities are diverse and include such examples as the Quakers (Society of Friends), Pennsylvania Dutch, and community groups such as churches and charities. The International Red Cross, recipient of the Nobel Peace Prize in 1963, is a global example, and perhaps one of the largest helping communities. It was founded by a committee of five Swiss citizens in 1863 as an international organisation to protect the sick and wounded during war (Nobelprize.org). As an organisation it has grown

Table 2 Community benefits: Texas border neighbourhood watch (Aud 2010)

Consistent audience	If it is on the Internet, someone will watch. The test run had over 230,000 subscribed watchers. There were over 5,000 subscribers in France and 9,000 in Germany. This is the power of the Long Tail.
Constant surveillance	If it is on the Internet, it will be watched around the clock. At any given time during the test run, there were over 1,000 watchers. Watchers were from around the planet, and by their local "prime time", participation ensured continuous observation.
Active participants	If watchers are given the means to respond, they will respond. Because a response/email button was included in the site, regardless of the hour, any event generated multiple responses from around the globe.
Self-vetting data	Because there were multiple simultaneous responses testifying to the same event, the responses were self-validating. Simultaneous emails detailing essentially the same witnessed event made the system all but impossible to spoof. The simultaneous delivery of messages with essentially the same content arriving within seconds was all but impossible to duplicate.

and developed to become a worldwide organisation dedicated to alleviating human suffering wherever it occurs.

A "helping community" is motivated by a number of factors including sympathetic identification with victims, individual sense of obligation, and the awareness that others are helping (norm) (Sebastian and Bui 2009). There are factors that can promote or impede these motivators. For example, Sebastian and Bui (2009) note that while positive social pressure can increase helping motivation, blaming victims for their suffering can be a demotivator. Other positive impacts include perceived severity of victims' deprivation, social randomness of deprivation, exposure in the media, direct contact with the victims, and positive social pressure. De-motivators include the number of victims and subjective deprivation counteracted by relative deprivation (Sebastian and Bui 2009). For an in-depth discussion of this, see Bui and Sebastian's chapter in this book (Chap. 8). For an earlier discussion of the confluence of factors that can result in a "therapeutic community response" or helping community see Barton (1969).

One can observe that many of the factors affecting helping communities, whether positive or negative, are very similar to some of the factors affecting regular disaster responders and can be categorised under the concept of threat rigidity. For example, a negative factor is the apparent lack of control in reducing negative consequences such as fatalities. This can lead people to have doubts about their ability to promote positive change. This can easily produce the effect of "blaming the victims" for such things as not leaving soon enough. Thus, understanding the factors influencing helping communities and disaster responders is necessary to develop ways to promote positive helping behaviours and ameliorate negative, blaming ones.

ICT support for these helping communities can help these true "first-responders" in their efforts. Templates have been suggested for use in an emergency management system (DERMIS) (Turoff et al. 2004a). The same concept can be used in preparing ICT for citizen participants. Sebastian and Bui (2009) suggest that workflow-based templates (which can be then filled in for the existing emergency) are one possible way to guide these emergent groups. The templates can help organise, represent and support action on relevant information. But, the focus should be on task completion rather than efficiency as the helping community may not have requisite expertise (Sebastian and Bui 2009).

Templates in disasters have to follow a metaphor of events-roles-actions-roles with other associated information (Turoff et al. 2004a). Events such as an accident or building collapse trigger the actions that many different roles have to take. Each of those actions, by its explicit choice, may in turn trigger other roles to take other actions. What these templates should allow for is the dynamic creation of decision tracking processes that include the alternative choices and the passing of the consequences to other such templates. The roles and action options chosen should be based upon the prior choice made. One needs to capture innovation as it occurs.

The same motivators identified by Sebastian and Bui (2009) for volunteers to participate in helping communities may be motivators for professional responders to join their organisations. Some of the factors are probably common to both volunteers and professionals for the response efforts as well (e.g., direct contact with the victims), but it must be remembered that, at the time of response, the professionals are likely to be very motivated by their obligations to the organisations to which they belong. Thus, the model of motivational factors would need to be modified to represent the factors impacting the response of the professional. However, the lesson of Katrina, when bus drivers and police failed in their duties because of competing obligations to their families, is that motivation is not a static thing but is fluid and can change given extreme situations. Personal motivators such as seen in helping communities may still be a factor for the professional when personal obligations conflict with professional ones.

5 Conclusion

Methods have been described in this chapter that can manage very large groups of individuals, be they PDET or traditionally collocated, crisis managers, large organisations or the public community. Given online systems and the Internet, these systems and methods have the potential to transform the way groups and organisations approach decision making from everyday tasks to new emergency response, all helping to network and foster these communities.

The landscape of collaboration support and technology is a rapidly changing one. For example, Open Source solutions are being developed by the government as a means to further support the needs of the community by developing software free for its citizens versus continuing to buy proprietary software that is costly to purchase and maintain. One of the most promising technologies for collaboration support in emergency management is that of social networking.

Social networks have great potential to support PDETs. Social networks are a recent phenomenon on the Web and are undergoing a rapid evolution. New concepts and ideas are emerging all the time and there is growing competition to attract and capture users. The collaborative functionality of social networking is expanding beyond the dedicated sites, such as Facebook, to other applications such as sites for sharing photographs and videos and even Google's new social networking application, Buzz. A primary objective of these systems is to capture the user and isolate him or her within the system. This will inevitably lead to confusion and information overload for those users who belong to a number of different social networks. In some cases, the functionality is limited and serves a narrow information transfer purpose (e.g., Twitter). Existing social networking sites can be general (e.g., Facebook) or serve a specific community (e.g., LinkedIn). In contrast to these silos of networking, the emergency management function ultimately requires integration across all phases of the process from planning through training and execution and into recovery. It requires the integration of those segments of the community that want to participate in any or all of these processes. Such functionality can only come from the addition of functionality specifically designed for this purpose. Thus, it is unlikely to be served by the social network systems being developed for general purpose and/or for profit.

It is interesting to observe that collaborative groups have been supported in the past in ways that are even richer than that offered by current social networks. For example, group collaboration has been supported by online learning systems; group decision support systems (GDSS); computerised mediated communications (CMC); computer supported cooperative work (CSCW); emergency management information systems; and online Delphi systems (White, Turoff, and Hiltz 2010). Developers and researchers would do well to examine those efforts and integrate concepts from them into the design of social networking sites for collaboration.

Thus, although the needs of the emergency domain are unlikely to be met by existing social networking sites, the concept is promising for supporting PDETs. What is needed is to design systems that focus on the more obvious capabilities initially and then evolve such systems in an incremental approach by carefully evaluating what is needed and how the system can evolve. The lack of current integration amongst different phases of emergency preparedness and management systems is a core problem that must also be addressed as part of bringing in citizen and community participation in these processes on a continuous basis and with integration in the command and control processes. The example of the Texas-Mexico border monitoring system previously described (Aud 2010) is an excellent example of the possibilities. Citizen watch groups have been tried around the country in various communities, but even with all the video monitoring that has been put into place, there has not be a movement to set up citizen-based monitoring in high crime areas despite the fact that such monitoring could be done safely from a distance with the use of technology. We need systems that can bring new users and organisations into participation using systems that are used on a continuous basis. This will overcome the classic problem that emergency systems that are not used on a regular basis don't work well when the actual emergency occurs (Turoff et al. 2004a). If these systems are to meet the needs of the users then, as suggested by media synchronicity theory (Dennis et al. 2009), a variety of communications channels (both synchronous and asynchronous) need to be included in the design.

Unfortunately, much of the sponsored research and development in this field is fragmented and focuses on different areas (e.g., law enforcement, fire fighting, public works, etc.) rather than on the collaborating community of responders. It is also subdivided by the phases of planning, detection, training, preparedness, response and recovery. This reductionist approach leads to a great deal of redundancy in R & D concerned with information systems in each of these areas. In part, this has led to the emergence of a new professional group that attempts to cut across these areas and focus on the general problems of the development of information systems for the emergency domain. Founded in 2004, Information Systems for Crisis Response and Management (ISCRAM.org) alternates its meetings every year between Europe and the United States. The yearly meeting is an affiliated meeting with the Association for Information Systems (AIS). ISCRAM also sponsors sessions at other conferences such as Hawaii's International Conference on Systems Sciences (HICSS) and Americas Conference on Information Systems (AMCIS). Through organisations and efforts of this sort, the need for more cross-organisational and integrated R & D can be highlighted which can ultimately lead to the development of systems suited for supporting PDETs. It is through this platform of communication and collaboration that real time science and engineering can be nurtured, information can be integrated and knowledge disseminated providing a new norm for group interaction and decision making.

The approaches described in this chapter for collaboration and the production of collective intelligence can be used to improve decision making during every day tasks but especially to support time critical situations. We defined a PDET as team of practitioners and/or administrators working together to manage an emergency such that the team has subteams, some of which are distributed from others geographically, functionally and/or organisationally, but within a subteam the members are working together on a common goal and have developed subteam identity. For PDETs we have extended the definition of a PDT such that for each subteam, at any given moment, members may or may not be physically collocated but they are working collaboratively on solving the same problem creating a faultline that distances the subteam from other subteams in the team. A subteam can be dealing with a number of problems and belong to different teams associated with each problem. In the emergency environment, the teams are usually more fluid and transitory than the subteams which can also exacerbate in-group/out-group effects that can impede the development of whole-team identity. However, with appropriate support, PDETs can provide a safer environment and lessen the potential destruction that can come from the immediate after effects of poor decision implementation.

References

Armstrong, D.J. and P. Cole, "Managing Distances and Differences in Geographically Distributed Work Groups," in Hinds, P.J. and Kessler, S. (eds), *Distributed Work: New Ways of Working Across Distance Using Technology*, MIT Press, Cambridge, MA 2002.

Aud, J., "TxMAP via LICONT," in *Proceedings of the Information Systems for Crisis Response and Management (ISCRAM)*, Seattle, WA 2010.

Banuals, V.A., M. Turoff and J. Lopez, "Clustering Scenarios Using Cross Impact Analysis," in *Proceedings of the Information Systems for Crisis Response and Management (ISCRAM)*, 2010.

Barton, A.H., *Communities in Disaster*, Doubleday, 1969.

Bos, N., J.S. Olsen, N. Nan, N.S. Shami, S. Hoch and E. Johnson, "Collocation Blindness' in Partially Distributed Groups: Is There a Downside to Being Collocated?" in *Proceedings of CHI*, Quebec, Canada 2006.

Coppola, N., S.R. Hiltz and N. Rotter, "Building Trust in Virtual Teams," *IEEE Transactions on Professional Communication*, 47, 2, June 2004, 95–104.

Danieisson, M. and K. Ohisson, "Decision Making in Emergency Management: A Survey Study," *International Journal of Cognitive Ergonomics*, 3, 2, 1999, 91–99.

Dennis, A.R., R.M. Fuller and S.S. Valacich, "Media, Tasks, and Communication Processes: A Theory of Media Synchronicity," *MIS Quarterly*, 32, 2, 2009, 575–600.

Hendela, A., X. Yao, M. Turoff, S.R. Hiltz and M. Chumer, "Virtual Emergency Preparedness Gaming: A Follow Up Study," in *Proceedings of the Information Systems for Crisis Response and Management (ISCRAM)*, Newark, NJ 2006.

Hiltz, S.R. and M. Turoff, *The Network Nation: Human Communication via Computer*, First edition 1978, Addison Wesley, Revised edition 1993, Cambridge, MA MIT Press.

Hinds, P. and M. Mortensen, "Understanding Conflict in Geographically Distributed Teams: An Empirical Investigation," *Organization Science*, 16, 3, 2005, 290–307.

Huang, H. and R. Ocker, "Preliminary Insights into the In-Group/Out-Group Effect in Partially Distributed Teams: An Analysis of Participant Reflections," in *Proceedings of SIGMIS-CPR'06*, Pomona, CA 2006.

Iacono, C.S. and W. Weisband, "Developing Trust in Virtual Teams," in *Proceedings of the 30th Hawaii International Conference on System Sciences (HICSS)*, Maui, HI 1997, 412–420.

International Committee of the Red Cross – History of Organization, URL = http://nobelprize.org/nobel_prizes/peace/laureates/1963/red-cross-history.html.

Kowalski-Trakofler, K., C. Vaught and T. Sharf, "Judgment and Decision Making Under Stress: An Overview for Emergency Managers," *International Journal of Emergency Management*, 1, 3, 2003, 278–289.

Meyerson, D., K.E. Weick and R.M. Kramer, "Swift Trust and Temporary Groups" in Kramer, R.M. and Tyler, T.R. (eds), *Trust in Organizations: Frontiers of Theory and Research*. Thousand Oaks: SAGE Publications, Inc., 1996, 166–195.

Mitchell, J.K., ed., *Crucibles of Hazard: Mega-Cities and Disasters in Transition*. Tokyo: United Nations University Press, 1999.

Palen, L., S.R. Hiltz and S. Liu, "Citizen Participation in Emergency Preparedness and Response," *Communications of the ACM, special issue*, March 2007, 54–58.

Panteli, N. and R.M. Davison, "The Role of Subgroups in the Communication Patterns of Global Virtual Teams," *IEEE Transactions on Professional Communication*, 48, 2, 2005, 191–200.

Plotnick, L, E.A. Gomez, C. White and M. Turoff, "Furthering Development of a Unified Emergency Scale Using Thurstone's Law of Comparative Judgment, A Progress Report," in *Proceedings of the Fourth International Conference on Information Systems for Crisis Response and Management (ISCRAM)*, Delft, the Netherlands 2007.

Plotnick, L., S.R. Hiltz and R.J. Ocker, "Trust in Partially Distributed Teams," in *Proceedings of the Thirtieth International Conference on Information Systems (ICIS)*, Phoenix, AZ 2009.

Plotnick, L., S.R. Hiltz, and R.J. Ocker, "Media Choices and Trust in Partially Distributed Teams," in *Proceedings of the 43rd Hawaii International Conference on System Sciences (HICSS)*, Kauai, HI 2010.

Polzer, J.T., B. Crisp, S.L. Jarvenpaa and J.W. Kim, "Expanding the Faultline Model to Geographically Dispersed Teams: How Collocated Subgroups Can Impair Group Functioning," *Academy of Management Journal*, 29, 4, 2006, 679–692.

Sebastian, I.M. and T.X. Bui, "Emergent Groups for Emergency Response – Theoretical Foundations and Information Design Implications," in *Proceedings of Americas Conference on Information Systems (AMCIS)*, San Fransisco, CA 2009.

Turoff, M., M. Chumer, B. Van de Walle and X. Yao, "The Design of a Dynamic Emergency Response Management Information System (DERMIS)," *Journal of Information Technology, Theory and Application (JITTA)*, 5, 4, 2004a, 1–35.

Turoff, M., M. Chumer, S.R. Hiltz, R. Klashner, M. Alles, M. Vararheyi and A. Kogan, "Assuring Homeland Security: Continuous Monitoring, Control & Assurance of Emergency Preparedness," *Journal of Information Technology, Theory and Application (JITTA)*, 6, 3, 2004b, 1–24.

Turoff, M., M. Chumer and S.R. Hiltz, "Emergency Planning As a Continuous Game," in *Proceedings of the 3th International Conference on Information Systems for Crisis Response and Management (ISCRAM)*, Newark, NJ 2006.

Vieweg, S., L. Palen, S. Liuk, A. Hughes and J. Sutton, "Collective Intelligence in Disaster: Examination of the Phenomenon in the Aftermath of the 2007 Virginia Tech Shooting," in *Proceedings of the Fifth International Conference on Information Systems for Crisis Response and Management (ISCRAM)*, Washington, DC 2008.

Wakefield, R.L., D.E. Leidner and G. Garrison, "A Model of Conflict, Leadership, and Performance in Virtual Teams, *Information Systems Research*, 19, 4, 2008, 434–455.

Weick, K. and K. Sutcliffe, *Managing the Unexpected: Assuring High Performance in an Age of Complexity.* Jossey-Bass, 2007.

White, C., L. Plotnick, M. Turoff and S.R. Hiltz, "A Dynamic Voting Wiki," in *Proceedings of the 13th Americas Conference on Information Systems (AMCIS)*, Keystone, CO 2007a.

White, C., M. Turoff and B. Van de Walle, "A Dynamic Delphi Process Utilizing a Modified Thurstone Scaling Method: Collaborative Judgment in Emergency Response," in *Proceedings of the 4th International Conference on Information Systems for Crisis Response and Management (ISCRAM)*, Delft, the Netherlands 2007b.

White, C., L. Plotnick, R. Addams-Moring, M. Turoff and S.R. Hiltz, "Leveraging a Wiki to Enhance Virtual Collaboration in the Emergency Domain," in *Proceedings of the 41st Hawaii International Conference on System Sciences (HICSS)*, Hawaii, Hawaii 2008.

White, C., M. Turoff, and S.R. Hiltz, "A Real Time Online Delphi Decision System, Version 2.0: Crisis Management Support During Extreme Events," in *Proceedings of the 7th International Conference on Information Systems for Crisis Response and Management (ISCRAM)*, Seattle, WA 2010.

Yao, X. and M. Turoff, "Using Task Structure to Improve Collaborative Scenario Creation," in *Proceedings of the 4th International Conference on Information Systems for Crisis Response and Management (ISCRAM)*, 2007.

Yao, X., M. Turoff, and M. Chumer, "Designing a Group Support System to Review and Practice Emergency Plans in Virtual Teams," in *Proceedings of the 6th International Conference on Information Systems for Crisis Response and Management (ISCRAM)*, 2009.

Zigurs, I., "Leadership in Virtual Teams: Oxymoron or Opportunity?" *Organizational Dynamics*, 31, 4, 2002, 339–351.

Chapter 11
Why Real-Time Transaction Processing Fails to Capture the Context Required for Decision Support

Fergal Carton[1], Frederic Adam[1], and Patrick Brézillon[2]

[1] Business Information Systems, University College Cork, Ireland
[2] Laboratoire d'Informatique de Paris 6, Université Pierre et Marie Curie, Paris, France

Abstract This chapter considers the problems in providing real-time decision support to managers using our observations of the distribution process in a case study of a multinational manufacturing firm. This firm is characterised by its reliance on an ERP (enterprise resource planning) package for transaction processing, but is also known for its use of more complex technical architectures for decision support. Our observations reveal that, despite the existence of a standardised and centralised ERP architecture, aligning this real-time transaction processing system with the reality of doing business is subject to constraints arising from both the business and virtual context of the firm. We explain the gradual and inevitable emergence of gaps between the inflexible ERP system and the decision support needs of managers. On the basis of the case studied, we conclude with a theoretical framework for the relationship between real-time transaction processing and decision support, differentiating between an information processing level and a decision process level.

Keywords Real-time decision support • ERP • Transaction processing • Case study • Middle managers • Impact of information systems.

1 Introduction

In the modern business world, the acceleration of business cycles and the increasing focus on short term objectives, particularly in multinational firms, are fundamentally changing the nature of the role of a large category of middle managers engaged in managing specialised business processes (Carton and Adam 2008). These changes have a significant impact on the type of decision support that should be provided to

F. Carton (✉)
Business Information Systems, University College Cork, Ireland
e-mail: f.carton@ucc.ie

F. Burstein et al. (eds.), *Supporting Real Time Decision-Making*,
Annals of Information Systems 13, DOI 10.1007/978-1-4419-7406-8_11,

these managers who, in many cases, only have access to an enterprise-wide system, e.g., an ERP (enterprise resource planning), in terms of decision support. Indeed, the type of information systems provided to middle managers in support of the decision making is also having an impact on the way they can or cannot contribute to their organisations (Pinsonneault and Kraemer 1993; Pinsonneault and Rivard 1998).

Some of the most fundamental changes in middle management decision making revolve around the acceleration of business cycles and the concentration on short term performance. In this chapter, we use a case study to illustrate the changing role of middle managers and the problems they encounter in effectively and efficiently running the segment of the business under their direct control, due to the lack of dedicated decision support. We take the example of the sales fulfilment process (referred to in the chapter as the deliver process) at SIT, a large multinational company in the high tech sector and show that the systems available to managers break down and provide no help at all when the process accelerates and decisions need to be made very rapidly, as is the case at the end of each accounting period. The case also illustrates that the difficulty in providing near real-time support at a decision making level raises very tangible and sometimes insurmountable technical and business issues. Indeed, even providing near real-time transaction processing is impossible in the case of large and complex firms. Critically, both technical and business issues are due to a large extent to the context in which managers and their organisations operate and the implications of this context for the way transactions are processed and the decision situations facing managers.

The chapter is organised as follows: firstly, we discuss the importance of context in providing decision support for managers. Then a methodology is presented that is suited to study the ability of ERP systems to capture context for decision support. Following this, the case study is presented and the intricacies of the deliver process are discussed to elicit the context in which decision making takes place and the related constraints. We then present our analysis of the case study and, leveraging our observations, we propose some conclusions about this case study. Finally, we consider what theoretical contributions can be drawn from the study in the form of an information processing architecture for decision support.

2 A Context-based Representation of the Decision Maker

Early MIS researchers suggested that the design of information systems should be influenced by the *decision* processes of the firm (Mason 1969; Earl and Hopwood 1980). Context is considered as the sum of two types of knowledge (Brézillon and Pomerol 1999), contextual knowledge and external knowledge. External knowledge may be the tacit knowledge known by the decision maker. Contextual knowledge is relevant to the step in the decision-making process and therefore depends on the decision at hand. A sub-set of the contextual knowledge may be proceduralised. Algorithms may be derived to trigger predefined responses to given stimuli. With the widespread adoption of highly proceduralised enterprise systems in organisations, management understanding of the basis of this proceduralisation is decreased, as the relevant business rules and workflow algorithms are embedded in the template processes of the ERP software. Some component of contextual knowledge is thus embedded in the software, and the manager loses the ability to apply his or her own discretion in decision making. Rather than providing a lens to help understand context, ERP systems can distort the perception of reality by providing managers with a poor virtual snapshot.

Furthermore, two types of change may influence the efficacy of the original system design. Changes or events in the real world context, such as a loss of a large customer or the introduction of a competing product, may influence the nature, urgency or focus of these processes. Secondly, changes may occur within the systems generating managerial data, such as a change in the calculation method for a key performance indicator or a change in the refresh cycle for a data warehouse. These changes may be instigated for reasons of technical efficiency, and managers may not be aware of either the changes or their significance. The combination of the system and the evolving business context can lead to blind spots in the decision process (Dechow and Mouristen 2005; Pomerol and Adam 2008).

In this chapter, we consider the relationship between transaction processing systems and the context awareness required for decision support by looking at one key business process at the sharp end of the supply chain: fulfilment of customer demand. We discuss the extent to which the incorporation of contextual knowledge in the business procedure has impacted decision-making capability of managers involved in the process.

3 Research Methodology

In this research, a case study of large multi-plant manufacturing multinational was carried out to explore the role of ERP in supporting managerial decision making. To support this objective, a framework of three research questions was designed, consisting of the following three questions. Research Question One was concerned with discovering the top-down goals to which the different functions work, the way in which these goals were "internalised" and disseminated throughout each functional organisation. Research Question Two was concerned with a more granular view of the execution of these goals, investigating what decisions were made by managers on a day-to-day basis, and what were the chief issues in making those decisions? Research Question Three drew on the output from Research Question Two by analysing the footprint of ERP in the decisional domains identified. In so doing, the research addresses the question of how ERP systems provide decision support (or hindrance) to managers in the different activity domains.

The SIT interviews were carried out in the period from April 2005 to August 2005 and involved meetings with 50 managers from different functions affected by the implementation of the ERP system. These interviews took place at two main manufacturing sites in Cork, Ireland, and Boston, USA. Table 1 shows the number

Table 1 Inventory of interviews by site and by function

Interview count	Cork	Boston	Total
Finance	5	9	14
Manufacturing/ distribution	13	6	19
Sales	4	3	7
IS	4	2	6
Engineering	2		2
HR	2		2
Total	30	20	50

Table 2 Coded observations for deliver process by function of interviewee

Function	RQ1	RQ2	RQ3	Total
Distribution	80	25	71	176
Finance	51	33	26	110
Information systems	30	20	15	65
Manufacturing	29	26	11	66
Materials	7	1		8
Total	197	105	123	425

of managers interviewed in each case, broken down by function and by site. An original facet of this research was that interviewees themselves were asked to define their *organisational goals*, and then describe their related *decision processes*. We also ensured that they related their observations to the key *business processes* of the firm. This ensured a rigorous sampling of the decision processes studied and a tight coupling with organisational objectives. Thus, our study was pertinent to the organisation as a whole and did not suffer from a manager centric vision of the impact of ERP.

All interviews were taped and transcribed verbatim in a set of electronic documents. Significant transcript fragments were then extracted into a set of spreadsheets using hyperlinks so that the linkage with the underlying raw data was never lost. Each extracted comment, together with demographic information indicating the identity and role of the interviewee, became a coded observation for inclusion in the data analysis. This gave rise to the recording of over 1,850 observations which were categorised by research question, by business process and by theme. The breakdown of these observations for the deliver process, which represents a subset of the total ($n = 425$), is shown in Table 2 below.

Triangulation of the findings was achieved through the diversity of backgrounds of managers interviewed. Comments on the deliver process were solicited from managers from different upstream and downstream functions. Managers in the materials and manufacturing functions are concerned with the upstream planning and execution processes which impact the deliver process. The distribution function includes managers directly responsible for the shipment of the product, thus the owners of the deliver process. Finance managers are dependent on the deliver process for revenue recognition procedures and invoicing procedures. Information systems managers have equally strong views on the deliver process as it represented the greatest technical challenge in terms of real-time information processing. Thus Table 2 shows that the comments regarding the deliver process came from a broad range of functions, and thus a measure of triangulation by functional area was achieved. Another validation approach used in this study was triangulation by organisational level. Comments on processes were recorded not just by colleagues in upstream or downstream functions at the local site, but also by peers at another US site.

Changes in the business context have a knock-on affect on control systems, but visibility of the original contextual evolution is often achieved from discussions about the system rather than the context. In the SIT case study, we uncovered a large number of such examples, not because managers told us about them, but because their impact surfaced in discussions regarding the role of ERP applications in supporting managerial decisions. Understanding the relationship between the business requirement for change and the perceived constraints of the system is a complex task. It justified the methodology adopted in terms of intensive interviewing and subsequent frequency counting to establish the intensity of the themes derived.

4 The Case of the Deliver Process at SIT

4.1 Context and Justification in Selecting This Case Study

SIT Ltd is a market-leading provider of data management solutions with products having evolved from mainframe storage systems in the late 1980's to platform independent network products by the mid-1990's. SIT's success is based on a winning formula of combining mass storage capacity with intelligent software that reliably manages large volumes of data securely and at high speed. Echoing the importance of the information managed by their products, SIT's highly pro-active field support is capable of diagnosing and rectifying a problem with one of its products before a customer realises there is an issue.

The company's rapid growth phase in the second half of the 1990's attracted much attention from the stock markets and analysts were drawn to the consistency of the company's performance. Demand for products was growing rapidly, with revenue growth consistently surpassing 30% per annum. In such a bullish market, the company simply had to decide what rate of production to aim for and then execute on that plan. Simultaneously, SIT began diversifying into content management software. Through a series of strategic acquisitions SIT increased its focus on commercial and medium-sized businesses, increasing transactional volumes tenfold (10,000 shipments per quarter as opposed to 1,000 in the past). Sales being driven by quarterly revenue targets, the company had always experienced the "hockey stick" effect of 80% of revenue being realised in the last 2 weeks of each quarter. The end of quarter stress was felt particularly by those at the distribution end of the business, where responsibility resides for converting the rush of late orders into shipments before the deadline of midnight on the last day of quarter. This is referred to in this chapter as the "deliver" process, which involves distribution, finance and manufacturing managers and operators.

The deliver process at SIT aims to ship all orders in the so-called backlog report. The distribution group is physically located near the shipping bay of each factory, and occupies a large area of the plant dedicated to finished goods. Shipping managers, although involved in relatively simple tasks such as picking, packing and shipping physical units, are key agents in the achievement of the corporate revenue goal, particularly at the crux point of quarter end. Key metrics for the deliver process are billings (shipped orders), backlog (approved orders ready to ship) and bookings (incoming orders). Executing on backlogged orders has become much more challenging as both the complexity of the product offering increases and volumes soar. Accustomed to a stretch goal mentality, this is an organisation where managers are rewarded accordingly. The "bust-relax" cycle of finishing each quarter with revenue targets achieved and no backlog is bemoaned but accepted.

We decided to concentrate on this process because stress builds on all elements of the sales order and distribution cycle, such that operators must operate in near real time in the last 2 weeks of each cycle, and the inefficiencies in the decision support provided to them by their transactional systems are rich in lessons for designers of real-time decision support tools. An additional incentive to focus on this process related to the fact that these 2 weeks were actually make or break for the company in terms of revenues – the decisions made by managers in the deliver process in that period of the cycle determine the margins achieved by the firm for the quarter, and quite simply decide whether the company reaches its revenue targets. Given the strong demand for its products, sales people were in the enviable position of being able to "cherry pick" from backlog (approved customer orders) those deals which best suited the requirements of the sales organisation in terms of maximising revenue, margin or achieving regional sales performance. Thus, the sales order allocation process was not so much allocating finished goods to a customer order, but selecting a customer order that best met the financial targets of SIT and allocating it to a product in finished goods. This involves both identifying the highest margin possible for each combination of a sales order and available inventory, but also trying to meet the corporate targets for product mix between the different categories of revenues.

At the same time, finishing the quarter with any orders left in backlog is considered a sign of under-performance in the deliver process, as this represents revenue "left on the shelf". In a key communication to shareholders in 1999, the CEO of the company highlighted that the key challenge for SIT was not generating business but in "execution", that is, the ability to deliver on commitments given to customers. It is this execution problem which is at the core of this chapter.

4.2 Information Systems Supporting the Process

A system developed and implemented with the help of a large consulting firm in the early 1990's was managing SIT's transactional workload. Sales orders, purchases and inventory were managed successfully on this system. There were two instances of this system, one in Boston at SIT's headquarters, and one in Cork. Two independent IS organisations existed in Cork and Boston, with a small number of local field support staff in every country. In 1998, a feasibility study recommended that SIT go ahead and implement an ERP application. In 1999 a software selection project resulted in the recommendation of Oracle™, principally for its flexibility in adapting to SIT's business processes. A single instance global ERP system based on Oracle™ applications was implemented in 2001. This "big bang" implementation addressed user requirements for transaction processing in back office activities such as sales order processing, materials, purchasing, manufacturing, distribution and finance. Covering over 43 geographies, the Oracle™-based system supported over 4,500 users worldwide. The first quarter end after implementation was successful, and by the second quarter end many of the transaction-related "wrinkles" had been ironed out. In the succeeding years, however, certain constraints imposed by the new ERP system began to bubble up to the surface as serious impediments to exploiting the full potential of the information stored within the ERP system. In relation to the deliver process, managers are supported on the one hand by the ERP application, which tells them line-by-line which sales order must be fulfilled. On the other, the production control system provides them with list of available inventory in terms of finished goods and their configuration, down to the level of the reference number on each electronic component. Matching supply and demand (the sales order to shipped components) is effected by shipping managers who instruct operators to make up the actual order to be shipped. This is reflected in the ERP application by a matching of shipped goods to each sales order.

5 Analysing the Case Study

In this section the main findings are presented, identifying the shortcomings of ERP systems in capturing the context required for decision support in the deliver process at SIT. Despite the investment in a highly integrated ERP system linking demand to supply, decisions relating to the deliver process at SIT remain manual. The constraints encountered are of two types – physical and virtual.

5.1 Decision Making Remains Manual

The core of operational decision making in the deliver process is the allocation of sales orders (representing demand) to available inventory (representing supply).

SIT has a manual sales order allocation process for the higher value products. The long production cycle, coupled with the complexity of the orders, means that products are effectively de-configured to order from the stock of finished goods on-hand. At the "Production Status" meeting, occurring daily as quarter end approaches, managers scan through a list of finished and semi-finished goods, making decisions on each unit's suitability for particular sales orders from backlog. The exact configuration of the order may not be available until extremely late in the quarter, as customers play a waiting game to secure the best price. The allocation of finished goods to many orders are initially made on a "best guess" basis, and then reviewed iteratively at this meeting. These product allocation decisions are typical of semi-structured decision making. The process relies to a large extent on managerial judgements, experience and relationships between the players. Due to the hockey stick effect on the pattern of quarterly sales, the allocation process at quarter end accelerates to such a speed that the ERP-based order administration system is left behind, and decision making becomes manual.

Backlog and booked orders are reported using a business intelligence (BI) tool to pull data from a data warehouse (DW) which itself extracts data from the sales order processing module of the ERP system. This BI extraction logic is required because the aggregation of sales orders in a manner that supports revenue related decisions is not possible to provide from native ERP reports.

Once the product has been allocated to these orders, the execution transactions – involving inventory release, picking and shipment – are automated on the ERP, with invoicing automatically triggered by shipment. To further emphasise the manual nature of allocation decisions, it is underlined that if suitable cabs are not found in finished goods, then distribution begins moving upstream to look at cabs coming through test. This means a product on its way through production may be allocated to a sales order several times over, because this *unofficial* allocation process is not recorded anywhere. SIT is conscious that the sustainability of such a process, which relies ultimately on people more than data, is doubtful as the shipment volumes increase exponentially.

The limited value of information systems to the deliver process arises from the marriage of a traditional focus on each and every order with a sophisticated but data hungry administration tool. The constraints arising from each party in the marriage are discussed in the next two sections.

5.2 Constraints Arising from the Physical Business Context

For the SIT deliver process, finishing the quarter with a backlog of orders is considered a sign of under-performance, as this represents revenue "left on the shelf". Distribution managers are responsible for honouring customer requirements, within the lead time specified on the sales order, no matter how late the orders are actually received. The approach of quarter end sees a radical shrinking of order turnaround time. Product allocation and shipment decisions made by managers at this point are made in a starkly different context to that in which the same decisions are made in the first 10 weeks of the quarter. This is because the decisions hinge on a rapidly shrinking window of opportunity to physically complete orders. This has two implications for decision making. Firstly, the exact value of individual sales orders in terms of revenue and profitability becomes critical for corporate level visibility of performance against targets. Secondly, the reconfiguration of an item in finished goods for one sales order represents an opportunity cost in terms of its potential for a different sales order. Managers must take a gamble that the re-work required is feasible within the timescales allowed. The decision context is altered simply by virtue of its timing in the quarter.

The joint pressures of an expanding product range and increased volumes have made the current way of manually allocating product untenable. Much of the lower end product requires no configuration, is fixed price, and therefore is suitable for automatic allocation. Furthermore, the concept of a global fulfilment process is emerging, where any customer could order any combination of hardware, software or service. These orders could be sourced from any one of seven or eight locations, including other field locations. Historically customers were associated with a specific plant by the "ship-to" address on the order. The US plant served US-based customers; the Cork plant served all others. Running over 40% of its business through the Cork plant allows SIT to benefit from the advantageous corporate tax rate in Ireland by centralising accounts receivable payments through the Irish set of books. Flexibility is key in this strategy as fiscal climates in the 50 different jurisdictions where SIT has a presence may evolve over time. Doing business in an evolving marketplace also necessitates flexibility in terms of the optimal configuration of plants, subsidiaries and revenue processes.

Cultural differences also account for variances in how similar information is aggregated and reported. For example, different sites have different versions of a key global metric such as backlog. According to one corporate IS manager, it is these cultural differences, stemming from an unwillingness to standardise local business processes to a corporate standard, that has bedevilled the usefulness of ERP to manufacturing. Manufacturing plants have strong local cultures, often identified with the style of leadership of their general managers, and although a common system may be imposed, users will find ways to "tune the transaction system" to the local way of doing things. Cultural differences also account for the level of trust shown by distribution in the sales organisation. Sales reps will vary in the reliability of the commitments they ask of manufacturing, and distribution managers are intuitively aware of the trustworthiness of the information they receive coming from the field.

This notion of demand trustworthiness introduces another discrepancy with respect to the ERP system. If a customer requirement is known about but the actual order has not been received, sales operations create a "planned order" which reserves a piece of inventory on behalf of the customer. Planners push these orders, known also as Build to Stock (BTS) orders, through to backlog to simulate the expected demand before the actual order has been received. This ensures the factory will secure the necessary manufacturing capacity in advance, but it may not be a good reflection of what the actual order will look like. Such allocations are made because as deadlines approach and in the absence of any harder information, Distribution has "to get something out". The tactic in effect increases the pull from the demand side (backlog), thereby reserving units from work in progress, which tends to increase the push from the supply side. However, it also corrupts the integrity of the data in the ERP system, as the BTS order has no link to actual demand.

These contextual factors provide some degree of illumination on the changing nature of the decision making scenarios for managers involved in the deliver process, demonstrating that these decisions are subject to external and internal influences on how business is carried out. The deliver process is where "the rubber meets the road" in terms of what the organisation promises to customers and shareholders versus what it can physically deliver. In the next section the constraints on distribution that arise from the use of the ERP system are examined.

5.3 *Constraints Arising from the Virtual Context (System Related)*

Allocation decisions are constrained by several factors arising from the use of ERP. Firstly, technical latency related to the reporting infrastructure impacts management decision making at the most critical point in the business cycle. High-level revenue attainment decisions can only be made with clear visibility of up-to-the-minute aggregated information for bookings (incoming sales orders), backlog (approved sales orders ready to ship), billings (shipped) and inventory. This information derives from the ERP system, as the only system of record for customer orders and their status. SIT employs a three-tier infrastructure for management information, mirroring live ERP data to a data warehouse, from where it is "published" via a business intelligence (BI) tool. As quarter end approaches and the system is dealing with heightened bookings activities, the single instance ERP system exhibits a degradation in response times. Its ability to keep backlog and billings up-to-date is impaired, in some cases resulting in the system running up to several hours behind the physical transactions. This means that despite shipment transactions being completed, management cannot see the corresponding orders moving off backlog, and therefore loses visibility of performance to target. This slowdown can have drastic consequences from a decision making perspective, as a corporate controller for revenue reporting iterated:

> ...that lag means people are making bad decisions, uninformed decisions, and having a disconnect in time between incoming and outgoing, people wasting their time with transactions that are incomplete....

The IT department has reacted to the technical latency issues by tuning the system for better performance, investing in higher processing power, but also by prioritising the processing power for the critical tasks. Native ERP reports, which would not suffer the same technical latency, were not considered adequate, as users are unable to filter or aggregate the information displayed. The abundance of the same level of detail on the standard backlog reports makes it difficult to answer questions that require an aggregated view, as confirmed by a Cork-based distribution supervisor:

> But it's not OK if you want to see how many orders you have now, what's the total backlog, how many Product As are there in the UK operating unit, how many Product B orders, how does it break down. You can't see any of that on Oracle...

Secondly, the flexibility in allocating (and re-allocating) product to sales orders proves difficult to incorporate into a generic ERP model, which considers that allocated inventory is "consumed", and therefore initiates a sequence of transactions that would be complicated, if not impossible, to roll-back in the event of a re-allocation. At the time of the case study, and with the benefit of hindsight, managers could see how customising the ERP system to their own local processes for the high margin product has ultimately limited its usefulness as the importance of that product line in revenue growth is diminishing.

Thirdly, using such a rigid process template for the administration of operational activities ignores the fact that the way of doing business evolves over time. Workarounds are implemented to adapt to the new business context, undermining data integrity. The growing volume of business with channel partners, for example, meant that the situation arose where SIT was shipping the same product via two different distribution channels, one direct from an SIT plant, the other via a channel partner. In order to differentiate between the two types of revenue, two different model numbers were used, without a second thought for the impact on data integrity.

Finally, distribution is witnessing high error rates on orders coming through to backlog for execution. Even for traditional high-end SIT products that are manufactured locally, orders coming through to distribution do not necessarily represent configurable and workable systems. This is more of an issue for the Cork plant, where orders are coming in from decentralised order administration groups in many different countries. In the USA, where plants have a centralised order administration group, orders that are incorrect are rejected outright. In Cork, a more tolerant approach is taken. A product configuration system (PCS), which interfaces to the Oracle sales order module, allows sales reps to build an order by compiling system components and calculating the associated price. The system will allow systems to be built that are not necessarily legitimate, as stated by a distribution supervisor in Cork:

> ...as long as it's buildable, the system will allow you to order it. The fact is, it might be buildable, but you can't plug the bloody thing in. You plug it in, it'll blow up...

Ultimate responsibility for the operability of the systems shipped rests with one highly skilled distribution employee. This person reviews the results of a configuration accuracy report, run just prior to shipment, and will decide whether to override the "Incorrect Configuration" flag or not. SIT acknowledges that the reliance of the entire fulfilment process on the manual intervention of one employee is clearly unsustainable. Equally, it is highly inefficient that many orders must be manually "interpreted into real product". Worse still, this lack of data integrity introduces latency in the process – at quarter end when distribution can least afford it.

In spite of the use of PCS to assist in the configuration and pricing of products by the sales organisation, according to a distribution manager in Cork, as many as 20% of the orders coming through to shipping have configuration errors. Inaccuracy in the master data is a possible reason for this. But erroneous sales orders are also a symptom of the seasonality of business activity as attention to detail is forfeited for speed of data entry in the last days of quarter. The configuration of the ERP system for international operations may also account for some of the inaccuracy. The set-up of each country in ERP involves the definition of different operating units, each with its own currency, chart of accounts and customers. Sales orders with currency problems form their own category of rejected orders, for example. On the other hand, customers in the US market are served by one operating unit, using one currency and with sales territories organised by state, area and district. A common gripe amongst Irish customer operations was that their US colleagues did not understand the complexity of doing business outside the US.

5.4 Decoupling the ERP System

The above constraints of technical latency, data integrity, workarounds, and process flexibility hamper the usefulness of ERP to the allocation and shipment process. The net effect of these constraints is that a slowdown in administrative processes threatens the actual physical execution of shipments. In reality, SIT has developed an ingenious customisation which puts the integration obligations of the system temporarily on hold. ERP-based transactions are put to one side during the final hours of the quarter while management, supervisors and technicians concentrate on the physical shipments to satisfy revenue goals. As long as the shipment takes place before midnight on the last day of quarter it can be considered recognisable for revenue. An auditor present on the loading bay at midnight ensures that the doors close promptly. Revenue recognition rules do not preclude, however, that the data entry involved with the shipping of the order can take place after the physical shipment of the goods. So, as long as the system date has not automatically rolled forward, the keying for previous day shipments can be continued into the next day of the new period, giving shipping clerks the vital 24 h they need to catch up with the last minute flurry of physical activity involved in packing and loading product onto the waiting trucks.

However, the downside of allowing reality and its virtual counterpart (the ERP system) to diverge is the ensuing manual workload in rectifying the variance. During the denouement of the frantic phase of shipping activity at quarter end, on Day 32, it is possible that a mismatch between a shipped order and the order in backlog will occur, as evidenced by one order to cash director:

> Now you come in the next day, to find out that the order doesn't quite line up with what you shipped, because you didn't have full visibility to the final detailed order.

The existence of such a feature and its importance in facilitating quarter end activity powerfully demonstrate the technical acrobatics required in order to make an integrated system adapt to the constraints of the real world. Attributable both to the limitations of the software and to the self-imposed constraints of a micro-managed distribution process, the result is that the value of an integrated tool for decision making is forfeited at the very moment it is most required. For managers and technicians in the deliver process, the data integrity issues caused by the imposition of a standard ERP template leave them responsible for customer critical configuration choices at the point of order execution.

The deliver process is the junction between a virtual customer requirement and a physical piece of inventory. A typical ERP system automates the administration of both sales orders and inventory movements. In this case, however, and our research suggests SIT is no exception, integration has been decoupled between supply and demand. The implications of this decoupling for decision support are discussed in the next section of this chapter.

6 Discussion

In seeking to learn from this case, we have endeavoured to formalise our observation in the model in Fig. 1.

Organisations implement ERP systems for reasons of co-ordination and control. The ERP system simultaneously standardises bureaucratic processes and centralises control of the information generated. The integration of ERP into the organisation introduces a high level of detail in data collection, resulting in an increase in data accuracy and consistency. Benefits of performance analysis and variation tracking

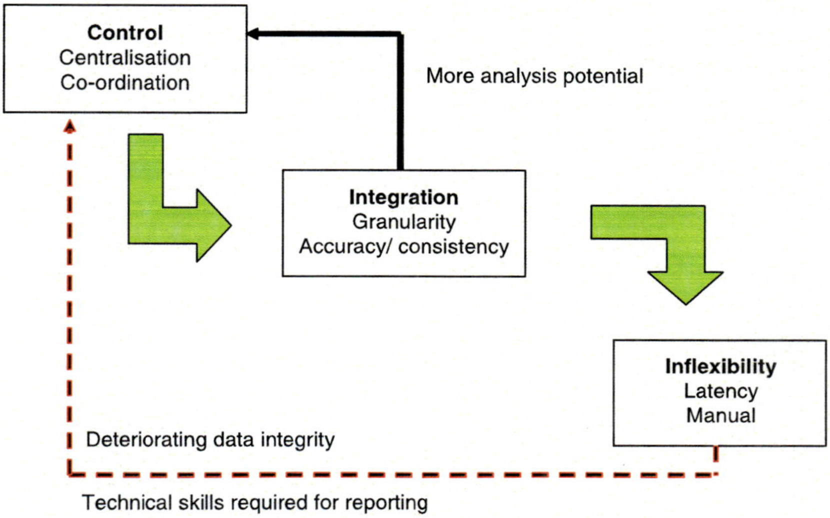

Fig. 1 How control objective of ERP integration is undermined by inflexibility

are derived. However, at the transactional interface, users find data collection cumbersome, and sometimes ill-adapted to their requirements. Modification of the ERP system is not considered, because the organisation wants to maintain its upgrade path to the next version of the ERP software. Because of this, users and managers begin to process information in an off-line manner. This in turn leads to slower and more complex decision processes and a deterioration of data integrity. Ultimately, the data integrity issues will undermine the control objectives of the ERP system.

Thus, many ERP implementations are characterised by functionality gaps between the logic coded in the ERP application and the reality of everyday business. Particularly at local sites within multinational corporations, resistance to template processes is a result of a strong cultural belief in a way of doing business that is specific to the local context. This is exemplified by the over-constrained decision process surrounding product shipment where the allocation decisions rely on input from three different sources of constraint. The configuration system (PCS) provides legitimate configurations from a commercial perspective, but this may be overruled by constraints arising from financial and inventory objectives. Shipments are made on the basis of both revenue targets and inventory utilisation, thus a manual satisficing model is the only option. Certainly the decision support capabilities of configuration tools needs to be re-evaluated in view of the increasing volume of standard configurations being sold.

The context specific nature of decision making is even more pertinent at a managerial level. Indeed, a recent study (André and Roy 2007) of environmental dashboards in total (a large multinational in the energy sector) that any dashboard tool designed to help managers to monitor parameters under their control must primarily be able to account for the specific context in which managers operate. In that case, as in many multinational companies, there is sometimes an opposition between central actors at headquarters level and local managers. Notwithstanding a heavily centralised and integrated IS infrastructure, dashboard tools must absolutely retain their ability to be customised locally, including in terms of the fine-tuning of the data that is injected into them. The success of dashboards of information for decision support relies on the fit between these tools and the level of understanding of the managers who are destined to use them (Adam and Pomerol 2008). A framework for classifying decision support requirements was defined according to the nature of the problem being looked at, moving from reporting facilities through support for managerial scrutiny and ultimately to serve problem discovery requirements (Adam and Pomerol 2008). On-line ERP systems certainly support the reporting of operational data, but their lack of support for managerial scrutiny and discovery explains the wealth of evidence of off-line data manipulation. The classification of such requirements should be an ongoing debate between developers and managers and one that takes into account both the shortcomings of the ERP architecture, including the multiple reporting layers used to interpret transactional data into business intelligence.

The final section of this chapter builds on this view of the relationship between real-time transactional systems and the decision support requirements for managers, using the empirical data gathered in the SIT case to propose a framework upon which further research may be based.

7 Conclusions and Guidelines for Technological Solutions

It is recommended that information systems practitioners and academics considering the use of integrated enterprise systems (such as ERP) for decision support use a framework to characterise the use of real-time information in the organisation in advance of the implementation of such complex solutions. The SIT case demonstrates the complexity of the technical architecture that had evolved to support managerial requirements for decision support. Based on this finding, and drawing on the work of DSS researchers (Adam and Pomerol 2008), a new framework is suggested, as shown in Fig. 2, to depict the cumulative value of information processing for decision makers in much the same sense that manufacturing can be thought of as a value adding process for the transformation of raw materials into finished products.

Starting with the capture of transactional data at the ERP level, information handling is automated by the rules and processes embedded in the ERP system. These rules might govern the processing of a sales order for example, such that legitimate data is entered for product configuration. The principle benefit for decision makers is the data integrity imposed by the use of the ERP system, as well as the workflow automation encapsulated in the system configuration. Data is typically extracted from the ERP system into a data warehouse (DW) for reporting purposes. The value to decision makers is in the reduction of information to those aspects of interest to the context of the decision, as well as allowing the correlation with data from other applications such as forecast and planning tools. A reclassification of data is required at this stage such that the operational data from the ERP system is recalibrated to match the parameters used by decision makers. For example, cost centre information might be manipulated to provide logical views of performance that correspond to organisational responsibilities. This re-classification may involve a mixture of data warehouse and business intelligence (BI) tools, and the benefit to the decision maker is the interpretation of data that arises from

Information processing layers	Software tools	Value to decision makers	DSS level
Discovery layer (interactive)	Spreadsheet	Interactivity	Decision process
Scrutiny layer (flexible presentation)	BI	Flexible presentation	
Reporting layer (pivots, broadcast rules, ...)	BI	Real-time visibility	
Consolidation logic and reconciliation (meta data)	DW and BI	Business focus	Information process
Interface layer (from planning systems)	DW	Correlation for control	
Extraction layer (which tables, when, where, ...)	DW	Data reduction	
Business rules and template processes	ERP	Efficient workflows	
Transaction layer	ERP	Data integrity	

Fig. 2 Information processing architecture for real-time decision support

operational ERP processes into a form that equates to the priorities of management control and performance measurement.

These first five layers of information processing, as shown in Fig. 2, are related to the manipulation of data into a format suitable for decision support. The next three layers correspond to the decision processes for which the information is used, and relate to reporting, scrutiny and discovery dimensions (Adam and Pomerol 2008). The use of BI tools and ultimately spreadsheets for the decision process level may introduce undesirable side affects such as latency and "multiple versions of the truth", as evidenced by the SIT case. Certainly the original value of data integrity derived from the ERP implementation is diluted by the use of data presentation and manipulation tools that take the user further from the real-time nature of the transaction layer.

It is not suggested that this framework will apply to all organisations, nor that the classification of software tools found in the SIT case can be generalised. However, it is recommended that both practitioners and academics would derive analytical benefit by viewing the processing of information in the enterprise according to the layers in this framework, identifying the technology and value-add at each level. At the very least, this would shed light on the role of information processing in real-time decision support, and the nature of the interface between these two domains.

References

Adam, F. and J.C. Pomerol, "Developing Practical Support Tools Using Dashboards of Information," in F. Burstein and C. Holsapple (Eds), *Handbook on Decision Support Systems, International Handbook on Information Systems Series*. London: Springer, 2008, 151–174.

André, S. and B. Roy, "Conception et mise en place d'un outil d'évaluation de la performance environnementale: le cas des raffineries de la société Total," *Journal of Decision Systems*, 16, 3, 2007, 335–367.

Brézillon, P. and J.C. Pomerol, "Contextual Knowledge Sharing and Cooperation in Intelligent Assistant Systems," *Le Travail Humain*, 62, 3, 1999, 223–246.

Carton, F. and F. Adam, "Investigating the Impact of ERP In Collaborative Decision Making – A Case Study in Distribution," in P. Zaraté et al. (Eds), *Collaborative Decision Making: Perspectives and Challenges*. Amsterdam: IOS, 2008, 295–307.

Dechow, N. and J. Mouristen, "Enterprise Resource Planning Systems, Management Control and the Quest for Integration," *Accounting, Organizations & Society*, 7, 8, October 2005, 691–733.

Earl, M.J. and A.G. Hopwood, "From Management Information to Information Management," in H. Lucas, F. Land, T. Lincoln and K. Supper (Eds), *The Information Systems Environment*. North-Holland: International Federal for Information Processing (IFIP), 1980, 133–143.

Mason, R., "Basic Concepts for Designing Management Information Systems," AIS research paper #8, October 1969.

Pinsonneault, A. and K.L. Kraemer, "The Impact of Information Technology on Middle Managers," *MIS Quarterly*, 17, 3, September 1993, 271–292.

Pinsonneault, A. and S. Rivard, "Information Technology and the Nature of Managerial Work: From the Productivity Paradox to the Icarus Paradox?" *MIS Quarterly*, 22, 3, September 1998, 287–311.

Pomerol, J.C. and F. Adam, "Understanding Human Decision Making – A Fundamental Step Towards Effective Intelligent Decision Support," in G. Wren (Ed.), *Intelligent Decision Making: An AI Based Approach*. London: Springer, 2008, 3–40.

Chapter 12
Continuous Auditing as a Foundation for Real Time Decision Support: Implementation Challenges and Successes

Robert Baksa and Murray Turoff

New Jersey Institute of Technology, Newark, New Jersey, USA

Abstract Continuous auditing has the potential to transform the existing audit paradigm from periodic reviews of a few accounting transactions to a continuous review of all transactions which thereby could vastly strengthen an organisation's risk management and business processes. Although some continuous auditing implementations are occurring now, their adoption is slower than expected. Continuous auditing systems require that human judgement be formalised and automated which can be a complex, costly and computationally intensive endeavour. However, continuous auditing systems have similarities with emergency management and response systems which integrate continuous auditing's detection and alerting functions with the tracking of decisions and decision options for situations that could be more effectively handled by human judgement. Emergency management and response systems could provide an effective prototype to help overcome some of the implementation obstacles that are impeding the implementation rate of continuous auditing systems.

With the goals of providing an empirical and methodological foundation for future continuous auditing systems and accelerating their rate of implementation, this chapter provides several definitions of continuous auditing, suggests possible architectures for these systems, lists some common implementation challenges and describes a few successful implementations.

Keywords Continuous auditing • Decision support • Emergency management

1 Introduction

Historically, organisations have relied on manual control testing to assess and mitigate risk in their operating environments. Control testing tends to be performed on a retrospective and cyclical basis, which often occurs many months after the

M. Turoff (✉)
New Jersey Institute of Technology, Newark, New Jersey, USA
e-mail: turoff@njit.edu

F. Burstein et al. (eds.), *Supporting Real Time Decision-Making*,
Annals of Information Systems 13, DOI 10.1007/978-1-4419-7406-8_12,

business activities were performed. The testing procedures employed have often been based on sampling methodologies and manual reviews of only a small percentage of the accounting transactions, policies and procedures, approvals, reconciliations, etc. Unfortunately, these antiquated testing procedures afford only a limited evaluation of an organisation's business processes and operational risks. In today's hyper-complex operating environment, these antiquated auditing and risk management techniques are becoming increasingly inadequate as evidenced by the dramatic recent increase in the number of financial crises plaguing the world's economy.

Increasingly, decision support systems are being harnessed to reinvent audit and risk management processes with the ultimate hope of preventing the next financial crisis by helping executives make informed decisions and maintain compliance with the perpetually evolving bodies of law and corporate policy. Inevitably, continuous auditing requires a type of decision support system that will help transform the audit paradigm from periodic reviews of a few transactions to a continuous review of all transactions.

Continuous auditing demands a complete formalisation of an organisation's business processes as well as their key control points, rules, metrics, and exceptions. When the processes of testing controls and identifying meaningful control exceptions are formalised, these processes generally can be automated, which can enable organisations to perform control and risk assessments in real time, analyse business processes for anomalies at the transaction level, and utilise system-generated alarms and data-driven indicators to identify control deficiencies and emerging risks. This type of automation will allow organisations unprecedented capabilities to respond to the demands of today's rapidly changing and hypercompetitive business environment as well as meet the growing regulatory compliance requirements (e.g., Sarbanes-Oxley, Basel II, etc.) in a cost effective manner.

However, to achieve this level of audit automation, human judgement would need to be totally replaced with a continuous auditing system which would be a complex, costly and computationally intensive endeavour. Some working in emergency management.-->have suggested a hybrid approach that would use both continuous auditing and human decision making. This method would integrate continuous auditing's detection and alerting functions with the tracking of decisions and decision options for situations that can be more effectively handled by human judgement (Turoff, Chumer, Hiltz, Klashner, Alles, Vasarhelyi, and Kogan 2004). Such an integrated approach may help overcome some of the implementation obstacles currently impeding continuous auditing implementations.

With the goal of providing an empirical and methodological foundation for future continuous auditing systems and accelerating their rate of implementation, the remaining sections of this chapter are organised as follows: Sect. 2 provides several definitions of continuous auditing; Sect. 3 suggests possible architectures for a continuous auditing system; Sect. 4 lists some common implementation challenges for a continuous auditing system; Sect. 5 describes some successful continuous auditing implementations; Sect. 6 is the conclusion.

2 Definition

An unequivocal continuous auditing definition would be an advantageous starting point in designing this type of system. However, the literature offers several overlapping and, sometimes competing, definitions for continuous auditing. Miklos Vasarhelyi, who is generally regarded as publisher of the first significant paper on continuous auditing in 1991, defines it as "an audit that happens immediately after or closely after a particular event" (McCann 2009). The Canadian Institute of Chartered Accountants (CICA) and the American Institute of Certified Public Accountants (AICPA) define continuous auditing as "a methodology that enables independent auditors to provide written assurance on the subject matter using a series of auditor's reports issued simultaneously with, or within a short time after, the occurrence of the events underlying the subject matter" (CICA/AICPA 1999). Rezaee defines continuous auditing as "a systematic process of gathering electronic evidence as a reasonable basis to render an opinion on fair presentation of financial statements prepared under the paperless, real-time accounting system" (Rezaee 2001). Helms and Mancino define continuous auditing as "software to detect auditors' specific exceptions from amongst all transactions that are processed either in real-time or near real-time environments. These exceptions could be investigated immediately or written to an auditor's log for subsequent work" (Helms, Mancino et al. 1999). The Global Technology Audit Guide (GTAG) defines continuous auditing as a method generally used by internal auditors to perform control and risk assessments automatically on a frequent basis. However, the GTAG's continuous auditing definition also includes other audit procedures that occur in real-time or near real-time including: continuous monitoring (a process that management puts in place to ensure the policies, procedures and business processes are operating effectively, which includes defining the control objectives and assurance assertions and establishing automated tests to highlight activities and transactions that fail to comply), continuous control assessment (a process that focuses on the early detection of control deficiencies) and continuous risk assessment (a process that detects processes or systems experiencing higher than expected levels of risk) (Coderre 2005). Although these definitions differ in semantics, they all share the notion of performing auditing processes very quickly.

3 Architecture

One approach to dramatically accelerating the audit process is to create a specialised decision support software system that automates the audit process. These new systems will require a distinctive software architecture defined as "the fundamental organisation of a system, embodied in its components, their relationships to each other and the environment, and the principles governing its design and evolution" (ANSI/IEEE 2000). In its simplest form, the continuous auditing system architecture requires only a digitised data source, well-defined data validation engine, and an alarm and/or reporting mechanism to alert the appropriate parties when these rules are violated.

Alles and Kogan formally define seven components of a continuous auditing system: (1) a layer of software for process control and monitoring, (2) an instantiation of the control and monitoring process for business process assurance by both internal and external assurors, (3) a constant stream of measurements (metrics) engineered out of key processes, (4) a sophisticated dynamic set of standards (models) to compare with the metrics, (5) a set of dynamic exception metrics to determine when an alarm is to be issued and its degree of importance, (6) an analytic layer to perform additional analysis related to several corporate functions (e.g., auditing, fraud evaluation, accounting rule compliance and estimate review), and (7) a new level of statutory reporting that may include reports to governmental agencies (Alles, Kogan et al. 2004).

Warren describes a Web-enabled software architecture that receives a continuous feed of data from a variety of enterprise systems and performs continuous monitoring, audits and control checks on this data (Warren 2005). Ye posits a service-oriented architecture would provide the most business value, rapid response capabilities and reuse for a continuous auditing system (Ye, Chen, Gaom and Y. He 2008). Woodroof adds the concept of continually combining data from multiple disparate organisations (Woodroof and Searcy 2001).

3.1 Digitised Data Source

A critical building block to a continuous auditing system is digitised data. As technologies such as electronic data interchange (EDI), electronic commerce (EC) and electronic funds transfer (EFT) increase the number of digitised audit trails, the possible reach of continuous auditing increases. Although today's organisations are not entirely paperless, much of their information has been digitised. Redgrave estimates that 93% of information created today is in a digital form, 70% of an organisation's records are stored electronically and 30% of electronically stored information is never printed (Redgrave 2005).

Alles et al. propose that a large relational database application would be an appropriate tool for an audit data repository. Such a repository would ideally contain and organise all the data needed from an audit perspective (Alles, Brennan et al. 2006a). Extract transform and load (ETL) tools could extract the data from the requisite systems, transform it to facilitate audit reporting and analytics, and then load it into the audit data repository. Data mining, which is a systematic process for extracting patterns from data (e.g., fraudulent transactions), could also be run against an audit data repository.

Alternatively, embedded audit modules (EAM) could be used to extract information of audit significance on a continuous basis to insert it into the audit data repository (Groomer and Murthy 1989). EAMs are generally application-level code specifically written to identify and continually extract data for certain key business events.

Because only data for key business events are extracted, this type of data extraction places minimal strain on the underlying systems in terms of processing time, disk I/O and network bandwidth.

Another view is that continuous auditing systems could leverage the data stored in an enterprise resource planning (ERP) system. Alles et al. describe how Siemens' continuous auditing system was built on top of the firm's ERP systems (Alles et al. 2006a). However, few organisations have a completely homogeneous information technology environment. The ACL (2006) survey of 858 audit executives in organisations with annual revenues in excess of $100 million illustrates this point. More than half of the respondents (58%) felt that fragmented and incomplete data structures constituted an extremely important issue facing their organisation; 28% felt it was important; 11% indicated it was slightly important; and only 3% of respondents felt this was not a key challenge in their organisation at this time (ACL 2006). Typically, large organisations have a complex information technology environment which could comprise a hodgepodge of ERPs or perhaps multiple instances of the same ERP, mainframe systems, off-the-shelf applications and legacy systems, all of which may contain valuable data for the auditor. In highly fragmented information technology environments, this approach may be impractical.

3.2 Data Validation Engine

The data validation engine takes as input the digitised data stream and outputs audit procedure exceptions that generally either sound an alarm (or alarms) and/or appear on an audit exception report. Many different types of algorithms have been suggested for the basis of the data validation engine: belief functions (Srivastava and Shafer 1992), continuity equations (Alles, Kogan, and Vasarhelyi 2006b), expert systems (Davis, Massey et al. 1997), neural nets (Coakley 1995) and regression-based statistical techniques (Vasarhelyi, Alles, and Kogan 2004). Theoretically, the same continuous auditing system could use multiple data validation engines for different situations or even for the same one. By using a programming language, these algorithms could be integrated together or supplemented with other arbitrarily complex handcrafted algorithms. However, these methods all share the following properties: they observe events in real or near real-time, generating alarms or reports when audit exceptions occur, and perform repeat tests quickly, continually and with low variable costs (Vasarhelyi et al. 2004).

4 Implementation Challenges

Although continuous auditing implementations are occurring, their adoption is slower than expected (Warren 2003). In general, current efforts have focused only on the detection part of a continuous audit and neglected the real-time response, which incorporates real-time human decisions, the measurement of the impact of those decisions and the determination of the effect of the responses. A continuous audit system that integrates detection and real-time response would represent the merger of the current concepts in continuous auditing and the objectives of modern emergency management and response systems (Turoff, de Walle, Van, and Xiang 2003).

The continuous auditing literature mentions five obstacles to a continuous auditing system implementation: difficulty in formalising business processes, cost, system acceptance test issues, information overload and system performance degradation. The following sections cover each of these implementation challenges in more detail.

4.1 Formalising Business Processes

Continuous auditing requires the formalisation of business processes, controls and audit exceptions. In general, this formalisation promotes precision and consistency, improves confidence in audit results and reduces long-run audit costs. Once a business process has been formalised, it can usually be automated. However, because many humans resist formal thinking, formalisation can be highly laborious and costly and some complex judgements are not amenable to formalisation. As Alles commented, formalising manual audit procedures to facilitate automation is much more difficult than what might have been anticipated (Alles et al. 2006a).

Moreover, complex business decisions may require multi-criteria decision making, which refers to decisions that have conflicting criteria and require implicit or explicit tradeoffs between competing objectives. These types of decisions generally require the aggregation of input from various disparate parties that very well may have sharply different views, responsibilities and objectives. Consequently, conventional audit programmes may not be designed for automation, because formalisation and judgemental procedures are often intermixed to make these complex business decisions. In order to optimally automate the audit process, the whole process may need to be reengineered. Wherever practical, continuous automated procedures should be relied on while manual methods and informal judgemental procedures should be eliminated (Alles, Kogan, Vasarhelyi, and Warren, Jr 2008).

One solution to the multi-criteria decision-making problem suggested by emergency management research is to combine a real-time decision support system that provides consistent and comprehensive information with a structured approach that allows experts to model decisions and their effects (Geldermann, Bertsch et al. 2009). Another possible approach to lessen the requisite formalisation taken from the emergency management research is to integrate human roles and human actions into a formal business process. For example, the resource interruption monitoring system developed for the US Office of Preparedness in 1972 had templated solutions to various situations (e.g., a shortage of fertilizer). This system defined generic "steps" for handling these situations. Each step had a designated owner responsible for performing an action on this step, as well as a set of possible actions. When the step owner performed an action, the owner of the next step was automatically notified. Each step had a configurable expected duration. If a particular step took longer than expected, the system would automatically send notifications to the relevant step owner as well as escalation notifications.

Using the above approach, audit processes that are difficult to formalise could still rely on human decision making. For example, the process for resolving an audit exception identified by a continuous auditing system could have a structured workflow ensuring the appropriate parties reviewed and acted on this exception. The workflow module would define and enforce the requisite resolution steps, the appropriate owners and actions for each step in the process, and the escalation procedures.

4.2 Cost

Continuous auditing systems tend to be perceived as expensive to implement. For example, in September 2008, the *Economist* asked 446 senior executives their views on the drawbacks of investing in automating their financial processes. The most frequently cited reason was the high level of investment required, cited by 48% of the respondents who answered. This answer was cited with twice the frequency of the next highest response: difficulty of modelling complex financial processes (Fedorowicz 2008). Unquestionably, these systems' perceived high implementation costs are a major obstacle currently impeding continuous auditing systems' implementation rate.

Moreover, only some of the benefits from a continuous auditing system are easily quantifiable: the cost savings associated with automating manual processes, consolidating systems and embedding controls into financial processes. Other possible benefits are difficult to quantify in terms of cost savings (e.g., fewer instances of noncompliance, better business decisions and risk management and reduced fraud risk). Because only some of the cost savings can be easily quantified, calculating a true total cost of ownership for a continuous auditing system is challenging, which could make justifying it purely from a cost perspective problematic.

However, one practical approach to containing the cost of a system is to limit the scope of the system implementation. Inevitably some auditing procedures will be more costly to formalise and automate than others. Consequently, one cost-effective implementation strategy is to limit the scope of the continuous auditing system to only the auditing procedures that can be easily formalised and automated. Alles suggests that formalisable auditing procedures should be separated from non-formalisable ones. Formalisable auditing procedure's controls are executed with high frequency (perhaps continuously), while non-formalisable ones can continue to be done manually and periodically (Alles et al. 2006a, b). Consequently, some audit procedures are either impossible or prohibitively expensive to formalise. One possible cost-effective approach to solving this design challenge is to use continuous auditing's detection and alerting functions for the formalisable auditing procedures, and use the tracking of decisions and decision options for the non-formalisable ones, which is the architecture recommended in some articles cited from the emergency management and response literature.

4.3 System Acceptance

In order for continuous auditing to become a mainstream application, it will have to overcome the user acceptance issues that plague all new information technology implementations. Venkatesh developed and tested a Unified Theory of Acceptance and Use of Technology (UTAUT), which can be used as a starting point to understand the potential system acceptance issues that could occur for a continuous auditing system. Four constructs were identified as direct determinants of user intention and usage behaviour: performance expectancy (the degree to which an individual believes that using the system will help attain gains in job performance), effort expectancy (the degree of effort associated with using and learning the system), social influence (the degree to which an individual perceives that important and/or powerful parties believe that the system should be used) and facilitating conditions (the degree to which an individual believes that an organisational and technical infrastructure exists to support system use). Gender, age, voluntariness and experience are key moderators of these four direct determinants. UTAUT predicts that behavioural intention to use a new continuous auditing system would be strongest when the end-users believe the continuous auditing system is supported by senior management, easy to use and well supported in terms of organisational and technical infrastructure, and will improve their efficiency and effectiveness at work (Venkatesh, Morris et al. 2003).

The UTAUT model's conclusions were supported by research conducted by Curtis. By surveying 331 members of the Institute of Management Accountants during the spring of 2009, Curtis concluded that accountants were more likely to champion continuous auditing systems that are perceived as easy to use and useful (i.e., producing demonstrative and visible results). Moreover, accountants supported less complex continuous auditing systems more frequently than very complex ones (Curtis 2009).

Fischer's observations during his interpretive field study with several large accounting firms indicate that inertia in these firms could be a barrier to continuous auditing acceptance. Fischer observed these accounting firms were reluctant to rely on more sophisticated and/or effective audit procedures even when they were readily available. Their preferences tended to be anchored on the audit procedures and processes regularly performed in the past (Fischer 1996). Finally, Hall and Khan suggest that adoption of a new invention might be slowed if it requires new and complex skills (Hall and Khan 2003).

However, Bailey James identified the five system attributes that lead to the highest user satisfaction with an information system: accuracy (the correctness of the system's output), reliability (the consistency and the dependability of the system's outputs), timeliness (the output of information in a time suitable for its use), relevance (the degree of congruence between what a user wants or requires and what is provided by the system) and confidence in the system (the user's feeling of assurance or certainty about the system) (Bailey James 1983). Therefore other things being equal, a continuous auditing system with a high degree of these attributes would be better accepted than one with a low degree of them.

4.4 Information Overload

Continuous auditing systems could increase the quantity of data available for analysis, which could trigger information overload. Information overload occurs when the volume of information supplied in a given unit of time exceeds the limited human information processing capacity, which tends to lead to confused and dysfunctional behaviour (Jacoby, Speller et al. 1974). Chewning and Harrell demonstrated that an overload of accounting data leads to decreased decision quality in accounting students (Chewning and Harrell 1990).

However, there are several possible technical solutions to the information overload problem: installing voting structures to evaluate information (Hiltz and Turoff 1985); using decision support systems (Cook 1993); deploying intelligent agents to limit alternatives (Edmunds and Morris 2000); providing flexible information organisation, filtering and routing options (Hiltz and Turoff 1985); utilising data visualisation tools (Chan 2001); creating a measurement system for information quality (Denton 2001); compressing, aggregating and categorising data (Grise and Gallupe 1999); defining decision models (Chewning and Harrell 1990); exception reporting (Ackoff 1967); and/or using search procedures (Olsen, Sochats et al. 1998).

4.5 System Performance

Adding continuous auditing controls and/or data extraction methods to an existing information technology system could negatively impact system performance. Hoxmeier concluded that user satisfaction with an information technology system decreases as response time increases (Hoxmeier and DiCesare 2000). In the best case, lengthy system response times would reduce user productivity and, in the worst case, render the system unusable.

Murthy examined the system performance implications of adding three types of controls (calculations, database lookups and aggregate function controls) to an e-commerce application. Calculation controls make comparisons between the current transaction and data retrieved from a single database lookup. Lookup controls are functionally equivalent to calculation controls. However, lookup controls require data from multiple tables. Aggregate function controls compare transaction values to the average, sum, maximum and/or minimum of a particular field. For example, one aggregate control compares the customer's current transaction amount to the customer's average historical amount. Murthy concluded calculation controls could be accommodated, regardless of system load. Lookup controls had a detrimental effect on system performance only during peak periods. Aggregate function controls had a dramatic negative impact on system performance irrespective of the system load (Murthy 2004).

5 Successful Implementations

In spite of the implementation obstacles, several continuous auditing systems have been successfully implemented and discussed in the literature. The following sections discuss and compare several aspects of these systems.

5.1 AT&T's Paperless Billing System

Vasarhelyi described the Continuous Process Auditing System (CPAS) that AT&T Bell Labs used to audit a large paperless billing system in real time. CPAS extracts audit data from the billing system, uses it to calculate operational analytics and standard metrics, activates alarms alerting an auditor to potential issues, and generates audit reports. When predefined system rules are violated, alarms are triggered, which call attention to these system anomalies. There are four types of alarms: Type 1 alarms are minor and deal with the functioning of the audit system. Type 2 alarms are low-level operational alarms designed for operating management. Type 3 alarms are higher-level exceptions sent directly to the auditors. Type 4 alarms warn auditors and top management of a serious crisis. Moreover, the auditor has an interactive environment to review operational reports, specify audit procedures for continuous repetition and define custom alarms (Vasarhelyi and Halper 1991).

5.2 Royal Canadian Mounted Police's Accounts Payable Departments

In the 2004–2005 fiscal year, the Royal Canadian Mounted Police (RCMP) implemented a continuous auditing system to assess its accounts payable (AP) control framework. The goals of this system were to provide reasonable assurance that the AP policies used by seven satellite offices complied with the central office's policies, the control framework effectively supported these AP activities and all financial transactions were processed consistent with these policies. The system used data extracted from the financial and human resources systems to compare cost, quality and time-based performance measures for each AP office. For example, labour cost for accounts payable, the average number of errors per invoice and the average number of days to pay an invoice were calculated and compared for each AP office. Using these data analysis techniques, the audit team uncovered control weaknesses and several instances of noncompliance with RCMP's policy (Coderre 2006).

When humans are involved in the decision-making process, tracking how long it takes for an action to occur has long been an integral part of emergency management and response systems. After a crisis occurs, evaluating the effectiveness of a crisis response to discover what could be improved in the process is an integral part of emergency management and response systems. For example, audiotapes of operators in emergency operations regularly receive time stamps so that post-mortems and precise analyses of who did what and when could be performed in an attempt to continually improve the process. Similarly, the continuous auditing literature describes a black box audit log, which is a confidential log of all of an organisation's germane audit procedures and other economic events. The black box log creates a permanent and non-updatable record of the most important audit procedures with an audit trail of its own, which is kept private and secure (Alles et al. 2004).

5.3 Siemens' SAP Security Settings

Siemens designed its continuous auditing system to monitor key security parameters (e.g., password complexity and expiration) for the firm's SAP systems. The system continually extracts information from SAPs' security tables and compares it to Siemens' security policies. When critical exceptions are identified, the system automatically generates alarms which are emailed to all relevant parties. To prevent alarm floods from sounding and hampering the ability to react to the underlying problems – or worse, having the alarm ignored altogether – a hierarchical alarm structure was implemented where each node has an enabled/disabled flag. Disabling the node prevents its children's alarms from sounding, thereby preventing alarm floods. Moreover, the system intelligently monitors alarms, waits a predefined period before re-sounding an alarm and initiates escalation procedures if an alarm is not resolved within a given time frame (Alles et al. 2006a).

5.4 Summary (Table 1)

Table 1 Summary of continuous auditing implementations

	AT&T	RCMP	Siemens
Purpose	Audit a large paperless billing system	Assess accounts payable control framework	Monitor the key security parameters for Siemens' SAP application
Validation engine	Predefined system rules	Compare cost, quality and time-based performance measures for seven satellite AP offices	Siemens' IT security policy
Data	Extracted from source billing system	Extracted from the satellite offices' financial and human resources systems	Extracted from SAP security tables
Alarms	Type 1 for minor system issues. Type 2 for operating management. Type 3 for higher-level exceptions for the auditor. Type 4 for warning auditors and top management of a serious crisis	None	Hierarchical email alarms that can be disabled at any level to prevent alarm floods and intelligent alarm monitors

6 Conclusion

Whether or not a continuous auditing system could be used to perform a consistent, credible and complete audit for an arbitrarily complex real-world organisation in a manner equaling or surpassing the capabilities of a human audit team remains an open research question and a source of much debate. Some argue it is not possible to fully automate the auditing process, because it requires human judgement and estimation, which can never be fully automated or performed continuously (Krass 2002). Although regulatory bodies painstakingly define standards and guidelines, and organisations spend significant resources defining their business policies and controls determining whether an organisation is in compliance with a particular standard, guideline or control still requires significant human judgement. Replacing human judgement tends to be difficult, costly and computationally intensive. Moreover, large-scale continuous auditing systems may be resisted because of their inscrutable complexity and novelty.

However, Sect. 5 illustrates that to date continuous auditing has achieved some modest real-world successes. This chapter suggests four practical recommendations that aspiring continuous auditing implementers could use to replicate these successes and, perhaps, improve on them. First, build the continuous auditing system on top of a solid architecture. Second, start on a small scale, focusing on the audit procedures that are easiest to formalise and automate, which may help mitigate the initial cost objection. Third, design the continuous auditing system to have acceptable system performance, produce demonstrative and visible results, and be easy to use and understand (e.g., consider using the techniques outlined in Sect. 4.4 to reduce information overload). Fourth, maximise social influence by getting the support of executive level champions, which may help overcome the natural reluctance to adopt a new system.

In some respects, the efforts to build emergency management and response systems seem transferable to continuous auditing systems. One promising area for future research is how to integrate continuous auditing's detection and alerting functions with the tracking of human decisions and decision options, which are features found in some emergency management and response systems. Combining these features into a coherent system that provides a structured decision methodology and flexible decision modelling may be the means to overcoming some of the implementation obstacles currently facing continuous auditing as well as the foundation of a revolutionary new management tool.

For example, after a major fiduciary disaster in an organisation, auditors are usually relied on to determine what caused this event. They must painstakingly reconstruct the decision trail from many different sources. However, if the concept of continuous auditing could be expanded to include the tracking of the organisational decision-making process that underlies the actual formulation, analysis and results supporting a particular decision, this system would become a central repository for the supporting details for all of an organisation's major decisions (Alles et al. 2004). This system would track what authorisations, documents and/or results were produced to justify and execute any decision at all levels in the organisation, which would impede the legal defenses used in cases like Enron where the high-level decision makers claimed they were completely unaware of some of the illegal and disastrous decisions being made. This type of continuous auditing system could make possible the accomplishment of the implicit goals of the Sarbanes-Oxley Act of 2002.

The ability to track the decision-making process at the highest levels of the firm would be a new concept for most organisations. The Sarbanes-Oxley Act holds an organisation's leaders accountable for the decision-making process and limits their ability to claim ignorance for illegal decisions for which they now risk being held criminally liable. One way the leadership of an organisation can protect itself from this risk is to define and track all types of decision processes that must occur at the upper levels of an organisation. To date, most organisations have only applied this tracking to lower-level decision processes. Tracking the process does not necessarily ensure the resulting decision is optimal. However, if the tracking process ensures the responsibilities for various reviews and analyses by the relevant parties were, in fact, carried out and documented, including who was involved and what documents were produced, there would be much less chance that anyone involved could claim ignorance. Another potential positive side effect of this tracking would be to reduce, or eliminate, the potential number of clearly ridiculous, rash or illegal decisions made within an organisation.

Moreover, decision modelling and tracking improve an organisation's ability to predict and manage the unexpected proactively in a cost-effective manner. Whether it is a clear emergency or the more normal unexpected events such as the loss of a prime customer, a significant problem with a product or sudden loss of skilled employees, tracking the decision process and its effects throughout the organisation provides the foundation to predict or, at least, quickly detect unexpected events at all levels of the organisation. This vigilance seeks to remove unexpected variability from an organisation's business processes and, if the unexpected does occur, detect it quickly before it has a chance to snowball into a catastrophic emergency (Weick and Sutcliffe 2001).

Acknowledgement from Robert Baksa I would like to thank Edison Properties L.L.C. and Gupton Marrs International for their financial support while pursuing this endeavour. I would also like to sincerely thank all my clients and colleagues for providing a challenging environment in which to grow and learn, my friends and wonderful family especially my wife, Sharon, and my two daughters, Rachel and Grace, for their continued support and encouragement, and the whole NJIT Information Systems Department, especially Professors Turoff and Hiltz, whose insight, patience and guidance have proven invaluable. Finally, a special thanks to my empathetic listeners, inspiring supporters, savants and those helpful in enabling research.

References

Ackoff, R.L., "Management Misinformation Systems," *Management Science* 14, 4, 1967b, 147–156.

ACL, "New Demands, New Priorities The Evolving Role of Internal Audit," 2006, URL = http://www.acl.com/PDFs/caesurvey_results06.pdf

Alles, M., G. Brennan, et al., "Continuous Monitoring of Business Process Controls: A Pilot Implementation of A Continuous Auditing System at Siemens," *International Journal of Accounting Information Systems*, 7, 2, 2006a, 137–161.

Alles M., A. Kogan, M.A. Vasarhelyi, and J.D. Warren, Jr., "Audit Automation as the Foundation of Continuous Auditing," in *16th World Continuous Auditing & Reporting Symposium*. Newark: Rutgers Business School, 2008.

Alles, M.G., A. Kogan, et al., "Restoring Auditor Credibility: Tertiary Monitoring and Logging of Continuous Assurance Systems," *International Journal of Accounting Information Systems*, 5, 2, 2004, 183–202.

Alles, M.G., A. Kogan, and M. Vasarhelyi, "Continuity Equations: Analytical Monitoring of Business Processes in Continuous Auditing", in *12th World Continuous Auditing & Reporting Symposium*. Newark: Rutgers Business School, 2006b.

ANSI/IEEE, *Recommended Practice for Architectural Description of Software-Intensive Systems*, 23, 2000.

Bailey James, S.W.P., "Development of a Tool for Measuring and Analyzing Computer User Satisfaction," *Management Science*, 29, 4, 1983, 17.

Chan, S.Y., "The Use of Graphs as Decision Aids in Relation to Information Overload and Managerial decision quality," *Journal of Information Science*, 27, 6, 2001, 417–426.

Chewning, E.G. and A.M. Harrell, "The Effect of Information Load on Decision Makers' Cue Utilization Levels and Decision Quality in A Financial Distress Decision Task," *Accounting, Organizations and Society*, 15, 6, 1990, 527–542.

CICA/AICPA, *Continuous Auditing, Research Report. T. C. I. o. C. Accountants*, Toronto, 1999.

Coakley, J.R., "Using Pattern Analysis Methods to Supplement Attention Directing Analytical Procedures," *Expert Systems with Applications*, 9, 4, 1995, 513–528.
Coderre, D., *Global Technology Audit Guide Continuous Auditing: Implications for Assurance, Monitoring, and Risk Assessment*, http://www.acl.com/pdfs/IIA_GTAG-May05.pdf 44, 2005.
Coderre, D., "A Continuous View of Accounts," *Internal Auditor*, 63, 2, 2006, 25–31.
Cook, G.J., "An Empirical Investigation of Information Search Strategies with Implications for Decision Support System Design," *Decision Sciences*, 24, 1993, 683–699.
Curtis, M.B., "Bottom-up Innovation – A Study of Intrepreneurship in Organizations," in *19th World Continuous Auditing & Reporting Symposium*. Newark: Rutgers Business School, 2009.
Davis, J.T., A.P. Massey, et al., "Supporting a Complex Audit Judgment Task: An Expert Network Approach," *European Journal of Operational Research*, 103, 2, 1997, 350–372.
Denton, D.K., "Better Decisions," *Industrial Management*, 43, 4, 2001, 21.
Edmunds, A. and A. Morris, "The Problem of Information Overload in Business Organisations: A Review of the Literature," *International Journal of Information Management*, 20, 1, 2000,17–28.
Fedorowicz, J., "Managing Risk through Financial Processes: Embedding Governance, Risk and Compliance," *The Economist*, 23, 2008.
Fischer, M.J., "'Real-izing' The Benefits of New Technologies as a Source of Audit Evidence: An Interpretive Field Study," *Accounting, Organizations and Society*, 21, 2–3, 1996, 219–242.
Geldermann, J., V. Bertsch, et al., "Multi-criteria Decision Support and Evaluation of Strategies for Nuclear Remediation Management," *Omega*, 37, 1, 2009, 238–251.
Grise, M.-L. and R.B. Gallupe, "Information Overload: Addressing the Productivity Paradox in Face-to-Face Electronic Meetings," *Journal of Management Information Systems*, 16, 3, 1999, 157–185.
Groomer, S.M. and U.S. Murthy, "Continuous Auditing of Database Applications: An Embedded Audit Module Approach," *Journal of Information Systems*, 3, 2, 1989, 53.
Hall, B. and B. Khan, *Adoption of New Technology*, vol. 22. Berkeley: University of California Department of Economics, 2003.
Helms, G.L., J.M. Mancino, et al., "Information Technology Issues for the Attest, Audit, and Assurance Services Functions," *CPA Journal*, 69, 5, 1999, 62.
Hiltz, S.R. and M. Turoff, "Structuring Computer-Mediated Communication Systems to Avoid Information Overload," *Communications of ACM*, 28, 7, 1985, 680–689.
Hoxmeier, J.A.D. and C. DiCesare, "System Response Time and User Satisfaction: An Experimental Study of Browser-Based Applications," in *Proceedings of the Association of Information Systems Americas Conference*, Long Beach, 2000.
Jacoby, J., D.E. Speller, et al., "Brand Choice Behavior as a Function of Information Load: Replication and Extension," *Journal of Consumer Research*, 1, 1, 1974, 33–42.
Krass, P., "The Never-ending Audit," *CFO*, 18, 10, 2002, 25.
McCann, D., "Internal Audit: The Continuous Conundrum," 2009, URL = http://www.cfo.com/article.cfm/14440838
Murthy, U.S., "An Analysis of the Effects of Continuous Monitoring Controls on e-Commerce System Performance," *Journal of Information Systems*, 18, 2, 2004, 29–47.
Olsen, K.A., K.M. Sochats, et al., "Full Text Searching and Information Overload," *The International Information & Library Review*, 30, 2, 1998, 105–122.
Redgrave, J., A. Prasad, J. Fliegel, T. Hiser, and C. Ragan, *The SEDONA Principles: Best Practices Recommendations & Principles for Addressing Electronic Document Production.* The SEDONA Conference, 2005.
Rezaee, Z.R.E. and A. Sharbatoghlie, "Continuous Auditing: The Audit of the Future," *Managerial Auditing Journal*, 16, 3, 2001, 150–158.
Srivastava, R.P. and G.R. Shafer, "Belief-Function Formulas for Audit Risk," *Accounting Review*, 67, 2, 1992, 249–283.
Turoff, M., M. Chumer, S.R. Hiltz, R. Klashner, M. Alles, M. Vasarhelyi, and A. Kogan, "Assuring Homeland Security: Continuous Monitoring, Control and Assurance of Emergency Preparedness," *Journal of Information Technology Theory and Application (JITTA)*, 6, 3, 2004, 24.

Turoff, M.C., M. de Walle, B. Van, and Y. Xiang, "The Design of a Dynamic Emergency Response Management Information System (DERMIS)," *Journal of Information Technology Theory and Application (JITTA)*, 5, 4, 2003.

Vasarhelyi, M.A., M.G. Alles, and A. Kogan, *Principles of Analytic Monitoring for Continuous Assurance*, 1, 2004.

Vasarhelyi, M.A. and F.B. Halper, "The Continuous Audit of Online Systems," *Auditing*, 10, 1, 1991, 110–125.

Venkatesh, V., M.G. Morris, et al., "User Acceptance of Information Technology: Toward a Unified View," *MIS Quarterly*, 27, 3, 2003, 425–478.

Warren, D., "Continuous Financial Controls Review Processes," *Sarbanes-Oxley Compliance Journal*, 2005.

Warren, D. and X. Parker, *Continuous Auditing: Potential for Internal Auditors*, The Institute of Internal Auditors Research Foundation, http://www.amazon.com/Continuous-Auditing-Potential-Internal-Auditors/dp/0894135155 2003.

Weick, K. and K. Sutcliffe, *Managing the Unexpected: Assuring High Performance in an Age of Complexity*. San Francisco: Jossey-Bass, 2001.

Woodroof, J. and D. Searcy, "Continuous Audit: Model Development and Implementation Within a Debt Covenant Compliance Domain," *International Journal of Accounting Information Systems*, 2, 3, 2001, 169–191.

Ye, H., S. Chen, F. Gao, and Y. He, "SOA-based Conceptual Model for Continuous Auditing: A Discussion," in *7th WSEAS International Conference on Applied Computer & Applied Computational Science (ACACOS '08)*, Hangzhou, 2008.

Chapter 13
Towards a "Just-in-Time" Distributed Decision Support System in Health Care Research

Ziad Kobti[2], Anne W. Snowdon[1], Robert D. Kent[2], Gokul Bhandari[1], Shamual F. Rahaman[2], Paul D. Preney[2], Carol A. Kolga[3], Barbara Tiessen[4], and Lichun Zhu[2]

[1] Odette School of Business, University of Windsor, Windsor, Ontario, Canada
[2] School of Computer Science, University of Windsor, Windsor, Ontario, Canada
[3] Kingston General Hospital, Kingston, Ontario, Canada
[4] Leamington District Memorial Hospital, Leamington, Ontario, Canada

Abstract The application of semi-automated decision support systems in health care faces challenging tasks mainly in generating evidence-based recommendations in a short critical time window. Traditional data collection and survey methodology to generate evidence for the decision support systems also suffers from a slow turn-around time. This chapter reports on a multi-disciplinary project between computer and health sciences to introduce a cumulative framework encapsulating innovative distributed data collection methodology, coupled with an intelligent multi-agent, socially driven decision support system. We report on the current design and implementation aspects of this integrated system with a case study in injury prevention to verify the initial model.

Keywords Cultural evolution • Health care • Multi-agent simulation • Wireless data collection • Social influence

1 Introduction

Health care is a highly complex and multidimensional system that has a social contract with societies to provide health care--> to citizens safely, effectively and in a timely manner. In clinical practice, health professionals make numerous complex decisions about managing illness or injury with patients in order to restore health and functional ability. At the health system level, leaders and policy makers are required to make complex decisions about health issues at the population level. In order for health professionals, health leaders or policy makers to make effective decisions, information that is current and accurate is critically important. Injury is currently the leading cause of death worldwide for individuals aged two to adult.

A.W. Snowdon (✉)
Odette School of Business, University of Windsor, Windsor, Ontario, Canada
e-mail: snowdon@uwindsor.ca

F. Burstein et al. (eds.), *Supporting Real Time Decision-Making*,
Annals of Information Systems 13, DOI 10.1007/978-1-4419-7406-8_13,

Currently, injury research provides important evidence regarding the prevalence, severity of injury, and factors that contribute to injury outcomes in populations. Yet, injury data is often difficult and time-consuming to collect, requiring health professionals and policy makers to make decisions and set policy based on evidence that may have been collected up to 5 years previously. Consider two examples of health system challenges related to injury that require effective, timely decisions based on current and accurate information.

The first example is the relatively high incidence of patient falls among hospitalised elderly and the need to develop intervention strategies to prevent these falls which so frequently result in serious injury and death. In hospitals, falls data is often collected on paper incident reports which are then entered into a database system. The analysis of the falls data often requires months to reach clinicians and is only reported in aggregate form which is then used to develop falls prevention programmes in clinical settings. The analysis of the falls data is retrospective and offers very little current information for those health professionals making decisions with regard to prevention. If falls information (i.e., risk factors, history of previous falls, existing co-morbidities) were available to the clinician in a just-in-time (JIT) manner for individual patients, the clinician would have the ability to examine the factors that place a particular patient at risk and then intervene to prevent a subsequent fall or injury.

The second example of a health system challenge related to injury is road crashes which are the leading cause of death of children in both Canada and the USA (Safe Kids Canada 2004). Population studies of injury and deaths due to road crashes are collected every 2–5 years, depending on the national policy of a specific country. Data is collected from roadside surveys whereby observers record the use of occupant restraints in vehicles as they drive through randomly selected intersections. The observation data is entered into a database and then analysed, up to 2 years following the observation studies, for trends in use of safety systems. Other injury data is collected at the scene of vehicle collisions whenever vehicle occupants are injured. These data sources are limited in scope and detail and require substantial time to produce meaningful analysis to support decision makers. Policy makers and health system leaders make decisions on prevention programmes based on retrospective data. The opportunity for evidence-based policy making (i.e., patterns and trends in injury due to road crashes) and evaluation of the impact of policy outcomes (i.e., legislation for correct use of child seats and seat belts, and information campaigns on road safety) is very slow, if not impossible, due to such infrequent monitoring of injury outcomes.

Evidence to support effective and accurate health care decisions is critically important in order for health care systems – and the professionals who work within those systems – to be effective and responsive to the needs of the populations they serve. However, the challenge remains in developing information systems that offer detailed and accurate analyses of "best evidence" that most accurately captures the magnitude, prevalence and severity of the health issue facing populations in a timely manner. This analysis is critically important for decision making by professionals in the health care system to create effective and timely interventions.

In this chapter, we discuss a collaborative research project conducted by an inter-professional team of researchers from health, computer science, and business (management science) at the University of Windsor. Dr. Anne Snowdon, her colleagues and their students at the University of Windsor pioneered this research. Their main objective was to empirically document the factors that contribute to persistent high rates of child fatalities and severe injuries due to road crashes in Canada. Ultimately, the goal was to identify effective strategies to improve correct use of child safety seats and to support the implementation of evidence-based legislation and injury prevention policies at the national level.

This large programme of research conducted several community-based surveys to identify parents' and drivers' perceptions and use of child safety seats for their children. The survey revealed widespread misuse of child seats, including child seats installed incorrectly, premature transition to seats that did not fit the child's height and weight, and premature use of seat belts for young children. The most prevalent misuse was found in school-aged children where as few as 28% of children in Canada were using booster seats while travelling in vehicles (Snowdon, Hussein, and Ahmed 2008a; Safe Kids Canada 2004). Almost half of Canadian children who die in vehicle crashes are four- to eight-year-old children wearing seat belts rather than using booster seats while travelling in vehicles (Chouinard 2005). Despite five Canadian provinces having booster seat legislation, rates of booster seats usage continue to remain very low in Canada (Snowdon, Hussein, Purc-Stevenson, Bruce, Kolga, and Boase, et al. 2008c). Intervention studies have been conducted to test the effectiveness of educational strategies in increasing parents' knowledge and use of safety systems for their children in vehicles (Snowdon, Hussein, High, Stamler, Polgar, and Patrick, et al, 2008b; Snowdon, Hussein, Purc-Stevenson, Follo, and Ahmed 2009). Longitudinal studies of education programmes were found to improve parents' knowledge of correct use of child seats, particularly knowledge of booster seat use. In all of these studies, the research team relied on traditional survey and intervention research methods which were able to identify parents' low rate of correct use of child seats and revealed their lack of knowledge of correct use. However, the research team needed a tool that could identify the dynamic and complex interplay of factors that influence how parents or other drivers make decisions about safely seating children in vehicles. To accomplish this, the research team engaged industry partners and decision support expertise to develop an innovative decision support system (DSS) for injury prevention initiatives in Canada.

A strategic partnership among the researchers, an industry partner – Research in Motion (RIM), and Transport Canada was the basis for the Decision Support System (DSS). The primary strategic partner was Transport Canada whose mandate is to set national road safety policy to achieve the vision for Canada to have the "safest roads in the world", referred to as Road Safety Vision 2010. The target established by Transport Canada was to achieve 95% correct use of seat belts and safety seats for child occupants in vehicles. Transport Canada conducts very large, national surveys to evaluate compliance with legislated use of seat belts and child seats for vehicle occupants on Canada's roadways. They collect observational data at randomly selected roadside sites throughout the country and the frequency of this survey varies widely. The last national child seat survey was conducted in 1995. The current survey involving this team of researchers was conducted in 2006. RIM was approached to collaborate on the data collection strategy required for the development of the DSS. This chapter first provides a review of the literature on injury prevention research, data collection methodologies at the population level, and the use of decision support systems in health care research. In Sect. 3, we describe a decision-making framework for building the DSS. Section 4 specifically discusses the design and development of our JIT artificial intelligence (AI)-based DSS and illustrates application of this system. The chapter concludes with a discussion in Sect. 5.

2 Literature Review

2.1 Health Research in Injury Prevention

Timely access to data is imperative to support injury prevention strategies at the population level. The World Health Organization estimates that over 1.18 million people are killed (3200 deaths/day) and more than 50 million injured or disabled as a result of motor vehicle crashes (MVC) annually. Without implementing effective prevention programmes, it is estimated that MVC injuries will become the third leading cause of the global burden of disease by 2020 (Krug, Sharma, and Lozano 2000; Peden, Scurfield, Sleet, Mohan, Hyder, and Jarawan, et al. 2004). In fact, MVC are the leading cause of death and serious injury for children under the age of 14 in Canada and the USA (NHTSA 2003; Safe Kids Canada 2004). Growing evidence suggests that the risk of death and serious injury due to MVC can be substantially reduced if children are properly restrained (Bedard, Guyatt, Stones, and Hirdes 2002; Glass, Segui-Gomez, and Graham 2000; Lund 2005).

In Canada, approximately two children die or are seriously injured every day as a result of road crashes (Transport Canada 2006). In the USA, six children die and 673 are seriously injured every day due to road crashes (National Highway Traffic Safety Administration 2003). Analysis of US crash data reveals that the risk of death can be reduced by as much as 74% and serious injury by as much as 67% with the correct use of child safety restraints (Weber 2003; Wegner and Girasek 2003). The rate of accurate use of such restraints has been reported as between 6% and 21% in American studies (Wegner and Girasek 2003). Correct use requires that the safety seat be appropriate for the child's height, weight and age (for infants only); be accurately installed and positioned correctly in the vehicle; and ensure that the child is securely fastened in the correct seat every time a child is transported in the vehicle. Various types of interventions have been designed and implemented to increase the correct use of child safety seats. Such interventions include, but are not limited to, child safety seat laws, community-based programmes, distribution and education programmes, incentive and education programmes, and education-only programmes. However, national car seat surveys designed to monitor and evaluate the safety of children travelling in vehicles are conducted approximately every 5 years due to the significant cost associated with these surveys. To date, a number of systematic reviews exploring the effectiveness of car safety seat interventions have been completed (Ehiri, Ejere, Magnussen, Emusu, King, and Osberg 2006; Turner, McClure, Nixon, and Spinks 2005; Zaza, Sleet, Thompson, Sosin, Bolen, and Task Force on Community Preventive Services, Atlanta, GA 2001). However, these reviews tend to be narrowly focused and include only a small number of US-based studies dating back to the late 1980s(2006). For example, Ehiri et al. reviewed five studies that focused on booster seat use for children aged 4–8 years, while Turner et al. (2005) reviewed only eight studies of community-based programmes. Zaza et al. (2001) examined the effectiveness of a broad range of car safety seat interventions for children aged birth to 4 years old, but the search strategy for this systematic review resulted in no Canadian studies being included in the review. Clearly, reviews of evidence that may be up to 20 years old or as recent as 10 years old, present significant challenges to policy and decision makers regarding the best evidence to support effective injury prevention programmes and legislation. The extent to which findings can be generalised to other populations is similarly problematic. Recent systematic reviews included studies conducted in countries outside of Canada, so it is very problematic to assume that even the findings in the US studies have application to the Canadian population. There is mounting pressure for health policy and injury prevention strategies to be based on strong empirical evidence, yet the evidence available to support policy decisions is retrospective and limited to research conducted in other countries.

Despite Road Safety Vision 2010's target of achieving the safest roads in the world, Canada's ranking for road safety has declined from 10th in the world to 22nd among other OECD countries in recent years (Leitch 2008). Despite substantial resources in injury prevention policy at the national level, and advanced technologies in vehicle safety systems by manufacturers, there has been no progress towards injury prevention targets in Canada to date. According to Transport Canada (2004), over 15,000 Canadians under the age of 14 were injured or killed in motor vehicle accidents in 2003. Though there is legislation for car seat usage already in effect in Canada, the high rate of child fatality continues in this country (Transport Canada 2004).

2.2 *Survey Approaches for Data Collection in Health Research*

A survey is a questionnaire consisting of a predetermined number of questions relating in whole or in part to a particular concept or phenomenon. Most surveys ask participants to respond to a number of questions that are designed specifically to elicit facts, perceptions, opinions, knowledge, or attitudes regarding the concept under study. Some surveys are purely observational and data is collected without direct contact with study participants (Wright 2005). In the context of health and safety, surveys of patients, medical practitioners and general populations are usually conducted against a background of archived data related to the matter under immediate study, as well as other data with possible relevance that may have to be data-mined. In all scenarios, however, surveys gather momentary snapshots of current information and provide a basis for studying evolving trends through reapplication of the same or associated surveys (Newsted, Huff and Munro 1998).

Surveys generally consist of three main steps: instrument design and testing, sampling and data collection, and extensive data analysis. Instrument development is the process of developing survey questions that are clear, theoretically sound, and which elicit intended data reflective of issues under study. Pilot testing of surveys is required to ascertain reliability of the survey and validity of findings.

Other considerations during this process include survey procedures, data management, ethics standards and expected costs (De Leeuw, Hox, and Dillman 2008; Newsted et al. 1998; Wright 2005). Data analysis involves data cleaning, multiple regression correlation analysis, trends analysis, and modelling of concepts and human and social behaviours leading to some limited ability to reason.

The majority of data collection approaches used in injury prevention research rely heavily on traditional "pen and paper" observation and self-report surveys. Observational surveys are typically conducted at randomly selected roadside intersections. The researchers record their observations of safety systems used by vehicle occupants while vehicles proceed through the selected intersection. Observational surveys are also conducted in parking lots or protected roadside areas whereby vehicles are stopped and occupants are asked to complete a self-report survey instrument. Observational data is collected while the vehicle is stopped at the designated area of the parking lot. These survey approaches are time-consuming, costly, and require significant time and resources for data entry and data analysis before results can be released to decision makers of injury professionals.

Recent advances in networking, communication and grid computing (Minoli 2005; Taylor 2005) have set the stage for rapid changes in health information collection and sharing (Bilykh, Bychkov, Dahlem, Jahnke, McCallum, and Obry, et al. 2003; Blanquer, Hernandez, Segrelles, Robles, Garcia, and Robledo 2005; Huang, Lanza, Rajasekaran, and Dubitzky 2005; Hwang and Aravamudham 2004; Lim, Choi, and Shin 2005; Smirnov, Pashkin, Chilov, and Levashova 2005; Srinivasan 2005). In particular, Web-based communication and wireless devices including sensors, cellular telephones and personal digital assistants (PDAs), have been found to be useful in health research and practice for distribution of information for teaching or patient care (Berry, Trigg, Lober, Karras, Galligan, and Austin-Seymour, et al. 2004; Kim, Kent, Aggarwal, and Preney 2005; Kopec, Eckhardt, Tamang, and Reinharth 2005; Paik, Kang, Choi, and Ham 2005; Sanderson, Goebel, and Munthe-Kaas 2005; Schaffers 2005; Skov and Hoegh 2006; Yao and Warren 2005). These advances provided the impetus for the research team to develop an innovative decision support system for injury prevention applications. A DSS that could achieve a simple and cost-effective method of collecting data using handheld devices could enter and analyse data quickly; using these advances in information system technology was the goal of this project.

Cost-effective data collection and analysis to support evidence-based decisions presented the team with a number of challenges. Increasingly, complex issues arise in the areas of data collection from static and mobile sensors and handheld devices, data flow across networks between storage and processing centres, all with high degrees of system and hardware heterogeneity, and support for decision making. In order to deal with these problems, techniques from distributed database and data mining (Lu, Naeem, and Stav 2006; Salem, Krishnaswamy, Loke, and Rakotonirainy 2005) and artificial intelligence, such as evolutionary computing, learning, and pattern recognition (Baqer, Khan, and Baig 2005; Hine, Judson, Ashraf, Arnott, Sixsmith, and Brown, et al. 2005; Kobti, Reynolds, and Kohler 2003; O'Hare, O'Gradym, Collier, and Keegan, 2005) were applied in the development of this system.

2.3 *Decision Support Systems in Health Care*

The concept of decision support systems (DSS) was first stated in the early 1970s in which DSS were called "interactive computer-based systems, which help decision makers utilise data and models to solve unstructured problems" (Gorry and Scott Morton 1971). A few years later, the definition of DSS became more nuanced as Keen and Scott Morton (1978) articulated, "Decision support systems couple the intellectual resources of individuals with the capabilities of the computer to improve the quality of decisions. It is a computer-based support system for management decision makers who deal with semi-structured problems." However, the concept of DSS has evolved significantly since its inception four decades ago and today DSS is more like an umbrella term referring to any kind of computerised information system capable of assisting individuals or organisations in their decision-making process.

The use of DSS in health care has a rich history in terms of both timeline and diversity of applications. In the early 1970s, an expert system called MYCIN was developed at Stanford University to identify bacteria causing infections and to recommend appropriate antibiotics. In health care, DSS have been used to assess the effectiveness of physicians' decisions (Wigton 1988), to improve quality of patient care (Bates and Gawande 2003), patient satisfaction (Kohli, Tan, Piontek, Ziege, and Groot 1999), to understand the role of hospitals (Conrad, Wickizer, Maynard, Klastorin, Lessler, Ross, Soderstrom, Sullivan, Alexander, and Travis 1996) and patient demographics (Bodenheimer 2005) on the quality of care among others. Artificial intelligence techniques such as agent-based simulation have been incorporated into health care DSS for over 40 years. Health care simulation refers to a process of mimicking a system for understanding the interactions between individuals and/or components of a system and how these interactions over time produce the behaviour observed in the health care system (Lyell, Sadsad, and Georgiou 2008). Regarding the application of simulation in health care, refer to these recent works of Homer and Hirsch (2006), Kuljis, Paul, and Stergioulas (2007), and Lyell et al. (2008).

3 A Framework for a Decision-Making Process

In this section, we describe a framework that was used for building our DSS. Simon (1977) suggested that a decision-making process consists of three phases: intelligence, design and choice. Figure 1, which is adapted from Turban and Aronson (2000, p. 42), depicts that a decision problem is abstracted from the reality "out there" based on some simplifications and assumptions. For the purpose of this study, the reality was that a high rate of severe injury of child occupants occurs due to the improper use, or nonuse of child safety seats in vehicles. These injuries account for more deaths in Canadian children annually than all other causes of death combined.

In the intelligence phase, we define the objectives and means of data collection. As shown in Fig. 1, the objective of this study was to prevent or reduce the injury

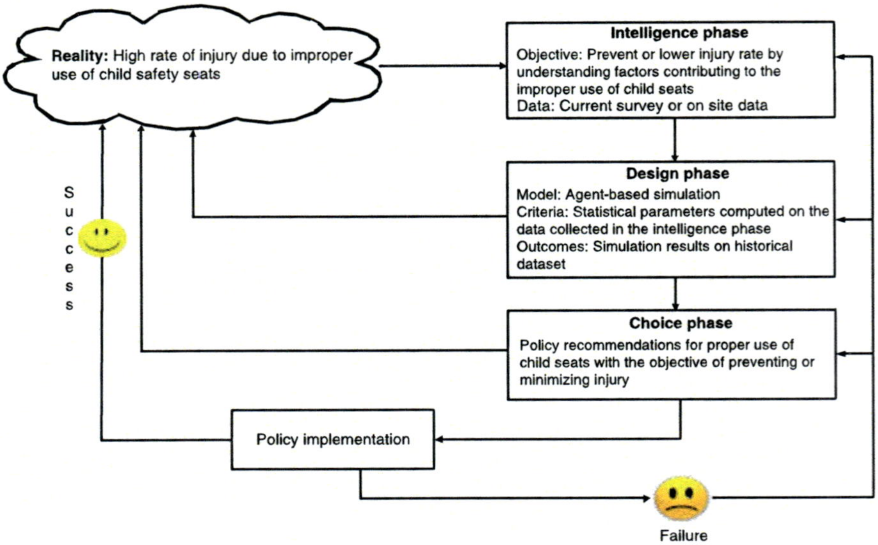

Fig. 1 A decision-making framework (Adapted from Turban and Aronson 2000)

rate of children by understanding various factors that contribute to the improper use of child seats. Data for the intelligence phase was obtained through survey and on-site data collection. The design phase involves formulating a model and setting criteria for choice and outcomes. In our research, we have primarily relied on an agent-based simulation model to examine the system. As outcomes from the design phase, we have considered results from the simulation run on a large historical database that evolved over the past decade. The choice phase involves providing solutions to the model, the ability to understand the sensitivity of the solution, and a plan for implementation of injury prevention strategies and approaches. In our study, the outcome from the choice phase is a list of policy recommendations regarding the proper use of child seats with the objective of minimising or preventing bodily injury. In the next section, we discuss in detail the design and development of our DSS-based on the framework depicted in Fig. 1.

4 Design and Development of the Just-in-Time AI-Based DSS

The JIT AI-based DSS consists of four components: the just-in-time data collection (JITDC) module, the artificial intelligence (AI) module, the persistent storage (PS), and the business logic and decision (BLD) module. As shown in Fig. 2, the JITDC module uploads and saves the collected field data into the PS. The PS is a repository for data and database schema for the DSS. The BLD module performs statistical analysis of the stored data and sends its results to the AI module for the purpose of initialising

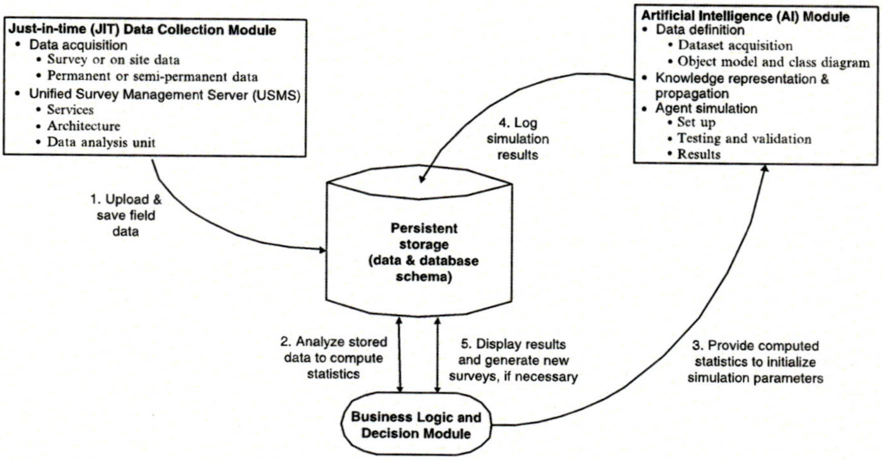

Fig. 2 A framework for the just-in-time AI-based DSS

agent-based simulation parameters. The AI module starts simulating its historical dataset after calibrating its model through two validation tests (Sect. 4.3.2.2). When the simulation results are aligned with the survey statistics computed by the BLD module, the model is considered stabilised and is initialised with these values to be used in actual production mode. The simulation data generated in the production mode are stored in the persistent storage. The BLD module displays the results in a graphical format to the user and generates new surveys if necessary. We now describe each module in detail.

4.1 *Just-in-Time Data Collection (JITDC) Module*

The overall objective of this module is to collect distributed data from various sources, extract and upload the collected data in the database, and attach semantics to the stored data for the purpose of statistical analysis and report generation. The JITDC module consists of two main components: data acquisition and the unified survey management server. Figure 3 depicts the organisation of the JITDC module.

4.1.1 Data Acquisition

Data acquisition refers to the process of collecting data via direct or indirect public communication. There are two kinds of data centres identified, the wireless data centre (*top left* component in Fig. 3) and the permanent or semi-permanent data centre (*top right* component in Fig. 3). The former consists of lightweight mobile

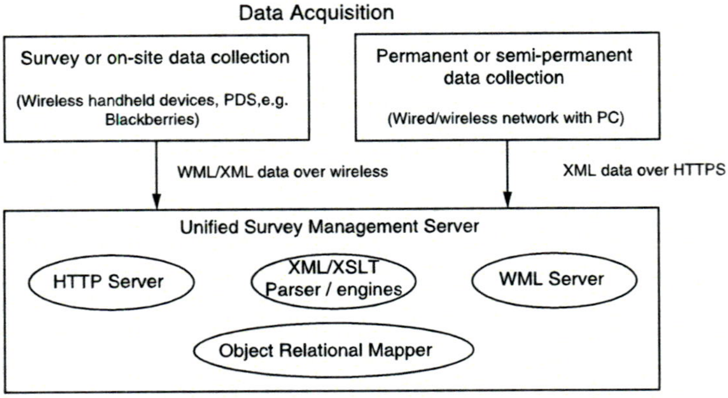

Fig. 3 The just-in-time data collection module

data centres (e.g., wireless handheld devices like Blackberry™, PDA, etc.) that would allow the surveyor to collect data from virtually any place where effective wireless Internet communication is available. Handheld devices were ideal for roadside observers since they were lightweight and easy to use. The latter is not intended to be mobile and thus can be equipped with power computation hardware. Such a centre may include the hospital or other public health care facilities.

4.1.2 Unified Survey Management System

The Unified Survey Management System (USMS) is a multi-tiered, distributed system for creating and deploying surveys online for data collection (Kent, Snowdon, Preney, Kim, Ren, and Aggarwal, et al. 2007; Snowdon, Kent, Kobti, and Howard 2006). USMS is also intended to provide analytical capabilities for post-survey statistical correlation studies as well as real-time trends analysis while field surveys are ongoing. Recent work involving agent-based modelling of social networks that use survey data suggested incorporating aspects of agent modelling support in order to provide an additional analytical framework for developing and testing intervention strategies using feedback. To accomplish these goals, the USMS was designed to support collaboration within a multidisciplinary research and strategic partnership context.

The core elements of a centralised USMS were developed initially as part of the 2006 national child seat survey conducted in collaboration with Transport Canada. The goal of this survey was to examine and document the use of child safety seat systems for child occupants on Canada's roadways (Snowdon et al. 2006). The child safety seat survey was designed based on previous Transport Canada surveys to elicit observational data on the use of restraint systems for children while travelling in vehicles. The survey also included a parking lot component whereby drivers were asked a number of questions about knowledge, perceptions and use of child safety seats in vehicles. Design and application of this highly detailed survey (with hundreds of questions) to a large population sample is a huge undertaking, but it is clear that a software approach was very useful.

Since 2006, the USMS has been undergoing further testing and development for application in a hospital setting to examine its utility for patient care reporting systems with nursing staff (Kent et al. 2007). Currently, the USMS has been extended to deal more effectively with these and similar application scenarios in health systems by redesigning and implementing an ad hoc, peer-to-peer based grid strategy using a service-oriented approach (Blanquer et al. 2005; Omar and Taleb-Bendiab 2006; Von Lubitz and Wickramasinghe 2006). This approach enables USMS to achieve local autonomy at each peer node while supporting secure data exchange and replication across the peer network, scalability of the network, shared access to resources and other features. Through these capabilities, it is possible to use USMS in other relevant areas, such as global health applications for epidemiology and disaster monitoring where "real-time" data collection and analysis are required to support rapid responses to natural disasters.

The USMS Web runs under OSes: Solaris 10, Linux (Debian, Fedora) using Apache web server 2.2. Open SSL 0.9.7d is used to create a self-signed certificate for SSL connection. Survey application has been rendered to Internet Explorer and Mozilla Firefox browsers, and to various Blackberry model browsers where we employed Blackberry™ development kits (Research in Motion). Language and scripting were accomplished using the following: Java (JDK, JVM), JXTA, Python, PHP 5, JpGraph 1.17, PHP 5, XML, XSLT-FO, WML, HTML. Network protocols include: HTTP, HTTPS, WAP, UDP, TCP. Database tools and applications include: PostgreSQL, Oracle 10g XE, MySQL, Datalog. For metadata work we use: Protégé, DAML+OIL, RDF, RDFS. Emerging standards support exists with OGSA/OGSI, OGSA-DAI/DQP (OGSA-DAI 3.0 documentation) and HL 7 health protocols. Our development work occurs within computer science laboratories using PC and server machines. The USMS Database System runs under Fedora core 4 Linux and Oracle 10 g XE with an Intel Pentium IV 2.8 GHz with 512 MB of RAM. All of the above machines are behind a firewall which provides a basic packet filtering facility to block "illegal" traffic specified by security policy. Authenticated access is provided through a secure HTTPS session.

4.1.2.1 Services Offered by the USMS

The USMS front end consists of an initial secure interface for logging onto the system. At this point, several views may be rendered, depending on role-based authorisation, including the full system (all capabilities) or restricted aspects (enact a specific survey only). The full system includes provisions for various tools, including data management, survey design, query and data mining, statistical analysis and modelling.

Management tools provide for access and security, user and device registry, approval by sponsors and ethics reviewers, and messaging between users. The survey design toolkit is comprised of a visual interface with point-and-click choice and text entry elements for defining number of questions (arbitrary), type of question (single choice, multiple choice with and without mutual exclusion, text, etc.), restrictions on responses (as an enforcement mechanism to assure correctness of input data and minimisation of data cleaning) and other inputs.

Once surveys have been designed, they must be approved. As a consequence of initial field testing, however, it is likely that surveys may be modified, so we have adopted a simple approach to retaining initial data to prevent loss and mark this data as pre-or post-approved. The generic query toolkit has been designed to facilitate production of user-oriented query interfaces for each survey (and more generic queries as well) and optimise the query logic for application to distributed query logic and data mining. The statistical analysis toolkit consists of a variety of simple analysis functions, but more importantly, provides an application interface to other packages for detailed analysis. We have adopted an open source development approach, but recognise that available proprietary tools, such as SPSS or SAS, may be required for some needs. Finally, the agent modelling toolkit provides for establishing appropriate data structures that agents may adopt for accessing survey data. Increasingly, survey data, particularly metadata, is expected to translate into conceptual knowledge; therefore, steps are underway to develop a knowledgebase that is commensurate with the survey database. From the user perspectives, the USMS affords the following capabilities:

(a) Local autonomy with built-in logic
(b) Easy to set up and manage for local IT staff; minimum training requirements for administrators and users
(c) Creation of surveys, with ability to edit data from survey questions, dynamically alter surveys during initial validation and testing phases, and lock surveys once validated
(d) Minimisation of data entry error
(e) Maintenance of data integrity
(f) Portability (cellular to desktops)
(g) Automatic download to servers and easy retrieval of data
(h) Flexible analysis and modelling features
(i) Real-time data analysis for efficient and effective decision making
(j) Meaningful data representation for multilevel (e.g., front line, managerial) interpretation and policy decision support

A partial list of services is summarised in Table 1.

4.1.2.2 Architecture of the USMS

The distributed core of the USMS system used a centralised architecture which split the system into multiple survey sites, data centres, and a centralised control centre. This architecture contained several drawbacks. First, the control centre was responsible for keeping all the metadata from various data sources updated and responded to all metadata queries which would place a heavy load on the control centre. Second, the control centre itself could have been a single point of failure.

Table 1 Services provided by the USMS

Module	Services offered
Task Management Services	Task analysis, service composition, choreography, resource planning, scheduling, load balancing
Survey Services	Creation, editing, approval (sponsor, ethics), policy implementation, data collection, query execution, interface and view rendering
Knowledge Services	Ontology design, creation, and integration
	Metadata and concept management
	Reasoning with simulation agents
Data Services	Survey storage, editing, transaction
	metadata, indexing, cataloguing, database federation and replication; survey data analysis, data mining, and reporting
Security Services	Registration (role-based), authentication, authorisation, encryption, auditing/assurance, accounting
Communication and Networking Services	Peer management, Web services, wireless, satellite

Third, heavy administration overheads needed to be applied to the entire architecture. Finally, research studies are typically ad hoc, are considered and developed quickly, need to be applied in diverse application contexts, and require rapid analyses to inform decisions. To overcome these limitations we have adopted a grid computing approach based on ad hoc, peer-to-peer (P2P) approaches (Chervenak and Cai 2006; Lim et al. 2005; Ulieru, Hadzic, and Chang 2006). P2P architecture offers good self-organisation and distributed control characteristics that help to overcome the aforementioned drawbacks. Therefore, we adopted a P2P-based architecture for USMS and combined the grid and P2P features. That is, each peer manages its own metadata (schema), and it queries and synchronises external metadata (schema that belong to the same peer group) using P2P services. The USMS query toolkit will use the schema to construct and evaluate queries. A complex query is reduced into atomic queries and then submitted to different data sources for execution via the data service, which is based on the Open Grid Services Architecture Data Access and Integration (OGSA-DAI) approach. In this way, we can still utilise the service-oriented data access and high throughput data delivery features provided by grids.

We have used JXTA to construct our distributed metadata management system. JXTA is an open-source, P2P protocol that provides for interoperability, platform independence, and ubiquity. In this architecture, on one hand, each peer acts as a fully functional USMS survey data collector and a data analysis unit. On the other hand, each peer is also a JATX peer and can be configured as one of the following peer types. *Normal Peer:* Peer that implements all of the core and standard JXTA services and can participate in all of the JXTA protocols to exchange metadata information. *Rendezvous Peer:* Peer that maintains global advertisement indexes and assists normal peers with advertisement searches. It also handles message broadcasting. *Relay Peer*: Peer that is used to store and forward messages between peers that do not have direct connectivity because of firewalls or network address translation (NAT).

A number of different peers can form a peer group for a common kind of survey service. Peers self-organise into peer groups, each uniquely identified by peer group identification (ID). JXTA supports each peer group establishing its own membership policy, ranging from open (anybody can join) to highly secure and protected (requiring credentials to gain membership). The communication within a peer group can be secured by a personal security environment membership service. Peers may belong to more than one peer group simultaneously. The USMS peer organisation is illustrated in Fig. 4. Figure 5 depicts the decentralised USMS with single peer architecture.

4.1.2.3 Data Analysis Unit

In order to analyse collected data, it is necessary to provide efficient, well-defined access to the data. The USMS imposes structure on the data model inferred through the survey structure itself. Thus, at the time of survey creation, many aspects of the data model structure can be accounted for and imposed to minimise the database development and administration overheads that would be otherwise required. We use XML to envelope surveys, survey questions and responses, while RDF and RDFS are used to describe metadata. The primary tool set components developed and adapted to USMS appear within the generic query toolkit (GQT) (Zhu, Ezeife, and Kent 2007) and a derivative generic query language (GQL). The following components are defined in detail.

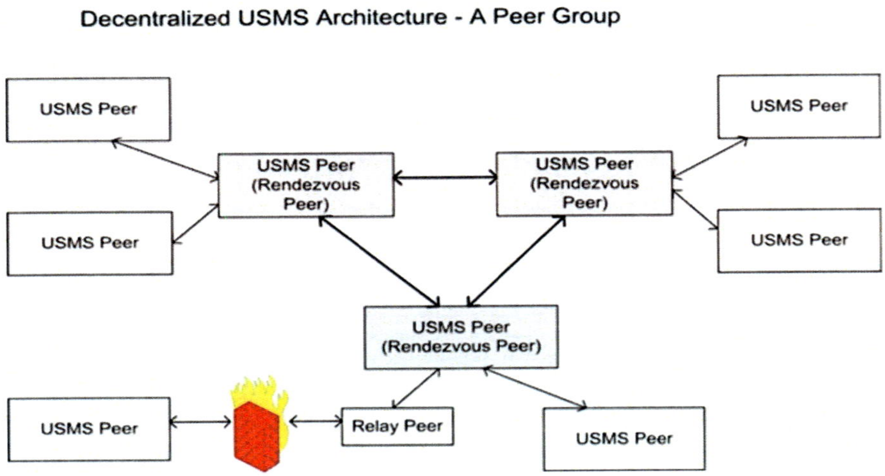

Fig. 4 The USMS peer group

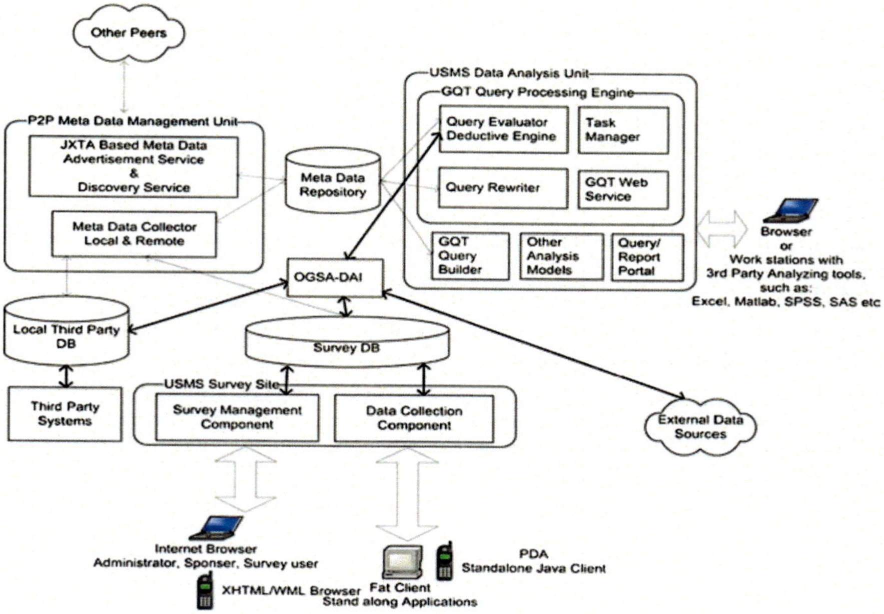

Fig. 5 Decentralised USMS, single peer architecture

(a) *Query builder*: Construct GQL script with the assistance of metadata repository. The schema that will be used in GQL will be global schema and survey schema.
(b) *Query rewriter*: Rewrites (extended) datalog query from using global schema to local schema (Liu 1995).
(c) *Query evaluator*: Processes (extended) datalog statements (after rewriting) by utilising either a top-down or bottom-down approach (Ullman 1990). This reduces the query into atomic simple queries and distributes them to various execution units.
(d) *Other analysis tools*: Multiple data analysis tools or algorithms can be integrated into this unit, such as agent modelling, statistical analysis, or data mining algorithms. GQL can be extended to provide a unified invocation interface for a data analysis process designer to utilise these tools.
(e) *Task Manager*: Maintains a task queue and invokes query evaluator to process submitted tasks. Sends notification upon task completion or failure.
(f) *GQT Web Service*: Web service interface for external applications to handle all the query processes (same function as current GQL Server).
(g) *Query/Report Portal*: Web-based user interface for query selection, submission, and viewing of results and data exports.
(h) *Metadata Repository*: It currently manages three types of metadata. (1) *Global Schema*: Logic level schema that represents the overall system model. In local-as-view (Ullman 1990) query rewriting approach, global schema is used to describe the local physical schema. This schema is likely to change, however.

(2) *Survey Schema*: Survey definitions that can be regarded as a kind of special relation that contains complex data types (nested sets and tuples). This is a fundamental aspect of developing a survey ontology. (3) *Local Physical Schema*: Schema extracted from relations or views from a local database, which may be subject to change.

4.2 Artificial Intelligence (AI) Module

As shown in Fig. 2, the AI module is a key component of our DSS which provides the intelligence to the DSS by means of a multi-agent-based modelling that simulates an artificial society using various evolutionary algorithm techniques. The AI module's multi-agent-based model is built around the cultural algorithm framework (Reynolds 2002). Cultural algorithm is a population-based evolutionary algorithm that provides a well-established framework for representing the population, culture and knowledge. It is also possible to include other evolutionary algorithms like particle swarm optimisation (PSO) (Ahmad, Yung-Chuan, Rahimi, and Gupta 2007; Coelho and Mariani 2006) or ant colony optimisation (ACO) (Dorigo, Birattari, and Stutzle 2006) into the cultural framework as alternate or hybrid evolutionary mechanisms. It is also suitable for simulating intelligent social beings as agents in an artificial society (Kobti et al. 2003).

4.2.1 Data Definition

The AI module of this JIT framework is itself a multi-agent model and constitutes its own stream of research, both in artificial intelligence applications in health care research (Kobti et al. 2003; Snowdon et al. 2006). The AI module is therefore referred to as the child safety model in the following text. The child safety model is built on top of a large dataset collected by a health research team over the last 10 years through numerous survey studies and interventions programmes. The surveys were specifically designed to empirically examine parent knowledge and use of child safety seats in vehicles. Therefore, the dataset includes substantial demographic data of the Canadian population of parents, such as education level, income level, age, gender, ethnicity and so on. Detailed information on the child's age, weight and height as well as patterns of use of child seats have been recorded in numerous survey type studies at the national level, which are still ongoing. In order to capitalise on the data effectively, the data was laid onto a relational database with database schema appropriate for the child safety model. Therefore, the model feeds on the database in order to initialise the object entities including driver, child and model properties. The dependency on the data and object model is conceptualised in Fig. 6.

We now describe the child safety model class diagram in terms of entities and relationships. The child safety model is tightly coupled with the survey data collected by health care researchers over the last 10 years. In addition to low level data structures, the agent model also requires a precise object-oriented model for its high

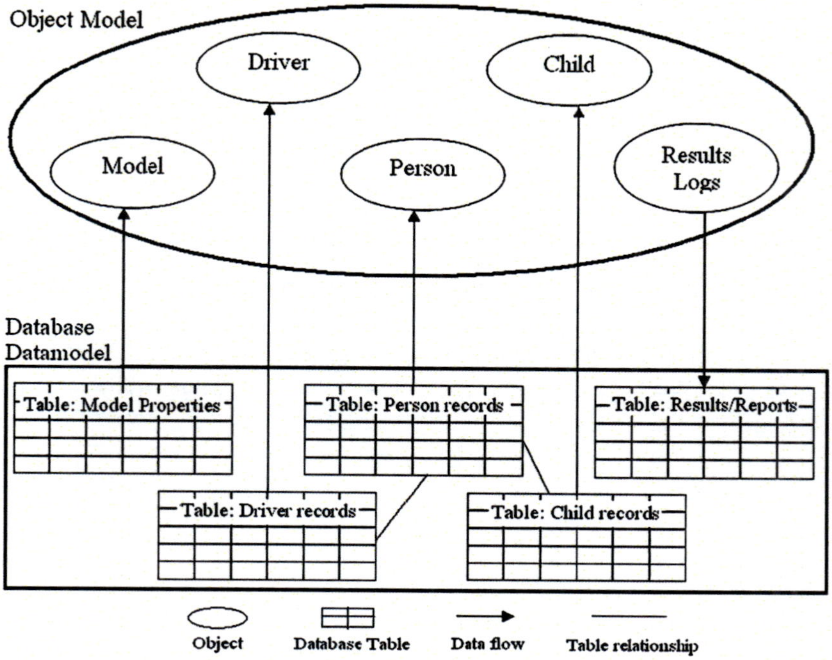

Fig. 6 AI module – the child safety model and its data source

level abstraction. The relationship among the objects and their respective data source must also be defined. In Fig. 7, all of the entities related to the model and their relationship are produced by means of a class diagram.

The implementation of this model used the Recursive Porous Agent Simulation Toolkit (Repast) (Collier, Howe, and North 2003). A detailed description, tutorial and features of Repast are available at their website. Each component of the model is described:

Model: Provides the environment of the agents. The model class is *AutoSimModel* that extends the Repast framework class *SimModelImpl.*

Person: Includes the concept of an adult person. Many demographic characteristics like gender, age, ethnicity and income level have been captured into this class. A person refers most often to the child's parent but may also refer to other family members or friends who transport children in a vehicle.

Child: This is an extension class to the *Person* class and represents the child entity conceptually in terms of the age, weight, and height measures of children that are used to determine correct use of child safety seats.

Family/Household: A collection of persons and children that constitutes a family. The social structure of the model is implemented through this class.

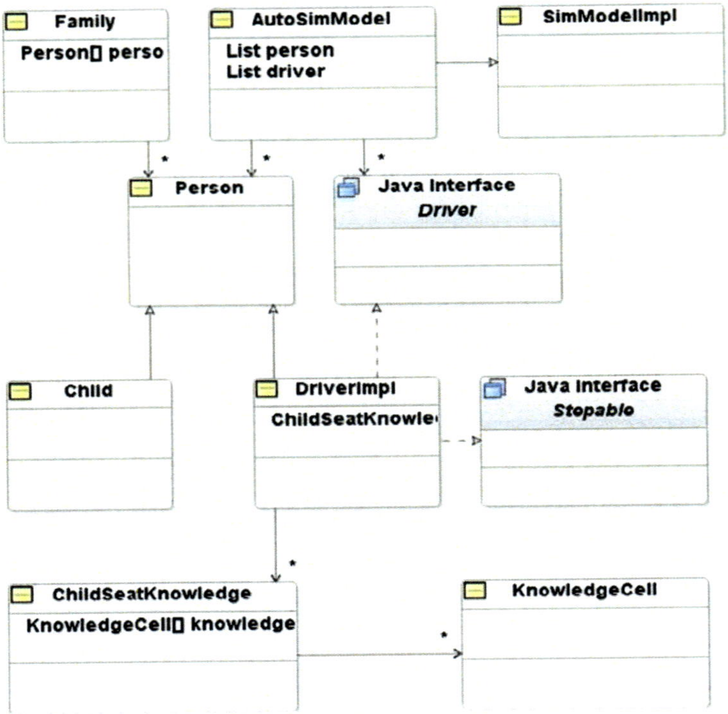

Fig. 7 Child safety model class diagram

Driver: Represents the intelligent, socially active agent of the *Model*. From the cultural algorithm point of view, a collection of the instances of this class forms the population space of the cultural algorithm. It implements the Repast interface *Stepable* for seamless integration into the repast model.

Child Seat Knowledge: This represents the percept of the driver's (or agent's) knowledge about child safety in vehicles. The knowledge representation component of the model is determined by this class. The implementation detail of this class follows in the next section.

Belief Space: Implements the belief space component of the cultural algorithm framework. This class accommodates different categories of knowledge and provides functionalities that influence the population (or the drivers).

4.2.2 Knowledge Representation and Propagation

The knowledge structure and its representation play a significant role in the child safety model. The concept of knowledge is also referred to as the strategy that each agent must be equipped with to effectively cope with the driving environment. With respect to this child safety model, the knowledge refers to the percept of the drivers about child safety, which in turn implies their knowledge of proper child seat usage. One of the major objectives of this model is to improve the drivers' percept, and to understand what and how improvement on drivers' knowledge and use of safety systems can be achieved. In order to formulate child seat knowledge, standards were adopted from different authoritative sources like Transport Canada, National Highway Traffic Safety Administration (NHTSA) of the USA, Safe Kids Canada, and injury prevention empirical literature.

The correct use of a child seat requires the accurate seat assignment of a child in a vehicle based on three criteria: age (for infants only), weight and height. The criterion for age is important only for children 1 year of age or less. For all other age groups, the importance of these criteria is equal and must be all satisfied for a child to be safely seated in a vehicle. Therefore, the percept of an individual is categorised based on these three criteria. Together, these three precepts define the overall knowledge of an individual agent.

Considering this pattern, it is then formalised that each agent has a set of three percepts respectively in terms of age, weight and height. Each category of percept again contains multiple sets of secondary percepts depending on the range of the unit of the child on that category. The secondary percepts are implemented as the class KnowledgeCell. The formal definition of knowledge is presented below.

$$\text{Driver's Knowledge} := \{K_{\text{Weight}}, K_{\text{Age}}, K_{\text{Heigh}}$$

where K_x is ChildSeatKowledge in terms of $x\}$

$$\text{ChildSeatKowledge} := \{\text{Cell}_i \mid$$

where $i = 0 \ldots n$, n being any number and each Cell_i is an instance of KnowledgeCell}

$$\text{KnowledgeCell} := \{\text{ lower range, upper range}, t,$$

where t € T and l € L}

T: = {rear facing seat, forward facing seat, booster seat, seat belt, sitting on adult's lap}

L: = {front seat, back middle, back side, centre middle, centre side}

According to this scheme, if a person thinks or knows that a child in the weight range (41–81 lb) may use a seat belt or booster seat and can be located in any seat other than the front seat, then this perception can be represented as follows:

$$\text{KnowledgeCell} := \left\{ \begin{array}{l} 41, 81, \{\text{Booster}, \text{Seatbelt}\}, \\ \{\text{back middle, back side, centre middle, centre side}\} \end{array} \right\}$$

As far as implementation is concerned, the T and L values are actually strings of 1s and 0s where the length of T is 5 (since there are five different types of seats) and the length of L is also 5 (for five different seat locations in a vehicle). Therefore, logically, we have the following:

If (someone has a choice of rear facing seat)
    $T[0]$ = "1", otherwise $T[0]$ = "0".
If (someone has a choice of forward facing seat)
    $T[1]$ = "1", otherwise $T[1]$ = "0".
If (someone has a choice of booster seat)
    $T[2]$ = "1", otherwise $T[2]$ = "0".
If (someone has a choice of seat belt)
    $T[3]$ = "1", otherwise $T[3]$ = "0".
If (someone has a choice of lap)
    $T[4]$ = "1", otherwise $T[4]$ = "0".

Similarly, the location string L is structured in the order of front, back, middle, back side, centre middle, centre side seat location. Therefore, the knowledge representation for the weight category of the person in the previous example would be:

$$\text{KnowledgeCell} = \; < 41, 81, 00110, 01111 >$$

A person may have multiple knowledge cells on a single category (such as age, weight, height, etc.) of knowledge. The collection of these cells for a given category represents the actual knowledge of this person on this category. This collection is implemented as the ChildSeatKnowledge class objects and the cells are implemented as KnowledgeCell class objects. According to this scheme, each person has three ChildSeatKnowledge objects: knowledge for Age K_A, Weight K_W and Height K_H. A complete set of percepts of a driver therefore can be represented as follows:

$$K_A := \{< 00, 13, 10000, 01111 >, < 13, 49, 01000, 01111 >, \\ < 49, 97, 00100, 01111 >, < 97, 145, 00010, 01111 >\}$$

$$K_W := \{< 00, 21, 10000, 01111 >, < 21, 41, 11000, 01111 >, \\ < 41, 81, 00100, 01111 >, < 81, 121, 00010, 01111 >\}$$

$$K_H := \{< 00, 27, 10000, 01111 >, < 27, 56, 01100, 01111 >, \\ < 56, 75, 00010, 01111 >\}$$

From the above set of percepts, the following can be concluded. The agent with this set of percepts believes that children in the age group 13–49 months (according to K_A) go only into forward facing seat and the child seat could be located anywhere in the car except for the front seat. Children in the weight group 41–81 lb (according to K_W) go to a booster seat and the seat can be located anywhere but the front seat.

A child in the height group 27–56 in. (according to K_H) may use a forward facing seat or a booster seat and could be located anywhere but the front seat.

For knowledge propagation, there is an innovative extension of cultural algorithm in the child safety model, which involves implementation of a social network among the agents. Practically, the agents that are being modelled in this simulation are artificial human drivers and child occupants with characteristics derived from real practical survey data. Therefore, the agents in this model are, by default, social in nature, and they tend to communicate and collaborate with each other. Therefore, the social network among them provides a communication channel among them. Each agent in the model is related to its kin and neighbours and it can influence its associates or be influenced by them. This influence mechanism of one agent by another is termed knowledge propagation. It is hypothesised that knowledge propagation and exploitation of other social network properties could lead to the development of more effective strategies to increase child safety and drivers' correct use of child safety seats.

4.2.3 Agent Simulation

The autonomous components of the model are the driver agents. The agents, or more precisely their knowledge, instances form the population space of the cultural model. The activity that an agent goes through during the run time of the simulation is presented in the following diagram.

Simulation Set Up

An agent can be in one of the three states after its initialisation and for the duration of the simulation run. The lifecycle of an agent is depicted in Fig. 8. The states are namely "Not Driving", "Driving" and in "Accident" state. The names of the states are self-explanatory and describe their activity, literally. As with any population-based algorithm with multi-agent modelling, this simulation also goes through a similar set of operations repeatedly until the terminating condition is achieved or the simulation is stopped. This set of repetitive processes is called "a step of the model." And the function that implements a step is called "step function." Therefore, a single execution or call to this function constitutes one step of the model. Various record keeping functions, result logging and display management operations are also involved in this function. We now describe some important model parameters and indexes used in the simulation.
Stress factor: The drivers use their knowledge while assigning a seat to the child passengers. However, his/her decision might be altered due to factors such as the child's resistance to use of safety restraints, experiencing an emergency situation, or the driver being in a rush to get children in the vehicle and travel to a destination, and so on. In order to incorporate these issues, the stress factor is introduced into the model which mutates the drivers' KnowledgeCell. This alteration may or may

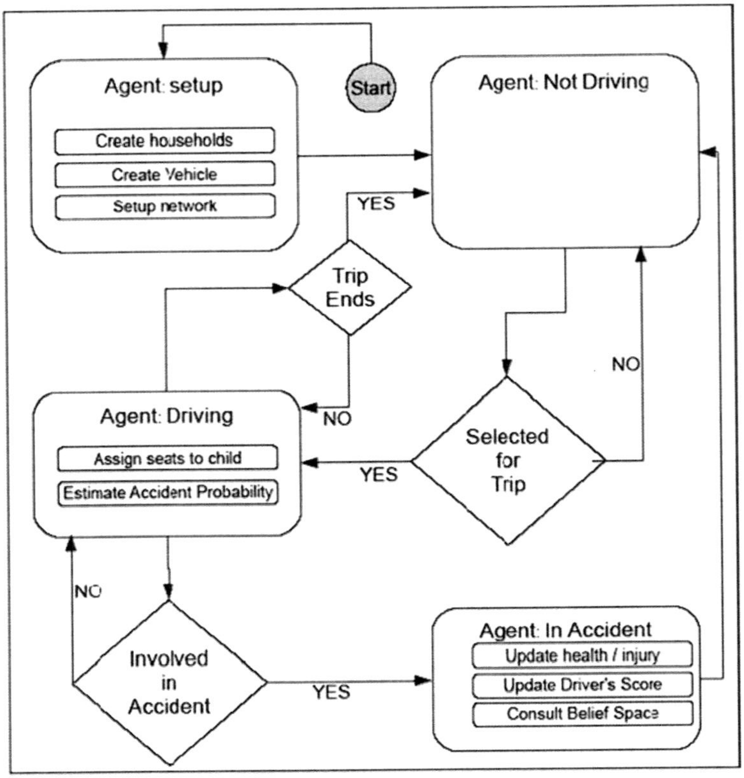

Fig. 8 Agent's life cycle

not affect the driver's decision. The stress factor is defined as a percentage, and stress factors 10%, 20% and 30% have been analysed and charted in the model. A higher stress factor implies higher level of dispersion or mutation from actual knowledge.

Learning Rate: Drivers' (i.e., the agents) are learning agents. They can learn new strategies from the belief space, from social networks or learn from safety education programmes. It is conceptualised that an agent may not be able to learn correctly from the source, and its perception may be slightly different than the information presented by the source. The learning rate defines the degree of accuracy with which an agent can learn from a given source. The learning rate is measured in percentage, where 100% implies accurate learning. The model has been tested for different learning rates.

Standard Knowledge Source and Complexity: The concept of standard knowledge source defines the sources from where parents or agents learn about child seat use in vehicles. The most commonly available sources of vehicle safety information are the manuals and booklets that come with the child seats when purchased and the information from health care professionals who educate families about safety seats in both hospitals and public health units. The knowledge the standard source provides is considered to be the most accurate. But at the same time, any standard source may offer a level of complexity which limits the parents' ability to absorb the knowledge perfectly. In fact, many child seat manuals were found to be very difficult to comprehend. The complexity level that a knowledge source may offer affects the performance of the agents in making the best decisions when seating their child in vehicles.

Correctness Index: The correctness index defines the level of accuracy with which a child is safely seated (assigned to a seat) in a vehicle. It can assume a value between 0 and 10. Each driver applies his/her knowledge strings to evaluate an assignment string. Another assignment string is evaluated using the standard knowledge and is matched bitwise against the previous one. The matching value is the number of matched bits, which could be, at most, 10. Usually, a matching score lower than five would imply wrong assignment and correct assignment would be greater than five. The correctness index, along with correct transition rate is one of the most important indexes used to evaluate the overall performance of the model.

Correct Seat Transition (CST) and Correct Transition Rate (CTR): As the simulation proceeds, the physical characteristics (e.g., age, weight, height of the children) change over time as the child grows older and gets taller and heavier. As the child's weight and height increase, parents or drivers must make correct decisions to transition their child into child seats that accommodate the child's increased height and weight. Therefore, the seat assignment for the child should also be changed accordingly. When a driver or parent decides on the correct set of seat assignments for a grown child, it is defined as correct seat transition (CST). On the other hand, correct transition rate (CTR) is defined as the percentage of children, among the total child population, who have been correctly transitioned to safety seats based on the child's height and weight. For example, when a child reaches 40 lb in weight and 40 in. in height, they are safely transitioned to a booster seat from a forward facing seat. The CTR is the percentage of children who are safely transitioned to booster seats when they reach this height and weight milestone. In this research model, the CTR is calculated over a period of 1 month each. The correctness indexes of all the seat assignments for each child are recorded over 1 month, and if the average of those indexes is over 6.0, then the transition for that child is deemed to be correct.

Testing and Validation

The reference implementation of the child safety model discussed above has been evaluated by performing some high level tests and outputs, verified against actual statistics and available data. These tests were termed as validation testing because they were designed to validate and calibrate the model. These were trial-and-error-based procedures and were performed several times until the model began to act rationally. Among these tests, the source complexity test and the stress factor test are described below. These tests, along with their counterparts, provide a well-calibrated and rational agent model.

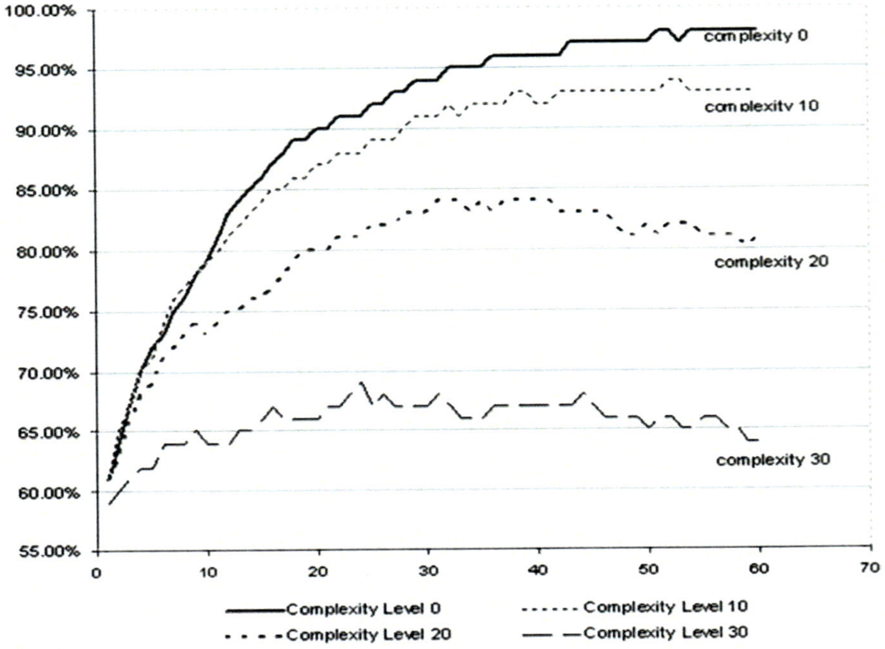

Fig. 9 Source complexity test

Source Complexity Test: This test of the model tests the response of the simulation when complexity is increased. A higher level of complexity offered by the standard knowledge source would be expected to lower the performance level of the model. Therefore maximum average CTR level should be lower, illustrated by the following charts in Fig. 9. For complexity level 0 (meaning no complexity), the average CTR reaches more than 95%, and as the complexity level goes up, the rate of transition correctness decreases, as one would expect in a valid simulation model.

Stress Factor Test: A variety of factors have a significant influence on correct use of child seats in vehicles (Snowdon et al. 2008a). The age of the child (ability of the child to resist), the availability of information, and the education of the parent all influence the rate of correct use of child safety seats. These factors are combined into a single factor termed as stress factor. It can assume a value between 0 and 100, with higher values implying higher levels of associated stress. Therefore, a higher stress factor would a result in lower safety system rate of correct use. In Fig. 10, the average rate of correct use is plotted over time for three different stress factors. The rate of correct use performance level decreased under conditions of higher stress in the validation testing.

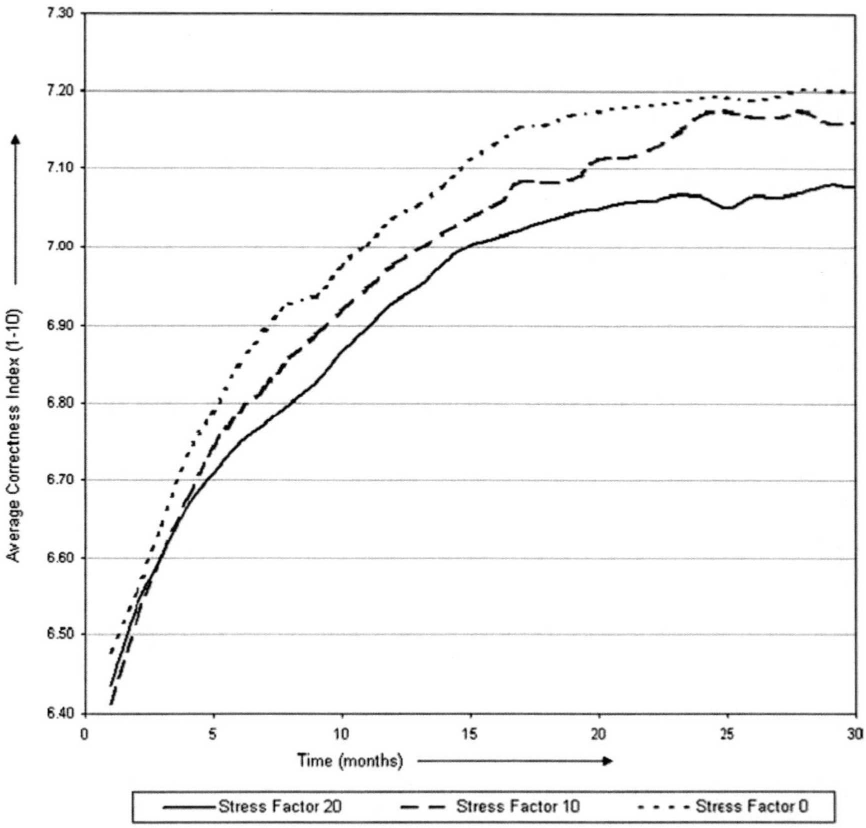

Fig. 10 Average correctness over time for different stress factors

Simulation Results

Once the model was verified as behaving rationally and its outputs were aligned with actual statistical research data, it was certified as usable for production use. Some of the recommendations or guidance from the model are presented in this section. Although the recommendations are not beyond any criticism, they clearly demonstrate the practical usability of the AI-based JIT framework to inform both policy development and to support health professional practice for injury prevention programme development.

Effect of Social Network

As described in an earlier section, the social network among the agents in the model acts as a communication channel and any new or different strategy achieved by an agent can be conveyed to another agent whereby proper capitalisation of this social behaviour may lead to improvements in average knowledge of correct use of safety systems in the whole population. Social networks typically exhibit the small world network topology, or six degrees of separation. It was hypothesised that the topology of the social network in place plays an overall role. In order to identify this effect, a test bed was designed that enables communication between connected agents. The knowledge exchanged over these neighbouring nodes can be observed by means of its manifested outcome. The simulations were executed several times, each with a different random topology supporting the neighbourhood relations. As a measure of topology, the number of relations, or edges, on the network was considered, and it was plotted against the maximum average correctness achieved. The edge in a social network represents a link between two agents if they are associated with one another and consequently enable an exchange route for knowledge. One chart was plotted for maximum average correctness attained in each run against numbers of edges in the network. And another was plotted against average of average correctness attained in each run against the numbers of edges in the network.

Figure 11 illustrates that the performance of correct use of safety seats increases with increasing number of edges but only up to a certain limit, at which point it begins to decline. Therefore, the model suggests that the effect of knowledge propagation on society affects the performance positively as the population density (in terms of edges) grows. But at a certain level of population density, the effect becomes negative.

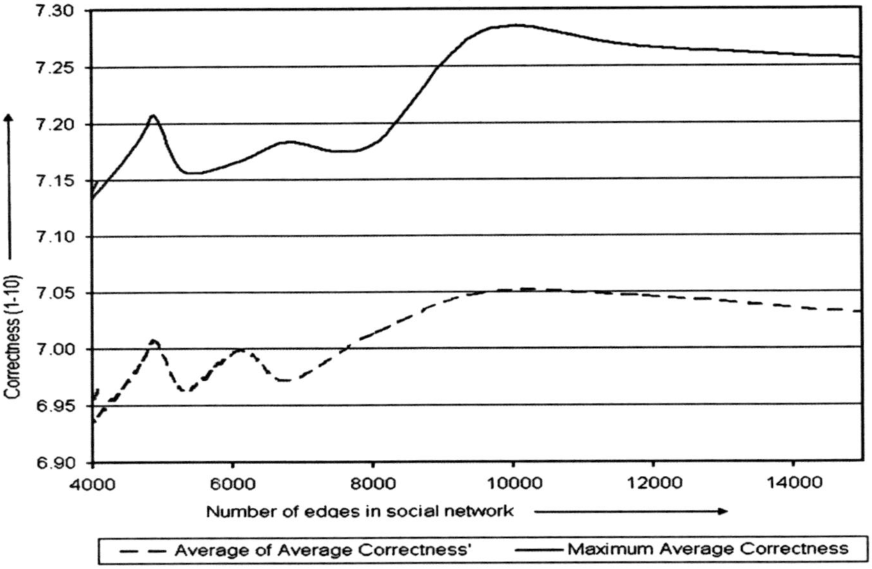

Fig. 11 The effect of network's edge count on performance

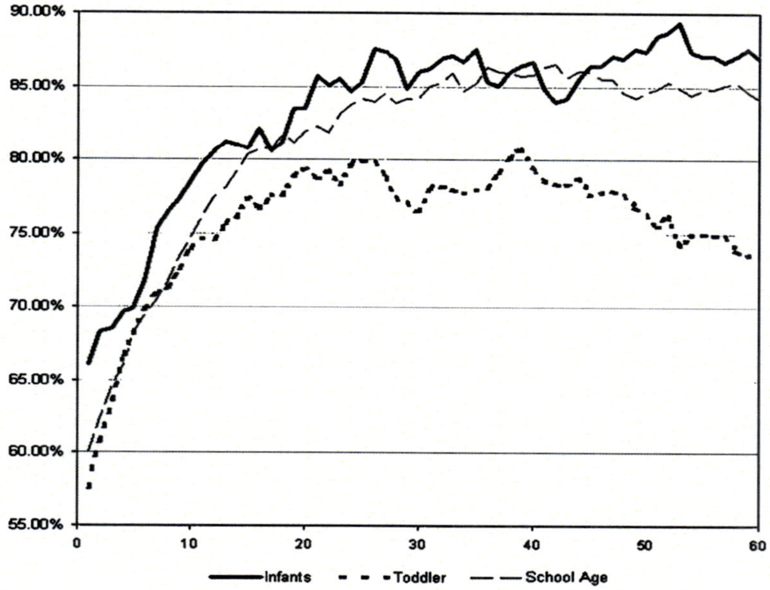

Fig. 12 Correct seat transition rate (%) over time for different age group of children

Effect of Age Group

In order to identify how parents or drivers change their strategy as their children's physical characteristics change with age, this test bed was designed. Here, CST rate is plotted over time for three different child age groups. The plots are shown in Fig. 12. It is obvious that as the toddlers grow up, their transfer rate to correct seat is inferior in comparison to other age groups. Infants and school age children are doing relatively better. Therefore, the model recommends special attention should be given towards parents with toddlers. It is noteworthy that in the 2006 national child seat survey, toddlers (aged 1–3 years) were the least likely to be correctly restrained in vehicles (Snowdon, Howard, and Boase 2007).

4.3 Persistent Storage

The persistent storage function is a relational database. Data is organised here with some predefined schema. The server component communicates with it by means of some object relational map that maintains consistency and meaning of the electronic records.

4.4 Business Logic and Decision Module

This component is primarily responsible for putting the collected data into some specific semantics so that another application can exploit the feed on it. Such application may include some statistical data analysis tool, reporting software or from the JIT Framework's point of view, it could be the AI Module of the framework. Another use of this component is that it is responsible for generating a new survey by creating the database schema, user interface component and business objects automatically.

5 Conclusion

Dr. Anne Snowdon, her colleagues and their students at the University of Windsor pioneered this research. Their main objective was to empirically document the factors that contribute to persistent, high rates of child fatalities and severe injuries due to road crashes in Canada. Ultimately, the goal was to identify effective strategies to improve correct use of child safety seats and to support the implementation of evidence-based legislation and injury prevention policies at the national level. In all of these studies, the research team relied on traditional survey and intervention research methods that were able to identify parents' low rate of correct use of child seats, and revealed their lack of knowledge of correct use. The health researchers' computational need for this research was twofold. First, they needed an efficient electronic survey system that could quickly organise survey records, particularly given that most data is collected in the communities where parents drive and interact with their social networks. An efficient data collection framework would allow for rapid analysis of population patterns and trends to support decisions for injury prevention programmes and strategies. Although statistical analysis offers many meaningful insights into the records, it suffers the following drawbacks:

(a) The statistical data and its analysis provide insight into only the surveyed locations and population and cannot explain the dynamic and evolutionary nature of its culture and society.
(b) The statistical surveys produce a static scenario of the population, which in reality is a dynamic and complex one.
(c) It is very difficult to identify how the economic, social, educational and regional background of the population affects the child safety seat knowledge and use. In short, the comprehensive effect of culture is difficult to identify using statistical techniques alone.
(d) Though statistical data produces a clear distribution of the population in terms of known parameters and issues, it fails to identify any unknown parameters that may exist. Therefore, it is easy to identify how car seats are being used, but difficult to come up with an effective plan to improve the perception of the parents and to understand why parents are making those decisions about car seat use in their vehicles.

To complement the traditional statistical approach to data analysis, an evolutionary multi-agent model of the problem domain was developed to function as an intelligent decision module with the following characteristics:

(a) A realistic model that very closely reflects the actual real life scenario of parents living in communities
(b) Scalable and applicable to a wide range of population demographics
(c) Takes into consideration the populations' financial, educational, ethnic and other cultural backgrounds
(d) An evolutionary model learns over time and evolves
(e) A representation of driver's knowledge on child safety issues
(f) Makes use of the available survey data efficiently and allows for testing and verification
(g) Allows graphic and visual presentation of geographic, spatial and statistical data
(h) Allows quick integration of new features

The development of a more dynamic model of how parents and drivers learn and make decisions about the use of safety seats for child occupants was not only fundamental to injury prevention policy and programme development, it was a logical next step in this programme of research. The JIT decision support system was able to capture the dynamic interaction of influences on children's safety in vehicles within their social networks. This dynamic decision support approach is an important tool that provides evidence to support policy and support the development of innovative approaches to injury prevention initiatives.

Road crashes remain the leading cause of death for children in both Canada and the USA. Despite Road Safety Vision 2010's target of achieving the safest roads in the world, Canada's ranking for road safety has declined from 10th in the world to 22nd among other OECD countries in recent years. This chapter reported on the development of a preliminary system for data collection and decision support applied to this national research strategy on injury prevention. The challenge of vehicle safety for children demonstrates the potential application of this DSS system for informing decisions of injury prevention practitioners and policy makers. Additional applications in hospital settings are currently underway. In this iteration, the entire process from data collection to decision support was executed successfully. Further developmental work for use in global health applications such as natural disasters will be undertaken. Much developmental work remains to be done in order to use the tool in large organisations which focus on population health, such as the World Health Organization.

Acknowledgement The authors acknowledge the work of the USMS team and volunteers who worked on collecting the survey data throughout Canada. RDK and AWS thank Research in Motion for providing Blackberry units for use in this research and NCE Auto21 and NSERC Discovery for funding support.

References

Ahmad, R., L. Yung-Chuan, S. Rahimi and B. Gupta, "A multi-agent based approach for particle swarm optimization," *International Conference on Integration of Knowledge Intensive Multi-Agent Systems (KIMAS 2007)*, Waltham, 2007, 267–271.

Baqer, M., A.I. Khan and Z.A. Baig, "Implementing a graph neuron array for pattern recognition within unstructured wireless sensor networks," *Lecture Notes in Computer Science*, 3823, 2005, 208–217.

Bates, D.W. and A.A. Gawande, "Patient safety: Improving safety with information technology," *New England Journal of Medicine*, 348(25), 2003, 2526–2534.

Bedard, M., G.H. Guyatt, M.J. Stones and J.P. Hirdes, "The independent contribution of driver, crash, and vehicle characteristics to driver fatalities," retrieved from Social Sciences Citation Index® (1965 to present) database, 2002.

Berry, D.L., L.G. Trigg, W.B. Lober, B.T. Karras, M.L. Galligan and M. Austin-Seymour, et al., "Computerized symptom and quality-of-life assessment for patients wtih cancer part I: Development and pilot testing," *Oncology Nursing Forum*, 31(5), 2004, 75–83.

Bilykh, I., Y. Bychkov, D. Dahlem, J.H. Jahnke, G. McCallum and C. Obry, et al., "Can GRID services provide answers to the challenges of national health information sharing?" *2003 Conference of the Centre for Advanced Studies on Collaborative Research*, Toronto, 2003, 39–53.

Blanquer, I., V. Hernandez, D. Segrelles, M. Robles, J.M. Garcia and J.V. Robledo, "Clinical decision support systems (CDSS) in GRID environments, from grid to healthgrid," *Healthgrid 2005*, 112, 2005, 80–89.

Bodenheimer, T., "High and rising health care costs. Part 1: Seeking an explanation," *Annals of Internal Medicine*, 142(10), 2005, 847–854.

Chervenak, A.L. and M. Cai, "Applying peer-to-peer techniques to grid replica location services," *Journal of Grid Computing*, 4(1), 2006, 1572–9814.

Chouinard, A., and B. Hurley, Towards the development of a national child restraint survey. In: Proceedings of Canadian Multidisciplinary Road Safety Conference XV, Fredericton, New Brunswick, June 6–9, 2005.

Coelho, L. and V.C. Mariani, "An efficient particle swarm optimization approach based on cultural algorithm applied to mechanical design," *IEEE Congress on Evolutionary Computation (CEC 2006)*, Vancouver, 2006, 1099–1104.

Collier, N., T. Howe and M. North, "Onward and upward: The transition to Repast 2.0," *Proceedings of First Annual North American Association for Computational Social and Organizational Science Conference*, Pittsburgh, 2003.

Conrad, D., T. Wickizer, C. Maynard, T. Klastorin, D. Lessler, A. Ross, N. Soderstrom, S. Sullivan, J. Alexander and K. Travis, "Managing care, incentives, and information: An exploratory look inside the "black box" of hospital efficiency," *Health Services Research*, 31(3), 1996, 235–259.

De Leeuw, E.D., J.J. Hox and D.A. Dillman, *International handbook of survey methodology*, European Association of Methodology. New York: Lawrence Erlbaum, 2008.

Dorigo, M., M. Birattari and T. Stutzle, "Ant colony optimization," *IEEE Computational Intelligence Magazine*, 1(4), 2006, 28–39.

Ehiri, J.E., H.O.D. Ejere, L. Magnussen, D. Emusu, W. King and J.S. Osberg, "Interventions for promoting booster seat use in four to eight year olds traveling in motor vehicles," *The Cochrane Database of Systematic Reviews*, 1, 2006, 1–45.

Glass, R.J., M. Segui-Gomez and J.D. Graham, "Child passenger safety: Decisions about seating location, airbag exposure, and restraint use," *Risk Analysis*, 20, 2000, 521–528.

Gorry, G.A. and M.S. Scott Morton, "A framework for management information systems," *Sloan Management Review*, 13, 1971, 1.

Hine, N., A. Judson, S. Ashraf, J. Arnott, A. Sixsmith and S. Brown, et al., "Modelling the behaviour of elderly people as a means of monitoring well being," *Lecture Notes in Computer Science*, 3538, 2005, 241–250.

Homer, J. and G. Hirsch, "System dynamics modeling for public health: Background and opportunities," *American Journal of Public Health*, 96 (3), 2006, 452–458.

Huang, C., V. Lanza, S. Rajasekaran and W. Dubitzky, "HealthGrid – Bridging life science and information technology," *Journal of Clinical Monitoring and Computing*, 19(4–5), 2005, 259–262.

Hwang, J. and P. Aravamudham, "Middleware services for P2P computing in wireless grid networks," *IEEE Internet Computing*, 8(4), 2004, 40–46

Keen, P.G.W. and M.S. Scott Morton, *Decision support systems: An organizational perspective*. Reading: Addison-Wesley, 1978.

Kent, R. D., A. Snowdon, P. Preney, D. Kim, J. Ren and A. Aggarwal, et al., "USMS: An open-source IT solution for effective health and safety data collection and decision support," *Halifax 7 (CPSI: Canadian Patient Safety Institute)*, Ottawa, 2007.

Kim, D., R. Kent, A. Aggarwal and P. Preney, "Flexible multi-layer virtual machine design for virtual laboratory in distributed systems and grids," *Proceeding of 1st WSEAS International Symposium on GRID COMPUTING*, Corfu Island, 2005.

Kobti, Z., R.G. Reynolds and T. Kohler, "A multi-agent simulation using cultural algorithms: The effect of culture on the resilience of social systems," *Proceedings of IEEE Conference on Evolutionary Computation, CEC '03*, 3, 2003, 1988–1995.

Kohli, R., J.K. Tan, F.A.D. Piontek, E. Ziege and H. Groot, "Integrating cost information with health management support system: An enhanced methodology to assess health care quality drivers," *Topics in Health Information Management*, 20(1), 1999, 80–95.

Kopec, D., R. Eckhardt, S. Tamang and D. Reinharth, "Towards a mobile intelligent information system with application to HIV/AIDS," *Studies in Health Technology and Informatics*, 114, 2005, 30–35.

Krug, E.G., G.K. Sharma and R. Lozano, "The global burden of injuries," *American Journal of Public Health*, 90(4), 2000, 523–526. URL = http://search.ebscohost.com/login.aspx?direct=true&db=cin20&AN=2001043079&site=ehost-live

Kuljis, J., L. Paul and K. Stergioulas, "Can health care benefit from modeling and simulation methods in the same way as business and manufacturing has?" *Proceedings of the 2007 Winter Simulation Conference*, Washington, DC, 2007.

Leitch, K., "Reaching for the top: A report by the advisor on health children and youth," Health Canada, 2008. URL = http://www.hc-sc.gc.ca/hl-vs/pubs/child-enfant/advisor-conseillere/index-eng.php

Lim, B., K. Choi and D. Shin, "A JXTA-based architecture for efficient and adaptive healthcare services," *Lecture Notes in Computer Science*, 3391, 2005, 776–785.

Liu, M., Relationlog: A Typed Extension to Datalog with Sets and Tuples (Extended Abstract). In Proceedings of the International Symposium on Logic Programming (ILPS '95, Portland, Oregon, Dec. 4–7). MIT Press, Cambridge, MA, 1995, 83–97.

Lu, J., T. Naeem, and J.B. Stav, "A distributed information system for healthcare web services," *Lecture Notes in Computer Science*, 3842, 2006, 783–790.

Lund, U.J., "The effect of seating location on the injury of properly restrained children in child safety seats," *Accident Analysis & Prevention*, 37, 2005, 435–439.

Lyell D, Sadsad R, Georgiou A., Health Systems Simulation. In N. Wickramasinghe & E. Geisler (Eds), Encyclopaedia of Healthcare Information Systems. Hershey, PA: *Medical Information Science Reference*, 2008, pp 646–655.

Minoli, D., *A networking approach to grid computing*. New Jersey: Wiley, 2005.

National Highway Traffic Safety Administration (NHTSA), *Traffic safety facts 2002: Occupant protection* No. DOT HS 809 610), 2003.

Newsted, P., S. Huff and M. Munro, "Survey instruments in IS," *MISQ Discovery*, December 1998.

OGSA-DAI 3.0 documentation. URL = http://people.ucalgary.ca/~newsted/tutor.htm

O'Hare, G.M.P., R.W. O'Grady, R.W. Collier and S. Keegan, "Agents as catalysts for mobile computing," *Lecture Notes in Computer Science*, 3508, 2005, 182–197.

Omar, W.M. and A. Taleb-Bendiab, "Service oriented architecture for E-health support services based on grid computing," *Proceedings of IEEE International Conference on Services Computing (SCC'06)*, Chicago, 2006, 135–142.

Paik, W., N.M. Kang, H. Choi and E. Ham, "Collaborative web-based nursing practice learning system," *Lecture Notes in Computer Science*, 3807, 2005, 152–161.

Peden, M., R. Scurfield, D. Sleet, D. Mohan, A.A. Hyder and E. Jarawan, et al., *World report on road traffic injury prevention*. Geneva: World Health Organization, 2004.

Reynolds, R.G., *Cultural algorithm: A tutorial*, 2002. URL = http://ai.cs.wayne.edu/ai/availablePapersOnLine/CULTURAL_ALGORITHMS_2002-05-03/CULTURAL_ALGORITHMS_2002-05-03.ppt

Safe Kids Canada, *Booster seat use in Canada: A national challenge*. Toronto: Safe Kids Canada, 2004.

Salem, F.D., S. Krishnaswamy, S.W. Loke and A. Rakotonirainy, "Context-aware ubiquitous data mining based agent model for intersection safety," *Lecture Notes in Computer Science*, 3823, 2005, 61–70.

Sanderson, N., V. Goebel and E. Munthe-Kaas, "Medtadata management for ad-hoc InfoWare – A rescue and emergency use case for mobile ad-hoc scenarios," *Lecture Notes in Computer Science*, 3761, 2005, 1365–1380.

Schaffers, H., "Innovation and systems change: The example of mobile, collaborative workplaces," *AI & Society*, 19(4), 2005, 334–347.

Simon, H., *The new science of management decision*. Englewood Cliffs: Prentice Hall, 1977.

Skov, M.B. and R.T. Hoegh, "Supporting information access in a hospital ward by a context-aware mobile electronic patient record," *Personal and Ubiquitous Computing*, 10(4), 2006, 205–214.

Smirnov, A., M. Pashkin, N. Chilov and T. Levashova, "Ontology-based knowledge repository support for healthgrids, from grid to healthgrid," *Healthgrid 2005*, 112, 2005, 47–56.

Snowdon, A., R. Kent, Z. Kobti and A. Howard, "Development of a wireless, web-services based survey for road to measure vehicle safety for Canadian children," *Proceedings of 8th World Conference on Injury Prevention and Safety Promotion*, Durban, 2006.

Snowdon, A., A. Howard and P. Boase, "The development of a protocol for a national study of Canadian children's safety in vehicles," Canadian Association of Road Safety Professionals, *Canadian Multidisciplinary Road Safety Conference Proceedings*, Montreal, June 2007.

Snowdon, A., A. Hussein and E. Ahmed, "Children at risk: Predictors of car seat safety misuse in Ontario," *Accident Analysis and Prevention*, 40, 2008a, 1418–1423.

Snowdon, A.W., A. Hussein, L. High, L. Stamler, J. Polgar and L. Patrick, et al., "The effectiveness of a multi-media intervention on parents' knowledge and use of vehicle safety systems for children," *Journal of Pediatric Nursing*, 23(2), 2008b, 126–139.

Snowdon, A.W., A. Hussein, R. Purc-Stevenson, B. Bruce, C. Kolga and P. Boase, et al., "Are we there yet? Canada's progress towards achieving road safety vision 2010 for children travelling in vehicles," *International Journal of Injury Control and Safety Promotion*, 16(4), 2008c, 231–237.

Snowdon, A.W., A. Hussein, R. Purc-Stevenson, G. Follo and E. Ahmed, "A longitudinal study of the effectiveness of a multi-media intervention on parents' knowledge and use of vehicle safety systems for children," *Accident Analysis & Prevention*, 41(3), 2009, 498–505. doi:10.1016/j.aap.2009.01.013.

Srinivasan, H., "Pervasive wireless grid architecture," *Proceedings of Second Annual Conference on Wireless on-Demand Network Systems and Services (WONS'05)*, St. Moritz, 2005, 83–88.

Taylor, I.J., *From P2P to web services and grids*. London: Springer, 2005.

Transport Canada, *Canadian motor vehicle traffic collision statistics* (No. T45-3/2003) Transport Canada, 2004.

Transport Canada, "Fatalities and injuries by age group, 2006," 2006, viewed February 15, 2009, URL = http://www.tc.gc.ca/eng/roadsafety/tp-tp3322-2006-page2-591.htm

Turban, E. and J.E. Aronson, *Decision support systems and intelligent systems*. Upper Saddle River: Prentice Hall, 2000.

Turner, C., R. McClure, J. Nixon and A. Spinks, "Community-based programs to promote car seat restraints in children 0–16 years – A systematic review," *Accident Analysis & Prevention*, 37, 2005, 77–83.

Ulieru, M., M. Hadzic and E. Chang, "Soft computing agents for e-health in application to the research and control of unknown diseases," *Information Sciences*, 176(9), 2006, 1190–1214.

Ullman, J.D., Chapter 12, *Principles of database and knowledge-base systems: Volume ii: The new technologies*. New York: W. H. Freeman, 1990.

Von Lubitz, D. and N. Wickramasinghe, "Network centric healthcare: Applying the tools, techniques, and strategies of knowledge management to create superior healthcare operations," *International Journal of Electronic Healthcare*, 2(4), 2006, 415–429.

Weber, K., "Crash protection for child passengers: A review of best practice," *UMTRI Research Review*, 31(3), 2003, 1–27. Retrieved from PAIS International database.

Wegner, M.V. and D.C. Girasek, "How readable are child safety seat installation instructions?" *Pediatrics*, 111, 2003, 588.

Wigton, R.S., "Use of linear-models to analyze physicians decisions," *Medical Decision Making*, 8(4), 1988, 241–252.

Wright, K.B., "Researching internet-based populations: Advantages and disadvantages of online survey research, online questionnaire authoring software packages, and web survey services," *Journal of Computer-Mediated Communication*, 10(3), 2005.

Yao, J. and S. Warren, "Applying the ISO/IEEE 11073 standards to wearable home health monitoring systems," *Journal of Clinical Monitoring and Computing*, 19(6), 2005, 427–436.

Zaza, S., D.A. Sleet, R.S. Thompson, D.M. Sosin, J.C. Bolen and Task Force on Community Preventive Services, Atlanta, GA, "Reviews of evidence regarding interventions to increase use of child safety seats," *American Journal of Preventive Medicine*, 21(4 Suppl), 2001, 31–47. doi:10.1016/S0749-3797(01)00377-4.

Zhu, L., C.I. Ezeife and R.D. Kent, "Generic query toolkit: A query interface generator integrating data mining," *Information Resources Management Association (IRMA)*, Vancouver, 2007.

Chapter 14
Context Modelling in Time-Critical Decision Support for Medical Triage

Shane Grigsby[1], Frada Burstein[1], and Nyree Parker[2]

[1] Centre for Organisational and Social Informatics, Monash University, Melbourne, Australia
[2] School of Nursing and Midwifery, Monash University
Peninsula Health, Frankston Vic, Australia

Abstract This chapter discusses the role of decision context within time-critical decision support in medical triage. Time-critical environments pose a challenge in the development of decision support systems in regards to the provision of relevant and timely information. Establishing context is used within a number of information technology fields as a means to improve the functionality of information systems. Likewise, establishing a decision context in time-critical decision support could assist in the provision of time-critical information to improve decision outcomes. This research proposes identifying contextual elements of a task being undertaken as a means to establish rules which can influence decision support provided. Through this, it is intended that a decision support system can refine contextual guidelines on the task being undertaken to act as a safety measure and for the purpose of risk mitigation within a clinical health care setting.

Keywords Medical triage • Knowledge context • Clinical decision support

1 Introduction

As decision support system capabilities continue to develop, the applicability of such systems to varying organisational environments increases. The development of new technologies provides new ways to improve operational processes to suit immediate needs of decision makers. Time-critical environments pose a challenge

F. Burstein (✉)
Centre for Organisational and Social Informatics, Monash University,
Melbourne, Australia
e-mail: Frada.Burstein@monash.edu

F. Burstein et al. (eds.), *Supporting Real Time Decision-Making*,
Annals of Information Systems 13, DOI 10.1007/978-1-4419-7406-8_14,

within decision support practice and research (Burstein and Cowie 2008). Time-critical environments are those in which the decision-making tasks have to be carried out within a short time frame. This time frame can vary depending on the operational environment; however, such systems generally operate in real time.

Time-critical environments require real-time access to information when and where it is needed. Availability of a decision support system at any time and consequently in any location requires deploying it on a mobile platform (Burstein, Cowie, Zaslavsky, and San Pedro 2008). Typically, decision support systems incorporate a search mechanism that allows users to locate relevant information. Use of mobile technology in time-critical environments presents new opportunities; however, it also presents challenges. The demands associated with continuous connectivity and the system's responsiveness to the context in which it is planned to be used, need to be considered. Thus, the new architectures for decision support on the move should consider which information can be pre-coded and then adapted to a specific context, and which one is better accessed on a once needed basis.

Access to timely and context-specific information is crucial for achieving the best decision outcomes in a timely manner. To accommodate time-critical environments, new methods of decision support information delivery and representation need to be explored. Such environments vary considerably and include some critical services such as health care. Medical errors pose a significant problem and finding a means to assist health care professionals when making decisions would be of significant benefit (Kohn, Corrigan, and Donaldson 2000).

This research involves the development of a mobile, time-critical decision support system for medical triage in an emergency department. The system incorporates knowledge alongside organisational standards and guidelines to identify characteristics of the task being undertaken. These characteristics can then be used to create a context. This context incorporates guiding rules that aim to establish safe operating ranges and assist triage nurses based on the particulars of the decision they are being faced with. This chapter discusses context in time-critical environments. Triage is an example of this and the chapter discusses the structure of time-critical context from a triage perspective. Its focus is the structure and contextual elements within triage, rather than the implementation of the system.

2 Context in Decision Making

Systems that apply a context are not new to information systems. Context information is utilised in context aware applications (Schot 1997; Skov and Høegh 2006; Morales-Aranda and Mayora-Ibarra 2007). These systems utilise context to control information display or behaviour of a system based on location. Context aware applications utilise inputs, normally from sensors, to determine the functional parameters of the system.

Grimshaw, Mott, and Roberts (1997) apply context as a filter between a user and database. Two types of context are defined, those being extension context and meta-data context. Extension context is described as amplifying or extending the data returned to a user. Meta-data context is described as transforming the data. These contexts are implemented as context classes and act as filters between the user and database, modifying the data retrieved from the database to suit the context of the user.

Brézillon and Brézillon (2008) discuss context by identifying and separating procedures and practices in which practices incorporate contextual cues. Decision-making processes are often embedded in procedures. They state that while this can allow the procedure to be applicable to a number of decision-making situations, it can often lead to sub-optimal solutions for specific decisions. Decision makers can often be faced with ill-defined situations. In such situations, a clear answer is not always evident and, as such, decisions are made through assessing advantages and disadvantages rather than complete decisions.

Generalised procedures are often created to assist in decision making. Decision makers, however, adapt these procedures to a decision problem along with contextual cues. The contextual cues used depend on the decision makers' experience and the situation characteristics. The modelling and inclusion of such contextual cues in a form of some rules can be critical for knowledge-based systems. Such rules can represent situational characteristics that can have a significant impact on a timely and relevant decision support.

Context-sensitive decision support incorporates a means to represent contextual elements and utilises them in decision support. In doing so, a decision support system is able to adapt the support information it provides to address specific characteristics of a given decision situation. Through this, the system can improve the decision support it is able to provide. By identifying a particular focus in a decision process, relevant contextual knowledge can be accessed and proceduralised. As Brézillon and Brézillon (2008) suggest, such proceduralised context provides a means to address the needs of specific situations.

For real-time decision support "on the move," the locality context can be of significant importance. Decision support systems can provide different forms of decision support based on the locations in which they are operating at any given time. The other component is the task being undertaken. The task component can be linked to the locality, whereby the locality changes the contextual elements relating to the task. Alternatively, the task may encounter many different contexts within a single locality. A context environment model for decision support is represented in Fig. 1.

Each locality and task could have many characteristics that individually identify that particular locality or task and, in doing so, differentiate it from the rest. These characteristics create a particular context for each locality or task, resulting in individual decision support requirements.

Decision support information is often tailored to a set of questions entered by a user and tailored to that user's profile. Task-focused, time-critical decision support instead needs a means to build these questions and profile via the task being undertaken and data being entered. Task-oriented, time-critical decision support differs in that it needs to be integrated into the decision-making process. Establishing a decision context provides a mechanism through which to identify and structure decision support information.

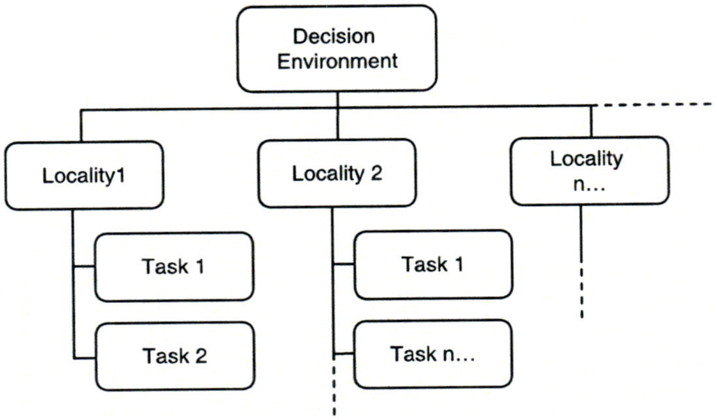

Fig. 1 Context environment model for decision support

3 Context Sensitive, Advisory Decision Support

This research proposes a context-sensitive advisory approach oriented towards addressing the challenges associated with mobile, knowledge-based, time-critical environments involving ill-defined decision situations. The approach proposes limited and concise guiding information in order to address small display screens associated with mobile devices and time-critical operations. Context is used to refer to contextual elements associated with a decision. These elements represent expert knowledge. A generalised context is proposed as a means to incorporate such information and address ill-defined decision situations.

The term "advisory system" encompasses a range of systems. These systems utilise a variety of decision support techniques. Beemer and Gregg (2008) classify such systems as providing guidance during the decision support process. In relation to techniques adopted for such decision support, Beemer and Gregg also refer to such systems as using case-based reasoning. While this appears to be a general rule, a range of systems utilising rule-based reasoning and other technologies are also identified as advisory systems.

This research uses a form similar, in some sense, to case-based reasoning through identification of generalised contextual cases; however, these cases are then formed into rules. Turban, Aronson, and Liang (2005) describe such cases as ossified cases. The system applies a category to each case/rule. This category is used for sorting purposes to locate the case that represents the most significant threat to the patient and assigns its category to the situation.

It appears some of the main distinctions between advisory systems and expert systems are that advisory systems are aimed at unstructured problem domains and act as decision support (Beemer and Gregg 2008). This research identifies advisory systems primarily through the distinction between an expert system as a decision maker and advisory as decision support. In that sense the system developed through this research is an advisory system, as it does not diagnose or provide a solution, instead suggesting appropriate courses of action based on procedural and contextual knowledge available. In terms of strict accordance to case-based reasoning, this research currently utilises ossified cases in the form of rules and, as such, could also be described as being based on an advisory system.

4 Context in Time-Critical Decision Support

A common problem in time-critical environments is a limited period during which to search for decision support information. If the problem domain is associated with a set of guidelines for a decision maker to follow, it is still expected that the specific context in which the decision maker operates brings some additional constraints. At the same time, some experiential knowledge can alter the way the final decision will be made. Required decision support information could alter the decision and an experiential knowledge could be derived by identifying the decision problem and modelling a context that is being faced in a generic way. After that, the relevant information can be specified from all these sources and displayed to guide the decision process in order to ensure safe operation, integrating formal guidelines as well as contextual information and experiential knowledge.

This research takes the approach of supplying decision support information as guidelines while a task is undertaken. The decision support information provided is based on data entered during the task, as well as the data derived from context model and expert knowledge built into the formal decision support procedure. The research proposes contextualising the decision being undertaken via task-related input. The research couples decision context with rule-based reasoning for representing expert knowledge, utilising the context identified to select appropriate rules, rule interpretations or rule boundaries for the task being undertaken.

This research identifies a decision context as a collection of identifiers. These identifiers represent aspects of the task that frame that task in a particular way. Such manipulation allows relevant rules or information to be identified in the knowledge base or the implementation of contextual rules to guide the decision. This is achieved by linking the contextual components identified to data in the knowledge base. Decision identifiers can be categorised and represented in a simple model. A model of the decision context and its components is represented in Fig. 2.

A decision context can be broken down into individual identifying factors which can be grouped under different categories. A significant number of identifiers may be required to adequately describe possible task contexts.

As the task is carried out, context-related information is entered either directly or inferred by task-related data entered. The context-related information is linked to particular identifiers that can then be incorporated into a context manager which represents the contextual elements of a task being undertaken. This manager can then be used by the system to link context identifiers to context-related rules. The context-related rules then influence the system's operation by either including or

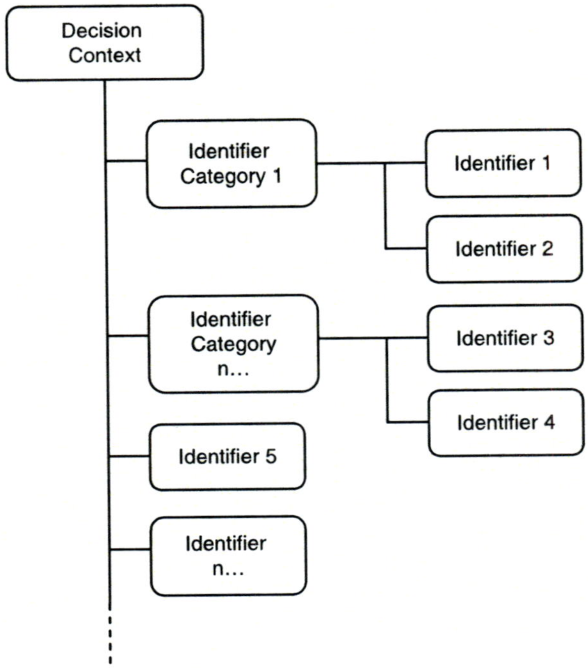

Fig. 2 Decision context components model

omitting procedural rules from the rule base, altering the interpretation of procedural rules or setting procedural rule value boundaries. Identifiers can be conceptually separated into generic identifiers that relate to the task or locality specific identifiers.

In decision-making environments where the nature of the task is unknown, a number of possible variations are possible. If the system does not adequately identify and provide a flexible means by which to accommodate these variations, it could lead to inadequate decision support provision. Context within a system provides a means by which the system can adapt to a task as it is undertaken.

5 Context in Medical Triage

This research treats context modelling in a way similar to the one suggested by Brézillon and Brézillon (2008), identifying procedures and contextual cues and modelling these to improve medical triage decision outcomes. Medical triage is a process of assessing the level of urgency of medical care based on a patient's condition. Triage nurses base their decisions on training and experience. Such nurses currently depend solely on their memory and state of mind to ensure they can adequately assign categories. Environments in which triage is undertaken are commonly unpredictable and stressful. Such environments can have a negative impact on the decision-making process. Medical triage in hospitals has yet to adopt any computer-aided decision support systems (DSS). This means decision support is currently restricted to their own notes or booklets, which detail what signs indicate a need for a particular category to be assigned. The adoption of a context sensitive DSS in triage could assist decision making and combat environmental distractions.

Medical triage utilises standard procedures to triage patients. However, these procedures do not always adequately address the triage situations encountered. Triage nurses incorporate their own knowledge and assess a patient based on potential risk through considering the full context for the presented case. Thus, when designing decision support systems, some contextual cues have to be proceduralised in order to incorporate them into the decision-making process and contribute to the decision support capabilities of a system.

A number of different standards frameworks are available and are generally taught to nurses in training programmes; however, currently nurses have to remember these frameworks or refer to written material (Mackway-Jones 1997; Beveridge 1999; ACEM 2000). These standards are descriptive in nature and open to interpretation. This interpretation usually incorporates specific considerations that relate to particular patient demographics or conditions. Where nurses have practiced, been trained, and are currently stationed can affect the categorisations being applied. It is possible nurses from separate hospitals can often have different interpretations prevalent to those localities, and as such, treat separate demographics or conditions differently (Durojaiye and O'Meara 2002; Crellin and Johnston 2003). Triage standards establish specific vital sign ranges or condition indicators, which are then related to particular ratings or categories.

In Australia, medical triage is implemented as the Australasian Triage Scale (ATS) (ACEM 2000). The ATS provides a guide through the process of triage. The standard is adopted by the Australian College of Emergency Medicine (ACEM) as part of its triage policy and used in emergency departments throughout Australia (ACEM 2001; Monash Institute of Health Services Research 2001). The ATS uses five possible categories represented by numerical values. The lower the numerical value, the higher the urgency for medical attention. Therefore, category one represents the highest need for medical attention, while category five represents non-severe cases. The ATS outlines possible conditions and indicates corresponding categories. In the process, the standard presents key signs that need to be considered.

Medical triage in Australia is already influenced by computer systems. These systems generally control the entry of data. However, they do not have any influence in the actual category assigned. No computer-aided decision support is currently being used in medical triage, apart from some research attempts in this area (Padmanabhan, Burstein, Churilov, Wassertheil, and Hornblower 2005; San Pedro, Burstein, Wassertheil, Arora, Churilov, and Zaslavsky 2005). Triage nurses are almost completely unassisted in this regard, apart from any textual references at hand. Influencing employees to conform to specific data representations is one method of influencing workplace operations. While data representation can be undertaken with relatively simple systems, influencing the decisions made within the workplace requires considerably more complex systems. DSSs provide a flexible means by which to access relevant operational information and in the process influence the decisions being made. DSSs are slowly being adopted into a clinical environment. Such systems include computerised physician order entry and computerised alert systems. These systems are concerned with reducing inverse reaction, incorrect medicine administration and notifying of clinical events. The use of such systems can provide significant benefits in relation to reducing medical errors (Bates, Cohen, Leape, and Overhage 2001).

In a similar manner to which DSSs are used in other medical departments, computerised systems could be introduced in medical triage, enforcing standards and consistency of common knowledge-based considerations. DSSs often attempt to determine what information would be relevant to the user's current context. They display information that the user can then take into account. Triage is a time-critical activity and as such any decision support provided must reflect this. As common data entry applications can influence the operations of users, a decision support system could be used to influence and direct triage nurses to comply with triage standards. In conjunction, through using knowledge-based rules to represent some experiential knowledge, such a system could also potentially assist in maintaining consistency through reducing varying interpretation.

Decision support needs to be concise and direct or the time commitment required could counteract time-related triage guidelines. Due to this, triage decision support needs to be integrated into the current triage process. Expert systems are concerned with tasks that require significant specialised knowledge (Turban et al. 2005). Such tasks are generally performed by experts who have accumulated the required knowledge associated with the task and have significant experience in the problem domain (Damiani, Khosla, and Sethi 2000; Turban et al. 2005). This description is applicable to triage nurses, as specialised knowledge and experience are required components in the triage decision-making process. In addition to the expert knowledge component of triage, multiple interconnected influences need to be considered. All of which can range in importance given a specific triage encounter. Triage does not specifically identify individual patients; however, characteristics associated with generalised patient populations are often relevant and used in the triage decision process.

5.1 Modelling Context in Medical Triage

This research utilised knowledge acquisition techniques to extract relevant information and form decision contexts that could be utilised by the system. The ATS indicates a list of risk factors that influence the categorisation of patients. Exactly how these factors affect the triage process is not explained; however, these risk factors can form a basis on which to structure a range of decision contexts for triage. The aim of the project was to acquire additional contextual knowledge from the experienced triage nurses, which they usually apply in making decisions in addition to ATS guidelines.

Knowledge acquisition involves extracting, interpreting and analysing problem-solving knowledge used by human experts. Knowledge acquisition can be a difficult and time consuming task (Milton 2007). A significant number of different knowledge acquisition techniques are available. Suitable knowledge acquisition techniques for the corresponding domain need to be adopted. Such techniques are required to ensure an adequate quantity and quality of knowledge is acquired. Sources of triage knowledge include triage nurses and standards documentation. Triage can be described as an intuitive process, based significantly on past experience, as well as factual knowledge.

Given that triage knowledge is often ambiguous and open to interpretation, it was assumed that knowledge acquisition techniques to allow adequate exploration of the decision process needed to be adopted. However, triage also utilises a set number of observations and results in a finite number of possible categories. Given a degree of structure, yet components open to interpretation, semi-structured interviews were used. This provided a degree of flexibility to explore how different factors influenced triage decisions while maintaining a manageable scope. Semi-structured interviews provide an effective and efficient manner through which to obtain expert knowledge from one or more experts (Milton 2007).

Knowledge acquisition can be a difficult and time-consuming task Milton (2007). Knowledge acquisition tools and "teachback" interviewing techniques were utilised to ensure correct interpretation and understanding of data. Knowledge acquisition was carried out through multiple semi-structured interviews involving a number of experienced triage nurses. The level of experience was determined via the number of years spent conducting triage. Knowledge acquisition sessions utilised an adaptation of the ATS and associated risk factors as knowledge acquisition tools to encourage and focus discussion during interviews. Five triage nurses were interviewed in order to provide an adequate information base. As the data is for a research-oriented prototype evaluating the effect of context, the total number of triage nurses utilised was limited in order to simplify knowledge acquisition. Future research would involve a more statistically significant number of triage nurses or triage nurse authorities before such information would be incorporated into a final system.

The knowledge acquisition involved five experts. To address potential inconsistency yet insure an adequate information collection, a primary and secondary expert setup was chosen (Turban et al. 2005). This setup provided a means to resolve inconsistency via the primary expert. A triage nurse with significant experience, training and involvement in triage education was used as the primary expert. Four secondary experts also took part providing additional information and rules that could then be evaluated by the primary expert. Knowledge acquisition identified a number of crucial decision considerations. These include:

- Risk factors which represent contextual elements,
- Automatic categorisation based on presenting case,
- Triage based on potentials, and
- Hospital-specific rules.

Table 1 Medical triage context categories and identifiers

Category	Identifiers
Impact/Mechanical	Penetrating Injury, Fall > 5m, MCA > 60 kph, MBA/Cyclist > 30 kph, Pedestrian Child, Pedestrian Adult, Ejection, Rollover, Prolonged Extrication, Death Same Car Occupant, Explosion
Co-morbidities	Respiratory Disease, Cardiovascular Disease, Renal Disease, Carcinoma, Diabetes, Substance Abuse, Immuno Compromised
Historical Variables	Apnoeic episode, Seizure Activity Before Presenting, Seizure Activity, Intermittent Altered Conscious State, Collapse
Cardiac Risk Factors	Smoker/Obesity, Diabetes, Positive Family History, Cholesterol/ High BP, Known Coronary Artery Disease, Other Vascular Disease
Victims of Violence	Domestic Violence, Sexual Assault, Neglect
Presenting Condition	Rash, Actual/Potential Effects of Drugs Alcohol, Chemical Exposure, Envenomation, Immersion, Hypothermic, Hyperthermic
Pregnancy	Over and Including 28 Weeks Pregnant, Less Than 28 Weeks Pregnant, Less Than 12 Weeks Pregnant
Age	Neonate (Child < 28 Days Old), Age > 65 Years, Age > 80 Years
Staff	Staff on Shift

All of the identified considerations can link to contextual considerations. The risk factors involved represent contextual elements relating to the decision. Automatic categorisation based on presenting case can be linked to contextual elements through risk factors and represents particular decision contexts that result in an automatic category assigned. Triage based on potentials is linked to risk factors as contextual elements and their potential effect on the patient's safety. Hospital specific-rules are a representation of locality-based contexts.

Knowledge acquisition also expanded on the risk factors identified in the ATS and formed an overall list of contextual elements. Medical triage contextual categories and identifiers are represented in Table 1 (ACEM 2000).

The context categories and identifiers listed represent a broad range of contextual elements that can influence a medical triage decision. These contextual components can influence the decision in a number of ways. Such contextual factors can establish safe category ranges given potential danger to a patient or potentially influence waiting times and reassessment.

6 Implementation

Implementation of the mobile, time-critical decision support system for emergency department triage utilised a personal digital assistant as a platform. The system was based on a previous prototype system that provided an advised category through evaluation of physiological discriminators (San Pedro et al. 2005).

Fig. 3 Prototype system screenshots

Building on the previous prototype, the new prototype incorporated contextual elements as risk factors. Risk factors implemented in the system provided a means to identify the context surrounding a patient's presentation at triage. Consequently, appropriate boundaries on categorisation can be incorporated into the triage encounter to improve patient safety. This provides a form of risk mitigation. Figure 3 provides a screenshot of some of the contextual elements within the system.

The system presented the contextual elements as checkable items. As these items were selected or de-selected, the system evaluated the effect on patient categorisation, attributing a minimum safe category given a particular context. Physiological discriminators were represented in combo boxes. The minimum context categories could be overwritten by the triage nurse operating the system or by entry of physiological discriminators that resulted in a higher category.

7 System Evaluation and Discussion

An empirical evaluation was undertaken to assess whether the system was able to address the challenges of real-time decision making in a triage environment. The evaluation included testing of correct operation of the system in relation to the rules derived from the knowledge acquisition, as well as qualitative study involving potential users of the system to ascertain the system's potential utility. The following section presents a brief discussion of evaluation results.

Five triage nurses took part in an empirical evaluation of the system. All five were female. Participant ages varied from under 30 up to 60 years. A spread was also evident in the range of triage nurse experience amongst the sample. Experience referred to actual time spent conducting triage. The range of triage nurse experience ranged from a minimum of 3 years to a maximum of 20. English was the primary language of all but one triage nurse. When it came to experience using handheld computing devices, three nurses responded with limited experience and two with no experience. The evaluation was aimed at establishing the importance of the contextual components of the system and whether it would potentially be suitable for the triage environment. The qualitative analysis was utilised given the novel domain, limited participant numbers and evaluation resources. This form of evaluation provided additional insight regarding the system's suitability.

The knowledge acquired was not detailed in official triage documentation and consequently a thorough evaluation against officially recognised material was not possible at this stage. A small selection of cases was found to be relevant and utilised as a means to establish the need for the contextual component and the important role contextual elements can play in triage decision support. Knowledge acquisition identified a significant number of risk factors, most of which were included in the ATS. Knowledge acquired from experts was utilised to form rules involving the identified risk factors. The results of the evaluation indicated that the system could include more risk factors. This was evident in that a number of participants identified a lack of information entry options.

Of importance was that the system only incorporated risk factors that were tied to rules, which affected the category that would be advised. This involved excluding some ATS risk factors to limit the amount of information that had to be displayed. The system was not designed to collect large amounts of statistical information. It only identified risk factors that had a significant influence on the category that was to be assigned. The evaluation highlighted a number of risk factors and information that the participants thought were relevant, but could not be entered into the device. These risk factors were not included within the ATS and were not previously presented during the knowledge acquisition.

The participants all agreed that the information to be entered into the system was up-to-date in accordance with triage standards. However, triage nurses were currently using a relatively new desktop system that incorporated information gathered for statistical purposes. Further investigation into the impact of identified risk factors and whether or how statistical the device could collect information will need to be investigated in future research. The results from the test cases indicated the contextual component provided safe categorisation support for the limited number of cases entered into the system.

Most participants did not perceive the device to be a potential hindrance and all indicated they would use the device again for triage if it were available. The general attitude of comments provided by the participants indicated interest and optimism towards the system. This reflects the general receptiveness of nurses towards computer technology as indicated by Eley, Fallon, Soar, Buikstra, and Hegney (2009).

All nurses utilised the menu navigation provided by the system; however, a split was noted in regards to finding relevant information and four of the five participants got lost while navigating the device. Despite this, participants provided supportive comments in regards to the chosen form of navigation, noting it as "easy," "useful," and "quicker (than current desktop systems)." Participant comments provided later indicated navigation troubles were likely due to a lack of familiarity with the device – "just me not knowing it," "not being familiar with it." This indicates the form of information input and delivery adopted was suitable for the intended environment. However, a lack of information entry options was also noted.

In regards to safety and accuracy, all participants indicated a positive response. In conjunction with the test case results this is a promising result in regards to system accuracy and safety. However, given that few test cases were available to evaluate the contextual component of the system, a more thorough assessment is still required. In regards to useful categorisation information provision, all participants responded positively. Positive responses were also noted in regards to ease of use-related questions. This indicates the advisory system architecture was a suitable deployment platform to provide support information in a form consistent with the needs of the problem domain.

Positive responses were provided by participants in regards to the contextual component of the system. This related to both perceived usefulness and entry of such information. All participants also indicated context support as an important feature of the system. One participant also perceived it as the best feature of the device – "I think the... risk factors [were] very good, best feature..." Positive responses were also provided in regards to the mobile platform on which the system was based, with some participants reporting portability as the best feature – "that it's portable," "It'd be good because it's portable." Most nurses also marked device mobility as an important feature of the device, supporting deployment of the system on a mobile platform. The participants also noted that in conjunction to general support, the system would be particularly useful for those learning the process of triage.

Overall, positive responses were provided in regards to the system design, finding relevant information, quality of information, ease of use and system features. This indicated the approach adopted and system developed was suitable for the mobile, knowledge-based, time-critical problem domain. The positive response in regards to quality of information and test case results are also of note. These results indicate the system was able to provide useful decision support for ill-defined decision situations associated with the problem domain.

8 Conclusions and Future Work

This chapter presented an approach to modelling decision context for time-critical decision support. A context- sensitive architecture based on the advisory decision support system architecture was proposed to deal with the complex and dynamic nature of an ill-defined domain. In such domains prior expert knowledge provided a useful source for context knowledge. Contextual knowledge was incorporated in a mobile decision support system prototype to address the knowledge-based nature of the medical triage environment. The researchers identified contextual elements and their representation within medical triage.

Context sensitive capabilities were introduced in the form of a context management component and contextual rules within the knowledge base. These components represented task characteristics and provided a means to control rule application and decision maker's behaviour during a task's execution. In this research the context management system provided real-time context modelling. This has the potential to allow a decision maker access to expert knowledge when required by formulating specific search criteria through task-specific data entry. Situation specific context was established through storage of selected risk factors within the contextual object.

Evaluating the effectiveness of the contextual elements in a time-critical environment is a future topic of research. The identification of context and inclusion of context-related rules in time-critical decision support has the potential to improve the decision support capabilities of a system.

The qualitative evaluation indicated the system provided decision support in a manner deemed useful by potential system users. It also established that the contextual component played a critical role within the system in that it addressed cases for which safe categories were not provided by a solely ATS standards-based implementation. Both these components, procedural and contextual, are required within the system to provide adequate and safe decision support. Overall the guiding form of decision support provided by the system received a positive response.

The modelling of the overall context is still relevant in relation to future work and expanding the system design. This research utilised user input to define the context. As health care systems continue to develop and gradually become interconnected, it may be possible for such contextual elements to be extracted from other systems such as a patient's electronic health care record or ambulance systems.

Context can play a vital role in decision support systems as it allows the system to accommodate locality and decision considerations based on expert knowledge in order to improve the provision of decision support information. There are a significant number of ways in which contextual considerations can be represented and incorporated into decision support.

Context can assist decision support systems to manage different localities as well as frame decision situations. Proceduralised context provides a means to incorporate contextual rules or reasoning into a system. In time-critical decision support, establishing a context can broaden the decision support capabilities of a system.

Decision context is an aspect of a time-critical decision support approach being utilised to develop a decision support system for medical triage. The broad contexts identified all have some impact in the triage process; however, not all have a direct influence on the rules or information to be displayed in the prototype developed. Future work will involve completing implementation of the prototype system and more detailed clinical evaluation. These are needed to ascertain the full scale of potential and the challenges of using such system to improve the process and outcomes of the medical triage specifically, as well as to produce some general conclusions about using mobile knowledge-based decision support in time-critical context.

References

ACEM, *Guidelines for the Implementation of the Australasian Triage Scale in Emergency Departments*, ACEM Policy Document, 2000.

ACEM, *Consistency of Triage in Victoria's Emergency Departments: Summary Report*. Melbourne, 2001.

Bates, D., M. Cohen, L. Leape and J. Overhage, "Reducing the frequency of errors in medicine using information technology," *American Medical Informatics Association* 8(4), 2001, 299–309.

Beemer, B. and D. Gregg, "Advisory systems to support decision making," *Handbook on Decision Support Systems 1 – Basic Themes*. F. Burstein and C. Holsapple (eds.). Berlin: Springer, 2008, 1: 511–527.

Beveridge, R., "Reliability of the Canadian emergency department triage and acuity scale: Interrater agreement," *Annals of Emergency Medicine* 32, 1999, 155–159.

Brézillon, P. and J. Brézillon, "Context sensitive decision support systems in road safety," *Handbook on Decision Support Systems 2 – Variations*. F. Burstein and C. Holsapple (eds.). Berlin: Springer, 2008, 2: 107–123.

Burstein, F. and J. Cowie, "Mobile decision support for time-critical decision making," *Encyclopedia of Decision Making and Decision Support Technologies*, F. Adam and P. Humphreys (eds.). New York: IGI Global, 2008, 2: 638–644.

Burstein, F., J. Cowie, A. Zaslavsky and J.C. San Pedro, "Support for real-time decision making in mobile financial applications," *Handbook on Decision Support Systems 2: Variations*, Frada Burstein and C. W. Holsapple (eds.). Berlin: Springer, 2008, 2: 81–106.

Crellin, D. and L. Johnston, "Poor agreement in application of the Australasian triage scale to paediatric emergency department presentations," *Contemporary Nurse* 15, 2003, 48–60.

Damiani, E., R. Khosla and I. Sethi, *Intelligent Multimedia Multi-Agent Systems – A Human-Centered Approach.* Norwell: Kluwer Academic, 2000.

Durojaiye, L. and M. O'Meara, "A study of triage of paediatric patients in Australia," *Emergency Medicine* 14, 2002, 67–76.

Eley, R., T. Fallon, J. Soar, E. Buikstra and D. Hegney, "Attitudes of Australian nurses to information technology in the workplace: A national survey," *Computers, Informatics, Nursing* 27(2), 2009, 114–121.

Grimshaw, D., P. Mott and S. Roberts, "The role of context in decision making: Some implications for database design," *European Journal of Information Systems* 6(2), 1997, 122–128.

Kohn, L., J. Corrigan and M. Donaldson, *To Err Is Human: Building a Safer Health System*, Institute of Medicine, 2000.

Mackway-Jones, K., *Emergency Triage*. London: BJM, 1997.

Milton, N.R., *Knowledge Acquisition in Practice: A Step-by-step Guide*. London: Springer, 2007.

Monash Institute of Health Services Research, "*Consistency of Triage in Victoria's Emergency Departments: Guidelines for Triage Education and Practice.*" Melbourne:Department of Human Services, 2001.

Morales-Aranda, A.H. and O. Mayora-Ibarra, "A context sensitive public display for adaptive multi-user information visualization," presented in the *Third International Conference on Autonomic and Autonomous Systems ICAS07*, Athens, June 19–25, 2007.

Padmanabhan, N., F. Burstein, L. Churilov, J. Wassertheil and B. Hornblower, "Experimental evaluation of mobile decision support prototype for emergency triage," in *Proceedings of the International Conference on DSS*, Porto Alegre, 2005.

San Pedro, J., F. Burstein, J. Wassertheil, N. Arora, L. Churilov and A. Zaslavsky, "On the development and evaluation of prototype mobile decision support for hospital triage," in *Proceedings of the 38th Hawaii International Conference on System Sciences*, Hawaii 2005.

Schot, J., "Communication in context: Exploring new mobile applications," in *Proceedings of the 1997 South African Symposium on Communications and Signal Processing*, 1997, 111–114.

Skov, B. and T. Høegh, "Supporting information access in a hospital ward by a context-aware mobile electronic patient record," *Personal and Ubiquitous Computing* 10(4), 2006, 205–214.

Turban, E., J. Aronson and T. Liang, *Decision Support Systems and Intelligent Systems*. Upper Saddle River: Pearson Education, Inc., 2005.

Chapter 15
Efficient Context Prediction for Decision Making in Pervasive Health Care Environments: A Case Study

Yves Vanrompay and Yolande Berbers

Department of Computer Science, Katholieke Universiteit Leuven, Leuven, Belgium

Abstract Mobile real-time decision support systems (RTDSS) find themselves deployed in a highly dynamic environment. Decision makers must be assisted, taking into account the various time-critical requirements. Perhaps even more important is the fact that the quality of the support given by the system depends heavily on the knowledge of the current and future contexts of the system. A DSS should exhibit inherent proactive behaviour and automatically derive the decision-making person (DMP)'s needs for specific information from the context that surrounds him/her. We propose to run a DSS on top of a middleware that helps the decision maker to contextualise information. Moreover, we give a set of requirements that the middleware should fulfil to learn, detect, and predict patterns in context to optimise the information flow to the decision maker. The approach is made concrete and validated in a case study in the domain of medical health care. Representative location prediction algorithms are evaluated using an existing dataset.

Keywords Decision support systems • Context awareness • Context prediction • Middleware • Learning

1 Introduction

Real-time decision support systems (RTDSS) assist decision-making persons (DMPs) in making decisions, based on real-time data. A DSS acts as an information system that can support the DMP in the decision-making process. An important aspect is the continuous monitoring of critical processes and the need to alarm the operator if certain situations occur. RTDSS can also give indication of corrective action that should be taken. The focus of a DSS is primarily on control, which is not the same as measuring and reporting. Control is exercised by a suitable

Y. Vanrompay (✉)
Department of Computer Science, Katholieke Universiteit Leuven, Leuven, Belgium
e-mail: yves.vanrompay@cs.kuleuven.be

F. Burstein et al. (eds.), *Supporting Real Time Decision-Making*,
Annals of Information Systems 13, DOI 10.1007/978-1-4419-7406-8_15,

information system directed to action (Harrison 1996). The correct action to take in a specific situation is dependent on the current context. The goal is to help DMPs to handle complex processes in conditions of rigid temporal restrictions.

Context management in the domain of real-time and mobile DSS is particularly challenging because in ubiquitous environments, context information is naturally dynamic and incomplete. Moreover, mobile devices like PDAs will typically be constrained in resources. A DSS should exhibit inherent proactiveness and automatically derive the DMP's needs for specific information from the context that surrounds him/her. Context can be defined as any information that can be used to characterise the situation of an entity such as a person, place, or object considered as relevant to the interaction between a user and an application (Dey 2001). Context-aware systems are able to adapt their operations to the current context, aiming at increasing usability and effectiveness by taking environmental context into account (Baldauf, Dustdar, and Rosenberg 2007). Context-aware DSS can learn what the right context is for making a good choice. By using the recorded history of situations (context), a context-aware DSS can achieve efficient context estimation. In this chapter, we investigate the requirements for modelling context and reasoning with context in order to infer higher-level context information (synthesis) and to predict future situations, enabling proactive behaviour of a DSS. Patterns in context can be learned by using the context history. Once learned, these patterns can be detected in real time when they occur. The detected pattern can then be used to infer higher-level information or to predict future behaviour of the system, thereby assisting the DMP in making correct decisions, taking into account the current context.

The learning and prediction algorithms are realised as plug-ins for middleware that enables context-aware self-adaptive applications. Such middleware provides support for all context management and distribution tasks, and automatically resolves dependencies between different types of context information needed by learning plug-ins or other context consumers. It also defines a common context model that can be used to represent context information. Thus, the middleware significantly reduces the burden on the developers, allowing them to concentrate on the functionalities of the decision-making support application.

This chapter is organised as follows: Sect. 2 presents a motivating health care application showing the need for context reasoning and prediction for a DSS. Section 3 presents the context middleware we propose for supporting context in DSS. Then, Sect. 4 presents the requirements for and realisation of context learning by operators, while Sect. 5 evaluates the approach. Finally, Sect. 6 gives an overview of related work and we conclude with some final remarks and future work in Sect. 7.

2 Motivating Application

Most high-level information cannot be directly sensed by sensors, but can only be inferred by analysing certain patterns of user activities in time. One of the most important kinds of contextual information is location information. A major context element influencing the other context elements is the current and predicted future location of the user because the activities of a user mainly depend on his/her location (e.g., in his/her office, at the shopping mall or in the sports centre). Moreover, available computing infrastructure like type of network will be different from one location to another. Finally, location-aware services like finding shops that could be of interest to the user are dependent on the current and future locations of the user.

To illustrate the importance of location prediction we present an example application with two scenarios in the domain of medical care. Mobile solutions for patient care are beginning to emerge. We envision a multifunctional integrated system for nurse call, logging, care registration and access control that supports and manages the daily workings of a hospital division. All relevant information needed to manage the division is shown in real time on screens in the central dispatch room. All actions are logged by the system and – at any time – data can be sorted or filtered to retrieve the information asked for by the operator. For instance, the average waiting time before treatment or the average time needed for each intervention can be used to tune the nurse organisation with the actual needs of the moment.

In normal conditions, the system is responsible for taking decisions like assigning a patient call for a nurse to the correct nurse without human intervention. However, in emergency situations (such as a sudden large influx of patients after a major accident), the decision system can be set on manual. The dispatcher will decide as to who is needed where and what the priorities are. The dispatcher makes decisions with support from and the context information shown on the screens.

Scenario 1. The nurse has a PDA on which she/he can consult information about the patient. The nurse can modify the data or enter new data. The current location of all nurses is known by the system through Radio Frequency Identification (RFID) readers in the environment. Figure 1 gives a representation of a typical environment the nurse is working in. There is a corridor with patient rooms with beds on both sides. However, full coverage of the environment by Wi-Fi is in most

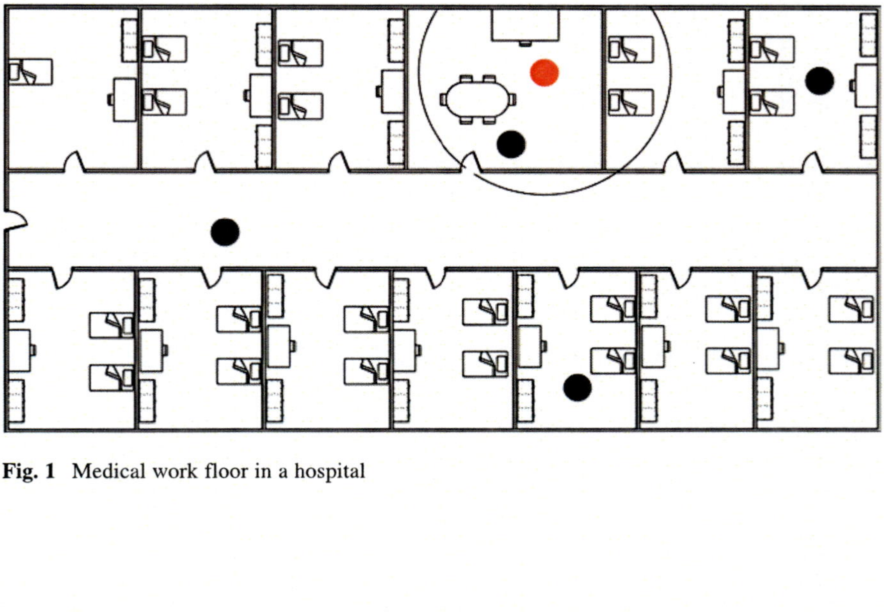

Fig. 1 Medical work floor in a hospital

cases not currently possible in a medical environment. The nurse's room is at a central location where a Bluetooth access point is located, represented by the black bullet with the circle around. It has a certain range illustrated by the circle. The patient data has to be synchronised on a regular basis to the central server for further processing by administrative and medical services. The goal is to make the data synchronisation completely transparent for the nurse.

The system has to determine autonomously the best time to synchronise. Because network connectivity must be available to do synchronisation, the time interval during which it is expected to have network connectivity must be predicted. First of all, static information can be used. At fixed times the nurse will be in the nurse's room to prepare medicine or to report to colleagues during a shift change. During these times we may expect network connectivity. Second, a model of the environment is used. The model consists primarily of a file that associates patients with rooms and a field that tells us the location of the Bluetooth access point. Last, the decision of the synchronisation timing depends on the evolution of network connectivity in time. This will be predicted by learning algorithms that use recent and past context information.

There are several advantages in knowing when to expect network availability. First, collaborative use of the network can be achieved in an environment where a number of mobile devices acting as alter egos of persons are active. When two mobile devices are in each other's reach and each device knows when it will have network connectivity, critical data can be transferred to the device that is predicted to have network connectivity at the earliest moment in the future. By implementing this data-hopping, a fast transfer of data to a central server can be achieved. Second, the high energy consumption related to the continuous polling for network discovery can be avoided. Efficient polling by doing network discovery only at time intervals when network availability is expected leads to a more efficient use of battery power.

Scenario 2. When a patient calls for a nurse, a decision has to be made in real time about which nurse is to be sent and then that nurse has to be notified by pager. This decision depends on a number of factors which are all part of the current context. The decision support system is part of the multifunctional integrated system and makes use of the middleware to obtain the context information it needs to make its decision. Relevant context consists of the current location of the nurse, her/his activity and whether her/his profile matches the possible needs of the specific patient. This leads to dynamic nurse planning, which takes into account the current situation in a hospital division and the intensity with which the nurse resource is being used at a specific time. For example, low-priority tasks can be delayed if a number of patients indicate, using the call system, that they need care.

3 The MUSIC Context Middleware

The middleware presented in this section is part of a larger initiative, the Mobile Users In Ubiquitous Computing Environments (MUSIC) project. The MUSIC project is a focused initiative aiming at the development of middleware-supporting, context-aware, self-adapting applications. The main target is to support both the development and run-time management of software systems that are capable of being adapted to highly dynamic user-and-execution context, and to maintain a high level of usefulness across context changes.

The MUSIC context system aims at a comprehensive solution for enabling context-aware applications. While part of a general adaptation-enabling middleware, the MUSIC context system can also be deployed independently.

The context system, of which the different concepts are shown in Fig. 2, allows for the development of the context sensing parts of an application independent of its context consuming parts. When a context-aware application is designed, its functional logic is defined independently of its context sensing logic. While designing the business logic of the application, its context dependencies need only be defined explicitly in a context query, or implicitly through a utility function – i.e., defined in its composition plan. The actual context sensing and processing can be defined independently via plug-ins, for which the middleware is responsible for managing. These context plug-ins are annotated with properties describing their required and provided context types. Thus, it is possible to dynamically and autonomously resolve context plug-ins and also to seamlessly manage their life cycles.

The design of the context system is based on a mutual context space, where data is stored and accessed via well-defined interfaces. The exact formatting of the context data in the context space is specified by a context ontology, which guarantees that independent context providers and consumers can seamlessly interoperate within the architecture. The context ontology provides information not only about the semantics of the abstracted context, but also about their representation. The context model consists of three basic layers of abstraction that correspond to the three main phases of context management: the conceptual layer, the exchange layer, and

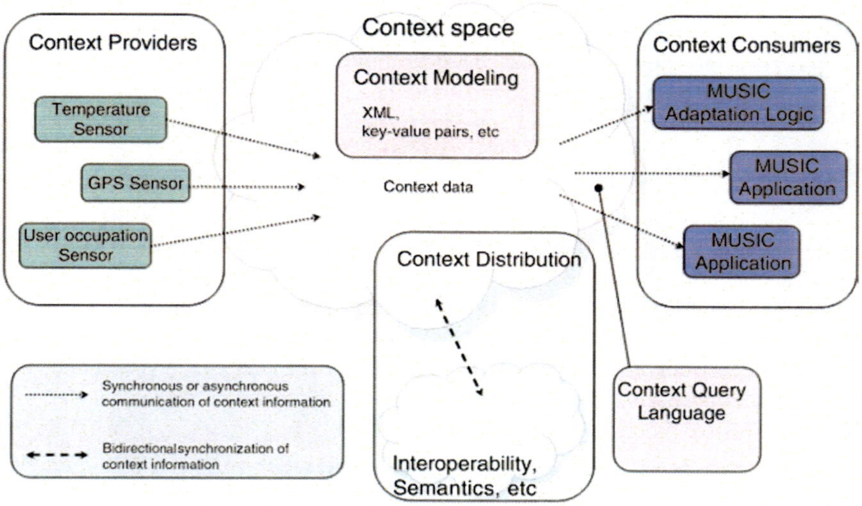

Fig. 2 The MUSIC context system

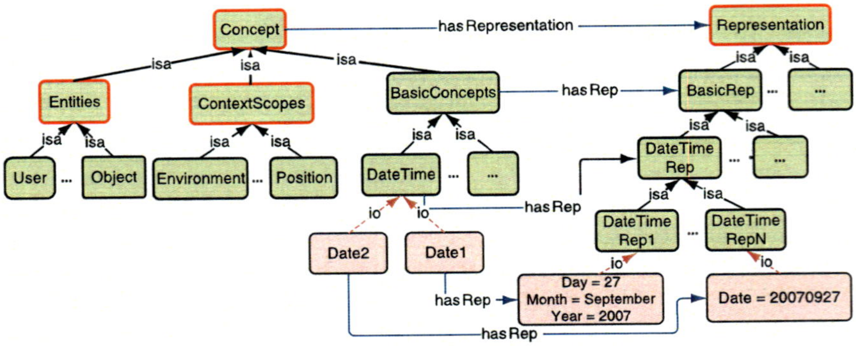

Fig. 3 The MUSIC context ontology

the functional layer. The conceptual layer enables the representation of context information in terms of *context elements*, which provide context information about *context entities* (the concrete subjects the context data refers to a user, a device, etc.) belonging to specific *context scopes*. The conceptual layer also incorporates the use of ontologies (Fig. 3) that are described in Ontology Web Language (OWL); the context scopes are intended as semantic concepts belonging to them. All the context scopes are associated with one or more *representations*, which are also specified in the ontology that describe the context data; the context information is structured in terms of parameters (*par* – attributes of context data or metadata associated with them), structures of parameters (*parS*), and an array of (structure of) parameters (*parA*). Moreover, the ontology is used to describe relationships between entities, e.g., a user has a brother or a device belongs to a user. Since ontology reasoning on mobile devices with limited resources can be onerous, we allow to reference context entities and context scopes also through predefined types. The type implicitly corresponds to a certain semantic concept and to a default representation of the context information.

In the context system architecture, the context plug-ins are dynamically attached to the mutual context space, and they push their sensed context data into the space according to their internal logic. The plug-ins can also access context data directly from the context space in order to process it and generate higher-level context data in return. Explicit access to the context data is provided by well-defined interfaces enabling both synchronous and asynchronous access to the context data. These interfaces are complemented with a context query language (CQL), providing a powerful and expressive structured query language (SQL)-like language for specifying and accessing context data (Reichle, Wagnar, Ullah Khan, Geihs, Valla, Fra, Paspallis, and Papadopoulos 2008). Finally, the context space is attached to a context storage, which allows for storing and accessing historical context data.

The architecture of the MUSIC context management system is based on two main abstractions: context sensors and context reasoners. Both of them correspond to pluggable components implementing an interface that specifies methods for activating and deactivating the individual plug-in components, as well as for accessing its associated metadata, even when inactive. Typically, the activation and deactivation methods delegate the events to the underlying machinery (e.g., in the case of hardware sensors) or detach themselves from a thread (e.g., in the case of a reasoner periodically probing a context value).

The plug-in metadata is defined at design-time from the context plug-in models. Most notably, the plug-in metadata reflect information on the context types provided and possibly required by the corresponding plug-in. In addition, Quality of Service (QoS) metadata can also be associated with plug-in components in a way similar to the one used for application components (e.g., freshness, accuracy, resource consumption, etc.). The plug-ins are packaged in self-contained files along with the applications. This is particularly useful in the case of application-specific context reasoners because the latter are platform independent (just like the context-aware applications) and can thus be packaged once and reused multiple times on different devices.

At deployment time, the plug-in components are automatically identified and their metadata is registered within the context management system. Besides the provided context types of the plug-in, the context system also evaluates its context needs. This is required because, in the case of context reasoners which dynamically synthesise complex context information based on more elementary types, it has to be verified that the needed context types are available. This is achieved using a context dependency resolution algorithm as described in Paspallis, Rouvoy, Barone, Papadopoulos, Eliassen and Mamelli (2008).

Finally, the context needs of the deployed applications are continuously evaluated at runtime by the context management system. Based on the running context needs, the required context plug-ins are activated, while the rest of them are deactivated to minimise the resource consumption. As new context-aware applications are deployed, started, stopped, and removed, the adaptation reasoner communicates the updated context needs to the context system, which dynamically activates and deactivates the deployed plug-ins accordingly.

4 Learning Algorithms and Operators

The components that learn, detect, and predict context patterns are implemented as dedicated plug-ins in the context middleware. The learning component makes use of the cache of historical values (context history base) to find patterns in the context information. The algorithms must be able to work on any type of context information. Therefore, we require the context representation to be generic and application-independent. This is achieved by explicitly making the representation of context part of the MUSIC context model and by offering a library of inter-representation transformations to the developers.

The learning operators can be instantiated as context plug-ins by specifying the plug-in metadata. This entails the context types required for learning (possibly accessed from the context storage) and the type of context patterns that will be learned, and thus provided by the plug-in. Additionally, QoS metadata like resources consumed by the learning algorithm and the degree of certainty of the resulting patterns can be added. Default parameters for the learning algorithms are set in the metadata but can be overridden by the developer.

Figure 4 exemplifies how a learning operator fits into the MUSIC context system. The learning operators are instantiated as context plug-ins by extending an abstract context plug-in class. The operator registers itself with the context middleware (1) by specifying plug-in metadata. That entails the context types required for learning (possibly accessed from the context storage) and the type of context patterns that will be learned and thus provided by the plug-in. Before the learning operator can be activated, the middleware checks whether a context plug-in for the specified required type is available and, if so, activates it if needed (2). After the learning operator has been activated (3), a listener is registered (4) which is notified if the required context types change their values (5 and 6). The learning algorithm is notified (7) and updates its output (8 and 9). It is worth mentioning that the context distribution support of the middleware allows for context plug-ins to be hosted on nodes in the network other than the context consumers. Also, the context sensors providing information to a learning operator plug-in can be located in other places in the network.

Learning involves finding classes of situations or patterns that are representative and on the basis of which newly detected patterns can be classified. The purpose of classification in general is to classify contextual information into a set of classes; it is usually used to decrease the dimensionality of input data. Unsupervised classification,

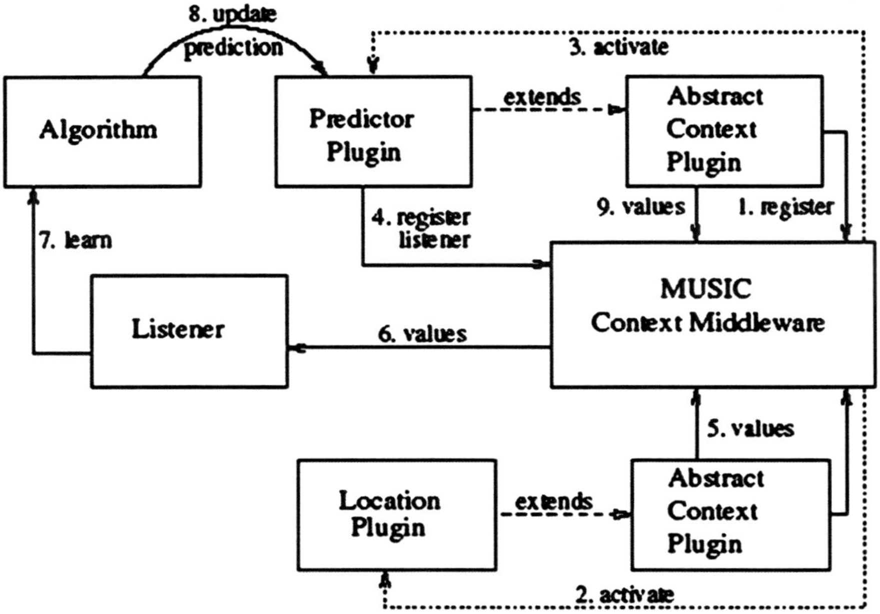

Fig. 4 Learning operators in the MUSIC context middleware

also named clustering, tries to find previously unknown classes, solely based on the given input data. Since we want a self-learning nonobtrusive system, supervised methods that demand an a priori definition of context classes or continuous questioning of the user cannot be applied.

We identified the following requirements for learning (classification):

- Online, in real time: bounds on processing time are known and deterministic.
- Adaptive: learning must never stop. The existing classification must be adapted to slowly changing input patterns. The learning rate depends on the level of dynamicity of the environment.
- Soft classification: more than one context (situation) can be active at the same time (e.g., "at work" and "on the phone"). Therefore, we need to specify the degree of membership to each context class.
- The learning approach has to be able to cope with limited (CPU and memory) resources typical of mobile devices such as PDAs.
- Uncertainty: the uncertainty of the learned results should be made explicit to the DMP or application.

Once patterns have been learned, they have to be detected in real-time as they occur. In order to guarantee boundaries on execution time to detect (possibly complex) patterns, they can be represented by a context pattern algebra similar to the event algebra proposed in Carlson (2007). A pattern represented by an expression with expression size x, which is a measure for the complexity of the pattern in this algebra, can be efficiently detected with known resources (memory and time). This is critical for the real-time (timing) requirements of a DSS.

Finally, context prediction involves a probabilistic scheme to deal with the uncertainty of future context situations. Since a predicted outcome will only occur with a specific probability, and different algorithms can give different probabilities, a measure must be defined that tells how confident an application can be in the predicted result. The algorithm should also be unsupervised. Several algorithms, which will be presented in the next section, meet these requirements (Mayrhofer 2004). To assist in the decision-making, event-condition-action (ECA) rules can be helpful. When a specific pattern is detected or predicted, the specified action should be performed if a condition is satisfied.

5 Evaluation

After describing how to fit the learning operators into the general MUSIC middleware, this section focuses on qualitatively and quantitatively evaluating the proposed approach. The qualitative evaluation shows that the MUSIC context middleware in combination with prediction capabilities suits the needs and addresses challenges posed by the motivating health care application. In order to assess the research quantitatively, we employ several representative context prediction algorithms and experiment with a realistic dataset.

5.1 Qualitative Evaluation

This section presents the approach taken to realise the first scenario of our motivating application in which the time of availability of network connectivity has to be predicted. We give an overview of the key context elements needed, the algorithm that was chosen to fulfil the requirements of the previous section and finally, some experimental results. More details can be found in Vanrompay, Rigole, and Berbers (2007).

The evolution in network connectivity is uncertain because a person can follow different paths in performing an activity. We use a probabilistic approach to model this uncertainty. Decisions are made based on the most probable evolution in time of network connectivity. Key context elements to be taken into account are time, place, and activity. The performed activity can depend on the time of the day. We assume that, at a certain fixed place, there is network connectivity. While performing activities a person walks around on the work floor visiting a number of places. The place where a person is located can be inferred from sensors (e.g., RFID) or it can be deduced from the person's current activities. Each activity has a path associated with it that can be recorded and used to learn movement patterns. So, essentially, we are doing path prediction. The context middleware is responsible for managing and distributing the context information from sensors to context reasoners and learners/predictors. DMPs or applications (which are context consumers,) can themselves ask for specific context information by sending a CQL query, or they can subscribe to context information and be notified by the context middleware in case of context changes. Dependencies between required and offered context types are automatically resolved by the middleware. For example, since the location predictor plug-in needs the current location, an appropriate location sensor is dynamically activated by the context middleware.

Key context elements in this case are time, activity, and location. Depending on the time of the day, certain activities are more likely to be performed than others. For example, around noon there is a high probability that the lunch distribution activity takes place. The followed path is dependent on the activity. Also, the amount of time spent on each patient depends on the activity. The current activity can be inferred by looking at the time and at what data is viewed or modified. For example, when the activity is parameter taking, parameters of the patient are entered in the PDA. By entering parameters of a certain patient and by using a patient-room association file (which is statically given information), the system can determine where the nurse is at the moment. Then the most probable path and the expected time interval during which the network will be available can be computed using Markov chains. Each activity will have its own associated Markov chain.

We evaluated the approach with some scenarios representing the daily movements of a nurse in a hospital division. First, we looked at the planning and daily tasks of a nurse. Representative paths followed by the nurse during her different activities were constructed. Also, real-life log data from nurse calls were obtained containing the time of call, the room, the duration to service every call and the nurse who got the call. This allowed us to mix typically followed paths with random nurse calls (from the log data) that had to be serviced. The effect in the training data is that at random moments in the normal path, a random room is added. After a few training cycles the probabilities of transitions from one room to another in the typical path outweigh the probabilities of the transitions caused by the random calls. Therefore, random calls are recognised because they have a small probability. The frequency of random calls also influences the predicted time of network connectivity. Initial experiments show a prediction accuracy of around 80%. This corresponds to the location prediction results for indoor movement of Petzold, Bagci, Trumler, and Ungerer (2003), where the Markov predictor gave results of prediction accuracy of 76.5%.

5.2 *Quantitative Evaluation*

For the evaluation of representative prediction algorithms we used the well-known dataset of the MavHome project (Cook, Youngblood, Heierman, Gopalratnam, Rao, Litvin, and Khawaja 2003). It is based on a person living for about a month in a house that is equipped with various sensors. We extracted the motion sensor data and grouped it according to the rooms in which the sensors were situated. This provided us with context information which was sufficiently abstract. The final dataset with about 85,000 entries was a time series of rooms where motion had been sensed.

A variety of algorithms for context prediction had been proposed, e.g., Petzold et al. (2003), Mayrhofer (2004), and Sigg, Haseloff, and David (2007). We have chosen first- and fifth-order Markov chains, the active Lempel-Ziv (ALZ) algorithm (Gopalratnam and Cook 2003), and a hidden Markov model (HMM) with five hidden states capable of online learning (Mongillo and Deneve 2008). The original ALZ algorithm violates the initial requirements because the memory consumption grows with the number of examples. Therefore, we restricted the internal tree to a maximum depth of $D = 5$. The predictions for the HMM are made by taking the sequence of the last O observations and using the Viterbi algorithm to find the most probable next observation.

The evaluation (Vanrompay, Mehlhase, and Berbers 2010) consists of requesting a prediction from the algorithm which is then compared to the actual next value. After the correctness has been assessed, the value is fed to the algorithm. Although the chosen algorithms do run in an online mode, we ignored the first 1,000 predictions in order to stabilise the results. The performance of the prediction algorithm was assessed by using the standard error rate "e" of the algorithm on the complete dataset.

Subsequently, we evaluated how good the predictions were, if we only consider those whose certainty value was higher than the given threshold of 0.8. Results are shown in Table 1. The error rate improved to about 8% (with the exception of the first-order Markov chain). This result rendered the predictions more usable than the results without using a threshold. Although the HMM had the best error rate in this case, it only made about 30,000 of the 85,000 predictions with this certainty. In contrast, the ALZ algorithm (and the fifth-order Markov chain) did more than 45,000 predictions above the threshold and had only a slightly worse error rate.

Table 1 Prediction algorithm error rates

Algorithm	Error rate w/o threshold	Error rate with threshold
Active Lempel-Ziv	0.2196	0.0881
First-order Markov chain	0.2442	0.1275
Fifth-order Markov chain	0.2218	0.0884
HMM	0.2711	0.0874

6 Related Work

The MUSIC middleware (Rouvoy, Barone, Ding, Eliassen, Hallsteinsen, Lorenzo, Mamelli, and Scholz 2009) aims at making context available to applications in an easy way and provides run-time support to adapt these applications. It abstracts context information from raw context sensors by context plug-ins. Context reasoners encapsulate operators that use raw sensor data to build more abstract context information like proposed in Paspallis et al. (2008). The MUSIC context middleware is designed to support dynamic activation and deactivation of these context plug-ins on demand to improve the resource utilisation of the target devices. Ranganathan and Campbell (2003) argues ubiquitous computing environments must provide middleware support for context-awareness. Their middleware is integrated in Gaia, an infrastructure for smart spaces and also employs different learning mechanisms to infer context information. However, the approach is agent-oriented and not integrated in an adaptation framework. Dey, Abowd, and Salber (2001) developed a toolkit enabling the rapid prototyping of context-aware applications. Unlike our work, it does not provide a generic mechanism to infer or predict high-level context information. The MoCoA framework (Senart, Cunningham, Bouroche, O'Connor, Reynolds, and Cahill 2006) is a flexible middleware framework for context-awareness targeting applications involving a large collection of mobile devices that adapt themselves. While learning is a part of the framework, collaborative reinforcement learning is the only technique considered.

Algorithms for context prediction have been proposed before. Mozer, Dodier and Vidmar (1997) used neural networks to create a thermostat that learns the user's behaviour and heats the house accordingly. Horvitz, Kochm Kadie, and Jacobs (2002) tried to forecast presence and availability of a user by analysing different features like the presence of other people in the office. Petzold et al. (2003) tried to infer which room a user will enter next by analysing the history of rooms. In common, all these approaches proposed algorithms that are specialised and may not work on more general domains. Cook et al. (2003) described a more general approach within the MavHome project that utilises different sensors and algorithms. A more complete overview about algorithms and their usage can be found in Mayrhofer (2004). More recent work has been done by Vanrompay et al. (2007) where Markov chains and HMMs are used, and Sigg et al. (2007) where statistical approaches are utilised. Boytsov, Zaslavsky, and Synnes (2009) extend the context spaces theory (Padovitz, Loke, and Zaslavsky 2004) by providing context prediction. A testbed is provided, allowing the evaluation of a variety of prediction methods. In our approach, several prediction algorithms (encapsulated in context plug-ins) can be active at the same time allowing an application to dynamically choose the predicted result with the highest confidence at runtime.

HMM have been used to learn movement patterns in a mobile network to perform Global System for Mobile Communications (GSM) tracking (Francois, Leduem and Martin 2004). Information related to the paths followed by mobile phones can be learned using HMMs and the prediction method allows for the anticipation of resource allocation. This means dynamic scheduling takes place. Chinchilla, Lindsey, and Papadopouli (2004) uses Markov chains to predict to which access point a wireless client will connect, given the last access point to which the client was connected. The goal is to improve the performance of the wireless infrastructures by load balancing, admission control, and resource reservation across access points. Mobility patterns of clients are learned from historical information. The system has been tested on a university campus with a wireless infrastructure. The next access point a wireless client connects to can be predicted with 86% accuracy according to experimental results. Papadopouli, Shen, and Spanakis (2005) presents a methodology that shows how mobility patterns and associations between users and access points evolve not only in space, but also in time. Therefore, wireless access patterns are characterised on the basis of stochastic parameters such as visit duration. Chakraborty, Yau, and Lui (2003) evaluates several heuristics that, based on the movement history of a mobile client, estimate an optimal time for communication. Time is optimal when the least energy will be used. The goal is thus to minimise the energy consumption necessary for wireless communication. Statistical information about a client's movement history is represented as heuristics based on Markov models.

7 Conclusions

In this chapter, we proposed to use a context middleware layer to enable context-awareness for mobile DSS. Specialised context plug-ins take care of learning and detecting patterns in context information to support the decision maker in a time-critical fashion. Moreover, the future evolution of the contextual information can be predicted, ensuring proactive behaviour of the DSS. Important requirements for dealing with patterns in information systems were derived and realised in a case study by the use of Markov chains. We focused on the potential advantages for real-time decision support of the combination of a middleware enabling context-aware application and the use of learning operators. The operators are generic and can be instantiated in context plug-ins, making it easier for developers to integrate context learning and prediction in their system. The MUSIC context middleware has a pluggable architecture, facilitating the dynamic (de)activation of the plug-ins and resolving the interdependencies between different context plug-ins. Several representative prediction algorithms were experimentally evaluated using an existing dataset.

Future work includes the investigation of a wider range of quality of context prediction measures, including certainty and cost (i.e., CPU, bandwidth). This will allow an application to assess the quality provided by different prediction components and make decisions based on these quality measures.

Acknowledgements The authors would like to thank their partners in the MUSIC-IST project and acknowledge the partial financial support given to this research by the European Union (6th Framework Programme, contract number 35166).

References

Baldauf, M., S. Dustdar and F. Rosenberg, "A survey on context-aware systems," in *International Journal of Ad Hoc and Ubiquitous Computing*, vol. 2, n. 4, 2007, 263–277.

Boytsov, A., A. Zaslavsky and K. Synnes, "Extending context spaces theory by predicting run-time context," in *Proceedings of NEW2AN/ruSMART 2009*, LNCS 5764. Berlin: Springer, 2009, 8–21.

Carlson, J., *Event pattern detection for embedded systems*, PhD thesis, Malardalen University Press, Dissertations no. 44, 2007.

Chakraborty, S., D. Yau and J. Lui, "On the effectiveness of movement prediction to reduce energy consumption in wireless communication," in *Joint International Conference on Measurement and Modeling of Computer Systems (SIGMETRICS)*, San Diego, June 2003.

Chinchilla, F., M. Lindsey and M. Papadopouli, "Analysis of wireless information locality and association patterns in a campus," *IEEE International Conference on Computer Communications (IEEE INFOCOM)*, Hong Kong, 2004.

Cook, D.J., M. Youngblood, E.O. Heierman, K. Gopalratnam, S. Rao, A. Litvin and F. Khawaja, "Mavhome: An agent-based smart home," in *Proceedings of the First IEEE International Conference on Pervasive Computing and Communications* (PerCom 2003), Fort Worth, 2003, 521–524.

Dey, A., "Understanding and using context," in *Personal and Ubiquitous Computing*, vol. 5, n. 1, 2001, 4–7.

Dey, A.K., G.D. Abowd and D. Salber, "A conceptual framework and a toolkit for supporting the rapid prototyping of context-aware applications," in *Human-Computer Interaction*, vol. 16, n. 2, 2001, 97–166.

Francois, J., G. Leduc and M. Martin, "Learning movement patterns in mobile networks: A generic method," in *European Wireless*, Barcelona, 2004, 128–134.

Gopalratnam, K. and D.J. Cook, "Active lezi: An incremental parsing algorithm for device usage prediction in the smart house," in *Proceedings of the Florida Artificial Intelligence Research Symposium*, St. Augustine, May 2003, 38–42.

Harrison, M., *Principles of Operations Management*. London: Pitman, 1996.

Horvitz, E., P. Koch, C.M. Kadie and A. Jacobs, "Coordinate: Probabilistic forecasting of presence and availability," in *Proceedings of the Eighteenth Conference on Uncertainty and Artificial Intelligence*, Edmonton, Morgan Kaufmann Publishers, San Francisco, 2002, 224–233.

Mayrhofer, R.M., *An architecture for context prediction*, PhD thesis, Johannes Kepler Universitat Linz, 2004.

Mongillo, G. and S. Deneve, "Online learning with hidden Markov models," in *Neural Computation*, vol. 20, 2008, 1706–1716.

Mozer, M.C., R.H. Dodier and L. Vidmar, "The neurothermosthat: Adaptive control of residential heating systems," in *Advances in Neural Information Processing Systems*, vol. 9, MIT Press, Cambridge, MA, 1997, 953–959.

MUSIC Consortium, "Self-adapting applications for mobile users in ubiquitous computing environments (MUSIC)," URL = http://www.ist-music.eu/

Padovitz, A., S.W. Loke and A. Zaslavsky, "Towards a theory of context spaces," in *Proceedings of the Second IEEE Annual Conference on Pervasive Computing and Communications Workshops*, Orlando, 2004, 38–42.

Papadopouli, M., H. Shen and M. Spanakis, "Characterizing the mobility and association patterns of wireless users in a campus," *11th European Wireless Conference*, Nicosia, 2005.

Paspallis, N., R. Rouvoy, P. Barone, G.A. Papadopoulos, F. Eliassen and A. Mamelli, "A pluggable and reconfigurable architecture for a context-aware enabling middleware system," in *10th International Symposium on Distributed Objects, Middleware, and Applications* (*DOA'08*), LNCS 5331. Monterrey: Springer, November 2008, 553–570.

Petzold, J., F. Bagci, W. Trumler and T. Ungerer, "Global and local state context prediction," in *Proceedings of the Workshop on Artificial Intelligence in Mobile Systems 2003* (*AIMS 2003*), Seattle, 2003.

Ranganathan, A. and R.H. Campbell, "A middleware for context-aware agents in ubiquitous computing environments," in *Middleware'03: Proceedings of the ACM/IFIP/USENIX 2003 International Conference on Middleware*, Rio de Janeiro. New York: Springer, 2003, 143–161.

Reichle, R., M. Wagner, M. Ullah Khan, K. Geihs, M. Valla, C. Fra, N. Paspallis and G. Papadopoulos, "A context query language for pervasive computing environments," in *Proceedings of 5th IEEE Workshop on Context Modeling and Reasoning*, at the *6th IEEE International Conference on Pervasive Computing and Communication* (*PerCom'08*), Hong Kong, 2008.

Rouvoy, R., P. Barone, Y. Ding, F. Eliassen, S. Hallsteinsen, J. Lorenzo, A. Mamelli and U. Scholz, "MUSIC: Middleware Support for Self-Adaptation in Ubiquitous and Service-Oriented Environments," in *Software Engineering for Self-Adaptive Systems (SEfSAS)*, LNCS 5525. Berlin: Springer, 2009.

Senart, A., R. Cunningham, M. Bouroche, N. O'Connor, V. Reynolds and V. Cahill, "MoCoA: Customisable middleware for context-aware mobile applications," in *Distributed Object Applications, Procedings of the 8th Internatinational Sympossion on Distibuted Objects and Application*, Montfellier, France, Nov 2006, 1722–1738.

Sigg, S., S. Haseloff and K. David, "Prediction of context time series," in *5th Workshop on Applications of Wireless Communications*, Lappeenranta, 2007, 31–45.

Vanrompay, Y., P. Rigole and Y. Berbers, "Predicting network connectivity for context-aware pervasive system with localized network availability," in *Proceedings of the 1st International Workshop on System Support for the Internet of Things*, Lisbon, March 2007.

Vanrompay, Y., S. Mehlhase and Y. Berbers, "An effective quality measure for prediction of context information," in *Proceedings of the Eighth Annual IEEE International Conference on Pervasive Computing and Communications and Workshops*, Mannheim, 2010.

Chapter 16
On-demand Assistance in Handling Ammunition: Development of a Mobile Ammo DSS

Supavich Pengnate[1], Ramesh Sharda[1], David Biros[1], Michael Hass[1], and Upton Shimp[2]

[1]The U.S. Army Defense Ammunition Center, OK, USA
[2]Department of Management Science and Information Systems, Oklahoma State University, OK, USA

Abstract Wireless technology and the emergence of handheld devices provide new ways to deliver and present information. For the military, availability of needed ammunition information is critical for decision making, especially in a war zone. This case study describes the extension of a Web-based ammunition multimedia encyclopedia (AME) developed for the U.S. Army Defense Ammunition Center (DAC). Mobile AME uses handheld technology to provide Quality Assurance Specialist Ammunition Surveillance (QASAS) personnel access to needed ammunition information via a personal digital assistant (PDA). The focus was to develop a highly usable system supporting QASAS decision making and training in choosing the best practices to properly handle ammunition items. This chapter discusses the motivation behind Mobile AME, design and development of the system, and future directions.

Keywords Mobile decision support • Handheld technology • Ammunition multimedia encyclopedia

1 Introduction

We have seen several mobile applications developed for organisations in the business domain. However, wireless technology and handheld devices can provide new channels to deliver and present information in military and government settings as well.

Mobile devices such as cell phones and personal digital assistants (PDAs) have gained increasing importance as systems and devices. Their use continues to improve capability to distribute Internet-based services to support the exchange and

---

S. Pengnate (✉)
Department of Management Science and Information Systems,
Oklahoma State University, OK, USA
e-mail: fone.pengnate@okstate.edu

F. Burstein et al. (eds.), *Supporting Real Time Decision-Making*,
Annals of Information Systems 13, DOI 10.1007/978-1-4419-7406-8_16,

sharing of data and services. Mobile computing represents a dynamic environment that enables a vast array of varying interfaces, contexts and automation (Abowd and Mynatt 2000). These technologies present an opportunity to offer the latest knowledge transfer to any worker in the field. For example, the development process, storage, and handling of modern ammunition has become increasingly more complex and thus, the challenge of developing dynamic training to maintain the quality of ammunition inspections is a significant problem for the U.S. Army Defense Ammunition Center (DAC).

DAC is an organisation within the Department of Defense (DOD) that prepares civilians, including former military personnel, to transport, manage, and supervise safe ammunition and explosives handling. DAC also supports the joint ammunition community worldwide through training, engineering logistics, explosives safety, and technical assistance. These civilians are in one of two career fields: Quality Assurance Specialist Ammunition Surveillance (QASAS) or Ammunition Managers (Kearney, Self, Bailey, Harris, Halcomb, Hill, and Shimp 2007).

In modern war, ammunition is one of the most necessary materials consumed on battlefields. The safety and reliability issues of ammunition are critical to the war fighters and are related to the optimal war-fighting capability of an armed force (Mullen 2002). Those issues are taken into account when a QASAS makes a decision about munitions viability to include discarded military munitions (DMM). DMM are typically abandoned in the field instead of returned back through the ammunition supply system. Ammunition stored improperly can cause components to deteriorate, which could lead to untimely detonation and irreversible tragedy. QASAS must evaluate the DMM and determine if it can be returned to ammunition inventories and thereby reduce waste, or if it must be processed for deactivation.

This case study presents a mobile application developed to support QASAS decision making for the best practice in handling any unfamiliar ammunition or DMM.

2 Background

2.1 Mobile Decision Support

The use of wireless technology and handheld devices enriches today's variety of e-services and extends opportunities for decision support. Users can get access to the most up-to-date information via wireless mobile devices and make real-time decisions. The application of handheld technology has been explored in various industries, in both private and public sectors. This allows mobile users to get access to required information and make decisions without geographic limitations. Table 1 presents examples of the use of mobile applications in different settings.

Mennecke and Strader (2002) categorised mobile devices into the laptop computer, handheld devices (PDA), telephone, hybrid (e.g., smart phone/pocket PC phone), wearable (e.g., jewellery, watches), vehicle-mounted, and enabling technologies such as global positioning system (GPS) devices. Even though many such portable

Table 1 Examples of research in mobile applications

Industry	Use of mobile device	Example references
Health care	Providing clinicians with patient information and communication to reduce medical errors	Chen, Mendonca, McKnightm Stetsin, Lei, and Cimino (2004)
Health care	Proposing a mobile agent to support emergency decision making of an ambulance service in real-time	Burstein, Zaslavsky, and Zrora (2005)
Education	Providing computer-supported collaborative learning activities in a museum	Cabrera, Frutos, Stoica, Dimitriadis, Fiotakis, and Liveri (2005)
Airport operations	Improving airport ground operations and preventing airport congestion in a crisis situation	Pestana, Silva, Casaca, and Nunes (2005)
Retail store	Using a mobile application to support a customer's evaluation of retail products	van der Heijden (2006)
Financial institute	Supporting real-time decision making for account management	Burstein, Cowie, Zaslavaky, and San Pedro (2008)

devices can provide decision support capability, PDAs and hybrid devices are of great relevance for the systems and are becoming increasingly popular for general users (Burstein et al. 2008). In this study, hybrid devices such as pocket PC phones (PPCs) were used for Mobile ammunition multimedia encyclopedia (AME).

2.2 Architectures of Mobile Decision Support

Generally, there are two main types of mobile applications: Web-based and local (Lee 2007). The first category of applications runs on a server, generally a Web server, and is accessed by mobile devices through the Internet. This category is typically developed in the client-server architecture. Examples would include applications on iPhone such as *New York Times* update. The second type includes stand-alone applications running on the devices themselves, with or without Internet access (Lee 2007). One example is Wikipedia on iPhone. This application includes 2 GB (current size) content on Wikipedia that is downloaded to an iPhone. The main idea is to have the information available in real time even when there is no phone or Internet connectivity. Enabling technologies such as JavaScript, XML, XHTML and Microsoft's.NET Framework – the.NET Compact Framework (.NET CF) – can be used to develop such applications.

Burstein et al. (2008) proposed different architectures in mobile decision support systems (DSS) according to the implementation of fundamental DSS components (database, analytical model, and user interface). A total of five possible mobile DSS architectures are presented in Table 2.

The mobile decision support architectures are distinguished by location of the resources and where computations are performed (Burstein et al. 2008). Advantages and disadvantages differ across architectures and the usefulness of each architecture

Table 2 Mobile decision support architectures (adapted from Burstein et al. 2008)

Architecture	Client Environment (User interface)	Server Environment (Server side)
(a) Client/server: Distributed functionality	Analytical Model, Database	Analytical Model, Database
(b) Client/server: Thick client-thin server	Analytical Model, Database	Analytical Model
(c) Client/server: Thin client-thick server		Analytical Model, Database
(d) Client/server: Client-proxy-server		Analytical Model, Database, Proxy
(e) Peer-to-peer (Standalone application)	Analytical Model, Database	

is determined by the purpose of the application, user requirements, and hardware requirements. Therefore, each component of mobile decision support is able to reside in a specific device or be distributed across server and client devices.

2.3 *Mobile AME's Context of Use*

Generally, mobile applications are different from more conventional information systems because they take into consideration the contexts of using mobile applications to adapt content and present it to users accordingly (Steiniger, Neun, and Edwardes 2006). Context of mobile application use can be classified in various ways, but the most common context distinctions are location of the mobile user, time of the mobile application use, and type of task or service requested. Nevertheless, mobile applications for decision making are not always designed for using them in real-time context. For example, GPS devices are used to make decisions regarding route choices by matching the user's location with map data stored in the device's internal memory and then presenting results to the user (Hofmann-Wellenhof, Lichtenegger, and Collins 1997). Several researchers have proposed context categorisations that are relevant to the user's environments (Schilit, Adams, and Want 1994; Abowd, Dey, Brown, Davies, Smith and Steggles 1999; Chen and Kotz 2000; Dey 2001). Furthermore, Nivala and Sarjakoski developed a map-based mobile context classification (2003). They classify mobile contexts into nine categories: system, purpose of use, time, physical surroundings, navigation history, orientation, cultural and social environments, and user (Nivala and Sarjakoski 2003).

It is imperative for QASAS to make quick and accurate decisions regarding the identification, maintenance, packaging, and transporting of ammunition all over the world. In many cases, QASAS find themselves in deployed locations with little or no Internet connectivity. Still they are required to make rapid decisions regarding ammunition safety. Most QASAS receive training early in their careers and acquire the rest of their knowledge and skills on the job. When QASAS deploy, they either bring a series of technical publications (in paper form) or rely on their own knowledge base to meet the demands of their jobs. This can lead to suboptimal decision-making.

In many cases, new ammunition has been introduced to the DOD that QASAS have never seen. In other cases, QASAS must deal with captured enemy ammunition with which they are not familiar. This makes it difficult for QASAS to identify the ammunition, much less make decisions with respect to the viability and safety of the materiel. In many cases, QASAS reported having to resort to making their best guess. They needed a portable decision-making tool that would enable them to (1) have an in-depth view of the ammunition, (2) access its specification data, (3) quickly ascertain its critical or major defects, and (4) decide on an appropriate course of action while deployed in austere environments. This is the objective of Mobile AME.

The major context of use for Mobile AME is accessing desired information in austere environments. In addition, there is a high likelihood of reduced or nonexistent wireless connectivity. Thus, Mobile AME was developed as a combination of standalone and server-client architecture as shown in Table 2. In the standalone mode, the ammunition data is stored in internal device memory. Therefore, the device does not have to establish a connection for retrieving ammunition information from the server. This can greatly reduce time for accessing the desired information. However, in the client-server mode, if Mobile AME is used in different contexts where the Internet connection is available, the Mobile AME user is able to get the most recent ammunition information updates by either downloading the database updates from the server to the internal ammunition database, or accessing Mobile AME system residing on the server via the mobile device's Web browser. Therefore, in contexts other than deployed environments, Mobile AME can be used to support QASAS training as well. Mobile AME's architecture is presented in the next section in more detail.

3 Mobile AME Design

In the design and development of Mobile AME, the two major concerns are content delivery and usability. The system must be able to offer decision support capability to QASAS where there is no Internet connectivity. Usability is another concern of Mobile AME. In designing the user interface, the screen should allow QASAS to navigate and read the content easily.

A related key factor for the success of Mobile AME is the human-computer interface (HCI) issue. Several studies have been conducted to correct a common problem of mobile applications – namely, giving mobile users access to computing services for complicated tasks and information presented via small displays. Mobile applications have small screens, poor audio interaction facilities, and limited input devices (Kristoffersen and Ljungberg 1999; Dunlop and Brewster 2002; Kjeldskov and Graham 2003; Kjeldskov, Skov, Als, and Hoegh 2004). According to Dunlop and Brewster the challenges for mobile HCI are categorised into five main areas (2002): (1) designing for mobility: a small working area such as in a mobile device limits working environment for mobile users (e.g., no notes on desk like typical working environments), (2) designing for a widespread population: lack of formal training for new mobile application users, (3) designing for limited input/output facilities – lack of keyboard input and poor quality of audio output, (4) designing for context information – mobile devices fit well with context-aware application, and (5) designing for user multitasking at levels more limited than in a desktop environment – for mobile applications, the degree of interruption when multitasking is likely to be much higher than that found in desktop designs (Dey, Abowd, and Salber 2001).

Several technologies have been developed to improve mobile device capability. Most mobile devices use a small built-in keyboard or a touch screen and stylus for input. Newer generations of PDAs include more advanced technologies such as multitouch (Apple, Inc. 2008), which allow designers more flexibility in designing interfaces. In order to achieve Mobile AME user interface goals, the system needs to deliver and present the content in an organised way under limitations of the wireless handheld environment such as screen size, memory storage capacity, and processor speed.

3.1 Device Independence

In this study, two major aspects of mobile computing are investigated: device independence and wireless device usability (Lum and Lau 2002; Venkatesh and Ramesh 2006). Consequently, those two approaches are used as development frameworks of Mobile AME.

Device independence refers to the device's capability to separate data and presentation to support the interchange of data between different platforms and heterogeneous computing systems (Germonprez, Germonprez, and Avital 2005). Device independence describes the presentation of information on different devices without changes made in the data, services, workflow, or personal computing preferences. Therefore, device independence provides access to the same information for different users. Data are independent from a particular device, irrespective of the device from which the request originates and the delivery and presentation of this data to a variety of devices running on different platforms with wide variations in screen sizes and technological capabilities as well as the rapid delivery of data over heterogeneous networks.

3.2 *Device usability*

Usability is a term that generally refers to the ease with which different people can employ a particular tool or other human-made object in order to achieve a particular goal (Nielsen 2000). In human-computer interaction, usability refers to the clarity with which a computer program or a website is designed. It is a critical factor for success in Web applications. Several studies identified the lack of usability as the key impediment for sites employed by mobile devices (Ramsay and Nielsen 2000; Jackson, Favier, and Stagia 2002). However, directly applying the principles of website design to a site used by portable devices may not produce desirable outcomes. Several researchers have studied the differences between the design of standard websites and sites used by mobile devices (Housel and Lindquist 1996; Jones, Marsden, Mohd-Nasir, Boone, and Buchanan 1999; Buyukkokten, Garcia-Molina, Paepcke, and Winograd 2000; Holzinger and Errath 2004; Tamminen, Oulasvirta, Toiskallio, and Kankainen 2004). Others (Lu, Yu, Liu, and Yaof 2003; Siau, Sheng, and Nah 2003; Fang, Chan, Brzezinski, and Xu 2005) have proposed a framework for designing sites used by mobile devices by employing the Technology Acceptance Model (TAM) (Davis, Bagozzim abd Warshaw 1989). However, Venkatesh and Ramesh proposed an alternative framework which follows the Microsoft Usability Guidelines (MUG) (Keeker 1997) that outperforms the TAM and provides a better understanding on the usability of mobile sites applications (Venkatesh and Ramesh 2006). Therefore in this study, the MUG framework for mobile sites proposed by Venkatesh and Ramesh was employed in Mobile AME development.

4 The Process of Decision Support for QASAS Personnel

This section presents frameworks of the process between QASAS' operations and Mobile AME (Fig. 1). As mentioned earlier, because the access to needed information is time-critical, Mobile AME was developed as a standalone application. Mobile AME provides QASAS with information so that they are able to properly handle ammunition with which they are unfamiliar. We note that QASAS only receive formal training early in their careers and typically they are not retrained to refine the knowledge before performing the operations. In addition, since there is an extensive inventory of ammunition, and since different ammunition variants are developed annually, it is unlikely that QASAS personnel are able to recognise all of the inspection points and procedures for all types of ammunition. Mobile AME's context of use is illustrated in Fig. 1.

As can be seen in Fig. 1, after updating Mobile AME from the base station where a desktop computer and Internet connectivity are available, the QASAS takes it into the field. There, QASAS use Mobile AME to inspect unfamiliar ammunition or DMM, retrieve ammunition information from Mobile AME, and identify inspection points and shipping and packaging information. Once the ammunition has been identified and its characteristics processed, QASAS can then decide whether the ammunition can be safely delivered to an ammunition storage facility or should be prepared for disposal.

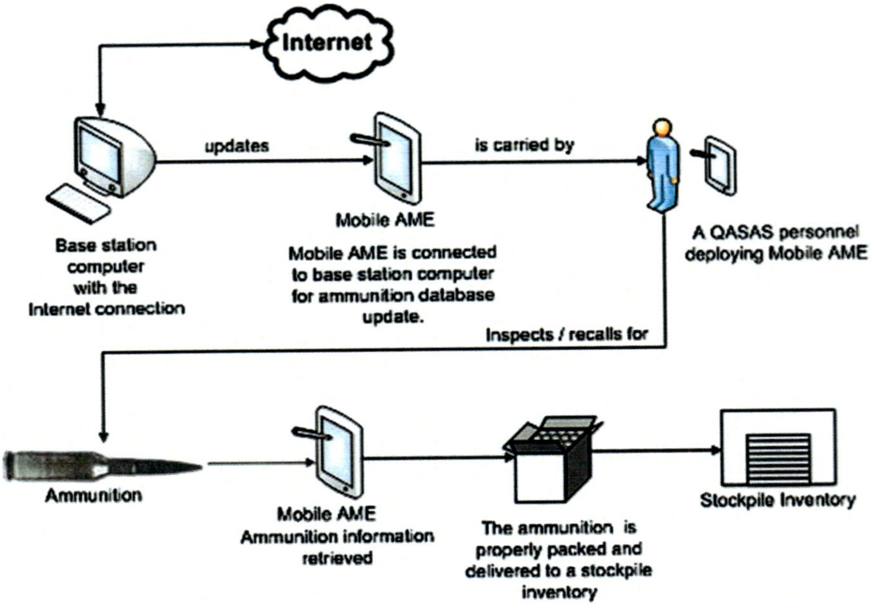

Fig. 1 Mobile AME context of use

5 Mobile AME System Architecture

As mentioned in the previous section, Mobile AME was developed under a client-server architecture framework. However, according to its context of use, Mobile AME works as a standalone application by storing presentation, logic, and data modules in its internal memory. In addition, the system can work using client-server architecture by connecting to the server through a base station with Internet connectivity or through its wireless capability. Figure 2 illustrates the system architecture of Mobile AME.

The major scripting technologies employed by the Mobile AME architecture include HTML document object model (HTML DOM), JavaScript, Extensible Markup Language (XML), and MySQL database on the server side. This solution functions on various handheld devices and operating platforms so that it achieves device independence requirements.

5.1 Mobile AME Data Source

Once the handheld device had been selected, software options for the data source were evaluated with the goal of device independence in mind. We decided to use XML as the database for ammunition content for Mobile AME.

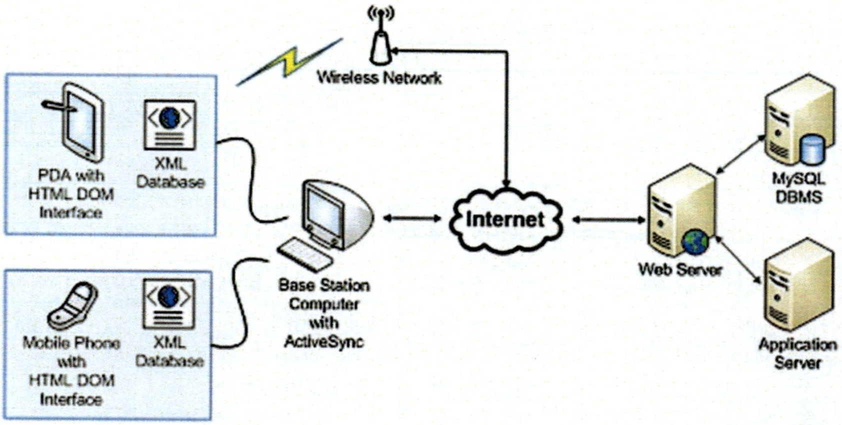

Fig. 2 Mobile AME architecture

XML has emerged as a powerful language that uses a structural approach to describe objects. It empowers content developers to define the tags used to provide the desired description of any object. In Table 3, XML tags used in Mobile AME to describe various attributes and elements of the ammunition are presented.

The main advantage of XML is that it is capable of working on most mobile device platforms. It also provides the flexibility to work in either standalone mode or from the server. The content alterations (add, update, or delete) are triggered when QASAS connect the mobile device to a computer running an application that enables data synchronisation between the mobile device and the computer.

In order to retrieve ammunition information from the XML file, we used JavaScript embedded in the HTML page to interact with the DOM. JavaScript is also used to perform navigation functions of the application.

5.2 *Server-Side Development*

On the server-side of Mobile AME, the server application transforms the ammunition data from MySQL to XML. XML is the data source of Mobile AME. In this state, several approaches that allow the transformation between MySQL and XML were examined. After the evaluation, the best solution for Mobile AME database transformation was to develop a PHP script that generates XML content from the MySQL database.

6 Mobile AME User Interface Design

In this section, Mobile AME's user interface is discussed. Mobile usability guidelines were used as a framework for Mobile HCI issues which include screen design, content presentation, and application navigation.

Table 3 XML structure for Mobile AME

Tag Name	Content Type	Description
<Ammunition>	Ammunition	Root tag that contains the collection of ammunition tags for different ammunition.
<Munition>	Munition	Contains collection of tags to describe single ammunition (DODIC).
<Category>	Category	Specifies the category details of the ammunition. It includes name, size, and image for every ammunition category.
<Sub-Category>	Sub-Category	Specifies the sub-category details of the ammunition. It includes name, size, and image for every ammunition sub-category.
<DODIC>	DODIC	Department of Defense Identification Code (DODIC). It is the unique indicator for every ammunition item.
<Name>	Name	Contains the name for the ammunition.
<Common Name>	Common Name	Contains alternate names used for the ammunition.
<Nomenclature>	Nomenclature	Contains the name of the ammunition as stated in the Ammunition Manual based on its DODIC.
<Use>	Use	Contains the brief description about the application or the use of particular ammunition.
<Description>	Description	Contains the brief description of the ammunition.
<Thumbnail>	Thumbnail Path	Contains the URL for thumbnail image of the ammunition.
<Videos>	Videos	Contains the collection of video URL for each ammunition item.
<Immersive>	Immersive Videos	Contains URL for immersive views.
<Specification>	Specification	Contains the URL for the specification details document in PDF format.
<Inspection>	Munition Inspection	Contains the URL for the ammunition inspection details document in PDF format.
<Packaging>	Packaging_Shipping	Contains the URL for the packaging and shipping details document in PDF format.
<Hotspots>	Hotspots	Contains collection of hotspot tags. Every hotspot tag includes Hotspot Name, URL Link (Links to the zoomed image of that hotspot), co-ordinates, related images, related videos related to a particular hotspot.

6.1 Screen Design

One of the critical issues of mobile devices is the limited amount of screen space on which to display information. This poses a challenge for handheld application developers to design the screen layout (Forman and Zahorjan 1994; Eisenstein, Vanderdonckt, and Puerta 2001; Brewster 2002). The screen in Mobile AME was originally based on the largest display on handheld devices available at the time the system was designed. The application display size was set to 240 pixels wide by 320 pixels high (Brown 2008).

Organising data via HTML tables is a technique for designing screen layout. However, the use of tables in mobile applications is not the same as in the desktop environment. Since all browsers do not support nested tables, the use of tables in a mobile environment is limited to a simple layout (MobileDesign 2008). In addition, all the tables are specified as percentages rather than fixed widths to dynamically present the content according to a variety of screen sizes across different devices.

6.2 *Presentation of the Content*

Mobile AME maintains consistency of the content presentation across different pages in the application by using cascading style sheets (CSS). The key characteristic of the style sheet is that it is a separate file from the HTML page. Every display element of Mobile AME is controlled by its style as defined in a style sheet file. Hence, pages in Mobile AME that refer to the same file have a consistent design.

7 Application Navigation

In Mobile AME, application navigation is another concern that extends functionality from the desktop version environment. Although connectivity, cursor navigation, and text input may be the same in both environments, the small screen in Mobile AME allows less information to be displayed. This is unlike the Web version of AME, which was developed under the desktop environment and allows several screens at different levels to display information. In addition, when the information is presented on a handheld device, any additional information must be altered or summarised to avoid overlong page scrolling.

As presented in Fig. 3, the basic navigation for Mobile AME is fairly standard. Upon launch, an ammunition type screen identifies major type of the ammunition in Mobile AME. Then users browse through the ammunition subcategories to get access to the desired ammunition.

Usually, mobile applications have two ways to use the Back function for navigation: a breadcrumb or history list, or as a path home as depicted in Fig. 4 (MobileDesign 2008).

The first approach, using a history list, allows users to jump across different functions of the application. Many users are familiar with this approach having encountered it through standard desktop Internet browsers. However, with the mobile application's small screen size, users may get lost. Mobile AME employs the second approach, a path home, in which the "Back" function takes the user back or "Up" one level. The advantage of this approach is that users are less likely to get lost and can return to known territory. This provides Mobile AME with ease of use. In addition, Mobile AME has a "Home" key on every page so users do not have to press "Back" several times to get to the main menu.

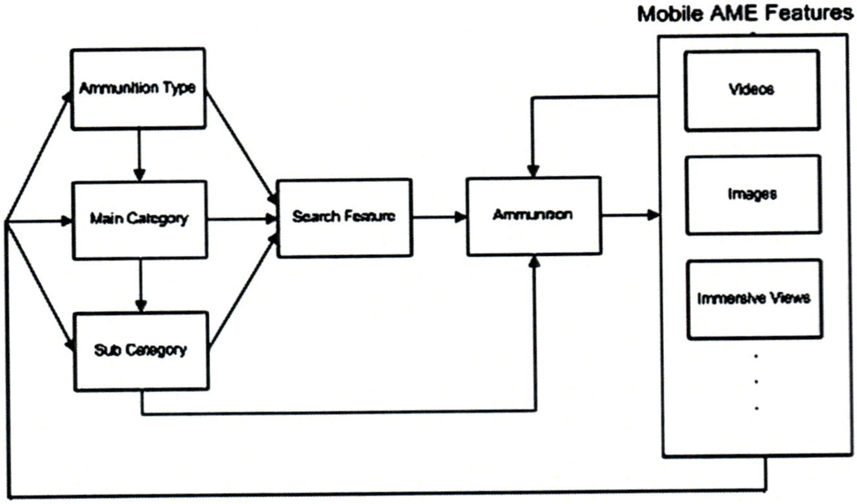

Fig. 3 Navigation architecture of Mobile AME

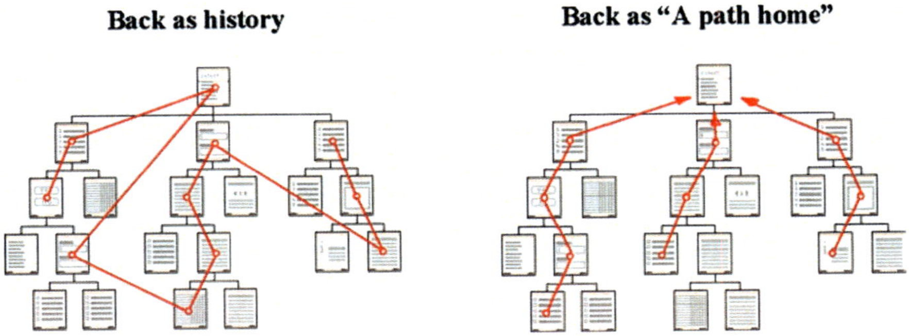

Fig. 4 Two major back functions for mobile applications (*Source*: MobileDesign 2008)

8 Mobile AME Functionality

Mobile AME provides QASAS with ammunition content in various presentations. The application consists of six major features: ammunition information, ammunition specification, inspection points, packaging and shipping information, three-dimensional immersive views, and visual inspection video clips.

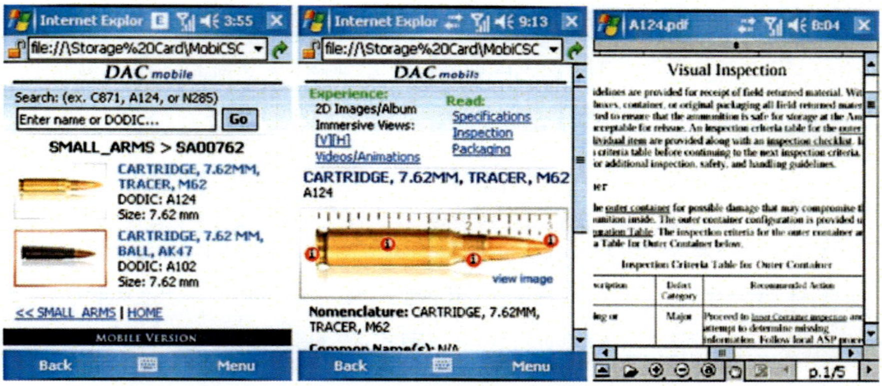

Fig. 5 Ammunition, specification, inspection, and packaging information

8.1 *Ammunition, Inspection Points, Specification, Packaging and Shipping Information*

When a desired ammunition item is selected, Mobile AME provides QASAS with general information and all the details of the specific item to include ammunition name, category, unique identification number, nomenclature, common name, use and description. The picture of each item includes inspection points or "hotspots", which show further details of a specific area when clicked. This feature enables QASAS to evaluate and visually inspect specific areas on the item as required by DOD ammunition inspection guidelines (Fig. 5).

Ammunition specification, inspection, and packaging information are stored in portable document formation (PDF) format. Storing the ammunition information as a PDF provides several advantages to Mobile AME. The PDF format is a platform-independent application used for representing two-dimensional documents in a manner independent of the application software, hardware, and operating system. PDF documents also allow QASAS to perform document encryption, document sharing, and document searches for desired information using keywords (Fig. 5).

8.2 *Three-Dimensional Immersive Views*

The immersive view is an advanced feature of Mobile AME that gives QASAS the virtual reality experience when they need to inspect any ammunition item residing in the database. This is particularly useful for items recently introduced to the community. The item is presented in three-dimensional interactive image-based animation that allows the user to manipulate the picture by rotating it vertically and horizontally (Fig. 6).

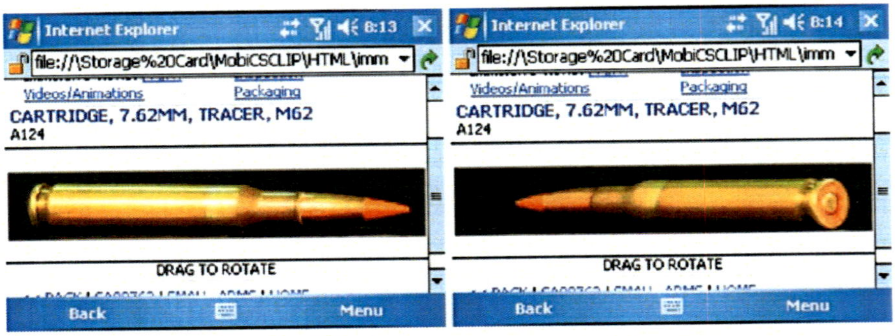

Fig. 6 Immersive view of an ammunition item in the horizontal orientation

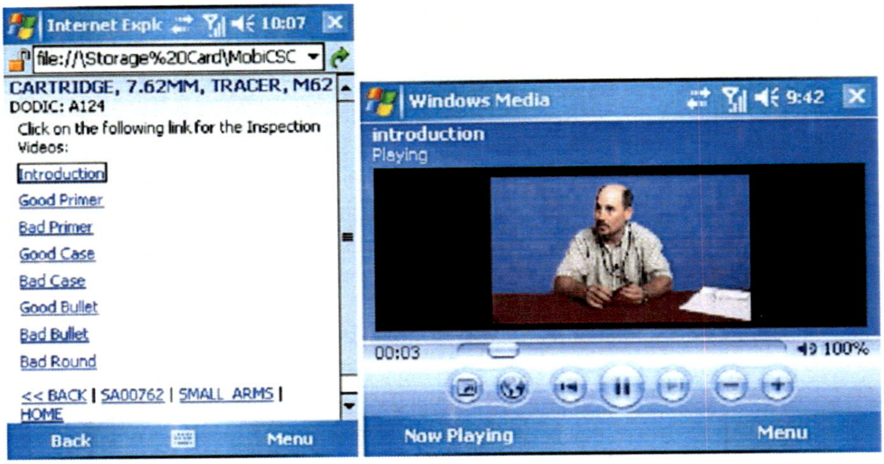

Fig. 7 Ammunition inspecting video clip

8.3 Inspection Point Video Clips

Another key feature of Mobile AME is the inspection point video clips. Video has become an important element of multimedia computing and communication environments in business, education, and military settings. For our system, video clips deliver instruction on visual inspections of ammunition to QASAS in the field. The video clips are organised into categories thereby allowing the user to watch only the video clip that applies to the situation at hand. The video clips were recorded in several formats (e.g., Windows Media Player, QuickTime or FLV) to allow viewing in different device platforms (Fig. 7).

9 Exploratory Evaluation of Mobile AME

Mobile AME was evaluated against attributes required by DAC to ascertain the overall feasibility, effectiveness, and efficiency of Mobile AME functionality.

Mobile AME was demonstrated to the subject matter experts (SMEs) at DAC and to senior leaders of the U.S. Army. The general reaction was that Mobile AME could provide ammunition information in an efficient and effective manner. There is enthusiastic support to implement this technology. Based on the feedback from the SMEs, we have refined the video presentations and presented content in both silent and sound-enabled modes. The common concern voiced by SMEs and leadership was the expense required to implement Mobile AME in a field. A field trial is necessary prior to full implementation.

The second stage of product evaluation, subject to proposal approval and funding, would be to provide some handheld devices to QASAS working in offices located in the U.S. These QASAS would evaluate Mobile AME functionality in ammunition storage areas. The system could be compared to the current means of obtaining ammunition information from an office computer located apart from the ammunition storage bays. After QASAS have used the devices for a predetermined period of time, we would request feedback through questionnaires and interviews. If Mobile AME is determined to be effective in these situations, approval will be requested to implement a field study at an overseas location.

10 Discussion

Wireless technology constantly evolves and improves. New capabilities such as higher processor performance, larger and better displays, and more storage capacity can significantly improve the capabilities and performance of Mobile AME.

The cost of the device was a common concern from the evaluation of Mobile AME. At the time of Mobile AME development, the cost of the device, HTC Tilt, was approximately $500. In addition, the major features of Mobile AME, the immersive views and the inspection point video clips, require higher performance device hardware and may consequently increase the cost for any device selected. One solution to reduce the implementation cost is to hold the hardware specification requirements constant while continuing to refine and improve the Mobile AME product. During the time it will take to refine Mobile AME, the cost of the devices will most likely fall.

Security and privacy are also of primary concern when dealing with ammunition information. Thus far, we have utilised user-level authentication to obtain access to Mobile AME application. However, we note this level of security will not be sufficient when dealing with actual deployment in a field setting. Therefore, further study would need to incorporate more comprehensive security features, to include the security of the XML database stored in the device's internal memory and the client-server data streams via encryption. We can evaluate physical security by protecting the handheld device itself. Most PDAs currently available have a built-in screen-locking feature that enables users to enter a password before using the device. More advanced security features available in newer PDAs include two-factor authentication employing biometric, token or proximity techniques. These features need to be evaluated for implementation on Mobile AME.

Mobile AME is a data retrieval system that provides its users with access to ammunition information in different multimedia formats. Future research will focus on a collaboration feature exploiting the wireless capabilities of the handheld devices to enable synchronous and asynchronous communication between users. Consequently, this new feature in Mobile AME will allow QASAS to share knowledge and information for more effective collaboration, education, and decision-making.

11 Conclusion

Wireless handheld applications used in military settings have the potential to alleviate the problem of inadequate ammunition information for QASAS in field settings. Mobile AME, as an extension to the Web-based ammunition multimedia encyclopaedia, enables its users to directly access the ammunition data repository via a portable device.

Our goal of Mobile AME development is to provide ammunition information to QASAS whenever and wherever they need it. Insufficient access to ammunition information and a lack of collaboration amongst QASAS are major causes of ammunition inspection errors. Handheld technology and portable DSS can mitigate such problems by providing QASAS with access to needed ammunition information in time-sensitive situations.

The handheld technology is used in the study to provide a new way for facilitating main operations for QASAS. According to the comments by subject-matter experts (SMEs) and senior military leaders, we have developed a wireless handheld solution that can reduce inspection errors. Our next steps are to incorporate security features to make Mobile AME field-worthy and to develop the collaboration system by which QASAS can share knowledge.

Due to the unique limitations of the wireless handheld environment, new challenges are presented to system developers for producing effective and efficient applications. We have taken these limitations into consideration when designing Mobile AME's architecture, its user interface, and its functionality. For Mobile AME, we have developed a usable and platform-independent mobile decision-support application that effectively and efficiently provides ammunition information to support decision making and operations of ammunition personnel. In addition, as technology in the mobile area improves and adapts to user requirements, it consequently provides us with opportunities to continue to identify, refine, and evaluate new capabilities for Mobile AME.

References

Abowd, G. and E. Mynatt, "Charting Past, Present, and Future Research in Ubiquitous Computing," *ACM Transactions on Computer-Human Interaction*, 7, 2000, 29–58.

Abowd, G., A. Dey, P. Brown, N. Davies, M. Smith and P. Steggles, "Toward a Better Understanding of Context and Context-Awareness," in *Proceedings of the First International Symposium on Handheld and Ubiquitous Computing*, Karlsruhe, 1999, 24–29.

Apple, Inc., iPhone Technology, 2008, http://www.apple.com/iphone/iphone-3gs/high-technology.html, accessed on November 25, 2008.

Brewster, S., "Overcoming the Lack of Screen Space on Mobile Computers," *Personal and Ubiquitous Computing*, 6, 3, 2002, 188–205.

Brown, J., "Display for Handheld Devices Issue," October 22, 2008. URL = http://www.informationdisplay.org/article.cfm?year=2008&issue=10&file=art6

Burstein, F., A. Zaslavsky and N. Zrora, "Context-Aware Mobile Agents for Decision-Making Support in Healthcare Emergency Applications," in *Proceedings of the Workshop on Context Modeling and Decision Support, CONTEXT'05* Paris, 2005.

Burstein, F., J. Cowie, A. Zaslavsky and J. San Pedro, "Support for Real-Time Decision Making in Mobile Financial Applications," in Burstein, F. and Clyde W. (eds.) *Handbook on Decision Support Systems*. Berlin: Springer, 2008.

Buyukkokten, O., H. Garcia-Molina, A. Paepcke and T. Winograd, "Power Browser: Efficient Web Browsing for PDAs," in *Proceedings of the Conference on Human Factor in Computing System (CHI'00)*, The Hague, 2000, 430–437.

Cabrera, J., H. Frutos, A. Stoica, Y. Dimitriadis, G. Fiotakis and K. D. Liveri, "Mystery in the Museum: Collaborative Learning Activities Using Handheld Devices," in *Proceedings of the 7th International Conference on Human Computer Interaction with Mobile Devices & Services, MobileHCI '05*, Salzburg, 2005, 19–22.

Chen, G. and D. Kotz, "A Survey of Context-Aware Mobile Computing Research," Tech. Report TR2000–381, Department of Computer Science, Dartmouth College, Hanover, 2000.

Chen, E., E. Mendonca, L. McKnight, P. Stetson, J. Lei and J. Cimino, "PalmCIS: A Wireless Handheld Application for Satisfying Clinician Information Needs," *Journal of the American Medical Information Association*, 11, 1, 2004, 19–28.

Davis, F. D., R. P. Bagozzi and P. R. Warshaw, "User Acceptance of Computer Technology: A Comparison of Two Theoretical Models," *Management Science*, 35, 8, 1989, 982–1002.

Dey, A., "Understanding and Using Context," *Personal and Ubiquitous Computing*, 5, 1, 2001, 4–7.

Dey, A.K., G.D. Abowd and D. Salber, "A Conceptual Framework and a Toolkit for Supporting the Rapid Prototyping of Context-Aware Applications," *Human-Computer Interaction*, 16, 2, 2001, 97–166.

Dunlop, M. and S. Brewster, "The Challenge of Mobile Devices for Human Computer Interaction," *Personal and Ubiquitous Computing*, 6, 2002, 235–236.

Eisenstein, J., J. Vanderdonckt and A. Puerta, "Applying Model-Based Techniques to the Development of UIs for Mobile Computers," in *Proceeding of the 6th International Conference on Intelligent User Interfaces*, Santa Fe, 2001, 69–76.

Fang, X., S. Chan, J. Brzezinski and S. Xu, "Moderating Effects of Task Type on Wireless Technology Acceptance," *Journal of Management Information Systems*, 22, 3, 2005, 123–157.

Forman, G. H. and J. Zahorjan, "The Challenges of Mobile Computing," *IEEE Computer*, 27, 4, 1994, 38–47.

Germonprez, M., N. Germonprez and M. Avital, "Using Interface Design Standards to Support Pervasive Computing," *Sprouts: Working Papers on Information Systems*, 5, 14, 2005.

Hofmann-Wellenhof, B., H. Lichtenegger and J. Collins, *Global Positioning System: Theory and Practice*, 4th edn. Wien: Springer, 1997.

Holzinger, A. and M. Errath, "Designing Web-Applications for Mobile Computers: Experiences with Applications to Medicine," in Stephanidis, C. and Stary, C. (eds.) *User-Centered Interaction Paradigms for Universal Access in the Information Society*. Lecture Notes of Computer Science, 3196. Berlin: Springer, 2004, 262–267.

Housel, B. C. and D. B. Lindquist, "WebExpress: A Client/Intercept Based System for Optimizing Web Browsing in a Wireless Environment," in *Proceedings of the Second Annual International Conference on Mobile Computing and Networking*, Rye, 1996, 419–431.

Jackson, P., J. Favier and I. Stagia, "Segmenting Europe's' Mobile Consumers," *Forrest Research Technographics Report*, 2002.

Jones, M, G. Marsden, N. Mohd-Nasir, K. Boone and G. Buchanan, "Improving Web Interaction on Small Displays," in *Proceeding of the Eighth International Conference on World Wide Web*, Toronto, 1999, 1129–1137.

Kearney, K., J. Self, L. Bailey, E. Harris, S. Halcomb, B. Hill and U. Shimp, "Building an Academic and Government Partnership in Workforce Education: Challenges and Possibilities," *Journal of Industrial Teacher Education*, 44, 3, 2007, 71–91.

Keeker, K., "Improving Web Site Usability and Appeal," 1997, URL = http://msdn.microsoft.com/en-us/library/cc889361%28office.11%29.aspx

Kjeldskov, J. and C. Graham, "A Review of Mobile HCI Research Methods," in *Proceedings of Mobile Human-Computer Interaction 2003*, 2003, 317–335.

Kjeldskov, J., M. B. Skov, B. S. Als, and R. T. Hoegh, "Is It Worth The Hassle? Exploring the Added Value of Evaluating the Usability of Context-Aware Mobile Systems in the Field," in *Proceedings of Mobile Human-Computer Interaction 2004*, 2004, 61–73.

Kristoffersen, S. and F. Ljungberg, "Making Place to Make IT Work: Empirical Explorations of HCI for Mobile CSCW," in *Proceedings of the International ACM SIGGROUP Conference on Supporting Group Work*, Phoenix, 1999, 276–285.

Lee, M-W., "Developing Mobile Applications Using the Microsoft Mobile Internet Toolkit," 2007, http://www.devx.com/wireless/Article/10148/1954, accessed on November 21, 2008.

Lu, J., C-S. Yu, C. Liu and J. E. Yao, "Technology Acceptance Model for Wireless Internet," *Internet Research*, 13, 3, 2003, 206–222.

Lum, W. Y. and F. C. M. Lau, "A Context-Aware Decision Engine for Content Adaptation," *IEEE Pervasive Computing*, 1, 3, 2002, 41–49.

Mennecke, B. E. and T. J. Strader, *Mobile Commerce: Technology, Theory, and Applications*. Hershey: Idea Group, 2002.

MobileDesign, "Mobile UI Design Resources, Patterns, Devices, and so Forth," December 2, 2008, URL = http://patterns.littlespringsdesign.com/index.php/Main_Page

Mullen, S., "Ammunition Readiness: Current problems and future implications for army transformation," *An Institution of Land Warfare Publication*, 2002, URL = http://www.ausa.org/SiteCollectionDocuments/ILW%20Web-ExclusivePubs/Landpower%20Essays/LPE02-1.pdf'.

Nielsen, J., *Designing Web Usability: The Practice of Simplicity*. Indianapolis: New Riders, 2000.

Nivala, A.-M. and L. T. Sarjakoski, "Need for Context-Aware Topographic Maps in Mobile Devices," in *Proceedings of ScanGIS 2003*, Espoo, 2003, 15–29.

Pestana, G., M. Silva, A. Casaca and J. Nunes, "Systems and Applications: An Airport Decision Support System for Mobiles Surveillance & Alerting," in *Proceedings of the 4th ACM International Workshop on Data Engineering for Wireless and Mobile Access*, Baltimore, 2005, 33–40.

Ramsay, M. and J. Nielsen, "WAP Usability Report – Deja vu: 1994 All Over Again," *Technical Report, Nielsen Norman Group*, 2000, URL = http://www.NNgroup.com/reports/wap, accessed on December 15, 2008.

Schilit, B., N. Adams and R. Want, "Context-Aware Computing Applications," in *Proceedings of IEEE Workshop on Mobile Computing Systems and Applications*, Santa Cruz, 1994, 85–90.

Siau, K., H. Sheng and F. Nah, "Development of a Framework for Trust in Mobile Commerce," *The Second Pre-ICIS Annual Workshop on Human-Computer Interaction Research in MIS*, Seattle, 2003.

Steiniger, S., M. Neun and A. Edwardes, "Foundations of Location Based Services," *Lecture Notes on LBS*, Department of Geography, University of Zurich, 2006.

Tamminen, S., A. Oulasvirta, K. Toiskallio and A. Kankainen, "Understanding Mobile Contexts," *Personal and Ubiquitous Computing*, 8, 2, 2004, 135–143.

van der Heijden, H., "Mobile Decision Support for In-Store Purchase Decisions," *Decision Support Systems*, 42, 2, 2006, 656–663.

Venkatesh, V. and V. Ramesh, "Web and Wireless Site Usability: Understanding Differences and Modeling Use," *MIS Quarterly*, 30, 1, 2006, 181–206.

Chapter 17
Development of a Mobile Situation Awareness Tool Supporting Disaster Recovery of Business Operations

Pedro Antunes[1], Claudio Sapateiro[2], Gustavo Zurita[3], and Nelson Baloian[4]

[1] Faculty of Sciences, University of Lisbon, Portugal
[2] Systems and Informatics Department, School of Technology, Polytechnic Institute of Setúbal, Portugal
[3] Management Control and Information Systems Department, Business School, Universidad de Chile, Chile
[4] Department of Computer Science, University of Chile, Santiago de Chile, Chile

Abstract Situation awareness (SA) is deemed essential when tackling situations that are characterised by complexity, hard-to-define causal relationships, dynamic changes, and lack of information. This chapter describes the development of a model and tool to support collaborative construction of SA. The proposed model organises awareness information elements according to situation dimensions, dimensional elements, and correlations between dimensional elements. The approach provides a strategic view of the situation and a structure supporting concurrent information updates. The developed tool supports collaborative information management using mobile devices and pen-based interaction. The chapter also reports a case study that has employed the model and tool to support the disaster recovery (DR) of business operations.The adopted research approach is exploratory and theory-driven. The evaluation task adopted the inspection method, employing experts in critical infrastructure maintenance. The obtained results indicate the model and tool are adequate to the types of disruptive events faced by critical infrastructure maintenance teams. The obtained results also indicate the proposed model and tool are regarded as mostly important to less experienced members; and also fundamental to the development of emergency plans.

Keywords Collaborative situation awareness • Disaster recovery • Mobility support • Decision support systems

P. Antunes (✉)
Faculty of Sciences, University of Lisbon, Portugal
e-mail: paa@di.fc.ul.pt

F. Burstein et al. (eds.), *Supporting Real Time Decision-Making*,
Annals of Information Systems 13, DOI 10.1007/978-1-4419-7406-8_17,

1 Introduction

The Cynefin framework has been developed with the purpose of understanding the impact of complexity on organisational decision making (Snowden and Boone 2007). This framework distinguishes four main decision-making contexts: simple, complicated, complex, and chaotic. Stable and straightforward relationships between causes and effects characterise the simple context. In these circumstances, the most adequate decision-making strategy is selecting an available plan. The complicated context is associated with multiple right answers for a known, albeit difficult, problem. Experts are necessary to analyse the concrete situation, find out the relationships between causes and effects, and develop a response plan.

The complex context deals with unpredictable and emergent situations where relationships between causes and effects are neither predefined nor easily analysed. Thus the best decision-making strategy consists in probing the system, obtaining feedback, and then deciding the most adequate course of action. The chaotic context is mainly characterised by turbulence, where the relationships between causes and effects may be unstable. The best decision-making strategy in this context recommends acting first and analysing the consequences later.

The simple and complicated contexts are associated with an ordered world and rational decision making. On the contrary, the complex and chaotic contexts concern lack of order in the world. Of course, we may find out that many organisations are operating mainly on one (simple) side of the world. The governmental bureaucracy would be exemplary of the simple, stable, and highly standardised context. But most organisations actually must deal with both worlds in order to maximise their chances of survivability.

One major challenge associated with shifting operations towards the unordered world concerns a cognitive function called situation awareness (SA). It may be loosely defined as knowing what is going on in the operating environment (Endsley 1995), dealing with a large amount of sensory cues to ultimately perceive what is important to the task at hand and how it may be effectively performed. SA is always associated with rich and dynamic environments such as piloting, air traffic control, and surgical operations. SA may be structured in three cognitive steps (Endsley 1995; Endsley 2003): (1) monitoring the contextual elements available in the environment, (2) diagnosing their meaning, and (3) projecting their near-future consequences.

SA may elucidate the cause-effect relationships established by the unordered world posited by the Cynefin framework. SA is crucial to explore a complex context since it serves to launch probes and perceive their effects in the environment while building a conceptual map of the situation. SA also supports the operations in a chaotic context, allowing proactively building patterns of reasonable action based on reflection over anticipated actions.

We emphasise that SA is both an individual and a collaborative function since very often multiple operators are necessary to disentangle asymmetric information. Therefore, besides the three cognitive steps mentioned above, we should also consider the interactions necessary to adjust individual and collective knowledge, share situation information, and anticipate the information needs of others (Shu and Futura 2005).

We seek to investigate how information technology may support collaborative SA. And we have a particular interest in one specific type of information technology – mobile devices such as personal digital assistants, mobile phones, and tablet computers. Mobile technology has seen a rapid development in the last few years. Following Moore's Law (Moore 1965), computing power is increasing rapidly, prices are decreasing, physical dimensions are becoming more adequate to mobile use, and its popularity is increasing. The development of networking and middleware technology supporting wireless communication, information synchronisation, and location awareness is also promoting the wide adoption of mobile technology in collaborative settings (Baloian, Zurita, Antunes, and Baytelman 2007).

People now have the prospect to work and collaborate everywhere, wandering in office buildings, visiting clients, commuting from home to office, staying at home and, of course, vacationing. Furthermore, by shifting the operations towards the unordered world, we are also finding very compelling application scenarios in which mobile technology may be critical to develop SA:

- In hospital environments, supporting a constant flow of information about patients' status amid health care personnel (Muñoz, Rodriguez, Favela, Martinez-Garcia, and González 2003; Tentori and Favela 2008)
- Beyond that, mediating health care information while being outside the hospital premises, considering both health care personnel and patients (Sá, Carriço, and Antunes 2007)
- Facilitating fieldwork and remote access to experts operating in remote areas (Antunes and André 2006; MacEachren 2005; Ochoa, Pino, Bravo, Dujovne, and Neyem 2008), and
- Supporting rescue efforts and emergency management in disaster areas (Cai, MacEachren, Brewer, McNeese, Sharma, and Fuhrmann 2005; Kwan and Lee 2005; Monares, Ochoa, Pino, Herskovic, and Neyam 2009).

This chapter reports exploratory research aiming to develop a SA tool on top of mobile technology. The specific application area is disaster recovery (DR) of business operations. In this context, the main goal of DR is preventing, mitigating, and containing the occurrence of major disruptions in critical business infrastructure, including networking, databases, and distributed services. The interest in DR has significantly increased since the occurrence of major business breakdowns in the United States of America caused by the terrorist attacks on the Twin Towers and hurricane Katrina (Hiles 2008).

The case reported in this chapter describes the initial trials of the SA tool in two organisations. We describe the preliminary study, requirements elicitation, and evaluation feedback obtained from the trials.

In the next section, we overview the related work. Section 3 describes the adopted research methodology. The SA model and tool are described in Sects. 4 and 5, respectively. The case study is presented in Sect. 6. The findings from the case study are presented in Sect. 7. Section 8 discusses the research outcomes and presents some concluding remarks.

2 Related Work

A wide number of situations may lead to lack of order in business operations, some emerging from inside the organisation (e.g., latent problems, failure of key resources, lack of flexibility, and the need to innovate) and many others emerging from the environment (e.g., market dynamics and natural hazards).

DR emerges as an organisational reaction to these situations. A simplified view of DR would consider the separation between disruptive and normal operations and the objective to move the operations from the disruptive towards the normal situation. DR is a complex process. It is affected by surprise, real-time constraints, spatial extension, number of involved stakeholders, risk and uncertainty, limitations of human perception, and cascading events (Wybo and Latiers 2006).

Of course, technology has always been considered a silver bullet capable of helping to resolve most organisational problems (Grint and Woolgar 1997). It is, therefore, natural that significant research effort has been applied to developing technology support for DR. But the complexity associated with DR challenges information systems development (ISD), mostly because the analysis and design activities may not realistically cover all the possible events, contexts, and dynamic interactions that may occur (Perrow 1999; Turoff, Chumer, Van de Walle, and Yao 2004).

This challenge is patent when we consider the ISD of work processes. We define work models with the objectives of automating recurrent activities and improving coordination and efficiency. But the support for unexpected exceptions, incomplete procedures, and dynamic changes is highly problematic (Mourão and Antunes 2007).

Markus, Majchrzak, and Gasser (2002) defend that a new approach to ISD is necessary to address the new class of systems falling outside what we previously referred to as the ordered world. This new class of systems is fundamentally characterised by being flexible, context-dependent, distributed, dynamically evolving, and collaborative. High reliability organisations (HRO), such as aviation and nuclear operations, clearly emphasise these characteristics (Weick and Sutcliffe 2001).

Interestingly, collaboration is regarded as a fundamental asset in HRO (Baker, Day, and Salas 2006). In complex and chaotic situations, the complete reliance on anticipated plans is quite difficult or even impossible (Bruinsma and Hoog 2006). Therefore, involved participants must orchestrate their interventions while adapting to unfolding events. Their decisions may lack full insight about the situation context. Information shortage, as well as information overload, may lead to initial unbalanced responses (e.g., prioritising less urgent actions) and mutual adjustments. Other factors emphasising the role of collaboration in complex and chaotic situations include the spatial extension of the situation, perception and knowledge gaps amongst the involved actors, and poor overall SA and representation (Wybo and Latiers 2006).

SA is key to understanding the impact of collaboration on DR, mostly because SA is an antecedent of sense making, collaboration, and collaborative decision-making (Weick 1995; Weick 2001). Businesses have a strong cognitive and heuristic character (Möller 2009) that must be supported with SA.

Based on a synthesis of 15 definitions found in the literature, Salmon, Stanton, Jenkins, Walker, Young, and Aujla (2007) define *individual SA* as the continuous extraction of environmental information and integration with previous knowledge to form a coherent mental picture and using that picture to direct and anticipate future events.

Since the late 1980s, a number of SA models have been proposed. The Ensdley's three-level model is the one that has received the utmost attention (1995). In level 1, training and experience directs attention to critical elements in the environment. Level 2 integrates elements that aid understanding the meaning of critical elements. And level 3 considers understanding the possible future scenarios.

Bedny and Meister (1999) rooted their model on activity theory and offer a more dynamic perspective over SA, considering a continuous loop in which SA directs interactions with the world, which in turn modifies SA. This continuous loop is motivated by the disparity between one's goals and the current perceived situation. It comprises three stages: orientational (development of an internal conceptual model), executive (moving towards a desired goal via decision making and action execution), and evaluative (assessing the feedback information and influencing the other stages).

Smith and Hancock (1995) proposed an ecological view of SA. The theory is that SA is neither resident in individuals nor in the world but rather in the interactions that are motivated by one's schemata; and that the outcome of that interaction will modify the existing schemata, which in turn directs further exploration.

All of the above models consider individual SA. The notion of *team SA* is more recent and currently lacks a universally accepted model (Salmon et al. 2007). Some literature on team cognition has been exploring the idea that team effectiveness may not only depend on an overlap of individual cognitions but also the construction of team cognition (Hayes 2006). Team SA combines individual SA (necessary to conduct individual tasks) with shared understanding of the situation amongst team members (Endsley and Jones 2001). Shu and Futura (2005) posit that team SA is collaborative and partially shared and partially distributed. Additionally, Salas, Prince, Baker, and Shrestha (1995) and Fiori, Salas, Cuevas, and Bowers (2003) highlight the importance of team processes as contributors to team SA, compensating the limitations of individual SA with information exchange and communication.

Stanton, Stewart, Harris, Houghton, Baber, McMaster, Salmon, Hoyle, Walker, Young, Linsell, Dymott, and Green (2006) suggest that in complex contexts, individuals rarely perform entirely independent activities. They are often coupled and tend to be coordinated. This focus on coordination changes the unit of analysis and affords analysing interactions at many different organisational levels. Thus, collaborative SA combines individual SA, distributed SA, shared SA, and team SA. This multidimensional view posits many challenges to SA research and development.

3 Research Methodology

This work assumes an engineering viewpoint aiming to improve collaborative SA through technology development. But the emphasis on cognition and collaboration mandate a user-centred approach to technology development. Therefore, in order to bring together these two different perspectives, we have adopted a research methodology combining exploratory with theory-based research.

On the one hand, the exploratory perspective seeks to obtain qualitative insights about the construction and maintenance of SA. This requires a strong focus on understanding the users' behaviour within a specific working context, which in our case is maintaining business operations after major breakdowns in technological infrastructure. The case study method (Gerring 2007) was selected to gather contextualised information from people highly experienced with DR of business operations.

On the other hand, our focus on technology development also mandates a positivistic approach to supporting SA in the selected application context and using a particular technological solution. Therefore, the theory-based approach (Briggs 2006) was adopted to ground the technology development on a sound engineering basis.

Consequently, the case study discussed in this chapter is also directed towards validating the SA model and tool we have been developing. As Briggs (2006) points out, a good theory can drive nonintuitive design choices that improve technology outcomes.

Because of this twofold approach, the adopted case study research is expected to provide hybrid outcomes. Being theory-driven, the outcomes are less open to surprise and the contextual information is less varied and insightful than usual. By also being exploratory, a rigorous validation of the proposed SA model is also less important than usual. Overall, the adopted research methodology seeks an early validation of the theoretical and practical constructs put forward regarding the use of mobile technology in support of collaborative SA. The defined research plan has the following major steps:

1. Develop SA theory and model
2. Implement the SA theory and model in a computational tool
3. Study the acceptance of theory and tool by practitioners
4. Go back to 1 until practitioners are satisfied

4 Situation Awareness (SA) Model

Our SA model proposes a representation of the key information elements involved in the DR process. Inspired by the "Swiss cheese" model (Reason 1997; Reason 2008) to organise SA information elements, the model posits that for an accident to occur an alignment of holes in different defence layers must occur.

We may characterise these defence layers according to a continuum of organisational strategies ranging from the sharp end to the blunt end (Hollnagel 2004; Woods and Hollnagel 2006). At the sharp end, we have operators and practitioners, the first-line of defence we usually find in a complex system. Towards the blunt end we may find line managers, administrative controls and regulations, designers and engineers, policy makers, and a myriad of other organisational factors and agents that indirectly contribute to the defence system.

Although the actual events that may lead to accidents tend to be highly intertwined and interdependent, the sharp end-blunt end view offers a simple way to conceptualise complex accident trajectories in a simple and linear way. We defend that this type of strategy may as well be adopted to construct SA. The main reasoning is the actors involved in DR may consider different SA layers in a way very similar to the one adopted by the "Swiss cheese" model. More specifically, our model defines a layered arrangement of the SA elements involved in the DR process, aligned from the sharp end to the blunt end.

Furthermore, we also adopt the perspective that information display is fundamental to support information analysis. We find in the literature many different forms to display qualitative data (e.g., concept clusters, empirical clusters, checklist matrixes, timelines, event listings, causal networks, and cognitive maps (Miles and Huberman 1994)).

One way to display awareness information is using situation matrixes (SM), allowing establishing correlations between several elements aligned according to dimensions of the situation. One typical SM is the goals/actions matrix, which correlates the defined goals with the actions perceived as necessary to accomplish those goals. Other examples of SM may include time/events, events/conditions, problems/solutions, actions/actors, and actors/resources. Observe three SM examples in Fig. 1.

We hypothesise that the combination of sharp end-blunt end layers with an SM offers the structure necessary to build and visualise SA. On the one hand, the layered matrixes provide a strategic view of the situation based on the dimensions perceived as necessary to understand the situation and act upon it. On the other hand, the correlations within each matrix provide a tactical view of the situation in its multiple dimensions. The proposed SA model is illustrated in Fig. 2.

Of course this SA model should be understood in a dynamic way. For a given application domain, an initial set of dimensions and SM may be available to support initial sense making, decision-making, planning, and action. But, as the situation evolves, new dimensions and SM may emerge in real time, while others may lose importance and disappear. We finally note the proposed SA model should be collaboratively managed. More details about this functionality will be presented in the next section.

5 Situation Awareness (SA) Tool

According to the proposed SA model, SA is structured with a collection of SM aligning with the various dimensions of the situation, including events, conditions, goals, resources, and actions. Let us start by describing the SA model in more detail.

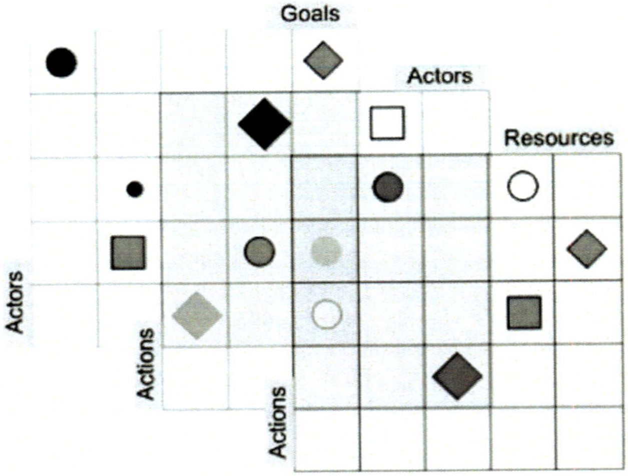

Fig. 1 Examples of situation matrixes. The correlations are represented with symbols

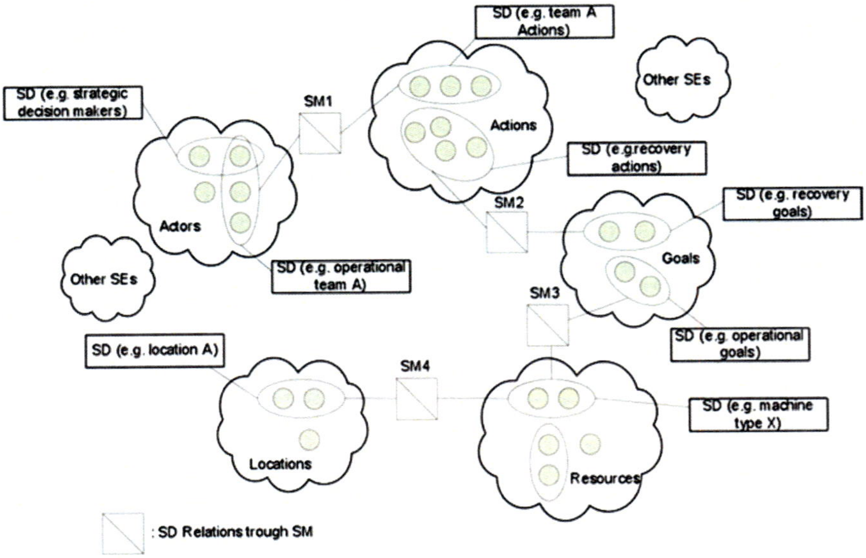

Fig. 2 Situation awareness model

The SM have two dimensions. Each dimension includes several entities that may be relevant to assess the situation. For instance, the goals dimension may include entities like mitigation, preparedness, response, and recovery. We note that, in this case, there is a sequence relationship between the entities that reproduces typical emergency handling stages (Harrald and Stoddard 1998). Another dimension may consider the actors involved in the DR process, a case where there may be no definite type of relationship between the entities. Therefore, the proposed tool should not define a priori the type of relationships between the elements defined for a dimension.

Regarding the SM correlations, their purpose is to express the strength of the relationships that contribute to assess the problem and delineate the solution. For instance, considering a SM with goals and actions, the correlations may express how much some actions contribute to some goals. The correlations should follow an ordinal scale (e.g., none, some, low, and high). But again the semantics depends on the specific application domain. What is fundamental is that the correlations should be expressed through different visual symbols (and attributes like colour) and convey an overall perspective of the several relationships established in an SM.

Of course, several SM are necessary to perceive the whole situation context. These SM are organised in a tree, a structure that is adequate to model the various dimensions of the situation (including time). Again, the relationships amongst the several SM are application dependent. In some cases, they may follow the sharp end-blunt end relationship previously discussed. In other cases they may closely follow chains of events, different levels of perception, projections of future events, or even a combination of all the above. Therefore, the implementation must be independent from any specific application domain but at the same time be flexible enough to accommodate the various configurations previously mentioned.

The developed tool supports the manipulation of SM using pen-based gestures. Interaction with the SM occurs in real time and using a small number of pen-based gestures. The gesture shown in Fig. 3a creates a new SM. The list of available dimensions is displayed when pointing towards the right side of the display, as shown in Fig. 3b. As illustrated in Fig. 3c, the selected dimensions may be dragged to the SM using the pen. Note again that currently the SM are bi-dimensional. Figure 4 shows a SM with two dimensions, actors, and actions.

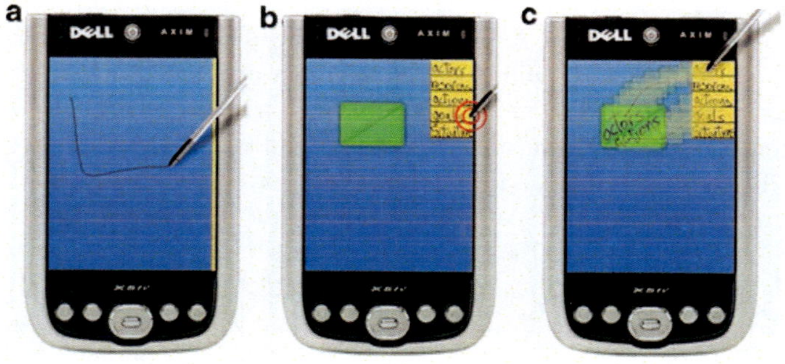

Fig. 3 Creating situation matrixes – (**a**) creation; (**b**) displaying dimensions; and (**c**) assigning dimensions

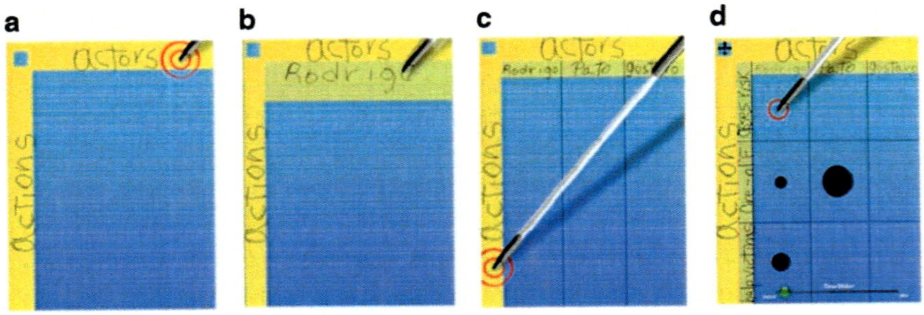

Fig. 4 Populating situation matrixes – (**a**) creating dimensional entities; (**b**) and (**c**) naming dimensional entities; and (**d**) defining correlations in the SM

After assigning dimensions to a SM, the users may start populating it with dimensional entities. One example is defining several actions and actors. This is accomplished by inserting lines and columns in the SM. To create lines and columns the user has to double click on the label (see Figs. 4a and 4c). After this, the user should name the dimensional element. Figure 4b shows how the " actors" dimension is populated with the "Rodriguez" element.

Figure 4d illustrates how correlations are established. The tool allows selecting correlations from a list of predefined values. We have currently implemented four correlation values: (a) empty cell, no importance given; (b) small dot, small importance; (c) medium dot, relative importance; and (d) big circle, high importance. Clicking on a cell will cause a pop-up menu to be displayed with the available options.

Since users may be interested in viewing different parts of the SM according to their context of action, the system allows hiding rows or columns by clicking on the respective label. Hidden rows and columns are displayed with thick lines. To show again a hidden column or row, the user just has to double click on the thick line.

Still regarding SM visualisation, the tool supports left-right and up-down scrolling, combined with zoom-in and zoom-out. These interactions are illustrated in Fig. 5. Note that, since display space in mobile devices is rather scarce, the above navigational capabilities rely on gestures instead of typical visual elements such as scrollbars.

We also note the mobile devices we have been using are capable of displaying one single SM, and with limitations since only a small number of dimensional elements may effectively be displayed without scrolling. The implemented interaction mechanism for navigating multiple SM is the hierarchical menu.

The SA tool adopts a fully replicated information architecture and supports concurrent updates of the SA model. Every mobile device maintains a replica of the SM tree and synchronises the updates whenever the network connection may be established. The users can thus modify or update the SM tree at every time, independently of the other users and the network connectivity. The adopted concurrency management approach has been coined "open floor" by the computer-supported collaborative work (CSCW) community (Lauwers and Lantz 1990; Reinhard, Schweitzer, Völksen, and Weber 1994). This approach does not define any rules governing the

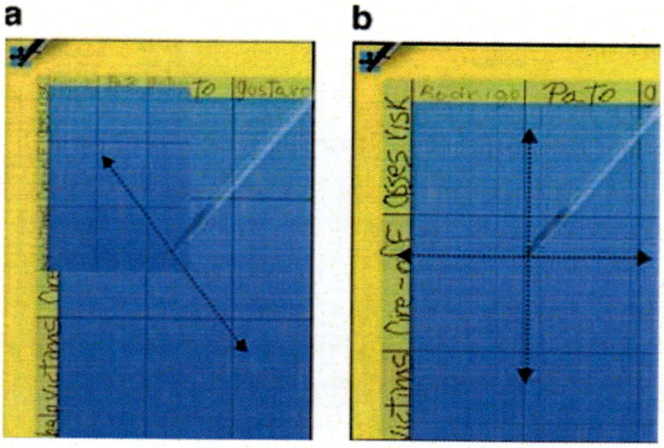

Fig. 5 SM navigation – (**a**) zoom-in and zoom-out; and (**b**) left-right and up-down scrolling

concurrent updates to shared information, delegating instead to the users any necessary social arrangements, which should be constructed during training.

The functionality described above was implemented on top of an existing mobile collaborative platform (Baloian et al. 2007). This platform has already been used to develop several mobile applications (e.g., Zurita, Antunes, Baloian, and Baytelman 2007; Zurita and Baloian 2005). The platform relies on ad-hoc networking to maintain collaboration under situations where structured networking infrastructure may fail, a characteristic that is particularly adequate to the DR context discussed in this chapter. More technical details about the mobile collaborative platform may be found in Baloian and Zurita (2009) and Zurita, Baloian, and Baytelman (2008).

6 Case Study

6.1 Definition

The case study concerns the support to DR in two information technology departments operating in two different organisations. These two departments are considered homogeneous for the purposes of the study.

The main responsibilities assigned to the selected departments include: installing and maintaining the networking and computing infrastructure, including network appliances, computers, printers, servers, backup units, etc; controlling the security threats to this infrastructure; and ensuring business continuity.

A large amount of the work accomplished by these departments concerns highly standardised activities such as reconfiguring routers, updating virus-scanning utilities, monitoring service levels, and responding to requests from single users and other departments. Our focus is not on these standardised activities but instead on the nonroutine activities necessary to maintain business continuity under abnormal conditions. These nonroutine activities are not solicited very often, but are highly pressed by time constraints and cognitive workload. This includes handling server failures, critical service failures (mail, Web proxy, domain naming), and large-scale networking failures, not to forget recovering from accidents such as fires, floods, and earthquakes.

Despite the existence of highly trained personnel, standardised business continuity plans and detailed procedures to address some disruptive situations, three main issues may strongly condition their effectiveness. Firstly, we should consider that standard procedures typically do not accommodate the whole variety of contextual and contingent factors affecting DR operations. Therefore, established plans and procedures serve more as information resources than actual operational processes (Suchman 1987). They may be an important asset but are not as critical as other assets, in particular highly knowledgeable human resources. Secondly, many DR operations require tacit knowledge, experience, decision making, and collaboration when assessing the situation and developing creative solutions and temporary workarounds. And thirdly, we should also consider the operation of large information technology infrastructure is typically distributed in two dimensions: spatially, regarding the various offices, buildings, cable networks, and technical spaces; and cognitively, since knowledge and skills tend to be widely distributed. This distributed nature emphasises the potential demand for collaborative SA.

What mobile technology may bring to these scenarios is empowering team members with collaborative SA. The envisioned functionality includes group communication and information sharing, synchronisation, and visualisation. More specifically, considering the defined SA model, the proposed functionality includes sharing the SM, allowing team members to collaboratively create, view and update SM, and their correlations in real time and on the move.

Based on the above premises, the main objective of the case study is exploring how the selected information technology departments may utilise mobile technology to recover from abnormal infrastructural conditions. The main factor of interest is SA.

6.2 Preliminary Study

To gain insights about DR of business operations, to verify our assertions, and to consolidate our goals, we conducted a preliminary study with the participating teams. The concrete objectives defined for the preliminary study were to (1) identify the types of incidents that emerge in these organisations and (2) identify the practices developed by the teams to overcome them. The participating teams were composed of one coordinator, two senior technicians, and two junior technicians; and one coordinator, one senior technician, and one junior technician.

Semistructured group interviews were utilised. The following open questions guided the interviews:

- Which situations may be described as incidents/accidents?
- Which preventive and diagnostic practices are currently being used?
- Which formal and informal procedures have been adopted?
- Which communication mechanisms are used during DR?

- Do you use any performance metrics?
- Do you use any plans with DR procedures?

The outcomes from the semistructured interviews indicate that the most critical incidents are related to server failures, mostly due to disk failures, and connectivity losses in specific network segments compromising a wide variety of services. A preoccupation with more untypical problems was also reported, "[...] like a flood in the basement where some of the equipment is located [...]"

As pointed out by both teams, the existing preventative practices rely heavily on monitoring active network components through control panels where alerts are displayed and emailed to the technicians. Many critical situations require the team members find out where the failing components are physically located. And they have to go to the physical locations to perceive the actual situation context. The diagnosis and recovery practices rely heavily on the field experience of each team member, which seems to be highly specialised, e.g., there are Windows, Mac, and LINUX specialists. The teams rely on quick informal meetings, phone calls, and chat-tools to share knowledge, coordinate activities, and make decisions. Besides performing maintenance actions, the teams also rely on service-level agreements with suppliers and a spare stock to overcome problems.

One key concern that emerged from the semistructured interviews was that teams find it important to document what has been done to diagnose and recover from incidents and accidents. This information was considered essential to support organisational learning, especially because human resources tend to rotate a lot in these units and thus past experience is often lost.

Although both teams use trouble ticket software in their routine maintenance operations, they also realised that trouble tickets are almost irrelevant during non-routine situations. Trouble tickets are sometimes used for incident opening and only occasionally for postmortem annotations to close incidents resulting in no significant impact on planning future responses.

Interestingly, one of the mentioned reasons for not using trouble tickets more often is they are not accessible where the incidents actually occur. The networking and computing infrastructure are distributed through several building and offices, while the trouble tickets are only available in desktop computers that may be inaccessible in these sites.

From the interviews we realised: (1) the selected application scenario concerns a mobile collaborative situation perceived as critical to the teams; and (2) the tasks perceived as important by the teams are related to decision-making support and organisational memory.

6.3 *Requirements Elicitation*

Having established the relevance of the selected application scenario, we proceeded with a more thorough analysis of the application requirements and their alignment with the developed SA theory and tool. We adopted the following method. First, we compiled a list of requirements from the related literature. We then requested the team members to analyse and prioritise the requirements according to their work context. And we finally established the list of requirements according to the perceived priorities.

The requirements compiled from the research literature consider four categories: collaborative technology (Steves, Morse, Gutwin, and Greenberg 2001), knowledge management (Vizcaíno, Martinez, Aranda, and Piattini 2005), team performance (Baeza-Yates and Pino 2006), and SA (Salmon, Stanton, Walker, and Green 2005). The first category addresses the main technological features necessary to provide collaboration support. The knowledge management category was selected because it has already been pointed out as important in the preliminary study. Team performance concerns the efficiency of technology support. And the last category was selected to specifically address the theoretical concerns associated with SA (Endsley 1995; Endsley 2003).

In Table 1 represents the compiled requirements list that was delivered to the participants for prioritisation. The participants (seven persons) were requested to individually rate the selected requirements with relevance to the teams' work context. The ratings scale was: 1 – Not perceived as important; 2 – Less important; 3 – Important; and 4 – Very important. The answers were received by email. The consolidated scores are shown in Table 2.

We defined a threshold of 3.0 for cutting off the less important requirements. As we may observe, the members rated eight requirements above the threshold (important or very important) and seven requirements below the threshold (less or not important). Interestingly, the four requirements categories are all evenly represented, although we find a slight advantage given to collaboration support and SA.

The obtained results clearly emphasise the importance given by the teams to immediacy of action (requirements 1, 4, and 13) and responsiveness to events (requirements 3, 5, 6, 8, 13). In our view, these results express the importance of

Table 1 Requirements list

#	Requirement	Area
1	Communication support through shared artefacts	Collaboration support
2	Transition between individual and team work	
3	Facilitate situation monitoring	
4	Minimum overhead	
5	Mobility support	
6	Help understanding situation context	Situation awareness
7	Help perceiving who is involved	
8	Assist situation size-up	
9	Assist overall situation representation	
10	Knowledge externalisation	Knowledge management
11	Knowledge transfer	
12	Document incident handling	
13	Improve diagnosis time	Performance
14	Improve recovery time	
15	Increase number of incidents simultaneously attended	

Table 2 Requirements priorities

#	1	2	3	4	AVG	STDEV
4			1	6	3.86	0.38
5			2	5	3.71	0.49
6			2	5	3.71	0.49
13			2	4	3.67	0.52
12		1	2	3	3.33	0.82
8			5	2	3.29	0.49
3			6	1	3.14	0.38
10		2	4	1	2.86	0.69
11		3	2	2	2.86	0.90
15	1		5	1	2.86	0.90
1		2	5		2.71	0.49
9		2	5		2.71	0.49
14		2	5		2.71	0.49
7		4	3		2.43	0.53
2		5	2		2.29	0.49

tight coupling (Perrow 1999) and actually elucidate how it may be obtained. Incident documentation was already mentioned in the semistructured interviews and emerged again as important (requirement 12).

And finally, it should also be emphasised that the teams validated the alignment with our research and their interests, especially concerning SA and mobility. Mobility was the second most rated requirement, while understanding the situation context appears in third place (although the other elements of SA were ranked lower). Overall, with this inquiry we validated our main research objectives and obtained important information necessary to adapt the tool to the target application domain and users.

6.4 Theory/Tool Evaluation

The evaluation of collaborative technology raises many methodological concerns that have received attention from researchers in the CSCW community (Herskovic, Pino, Ochoa, and Antunes 2007). Different evaluation techniques may be adopted according to emphasis on technical (e.g., interoperability), human (e.g., usability), and organisational (e.g., effects on task performance) issues (Gauducheau, Soulier, and Lewkowicz 2005; Vyhmeister, Mondelo, and Novella. 2006).

An evaluation strategy well adapted to case studies and complex collaborative settings uses field methods in actual working environments (Hughes, King, Rodden, and Andersen 1994). Although this approach allows capturing very rich data, it is also difficult to accomplish for various reasons: requirement of a large amount of time investment, necessity of using a fully working prototype, requirements of high commitment from the organisation, and access to actual or simulated disaster situations.

Inspection techniques (Nielsen 1994) may also be employed in case studies. Inspection techniques rely on domain experts to analyse the technology and expose possible problems and drawbacks of technology use. Inspection techniques are less costly than field methods and may be used earlier and more frequently in the development cycle.

Steves et al. (2001) defend that inspection techniques should be employed in early development stages when prototypes are still immature and field methods should be employed afterwards. Based on this perspective, our evaluation approach was based on inspection.

The evaluation process evolved in the following way. First, we requested the team leaders to develop a common use-scenario. Use-scenarios have been employed in conjunction with inspection techniques to bring more context to the evaluation task (Carroll 2000; Haynes, Purao, and Skattebo 2004). The developed scenario is shown in Fig. 6 (left).

We then conducted workshops with the teams, requesting them to inspect the tool in the context of the predefined scenario. Three interconnected devices purposely configured for the specific evaluation teams were supplied. The teams were given sufficient time to experience the tool and discuss its implications to their work. They were able to create SM, create dimensions and dimensional entities, define correlations, and navigate through the various SM, observing how the various devices use the ad-hoc network to synchronise information. The teams also had the opportunity to experience the collaborative nature of the tool, supporting concurrent updates to correlations. In Fig. 6 (right), we show the tool running on one mobile device during the workshops.

From these workshops we obtained qualitative data consisting of comments and suggestions. They revealed that when a nonroutine situation occurs, the personal

Scenario

"From several rooms, we received reports of network connectivity losses. Some technicians were notified by email, while others received several complaints by phone. The senior technician that received some of these complaints suspects the central switch located in the main building."

How the proposed tool may help diagnosing, planning and coordinating recovery actions?

Fig. 6 Inspection: (left) scenario, and (right) tool

experience of the involved operators strongly influences team SA. For example, when highly experienced operators happen to be available during the problematic situation, it was easier to collectively understand the causes, implications, and consequences of the event. The tool was perceived as the most relevant one to establish collaborative SA when the less-experienced operators were confronted with the situation. Knowledge transfer and incident documentation were considered very important to the team leaders, while knowledge representation and externalisation was revealed as most important to junior technicians.

The workshop participants also analysed the SA model and its impact on the DR strategy. From the discussions that took place in both workshops, the highly informal and unstructured work practices were obvious to both teams. The courses of action varied according to the involved actors and some discussions took place on the more efficient ways to address various occurrences. The participants drafted several SM in paper prototypes expressing the best ways to address some incidents. Figure 7 shows some examples of these paper prototypes.

This way the teams defined the most adequate set of SM to their work context. The dimensions they considered more relevant were: equipment, actors, locations, actions and steps. These dimensions would then be correlated in the following SM:

- Actions-Steps, detailing operational activities (e.g., check router X, reboot switch Y),
- Actors-Steps, defining responsibilities,
- Equipment-Actors, expressing who is responsible for the equipment (e.g., who may activate a supplier warranty and who has the skills necessary to inspect a LINUX server), and
- Equipment-Locations, allowing junior team members to find out the equipment locations (e.g., main gateway of building C6 is located in room 6.3.0.1).

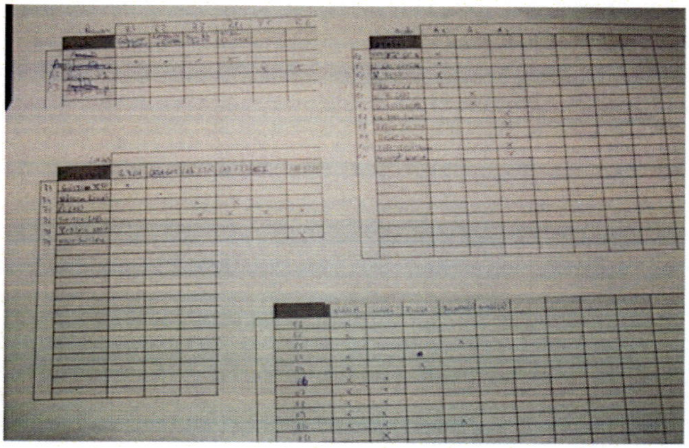

Fig. 7 Situation matrixes drafted during the workshops

Of course, the team members discussed a large set of usability problems they found in the tool. They recommended the SM should be easily reused across multiple DR processes. They also considered having an overview of the whole situation important, displaying all of the SM and existing correlations, something that is quite difficult to accomplish considering the small display size of the used devices.

A better support for navigating the SM was highly recommended. The participants also regarded keeping awareness information up-to-date a major challenge, emphasising the potential problems of either having "aged" information or, alternatively, having overhead introducing current information in the tool. The participants suggested asking for the validity of correlations. As correlations age, the users could be prompted to report their validity; they also suggested using visualisation techniques to express the ageing of correlations. And finally, both teams pointed the proposed model was aligned with the requirements they considered relevant for DR of business operations.

6.5 Results from the Case Study

It was possible to confirm with the case study that SA is influential whenever the teams must coordinate nonstandard activities since activities are distributed throughout the physical space and expertise is evenly distributed. SA seems to be more important to inexperienced workers.

By the end of the workshops, both teams reported the evaluation sessions revealed something they were only suspicious about: the individuals' experience strongly conditions the team's performance. The issue was not completely new to them, and they were trying to address it by compiling contingency plans externalising and optimising such knowledge. But due to lack of time, they have given low priority to this goal and so the available list of contingency plans is short in one organisation and nonexistent in the other. Both teams perceived the SA tool as an opportunity to define contingency plans. Thus, one interesting outcome of this case study was that, unlike what we were expecting, the SA tool seemed more useful to indirectly document DR strategies rather than supporting direct human interventions.

The teams' appropriation of the SA tool was patent. The workshop sessions served to define a template for contingency plans that could be used in the future. The template uses the proposed SA model and organises the overall response according to a set of SM and dimensions, including equipment, actors, locations, actions, and activities.

Finally, regarding the adopted research approach, some considerations were also worth noting. The first interview revealed crucial to establish a common ground for a richer discussion in the requirements and evaluation phases. The prototype was fundamental to develop a pragmatic view of the tools' advantages (e.g., mobility) and drawbacks (e.g., interaction problems and small display size), thus facilitating a realistic assessment of its utility. Overall, the evaluation process was adequate to an exploratory research focused on a specific theory and model based on expert evaluation.

7 Discussion

The main organisational problems dealing with the unordered world seemed to be rooted in a lack of collective awareness about the ongoing situation, plus communication and information management problems (Kanno and Furuta 2006; McManus, Seville, Brunsdon, and Vargo 2007; Milis and Walle 2007). Therefore, we concluded increasing the level of collaborative SA as a fundamental requirement for DR. The teams that participated in our research also supported this view.

To accomplish this endeavour, we articulated the main information elements necessary for collaborative SA with a model. The model, which was inspired by the "Swiss-cheese" model (Reason 1997, 2008), organises the information elements necessary for collaborative SA in a strategic view of the situation ranging from the sharp end to the blunt end. Each view brings together two dimensions of the sproblem and several correlations between the defined dimensional elements. The model may be constantly updated in runtime thus supporting information sharing, coordination, and collaboration.

Events, awareness and actions are often difficult to disentangle in the unordered world. The traditional linear models (e.g., Domino model (Heinrich 1931)) of accident trajectory suggest there is some intrinsic order over time, from event to awareness and action, but the reality is that chaos is what mostly defines disastrous conditions (Kelly 1998). The typical approaches to DR rooted on linear models have been criticised for only distinguishing the major stages in accident trajectories (Kelly 1998), forgetting many nonlinear relationships between the various elements that make up the accident context. Overall, the linear models seem to provide few insights about the actual unfolding of a disaster.

Others suggest that DR should instead focus on systemic views of the situation (Hollnagel and Woods 2005a, b). These new approaches emphasise contextual, situational, contingencial, and interactive relationships amongst multiple information elements. The model and tool we developed adopt the latter perspective. The main objective is maintaining collaboratively and in real time the multiple interdependencies of events, actions, actors, contexts, plans and many other factors involved in DR.

The model and tool are generic offering a common strategy to build a shared view of the situation using SM, situation dimensions, dimensional elements, and correlations. Predefined SM, situation dimensions, and dimensional elements may be tailored to suit specific domains and facilitate the first approach to the situation. But depending on the involved organisation and emergent situation, this information structure may have to be redefined in run time. Therefore, a significant effort has been made in order to accommodate dynamic changes in the information structure.

Another characteristic of the proposed model and tool is the support to concurrent changes in the information structure. This approach is quite distinct from others emphasising the chain of command and control. The hierarchical control has been criticised for favouring a concentration of decision making and putting too much emphasis on vertical communication (Drabek and McEntire 2003). Instead, several disaster sociologists emphasise that critical responses should be organised with decentralised structures and cooperation between actors (Drabek and McEntire 2003). The proposed model and tool also adopt this latter view.

The preliminary results from the case study indicate that the model and tool are influential whenever the teams have to coordinate nonstandard activities, especially when less-experienced workers are involved in the process. The results also indicate the importance of constructing and maintaining organisational memory, which may be supported with the proposed tool. Nevertheless, more qualitative and quantitative experiments are necessary to assess the model/tool contributions. Our research work is currently focused on: (1) developing metrics adequate for collaborative SA, which may be employed to quantitatively assess the tool's impact on team performance; and (2) developing experimental scenarios that could be used in laboratory to qualitatively assess the teams' construction and use of the SM in disaster situations.

8 Conclusions

The scenarios characterised by complexity, hard-to-define causal relationships, dynamic changes, and lack of information necessitate important changes in organisational decision making. Instead of predefined and structured approaches, we find strategies based on exploring, probing, and acting while trying to understand the situation.

The model and tool discussed in this chapter address these new strategies. The focus is on the support to the collaborative construction of SA by the involved users, allowing them to dynamically and concurrently manipulate the information structure. Furthermore, the proposed model organises the information structure according to multiple types of relationships, such as problems-solutions, causes-effects and actions-actors. This structure aims at facilitating information interaction and visualisation.

These conclusions are based on feedback from teams with high expertise in DR of business operations drawing from evaluations of our model and tool. Because inspection was the adopted evaluation method, further research should be conducted to validate the model and tool in real disaster situations. Nevertheless, the evaluation data already obtained indicate that the model and tool are capable of responding to the most significant problems faced by the teams. The participants' feedback also points towards the need to improve information visualisation and interaction in mobile devices.

Acknowledgements This work was partially funded by Fondecyt (project 1085010) and the Portuguese Foundation for Science and Technology (projects PTDC/EIA 67589/2006 and 102875/2008).

References

Antunes, P. and P. André, "A Conceptual Framework for the Design of Geo-Collaborative Systems," *Group Decision and Negotiation*, 15, 2006, 273–295.

Baeza-Yates, R. and J. Pino, "Towards Formal Evaluation of Collaborative Work and Its Application to Information Retrieval," *Information Research*, 11, 4, 2006, 271.

Baker, D., R. Day and E. Salas, "Teamwork as an Essential Component of High-Reliability Organizations," *Health Services Research*, 41, 4, 2006, 1576–1598.

Baloian, N. and G. Zurita, "Mc-Supporter: Flexible Mobile Computing Supporting Learning Though Social Interaction," *Journal of Universal Computer Science*, 15, 9, 2009, 1833–1851.

Baloian, N., G. Zurita, P. Antunes and F. Baytelman, "A Flexible, Lightweight Middleware Supporting the Development of Distributed Applications across Platforms," *The 11th International Conference on CSCW in Design*, Melbourne, 2007.

Bedny, G. and D. Meister, "Theory of Activity and Situation Awareness," *International Journal of Cognitive Ergonomics*, 3, 1, 1999, 63–72.

Briggs, R., "On Theory-Driven Design and Deployment of Collaboration Systems," *International Journal of Human-Computer Studies*, 64, 7, 2006, 573–582.

Bruinsma, G. and R. Hoog, *Third International Conference on Information Systems for Crisis Response and Management (ISCRAM)*, Newark, 2006, 53–65.

Cai, G., A. MacEachren, I. Brewer, M. McNeese, R. Sharma and S. Fuhrmann, "Map-Mediated Geocollaborative Crisis Management," *Intelligence and Security Informatics*, Heidelberg: Springer, 2005, 429–435.

Carroll, J., *Making Use: Scenario-Based Design of Human-Computer Interactions*. Cambridge: MIT Press, 2000.

Drabek, T. and D. McEntire, "Emergent Phenomena and the Sociology of Disaster: Lessons, Trends and Opportunities from Research Literature," *Disaster Prevention and Management*, 12, 2003, 97–112.

Endsley, M., "Toward a Theory of Situation Awareness in Dynamic Systems," *Human Factors*, 31, 7, 1995, 32–64.

Endsley, M., *Designing for Situation Awareness*. London: Taylor & Francis, 2003.

Endsley, M. and W. Jones, "A Model of Inter and Intra Team Situation Awareness: Implications for Design, Training And Measurement" in M. McNeese, E. Salas and M. Endsley, (eds.), *New Trends in Cooperative Activities: Understanding System Dynamics in Complex Environments*. Santa Monica: Human Factors and Ergonomics Society, 2001, 46–67.

Fiori, S., E. Salas, H. Cuevas and C. Bowers, "Distributed Coordination Space: Toward a Theory of Distributed Team Process and Performance," *Theoretical Issues in Ergonomics Science*, 4, 3 and 4, 2003, 340–364.

Gauducheau, N., E. Soulier and M. Lewkowicz, "Design and Evaluation of Activity Model-Based Groupware: Methedological Issues," in *Proceedings of the 14th IEEE International Workshops on Enabling Technologies: Infrastructure for Collaborative Enterprise*. Washington, DC: IEEE Computer Society, 2005, 226–234.

Gerring, J., *Case Study Research Principles and Practices*. Cambridge: Cambridge University Press, 2007.

Grint, K. and S. Woolgar, *The Machine at Work*. Cambridge: Blackwell, 1997.

Harrald, J. and L. Stoddard, "Scenario Based Identification and Structuring of Information Needs for the Response to Complex International Crisis," in *Proceedings of the 5th Annual Conference of the Emergency Management Society*, Washington, DC, 1998, 295–306.

Hayes, J., *Safety Decision Making in High Hazard Organisations at the Production/Maintenance Interface – A Literature Review*. Canberra: The Australian National University, National Research Centre for OHS Regulation, 2006.

Haynes, S., S. Purao and A. Skattebo, "Situating Evaluation in Scenarios of Use," in *Proceedings of the 2004 ACM conference on Computer Supported Cooperative Work*. Chicago: ACM Press, 2004, 92–101.

Heinrich, H., *Industrial Accident Prevention*. New York: McGraw-Hill, 1931.

Herskovic, V., J. Pino, S. Ochoa and P. Antunes, "Evaluation Methods for Groupware Systems" in Haake, J., S. Ochoa, and A. Cechich (eds.), *Groupware: Design, Implementation, and Use, Proceedings of the 13th International Workshop, CRIWG 2007*, Bariloche, September 2007. Heidelberg: Springer, 2007, 328–336.

Hiles, A., *The Definitive Handbook of Business Continuity Management*. West Sussex: Wiley, 2008.

Hollnagel, E., *Barriers and Accident Prevention*. Hampshire: Ashgate, 2004.

Hollnagel, E. and D. Woods, *Joint Cognitive Systems: Foundations of Cognitive Systems Engineering*. Boca Raton: CRC, 2005a.

Hollnagel, E. and D. Woods, *Joint Cognitive Systems: Introduction to Cognitive Systems Engineering*. Boca Raton: CRC, 2005b.

Hughes, J., V. King, T. Rodden and H. Andersen, "Moving out from the Control Room: Ethnography in System Design," *Proceedings of the 1994 ACM Conference on Computer Supported Cooperative Work*. Chapel Hill: ACM, 1994, 429–439.

Kanno, T. and K. Furuta, "Resilience of Emergency Response Systems" in E. Hollnagel and E. Rigaud (eds.), *Proceedings of the Second Resilience Engineering Symposium*. Antibes: Les Presses, 2006.

Kelly, C., "Simplifying Disasters: Developing a Model for Complex Non-Linear Events," *Australian Journal of Emergency Management*, 14, 1, 1998, 25–27.

Kwan, M. and J. Lee, "Emergency Response after 9/11: The Potential of Real-Time 3d Gis for Quick Emergency Response in Micro-Spatial Environments," *Computers, Environment and Urban Systems*, 29, 2, 2005, 93–113.

Lauwers, J. and K. Lantz, "Collaboration Awareness in Support of Collaboration Transparency: Requirements for the Next Generation of Shared Window Systems," in *Proceedings of the SIGCHI conference on Human Factors in Computing Systems: Empowering People*. Seattle: ACM, 1990, 303–311.

MacEachren, A., "Moving Geovisualization Toward Support for Group Work" in J. Dykes, A. MacEachren and M. Kraak (eds.), *Exploring Geovisualization*. Amsterdam: Elsevier, 2005, 445–462.

Markus, M., A. Majchrzak and L. Gasser, "A Design Theory for Systems That Support Emergent Knowledge Processes," *Management Information Systems Quarterly*, 26, 3, 2002, 179–212.

McManus, S., E. Seville, D. Brunsdon and J. Vargo, "Resilience Management: A Framework for Assessing and Improving the Resilience of Organizations," *Resilient Organizations*, 2007.

Miles, M. and A. Huberman, *Qualitative Data Analysis*. Thousand Oaks: Sage, 1994.

Milis, K. and B. Walle, "IT for Corporate Crisis Management: Findings from a Survey in 6 Different Industries on Management Attention, Intention and Actual Use," *40th Hawaii International Conference on Systems Science*. Waikoloa: IEEE Computer Society, 2007.

Möller, K., "Sense-Making and Agenda Construction in Emerging Business Networks – How to Direct Radical Innovation," *Industrial Marketing Management*, 2009.

Monares, A., S. Ochoa, J. Pino, V. Herskovic and A. Neyem, "Mobilemap: A Collaborative Application to Support Emergency Situations in Urban Areas," *13th International Conference on Computer Supported Cooperative Work in Design*. Santiago: IEEE, 2009, 565–570.

Moore, G., "Cramming More Components onto Integrated Circuits," *Electronics*, 38, 8, April 19, 1965.

Mourão, H. and P. Antunes, "Supporting Effective Unexpected Exceptions Handling in Workflow Management Systems," *Proceedings of the 22nd Annual ACM Symposium on Applied Computing, Special Track on Organizational Engineering*. Seoul: ACM, 2007, 1242–1249.

Muñoz, M., M. Rodriguez, J. Favela, A. Martinez-Garcia and V. González, "Context-Aware Mobile Communication in Hospitals," *Computer*, 36, 9, 2003, 38–46.

Nielsen, J., "Usability Inspection Methods," *Conference on Human Factors in Computing Systems*. Boston: ACM, 1994, 413–414.

Ochoa, S., J. Pino, G. Bravo, N. Dujovne and A. Neyem, "Mobile Shared Workspaces to Support Construction Inspection Activities" in P. Zarate, J. Belaud, G. Camileri and F. Ravat (eds.), *Collaborative Decision Making: Perspectives and Challenges*. Amsterdam: IOS, 2008, 211–220.

Perrow, C., *Normal Accidents, Living with High-Risk Technologies*. Princeton: Princeton University Press, 1999.

Reason, J., *Managing the Risks of Organizational Accidents*. Surrey: Ashgate, 1997.

Reason, J., *The Human Contribution: Unsafe Acts, Accidents and Heroic Recoveries*. Surrey: Ashgate, 2008.

Reinhard, W., J. Schweitzer, G. Völksen and M. Weber, "CSCW Tools: Concepts and Architectures," *Computer*, 27, 5, 1994, 28–36.

Sá, M., L. Carriço and P. Antunes, "Ubiquitous Psychotherapy," IEEE *Pervasive Computing*, 6, 1, 2007, 20–27.

Salas, E., C. Prince, D. Baker and L. Shrestha, "Situation Awareness in Team Performance: Implications for Measurement and Training," *Human Factors*, 37, 1, 1995, 123–126.

Salmon, P., N. Stanton, D. Jenkins, G. Walker, M. Young and A. Aujla, "What Really Is Going On? Review, Critique and Extension of Situation Awareness Theory," *Engineering Psychology and Cognitive Ergonomics*. Heidelberg: Springer, 2007, 407–416.

Salmon, P., N. Stanton, G. Walker and D. Green, "Situation Awareness Measurement: A Review of Applicability for C4i Environments," *Applied Ergonomics*, 37, 2, 2005, 225–238.

Shu, Y. and K. Futura, "An Inference Method of Team Situation Awareness Based on Mutual Awareness," *Cognition, Technology & Work*, 7, 2005, 272–287.

Smith, K. and P. Hancock, "Situation Awareness Is Adaptive, Externally Directed Consciousness," *Human Factors*, 37, 1995, 137–148.

Snowden, D. and M. Boone, "A Leader's Framework for Decision Making," *Harvard Business Review*, November 2007, 69–76.

Stanton, N., R. Stewart, D. Harris, R. Houghton, C. Baber, R. McMaster, P. Salmon, G. Hoyle, G. Walker, M. Young, M. Linsell, R. Dymott and D. Green, "Distributed Situation Awareness in Dynamic Systems: Theoretical Development and Application of an Ergonomics Methodology," *Ergonomics*, 49, 12–13, 2006, 1288–1311.

Steves, M., E. Morse, C. Gutwin and S.A. Greenberg, "Comparison of Usage Evaluation and Inspection Methods for Assessing Groupware Usability," in *Proceedings of the 2001 International ACM SIGGROUP Conference on Supporting Group Work*, Boulder, 2001, 125–134.

Suchman, L., *Plans and Situated Actions: The Problem of Human-Machine Communication*. New York: MIT Press, 1987.

Tentori, M. and J. Favela, "Activity-Aware Computing for Healthcare," IEEE *Pervasive Computing*, 7, 2, 2008, 51–57.

Turoff, M., M. Chumer, B. Van de Walle and X. Yao, "The Design of a Dynamic Emergency Response Management Information System (Dermis)," *Journal of Information Technology Theory and Application*, January 2004.

Vizcaíno, A., M. Martinez, G. Aranda and M. Piattini, "Evaluating Collaborative Applications from a Knowledge Management Approach," *14th IEEE International Workshops on Enabling Technologies: Infrastructure for Collaborative Enterprise (WETICE'05)*. Washington, DC: IEEE CS Press, 2005, 221–225.

Vyhmeister, R., P. Mondelo and M. Novella, "Towards a Model for Assessing Workers' Risks Resulting from the Implementation of Information and Communication Systems and Technologies," *Human Factors in Ergonomics & Manufacturing*, 16, 1, 2006, 39–59.

Weick, K., *Sensemaking in Organizations*. Thousand Oaks: Sage, 1995.

Weick, K., *Making Sense of the Organization*. Oxford: Blackwell, 2001.

Weick, K. and K. Sutcliffe, *Managing the Unexpected: Assuring High Performance in an Age of Complexity*. San Francisco: Jossey-Bass, 2001.

Woods, D. and E. Hollnagel, *Joint Cognitive Systems: Patterns in Cognitive Systems Engineering*. Boca Raton: CRC, 2006.

Wybo, J. and M. Latiers, "Exploring Complex Emergency Situations' Dynamic: Theoretical, Epistemological and Methodological Proposals," *International Journal of Emergency Management*, 3, 1, 2006, 40–51.

Zurita, G., P. Antunes, N. Baloian and F. Baytelman, "Mobile Sensemaking: Exploring Proximity and Mobile Applications in the Classroom," *Journal of Universal Computer Science*, 13, 10, 2007, 1434–1448.

Zurita, G. and N. Baloian, "Handheld-Based Electronic Meeting Support," *Lecture Notes in Computer Science*, 3706, 2005, 341–350.

Zurita, G., N. Baloian and F. Baytelman, "A Collaborative Face-to-Face Design Support System Based on Sketching and Gesturing," *Advanced Engineering Informatics*, 22, 3, 2008, 340–349.

Index

F. Burstein et al. (eds.), *Supporting Real Time Decision-Making*, Annals of Information Systems 13, DOI 10.1007/978-1-4419-7406-8,

N

O

P

R

S

T

V

W